Garfield's Sunday Finest

35 YEARS OF MY BEST SUNDAY FUNNIES

Garfield's Sunday Finest

35 YEARS OF MY BEST SUNDAY FUNNIES

BY JIM DAVIS

BALLANTINE BOOKS • NEW YORK

Credits

EDITORS

Mark Acey, Scott Nickel

DESIGN AND PRODUCTION

Thomas Howard, Brad Hill

CREATIVE SUPPORT

Brett Koth, Lynette Nuding,

Larry Fentz, Sheila Bolduc

A Ballantine Books Trade Paperback Original

Published in the United States by Ballantine Books, an imprint of
Random House, LLC, New York, a Penguin Random House Company

BALLANTINE and the HOUSE colophon are registered trademarks of Random House, LLC

ISBN 978-0-345-52597-0

Printed in China on acid-free paper

www.ballantinebooks.com

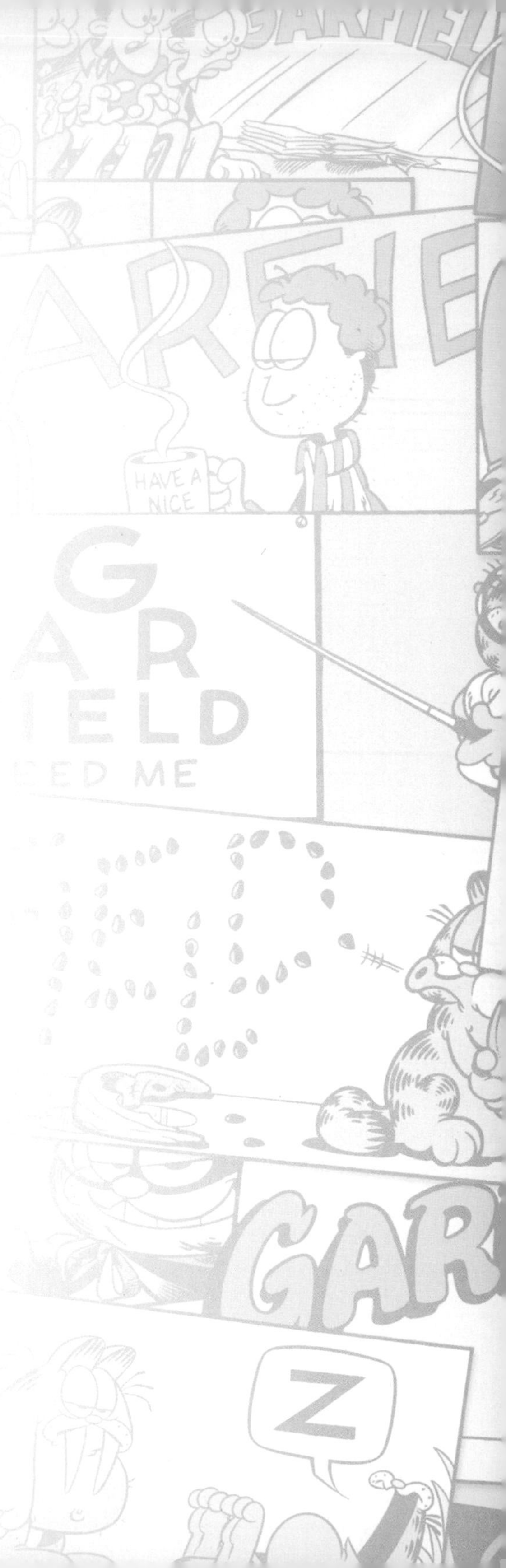
HAVE A NICE
GAR
Z

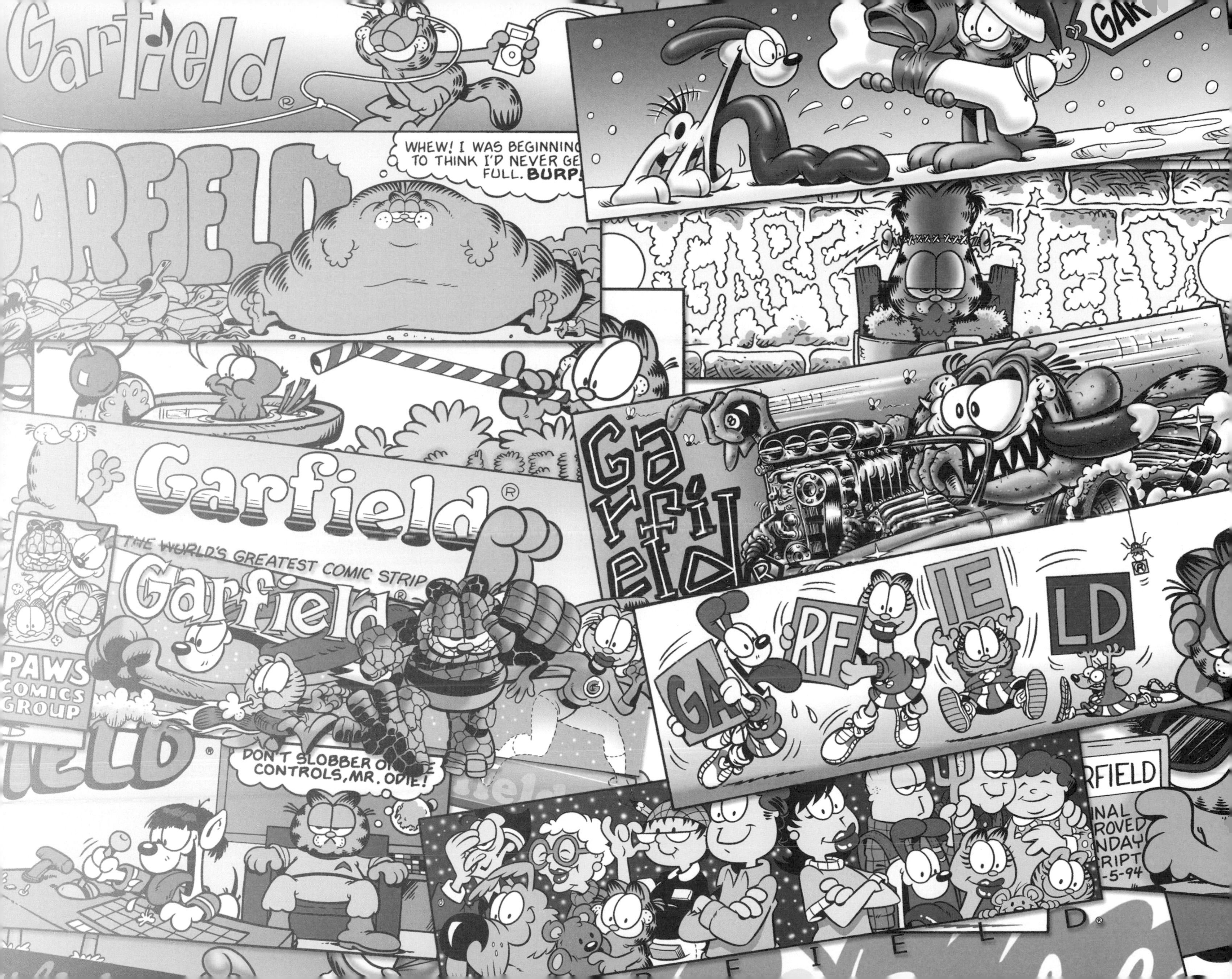

Garfield
WHEW! I WAS BEGINNING TO THINK I'D NEVER GE FULL. BURP!
Garfield
THE WORLD'S GREATEST COMIC STRIP
Garfield
PAWS COMICS GROUP
DON'T SLOBBER O E CONTROLS, MR. ODIE!
GA RF IE LD
RFIELD

This one is a sentimental favorite. It's my first Sunday.
I wanted to start Garfield's career with something classic.

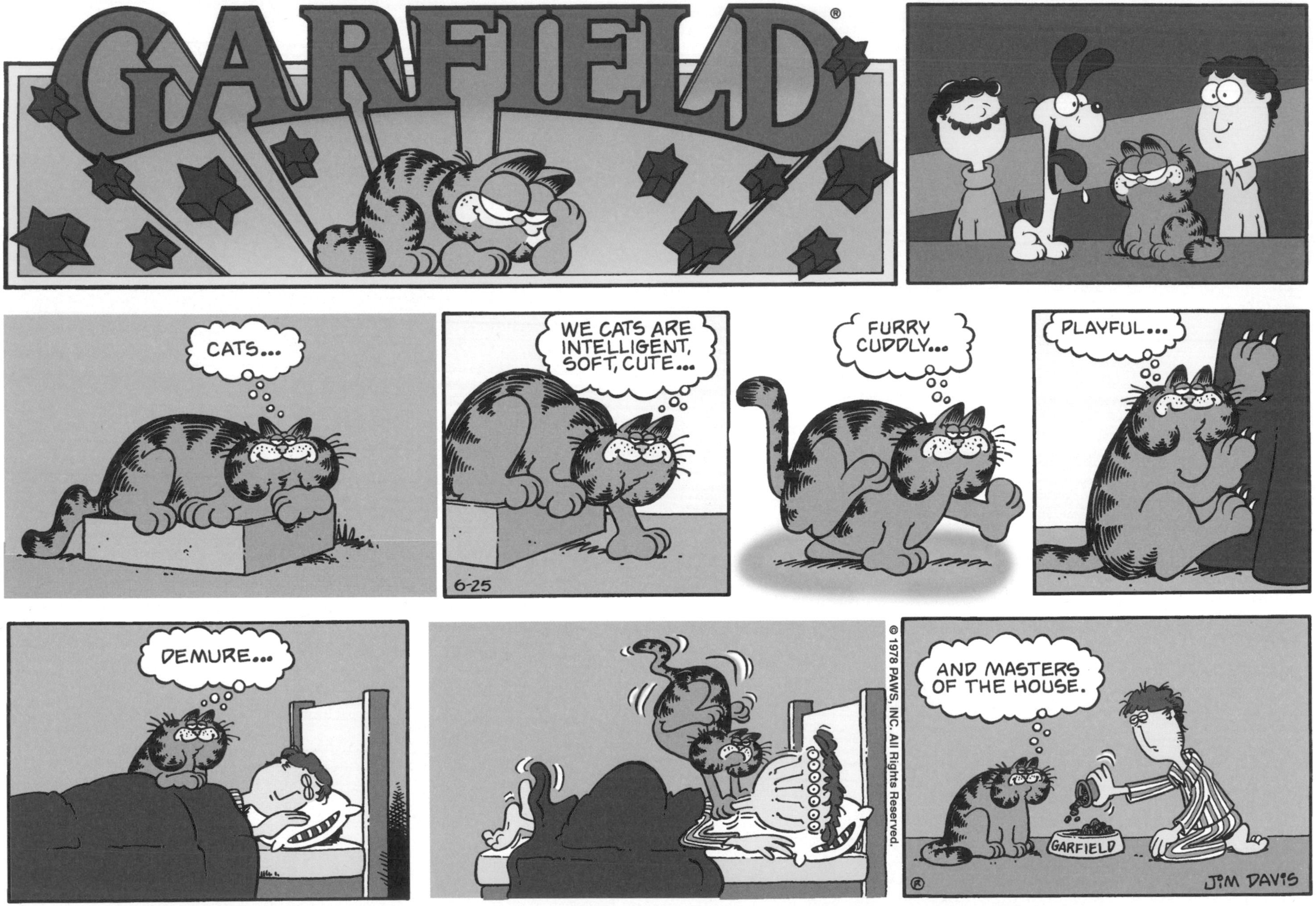
GARFIELD®
CATS...
WE CATS ARE INTELLIGENT, SOFT, CUTE...
6-25
FURRY CUDDLY...
PLAYFUL...
DEMURE...
© 1978 PAWS, INC. All Rights Reserved.
AND MASTERS OF THE HOUSE.
GARFIELD
JIM DAVIS

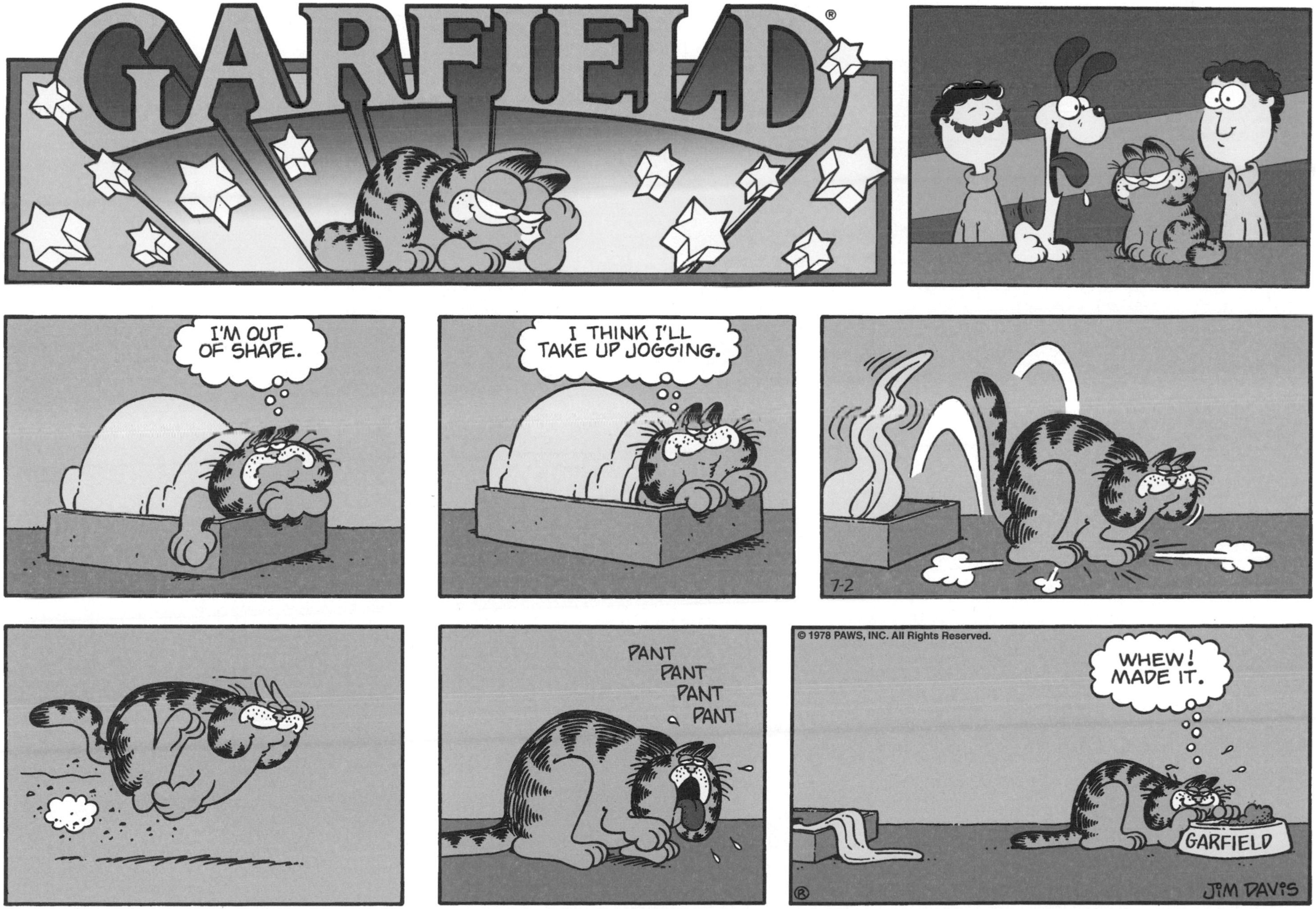
GARFIELD®
I'M OUT OF SHAPE.
I THINK I'LL TAKE UP JOGGING.
7-2
PANT PANT PANT PANT
© 1978 PAWS, INC. All Rights Reserved.
WHEW! MADE IT.
GARFIELD
JIM DAVIS

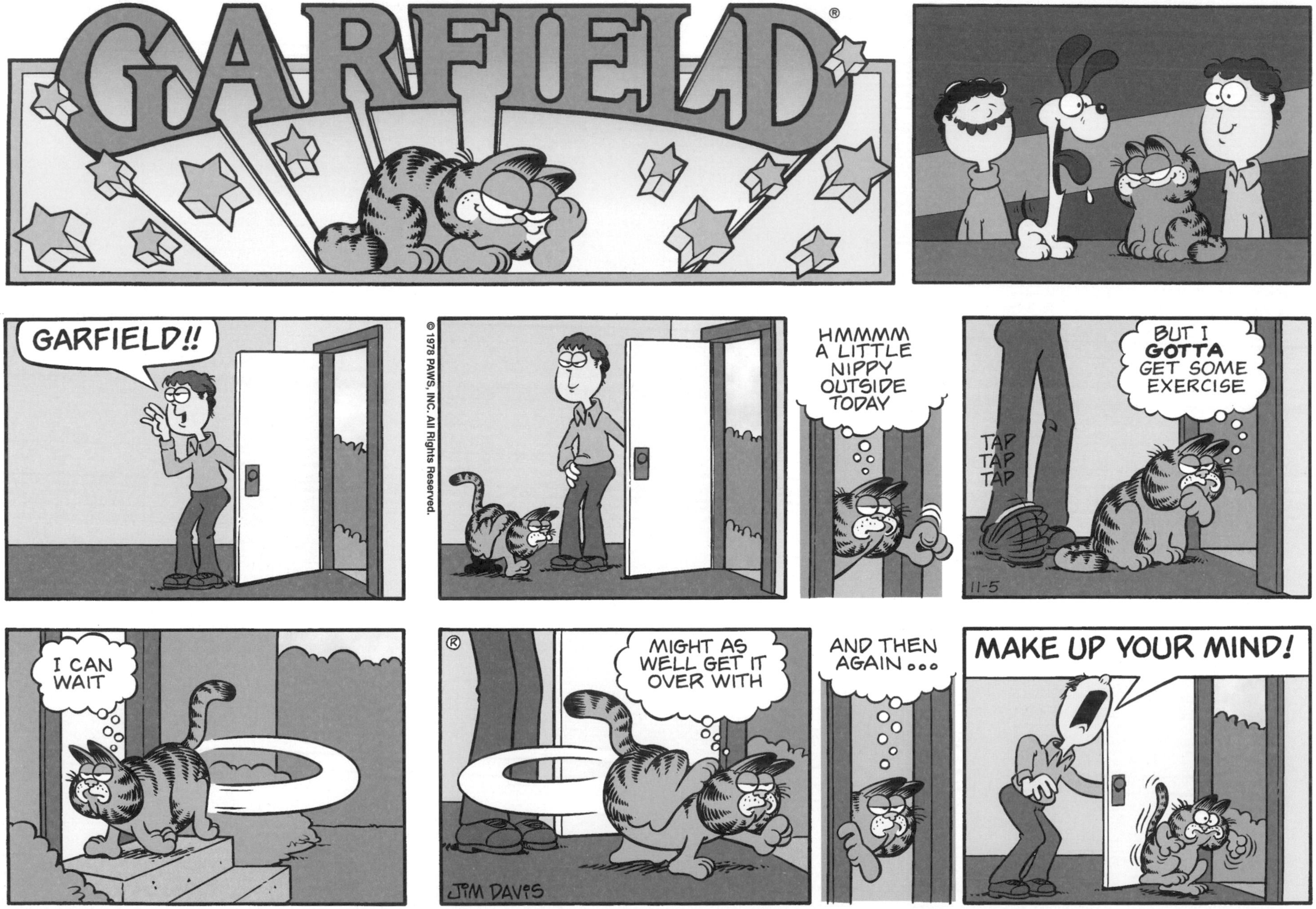
GARFIELD®
GARFIELD!!
© 1978 PAWS, INC. All Rights Reserved.
HMMMM A LITTLE NIPPY OUTSIDE TODAY
TAP TAP TAP
BUT I **GOTTA** GET SOME EXERCISE
11-5
I CAN WAIT
®
MIGHT AS WELL GET IT OVER WITH
JIM DAVIS
AND THEN AGAIN...
MAKE UP YOUR MIND!

I thought that I'd get all the cat clichés out of the way in one strip and get it over with.

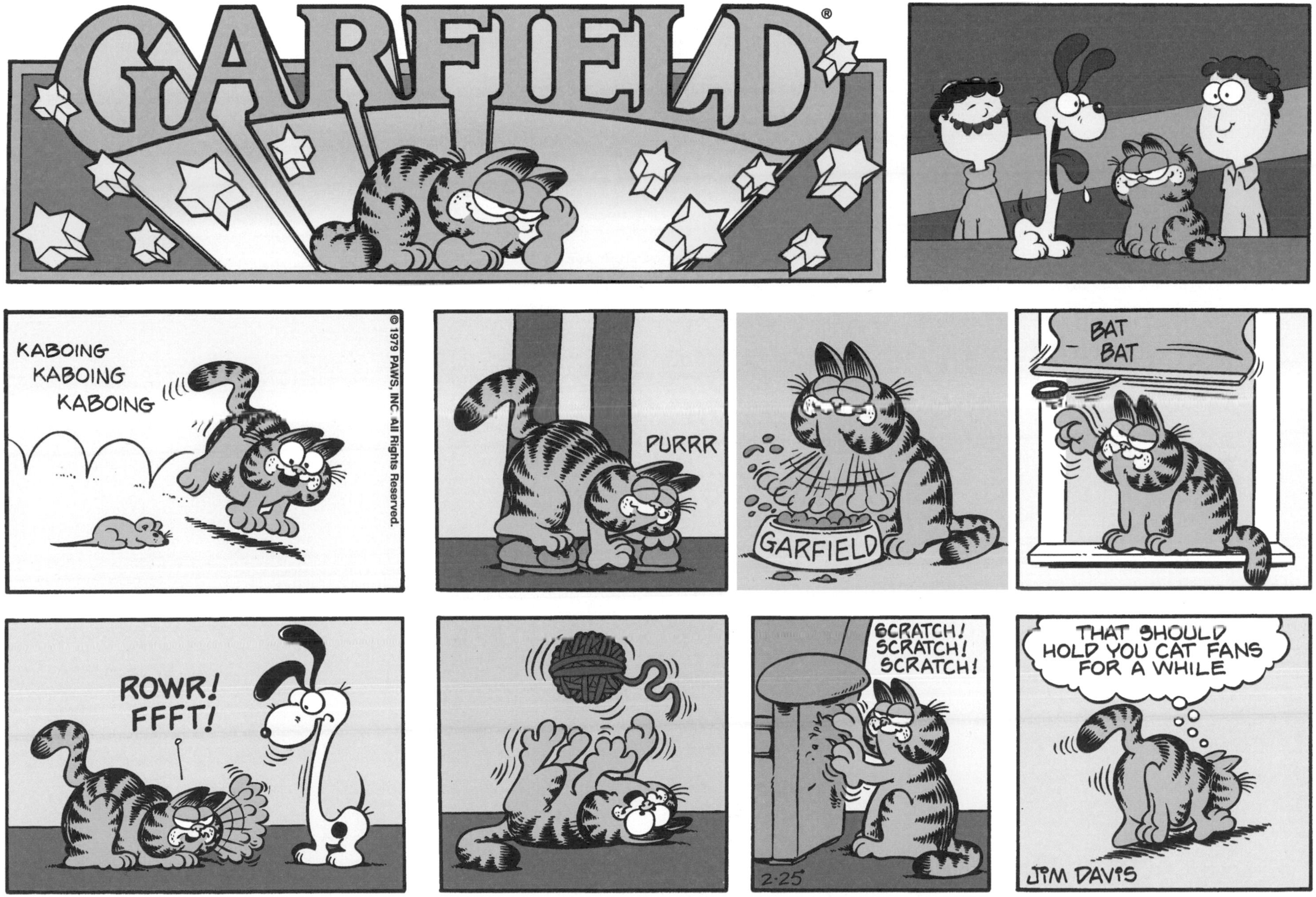
GARFIELD®
© 1979 PAWS, INC. All Rights Reserved.
KABOING
KABOING
KABOING
PURRR
GARFIELD
BAT
BAT
ROWR!
FFFT!
SCRATCH!
SCRATCH!
SCRATCH!
2-25
THAT SHOULD
HOLD YOU CAT FANS
FOR A WHILE
JIM DAVIS

I think that many pet owners harbor the suspicion that their pets think and feel in human terms. This strip throws more fuel on the fire.

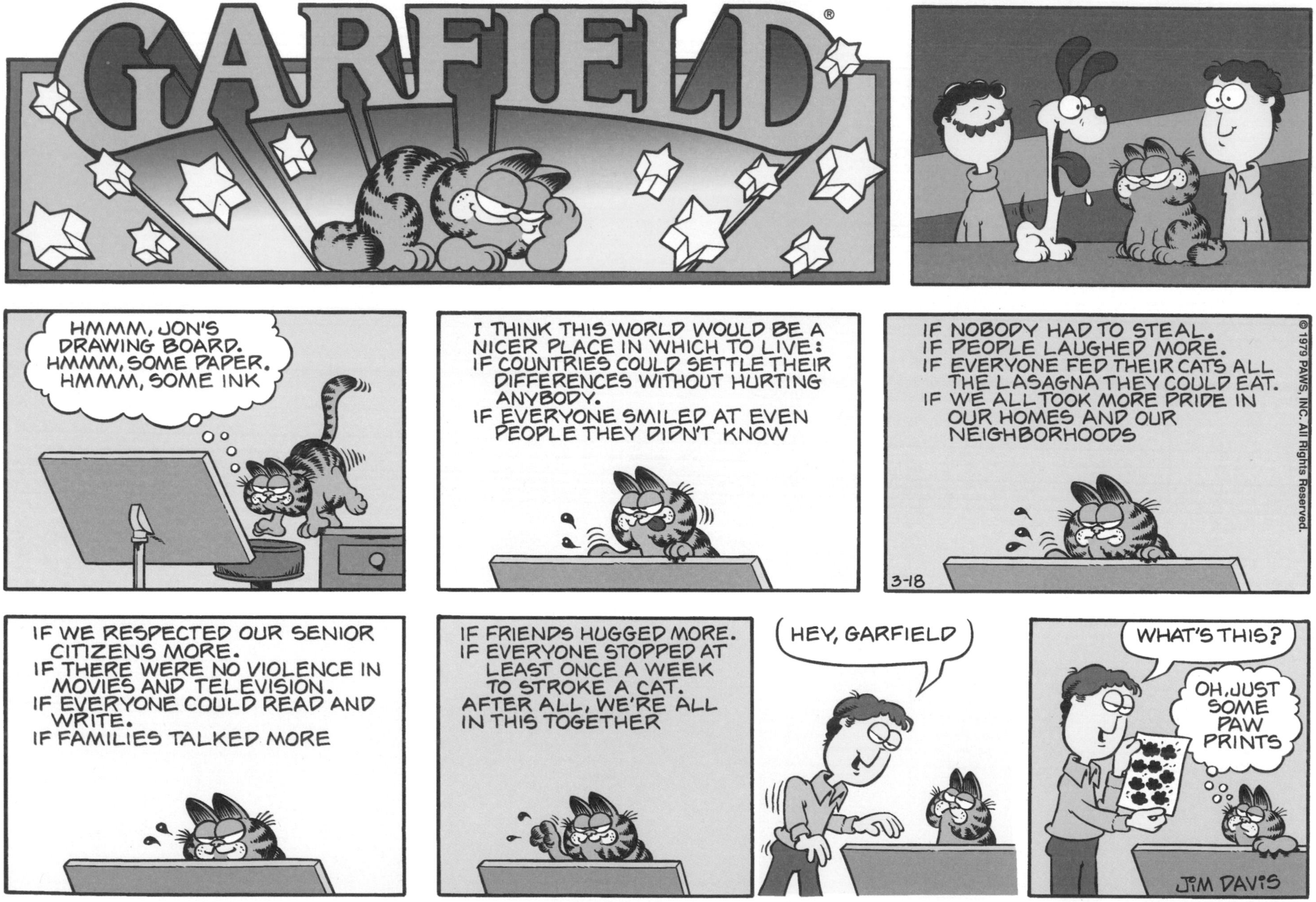
GARFIELD®
HMMM, JON'S DRAWING BOARD. HMMM, SOME PAPER. HMMM, SOME INK
I THINK THIS WORLD WOULD BE A NICER PLACE IN WHICH TO LIVE: IF COUNTRIES COULD SETTLE THEIR DIFFERENCES WITHOUT HURTING ANYBODY. IF EVERYONE SMILED AT EVEN PEOPLE THEY DIDN'T KNOW
IF NOBODY HAD TO STEAL. IF PEOPLE LAUGHED MORE. IF EVERYONE FED THEIR CATS ALL THE LASAGNA THEY COULD EAT. IF WE ALL TOOK MORE PRIDE IN OUR HOMES AND OUR NEIGHBORHOODS
© 1979 PAWS, INC. All Rights Reserved.
3-18
IF WE RESPECTED OUR SENIOR CITIZENS MORE. IF THERE WERE NO VIOLENCE IN MOVIES AND TELEVISION. IF EVERYONE COULD READ AND WRITE. IF FAMILIES TALKED MORE
IF FRIENDS HUGGED MORE. IF EVERYONE STOPPED AT LEAST ONCE A WEEK TO STROKE A CAT. AFTER ALL, WE'RE ALL IN THIS TOGETHER
HEY, GARFIELD
WHAT'S THIS?
OH, JUST SOME PAW PRINTS
JIM DAVIS

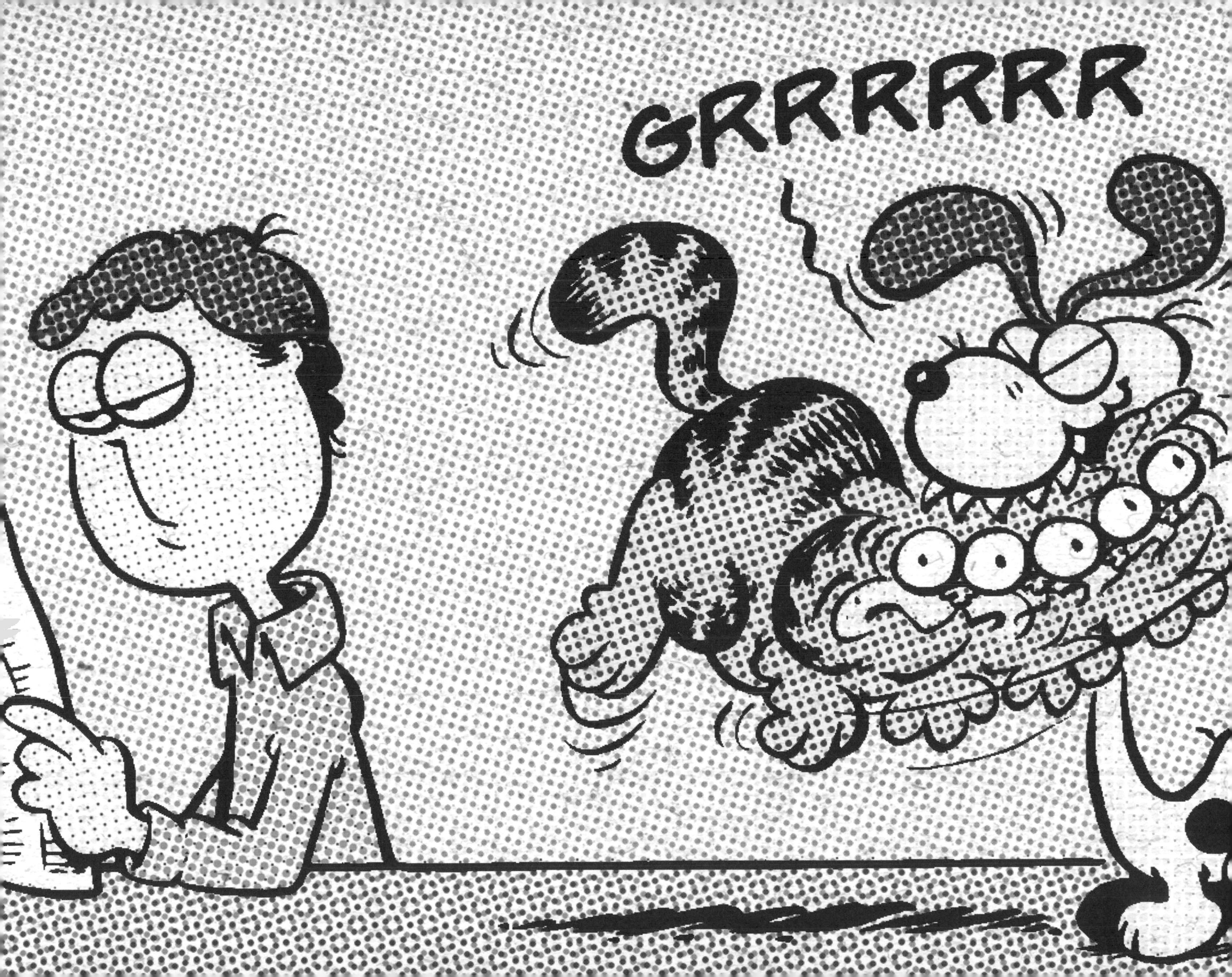
GRRRRRRR

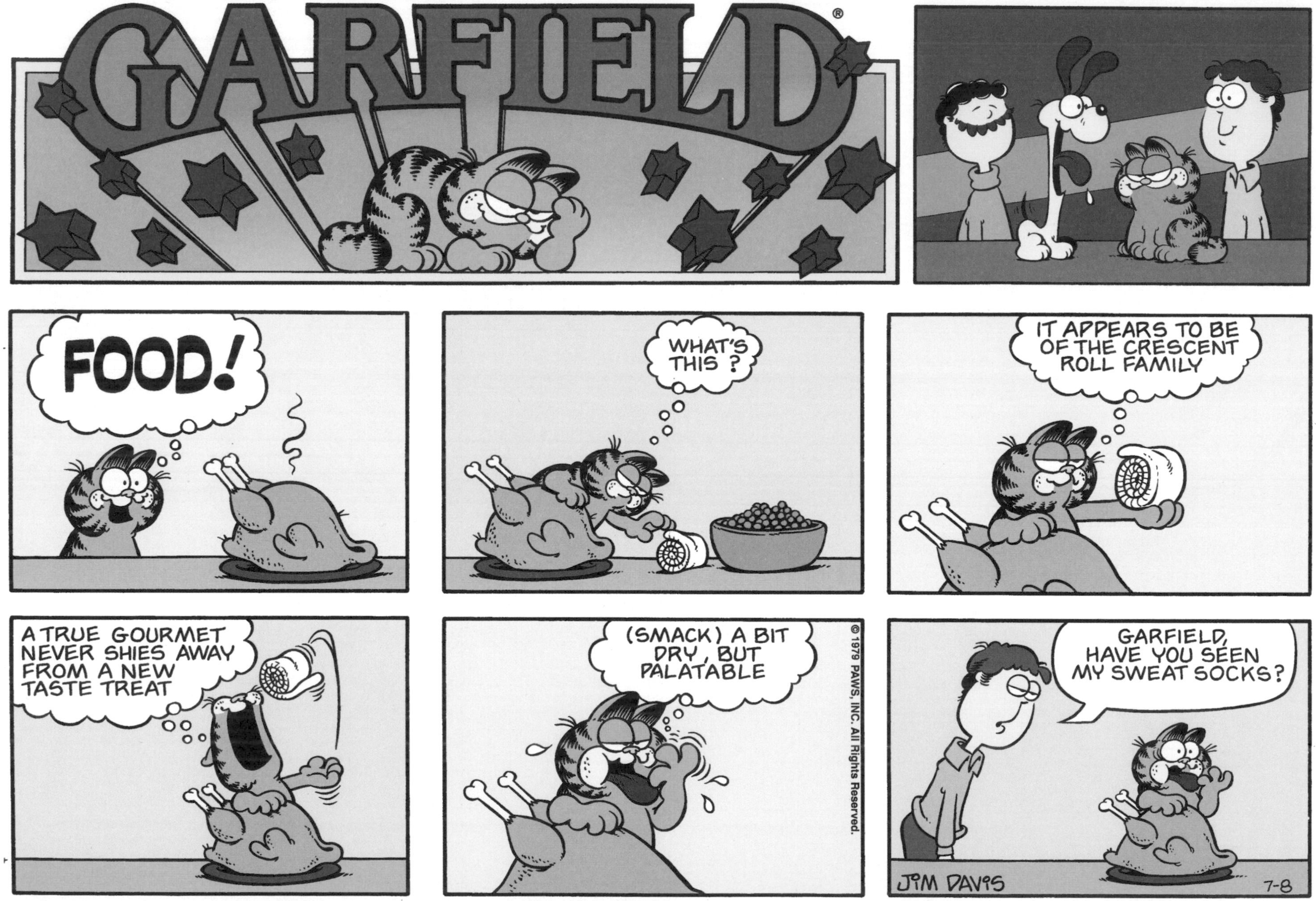
GARFIELD®
FOOD!
WHAT'S THIS ?
IT APPEARS TO BE OF THE CRESCENT ROLL FAMILY
A TRUE GOURMET NEVER SHIES AWAY FROM A NEW TASTE TREAT
(SMACK) A BIT DRY, BUT PALATABLE
© 1979 PAWS, INC. All Rights Reserved.
GARFIELD, HAVE YOU SEEN MY SWEAT SOCKS?
JIM DAVIS
7-8

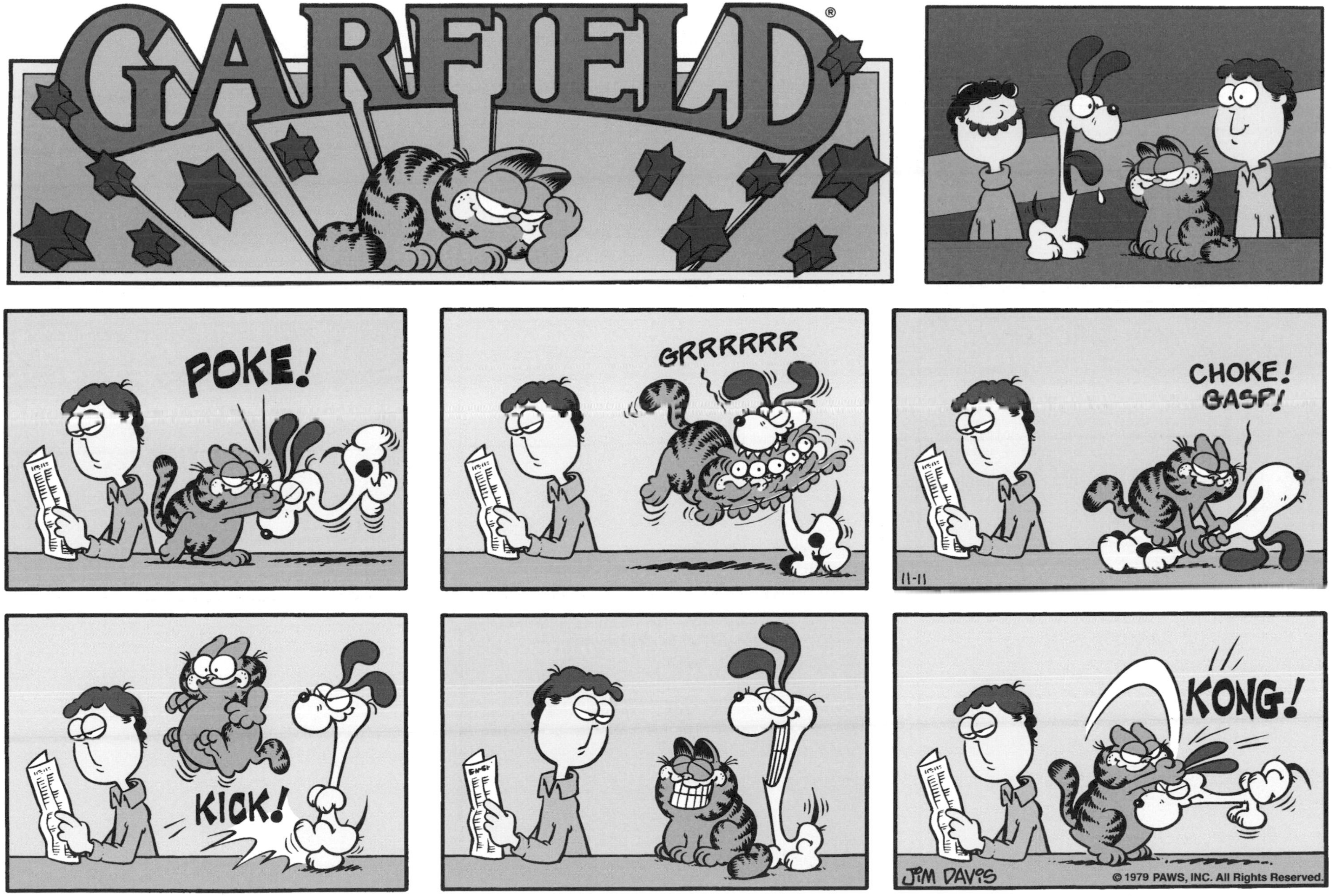
GARFIELD®
POKE!
GRRRRRR
CHOKE! GASP!
11-11
KICK!
KONG!
JIM DAVIS
© 1979 PAWS, INC. All Rights Reserved.

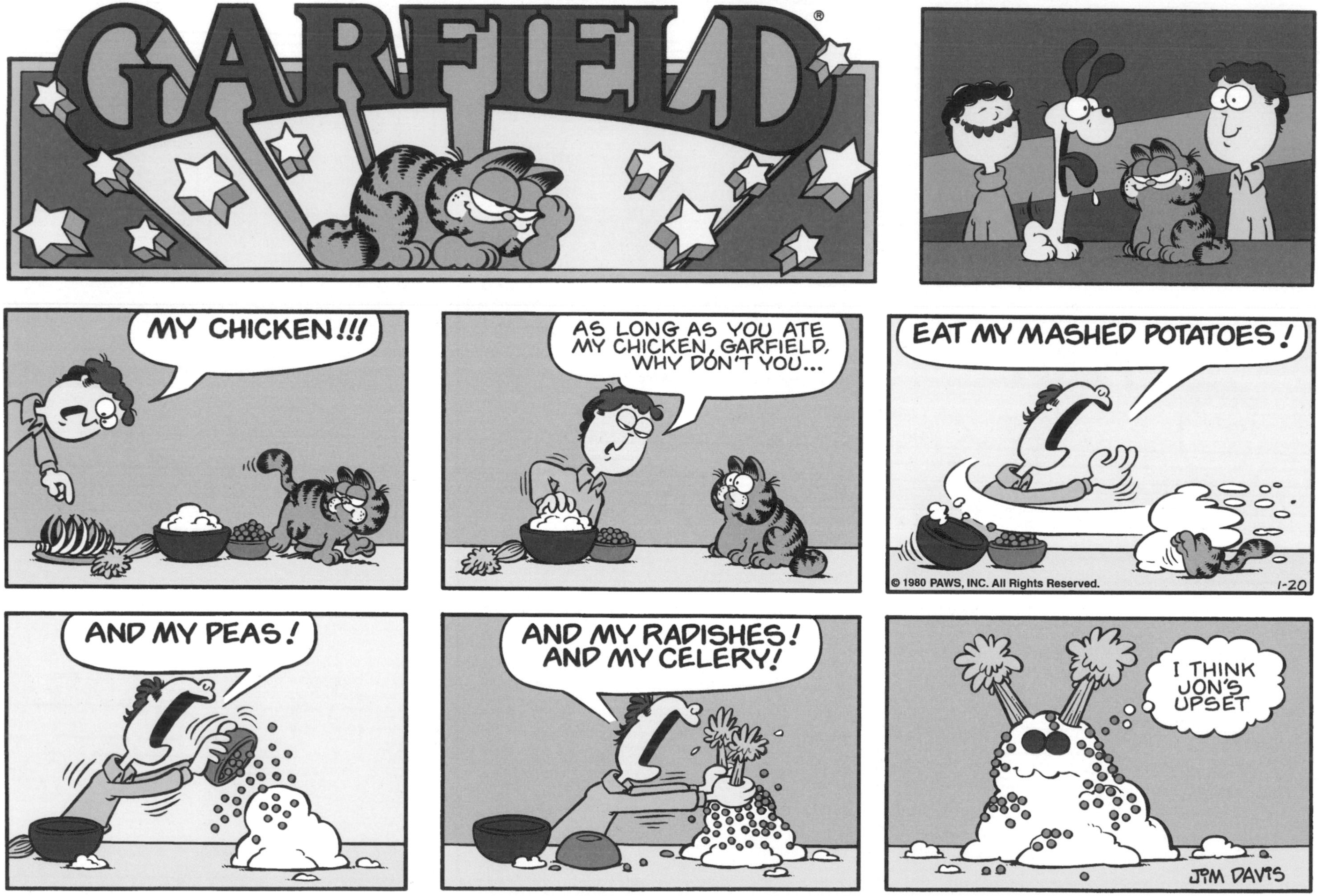
GARFIELD®
MY CHICKEN!!!
AS LONG AS YOU ATE MY CHICKEN, GARFIELD, WHY DON'T YOU...
EAT MY MASHED POTATOES!
© 1980 PAWS, INC. All Rights Reserved.
1-20
AND MY PEAS!
AND MY RADISHES! AND MY CELERY!
I THINK JON'S UPSET
JIM DAVIS

I love punch lines that come out of left field. This is a silly gag that pokes fun at itself.

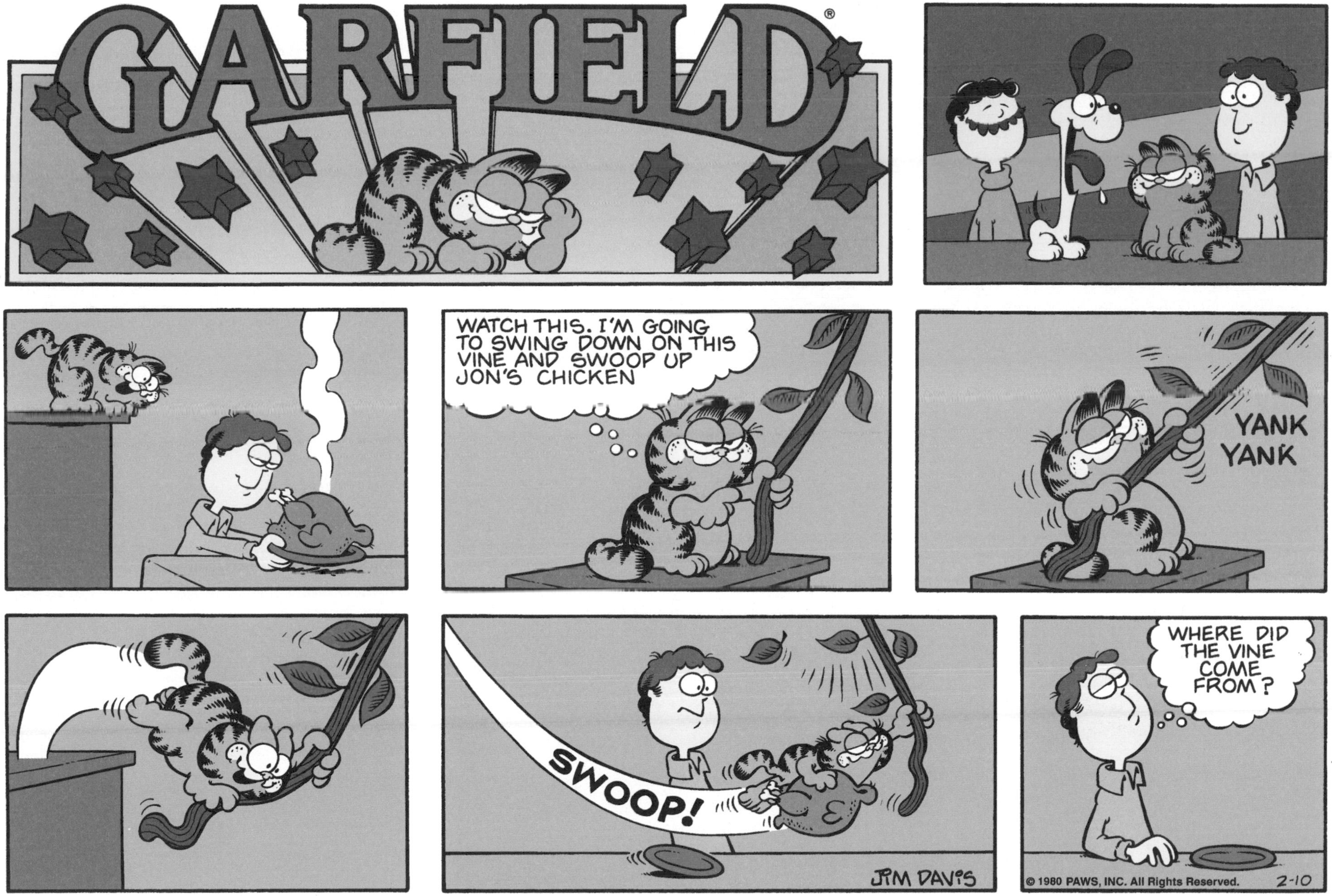

GARFIELD®
WATCH THIS. I'M GOING TO SWING DOWN ON THIS VINE AND SWOOP UP JON'S CHICKEN
YANK YANK
SWOOP!
JIM DAVIS
WHERE DID THE VINE COME FROM?
© 1980 PAWS, INC. All Rights Reserved.
2-10

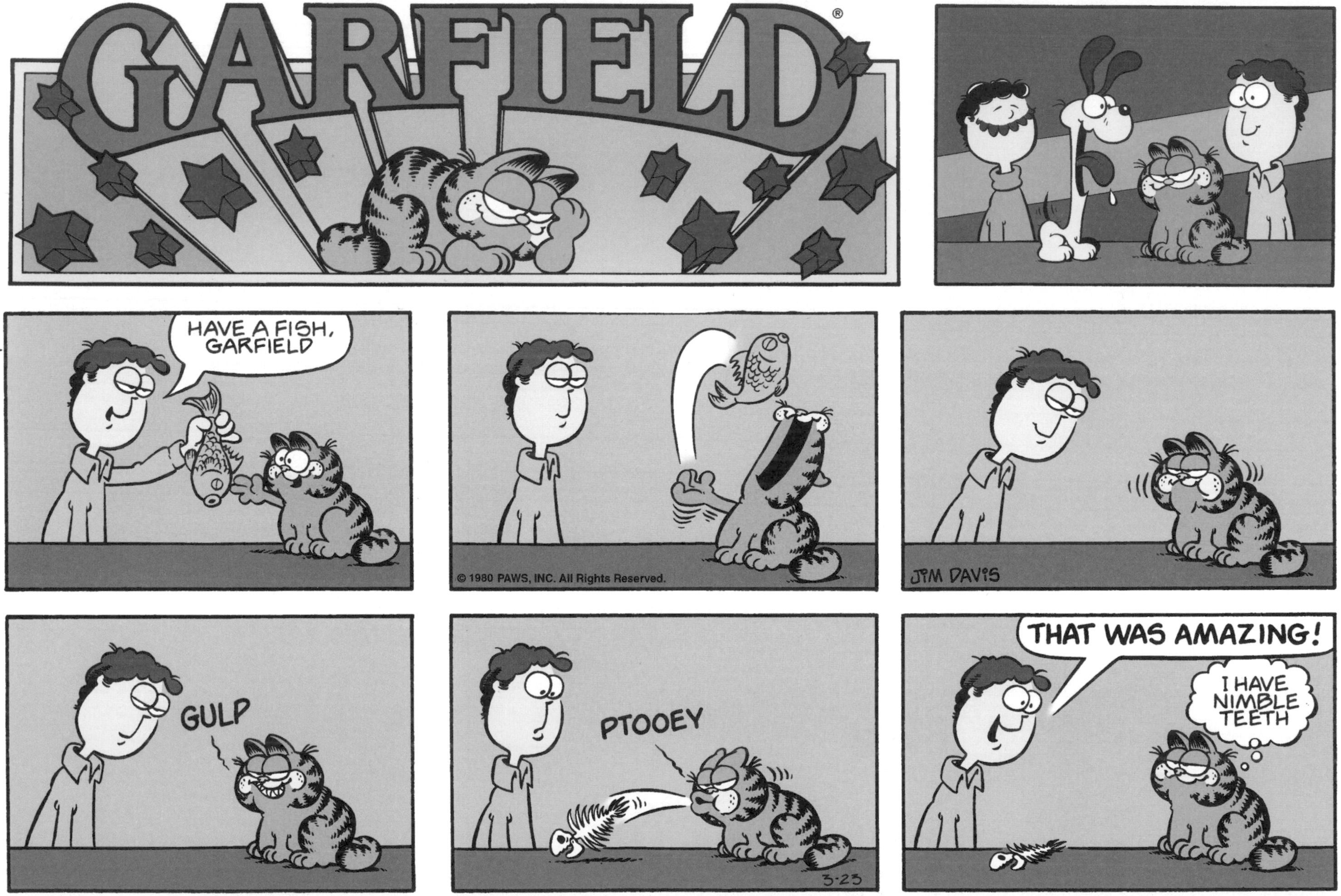
GARFIELD®
HAVE A FISH, GARFIELD
© 1980 PAWS, INC. All Rights Reserved.
JIM DAVIS
GULP
PTOOEY
3-23
THAT WAS AMAZING!
I HAVE NIMBLE TEETH

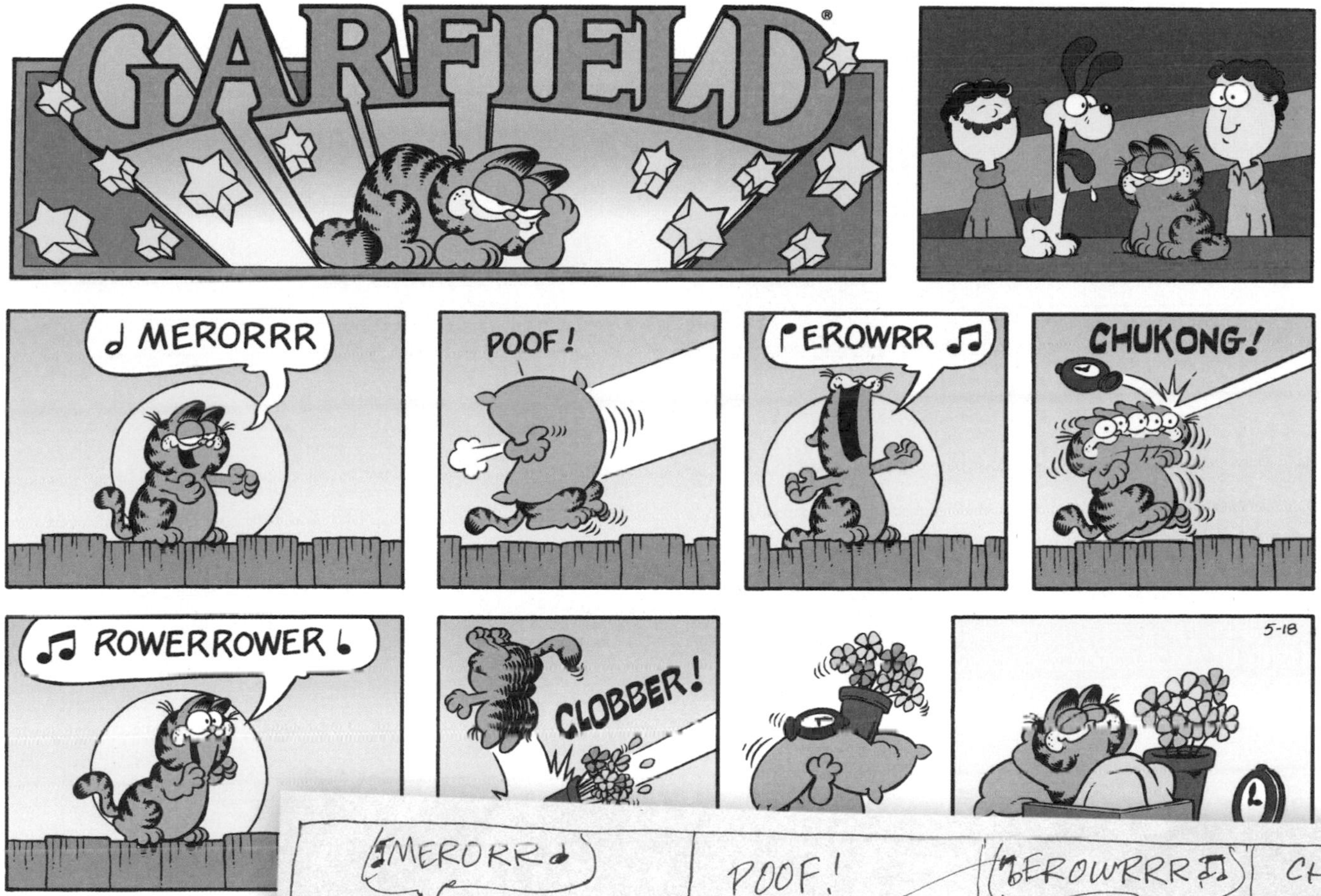
GARFIELD
MERORRR
POOF!
EROWRR
CHUKONG!
ROWERROWER
CLOBBER!
5-18

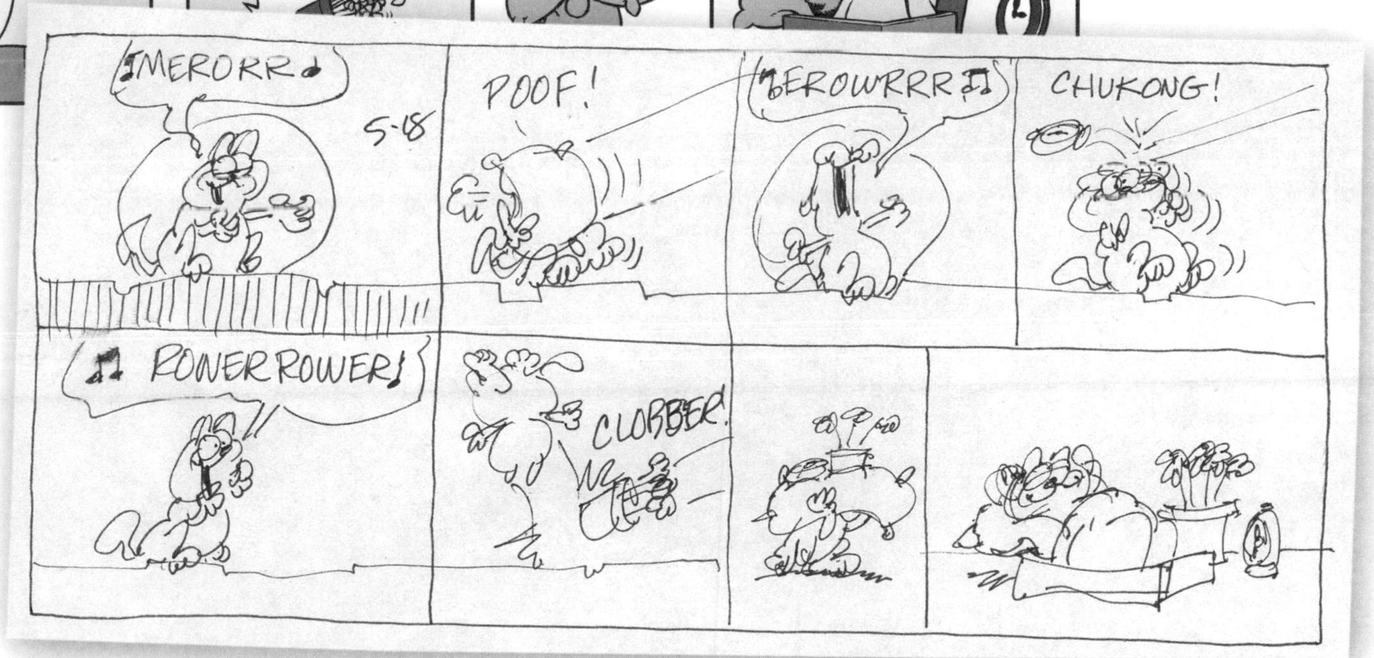
MERORR
5-18
POOF!
EROWRRR
CHUKONG!
ROWERROWER
CLOBBER!

original rough

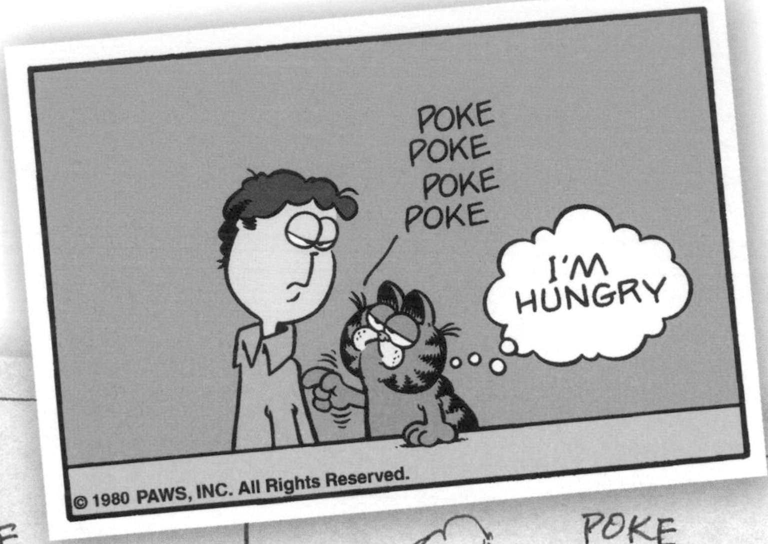
POKE
POKE
POKE
POKE
I'M HUNGRY
© 1980 PAWS, INC. All Rights Reserved.

This strip is historic in that it's the only time that odie has ever spoken!

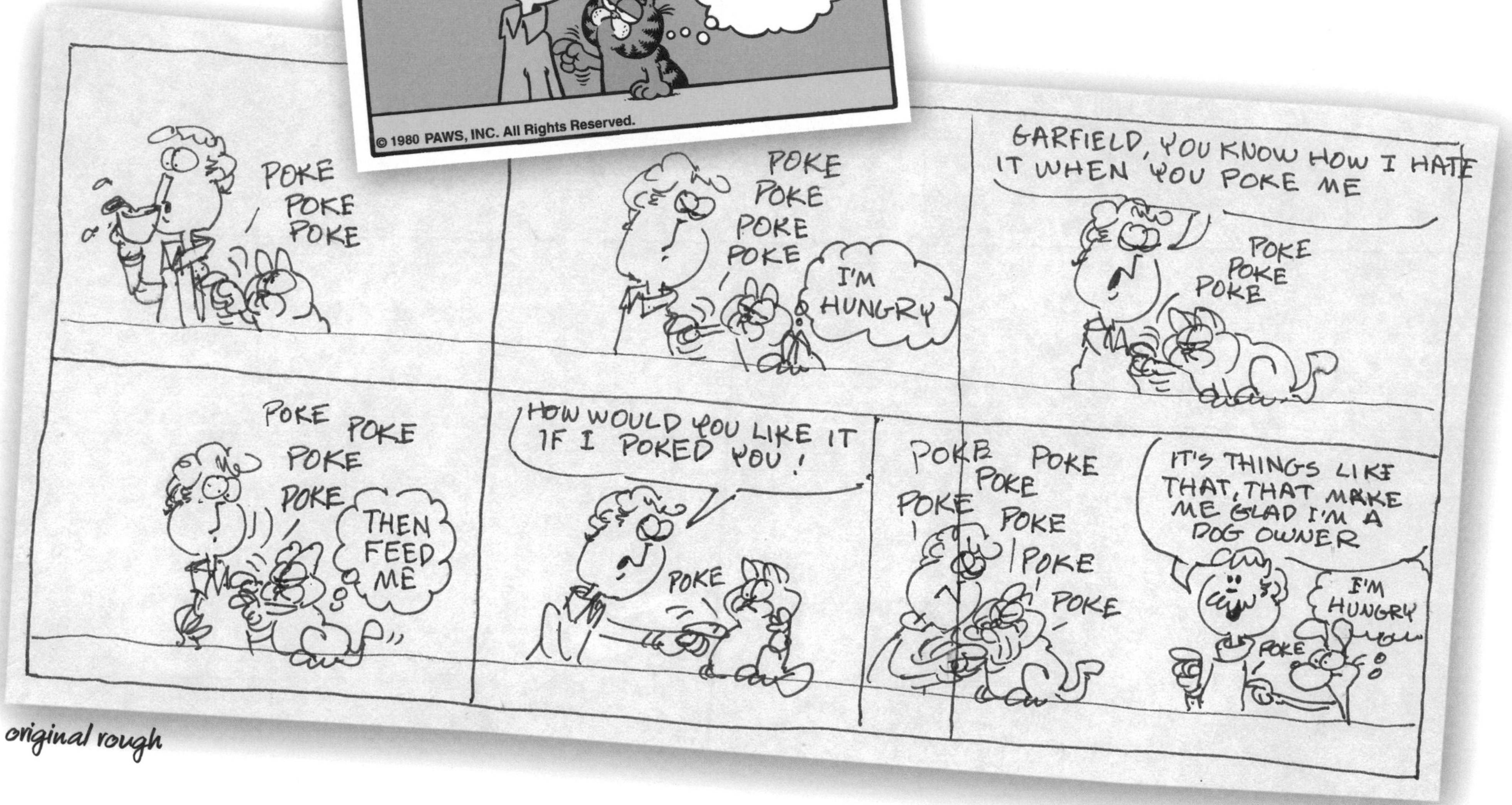
POKE
POKE
POKE
POKE
POKE
POKE
POKE
I'M HUNGRY
GARFIELD, YOU KNOW HOW I HATE IT WHEN YOU POKE ME
POKE
POKE
POKE
POKE
POKE
POKE
POKE
THEN FEED ME
HOW WOULD YOU LIKE IT IF I POKED YOU!
POKE
POKE
POKE
POKE
POKE
POKE
POKE
POKE
IT'S THINGS LIKE THAT, THAT MAKE ME GLAD I'M A DOG OWNER
I'M HUNGRY
POKE

original rough

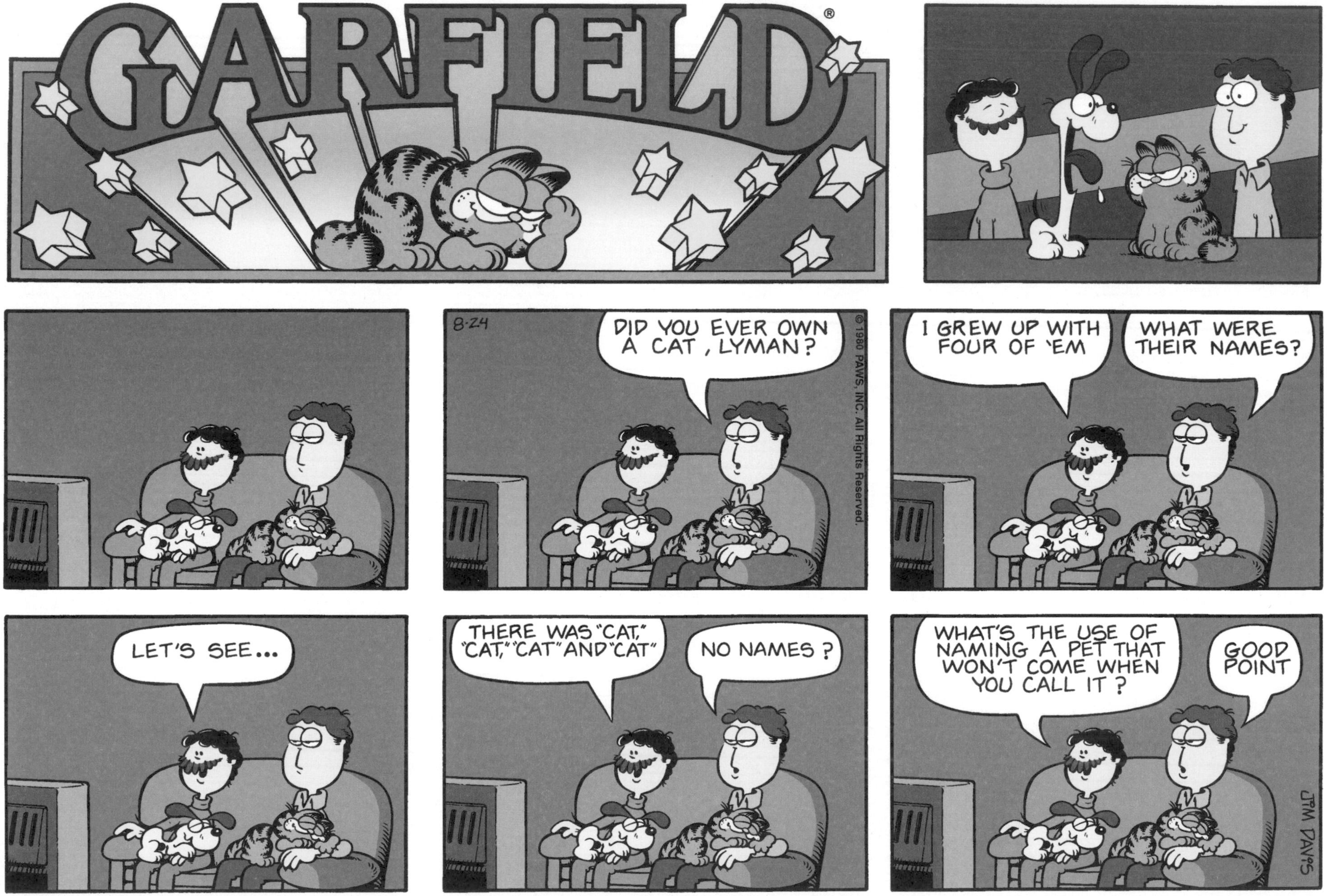
GARFIELD®
8-24
© 1980 PAWS, INC. All Rights Reserved.
DID YOU EVER OWN A CAT, LYMAN?
I GREW UP WITH FOUR OF 'EM
WHAT WERE THEIR NAMES?
LET'S SEE...
THERE WAS "CAT," "CAT," "CAT" AND "CAT"
NO NAMES?
WHAT'S THE USE OF NAMING A PET THAT WON'T COME WHEN YOU CALL IT?
GOOD POINT
JIM DAVIS

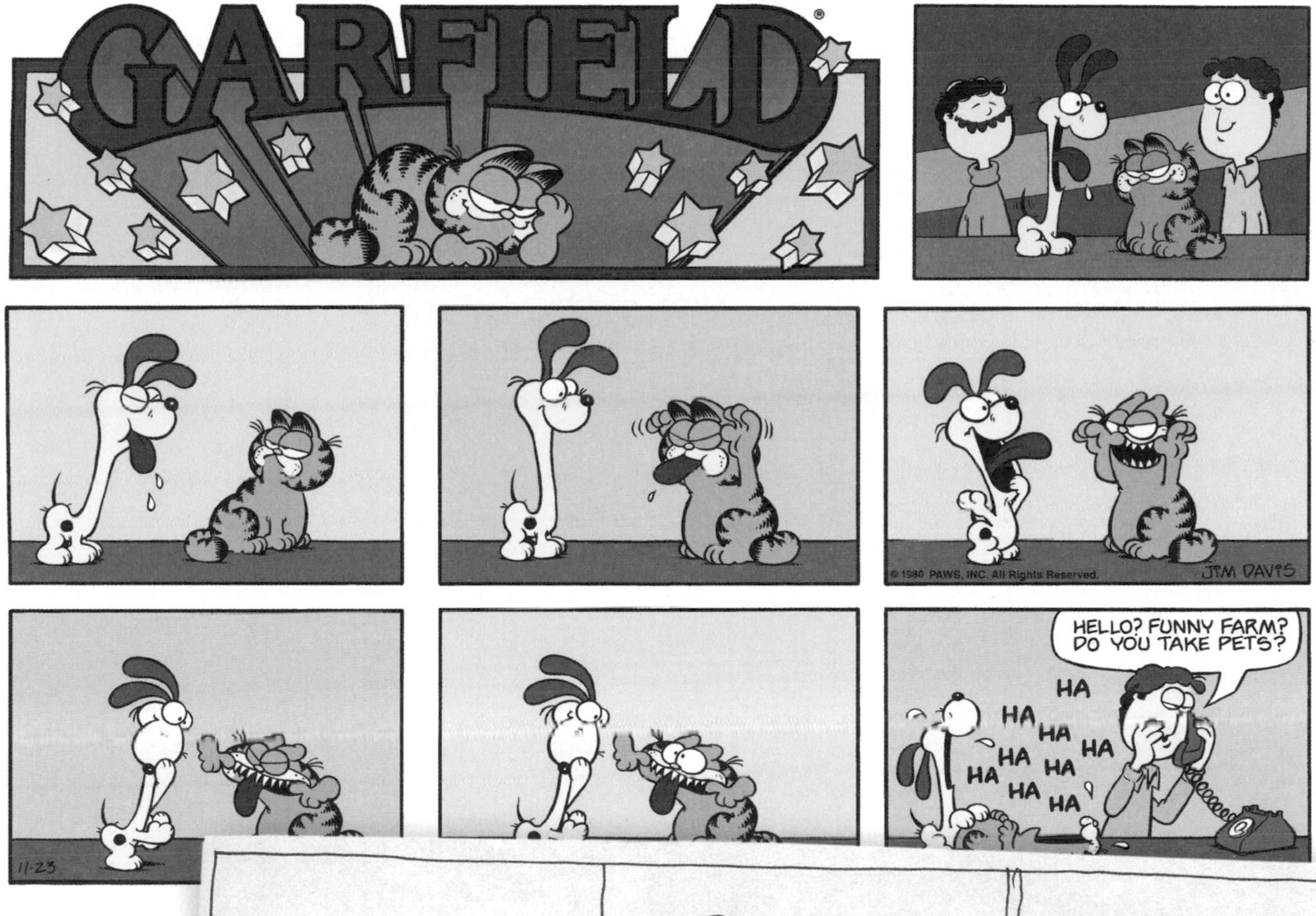
GARFIELD
© 1980 PAWS, INC. All Rights Reserved.
JIM DAVIS
11-23
HELLO? FUNNY FARM? DO YOU TAKE PETS?
HA HA HA HA HA HA HA HA HA

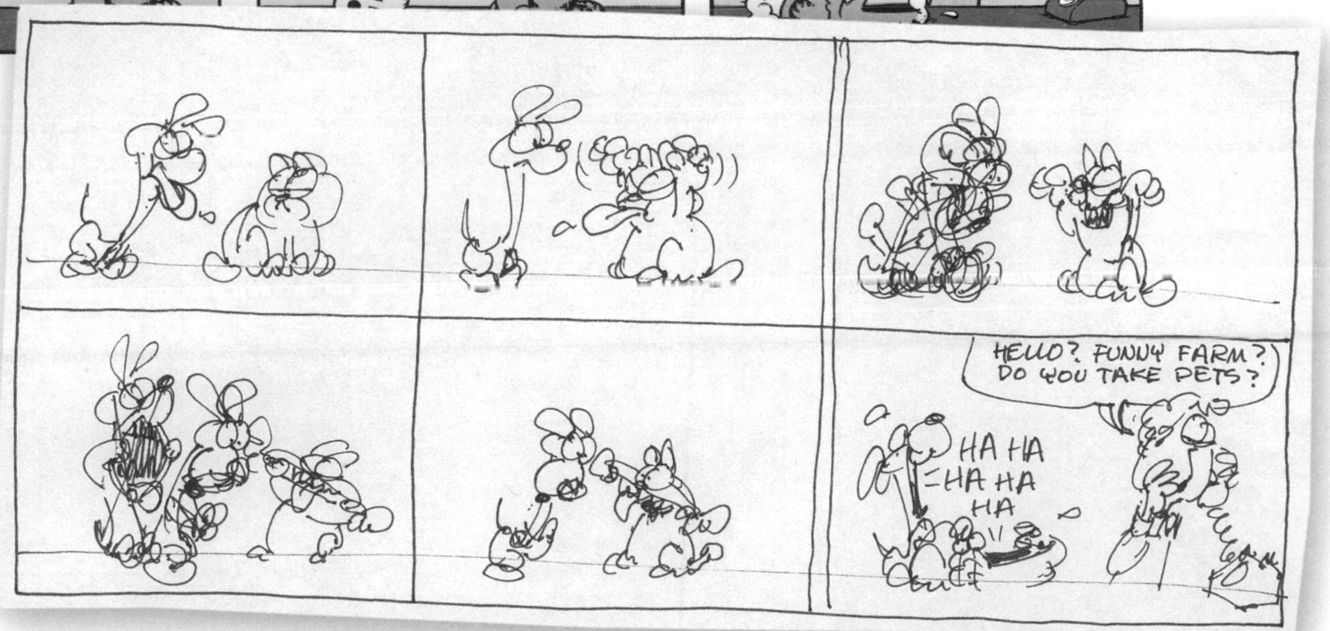
HELLO? FUNNY FARM? DO YOU TAKE PETS?
HA HA
HA HA
HA

original rough

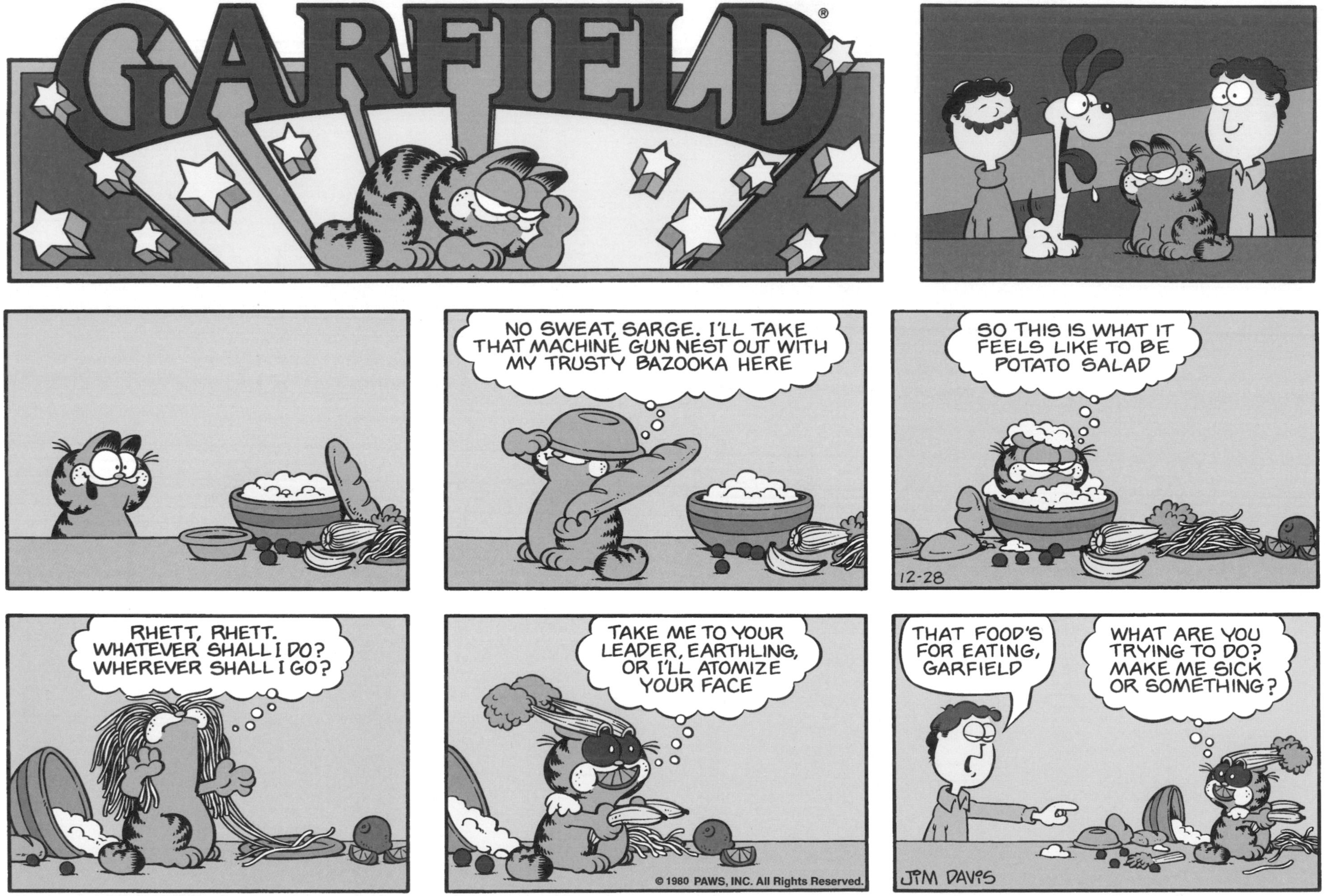
GARFIELD®
NO SWEAT, SARGE. I'LL TAKE THAT MACHINE GUN NEST OUT WITH MY TRUSTY BAZOOKA HERE
SO THIS IS WHAT IT FEELS LIKE TO BE POTATO SALAD
12-28
RHETT, RHETT. WHATEVER SHALL I DO? WHEREVER SHALL I GO?
TAKE ME TO YOUR LEADER, EARTHLING, OR I'LL ATOMIZE YOUR FACE
© 1980 PAWS, INC. All Rights Reserved.
THAT FOOD'S FOR EATING, GARFIELD
WHAT ARE YOU TRYING TO DO? MAKE ME SICK OR SOMETHING?
JIM DAVIS

My son, the one with perfect pitch, was always correcting me when I sang off-pitch, which was . . . always.

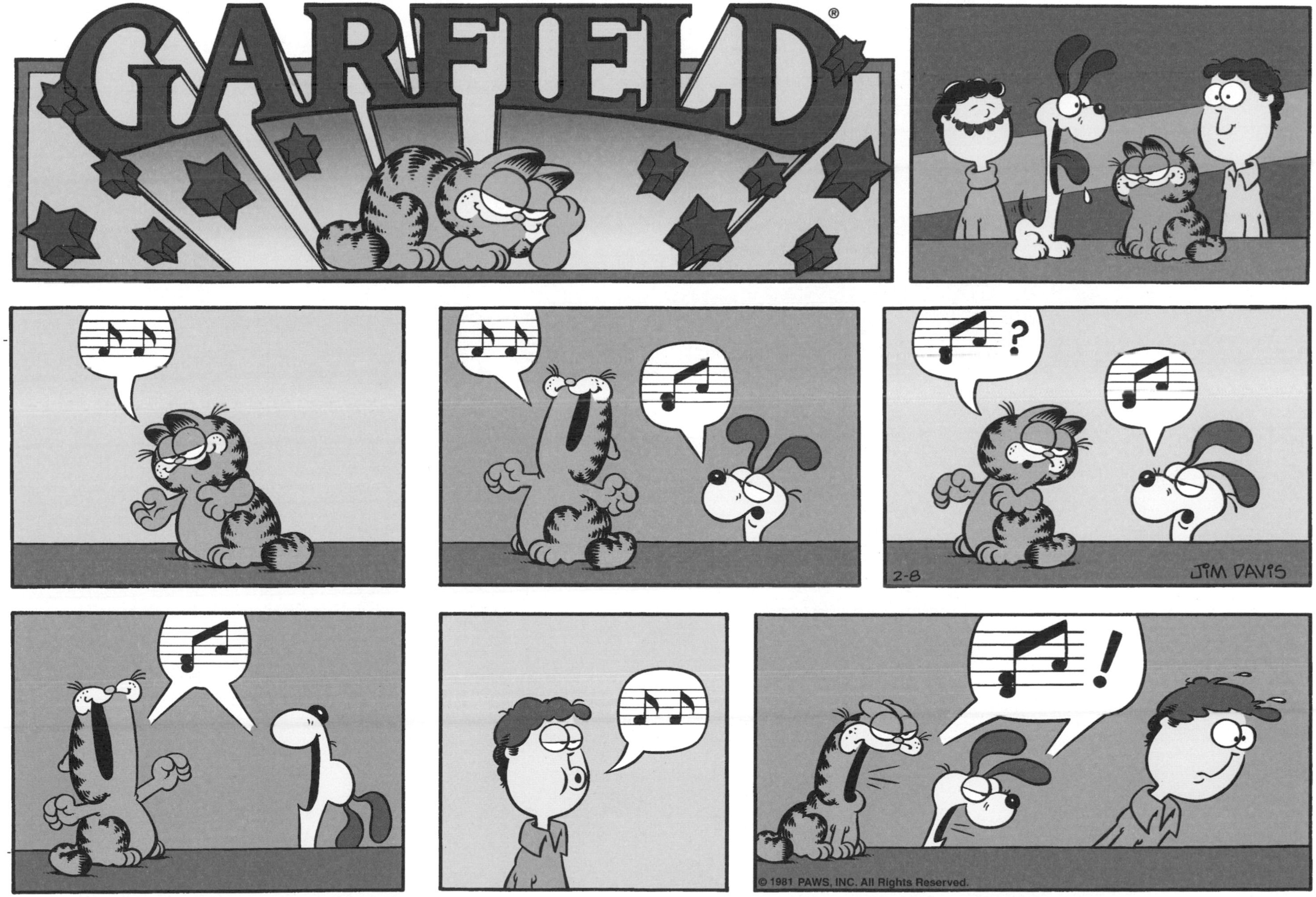
GARFIELD®
?
2-8
JIM DAVIS
!
© 1981 PAWS, INC. All Rights Reserved.

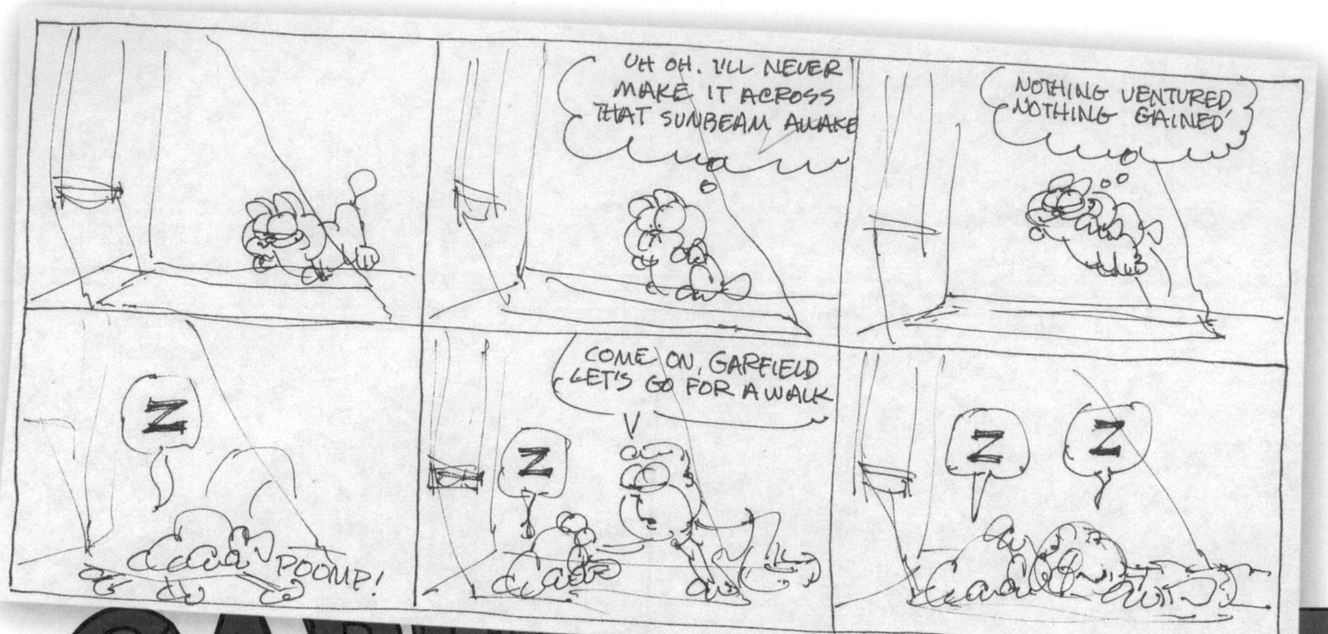
UH OH. I'LL NEVER MAKE IT ACROSS THAT SUNBEAM AWAKE
NOTHING VENTURED NOTHING GAINED
Z
POOMP!
Z
COME ON, GARFIELD LET'S GO FOR A WALK
Z
Z

original rough

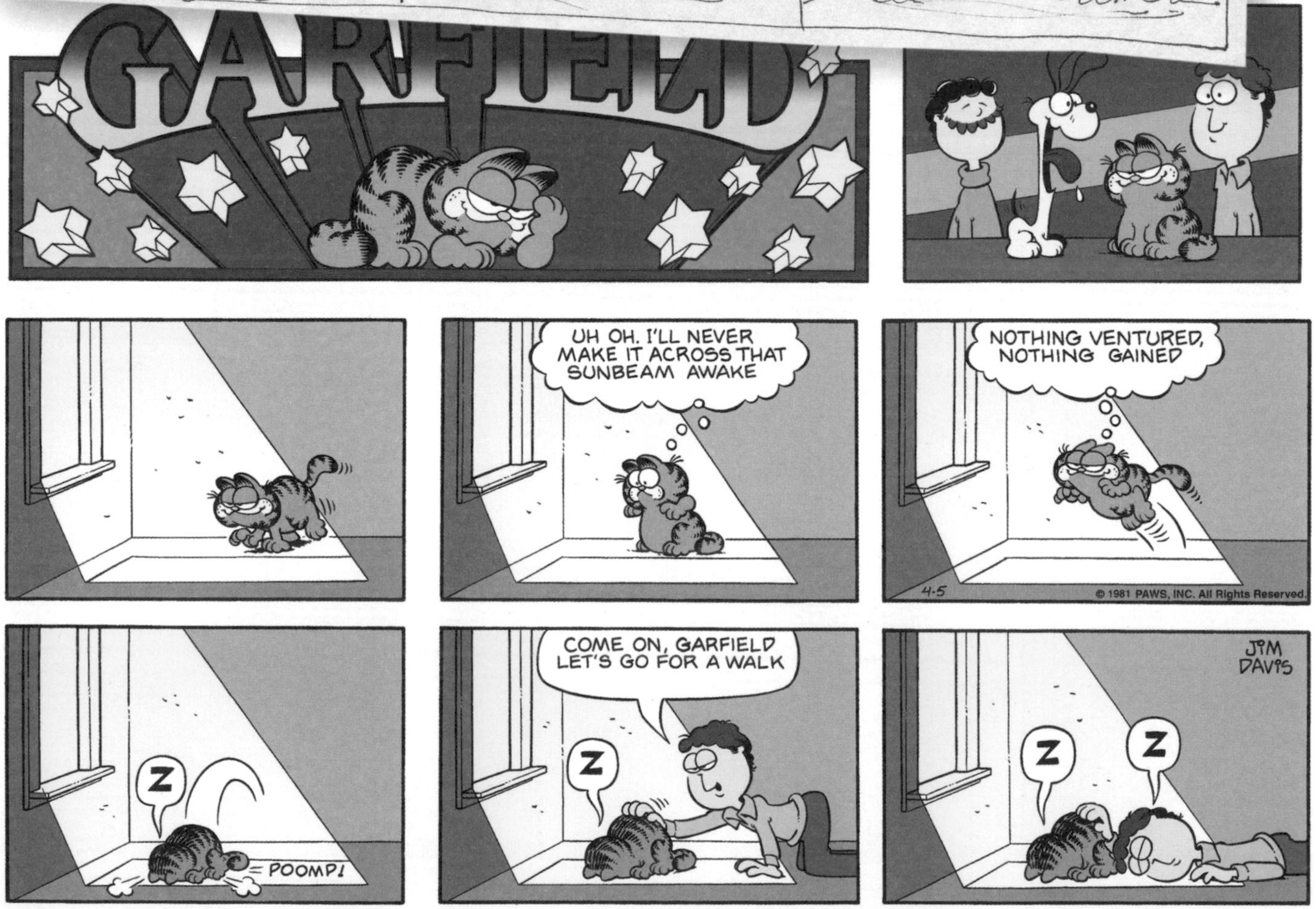
GARFIELD
UH OH. I'LL NEVER MAKE IT ACROSS THAT SUNBEAM AWAKE
NOTHING VENTURED, NOTHING GAINED
4-5
© 1981 PAWS, INC. All Rights Reserved.
Z
POOMP!
COME ON, GARFIELD LET'S GO FOR A WALK
Z
JIM DAVIS
Z
Z

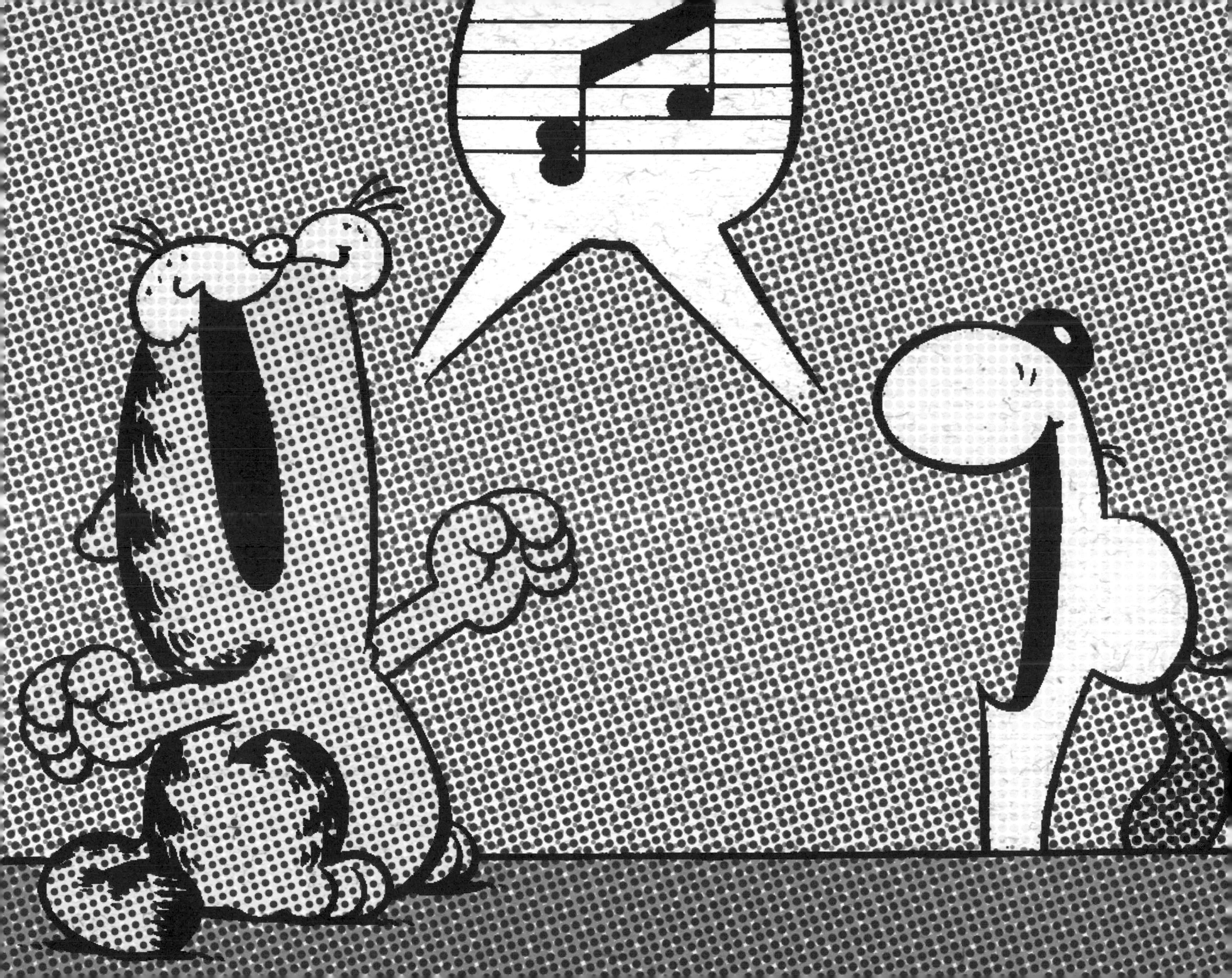

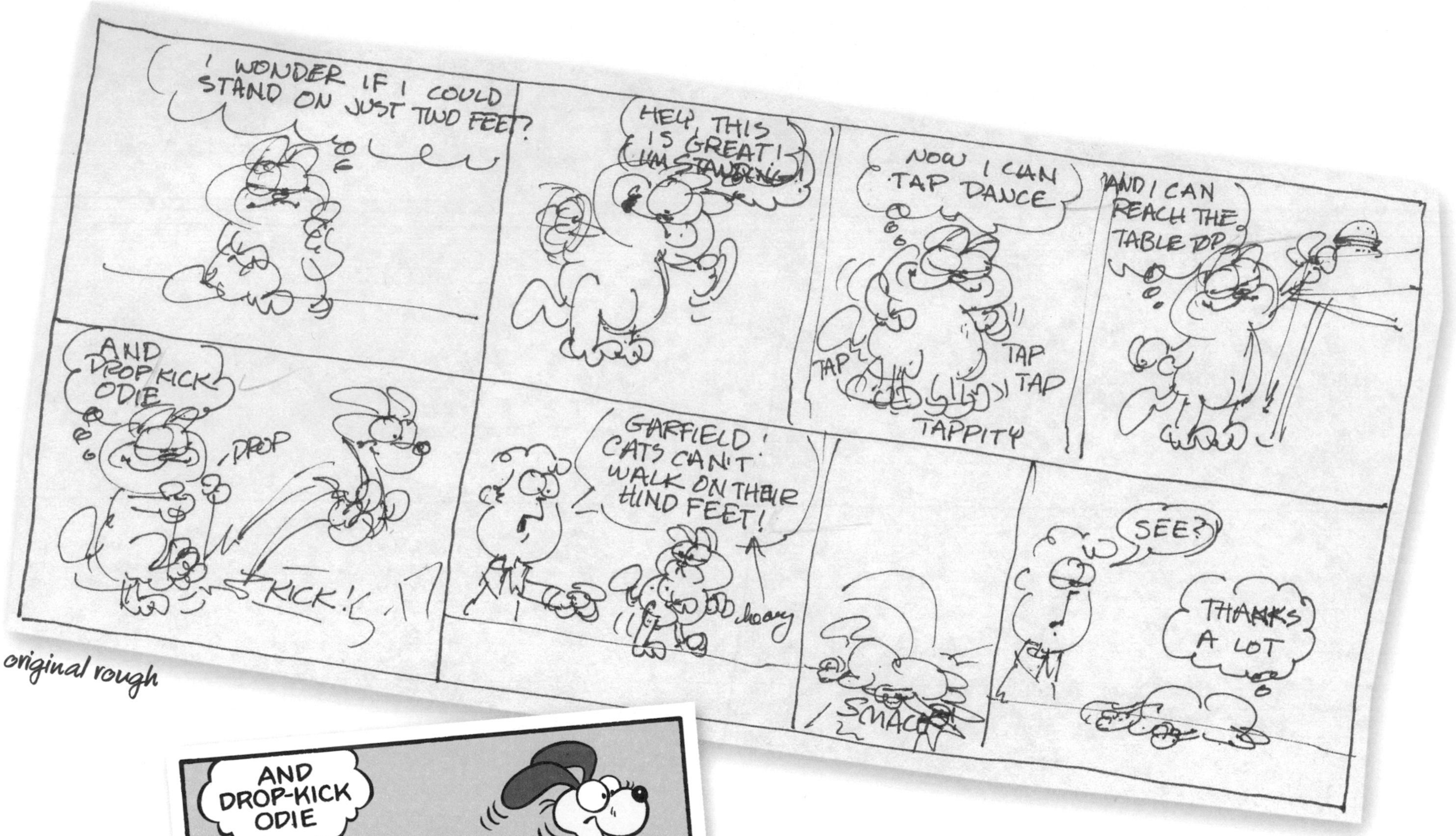
I WONDER IF I COULD STAND ON JUST TWO FEET?
HEY, THIS IS GREAT!
NOW I CAN TAP DANCE
TAP
TAP
TAP
TAPPITY
AND I CAN REACH THE TABLE TOP
AND DROP KICK ODIE
DROP
KICK!
GARFIELD! CATS CAN'T WALK ON THEIR HIND FEET!
SMACK
SEE?
THANKS A LOT

original rough

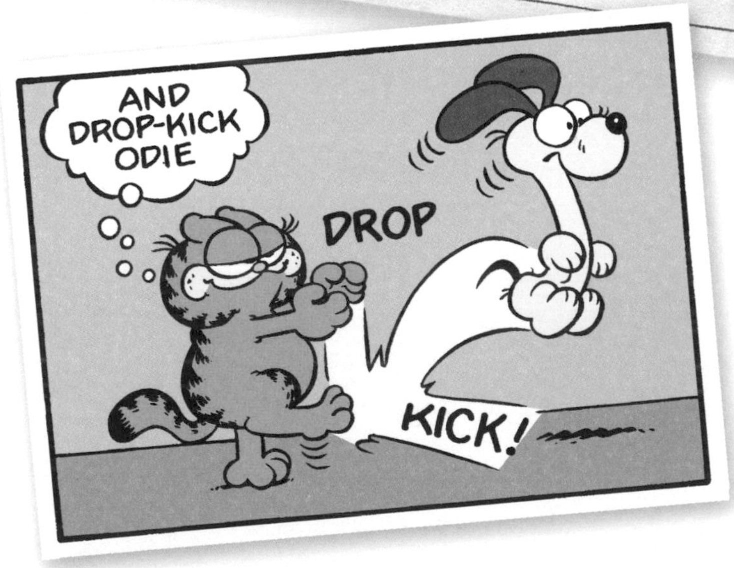
AND DROP-KICK ODIE
DROP
KICK!

This is the first time Garfield stood on two feet. Notice how small his feet are. I later made them bigger at the suggestion of a guy named Charles Schulz.

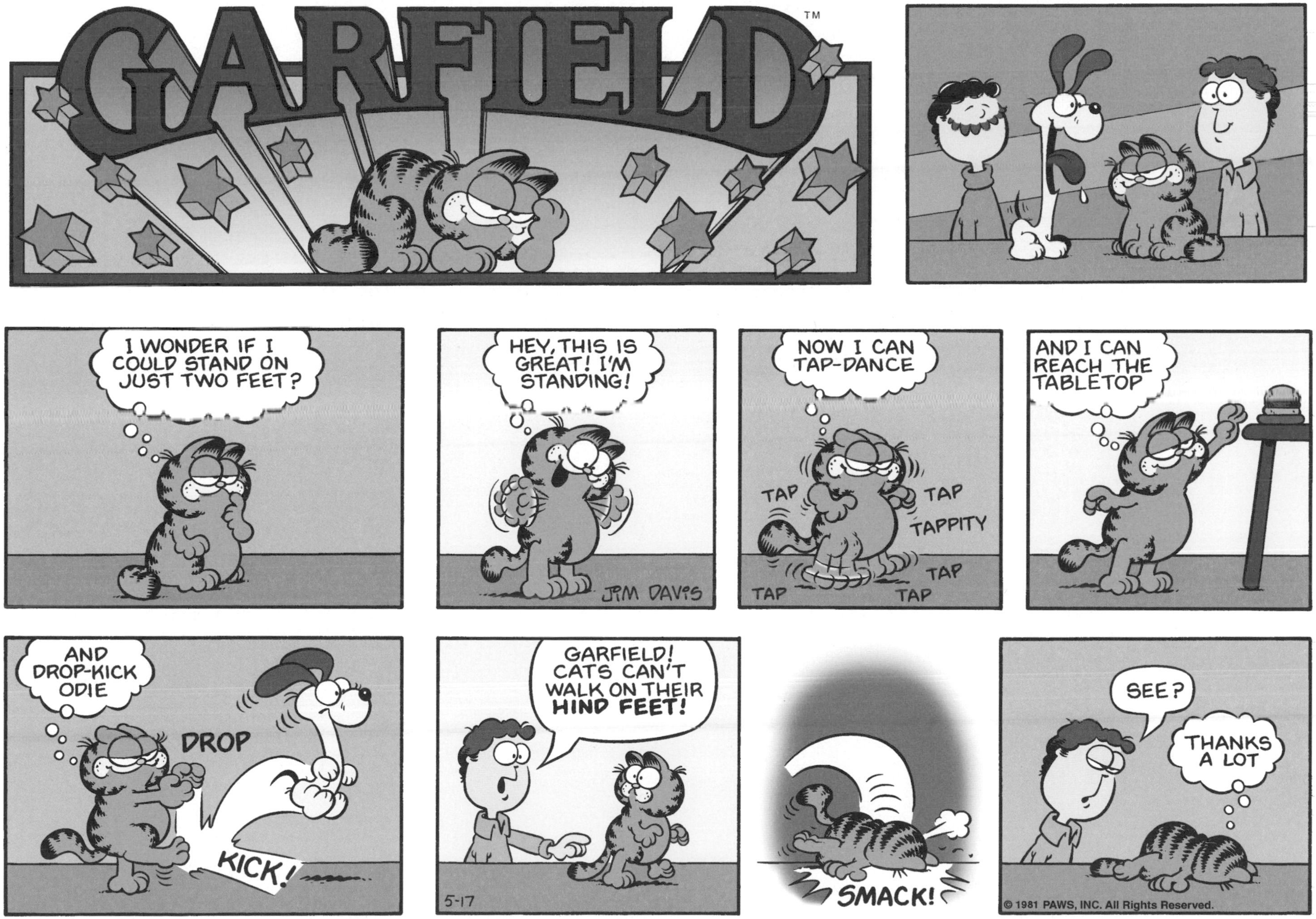
GARFIELD™
I WONDER IF I COULD STAND ON JUST TWO FEET?
HEY, THIS IS GREAT! I'M STANDING!
JIM DAVIS
NOW I CAN TAP-DANCE
TAP
TAP
TAPPITY
TAP
TAP
TAP
AND I CAN REACH THE TABLETOP
AND DROP-KICK ODIE
DROP
KICK!
GARFIELD! CATS CAN'T WALK ON THEIR **HIND FEET!**
5-17
SMACK!
SEE?
THANKS A LOT
© 1981 PAWS, INC. All Rights Reserved.

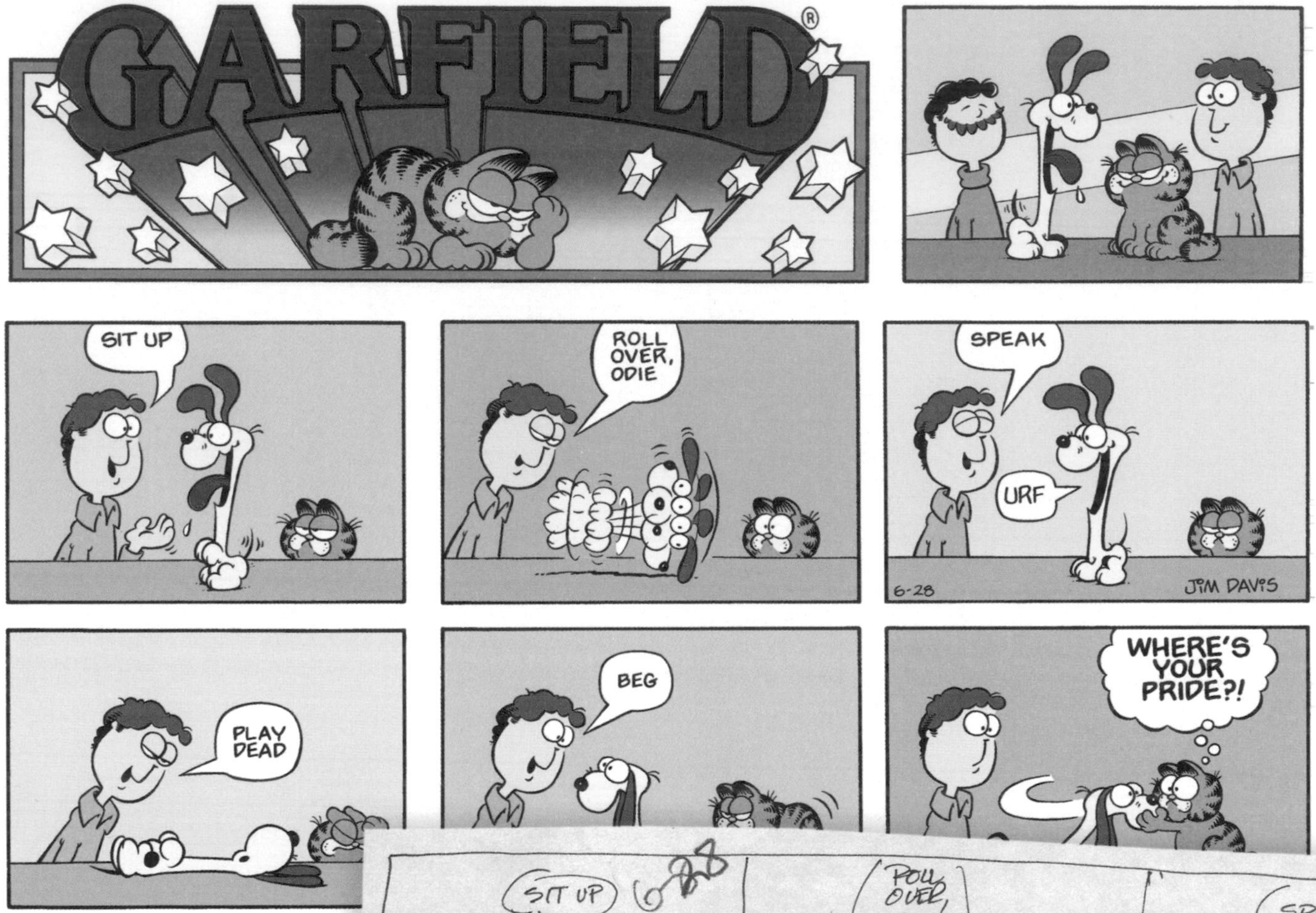
GARFIELD
SIT UP
ROLL OVER, ODIE
SPEAK
URF
6-28
JIM DAVIS
PLAY DEAD
BEG
WHERE'S YOUR PRIDE?!

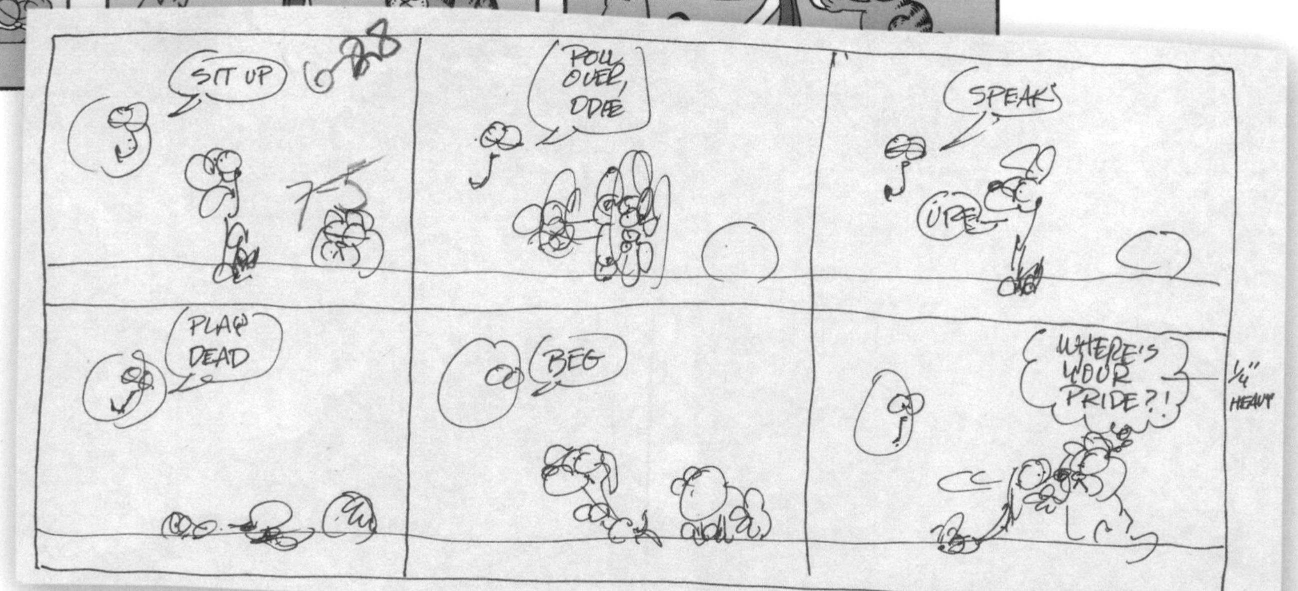
SIT UP
ROLL OVER, ODIE
PLAY DEAD
BEG
WHERE'S YOUR PRIDE?!

original rough

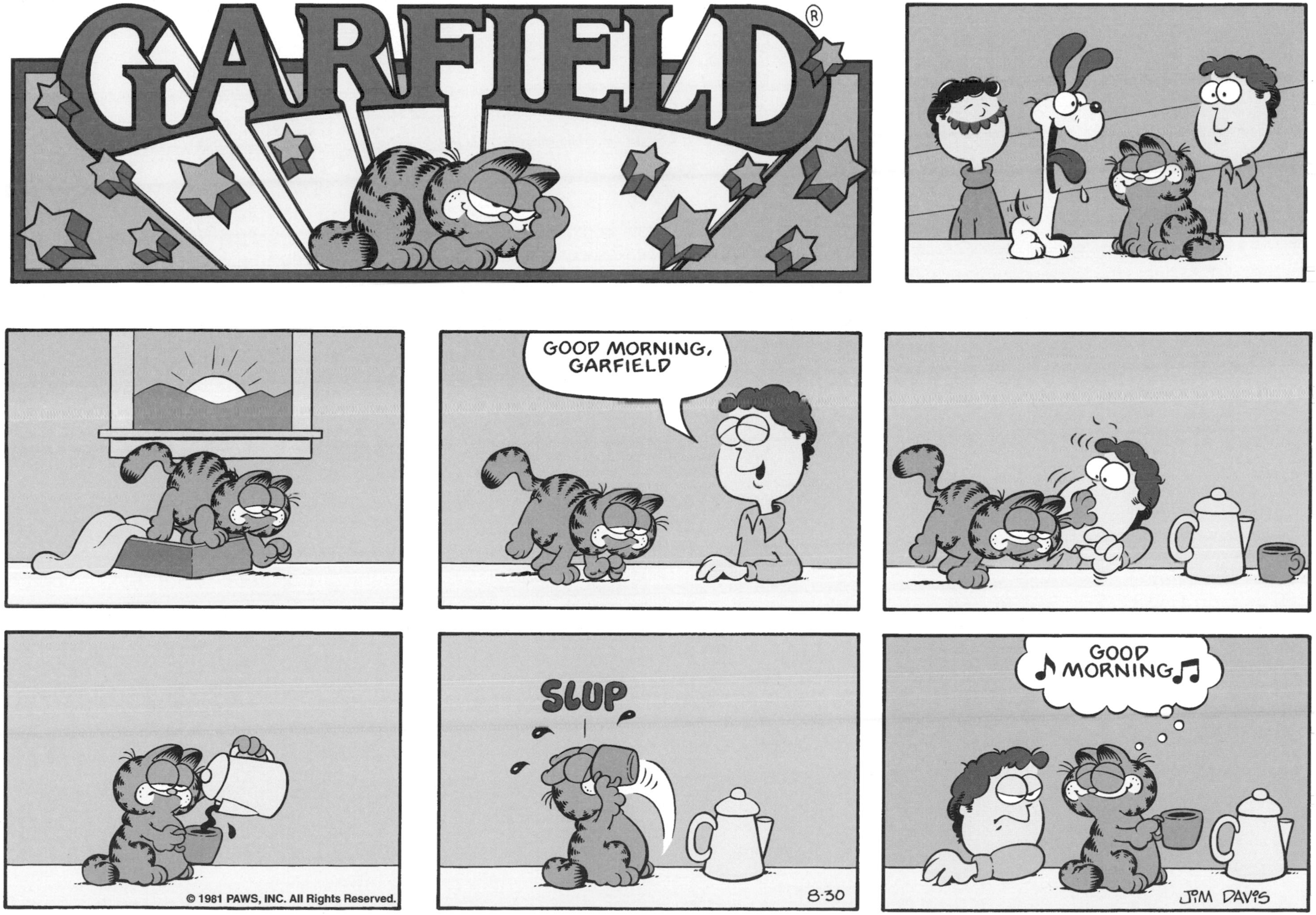
GARFIELD®
GOOD MORNING, GARFIELD
© 1981 PAWS, INC. All Rights Reserved.
SLUP
8·30
GOOD ♪ MORNING ♫
JIM DAVIS

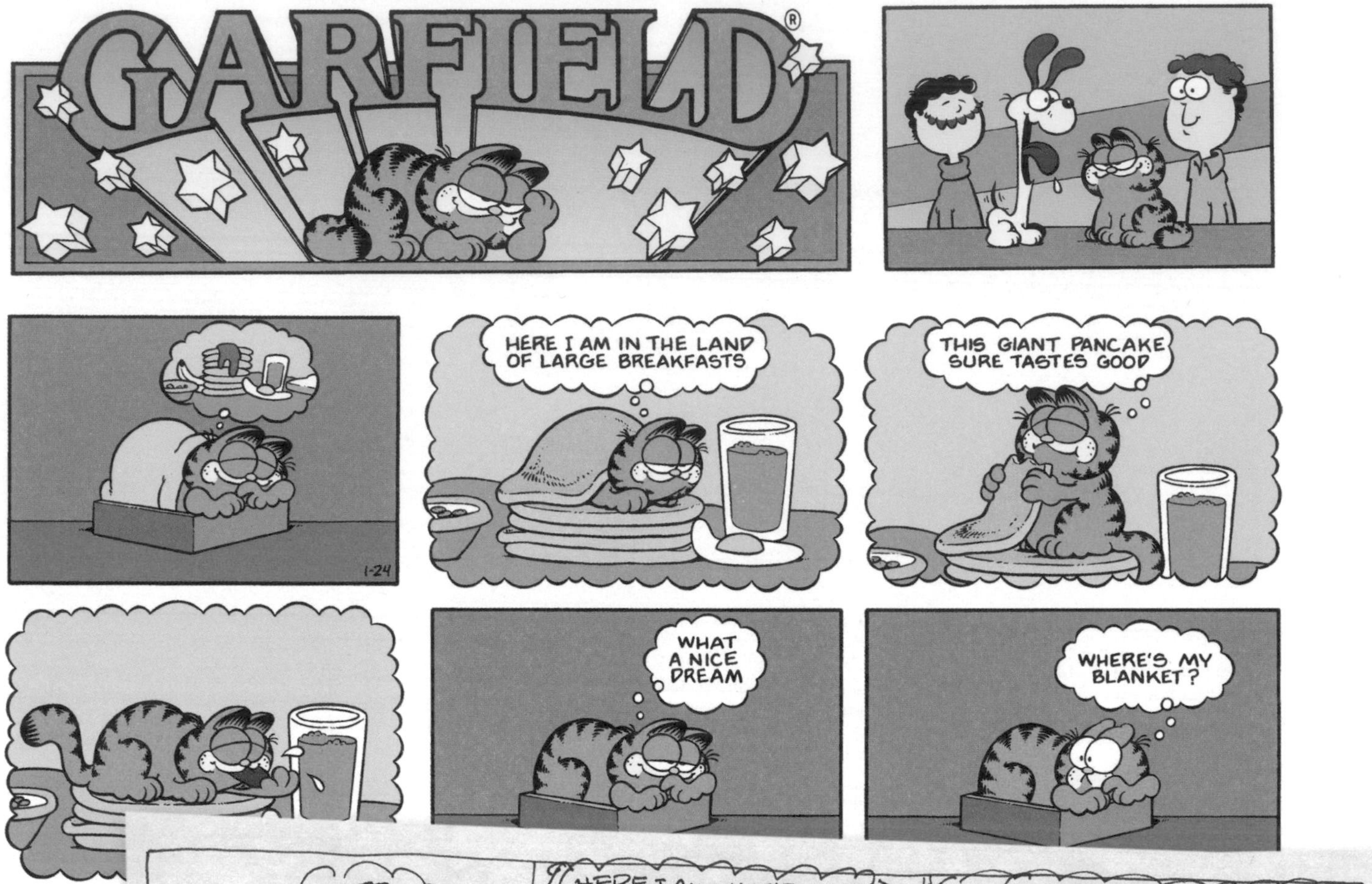
GARFIELD®
HERE I AM IN THE LAND OF LARGE BREAKFASTS
THIS GIANT PANCAKE SURE TASTES GOOD
1-24
WHAT A NICE DREAM
WHERE'S MY BLANKET?

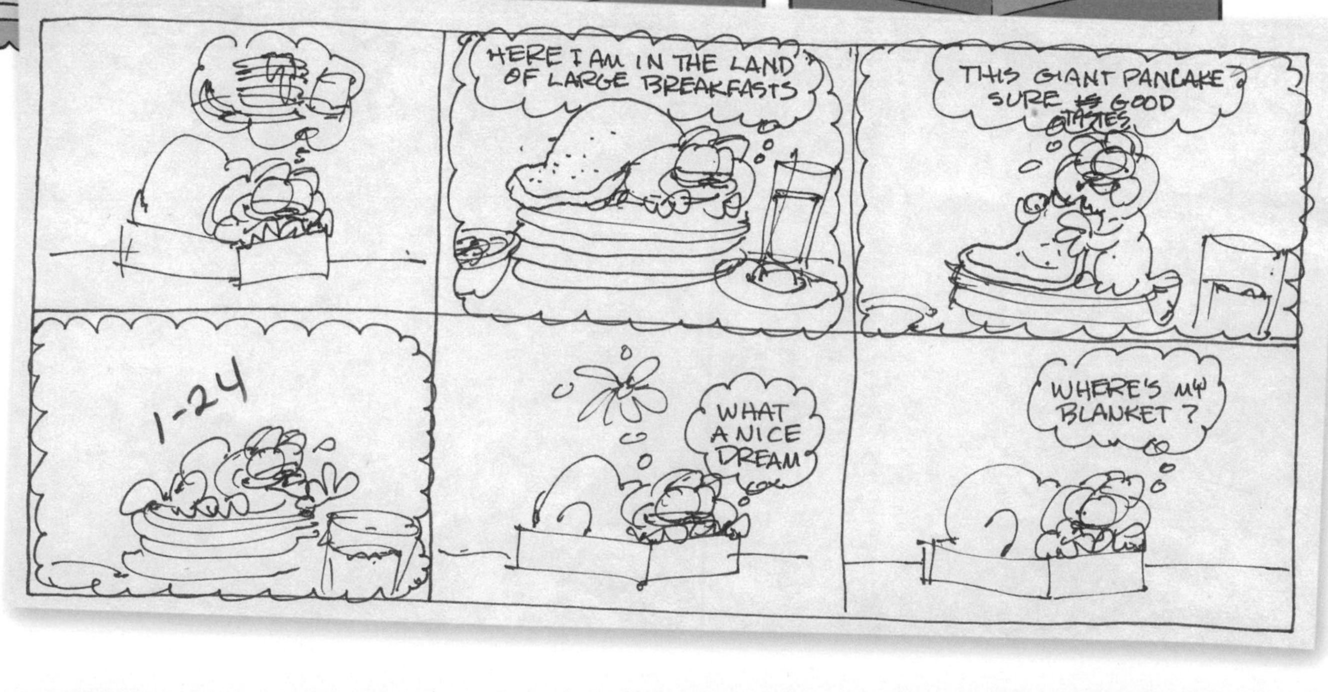
HERE I AM IN THE LAND OF LARGE BREAKFASTS
THIS GIANT PANCAKE SURE TASTES GOOD
1-24
WHAT A NICE DREAM
WHERE'S MY BLANKET ?

original rough

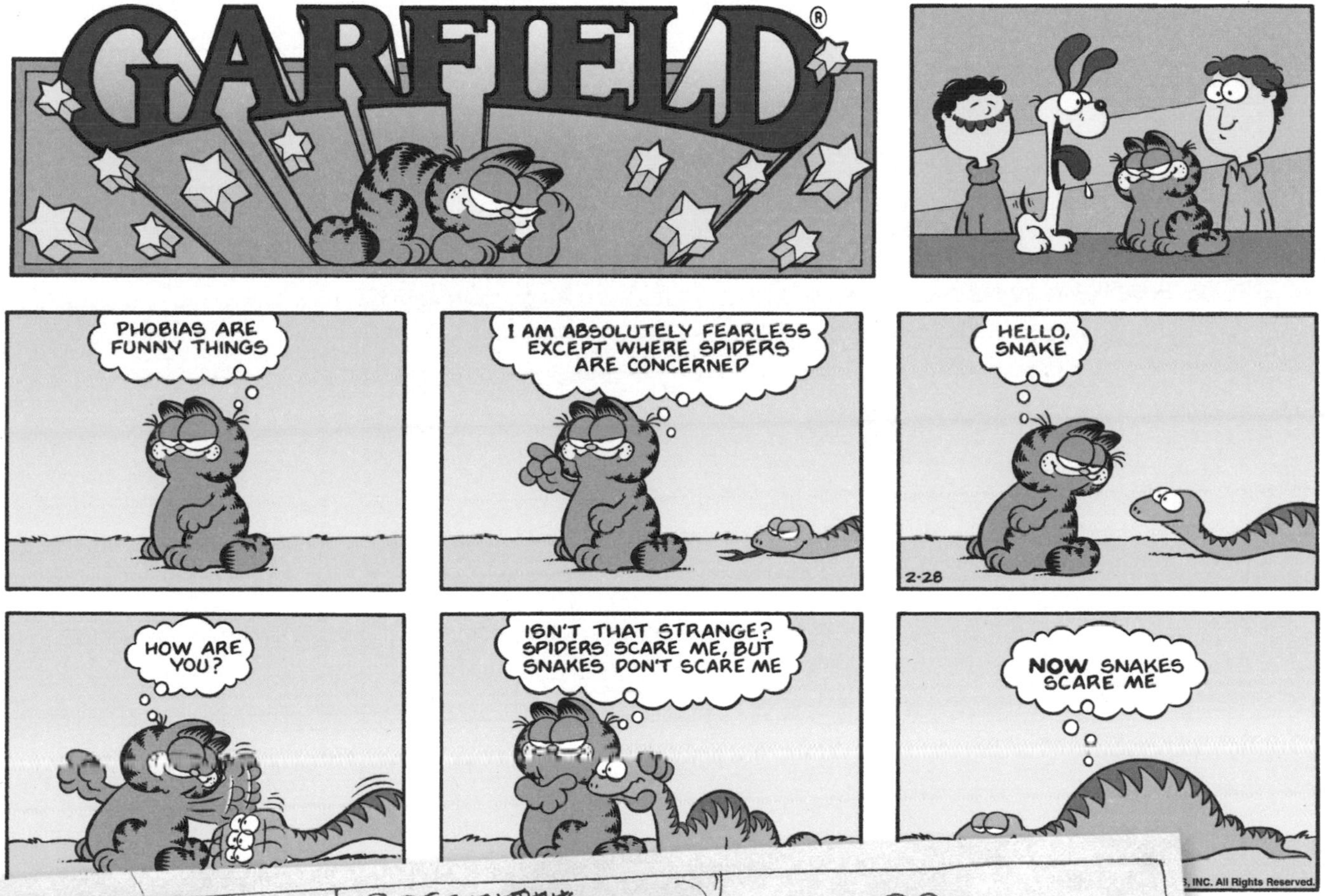
GARFIELD®
PHOBIAS ARE FUNNY THINGS
I AM ABSOLUTELY FEARLESS EXCEPT WHERE SPIDERS ARE CONCERNED
HELLO, SNAKE
2-28
HOW ARE YOU?
ISN'T THAT STRANGE? SPIDERS SCARE ME, BUT SNAKES DON'T SCARE ME
NOW SNAKES SCARE ME
S, INC. All Rights Reserved.

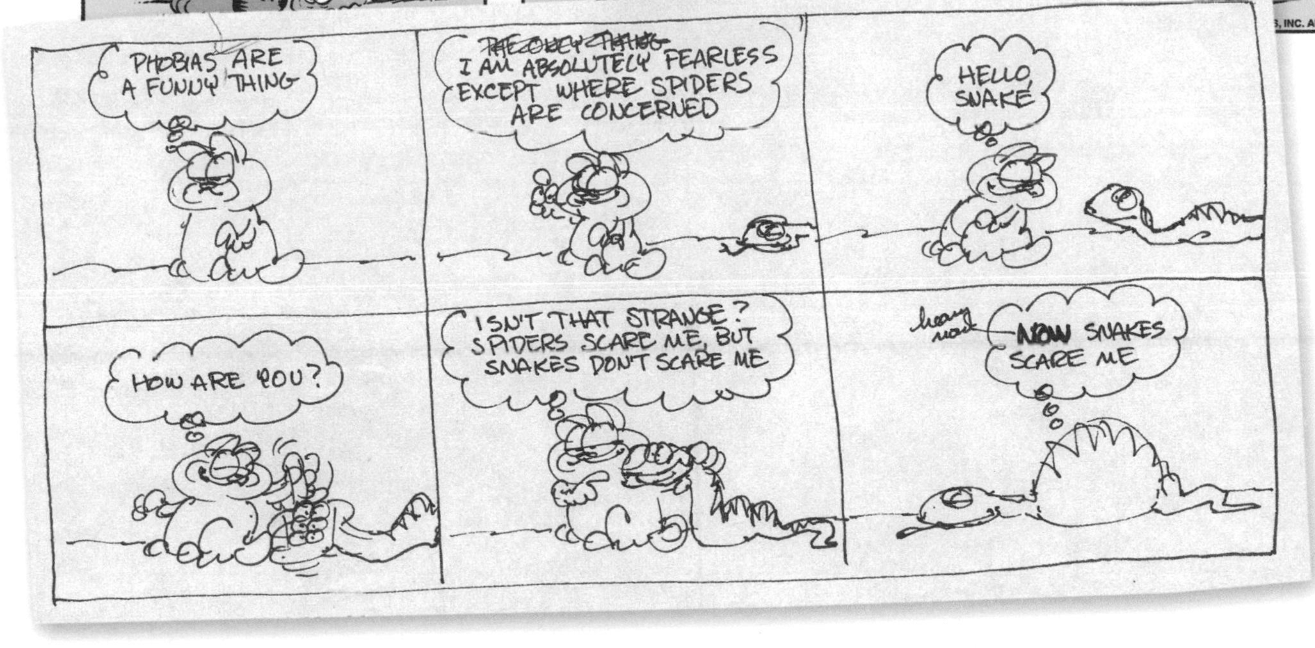
PHOBIAS ARE A FUNNY THING
I AM ABSOLUTELY FEARLESS EXCEPT WHERE SPIDERS ARE CONCERNED
HELLO, SNAKE
HOW ARE YOU?
ISN'T THAT STRANGE? SPIDERS SCARE ME, BUT SNAKES DON'T SCARE ME
NOW SNAKES SCARE ME

original rough

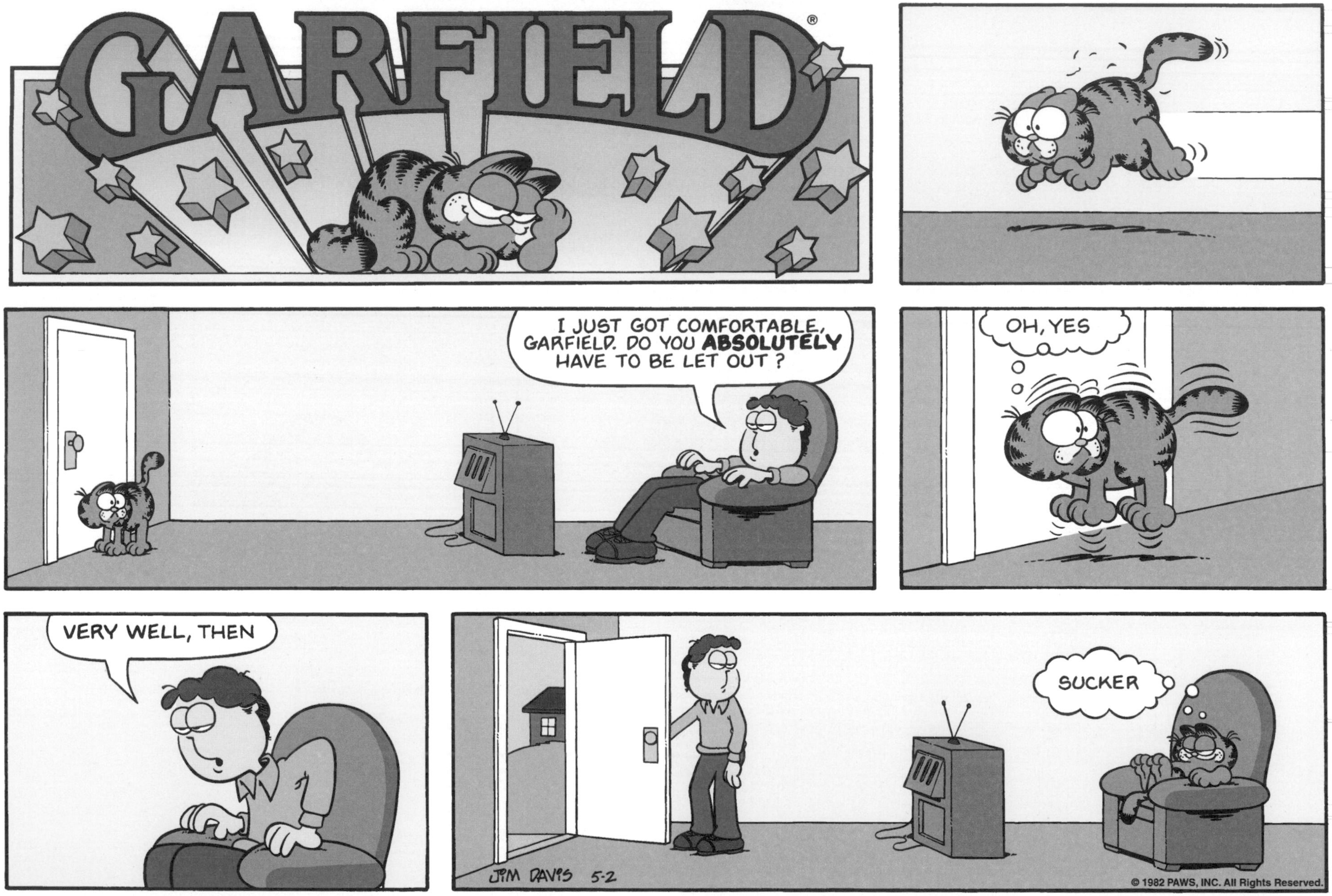
GARFIELD®
I JUST GOT COMFORTABLE, GARFIELD. DO YOU **ABSOLUTELY** HAVE TO BE LET OUT ?
OH, YES
VERY WELL, THEN
SUCKER
JIM DAVIS 5-2
© 1982 PAWS, INC. All Rights Reserved.

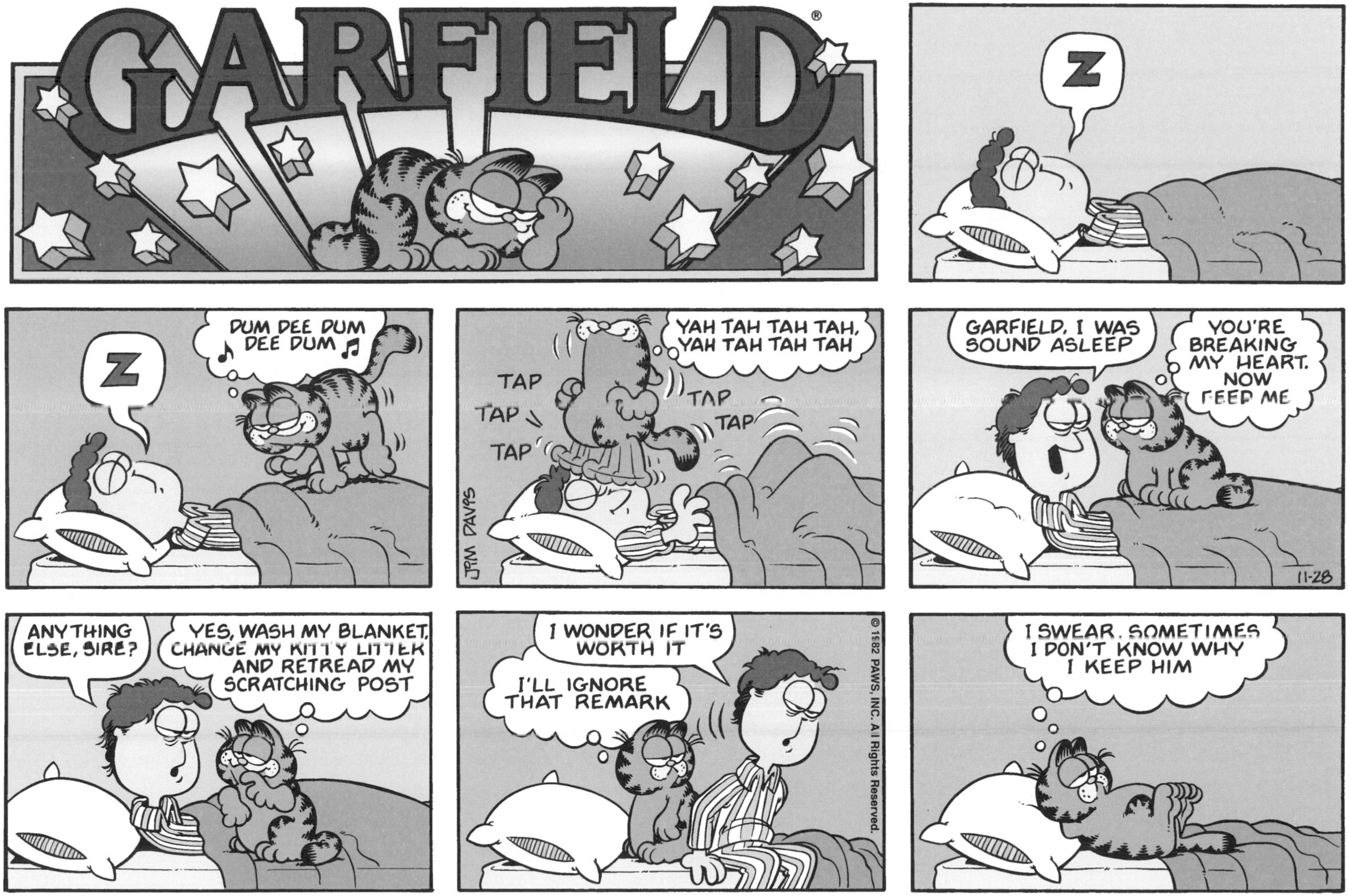
GARFIELD®
Z
Z
DUM DEE DUM DEE DUM
YAH TAH TAH TAH, YAH TAH TAH TAH
TAP
TAP
TAP
TAP
TAP
GARFIELD, I WAS SOUND ASLEEP
YOU'RE BREAKING MY HEART. NOW FEED ME
11-28
ANYTHING ELSE, SIRE?
YES, WASH MY BLANKET, CHANGE MY KITTY LITTER AND RETREAD MY SCRATCHING POST
I WONDER IF IT'S WORTH IT
I'LL IGNORE THAT REMARK
© 1982 PAWS, INC. All Rights Reserved.
I SWEAR. SOMETIMES I DON'T KNOW WHY I KEEP HIM

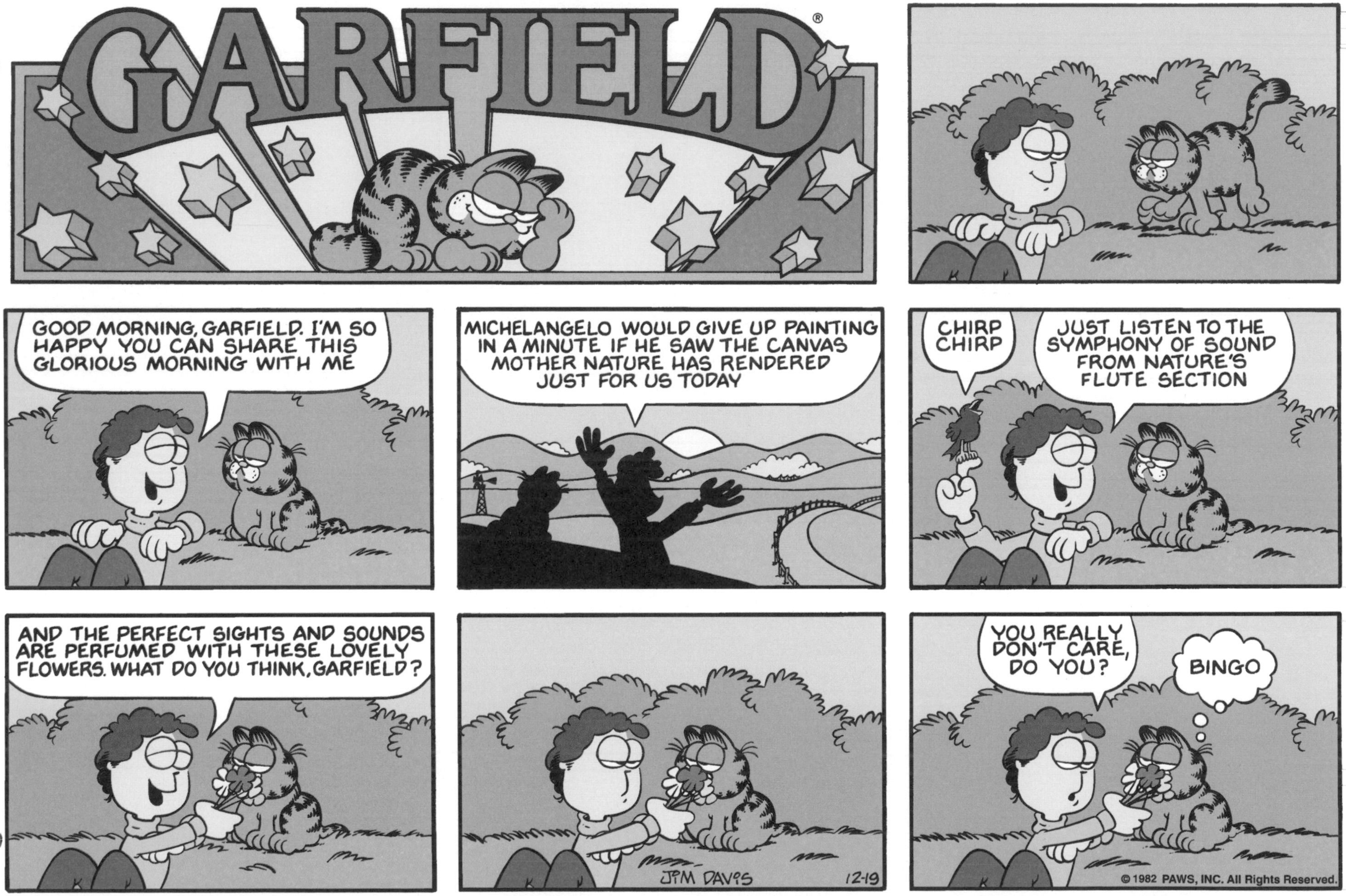
GARFIELD®
GOOD MORNING, GARFIELD. I'M SO HAPPY YOU CAN SHARE THIS GLORIOUS MORNING WITH ME
MICHELANGELO WOULD GIVE UP PAINTING IN A MINUTE IF HE SAW THE CANVAS MOTHER NATURE HAS RENDERED JUST FOR US TODAY
CHIRP CHIRP
JUST LISTEN TO THE SYMPHONY OF SOUND FROM NATURE'S FLUTE SECTION
AND THE PERFECT SIGHTS AND SOUNDS ARE PERFUMED WITH THESE LOVELY FLOWERS. WHAT DO YOU THINK, GARFIELD?
JIM DAVIS
12-19
YOU REALLY DON'T CARE, DO YOU?
BINGO
© 1982 PAWS, INC. All Rights Reserved.

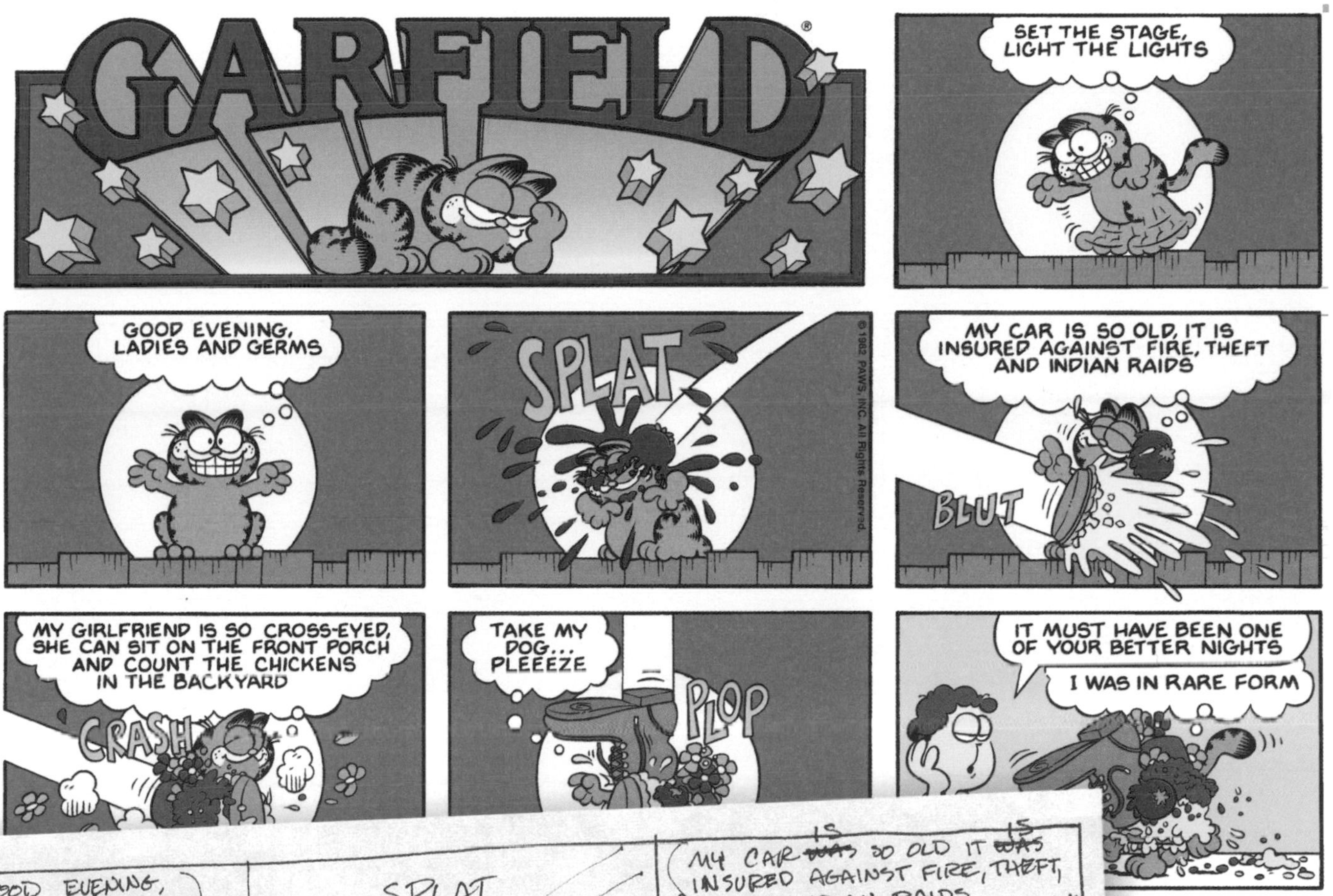
GARFIELD
SET THE STAGE, LIGHT THE LIGHTS
GOOD EVENING, LADIES AND GERMS
SPLAT
© 1982 PAWS, INC. All Rights Reserved.
MY CAR IS SO OLD, IT IS INSURED AGAINST FIRE, THEFT AND INDIAN RAIDS
BLUT
MY GIRLFRIEND IS SO CROSS-EYED, SHE CAN SIT ON THE FRONT PORCH AND COUNT THE CHICKENS IN THE BACKYARD
CRASH
TAKE MY DOG... PLEEEZE
PLOP
IT MUST HAVE BEEN ONE OF YOUR BETTER NIGHTS
I WAS IN RARE FORM

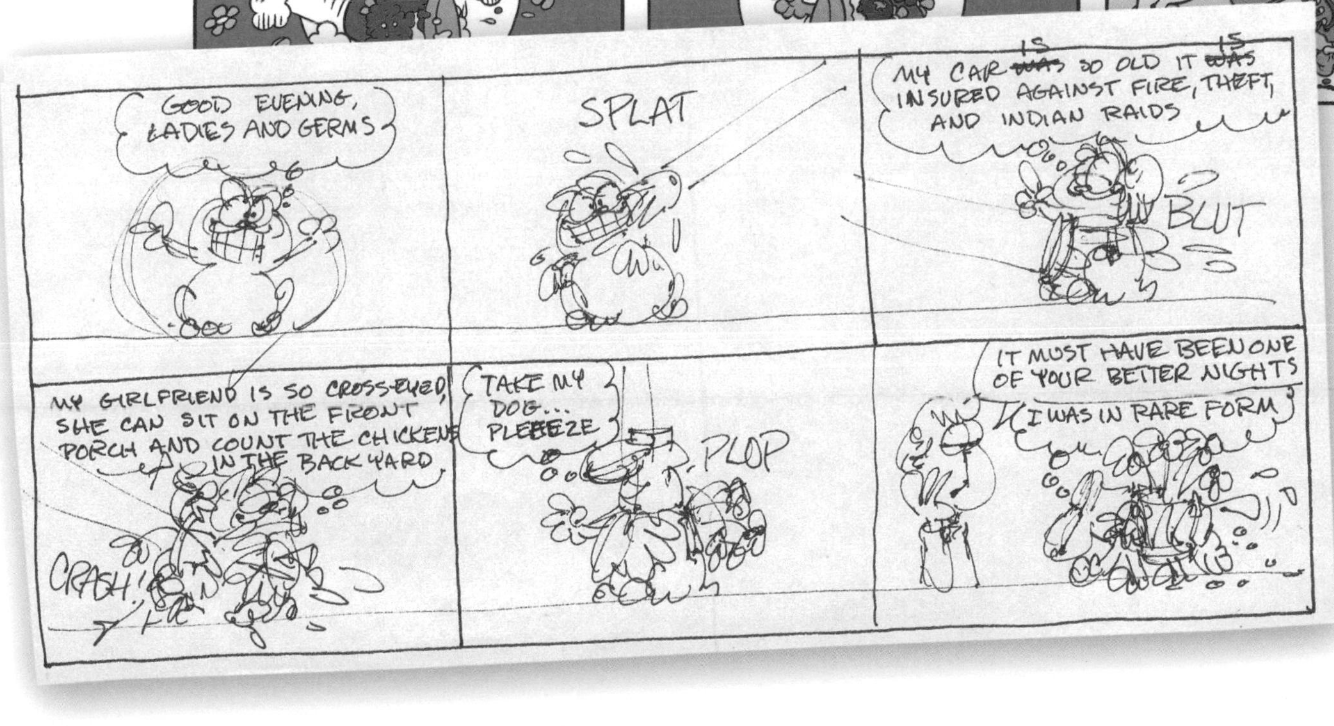
GOOD EVENING, LADIES AND GERMS
SPLAT
MY CAR ~~WAS~~ IS SO OLD IT ~~WAS~~ IS INSURED AGAINST FIRE, THEFT, AND INDIAN RAIDS
BLUT
MY GIRLFRIEND IS SO CROSS-EYED, SHE CAN SIT ON THE FRONT PORCH AND COUNT THE CHICKENS IN THE BACK YARD
CRASH!
TAKE MY DOG... PLEEEEZE
PLOP
IT MUST HAVE BEEN ONE OF YOUR BETTER NIGHTS
I WAS IN RARE FORM

original rough

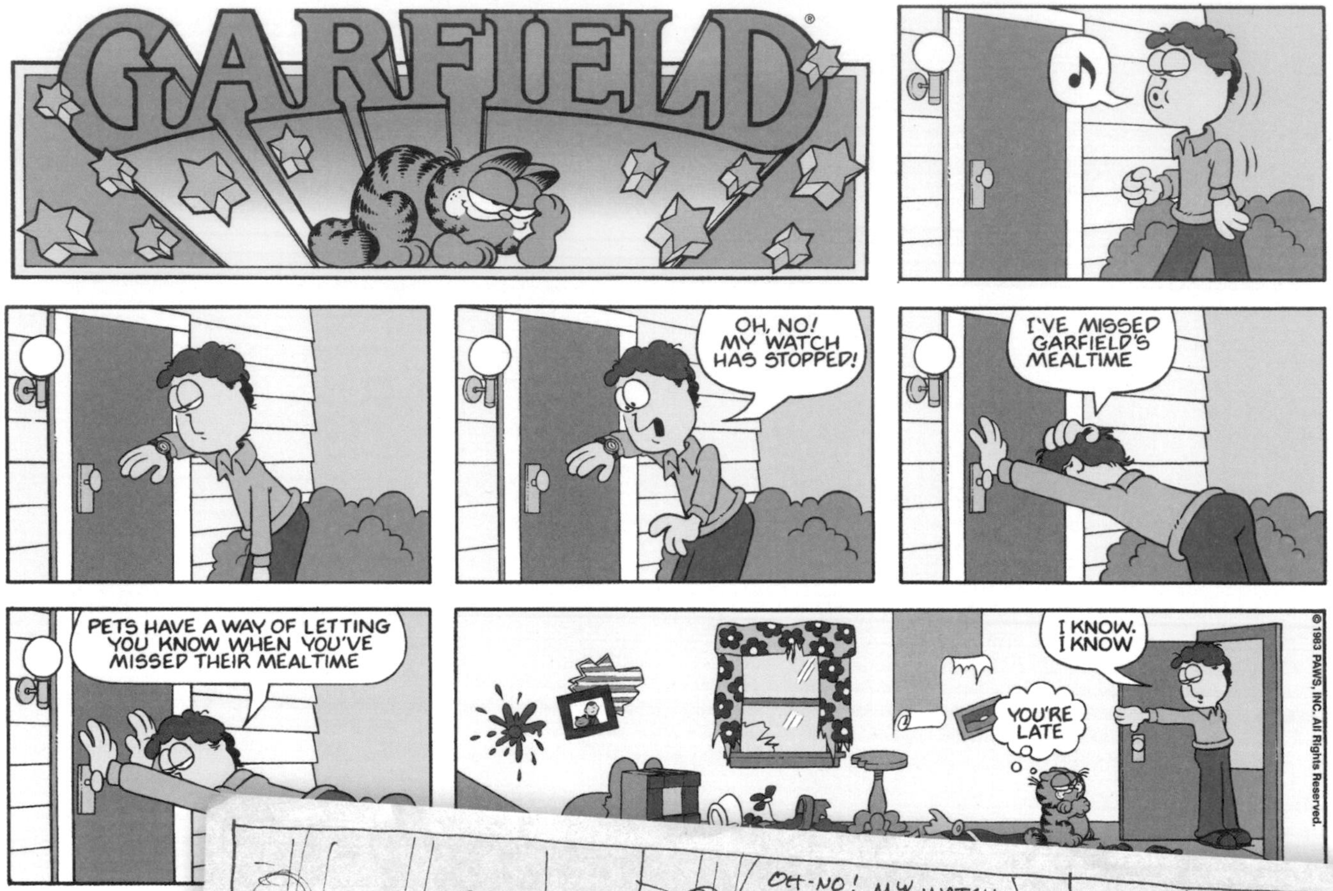
GARFIELD
♪
OH, NO! MY WATCH HAS STOPPED!
I'VE MISSED GARFIELD'S MEALTIME
PETS HAVE A WAY OF LETTING YOU KNOW WHEN YOU'VE MISSED THEIR MEALTIME
I KNOW. I KNOW
YOU'RE LATE
© 1983 PAWS, INC. All Rights Reserved.

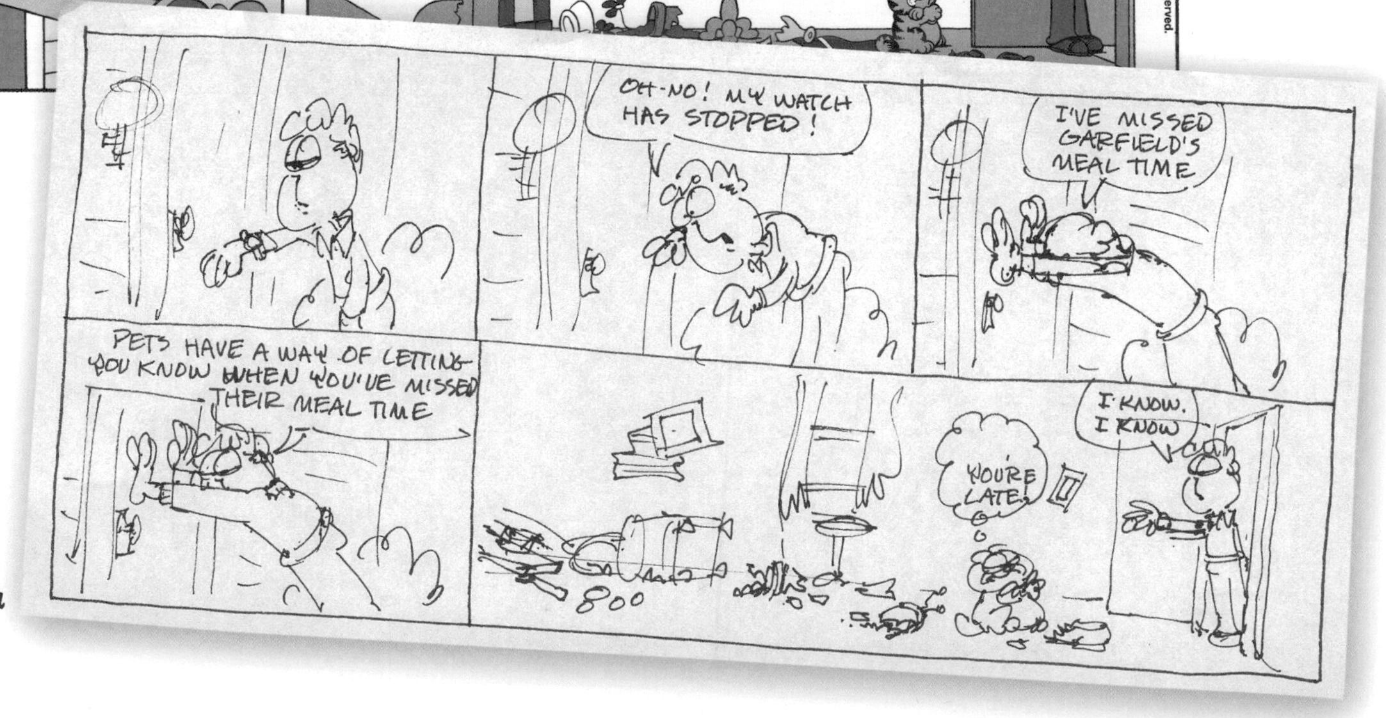
OH-NO! MY WATCH HAS STOPPED!
I'VE MISSED GARFIELD'S MEAL TIME
PETS HAVE A WAY OF LETTING YOU KNOW WHEN YOU'VE MISSED THEIR MEAL TIME
YOU'RE LATE!
I KNOW. I KNOW

original rough

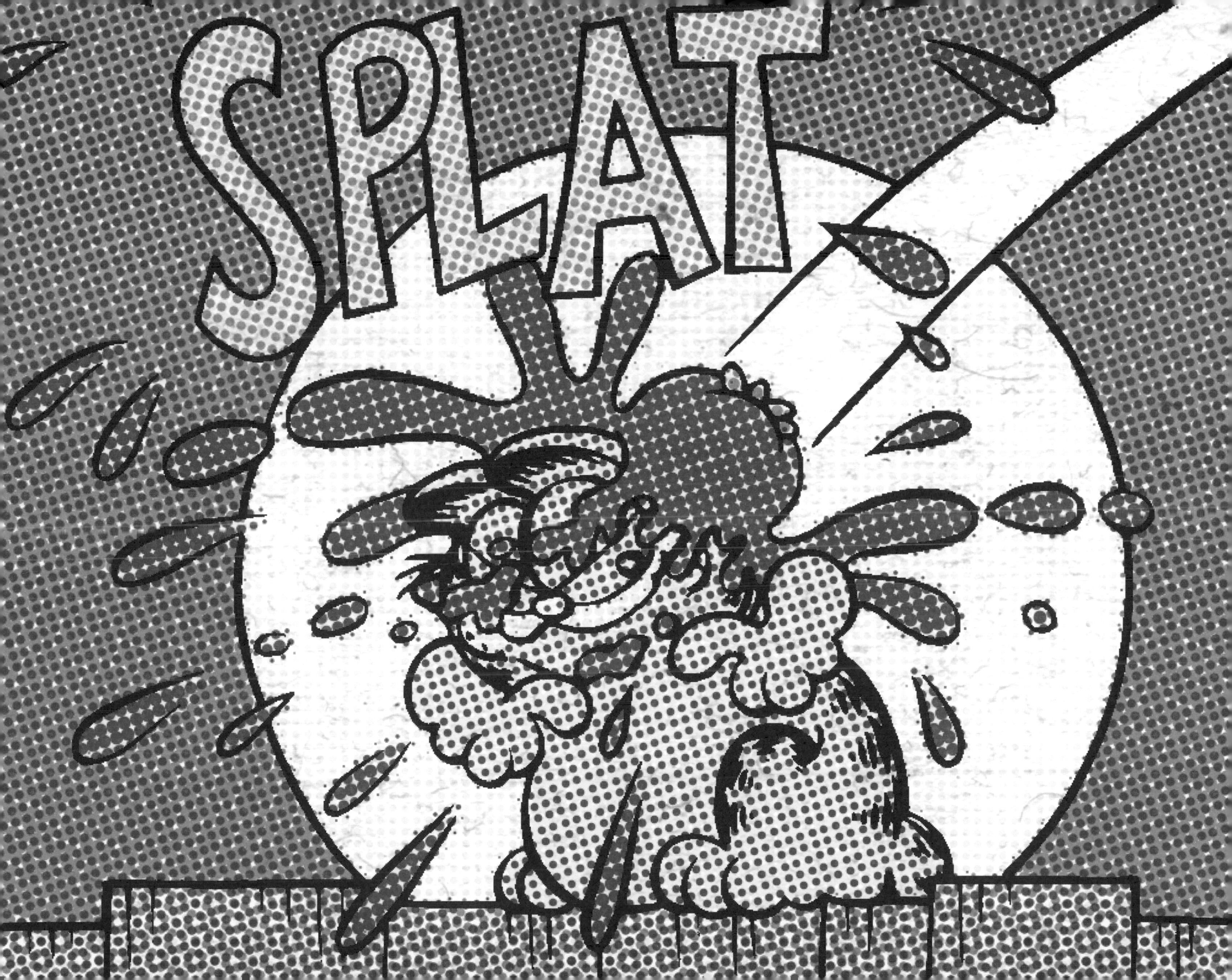
SPLAT

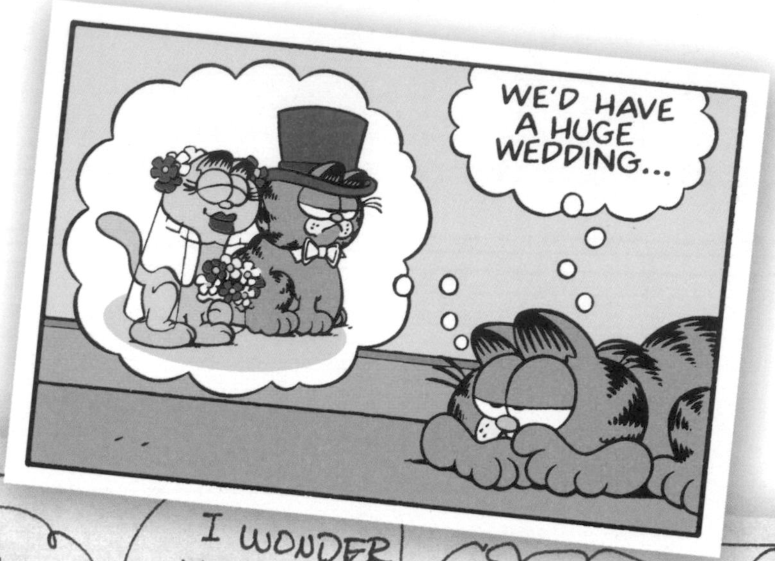
WE'D HAVE A HUGE WEDDING...

As strange as it sounds, there are some things that I'd like to do with Garfield, but he won't let me.

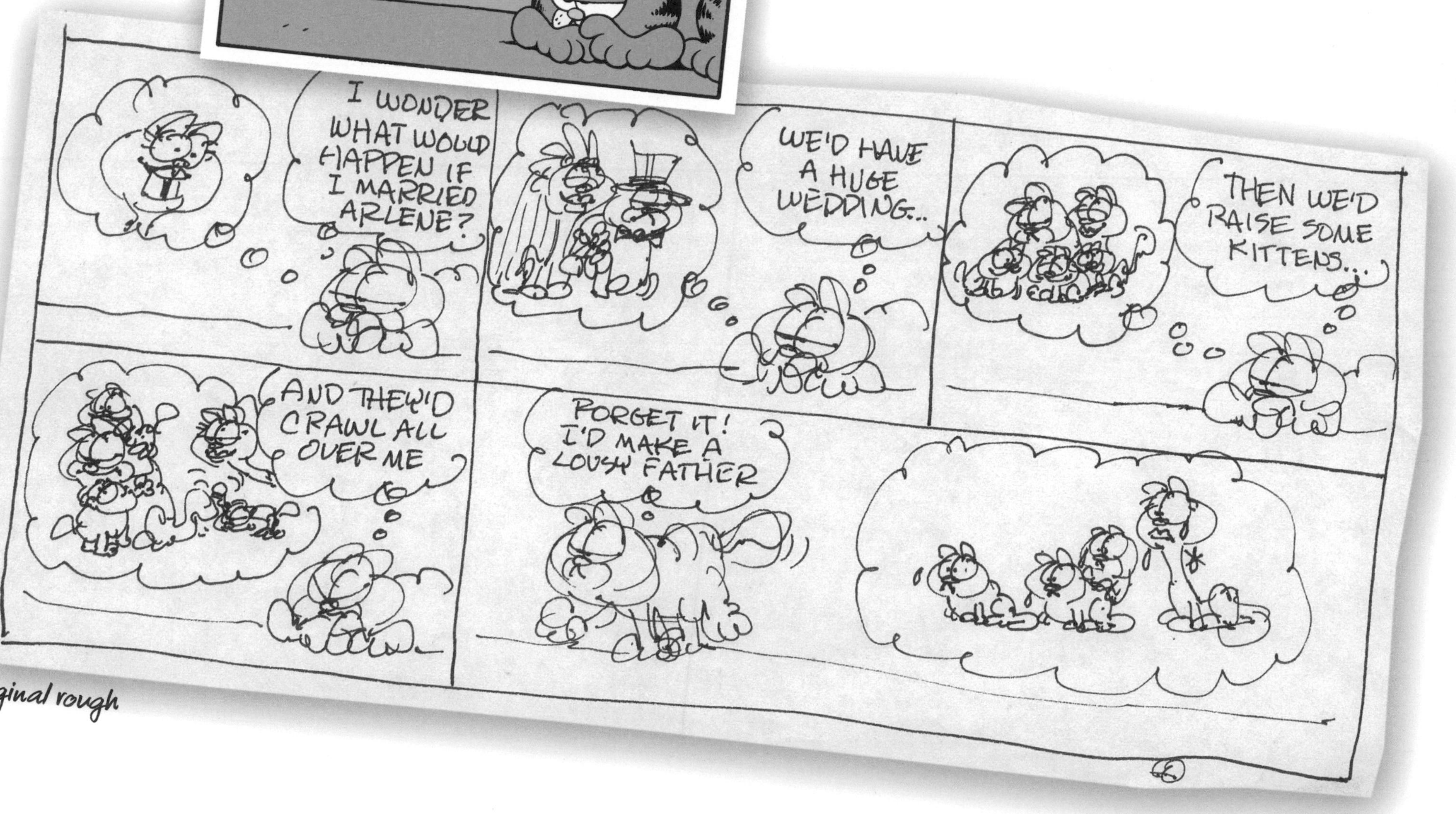
I WONDER WHAT WOULD HAPPEN IF I MARRIED ARLENE?
WE'D HAVE A HUGE WEDDING...
THEN WE'D RAISE SOME KITTENS...
AND THEY'D CRAWL ALL OVER ME
FORGET IT! I'D MAKE A LOUSY FATHER

original rough

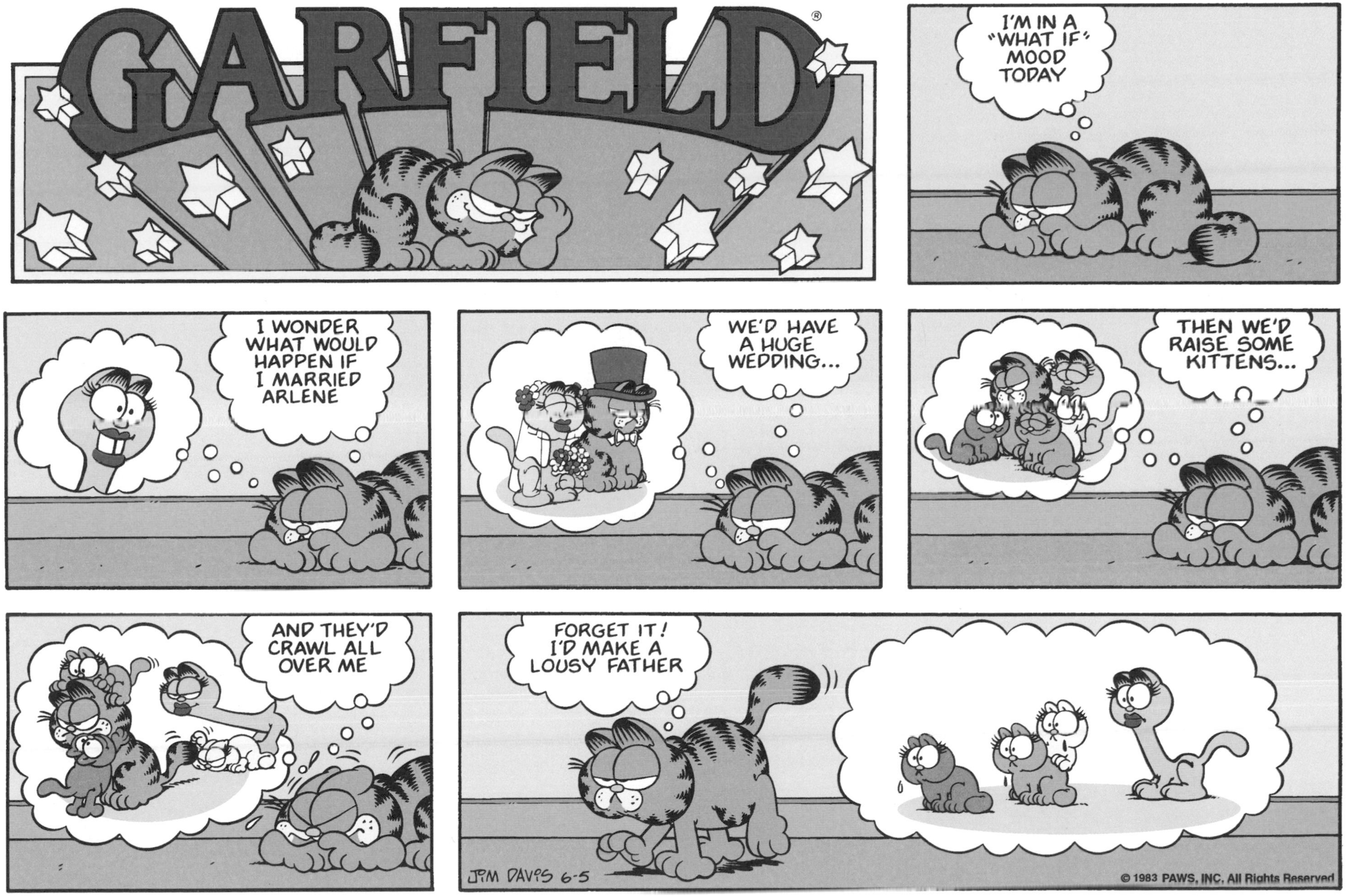
GARFIELD®
I'M IN A "WHAT IF" MOOD TODAY
I WONDER WHAT WOULD HAPPEN IF I MARRIED ARLENE
WE'D HAVE A HUGE WEDDING...
THEN WE'D RAISE SOME KITTENS...
AND THEY'D CRAWL ALL OVER ME
FORGET IT! I'D MAKE A LOUSY FATHER
JIM DAVIS 6-5
© 1983 PAWS, INC. All Rights Reserved

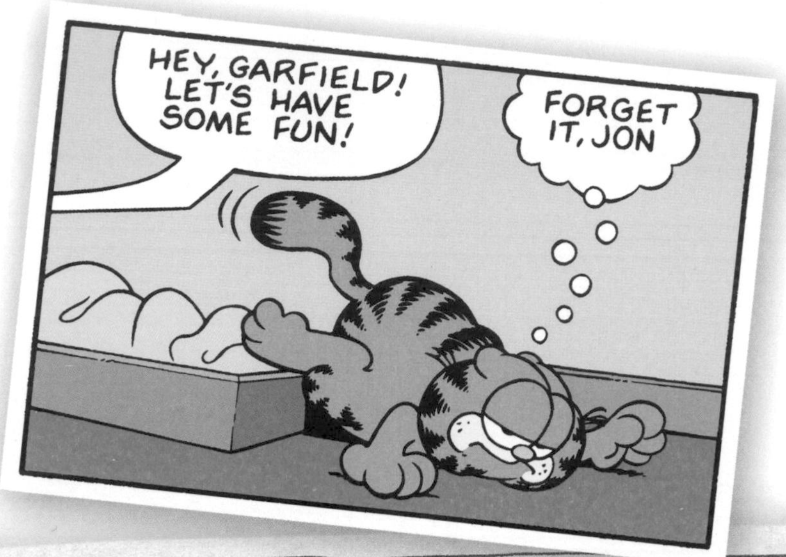

HEY, GARFIELD! LET'S HAVE SOME FUN!
FORGET IT, JON

One of life's mysteries . . .

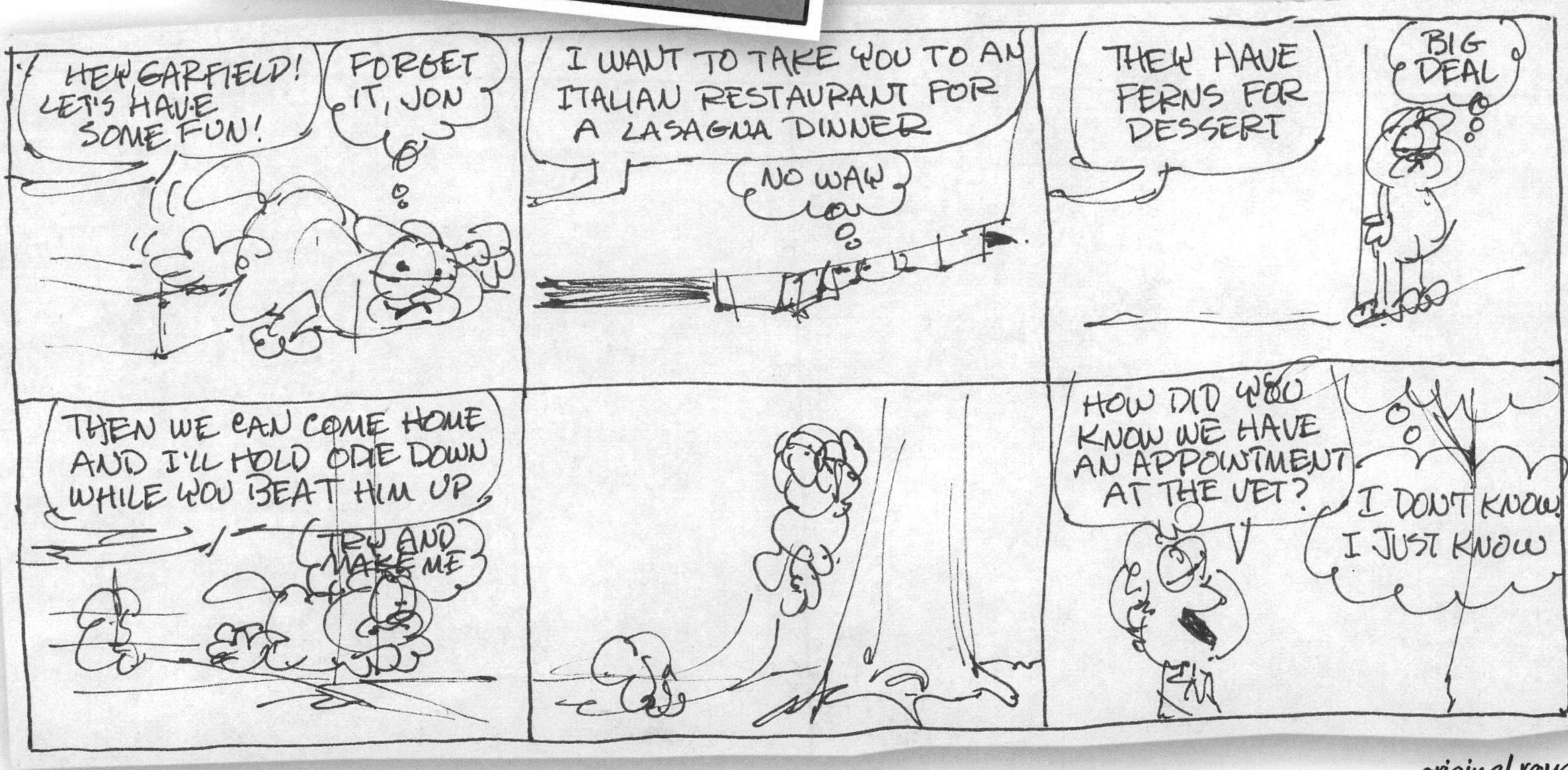

HEY GARFIELD! LET'S HAVE SOME FUN!
FORGET IT, JON
I WANT TO TAKE YOU TO AN ITALIAN RESTAURANT FOR A LASAGNA DINNER
NO WAY JON
THEY HAVE FERNS FOR DESSERT
BIG DEAL
THEN WE CAN COME HOME AND I'LL HOLD ODIE DOWN WHILE YOU BEAT HIM UP
TRY AND MAKE ME
HOW DID YOU KNOW WE HAVE AN APPOINTMENT AT THE VET?
I DONT KNOW. I JUST KNOW

original rough

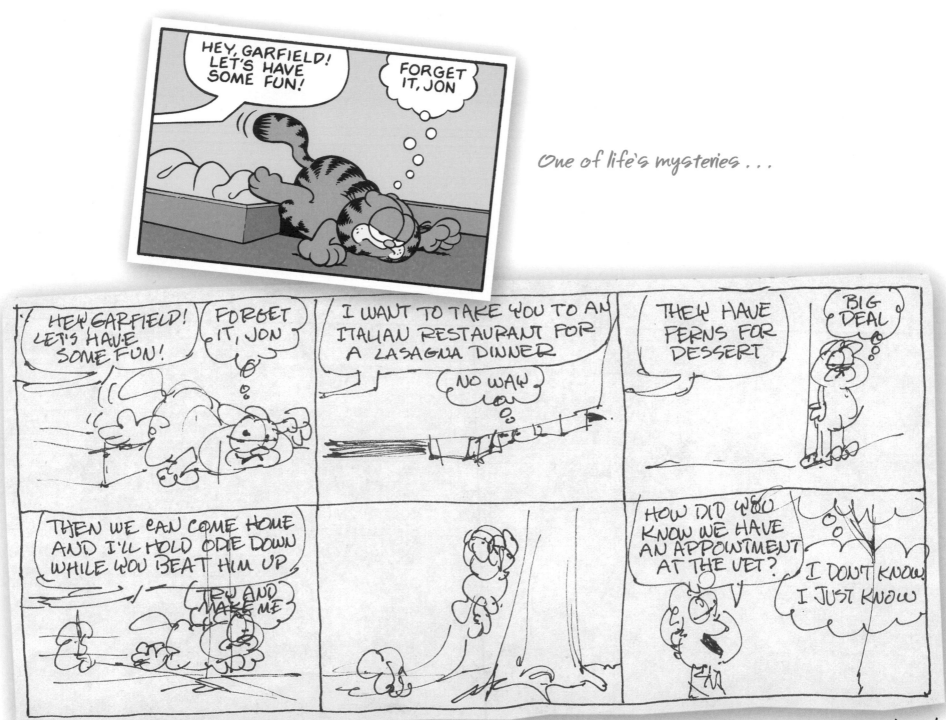

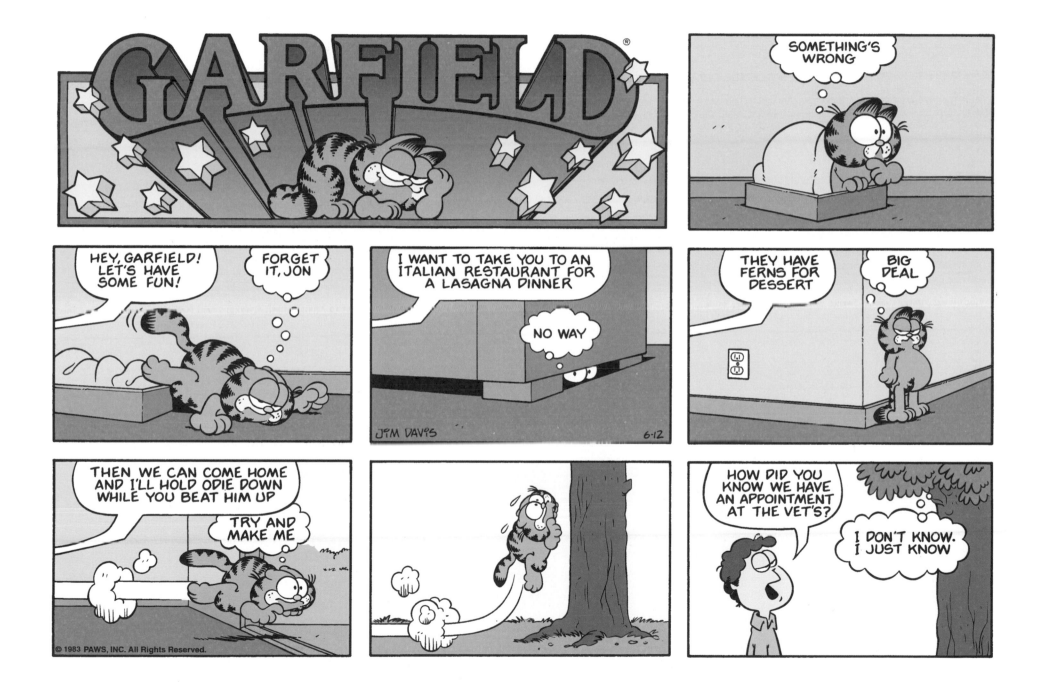

GARFIELD
SPLUT
PLIK
BAT
8-28
© 1983 PAWS, INC. All Rights Reserved.
SCRATCH
DRIP
BORED, GARFIELD?
SOME DAYS I GET TIRED OF BEING A CAT

SPLUT
PLIK
DRIP
WATER
BORED, GARFIELD?
SCRATCH
BAT
SOME DAYS I GET TIRED OF BEING A CAT

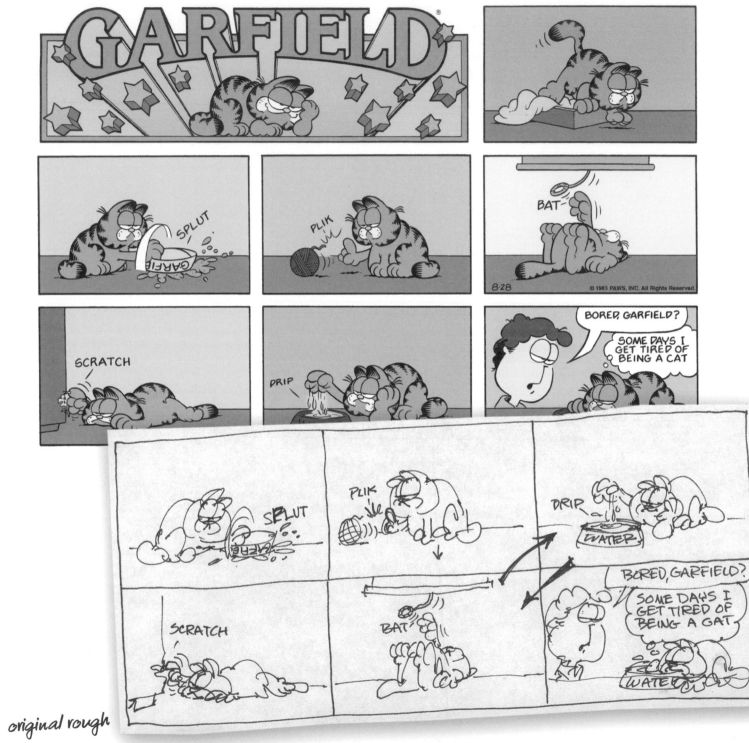

original rough

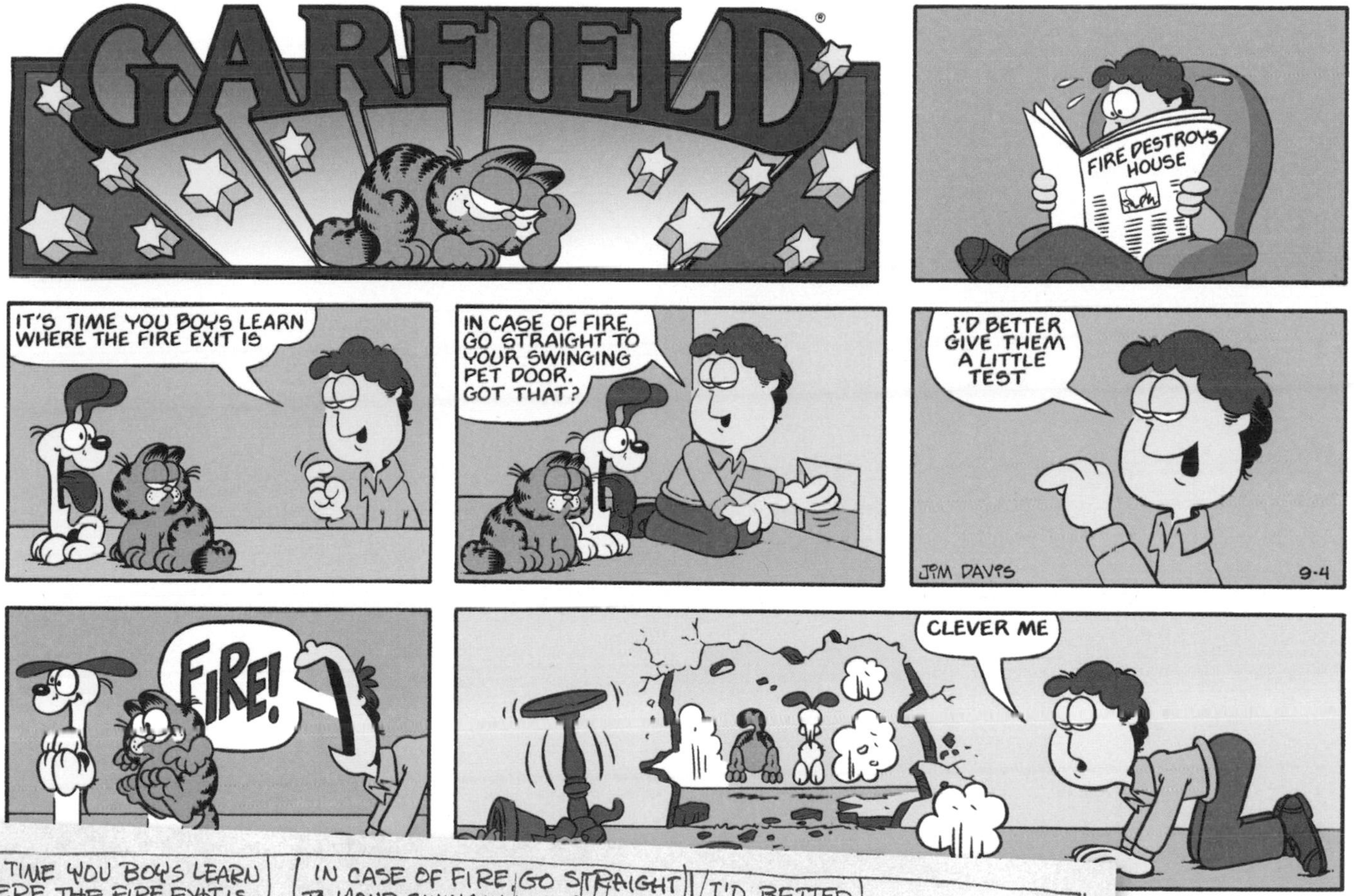
GARFIELD
FIRE DESTROYS HOUSE
IT'S TIME YOU BOYS LEARN WHERE THE FIRE EXIT IS
IN CASE OF FIRE, GO STRAIGHT TO YOUR SWINGING PET DOOR. GOT THAT?
I'D BETTER GIVE THEM A LITTLE TEST
JIM DAVIS 9-4
FIRE!
CLEVER ME

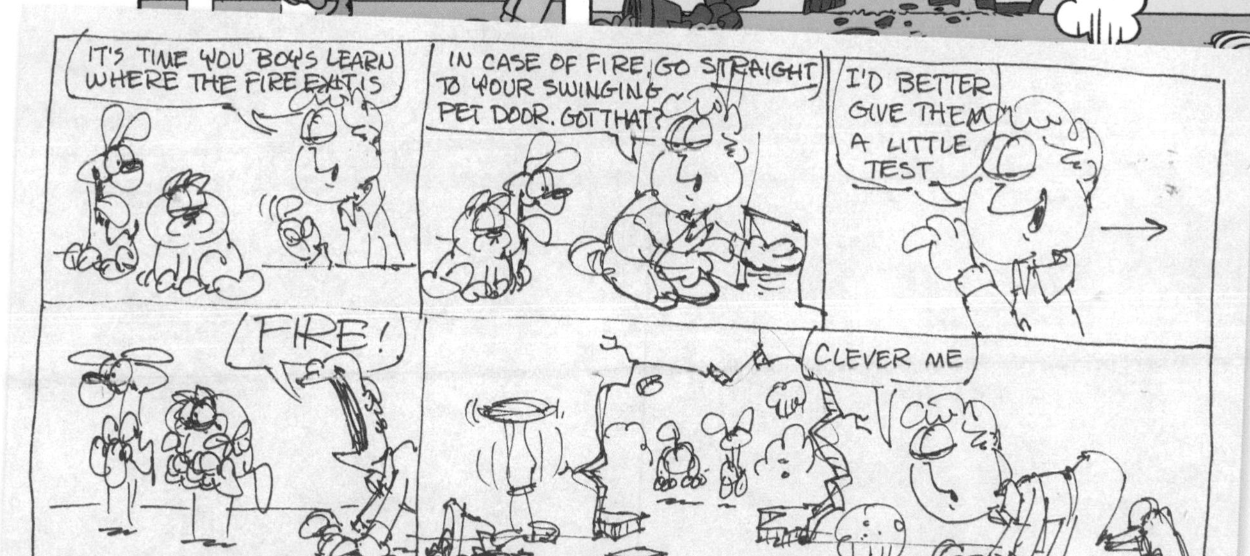
IT'S TIME YOU BOYS LEARN WHERE THE FIRE EXIT IS
IN CASE OF FIRE, GO STRAIGHT TO YOUR SWINGING PET DOOR. GOT THAT?
I'D BETTER GIVE THEM A LITTLE TEST
FIRE!
CLEVER ME

original rough

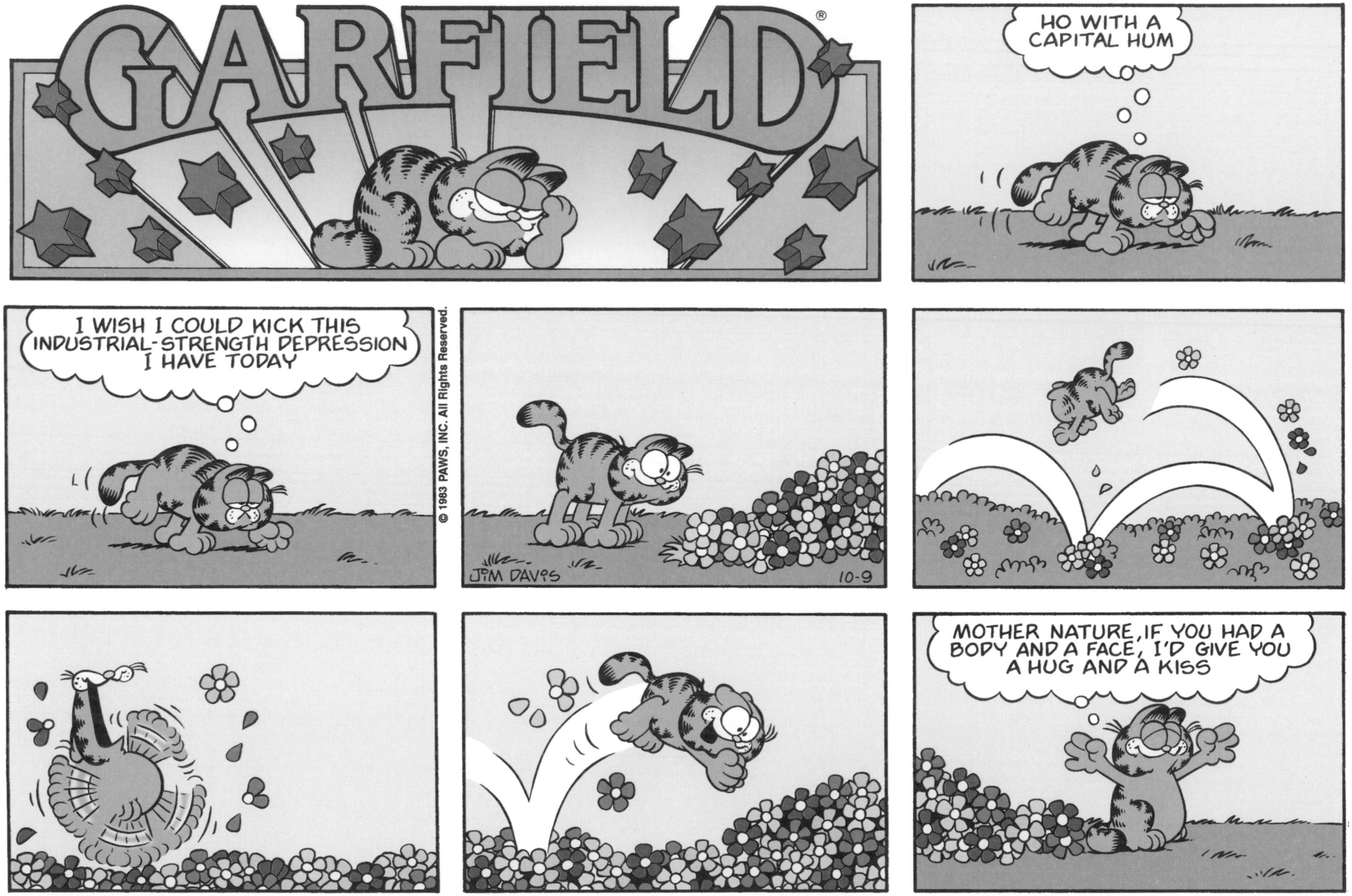
GARFIELD®
HO WITH A CAPITAL HUM
I WISH I COULD KICK THIS INDUSTRIAL-STRENGTH DEPRESSION I HAVE TODAY
© 1983 PAWS, INC. All Rights Reserved.
JIM DAVIS 10-9
MOTHER NATURE, IF YOU HAD A BODY AND A FACE, I'D GIVE YOU A HUG AND A KISS

Even a world-class cynic like Garfield allows himself an honest moment.

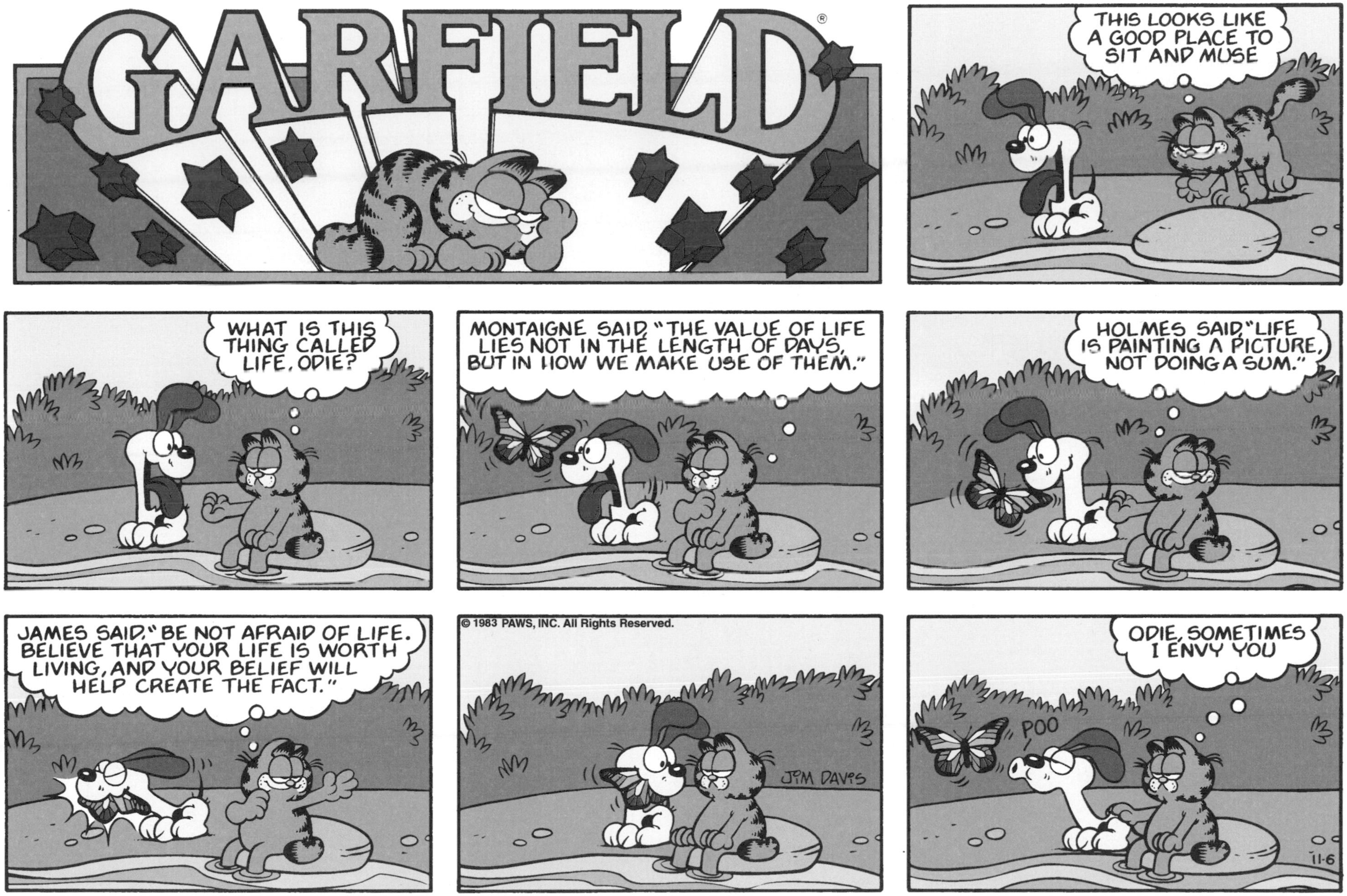
GARFIELD®
THIS LOOKS LIKE A GOOD PLACE TO SIT AND MUSE
WHAT IS THIS THING CALLED LIFE, ODIE?
MONTAIGNE SAID, "THE VALUE OF LIFE LIES NOT IN THE LENGTH OF DAYS, BUT IN HOW WE MAKE USE OF THEM."
HOLMES SAID, "LIFE IS PAINTING A PICTURE, NOT DOING A SUM."
JAMES SAID, "BE NOT AFRAID OF LIFE. BELIEVE THAT YOUR LIFE IS WORTH LIVING, AND YOUR BELIEF WILL HELP CREATE THE FACT."
© 1983 PAWS, INC. All Rights Reserved.
JIM DAVIS
ODIE, SOMETIMES I ENVY YOU
POO
11-6

The strips with heart are among my favorites. maybe, someday, these two will get together.

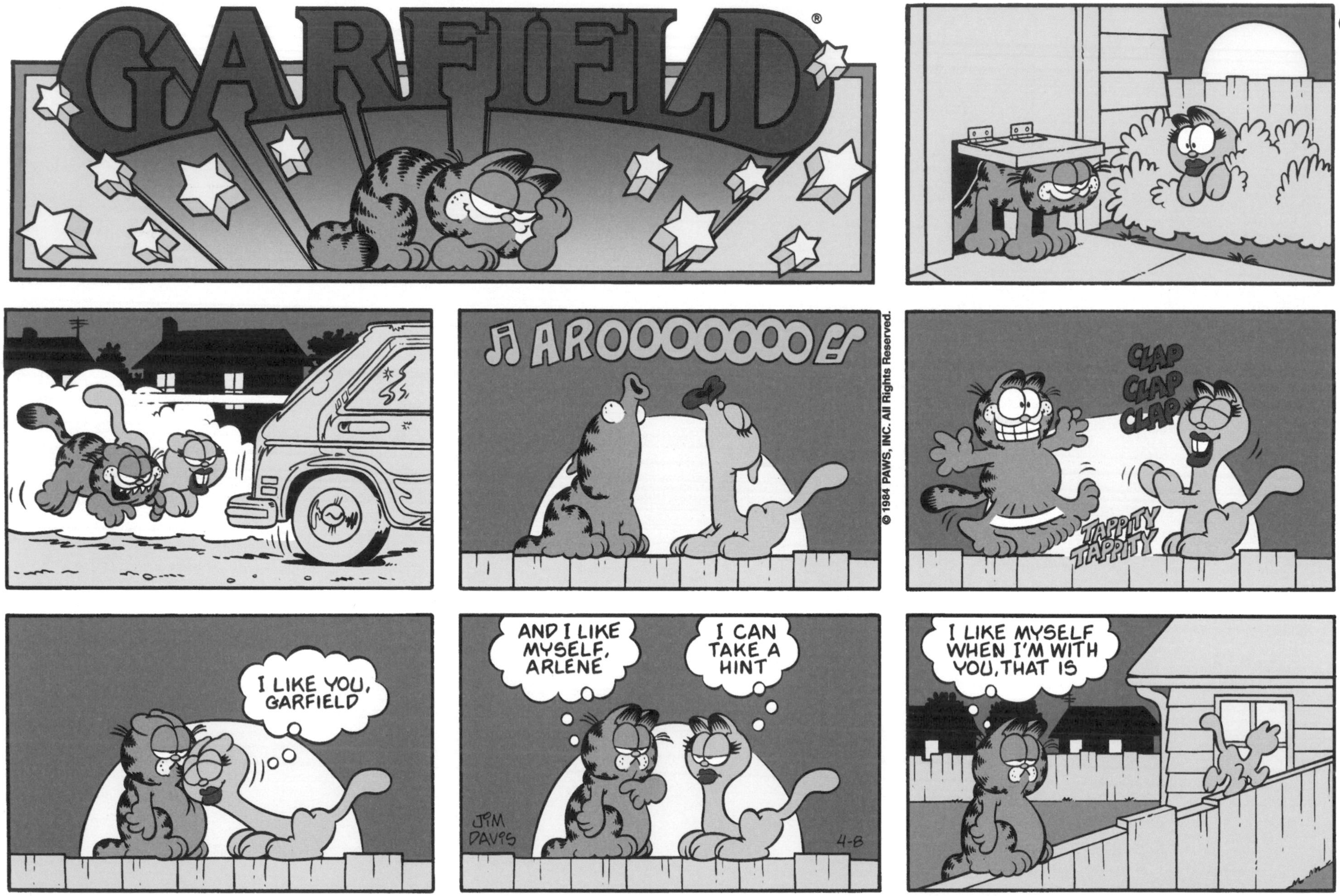
GARFIELD®
AROOOOOOO
CLAP
CLAP
CLAP
TAPPITY
TAPPITY
© 1984 PAWS, INC. All Rights Reserved.
I LIKE YOU, GARFIELD
AND I LIKE MYSELF, ARLENE
I CAN TAKE A HINT
JIM DAVIS
4-8
I LIKE MYSELF WHEN I'M WITH YOU, THAT IS

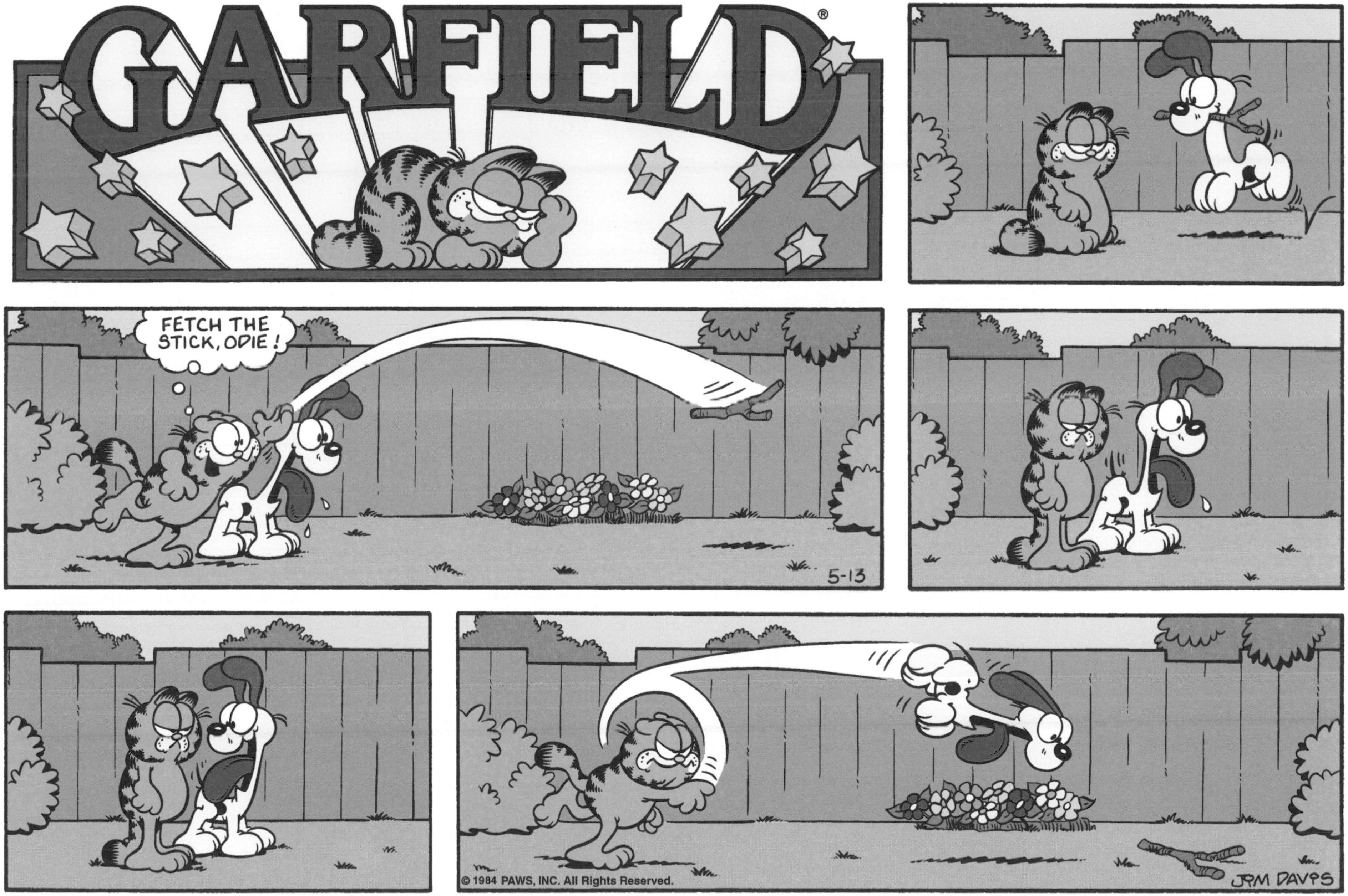
GARFIELD®
FETCH THE STICK, ODIE!
5-13
© 1984 PAWS, INC. All Rights Reserved.
JIM DAVIS

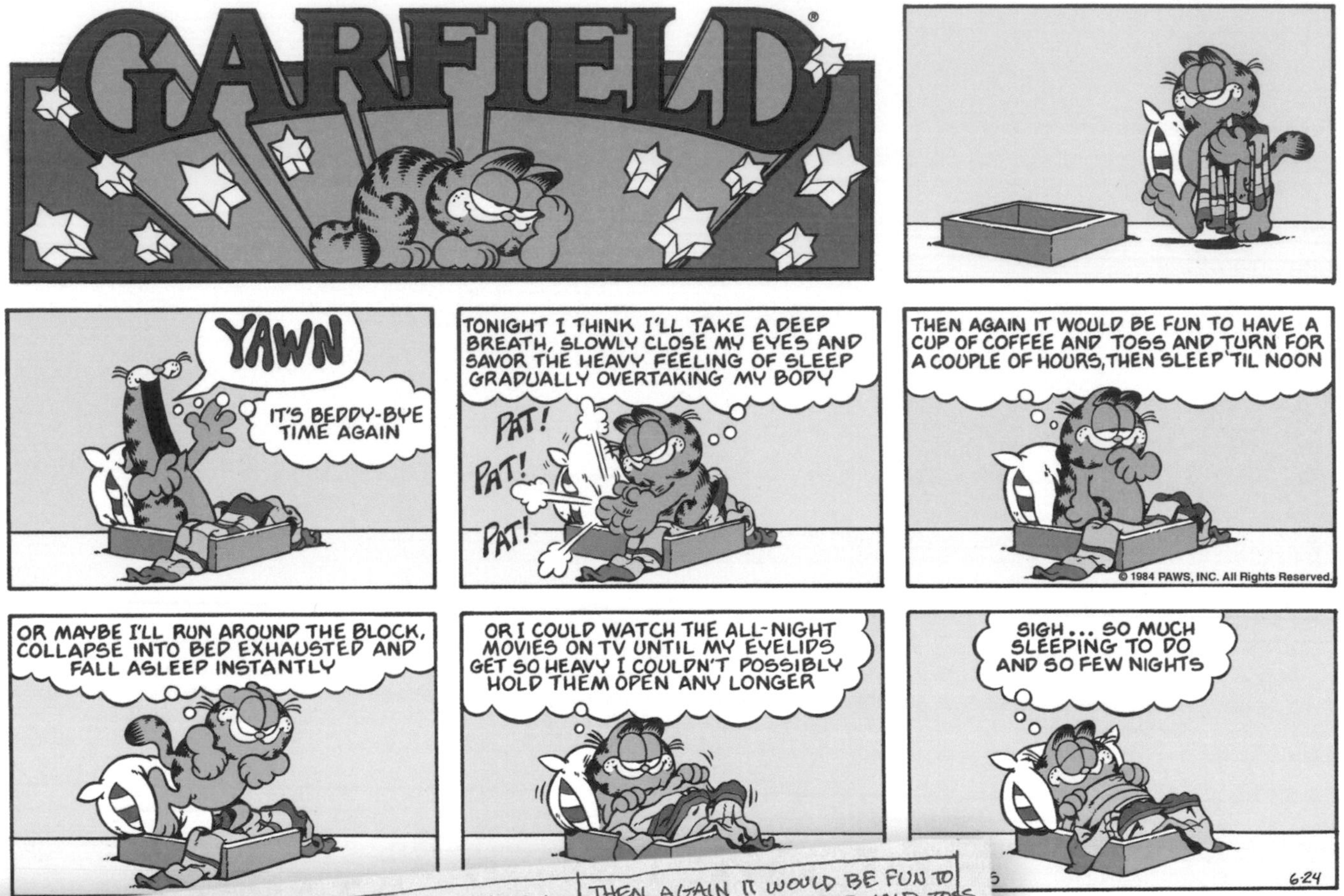
GARFIELD®
YAWN
IT'S BEDDY-BYE TIME AGAIN
TONIGHT I THINK I'LL TAKE A DEEP BREATH, SLOWLY CLOSE MY EYES AND SAVOR THE HEAVY FEELING OF SLEEP GRADUALLY OVERTAKING MY BODY
PAT! PAT! PAT!
THEN AGAIN IT WOULD BE FUN TO HAVE A CUP OF COFFEE AND TOSS AND TURN FOR A COUPLE OF HOURS, THEN SLEEP 'TIL NOON
© 1984 PAWS, INC. All Rights Reserved.
OR MAYBE I'LL RUN AROUND THE BLOCK, COLLAPSE INTO BED EXHAUSTED AND FALL ASLEEP INSTANTLY
OR I COULD WATCH THE ALL-NIGHT MOVIES ON TV UNTIL MY EYELIDS GET SO HEAVY I COULDN'T POSSIBLY HOLD THEM OPEN ANY LONGER
SIGH... SO MUCH SLEEPING TO DO AND SO FEW NIGHTS
6·24

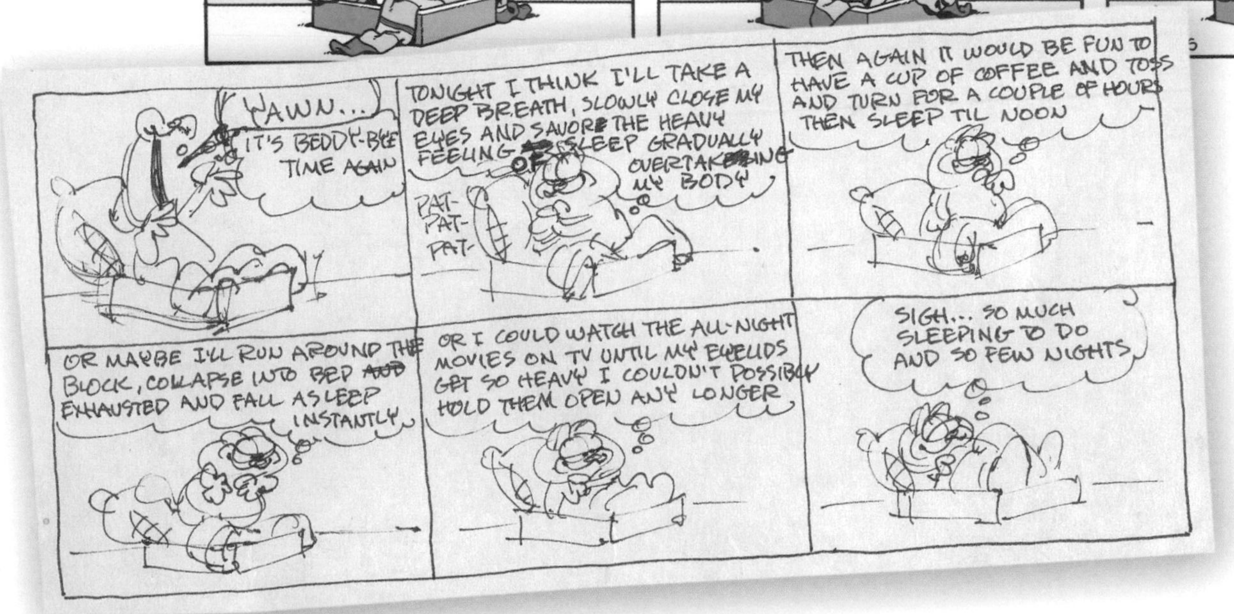
YAWN...
IT'S BEDDY-BYE TIME AGAIN
TONIGHT I THINK I'LL TAKE A DEEP BREATH, SLOWLY CLOSE MY EYES AND SAVOR THE HEAVY FEELING OF SLEEP GRADUALLY OVERTAKING MY BODY
PAT- PAT- PAT-
THEN AGAIN IT WOULD BE FUN TO HAVE A CUP OF COFFEE AND TOSS AND TURN FOR A COUPLE OF HOURS THEN SLEEP TIL NOON
OR MAYBE I'LL RUN AROUND THE BLOCK, COLLAPSE INTO BED EXHAUSTED AND FALL ASLEEP INSTANTLY
OR I COULD WATCH THE ALL-NIGHT MOVIES ON TV UNTIL MY EYELIDS GET SO HEAVY I COULDN'T POSSIBLY HOLD THEM OPEN ANY LONGER
SIGH... SO MUCH SLEEPING TO DO AND SO FEW NIGHTS

original rough

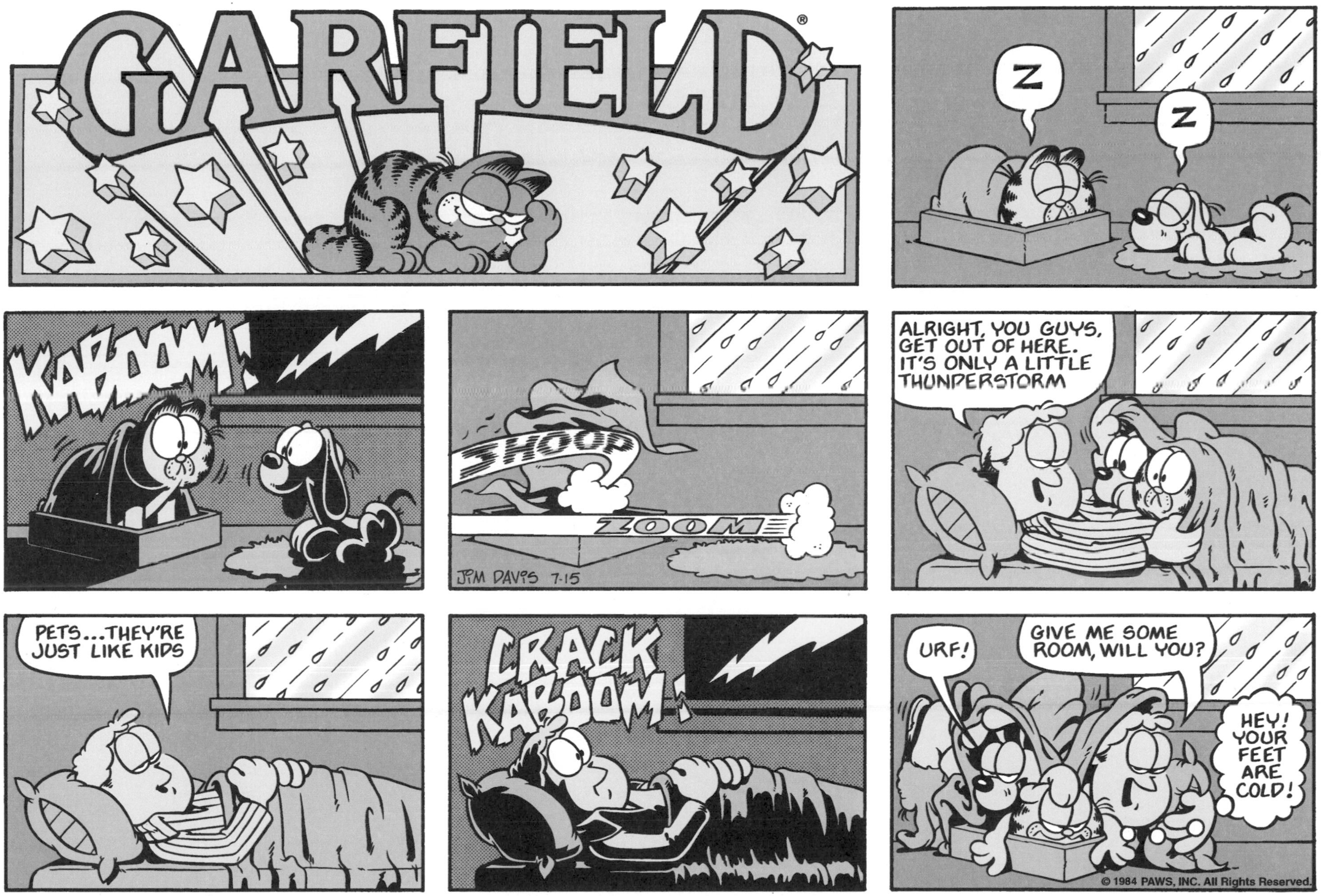
GARFIELD
Z
Z
KABOOM!
SHOOP
ZOOM
JIM DAVIS 7-15
ALRIGHT, YOU GUYS, GET OUT OF HERE. IT'S ONLY A LITTLE THUNDERSTORM
PETS...THEY'RE JUST LIKE KIDS
CRACK KABOOM!
URF!
GIVE ME SOME ROOM, WILL YOU?
HEY! YOUR FEET ARE COLD!
© 1984 PAWS, INC. All Rights Reserved.

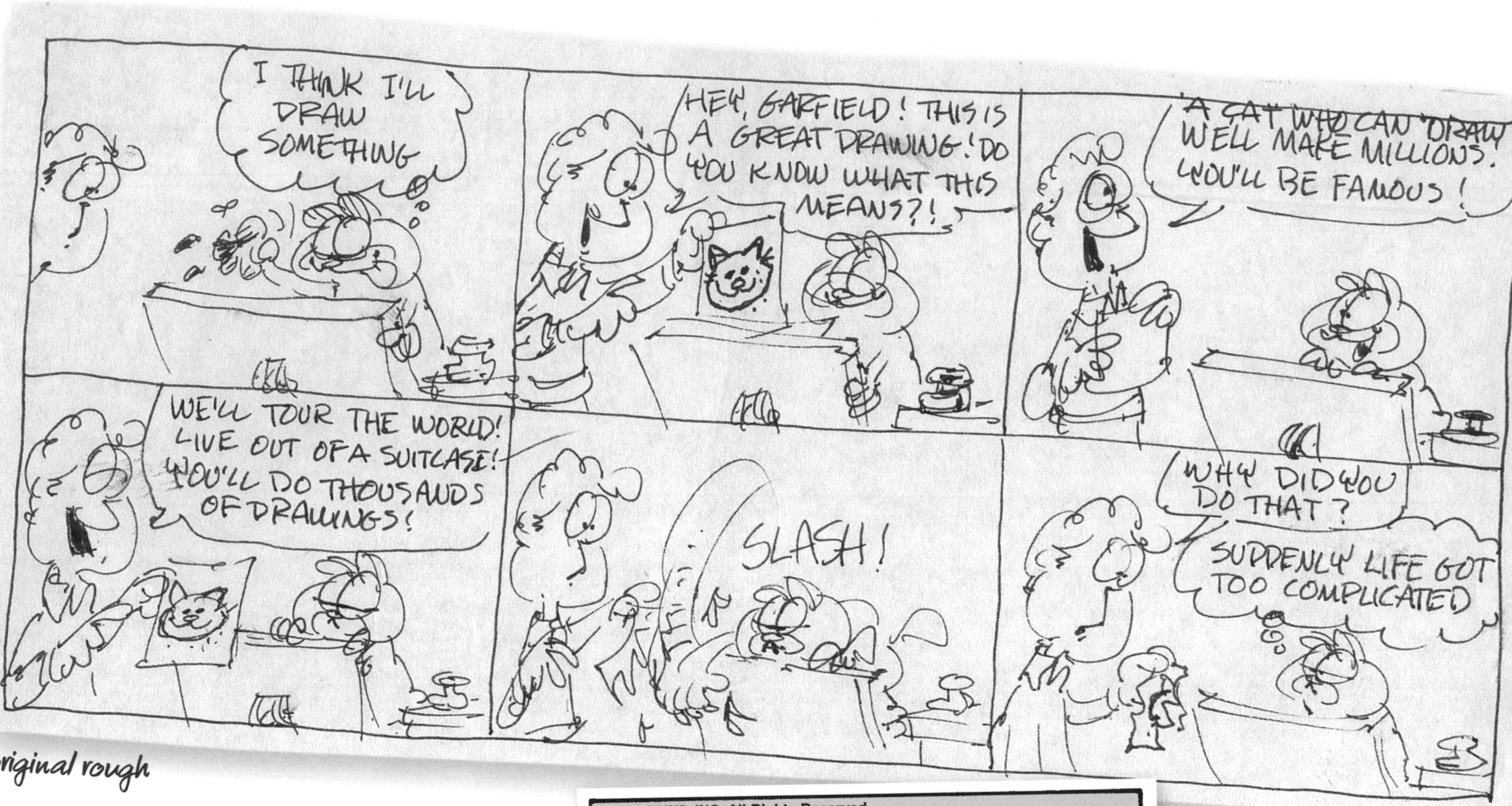
I THINK I'LL DRAW SOMETHING
HEY, GARFIELD! THIS IS A GREAT DRAWING! DO YOU KNOW WHAT THIS MEANS?!
A CAT WHO CAN DRAW WILL MAKE MILLIONS. YOU'LL BE FAMOUS!
WE'LL TOUR THE WORLD! LIVE OUT OF A SUITCASE! YOU'LL DO THOUSANDS OF DRAWINGS!
SLASH!
WHY DID YOU DO THAT?
SUDDENLY LIFE GOT TOO COMPLICATED

original rough

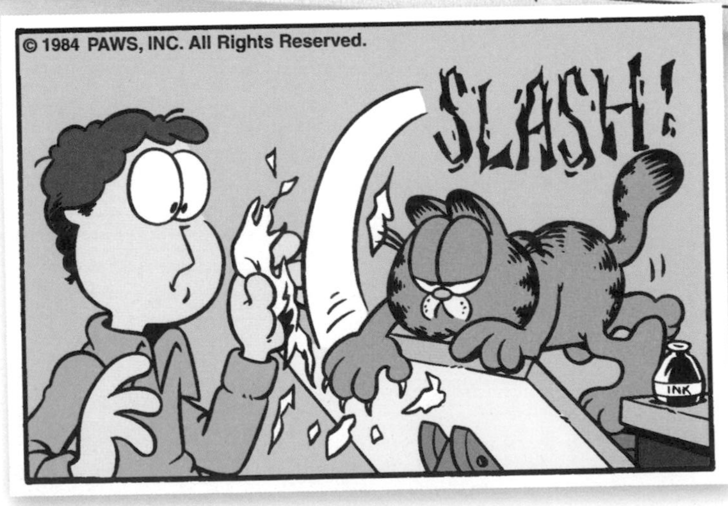
© 1984 PAWS, INC. All Rights Reserved.
SLASH!
INK

Cats may very well have
life figured out.

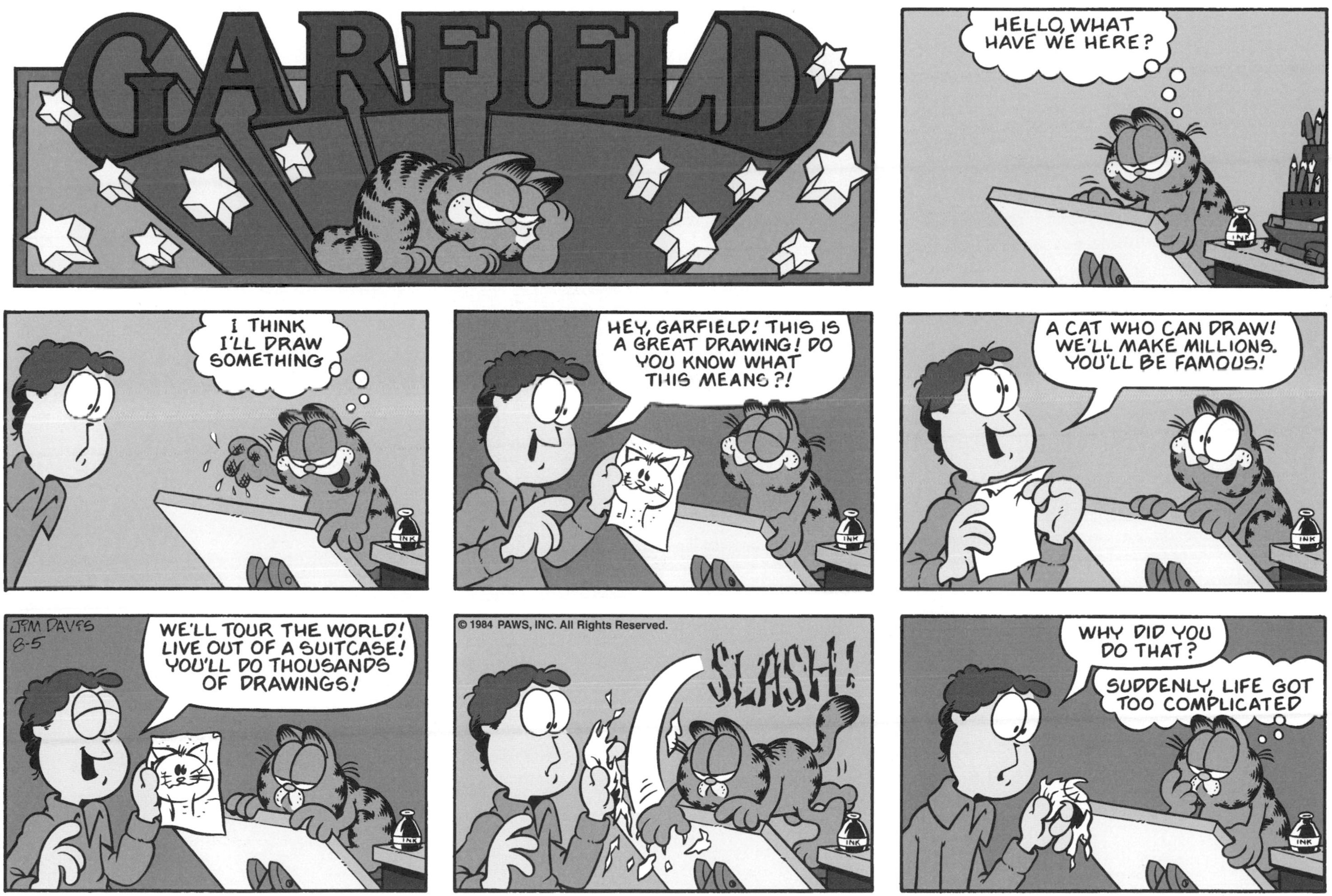

GARFIELD
HELLO, WHAT HAVE WE HERE?
I THINK I'LL DRAW SOMETHING
HEY, GARFIELD! THIS IS A GREAT DRAWING! DO YOU KNOW WHAT THIS MEANS?!
A CAT WHO CAN DRAW! WE'LL MAKE MILLIONS. YOU'LL BE FAMOUS!
JIM DAVIS 8-5
WE'LL TOUR THE WORLD! LIVE OUT OF A SUITCASE! YOU'LL DO THOUSANDS OF DRAWINGS!
© 1984 PAWS, INC. All Rights Reserved.
SLASH!
WHY DID YOU DO THAT?
SUDDENLY, LIFE GOT TOO COMPLICATED

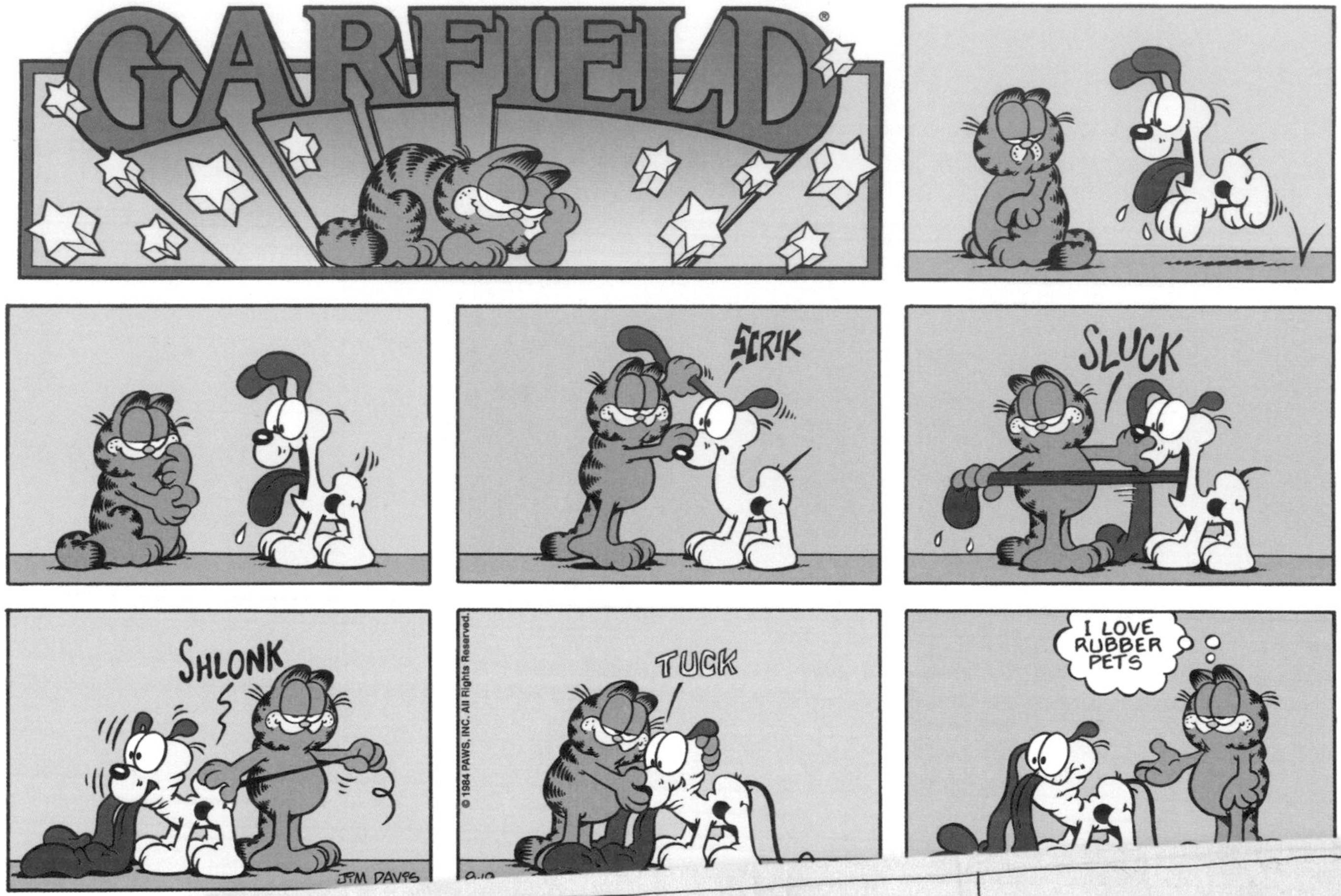
GARFIELD
SCRIK
SLUCK
SHLONK
© 1984 PAWS, INC. All Rights Reserved.
TUCK
I LOVE RUBBER PETS
JIM DAVIS

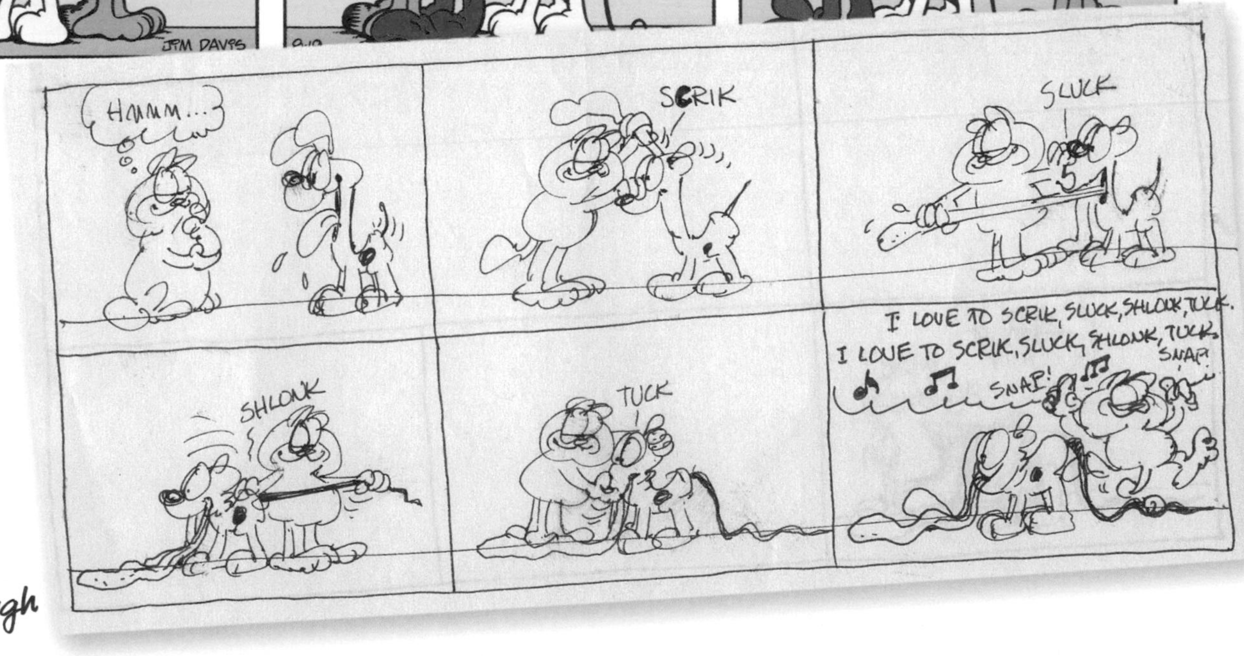
HMMM...
SCRIK
SLUCK
SHLONK
TUCK
I LOVE TO SCRIK, SLUCK, SHLOCK, TUCK.
I LOVE TO SCRIK, SLUCK, SHLONK, TUCK,
SNAP!
SNAP!

original rough

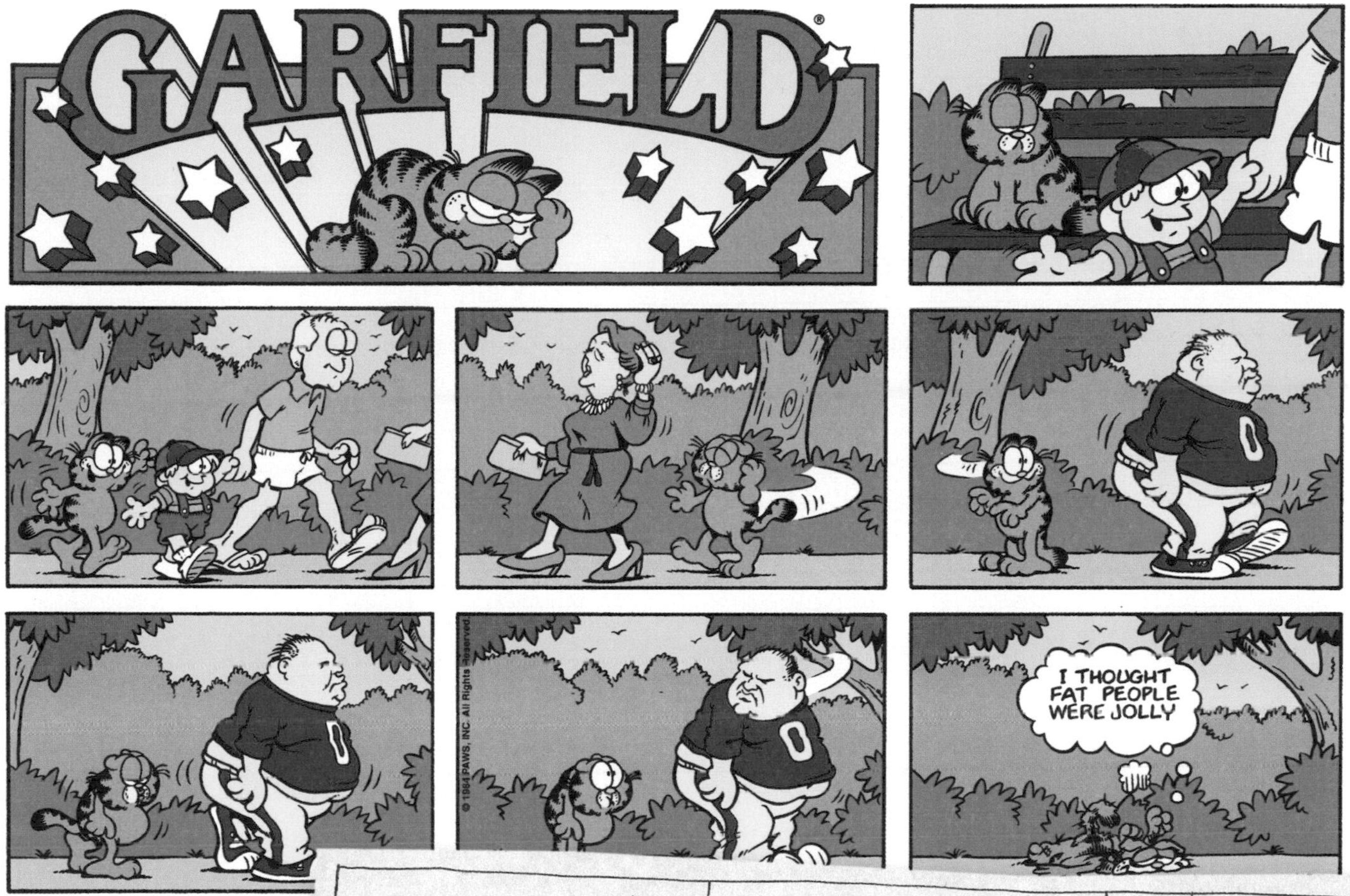
GARFIELD
© 1984 PAWS, INC. All Rights Reserved.
I THOUGHT FAT PEOPLE WERE JOLLY

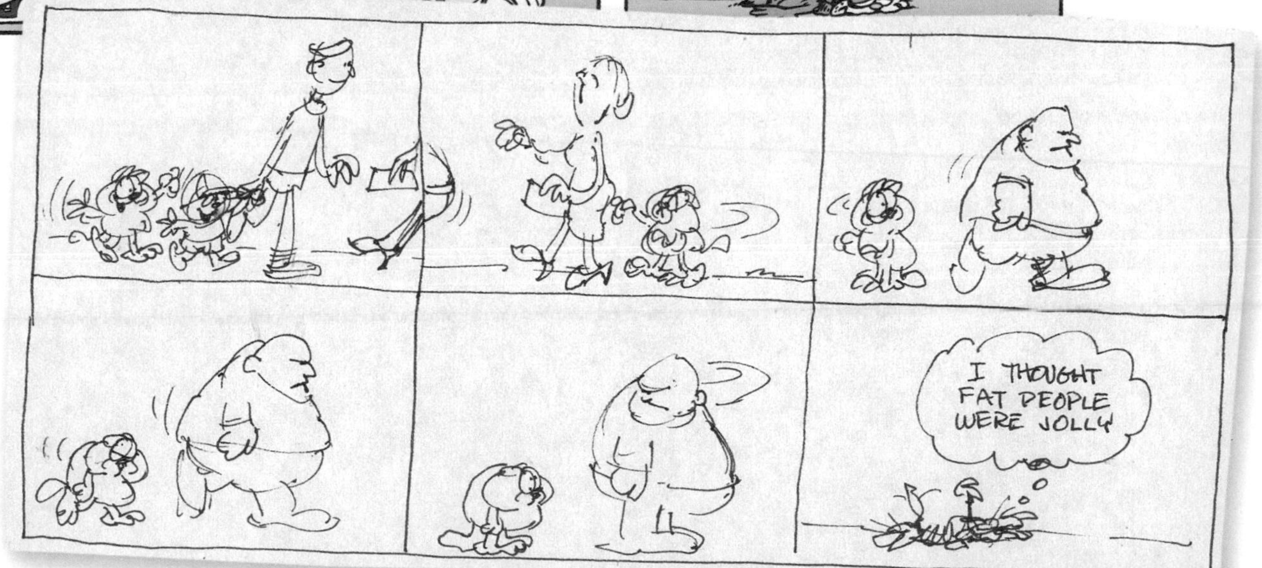
I THOUGHT FAT PEOPLE WERE JOLLY

original rough

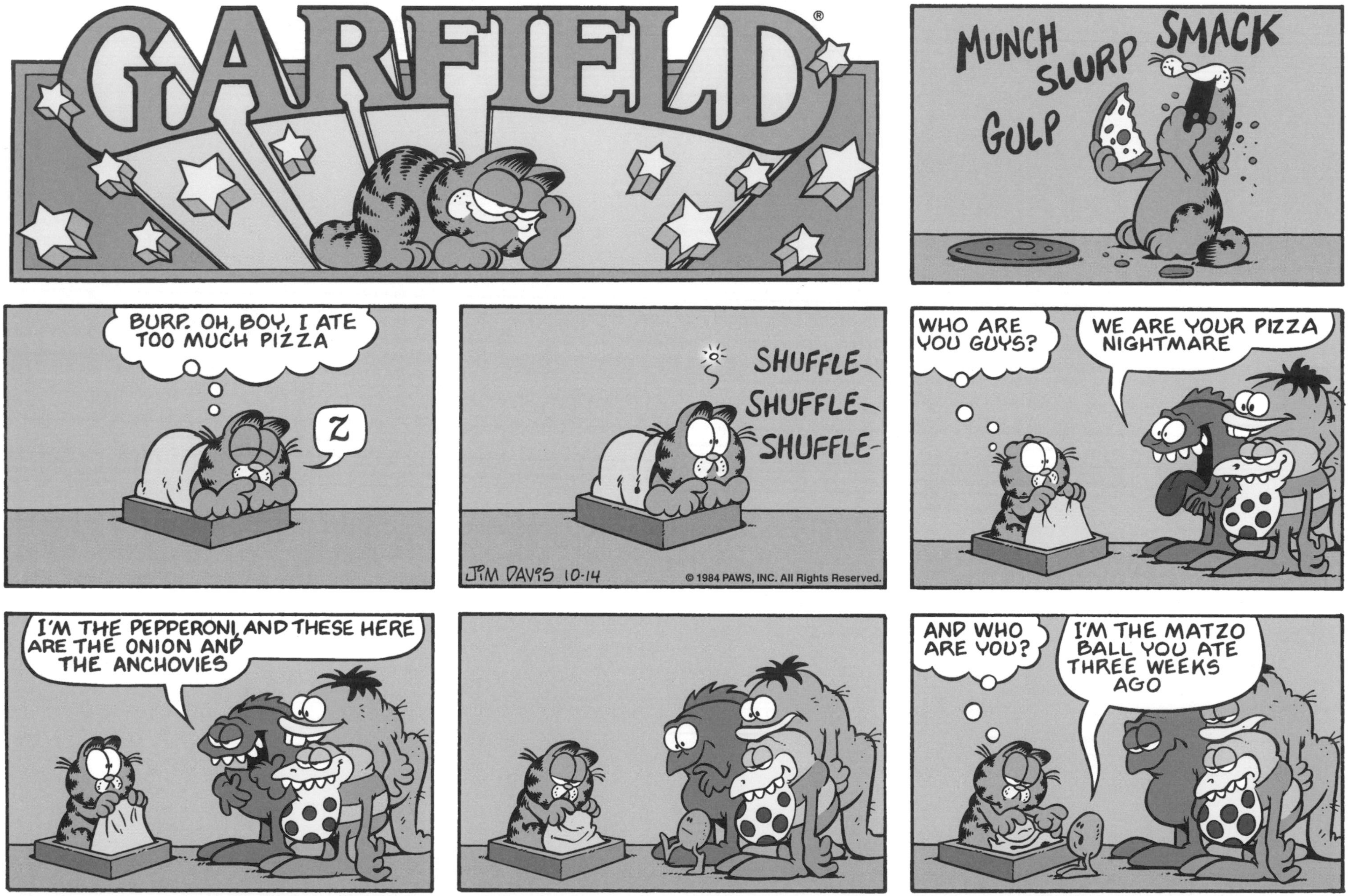
GARFIELD®
MUNCH
SLURP
SMACK
GULP
BURP. OH, BOY, I ATE TOO MUCH PIZZA
Z
SHUFFLE
SHUFFLE
SHUFFLE
JIM DAVIS 10-14
© 1984 PAWS, INC. All Rights Reserved.
WHO ARE YOU GUYS?
WE ARE YOUR PIZZA NIGHTMARE
I'M THE PEPPERONI, AND THESE HERE ARE THE ONION AND THE ANCHOVIES
AND WHO ARE YOU?
I'M THE MATZO BALL YOU ATE THREE WEEKS AGO

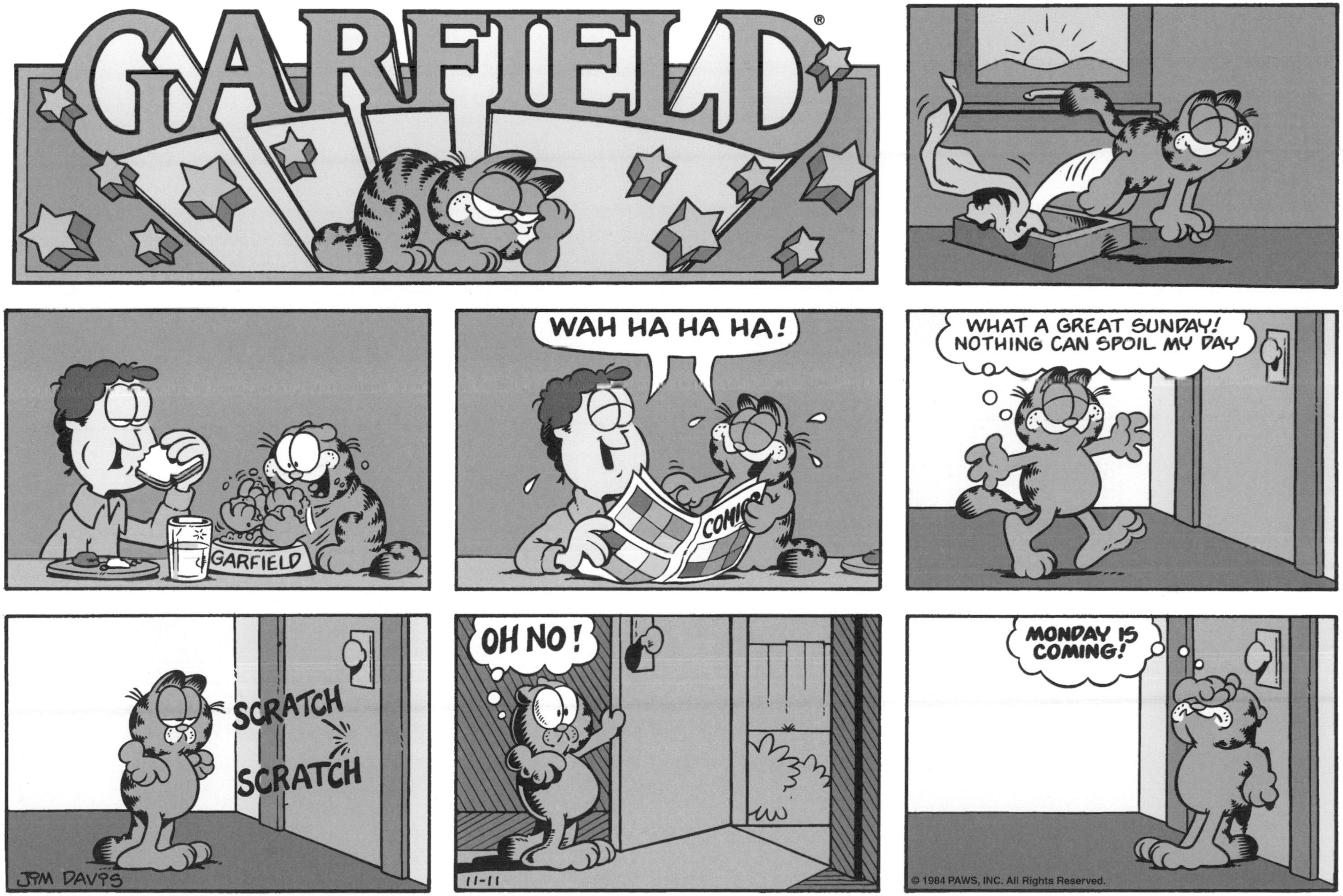
GARFIELD®
WAH HA HA HA!
COMICS
WHAT A GREAT SUNDAY! NOTHING CAN SPOIL MY DAY
SCRATCH
SCRATCH
JIM DAVIS
OH NO!
11-11
MONDAY IS COMING!
© 1984 PAWS, INC. All Rights Reserved.

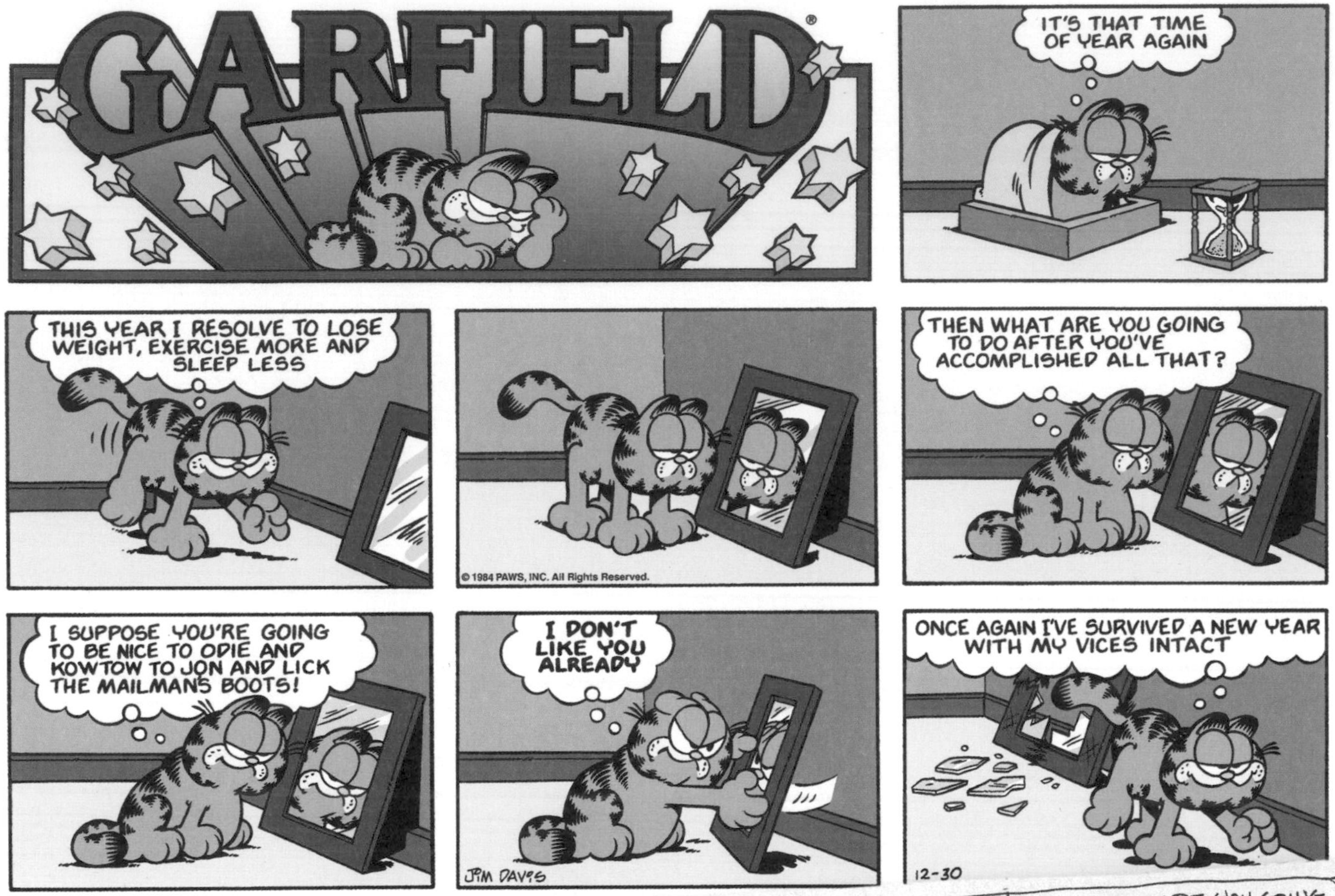
GARFIELD
IT'S THAT TIME OF YEAR AGAIN
THIS YEAR I RESOLVE TO LOSE WEIGHT, EXERCISE MORE AND SLEEP LESS
THEN WHAT ARE YOU GOING TO DO AFTER YOU'VE ACCOMPLISHED ALL THAT?
© 1984 PAWS, INC. All Rights Reserved.
I SUPPOSE YOU'RE GOING TO BE NICE TO ODIE AND KOWTOW TO JON AND LICK THE MAILMAN'S BOOTS!
I DON'T LIKE YOU ALREADY
ONCE AGAIN I'VE SURVIVED A NEW YEAR WITH MY VICES INTACT
JIM DAVIS
12-30

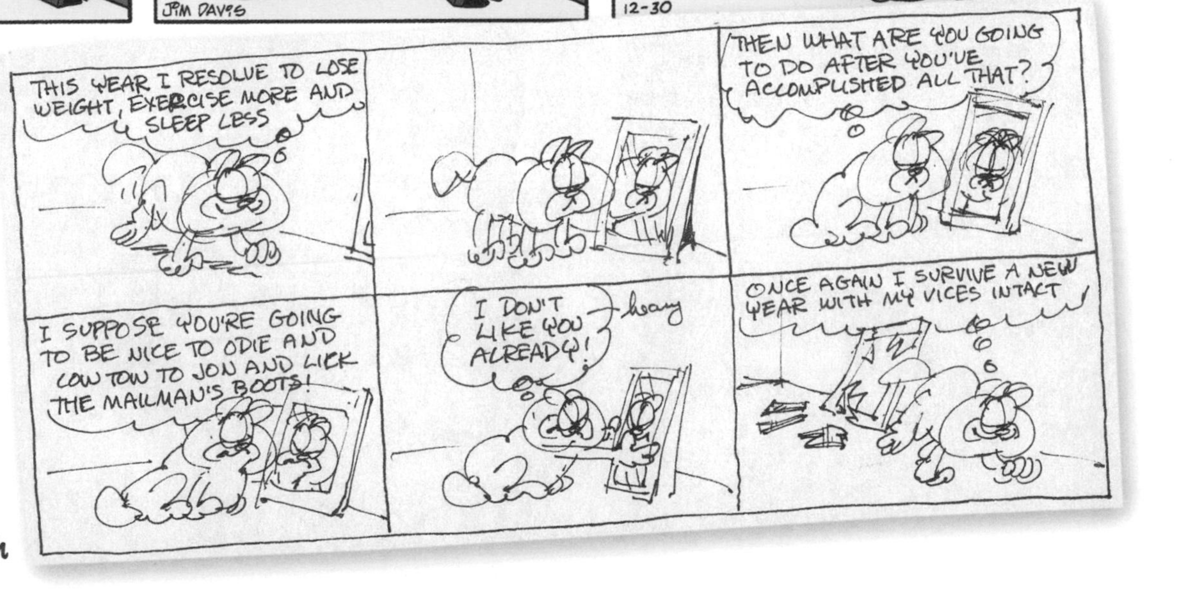
THIS YEAR I RESOLVE TO LOSE WEIGHT, EXERCISE MORE AND SLEEP LESS
THEN WHAT ARE YOU GOING TO DO AFTER YOU'VE ACCOMPLISHED ALL THAT?
I SUPPOSE YOU'RE GOING TO BE NICE TO ODIE AND COW TOW TO JON AND LICK THE MAILMAN'S BOOTS!
I DON'T LIKE YOU ALREADY!
heavy
ONCE AGAIN I SURVIVE A NEW YEAR WITH MY VICES INTACT

original rough

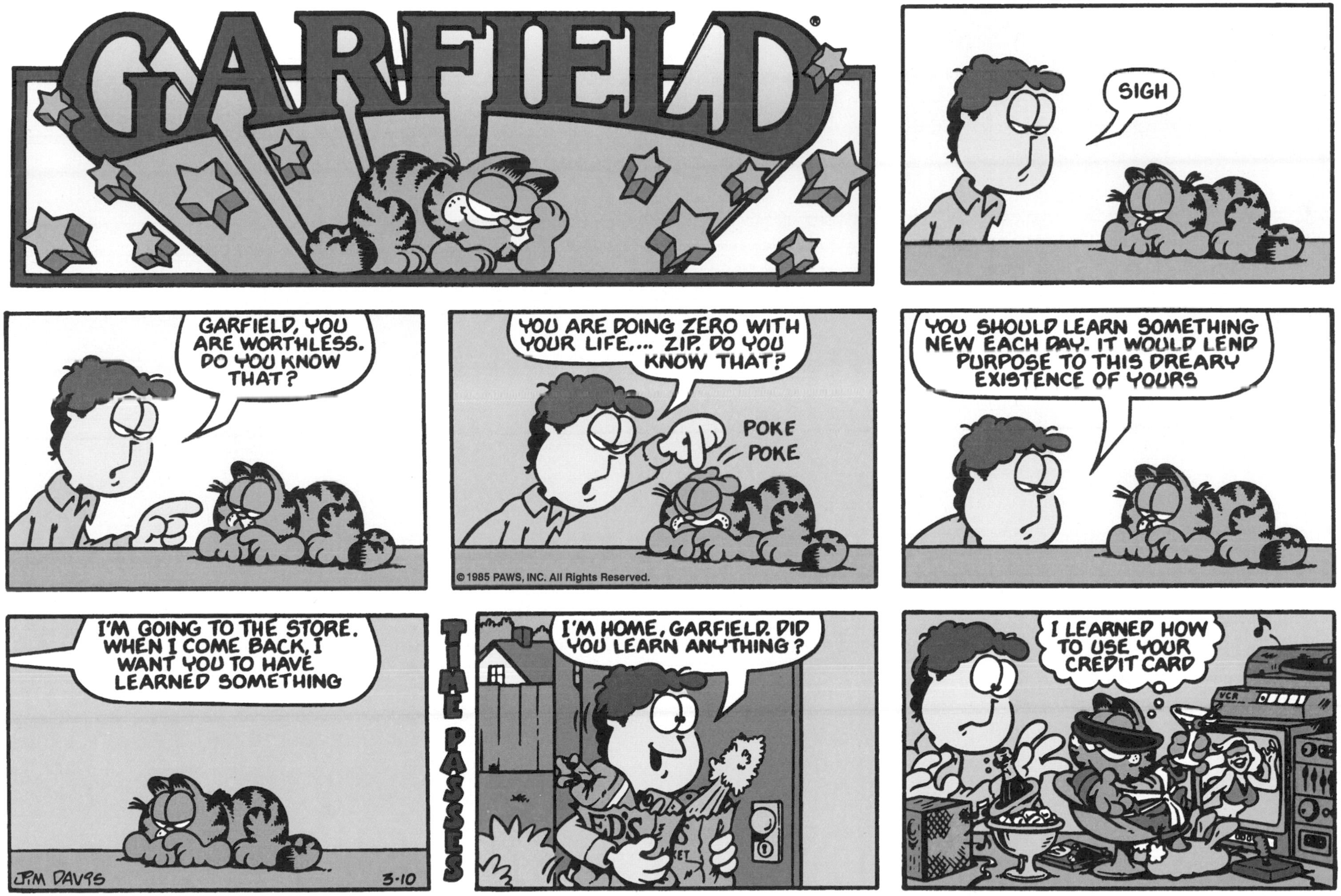
GARFIELD
SIGH
GARFIELD, YOU ARE WORTHLESS. DO YOU KNOW THAT?
YOU ARE DOING ZERO WITH YOUR LIFE.... ZIP. DO YOU KNOW THAT?
POKE POKE
© 1985 PAWS, INC. All Rights Reserved.
YOU SHOULD LEARN SOMETHING NEW EACH DAY. IT WOULD LEND PURPOSE TO THIS DREARY EXISTENCE OF YOURS
I'M GOING TO THE STORE. WHEN I COME BACK, I WANT YOU TO HAVE LEARNED SOMETHING
JIM DAVIS
3-10
TIME PASSES
I'M HOME, GARFIELD. DID YOU LEARN ANYTHING?
I LEARNED HOW TO USE YOUR CREDIT CARD

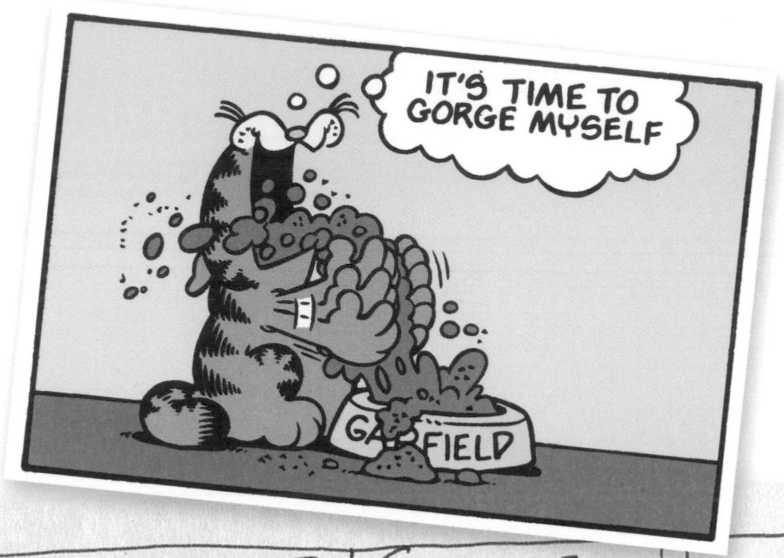
IT'S TIME TO GORGE MYSELF
GARFIELD

Some of the strips endure because they end with what I call a "quotable quote."

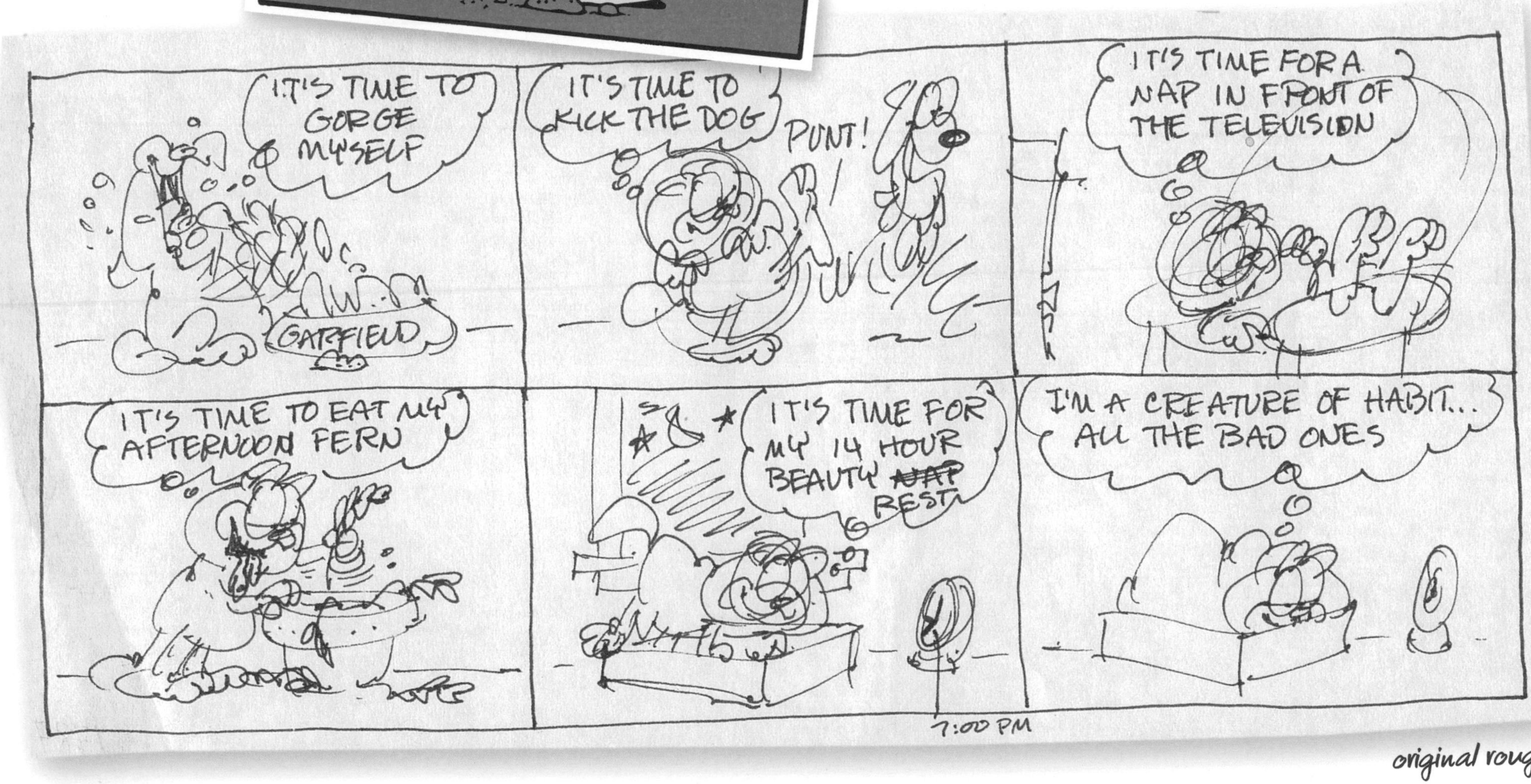
IT'S TIME TO GORGE MYSELF
GARFIELD
IT'S TIME TO KICK THE DOG
PUNT!
IT'S TIME FOR A NAP IN FRONT OF THE TELEVISION
IT'S TIME TO EAT MY AFTERNOON FERN
IT'S TIME FOR MY 14 HOUR BEAUTY ~~NAP~~ REST
I'M A CREATURE OF HABIT... ALL THE BAD ONES
7:00 PM

original rough

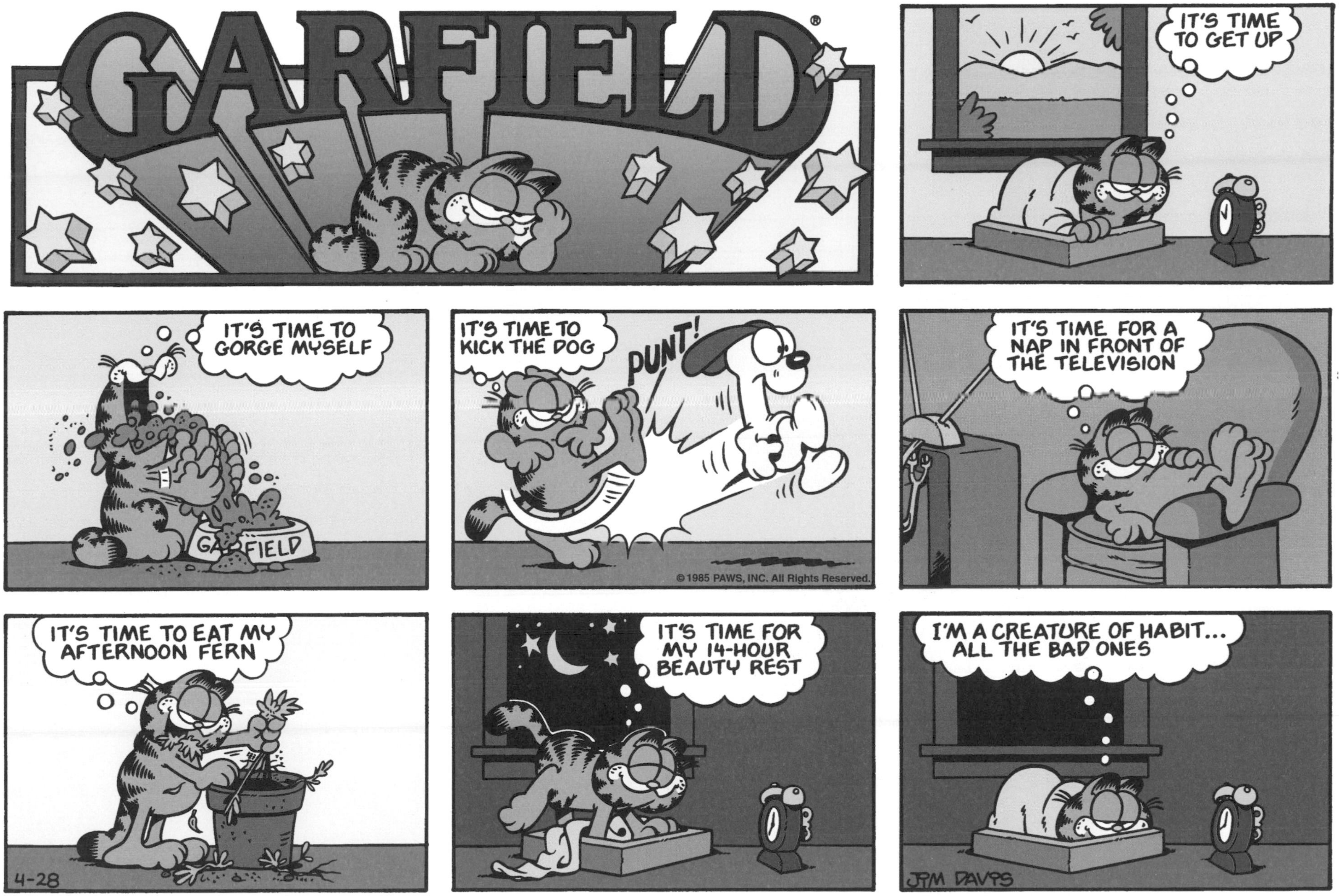
GARFIELD®
IT'S TIME TO GET UP
IT'S TIME TO GORGE MYSELF
GARFIELD
IT'S TIME TO KICK THE DOG
PUNT!
© 1985 PAWS, INC. All Rights Reserved.
IT'S TIME FOR A NAP IN FRONT OF THE TELEVISION
IT'S TIME TO EAT MY AFTERNOON FERN
4-28
IT'S TIME FOR MY 14-HOUR BEAUTY REST
I'M A CREATURE OF HABIT... ALL THE BAD ONES
JIM DAVIS

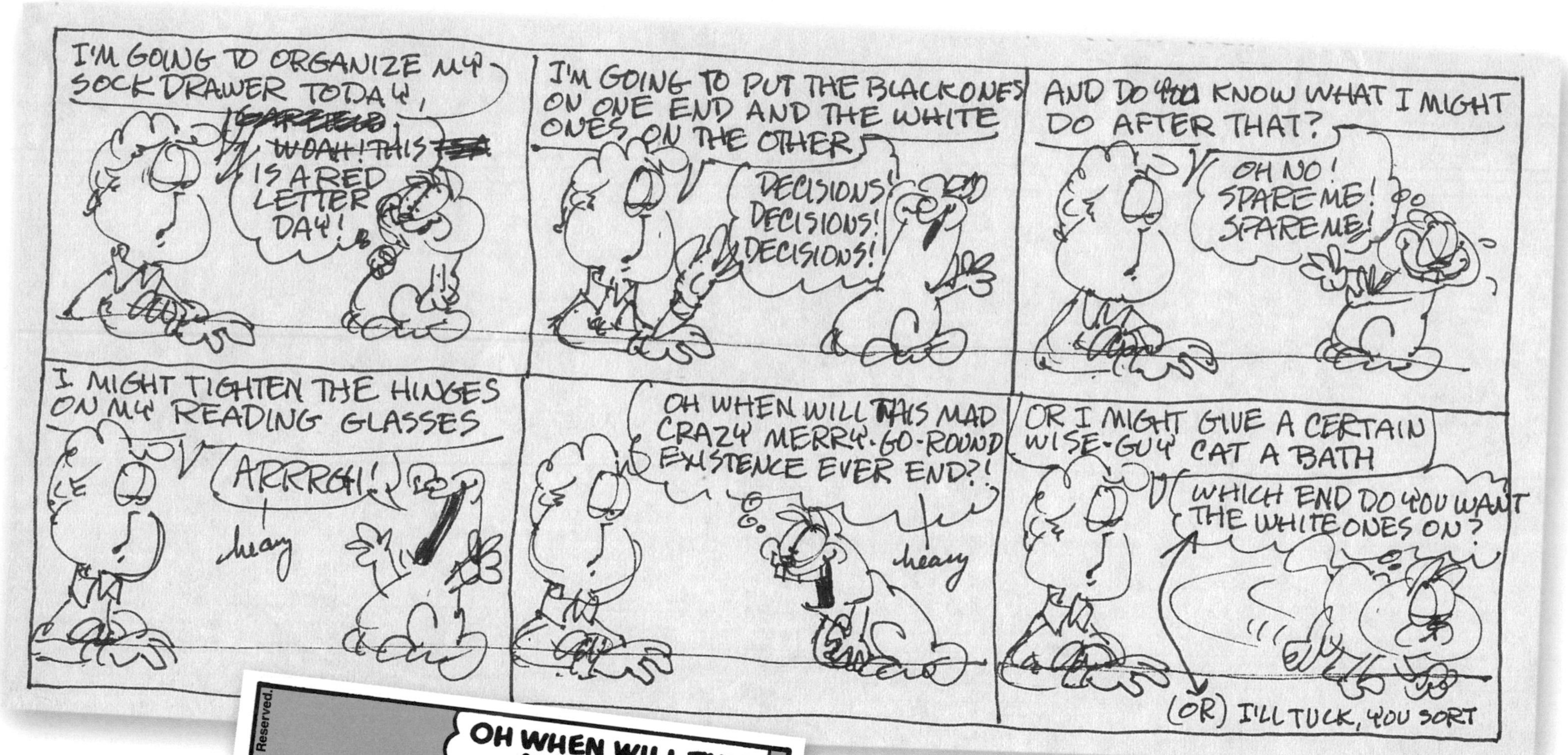
I'M GOING TO ORGANIZE MY SOCK DRAWER TODAY,
WOAH! THIS IS A RED LETTER DAY!
I'M GOING TO PUT THE BLACK ONES ON ONE END AND THE WHITE ONES ON THE OTHER
DECISIONS! DECISIONS! DECISIONS!
AND DO YOU KNOW WHAT I MIGHT DO AFTER THAT?
OH NO! SPARE ME! SPARE ME!
I MIGHT TIGHTEN THE HINGES ON MY READING GLASSES
ARRRGH!
heavy
OH WHEN WILL THIS MAD CRAZY MERRY-GO-ROUND EXISTENCE EVER END?!
heavy
OR I MIGHT GIVE A CERTAIN WISE-GUY CAT A BATH
WHICH END DO YOU WANT THE WHITE ONES ON?
(OR) I'LL TUCK, YOU SORT

original rough

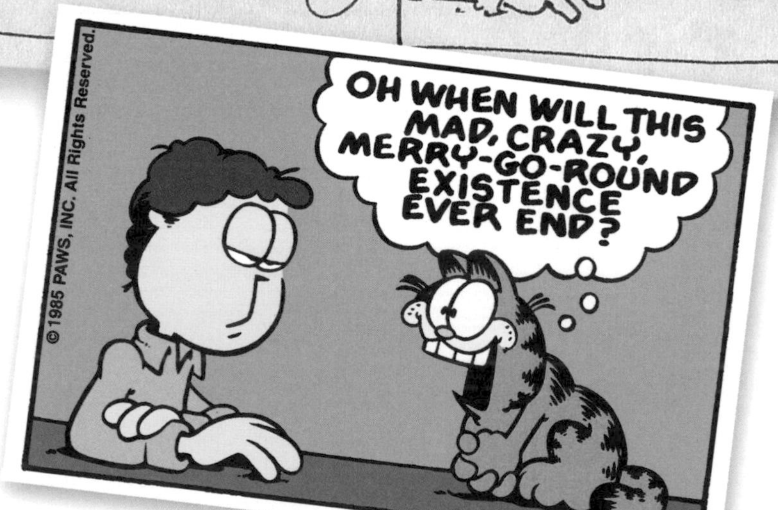
OH WHEN WILL THIS MAD, CRAZY, MERRY-GO-ROUND EXISTENCE EVER END?
© 1985 PAWS, INC. All Rights Reserved.

Even though Garfield can't talk, I still marvel at how well he and Jon communicate.

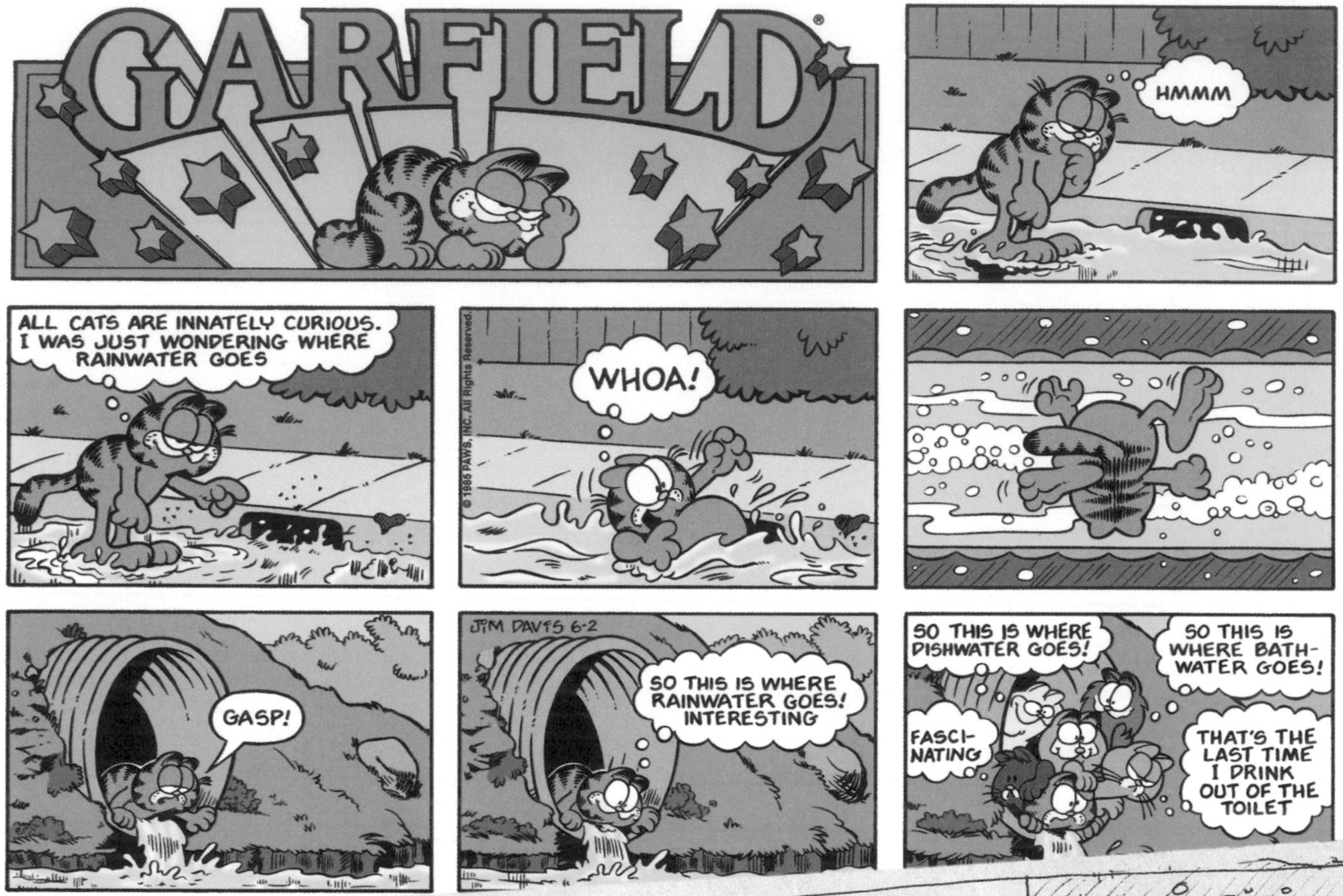
GARFIELD
HMMM
ALL CATS ARE INNATELY CURIOUS. I WAS JUST WONDERING WHERE RAINWATER GOES
© 1985 PAWS, INC. All Rights Reserved.
WHOA!
GASP!
JIM DAVIS 6-2
SO THIS IS WHERE RAINWATER GOES! INTERESTING
SO THIS IS WHERE DISHWATER GOES!
SO THIS IS WHERE BATH-WATER GOES!
FASCI-NATING
THAT'S THE LAST TIME I DRINK OUT OF THE TOILET

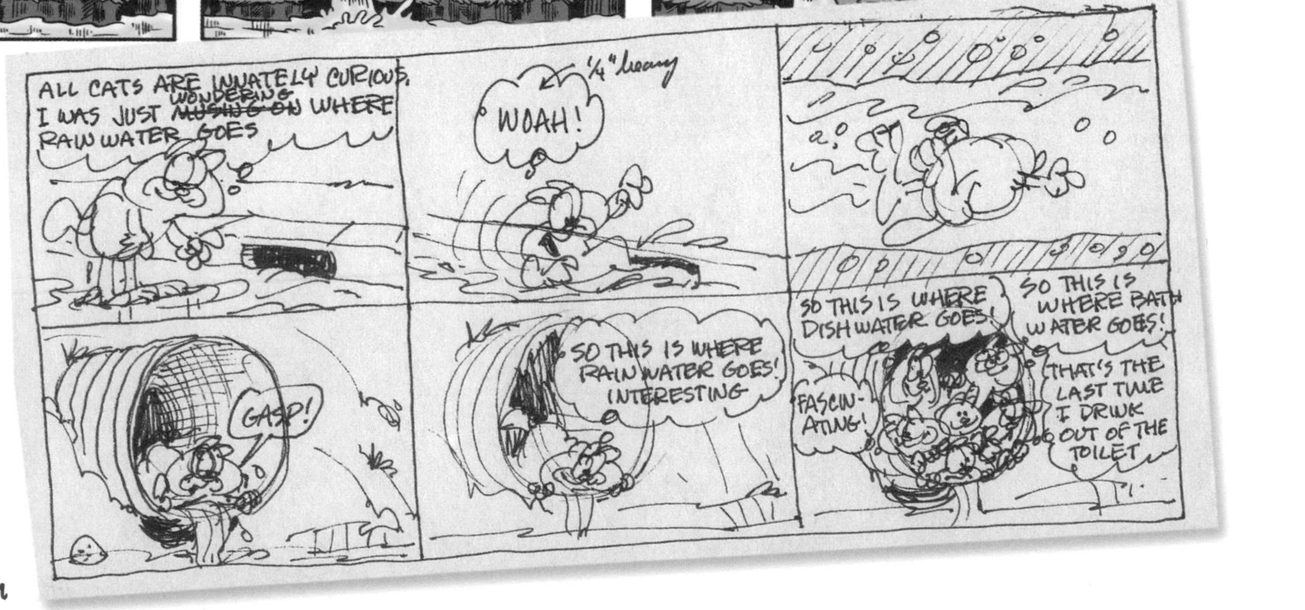
ALL CATS ARE INNATELY CURIOUS. I WAS JUST ~~MUSING ON~~ WONDERING WHERE RAINWATER GOES
1/4" heavy
WOAH!
GASP!
SO THIS IS WHERE RAINWATER GOES! INTERESTING
SO THIS IS WHERE DISHWATER GOES!
SO THIS IS WHERE BATH WATER GOES!
FASCIN-ATING!
THAT'S THE LAST TIME I DRINK OUT OF THE TOILET

original rough

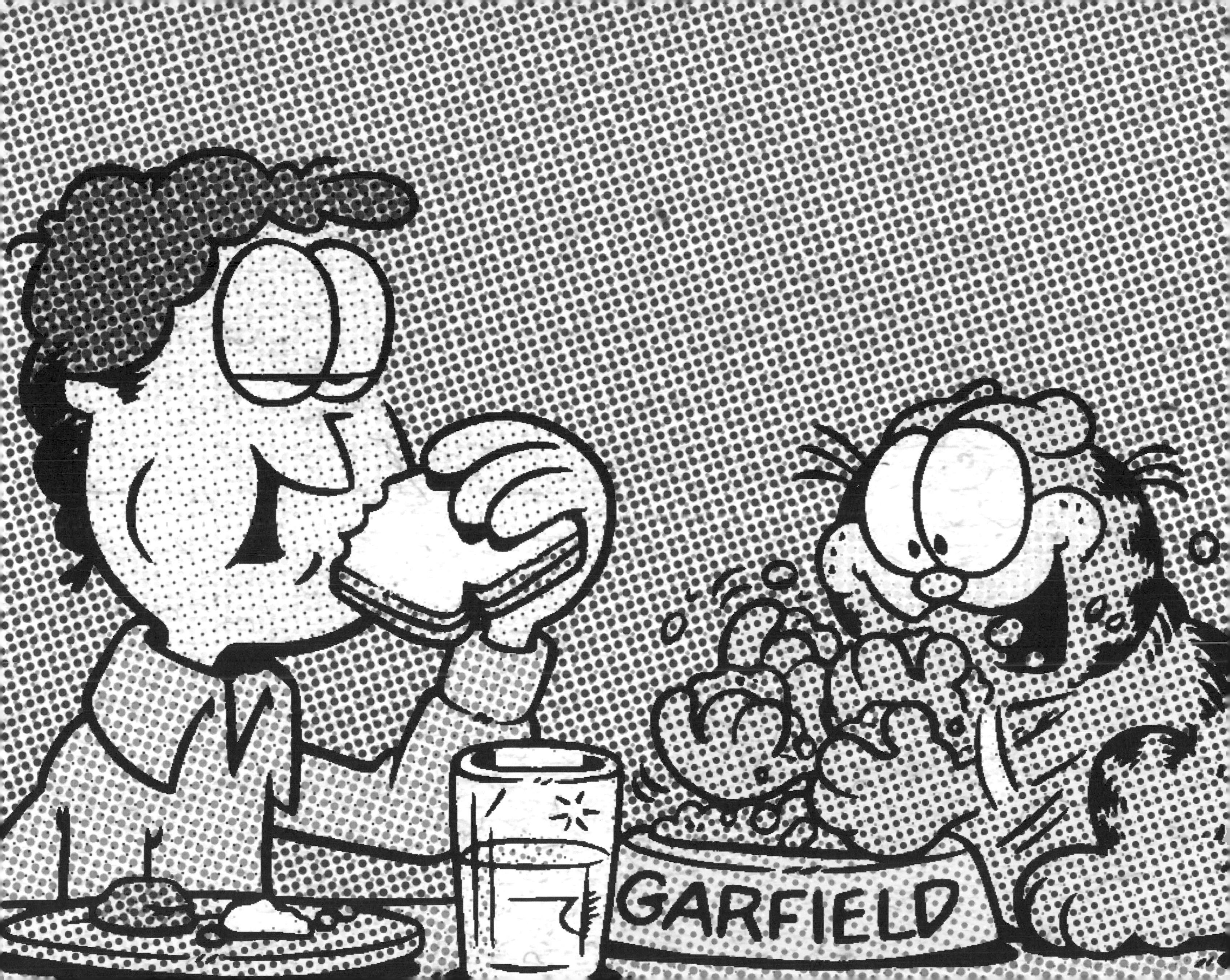
GARFIELD

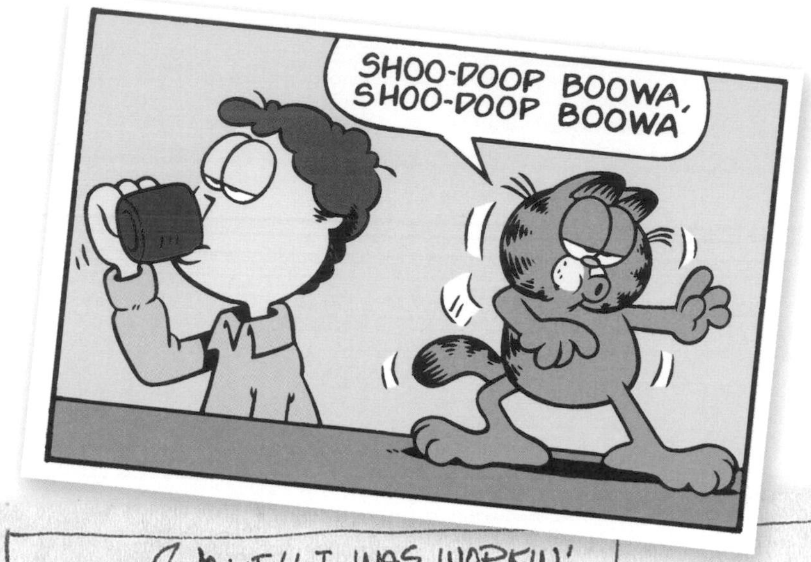
SHOO-DOOP BOOWA, SHOO-DOOP BOOWA

I must confess that these lyrics aren't original. They were penned by a college classmate for his band. Since then, I've often wondered whatever became of David Letterman.

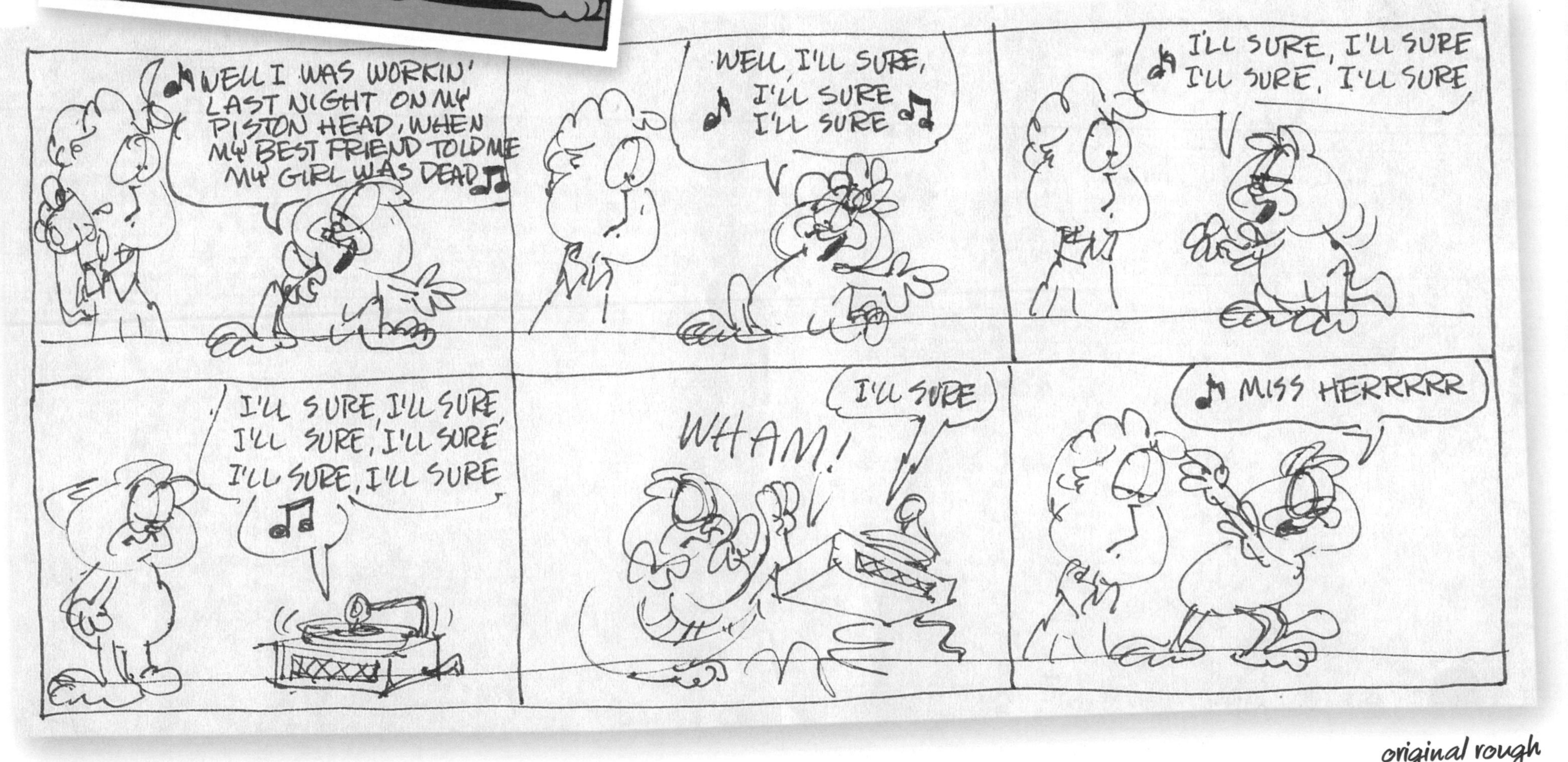
WELL I WAS WORKIN' LAST NIGHT ON MY PISTON HEAD, WHEN MY BEST FRIEND TOLD ME MY GIRL WAS DEAD
WELL, I'LL SURE, I'LL SURE I'LL SURE
I'LL SURE, I'LL SURE I'LL SURE, I'LL SURE
I'LL SURE, I'LL SURE, I'LL SURE, I'LL SURE I'LL SURE, I'LL SURE
I'LL SURE
WHAM!
MISS HERRRRR

original rough

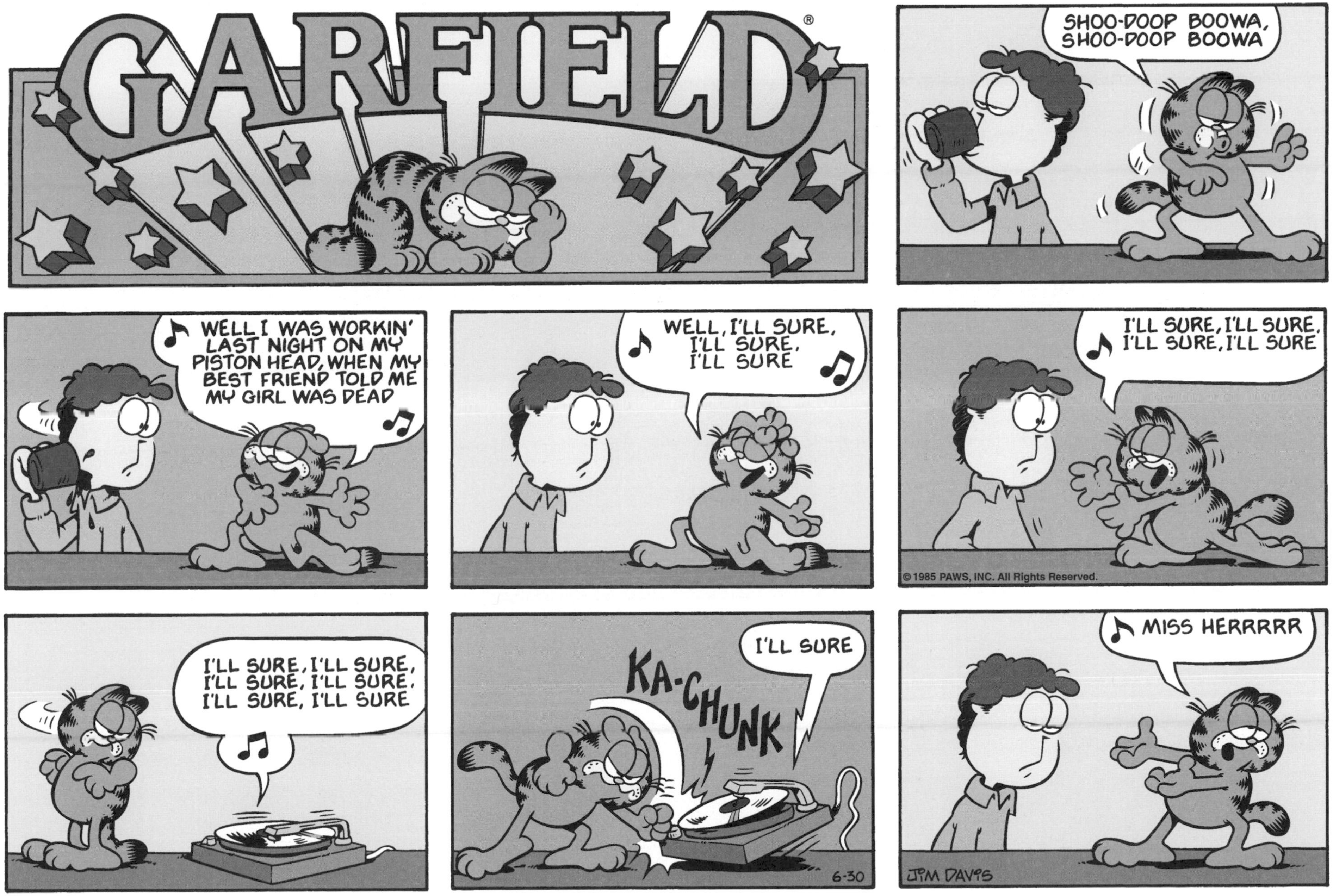
GARFIELD®
SHOO-DOOP BOOWA, SHOO-DOOP BOOWA
WELL I WAS WORKIN' LAST NIGHT ON MY PISTON HEAD, WHEN MY BEST FRIEND TOLD ME MY GIRL WAS DEAD
WELL, I'LL SURE, I'LL SURE, I'LL SURE
I'LL SURE, I'LL SURE, I'LL SURE, I'LL SURE
© 1985 PAWS, INC. All Rights Reserved.
I'LL SURE, I'LL SURE, I'LL SURE, I'LL SURE, I'LL SURE, I'LL SURE
KA-CHUNK
I'LL SURE
6-30
MISS HERRRRR
JIM DAVIS

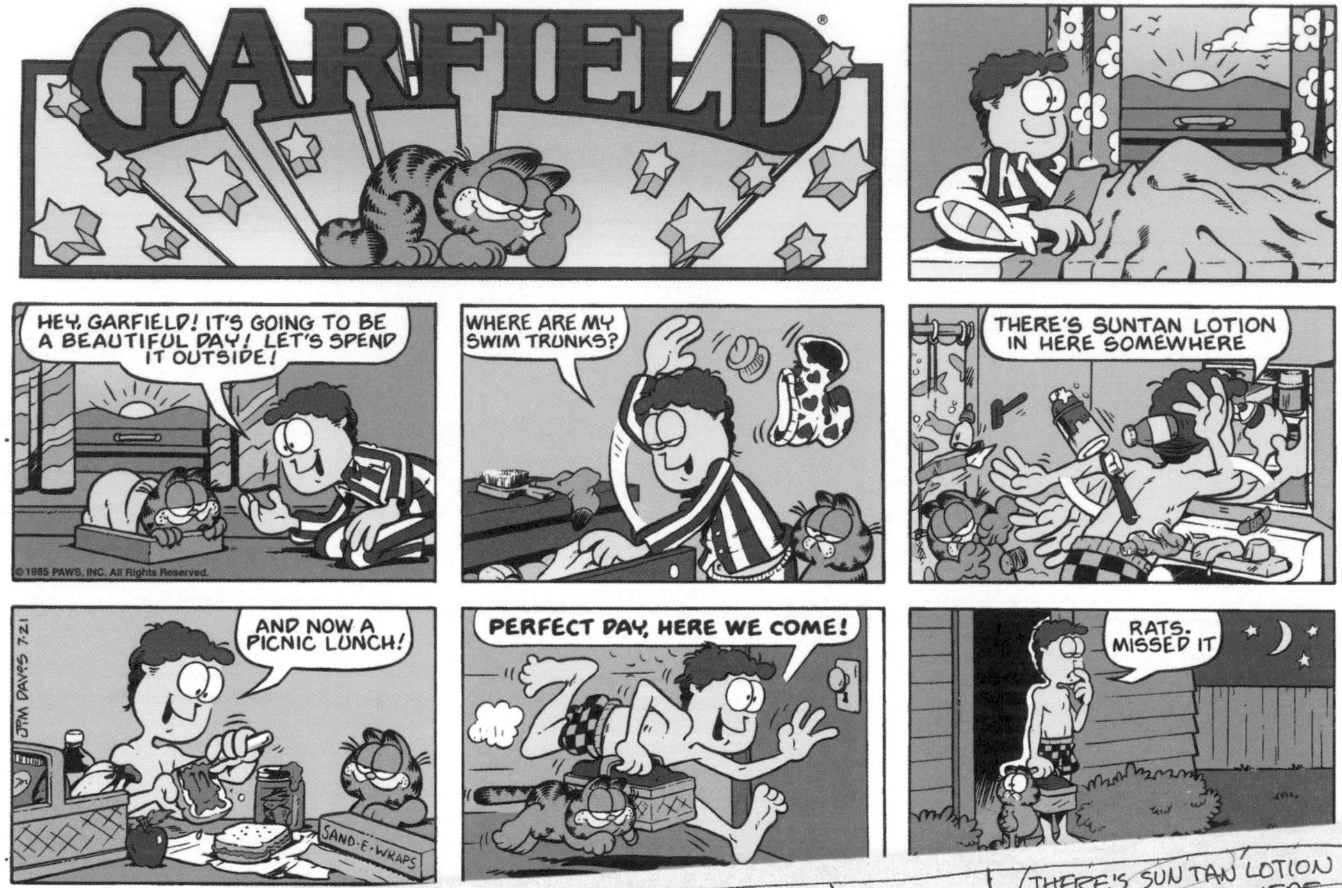
GARFIELD
HEY, GARFIELD! IT'S GOING TO BE A BEAUTIFUL DAY! LET'S SPEND IT OUTSIDE!
© 1985 PAWS, INC. All Rights Reserved.
WHERE ARE MY SWIM TRUNKS?
THERE'S SUNTAN LOTION IN HERE SOMEWHERE
JIM DAVIS 7-21
AND NOW A PICNIC LUNCH!
SAND-E-WRAPS
PERFECT DAY, HERE WE COME!
RATS. MISSED IT

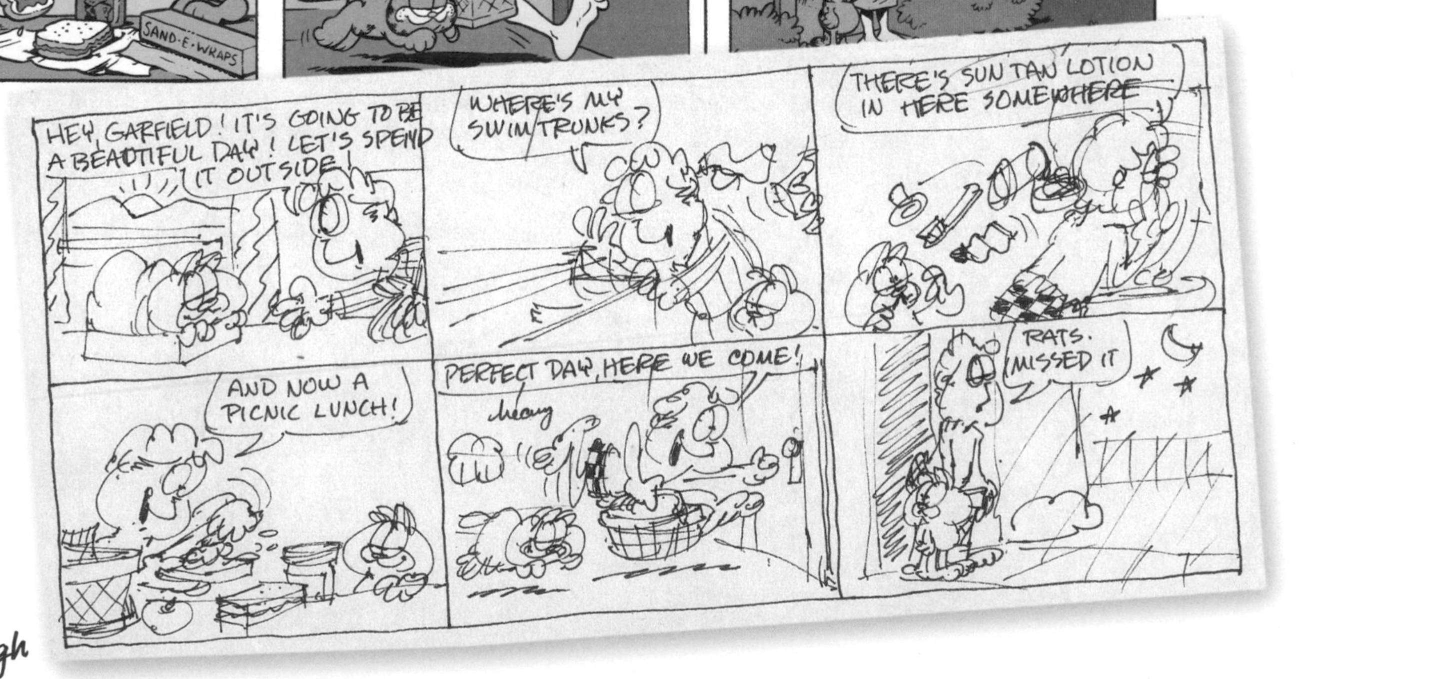
HEY, GARFIELD! IT'S GOING TO BE A BEAUTIFUL DAY! LET'S SPEND IT OUTSIDE!
WHERE'S MY SWIM TRUNKS?
THERE'S SUN TAN LOTION IN HERE SOMEWHERE
AND NOW A PICNIC LUNCH!
PERFECT DAY, HERE WE COME!
RATS. MISSED IT

original rough

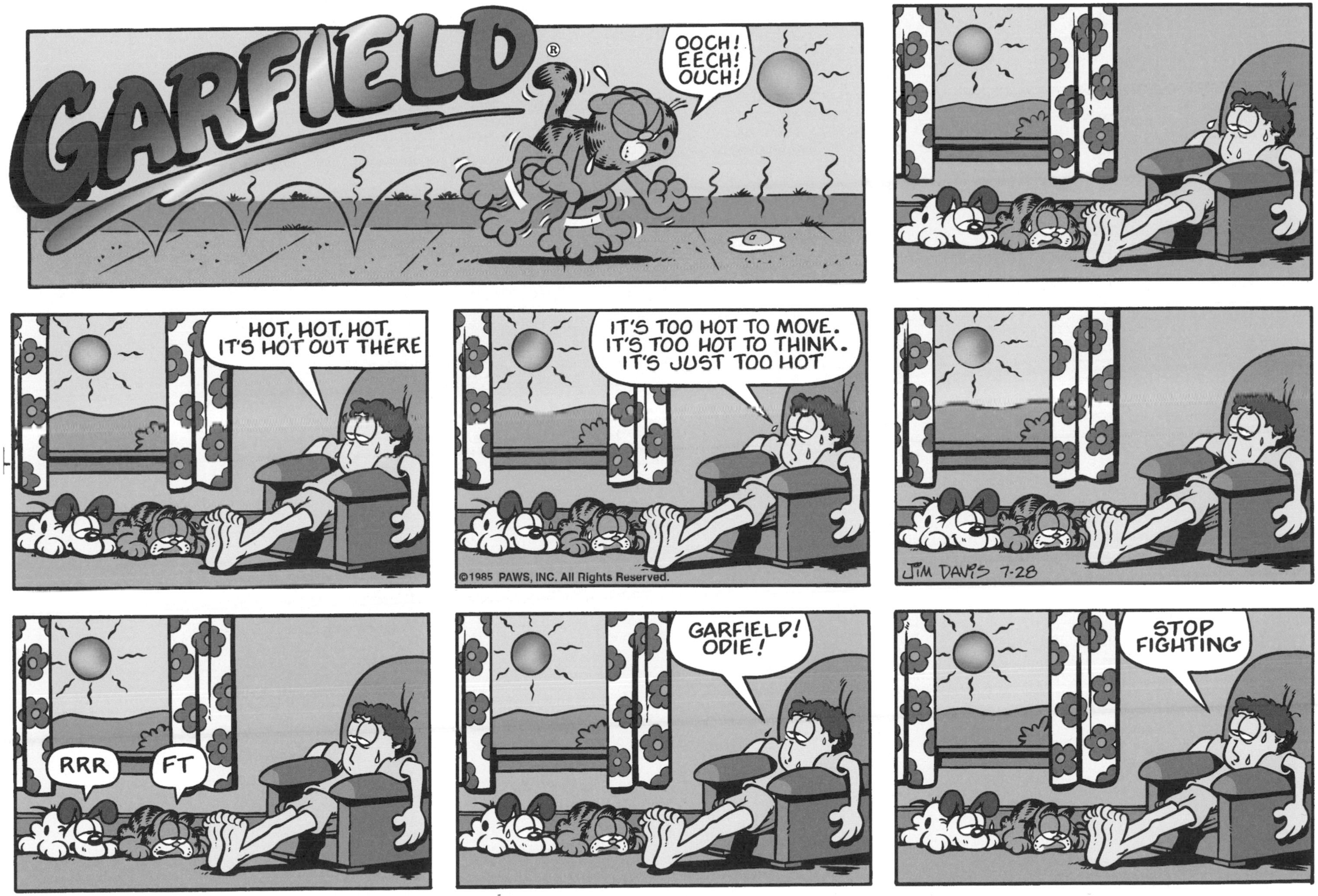
GARFIELD®
OOCH! EECH! OUCH!
HOT, HOT, HOT. IT'S HOT OUT THERE
IT'S TOO HOT TO MOVE. IT'S TOO HOT TO THINK. IT'S JUST TOO HOT
©1985 PAWS, INC. All Rights Reserved.
JIM DAVIS 7-28
RRR
FT
GARFIELD! ODIE!
STOP FIGHTING

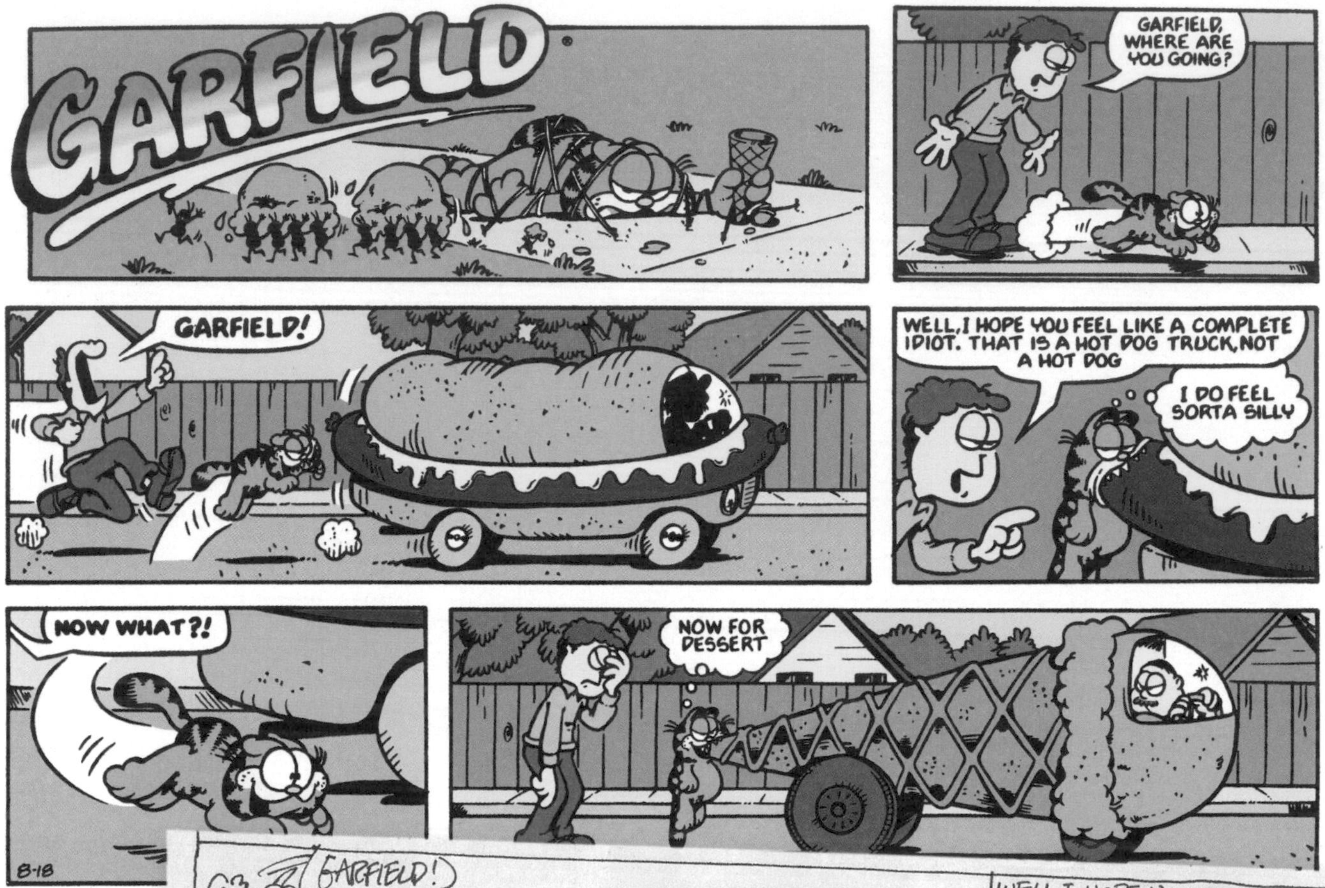
GARFIELD
GARFIELD, WHERE ARE YOU GOING?
GARFIELD!
WELL, I HOPE YOU FEEL LIKE A COMPLETE IDIOT. THAT IS A HOT DOG TRUCK, NOT A HOT DOG
I DO FEEL SORTA SILLY
NOW WHAT?!
NOW FOR DESSERT
8-18

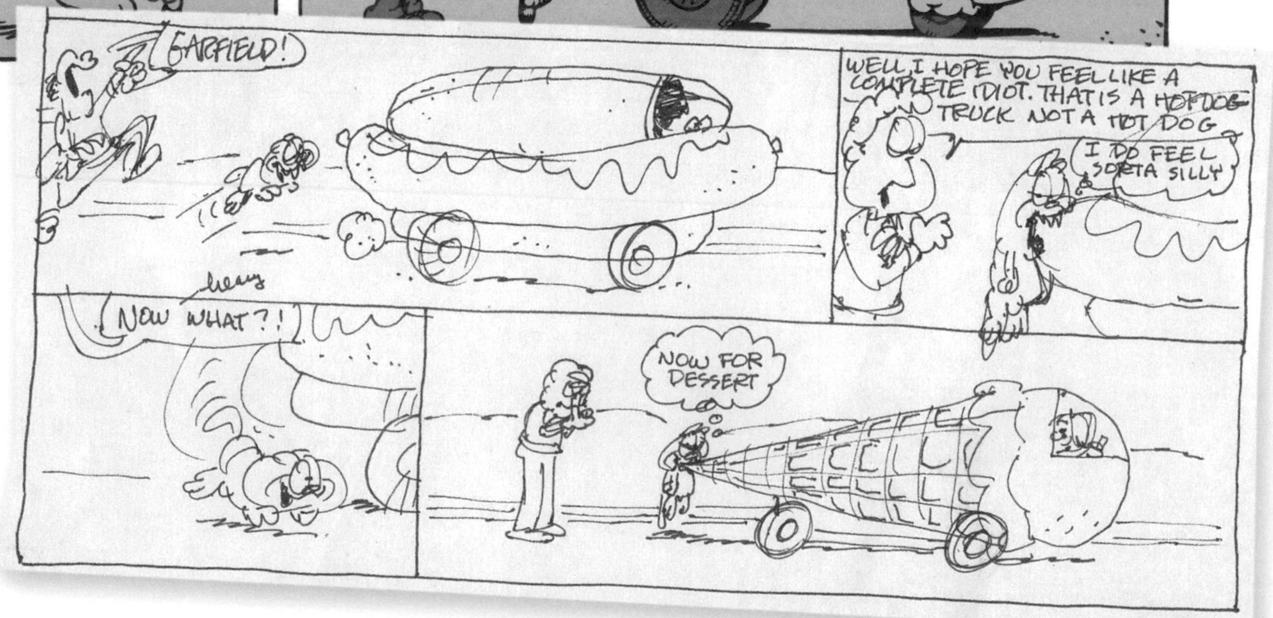
GARFIELD!
WELL, I HOPE YOU FEEL LIKE A COMPLETE IDIOT. THAT IS A HOT DOG TRUCK NOT A HOT DOG
I DO FEEL SORTA SILLY
heavy
NOW WHAT?!
NOW FOR DESSERT

original rough

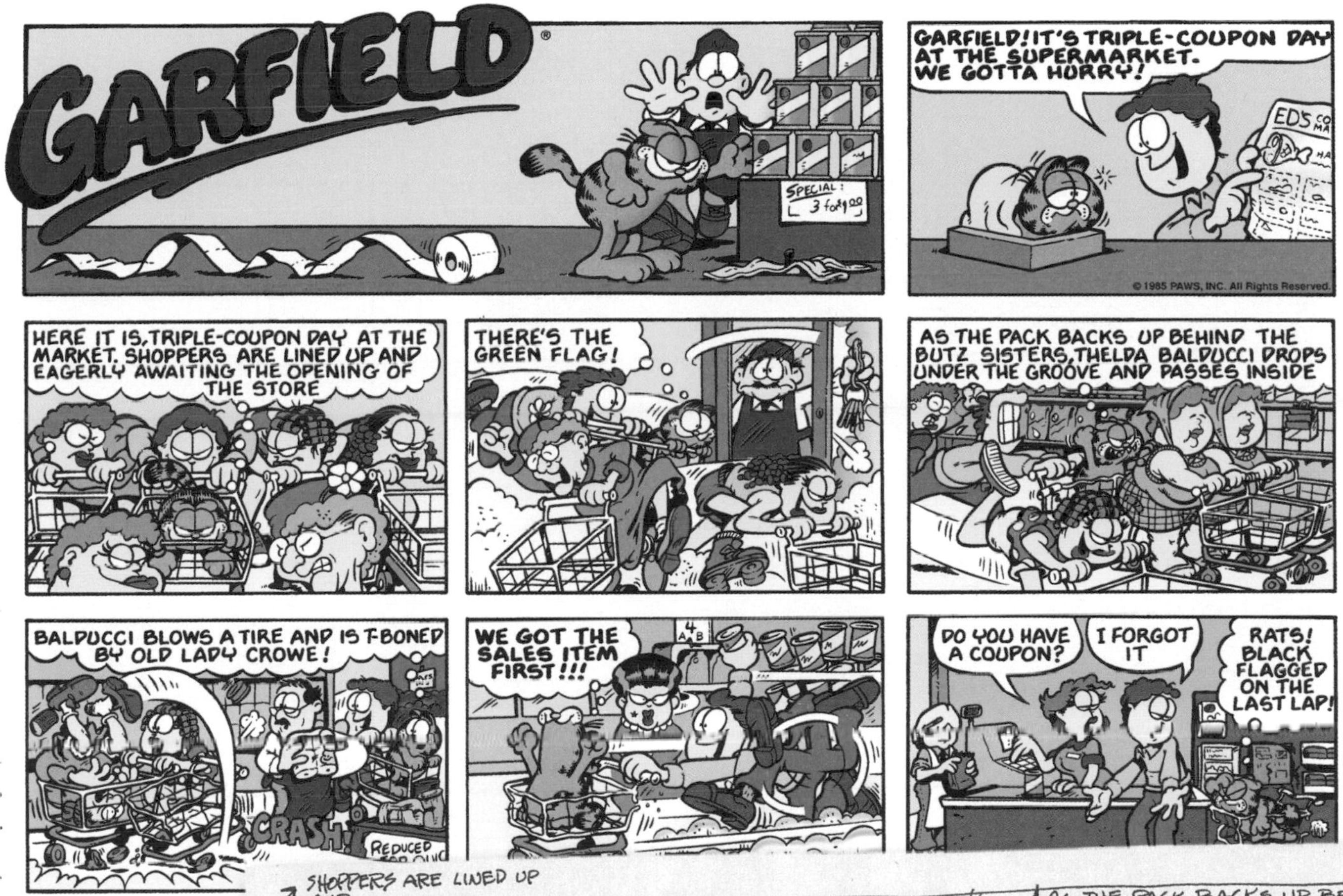
GARFIELD®
SPECIAL: 3 for $1.00
GARFIELD! IT'S TRIPLE-COUPON DAY AT THE SUPERMARKET. WE GOTTA HURRY!
ED'S
© 1985 PAWS, INC. All Rights Reserved.
HERE IT IS, TRIPLE-COUPON DAY AT THE MARKET. SHOPPERS ARE LINED UP AND EAGERLY AWAITING THE OPENING OF THE STORE
THERE'S THE GREEN FLAG!
AS THE PACK BACKS UP BEHIND THE BUTZ SISTERS, THELDA BALDUCCI DROPS UNDER THE GROOVE AND PASSES INSIDE
BALDUCCI BLOWS A TIRE AND IS T-BONED BY OLD LADY CROWE!
CRASH!
WE GOT THE SALES ITEM FIRST!!!
DO YOU HAVE A COUPON?
I FORGOT IT
RATS! BLACK FLAGGED ON THE LAST LAP!

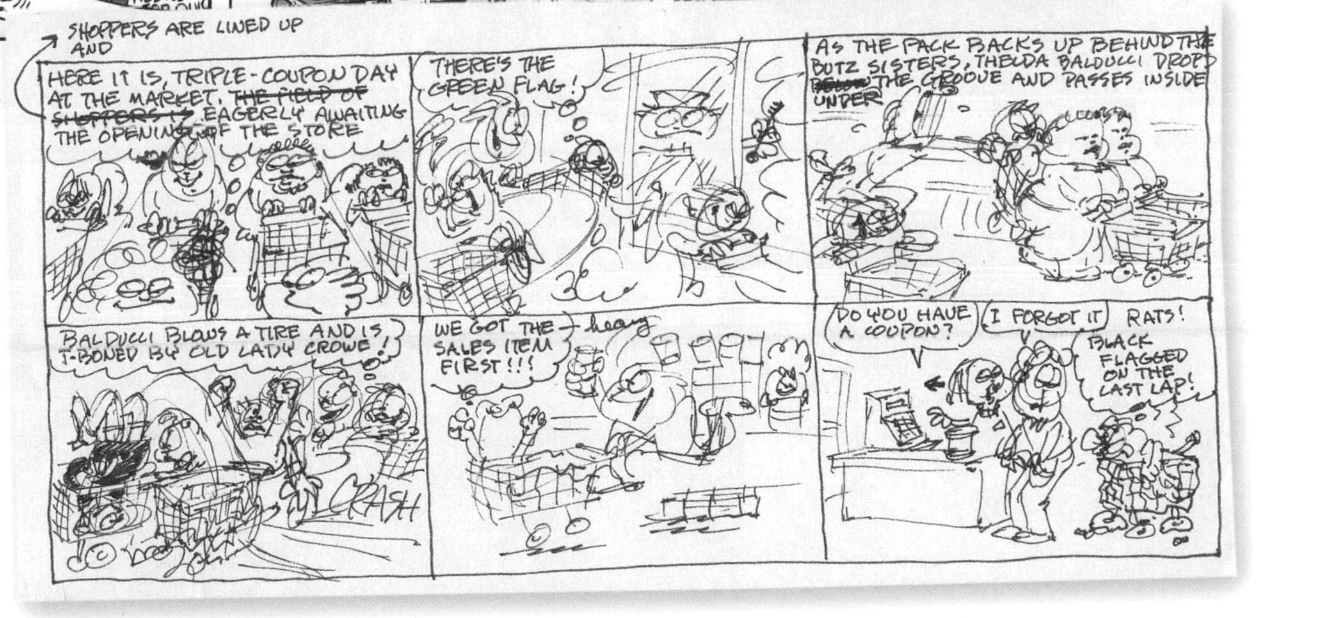
SHOPPERS ARE LINED UP AND
HERE IT IS, TRIPLE-COUPON DAY AT THE MARKET. THE FIELD OF SHOPPERS IS EAGERLY AWAITING THE OPENING OF THE STORE
THERE'S THE GREEN FLAG!
AS THE PACK BACKS UP BEHIND THE BUTZ SISTERS, THELDA BALDUCCI DROPS BELOW UNDER THE GROOVE AND PASSES INSIDE
BALDUCCI BLOWS A TIRE AND IS T-BONED BY OLD LADY CROWE!
CRASH
WE GOT THE SALES ITEM FIRST!!!
DO YOU HAVE A COUPON?
I FORGOT IT
RATS! BLACK FLAGGED ON THE LAST LAP!

original rough

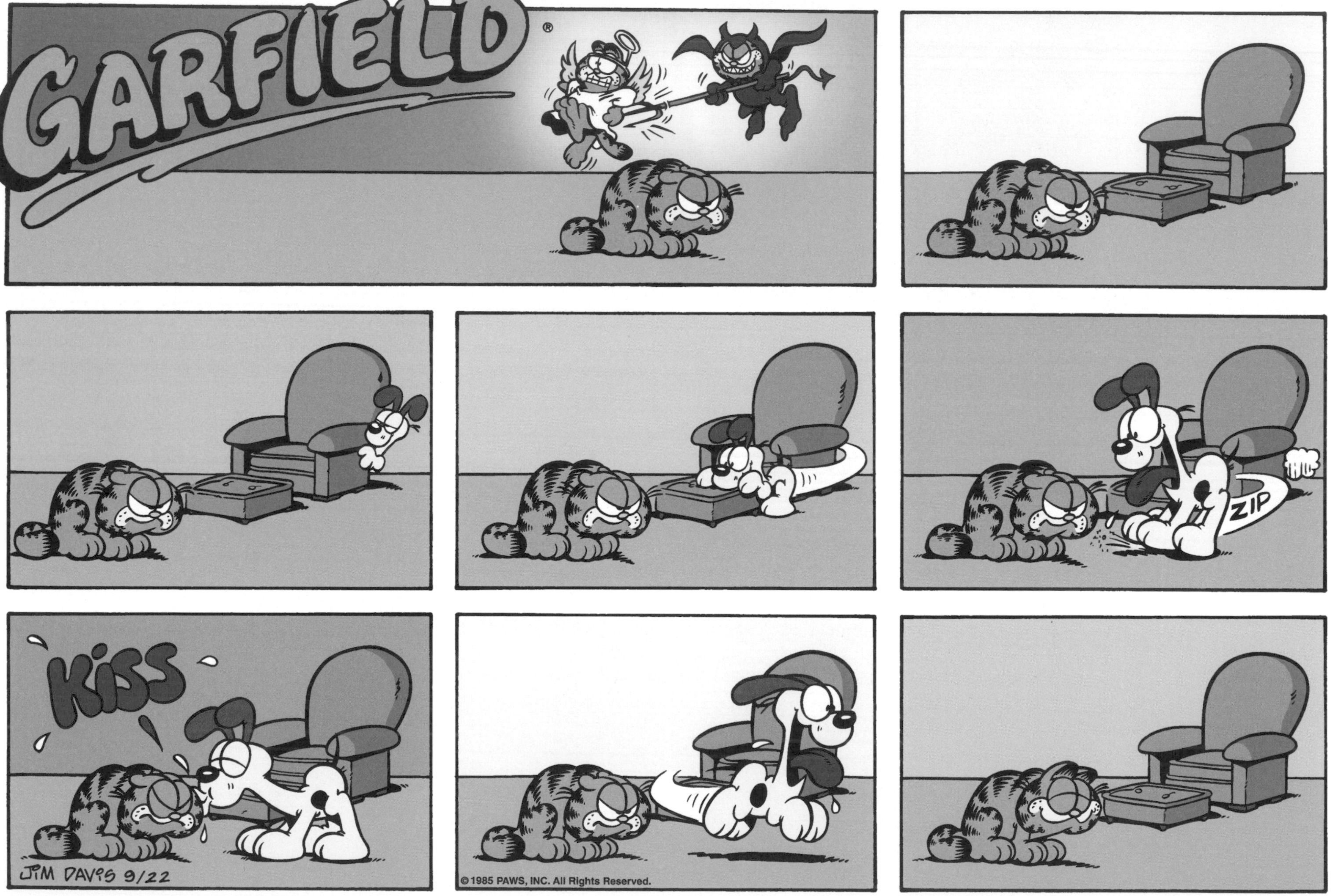
GARFIELD®
ZIP
KISS
JIM DAVIS 9/22
© 1985 PAWS, INC. All Rights Reserved.

I had an assistant who would blurt these gems out during long afternoons at our drawing boards. You can't improve on real life.

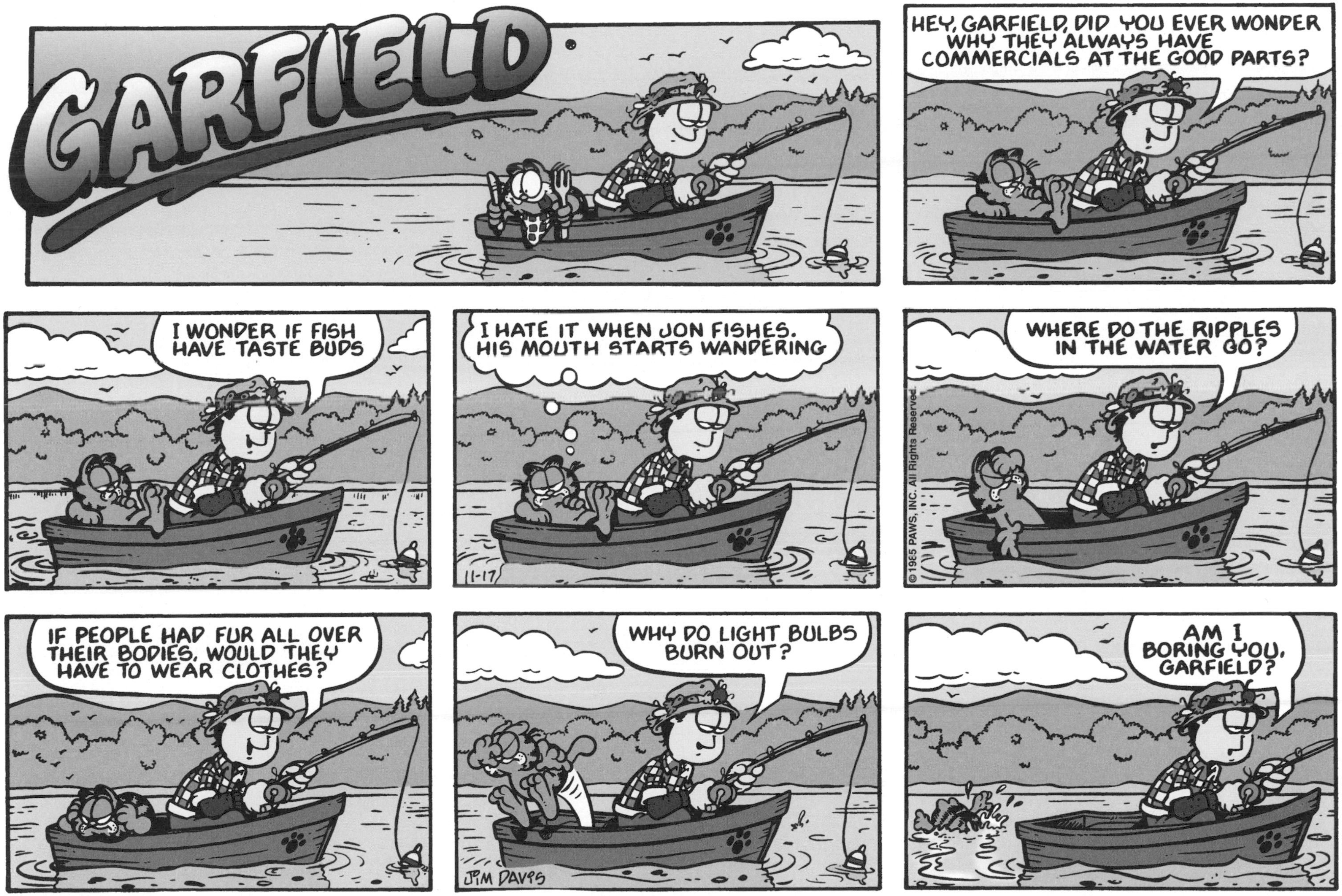
GARFIELD
HEY, GARFIELD, DID YOU EVER WONDER WHY THEY ALWAYS HAVE COMMERCIALS AT THE GOOD PARTS?
I WONDER IF FISH HAVE TASTE BUDS
I HATE IT WHEN JON FISHES. HIS MOUTH STARTS WANDERING
11-17
WHERE DO THE RIPPLES IN THE WATER GO?
© 1985 PAWS, INC. All Rights Reserved.
IF PEOPLE HAD FUR ALL OVER THEIR BODIES, WOULD THEY HAVE TO WEAR CLOTHES?
WHY DO LIGHT BULBS BURN OUT?
JIM DAVIS
AM I BORING YOU, GARFIELD?

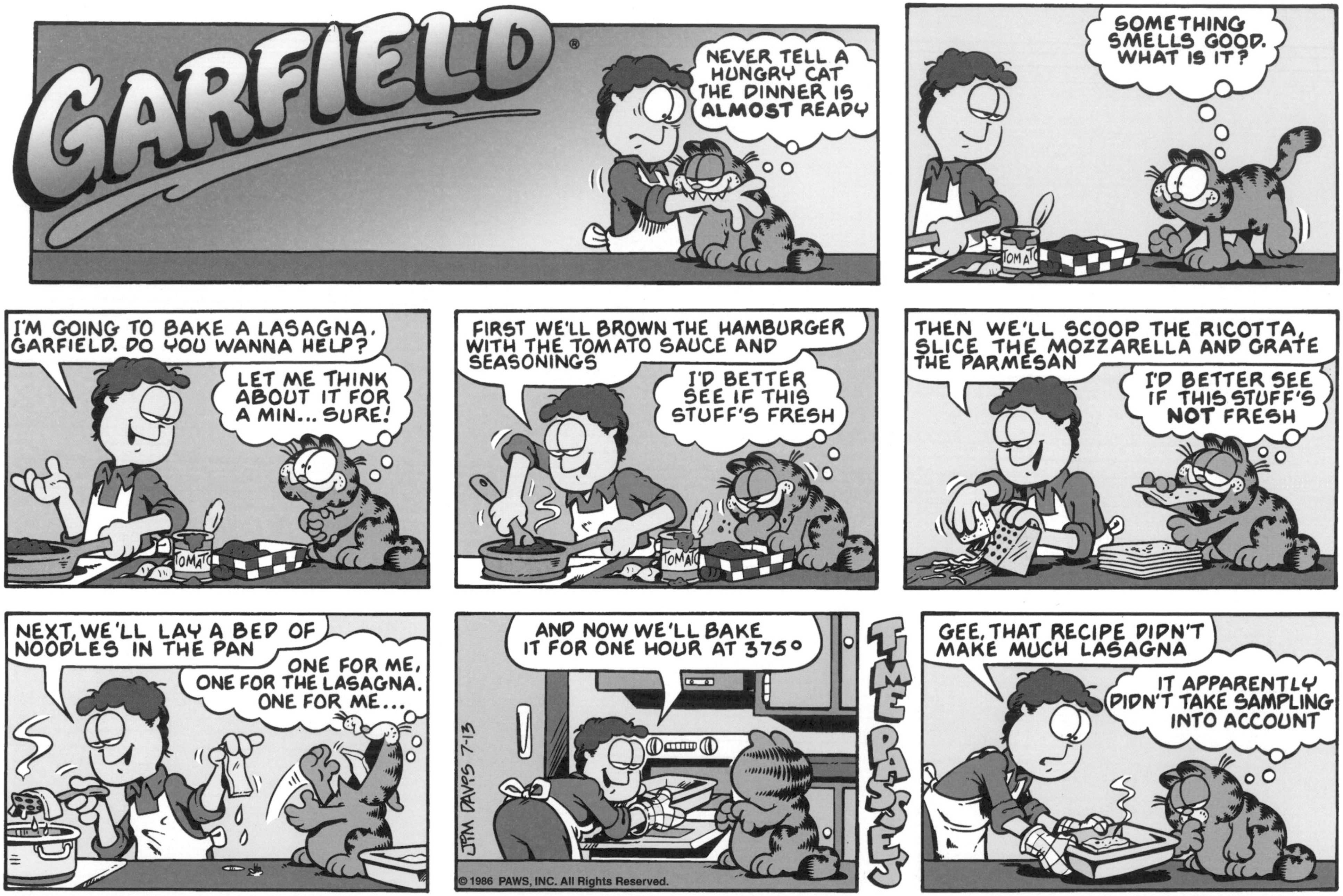
GARFIELD®
NEVER TELL A HUNGRY CAT THE DINNER IS ALMOST READY
SOMETHING SMELLS GOOD. WHAT IS IT?
TOMATO
I'M GOING TO BAKE A LASAGNA, GARFIELD. DO YOU WANNA HELP?
LET ME THINK ABOUT IT FOR A MIN... SURE!
FIRST WE'LL BROWN THE HAMBURGER WITH THE TOMATO SAUCE AND SEASONINGS
I'D BETTER SEE IF THIS STUFF'S FRESH
THEN WE'LL SCOOP THE RICOTTA, SLICE THE MOZZARELLA AND GRATE THE PARMESAN
I'D BETTER SEE IF THIS STUFF'S NOT FRESH
NEXT, WE'LL LAY A BED OF NOODLES IN THE PAN
ONE FOR ME, ONE FOR THE LASAGNA. ONE FOR ME...
AND NOW WE'LL BAKE IT FOR ONE HOUR AT 375°
JIM DAVIS 7-13
© 1986 PAWS, INC. All Rights Reserved.
TIME PASSES
GEE, THAT RECIPE DIDN'T MAKE MUCH LASAGNA
IT APPARENTLY DIDN'T TAKE SAMPLING INTO ACCOUNT

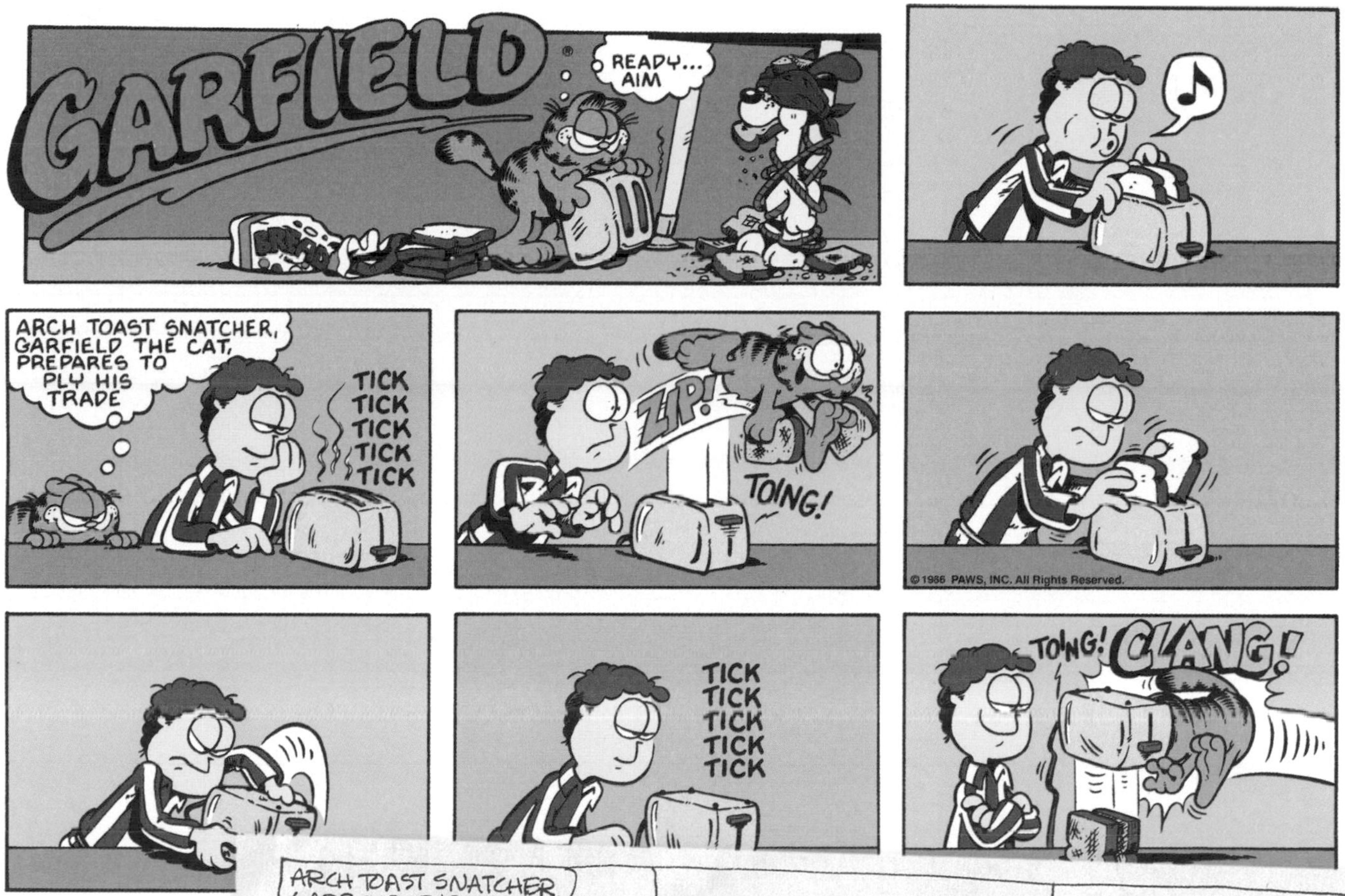
GARFIELD®
READY... AIM
♪
ARCH TOAST SNATCHER, GARFIELD THE CAT, PREPARES TO PLY HIS TRADE
TICK TICK TICK TICK TICK
ZIP!
TOING!
© 1986 PAWS, INC. All Rights Reserved.
TICK TICK TICK TICK TICK
TOING! CLANG!

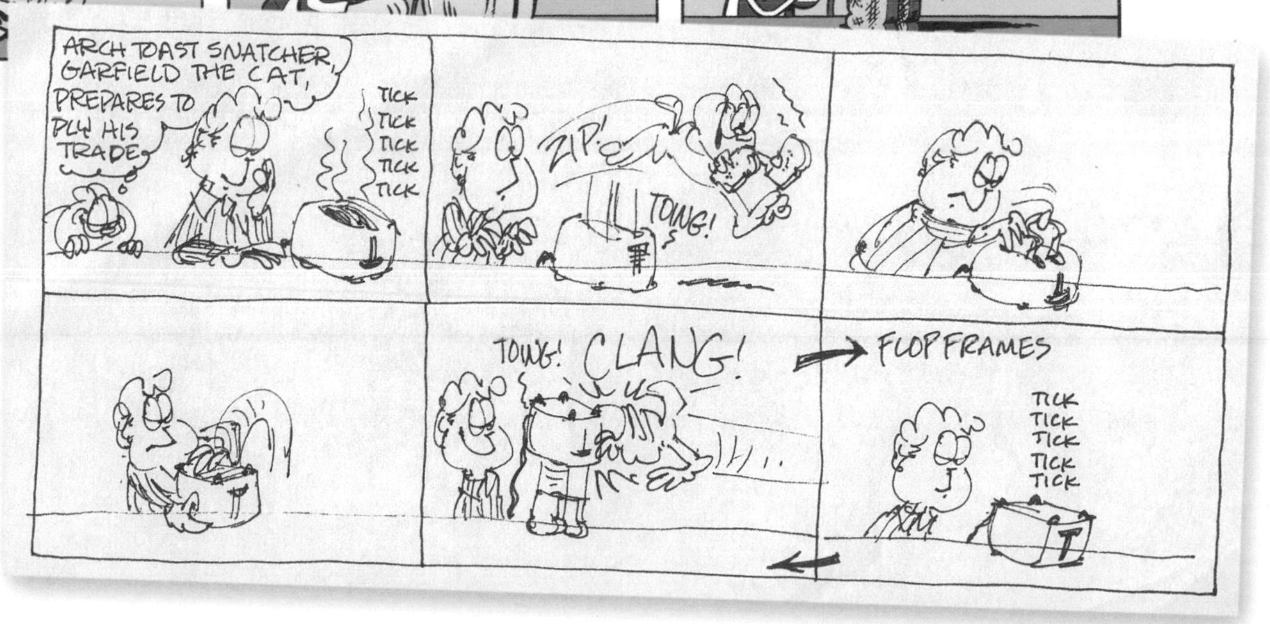
ARCH TOAST SNATCHER, GARFIELD THE CAT, PREPARES TO PLY HIS TRADE
TICK TICK TICK TICK TICK
ZIP!
TOING!
TOING! CLANG!
FLOP FRAMES
TICK TICK TICK TICK TICK

original rough

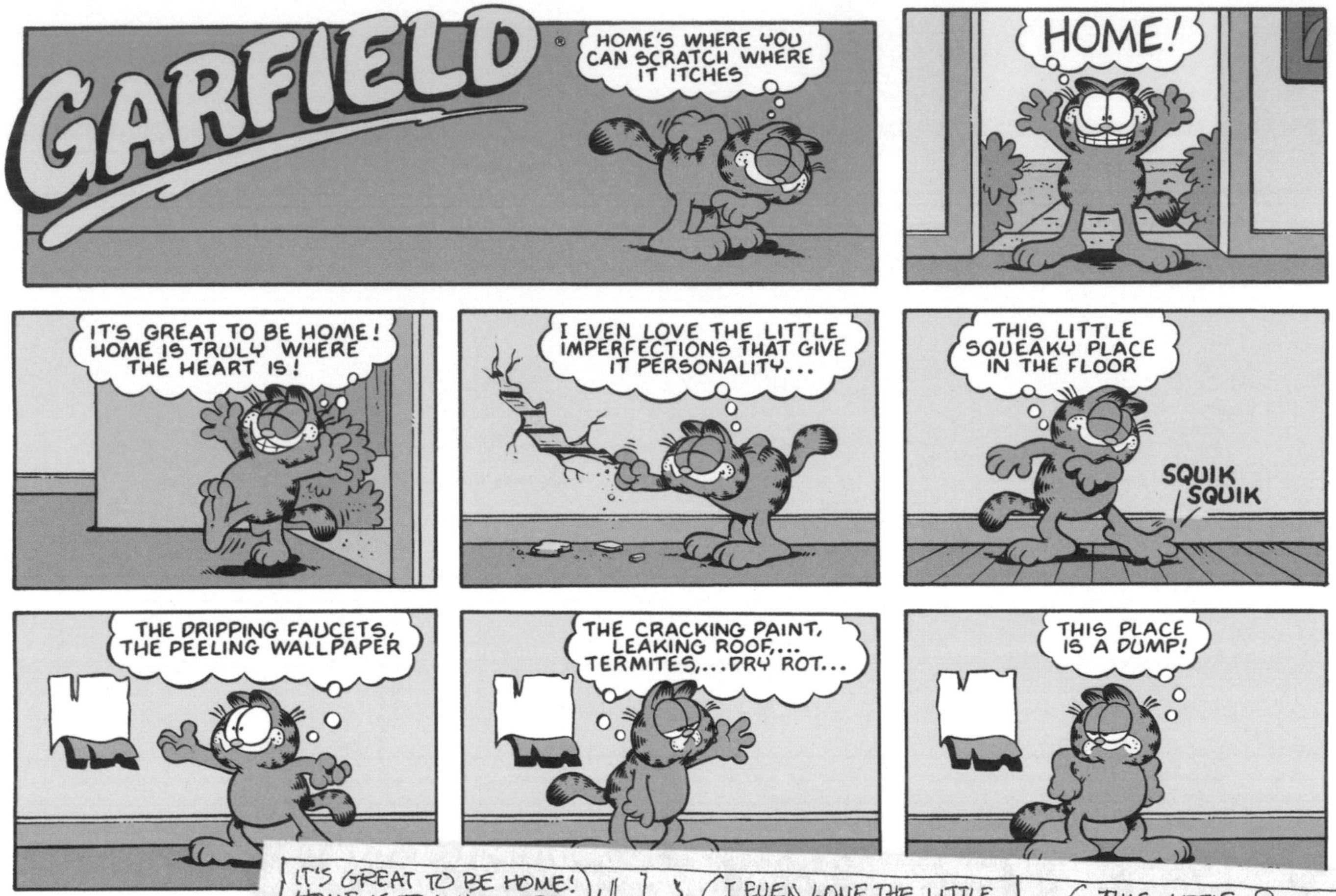
GARFIELD
HOME'S WHERE YOU CAN SCRATCH WHERE IT ITCHES
HOME!
IT'S GREAT TO BE HOME! HOME IS TRULY WHERE THE HEART IS!
I EVEN LOVE THE LITTLE IMPERFECTIONS THAT GIVE IT PERSONALITY...
THIS LITTLE SQUEAKY PLACE IN THE FLOOR
SQUIK SQUIK
THE DRIPPING FAUCETS, THE PEELING WALLPAPER
THE CRACKING PAINT, LEAKING ROOF,... TERMITES,...DRY ROT...
THIS PLACE IS A DUMP!

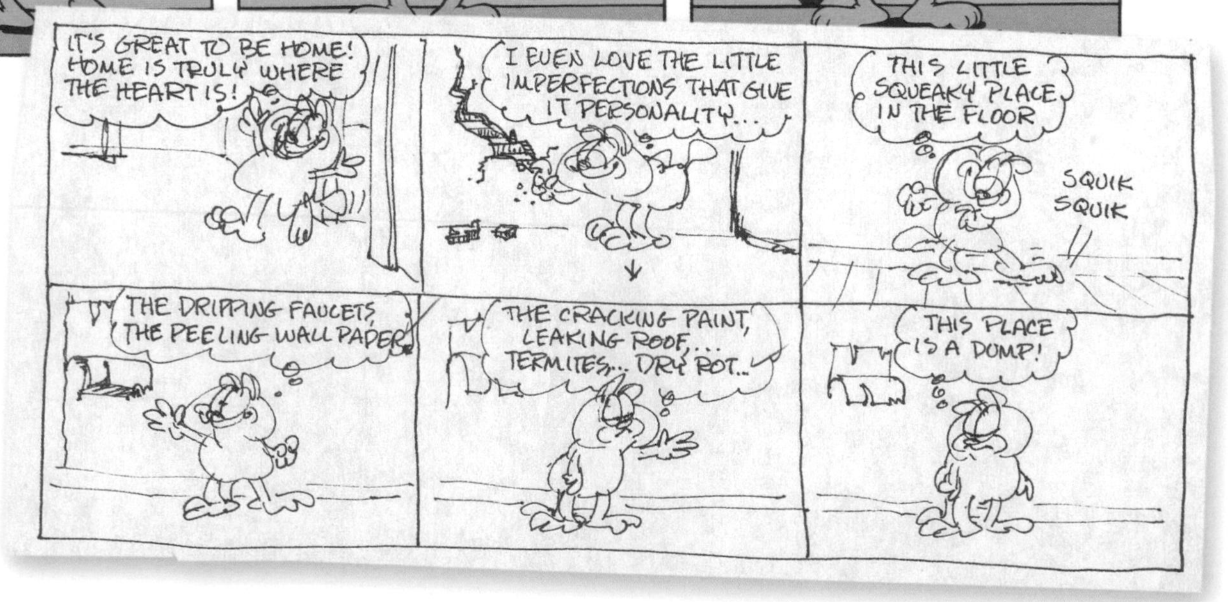
IT'S GREAT TO BE HOME! HOME IS TRULY WHERE THE HEART IS!
I EVEN LOVE THE LITTLE IMPERFECTIONS THAT GIVE IT PERSONALITY...
THIS LITTLE SQUEAKY PLACE IN THE FLOOR
SQUIK SQUIK
THE DRIPPING FAUCETS, THE PEELING WALLPAPER
THE CRACKING PAINT, LEAKING ROOF,... TERMITES,... DRY ROT..
THIS PLACE IS A DUMP!

original rough

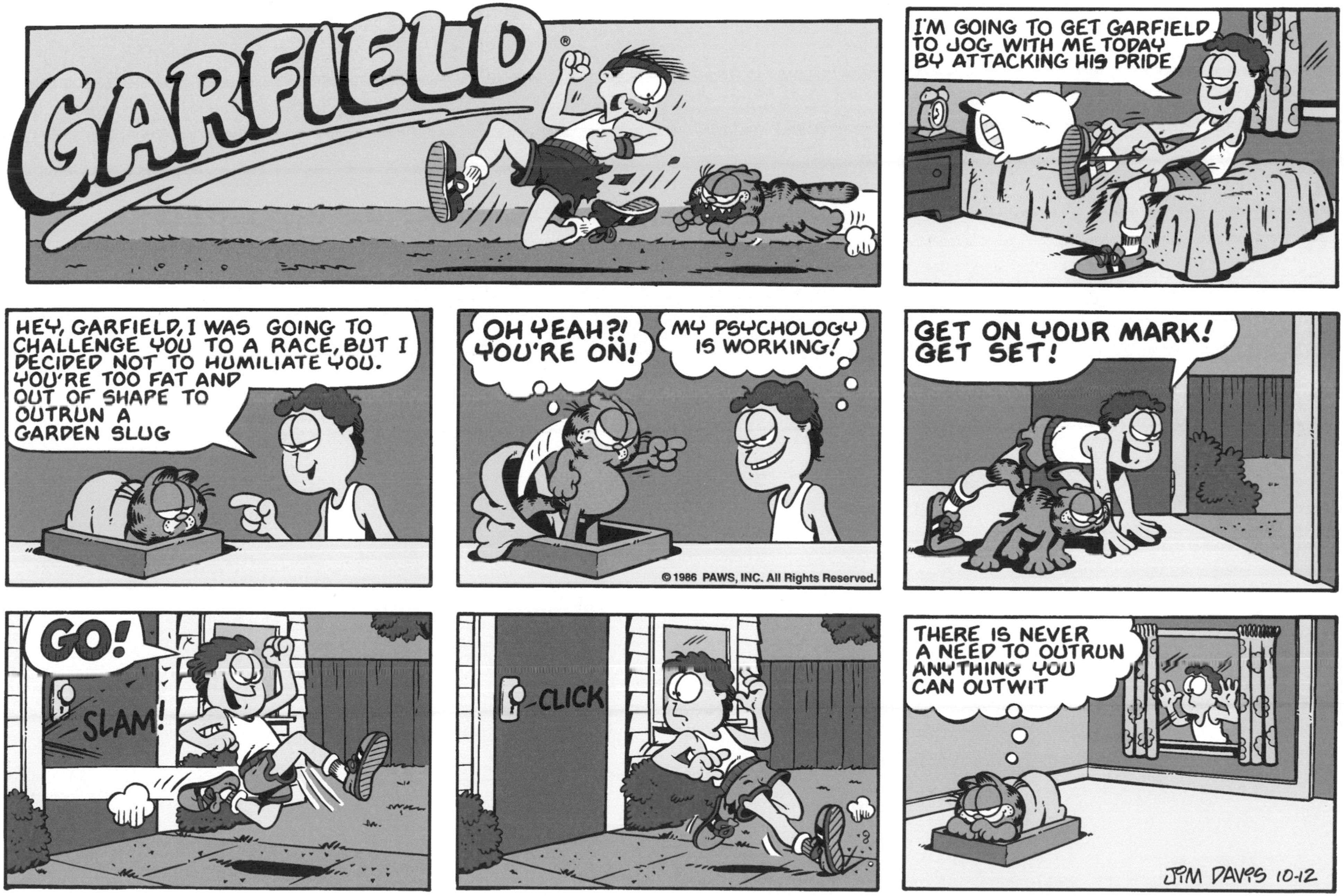

GARFIELD®
I'M GOING TO GET GARFIELD TO JOG WITH ME TODAY BY ATTACKING HIS PRIDE
HEY, GARFIELD, I WAS GOING TO CHALLENGE YOU TO A RACE, BUT I DECIDED NOT TO HUMILIATE YOU. YOU'RE TOO FAT AND OUT OF SHAPE TO OUTRUN A GARDEN SLUG
OH YEAH?! YOU'RE ON!
MY PSYCHOLOGY IS WORKING!
© 1986 PAWS, INC. All Rights Reserved.
GET ON YOUR MARK! GET SET!
GO!
SLAM!
CLICK
THERE IS NEVER A NEED TO OUTRUN ANYTHING YOU CAN OUTWIT
JIM DAVIS 10-12

This gag was a shameless vehicle to let my assistant Gary Barker draw those weird people he loves to draw! That's Gary, second from the left in the back, in his Captain Cartoon costume.

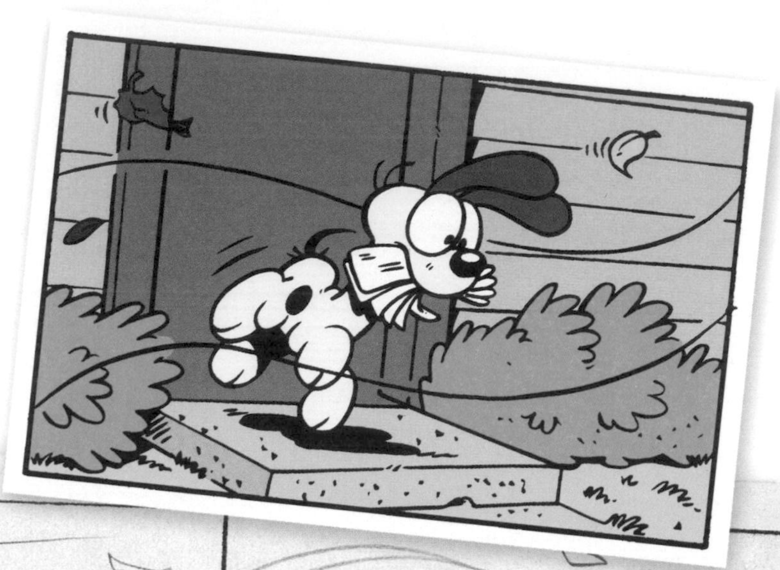

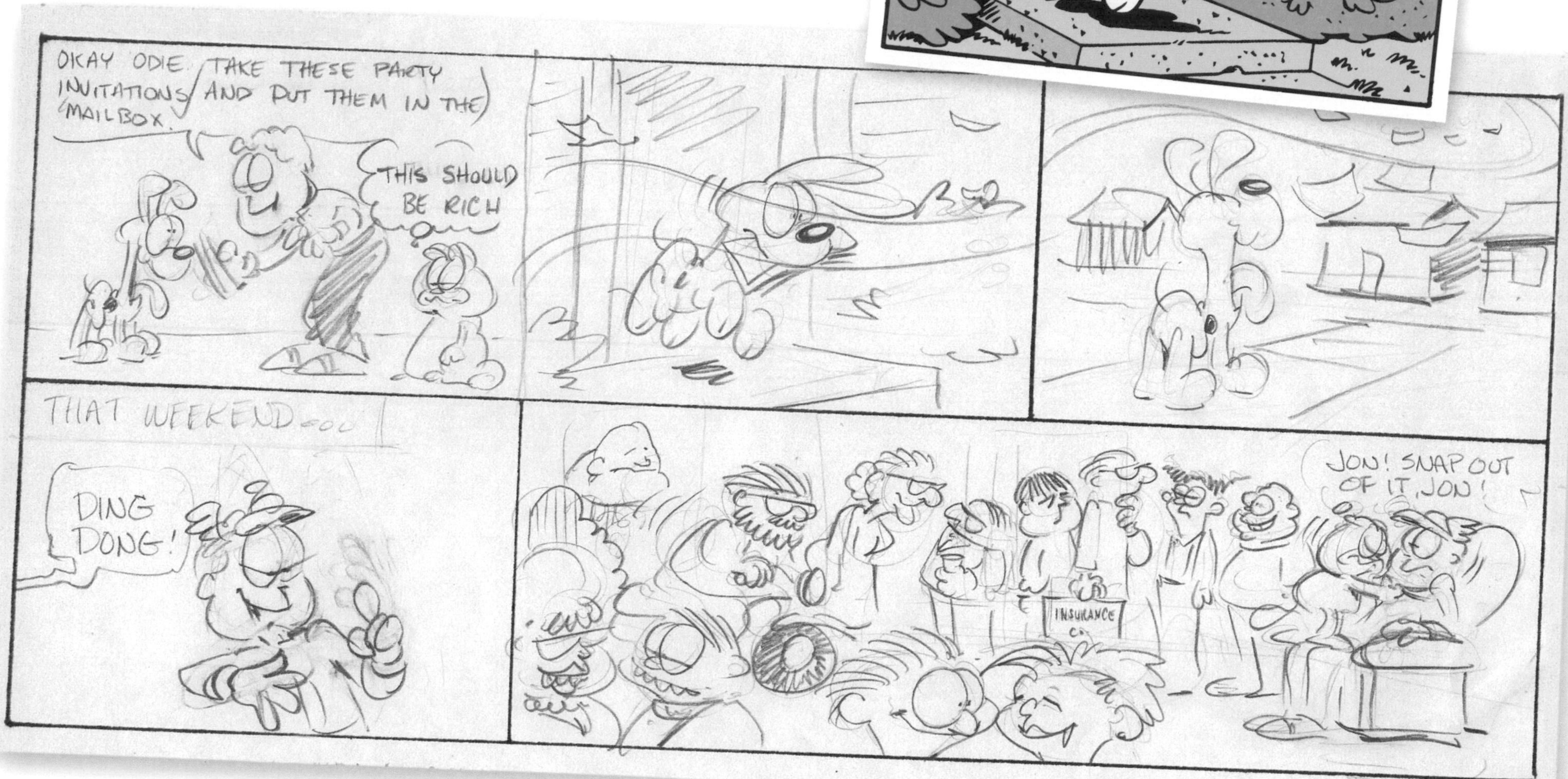

OKAY ODIE, TAKE THESE PARTY INVITATIONS AND PUT THEM IN THE MAILBOX.
THIS SHOULD BE RICH
THAT WEEKEND...
DING DONG!
INSURANCE CO.
JON! SNAP OUT OF IT, JON!

original rough

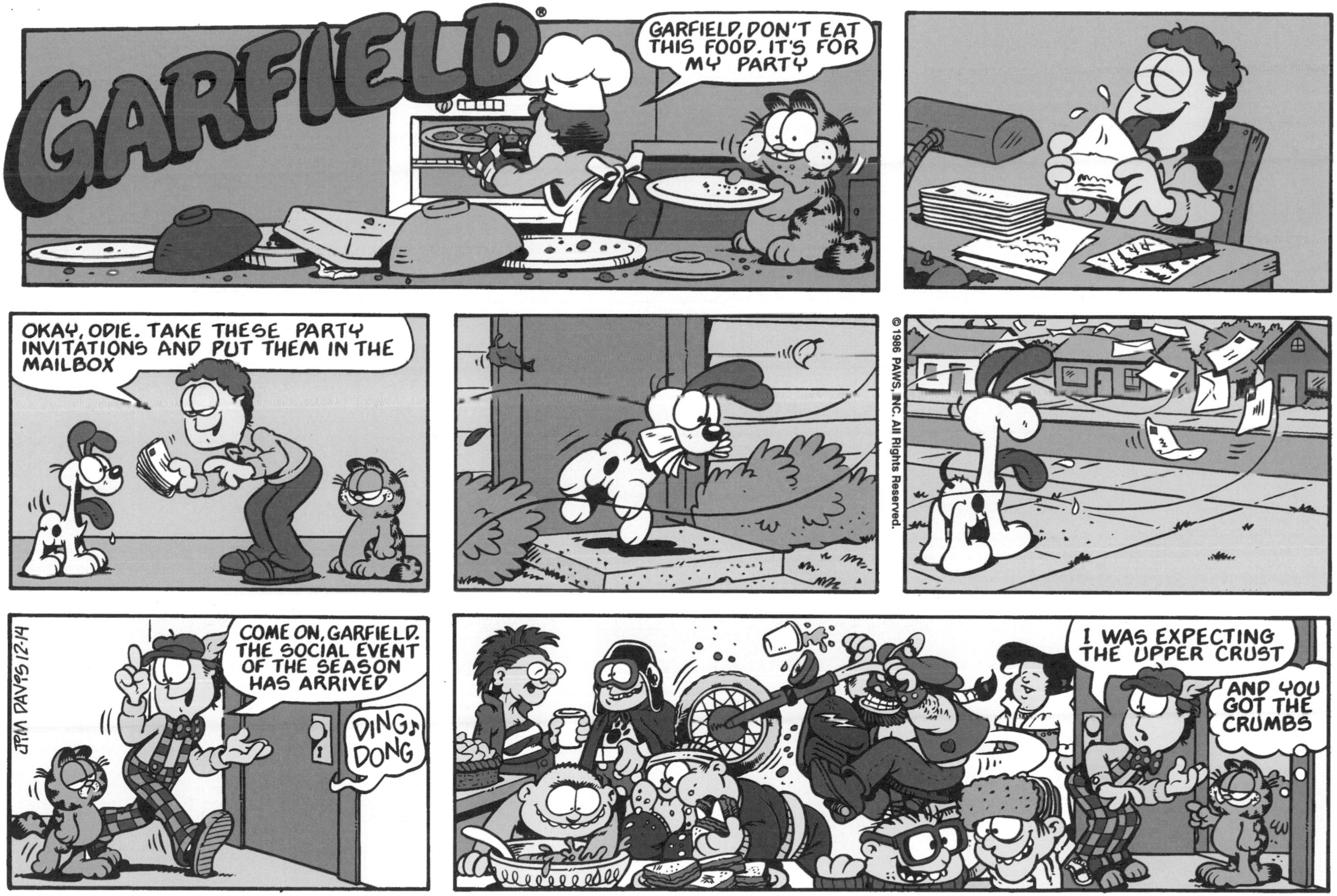
GARFIELD®
GARFIELD, DON'T EAT THIS FOOD. IT'S FOR MY PARTY
OKAY, ODIE. TAKE THESE PARTY INVITATIONS AND PUT THEM IN THE MAILBOX
© 1986 PAWS, INC. All Rights Reserved.
JPM DAVPS 12·14
COME ON, GARFIELD. THE SOCIAL EVENT OF THE SEASON HAS ARRIVED
DING♪ DONG
I WAS EXPECTING THE UPPER CRUST
AND YOU GOT THE CRUMBS

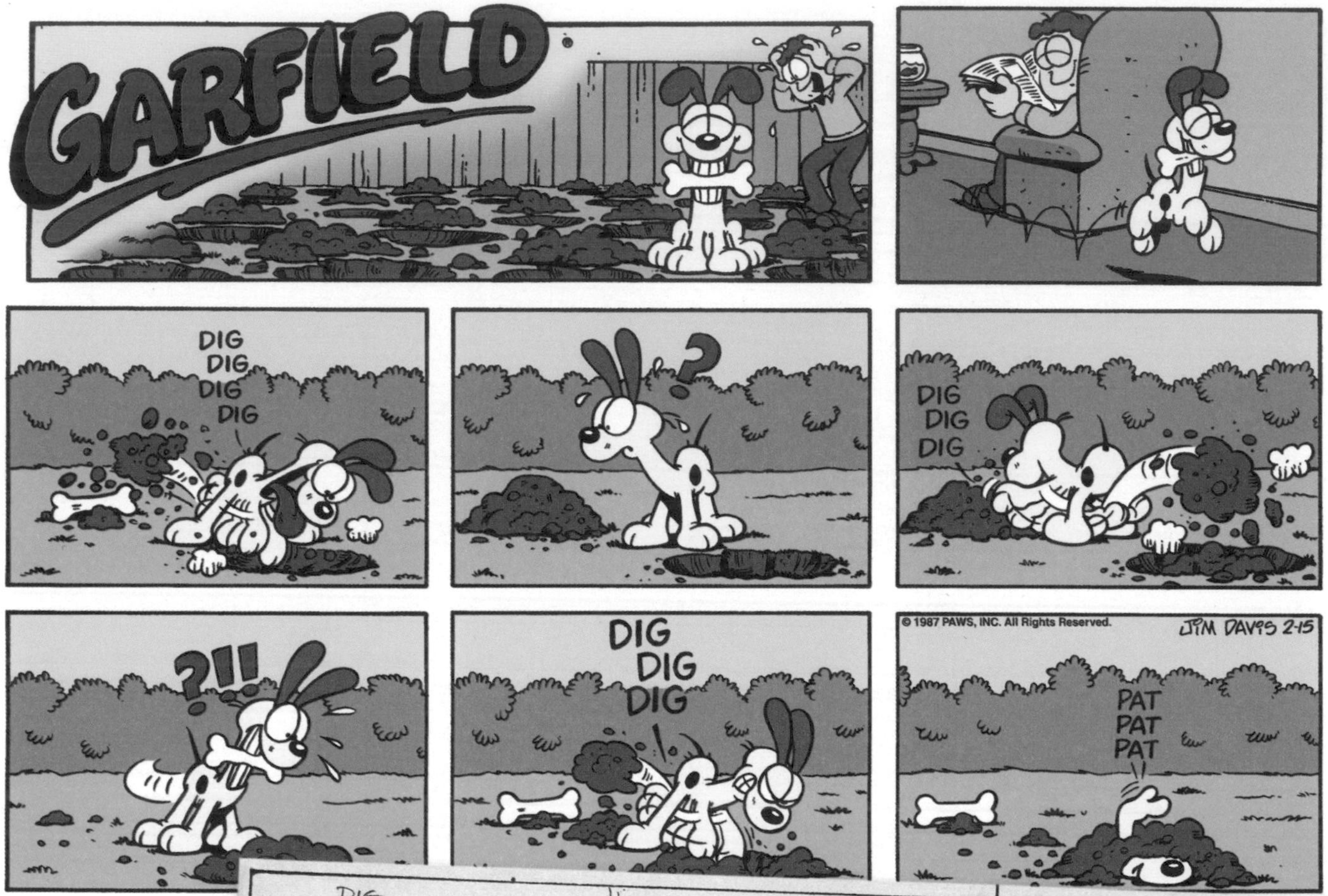
GARFIELD
DIG
DIG
DIG
DIG
?
DIG
DIG
DIG
?!!
DIG
DIG
DIG
© 1987 PAWS, INC. All Rights Reserved.
JIM DAVIS 2-15
PAT
PAT
PAT

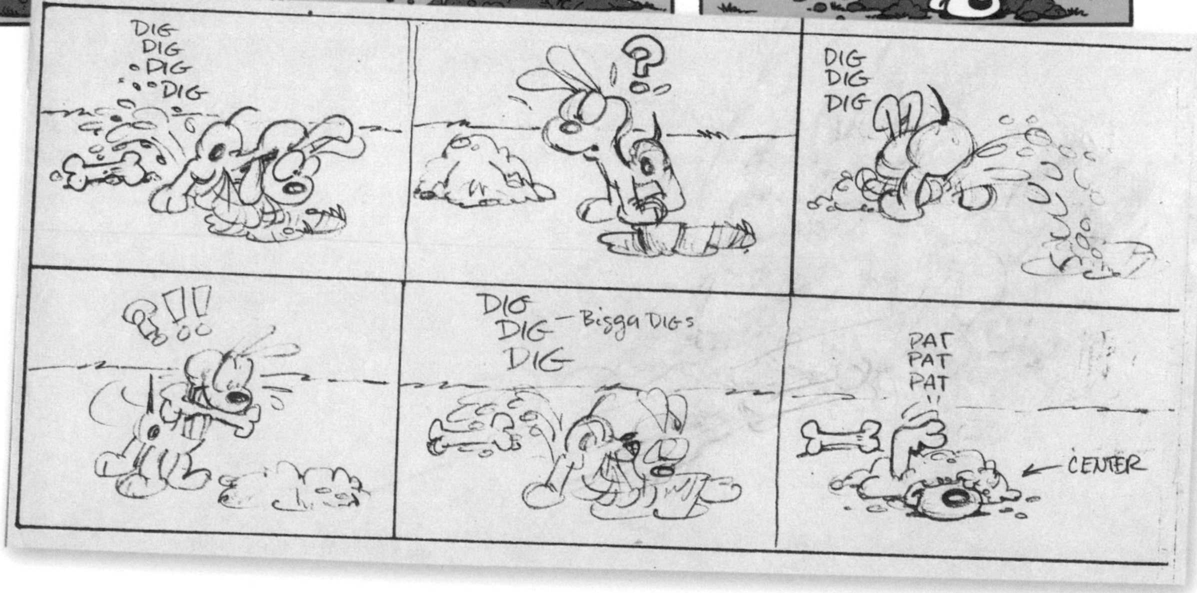
DIG
DIG
DIG
DIG
?
DIG
DIG
DIG
?!!
DIG
DIG
DIG
— Bigga DIGS
PAT
PAT
PAT
← CENTER

original rough

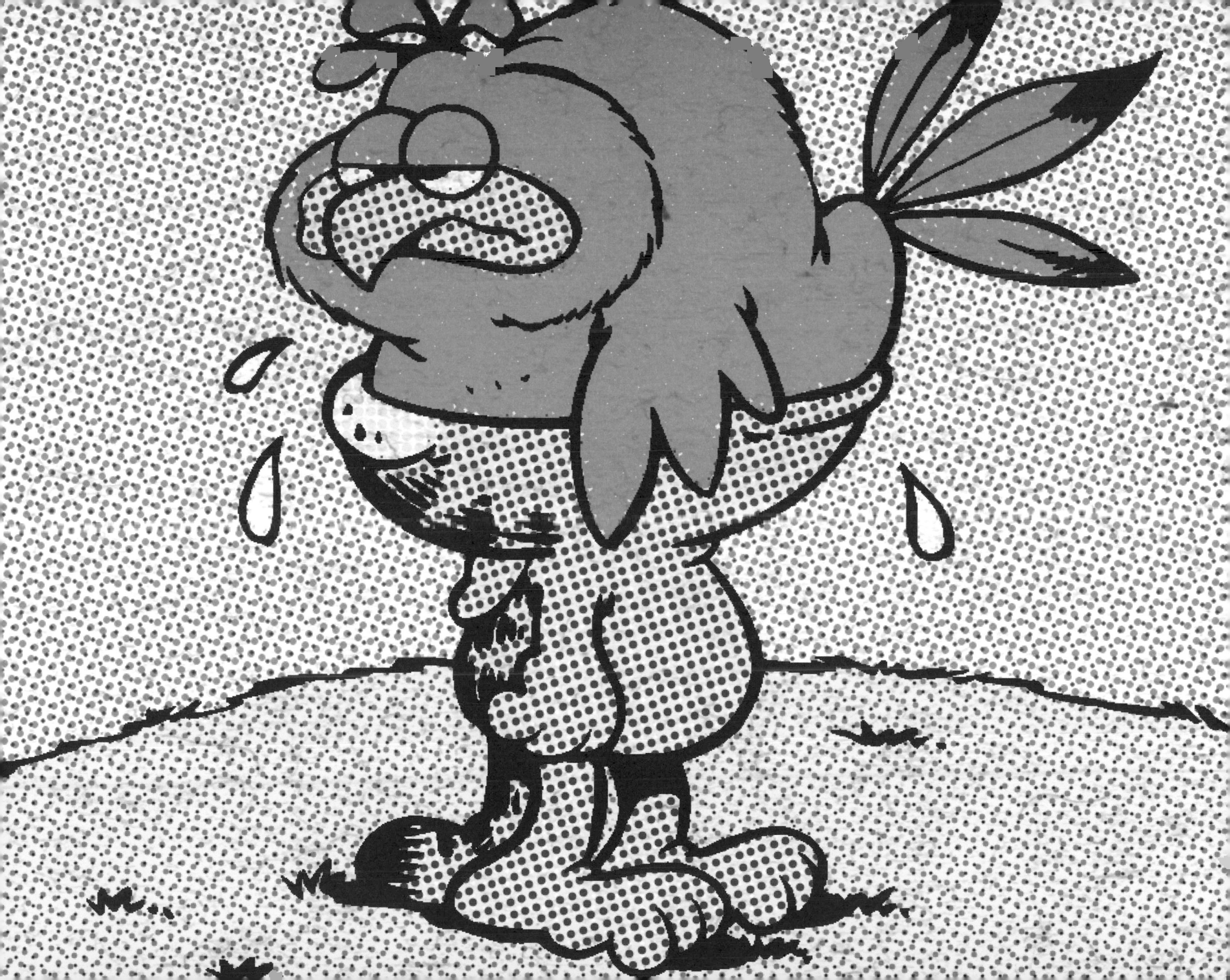

Be honest now.
You've all had these dreams.

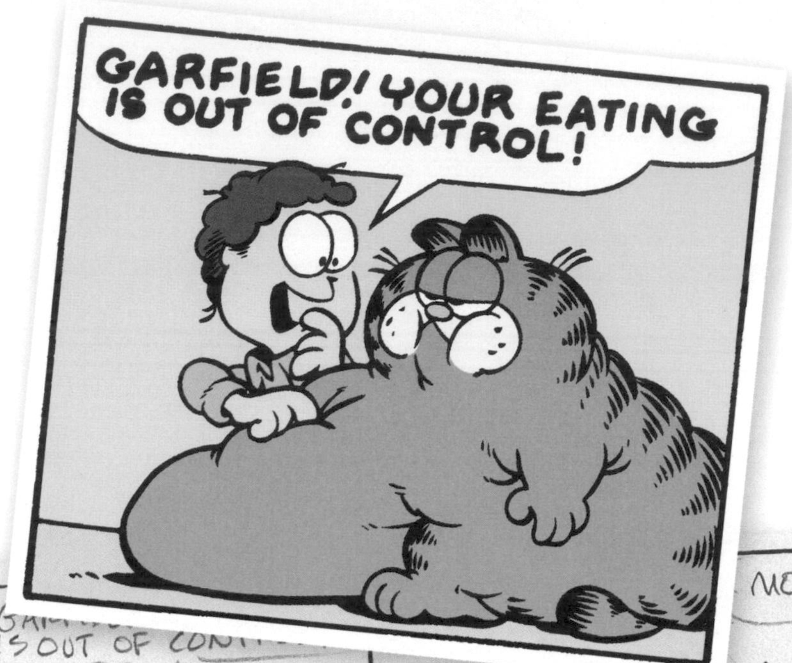
GARFIELD! YOUR EATING IS OUT OF CONTROL!

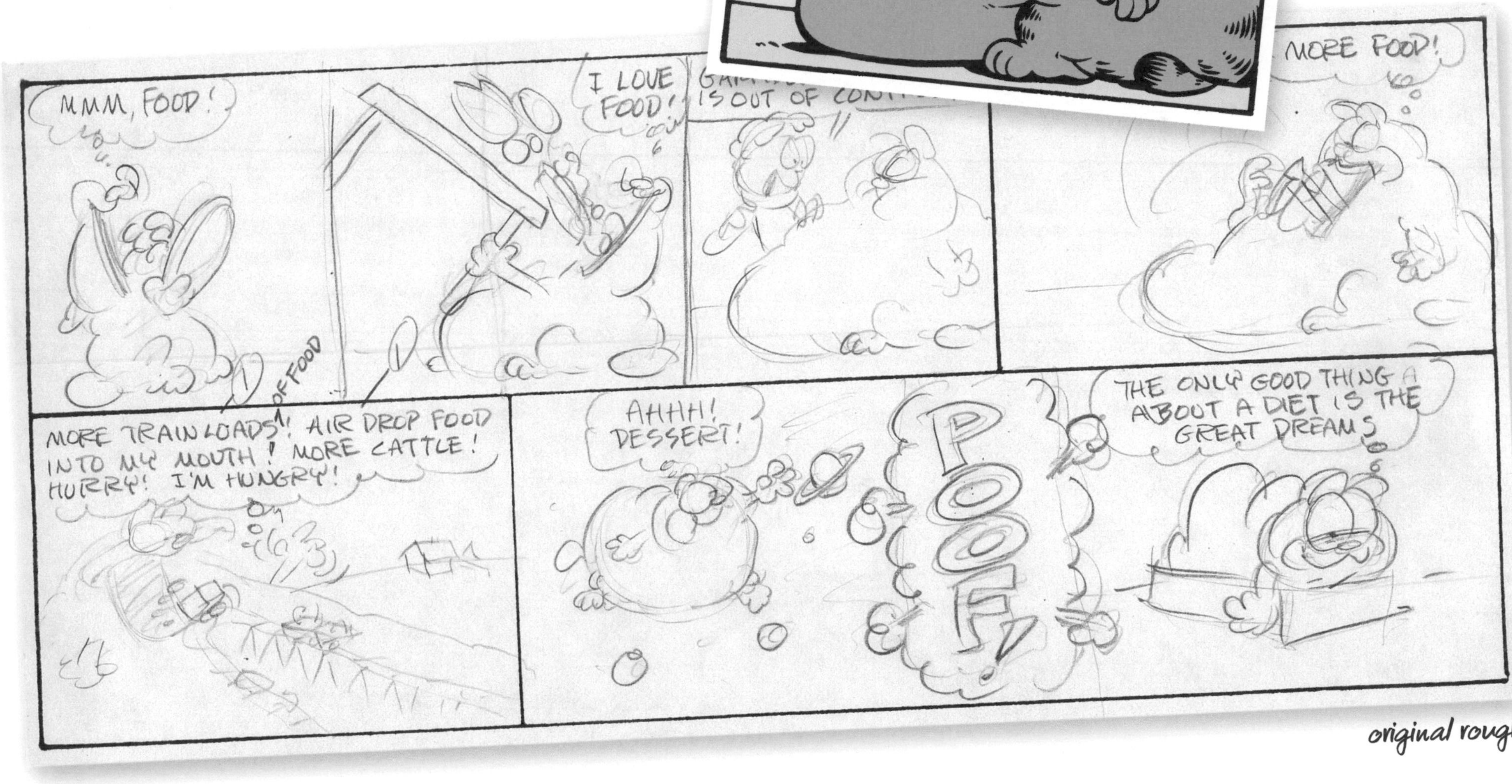
MMM, FOOD!
I LOVE FOOD!
IS OUT OF
MORE FOOD!
MORE TRAINLOADS OF FOOD! AIR DROP FOOD INTO MY MOUTH! MORE CATTLE! HURRY! I'M HUNGRY!
AHHH! DESSERT!
POOF
THE ONLY GOOD THING ABOUT A DIET IS THE GREAT DREAMS

original rough

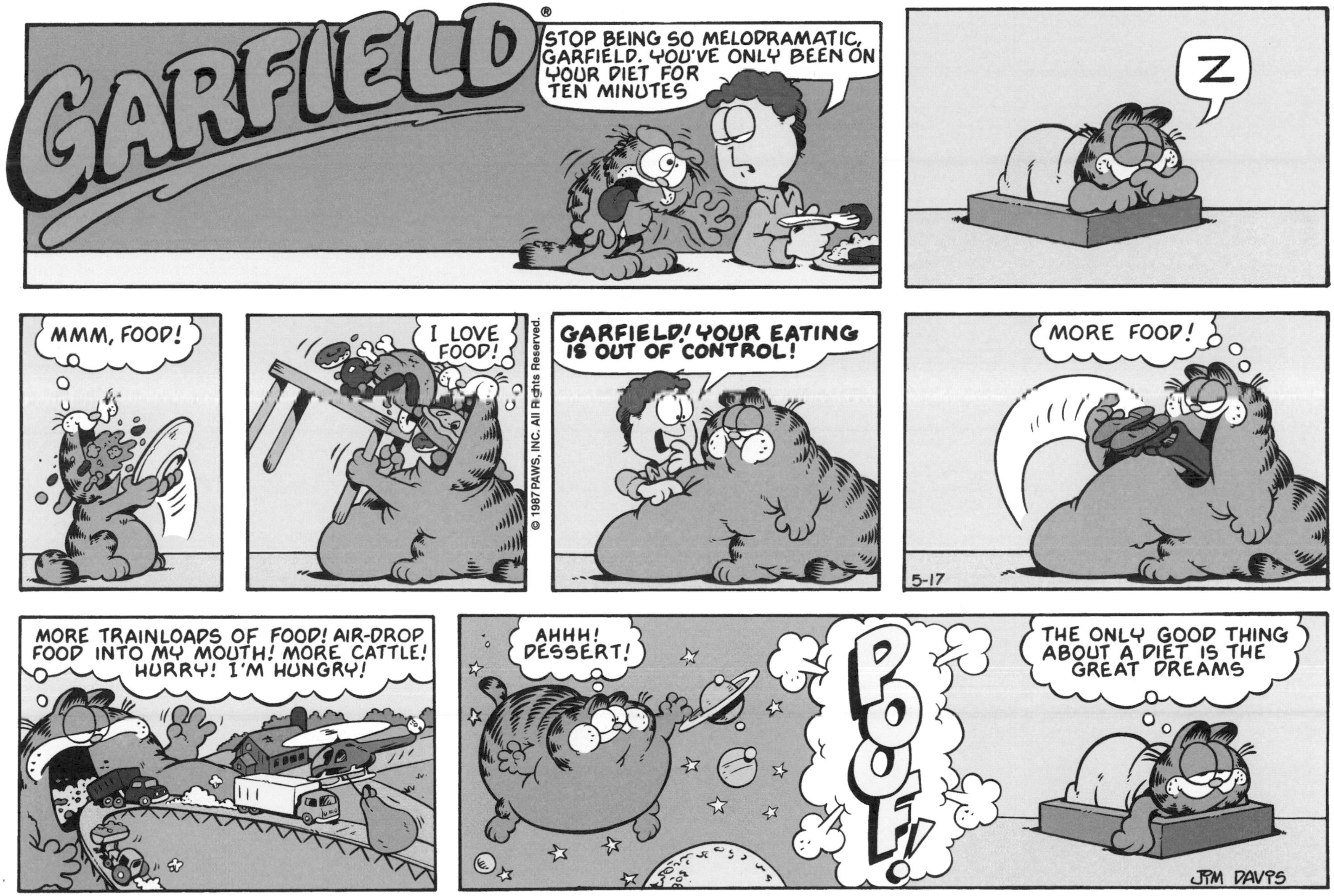
GARFIELD®
STOP BEING SO MELODRAMATIC, GARFIELD. YOU'VE ONLY BEEN ON YOUR DIET FOR TEN MINUTES
Z
MMM, FOOD!
I LOVE FOOD!
© 1987 PAWS, INC. All Rights Reserved.
GARFIELD! YOUR EATING IS OUT OF CONTROL!
MORE FOOD!
5-17
MORE TRAINLOADS OF FOOD! AIR-DROP FOOD INTO MY MOUTH! MORE CATTLE! HURRY! I'M HUNGRY!
AHHH! DESSERT!
POOF!!
THE ONLY GOOD THING ABOUT A DIET IS THE GREAT DREAMS
JIM DAVIS

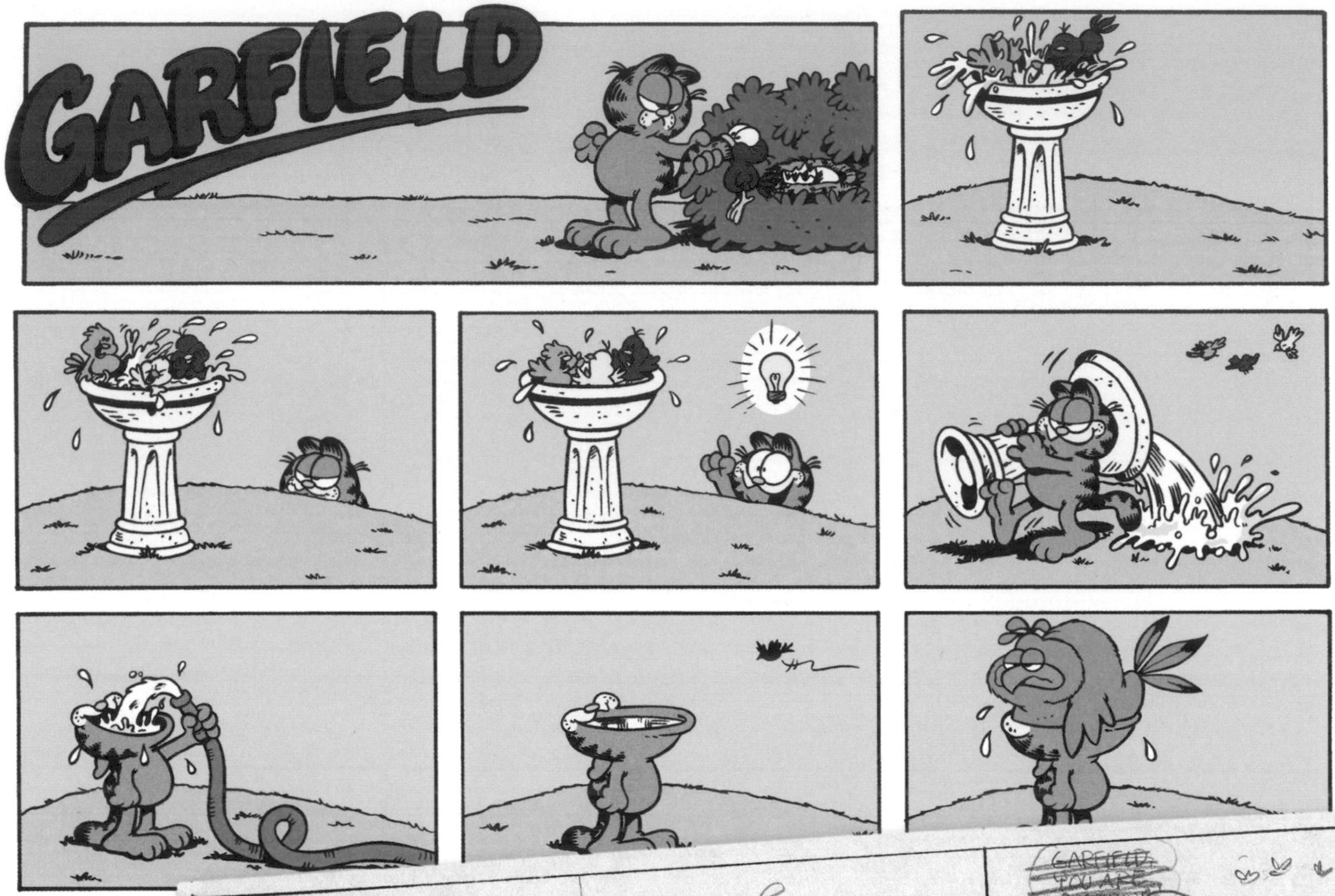
GARFIELD

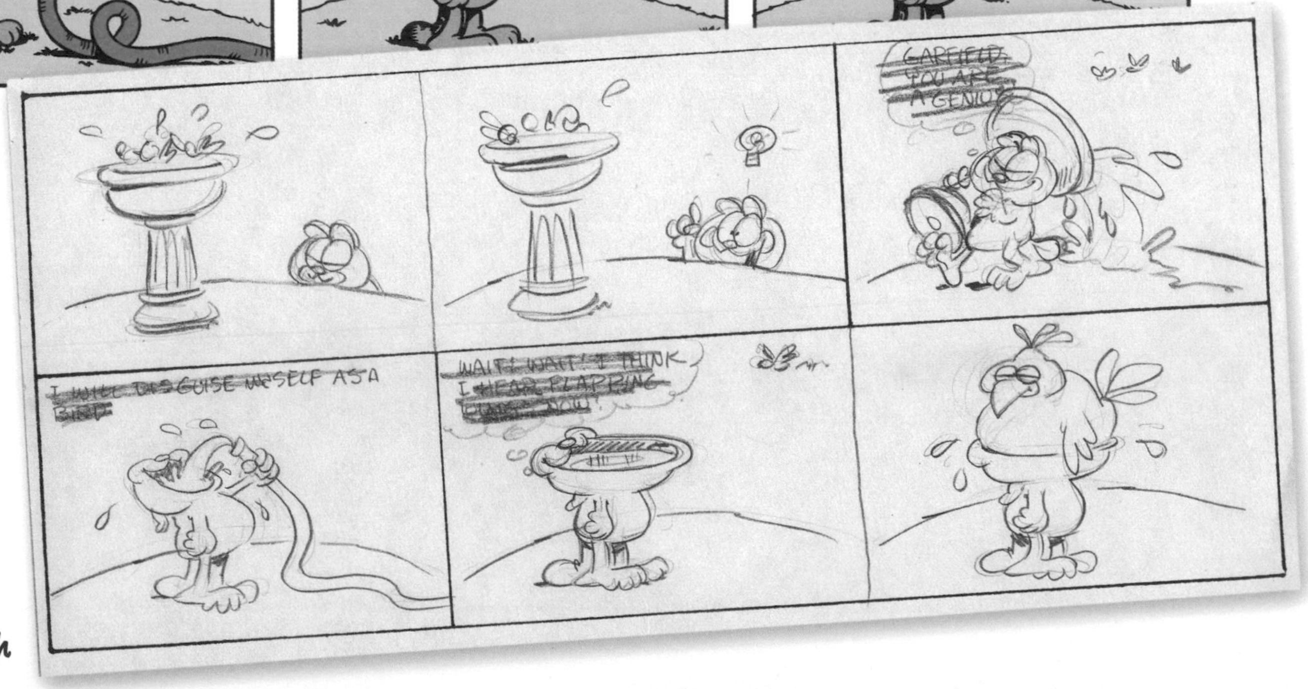
GARFIELD, YOU ARE A GENIUS
I WILL DISGUISE MYSELF AS A BIRD
WAIT! WAIT! I THINK
I HEAR FLAPPING

original rough

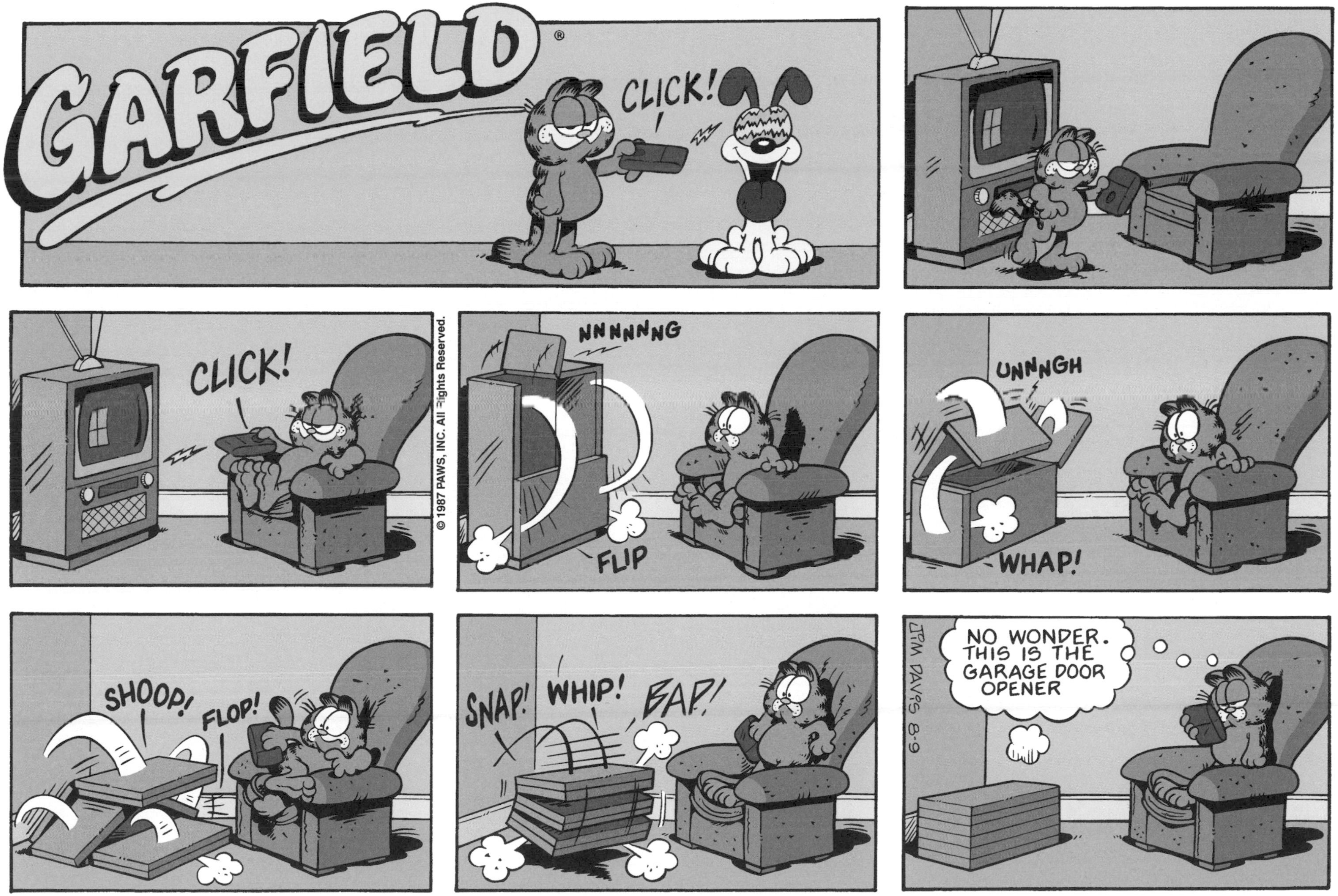
GARFIELD®
CLICK!
© 1987 PAWS, INC. All Rights Reserved.
CLICK!
NNNNNNG
FLIP
UNNNGH
WHAP!
SHOOP!
FLOP!
SNAP!
WHIP!
BAP!
JIM DAVIS 8-9
NO WONDER. THIS IS THE GARAGE DOOR OPENER

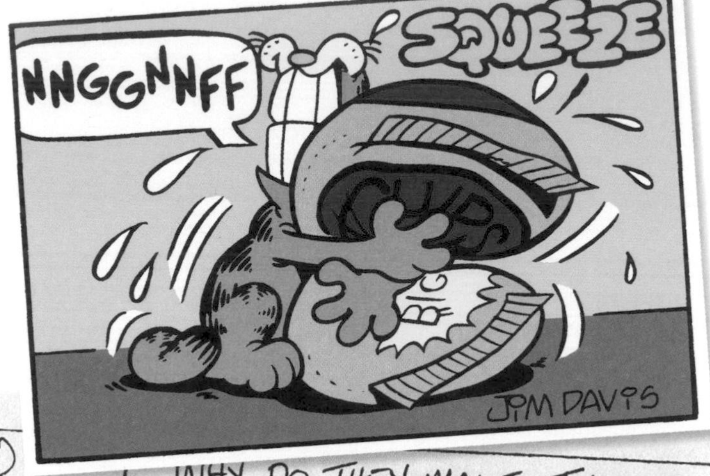
NNGGNNFF
SQUEEZE
CHIPS
JIM DAVIS

Sometimes I step away from humor and do editorial comment.

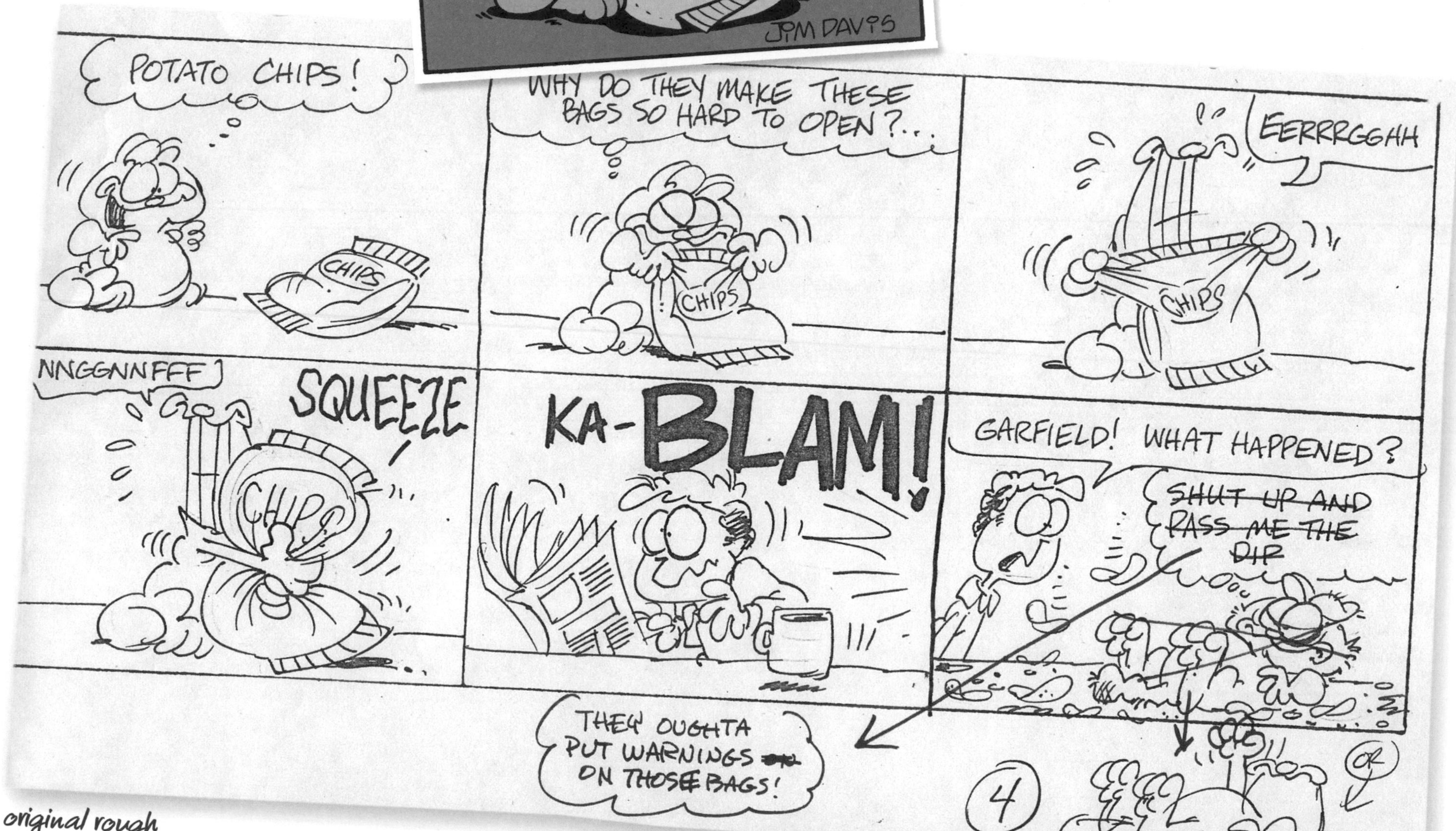
POTATO CHIPS!
CHIPS
WHY DO THEY MAKE THESE BAGS SO HARD TO OPEN?...
CHIPS
EERRRGGAH
CHIPS
NNGGNNFFF
SQUEEZE
CHIPS
KA-BLAM!
GARFIELD! WHAT HAPPENED?
~~SHUT UP AND PASS ME THE DIP~~
THEY OUGHTA PUT WARNINGS ON THOSE BAGS!
4
OR

original rough

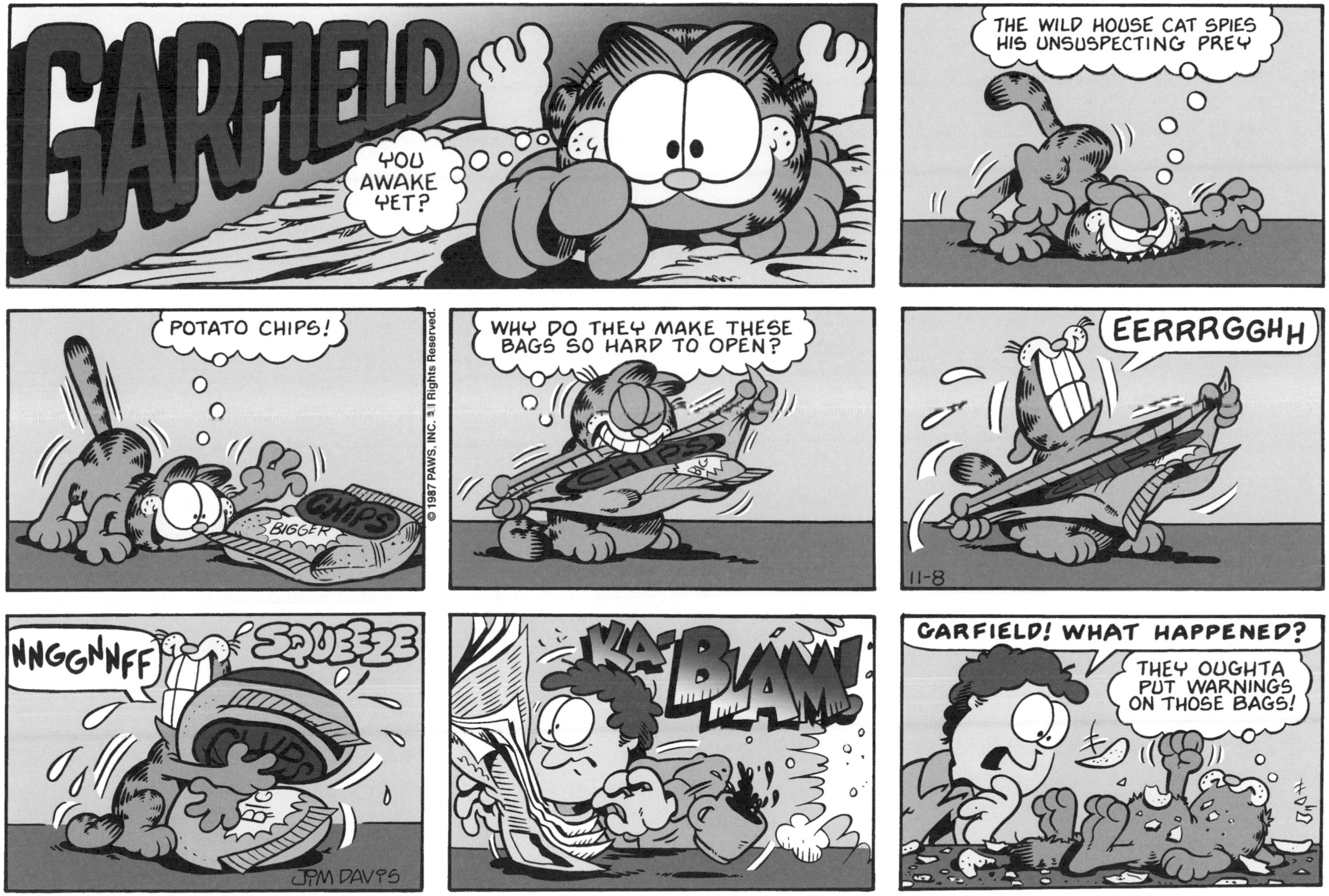
GARFIELD
YOU AWAKE YET?
THE WILD HOUSE CAT SPIES HIS UNSUSPECTING PREY
POTATO CHIPS!
CHIPS
BIGGER
© 1987 PAWS, INC. All Rights Reserved.
WHY DO THEY MAKE THESE BAGS SO HARD TO OPEN?
CHIPS
EERRRGGHH
11-8
NNGGNNFF
SQUEEZE
JPM DAVPS
KA-BLAM!
GARFIELD! WHAT HAPPENED?
THEY OUGHTA PUT WARNINGS ON THOSE BAGS!

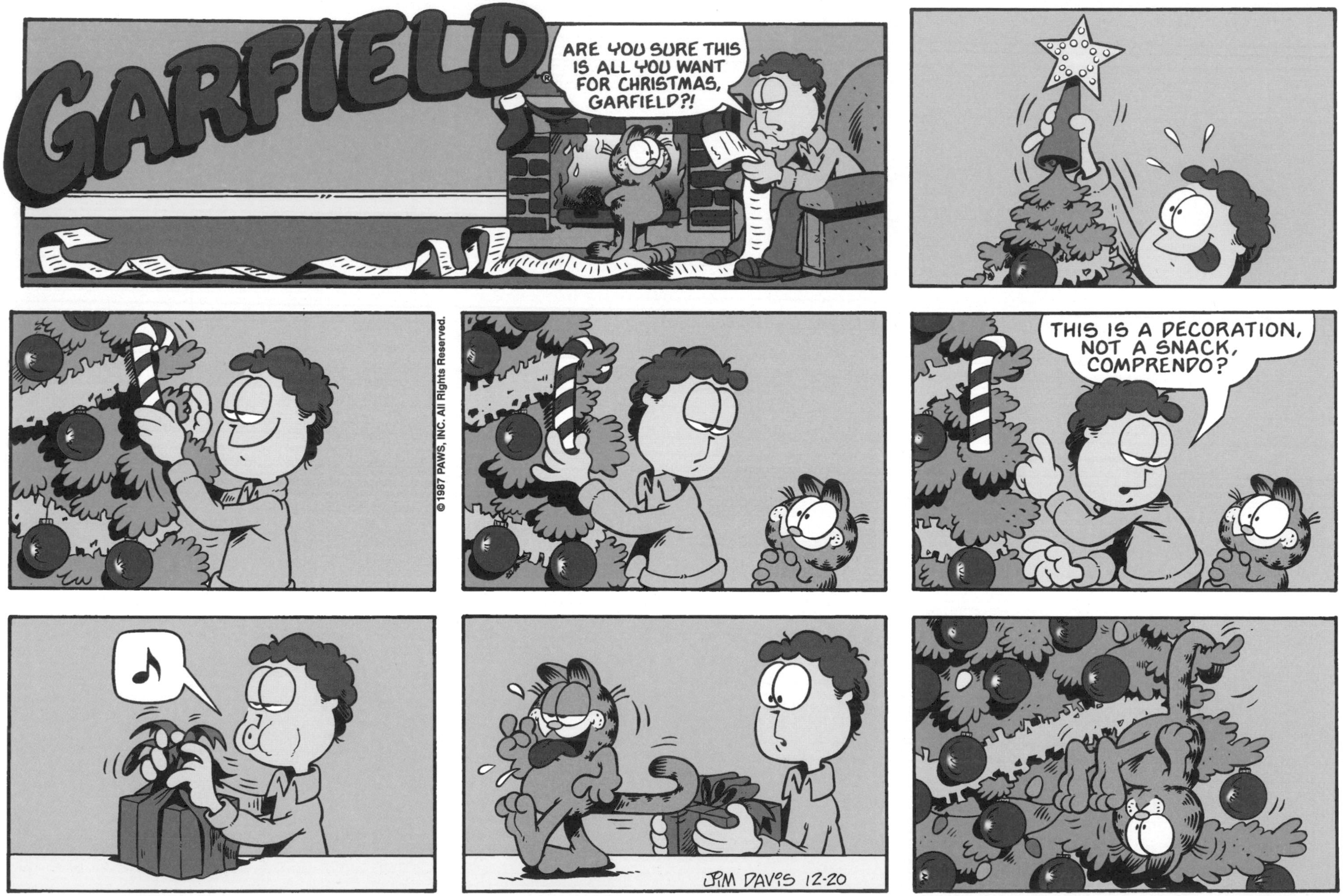
GARFIELD
ARE YOU SURE THIS IS ALL YOU WANT FOR CHRISTMAS, GARFIELD?!
THIS IS A DECORATION, NOT A SNACK, COMPRENDO?
♪
JIM DAVIS 12-20

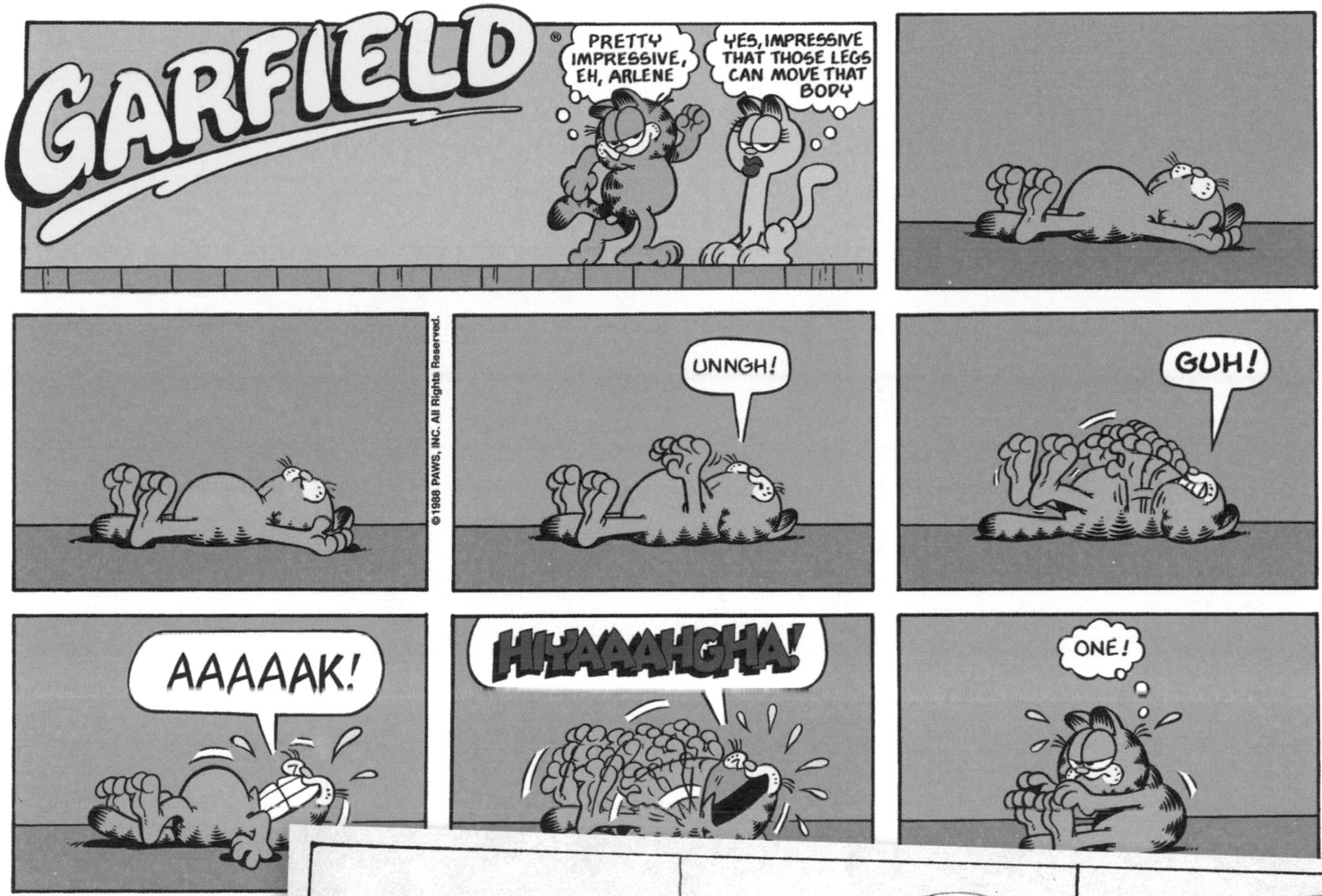
GARFIELD
PRETTY IMPRESSIVE, EH, ARLENE
YES, IMPRESSIVE THAT THOSE LEGS CAN MOVE THAT BODY
©1988 PAWS, INC. All Rights Reserved.
UNNGH!
GUH!
AAAAAK!
HIYAAAHGHA!
ONE!

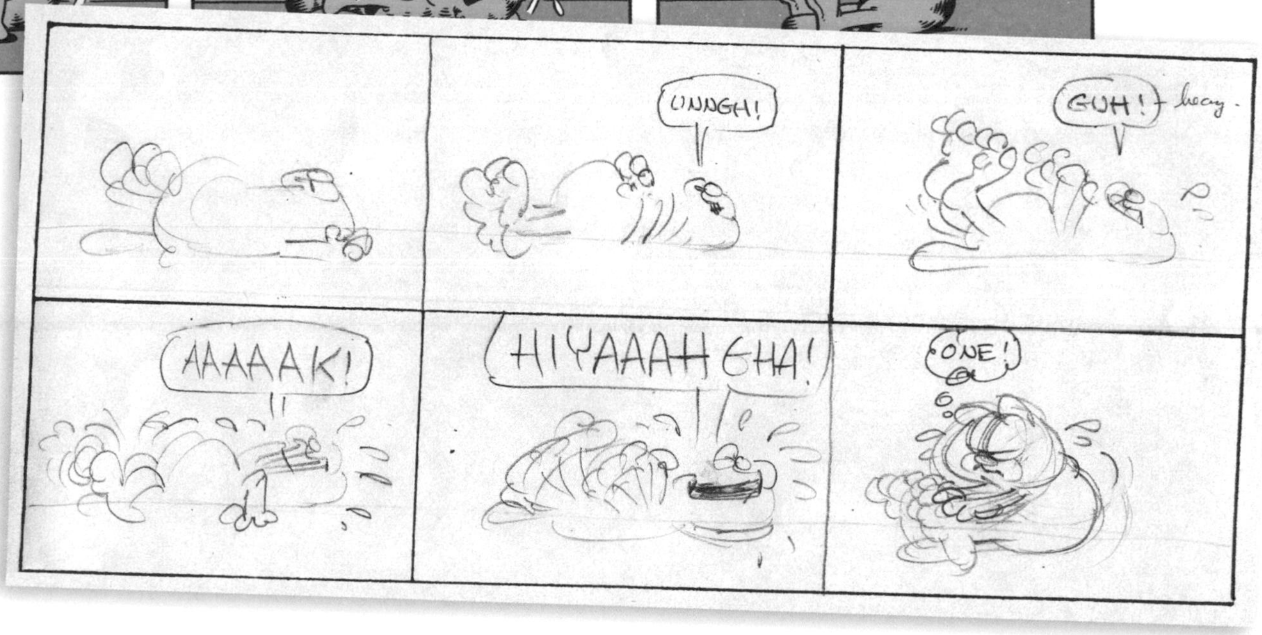
UNNGH!
GUH!
AAAAAK!
HIYAAAH GHA!
ONE!

original rough

I decided to have Garfield ship Nermal to Abu Dhabi
because it's a really funny-sounding place . . .
and Tierra del Fuego was too long for the balloons.

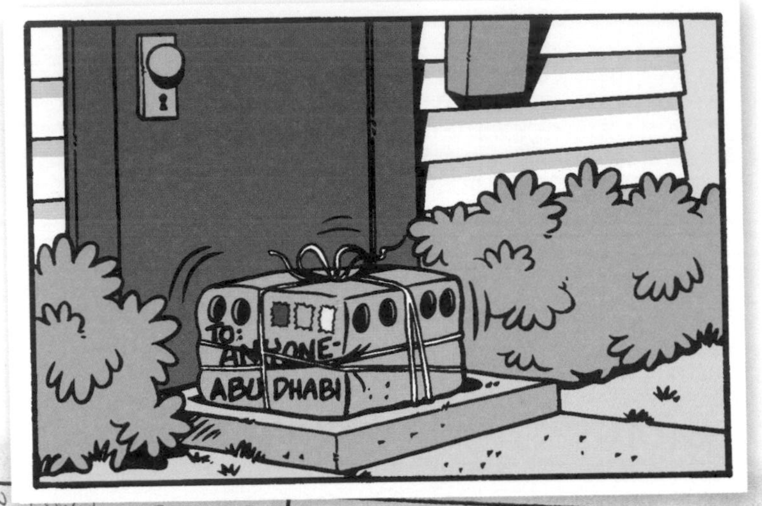
TO:
ANYONE-
ABU DHABI

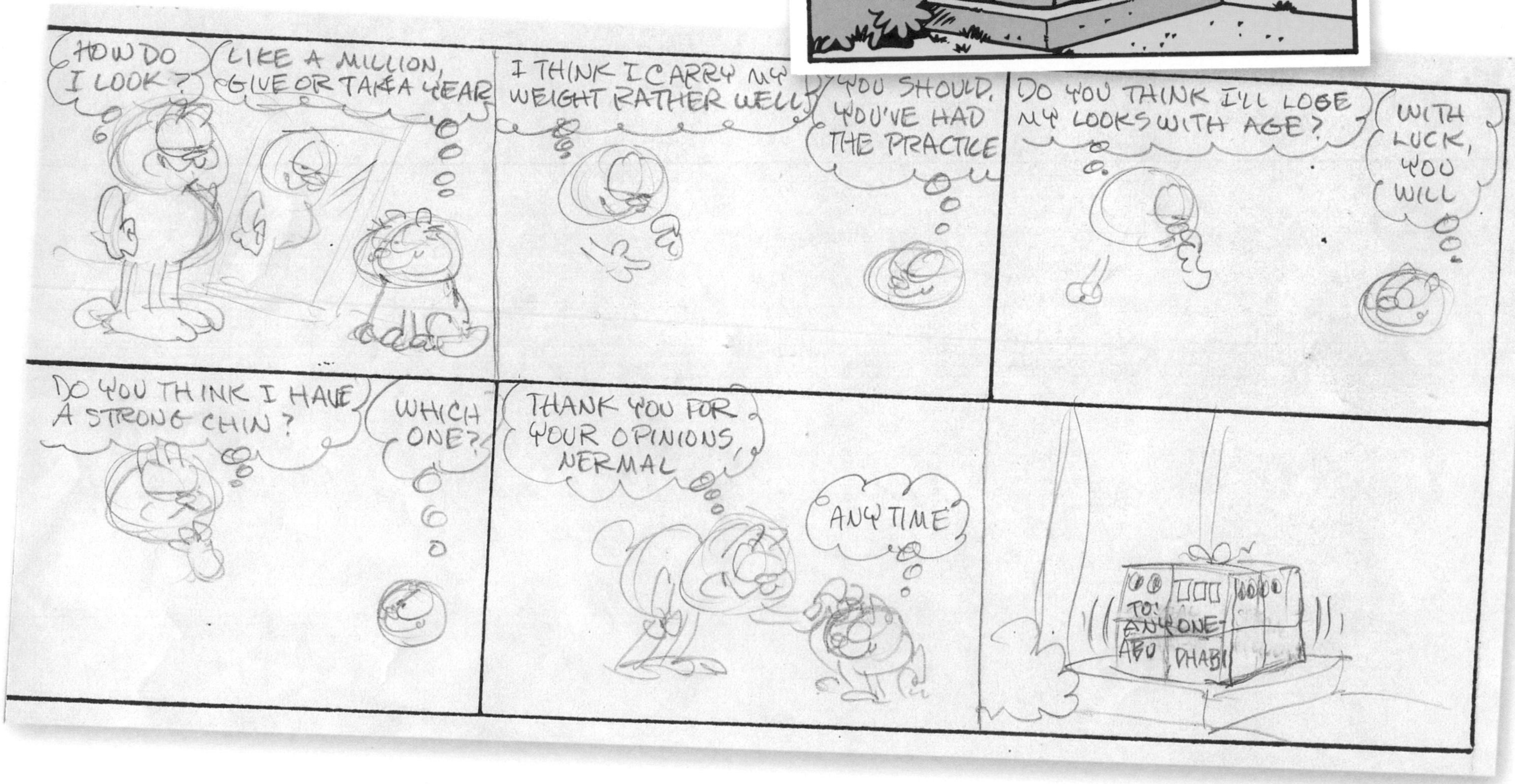
HOW DO I LOOK?
LIKE A MILLION, GIVE OR TAKE A YEAR
I THINK I CARRY MY WEIGHT RATHER WELL
YOU SHOULD. YOU'VE HAD THE PRACTICE
DO YOU THINK I'LL LOSE MY LOOKS WITH AGE?
WITH LUCK, YOU WILL
DO YOU THINK I HAVE A STRONG CHIN?
WHICH ONE?
THANK YOU FOR YOUR OPINIONS, NERMAL
ANYTIME
TO:
ANYONE-
ABU DHABI

original rough

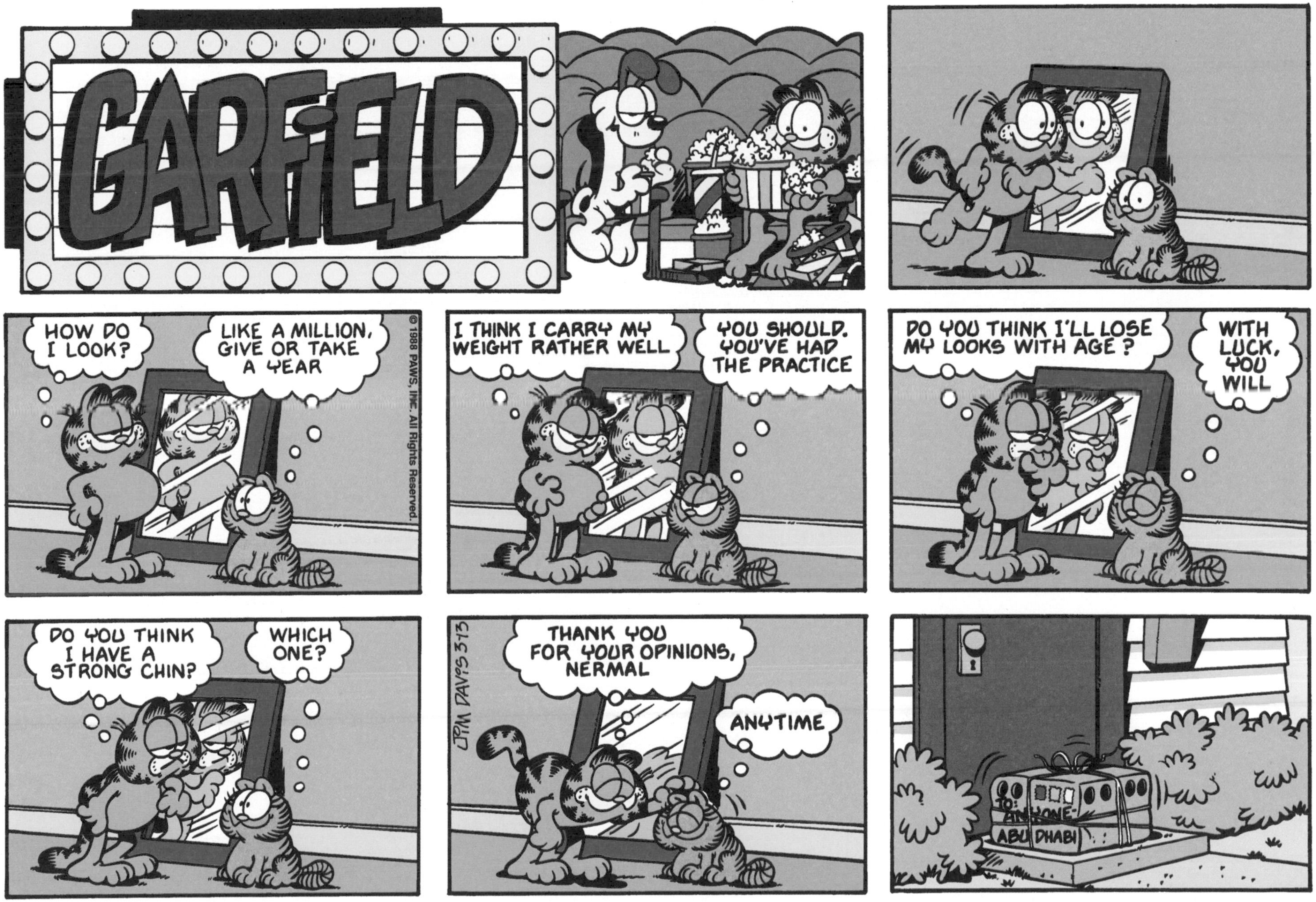
GARFIELD
HOW DO I LOOK?
LIKE A MILLION, GIVE OR TAKE A YEAR
© 1988 PAWS, INC. All Rights Reserved.
I THINK I CARRY MY WEIGHT RATHER WELL
YOU SHOULD. YOU'VE HAD THE PRACTICE
DO YOU THINK I'LL LOSE MY LOOKS WITH AGE?
WITH LUCK, YOU WILL
DO YOU THINK I HAVE A STRONG CHIN?
WHICH ONE?
JIM DAVIS 3-13
THANK YOU FOR YOUR OPINIONS, NERMAL
ANYTIME
TO: ANYONE- ABU DHABI

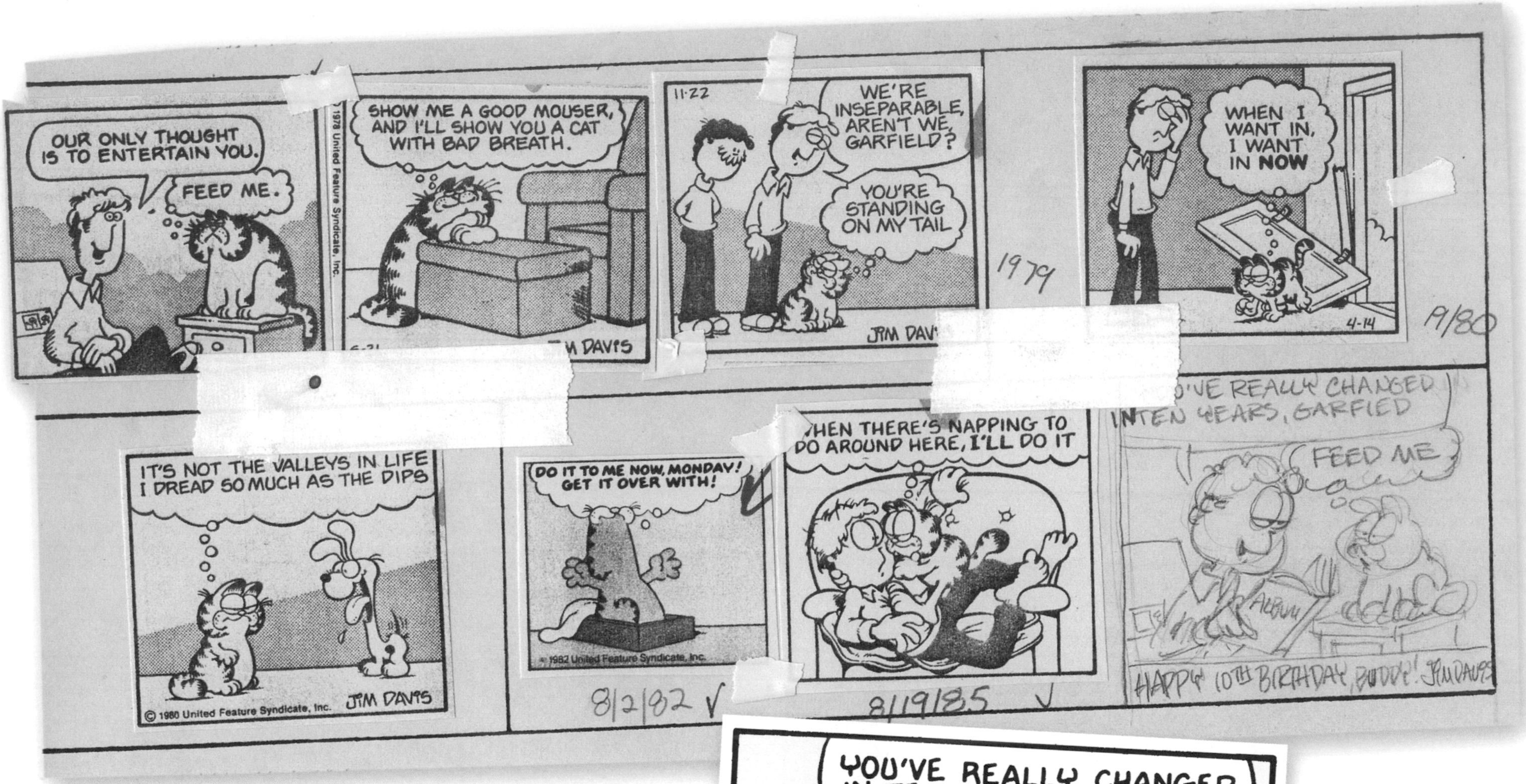
OUR ONLY THOUGHT IS TO ENTERTAIN YOU.
FEED ME.
SHOW ME A GOOD MOUSER, AND I'LL SHOW YOU A CAT WITH BAD BREATH.
© 1978 United Feature Syndicate, Inc.
11·22
WE'RE INSEPARABLE, AREN'T WE, GARFIELD?
YOU'RE STANDING ON MY TAIL
1979
WHEN I WANT IN, I WANT IN NOW
4-14
9/80
IT'S NOT THE VALLEYS IN LIFE I DREAD SO MUCH AS THE DIPS
© 1980 United Feature Syndicate, Inc.
JIM DAVIS
DO IT TO ME NOW, MONDAY! GET IT OVER WITH!
© 1982 United Feature Syndicate, Inc.
8/2/82
WHEN THERE'S NAPPING TO DO AROUND HERE, I'LL DO IT
8/19/85
YOU'VE REALLY CHANGED IN TEN YEARS, GARFIED
FEED ME
ALBUM
HAPPY 10TH BIRTHDAY, BUDDY! JIM DAVIS

original rough

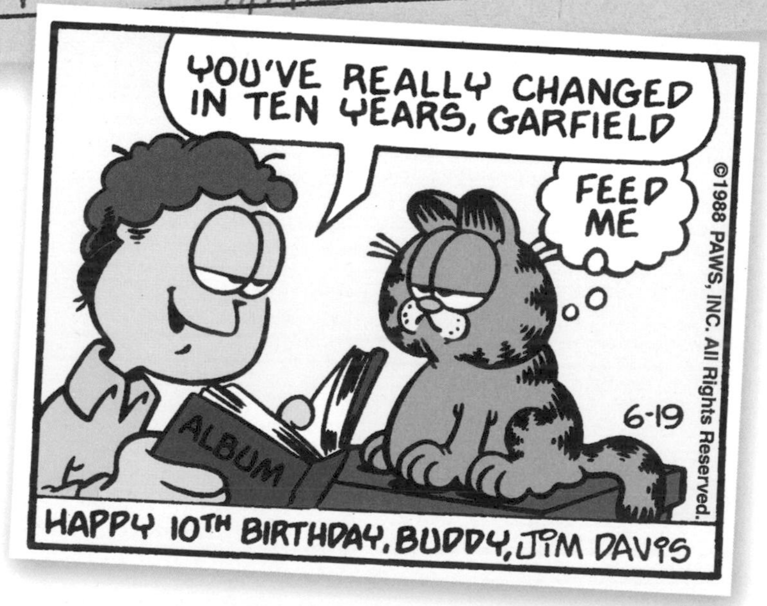
YOU'VE REALLY CHANGED IN TEN YEARS, GARFIELD
FEED ME
ALBUM
6-19
©1988 PAWS, INC. All Rights Reserved.
HAPPY 10TH BIRTHDAY, BUDDY, JIM DAVIS

Look at how much Garfield changed. Ten years is a really long time to do a comic strip.

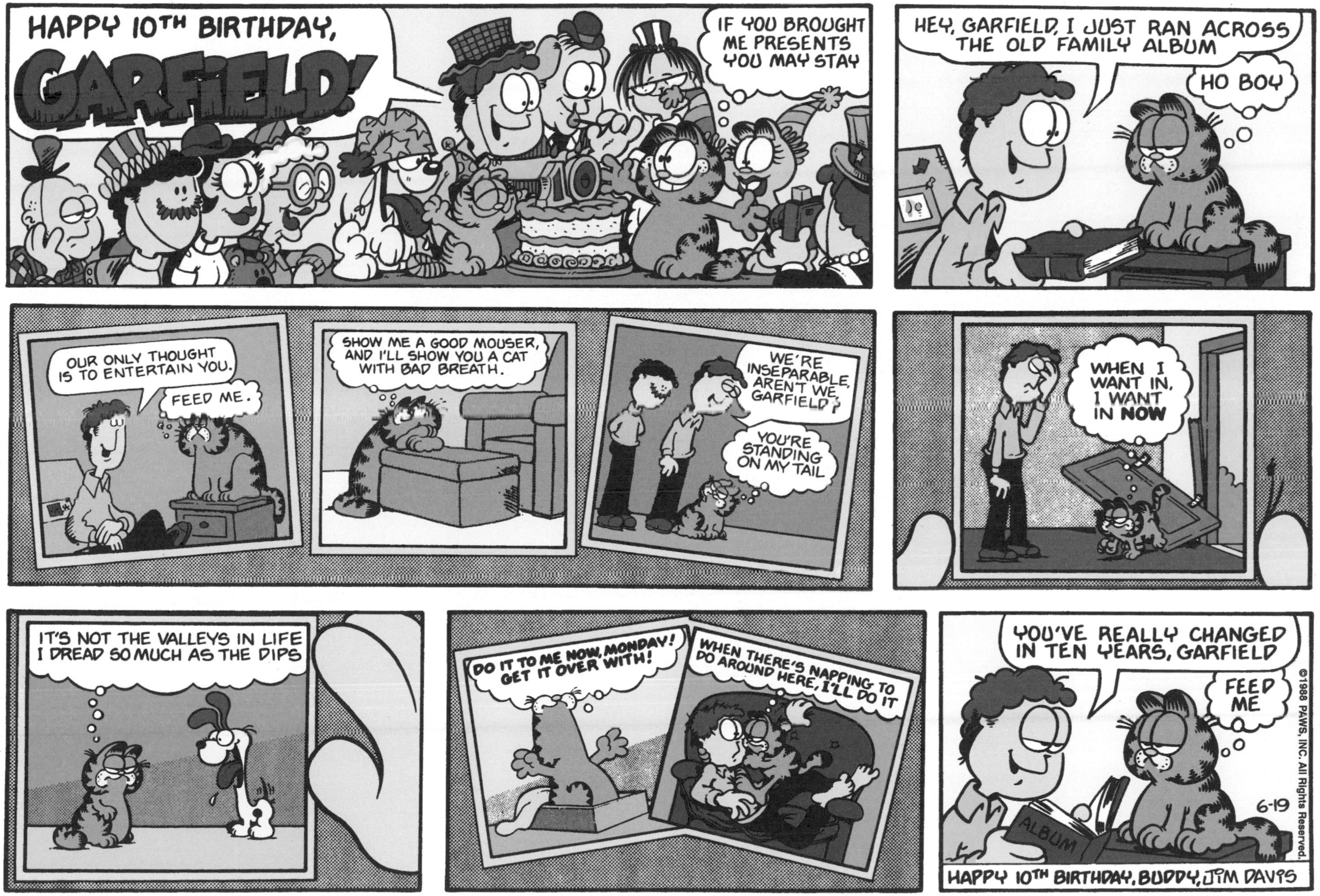

HAPPY 10TH BIRTHDAY, GARFIELD!
IF YOU BROUGHT ME PRESENTS YOU MAY STAY
HEY, GARFIELD, I JUST RAN ACROSS THE OLD FAMILY ALBUM
HO BOY
OUR ONLY THOUGHT IS TO ENTERTAIN YOU.
FEED ME.
SHOW ME A GOOD MOUSER, AND I'LL SHOW YOU A CAT WITH BAD BREATH.
WE'RE INSEPARABLE, AREN'T WE, GARFIELD?
YOU'RE STANDING ON MY TAIL
WHEN I WANT IN, I WANT IN NOW
IT'S NOT THE VALLEYS IN LIFE I DREAD SO MUCH AS THE DIPS
DO IT TO ME NOW, MONDAY! GET IT OVER WITH!
WHEN THERE'S NAPPING TO DO AROUND HERE, I'LL DO IT
YOU'VE REALLY CHANGED IN TEN YEARS, GARFIELD
FEED ME
ALBUM
6-19
©1988 PAWS, INC. All Rights Reserved.
HAPPY 10TH BIRTHDAY, BUDDY, JIM DAVIS

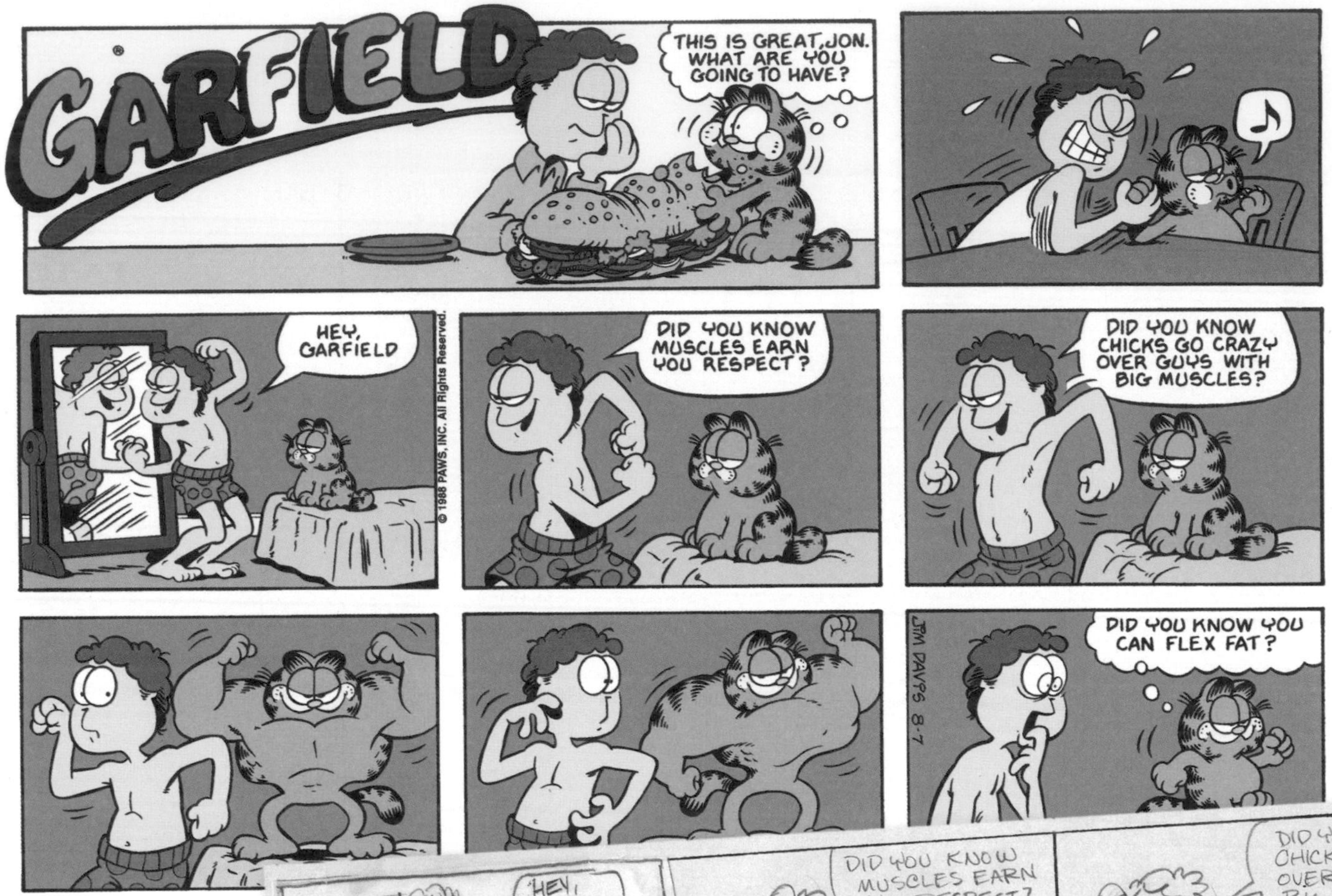
GARFIELD
THIS IS GREAT, JON. WHAT ARE YOU GOING TO HAVE?
♪
HEY, GARFIELD
© 1988 PAWS, INC. All Rights Reserved.
DID YOU KNOW MUSCLES EARN YOU RESPECT?
DID YOU KNOW CHICKS GO CRAZY OVER GUYS WITH BIG MUSCLES?
JIM DAVIS 8-7
DID YOU KNOW YOU CAN FLEX FAT?

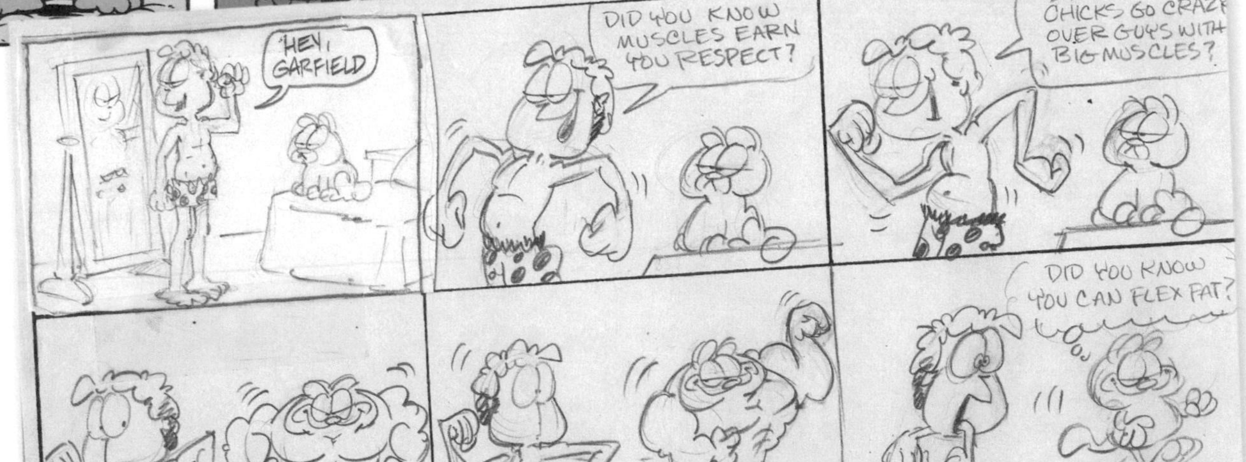
HEY, GARFIELD
DID YOU KNOW MUSCLES EARN YOU RESPECT?
DID YOU KNOW CHICKS GO CRAZY OVER GUYS WITH BIG MUSCLES?
DID YOU KNOW YOU CAN FLEX FAT?

original rough

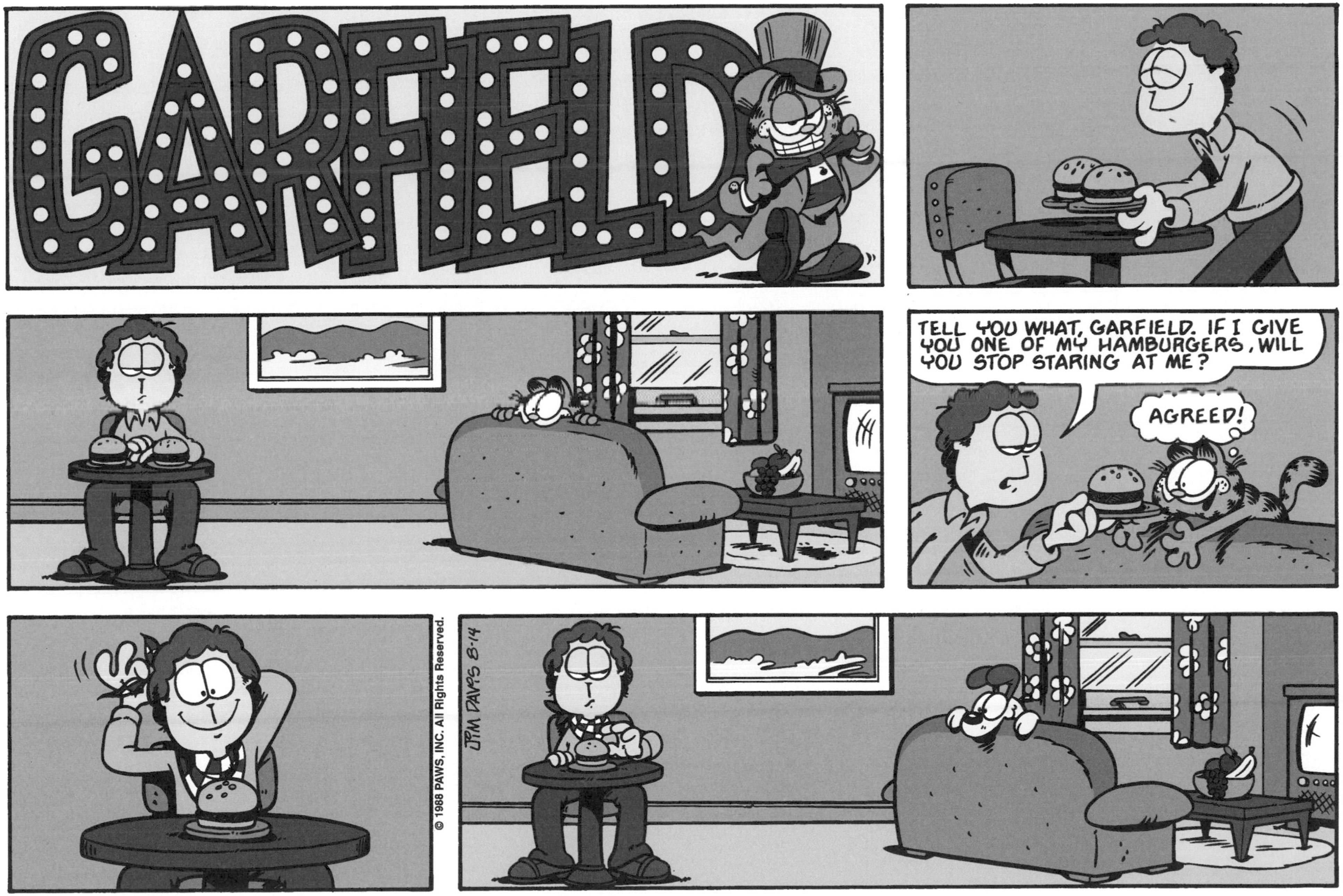
GARFIELD
TELL YOU WHAT, GARFIELD. IF I GIVE YOU ONE OF MY HAMBURGERS, WILL YOU STOP STARING AT ME?
AGREED!
© 1988 PAWS, INC. All Rights Reserved.
JIM DAVIS 8-14

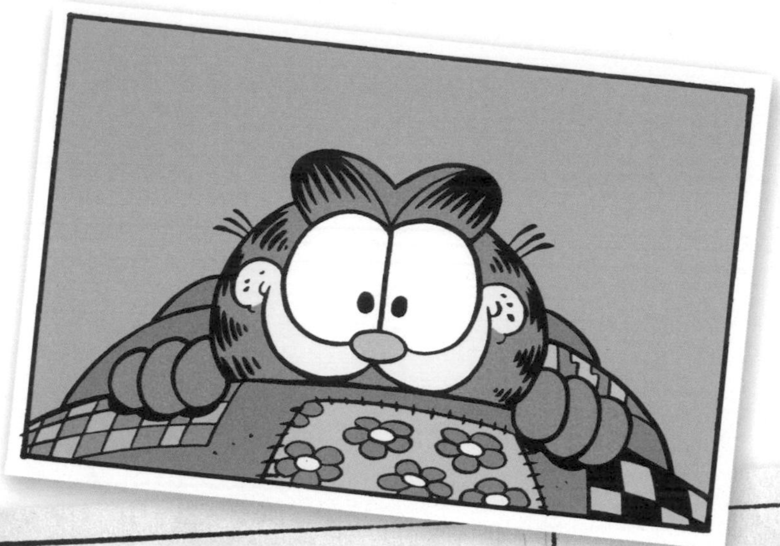

Every now and then I have to do a gag just for the cat lovers. Waking up to cat breath is just one of the many joys of cat ownership.

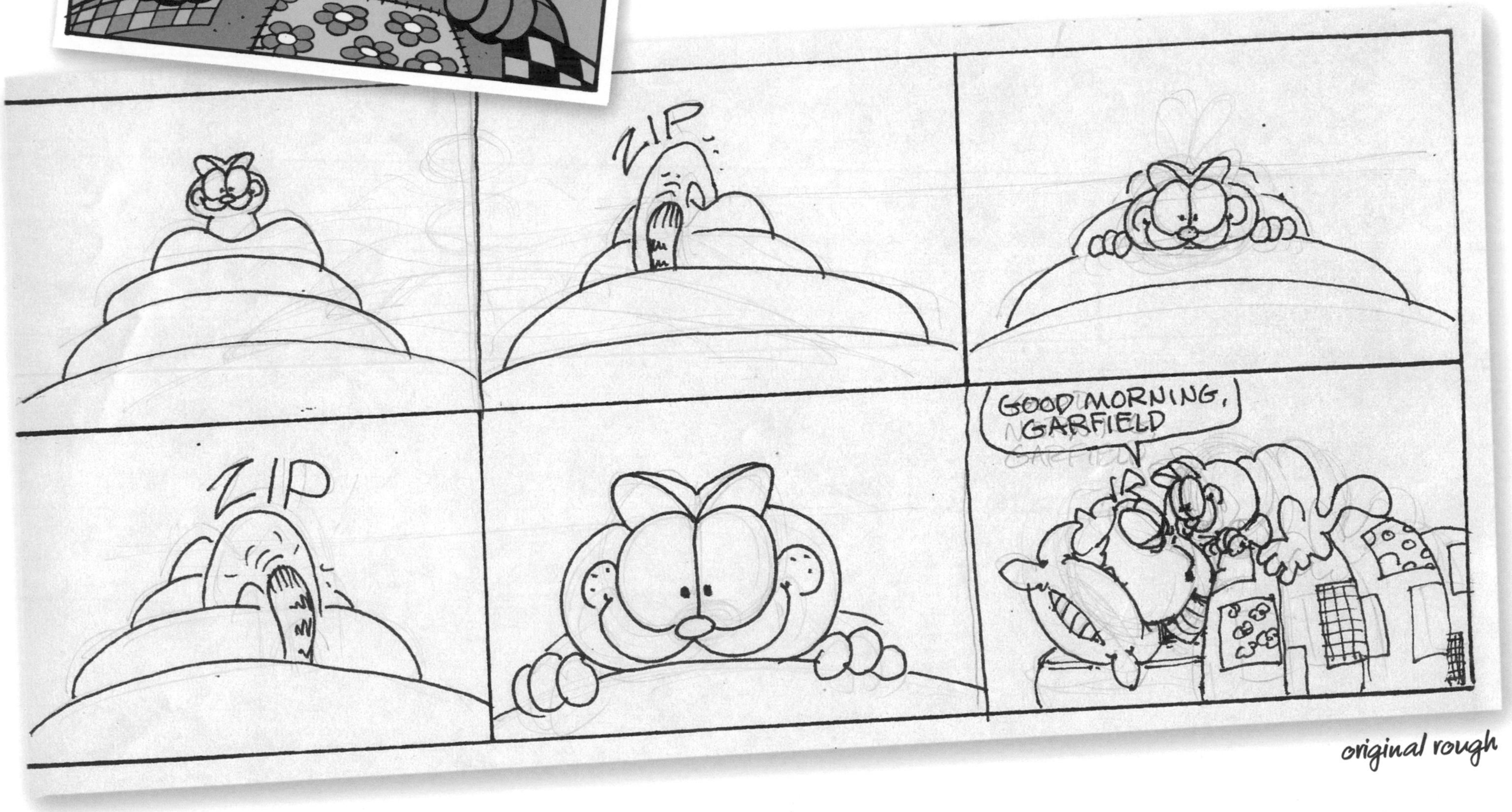
ZIP
ZIP
GOOD MORNING, GARFIELD

original rough

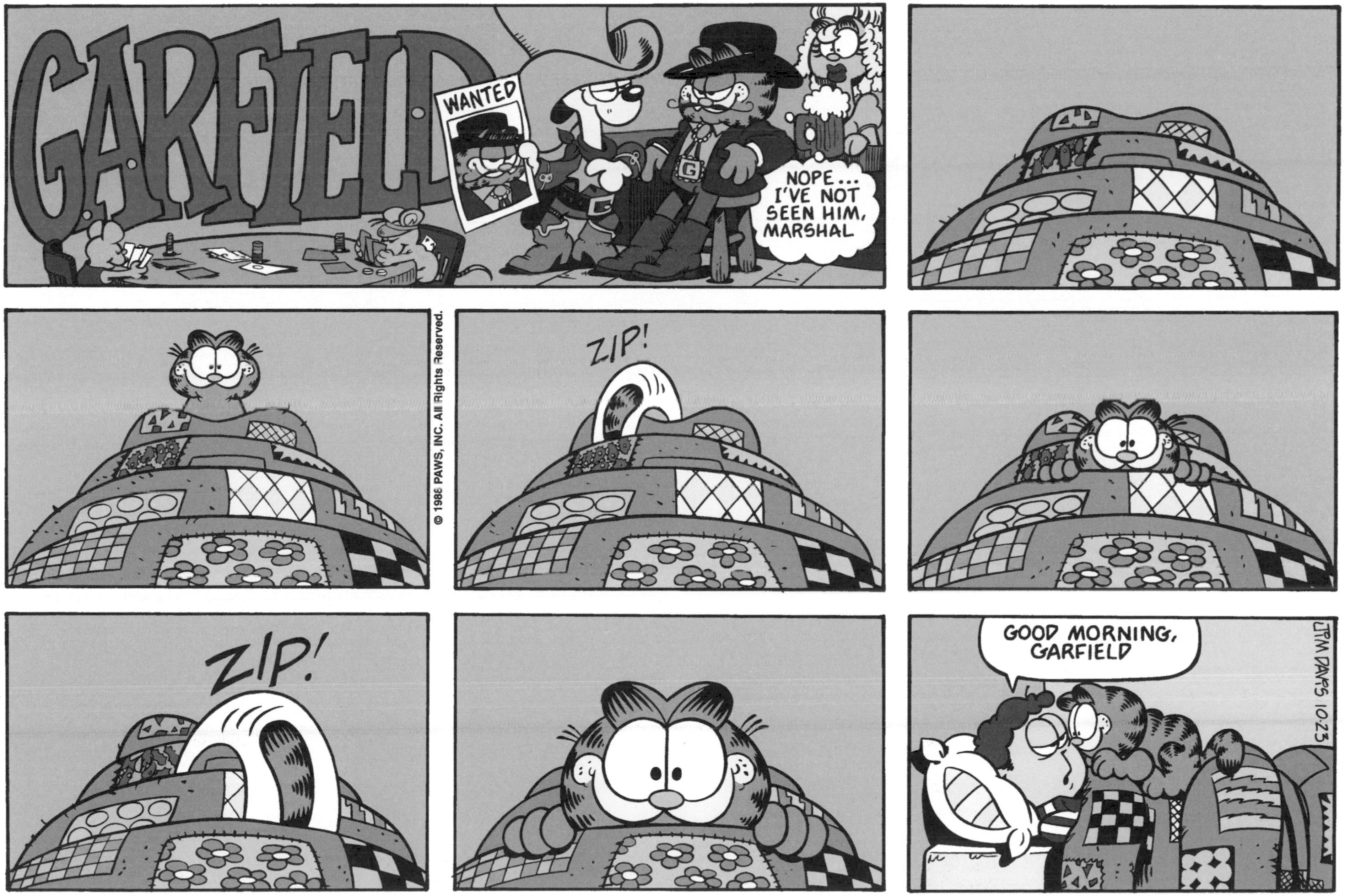

GARFIELD
WANTED
NOPE... I'VE NOT SEEN HIM, MARSHAL
© 1988 PAWS, INC. All Rights Reserved.
ZIP!
ZIP!
GOOD MORNING, GARFIELD
JPM DAVIS 10-23

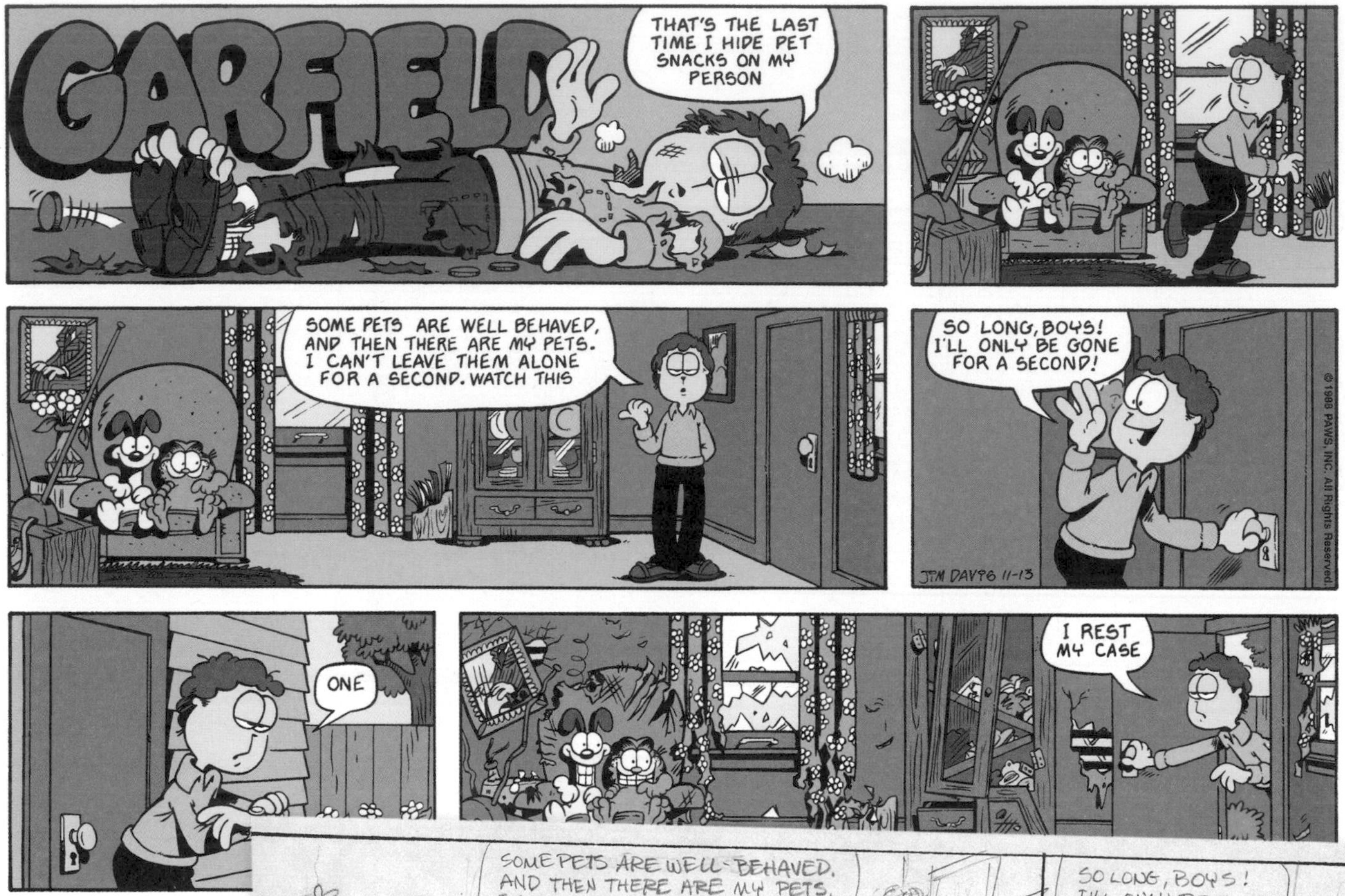
GARFIELD
THAT'S THE LAST TIME I HIDE PET SNACKS ON MY PERSON
SOME PETS ARE WELL BEHAVED, AND THEN THERE ARE MY PETS. I CAN'T LEAVE THEM ALONE FOR A SECOND. WATCH THIS
SO LONG, BOYS! I'LL ONLY BE GONE FOR A SECOND!
JIM DAVIS 11-13
© 1988 PAWS, INC. All Rights Reserved
ONE
I REST MY CASE

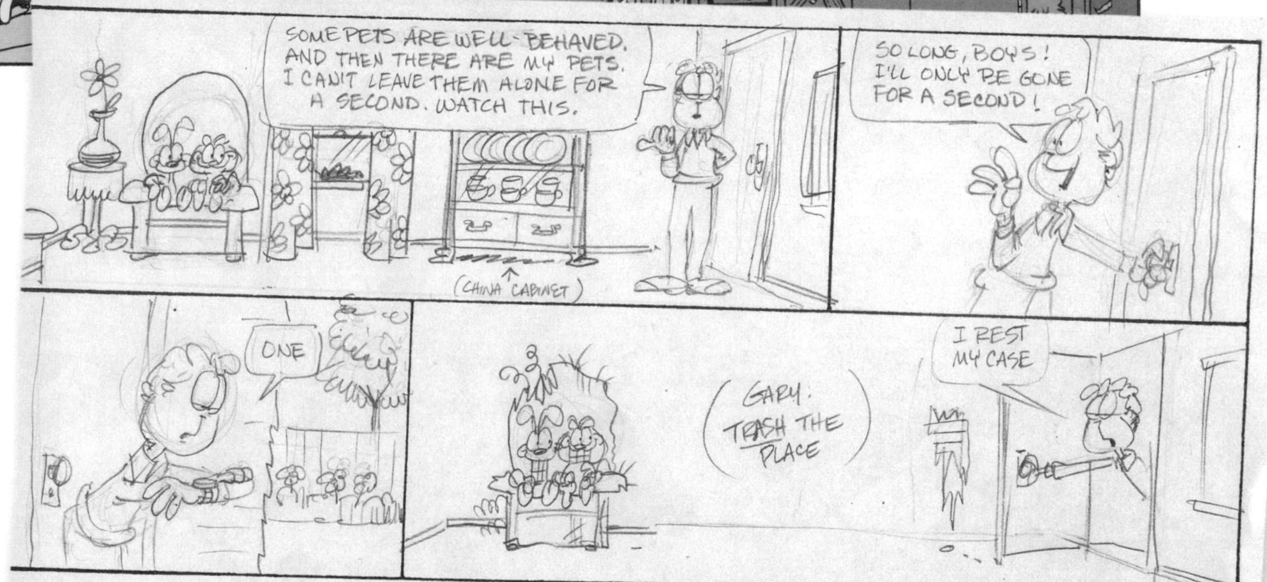
SOME PETS ARE WELL-BEHAVED. AND THEN THERE ARE MY PETS. I CAN'T LEAVE THEM ALONE FOR A SECOND. WATCH THIS.
(CHINA CABINET)
SO LONG, BOYS! I'LL ONLY BE GONE FOR A SECOND!
ONE
(GARY: TRASH THE PLACE)
I REST MY CASE

original rough

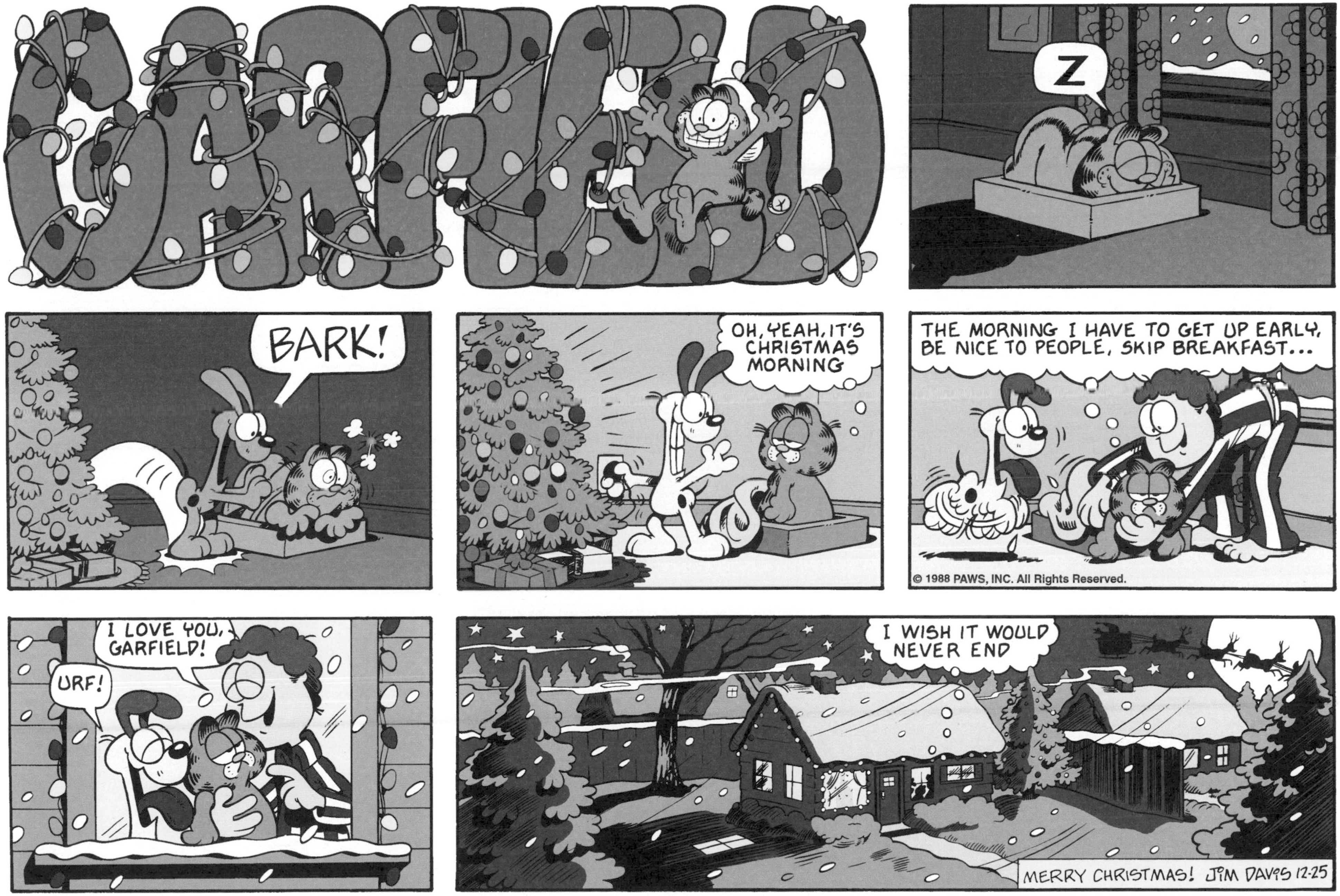
GARFIELD
Z
BARK!
OH, YEAH, IT'S CHRISTMAS MORNING
THE MORNING I HAVE TO GET UP EARLY, BE NICE TO PEOPLE, SKIP BREAKFAST...
© 1988 PAWS, INC. All Rights Reserved.
I LOVE YOU, GARFIELD!
URF!
I WISH IT WOULD NEVER END
MERRY CHRISTMAS! JIM DAVIS 12-25

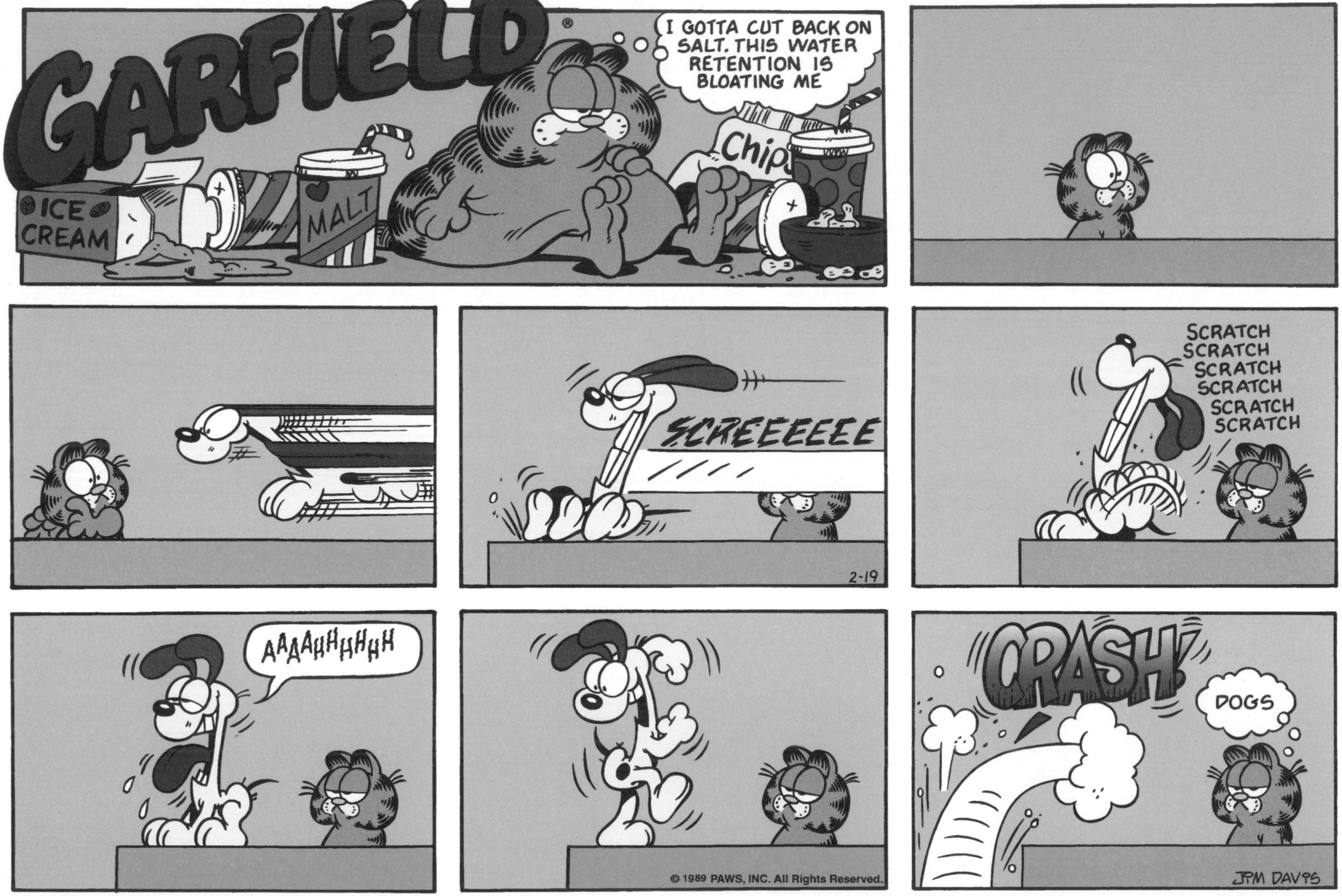
GARFIELD®
ICE CREAM
MALT
Chips
I GOTTA CUT BACK ON SALT. THIS WATER RETENTION IS BLOATING ME
SCREEEEEEE
2-19
SCRATCH SCRATCH SCRATCH SCRATCH SCRATCH SCRATCH
AAAAHHHHHH
CRASH!
DOGS
JPM DAVPS

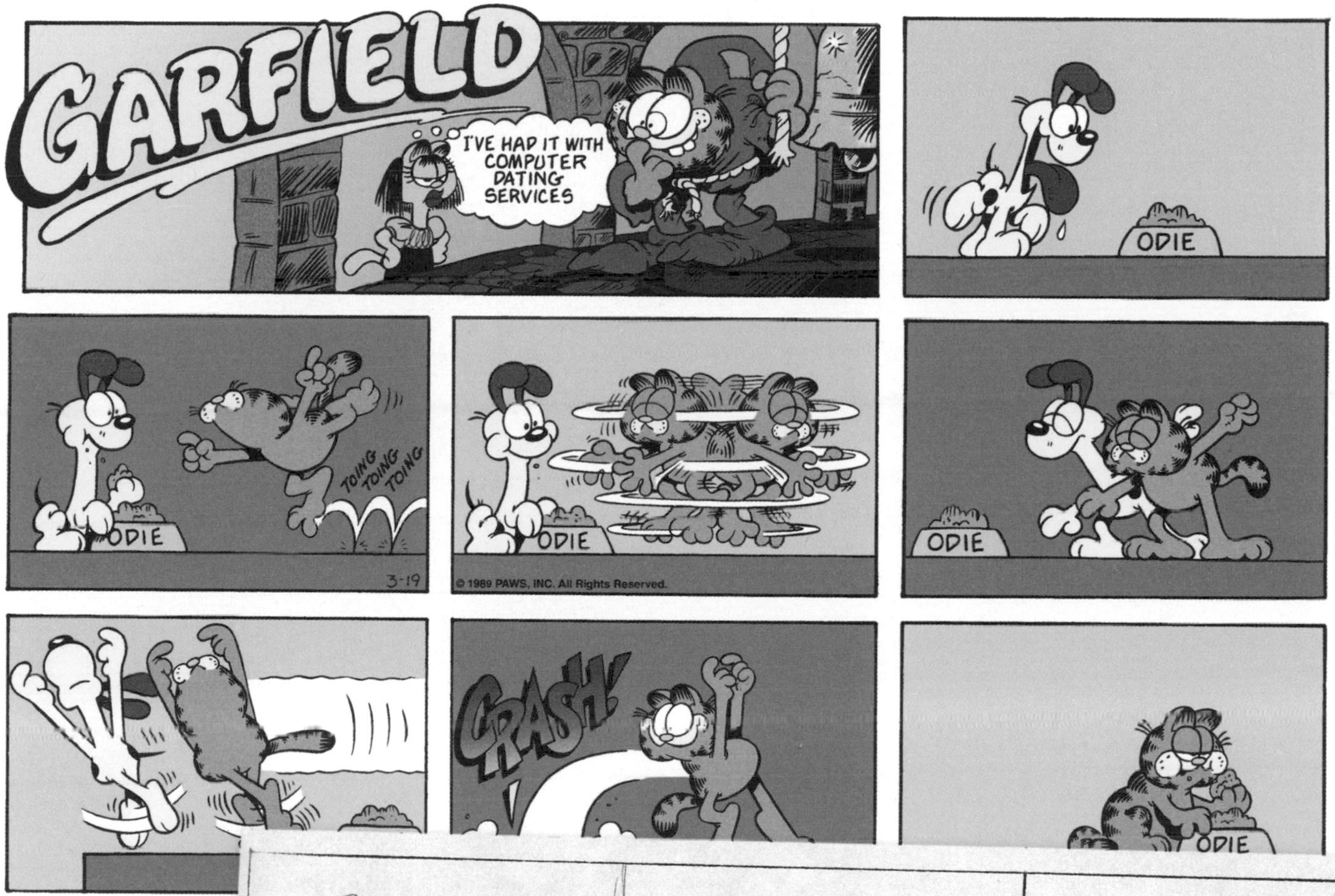
GARFIELD
I'VE HAD IT WITH COMPUTER DATING SERVICES
ODIE
ODIE
TOING TOING TOING
3-19
ODIE
© 1989 PAWS, INC. All Rights Reserved.
ODIE
CRASH!
ODIE

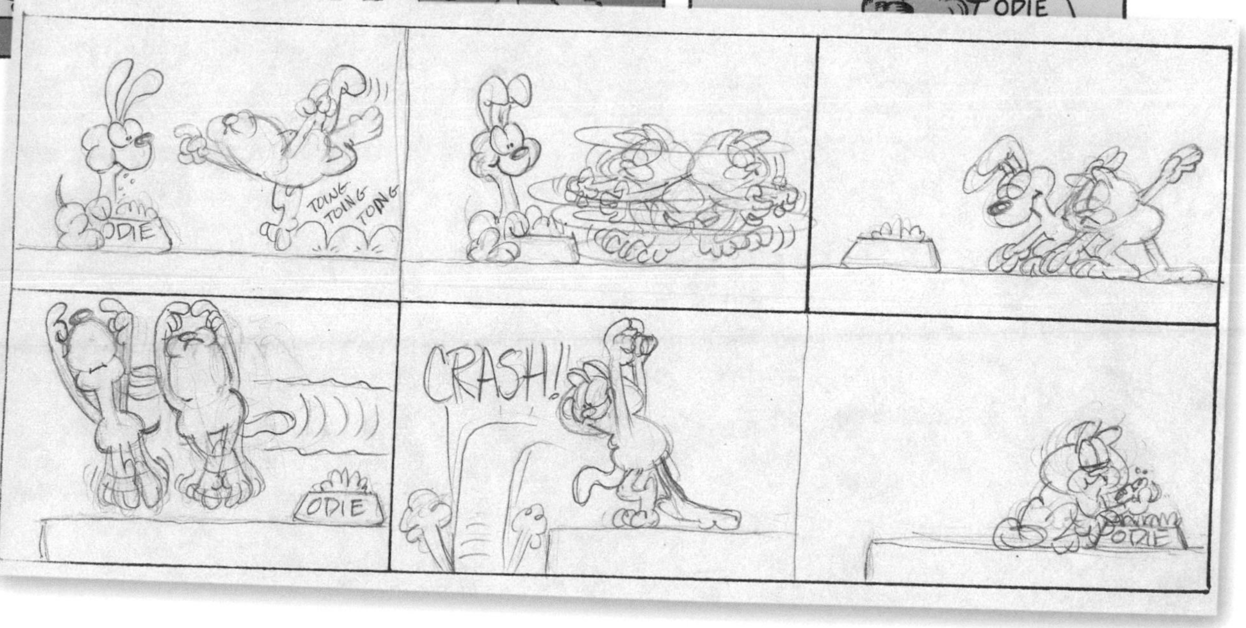
ODIE
TOING TOING TOING
ODIE
CRASH!
ODIE

original rough

I've discovered that the age gags are getting less funny as they're getting more biographical.

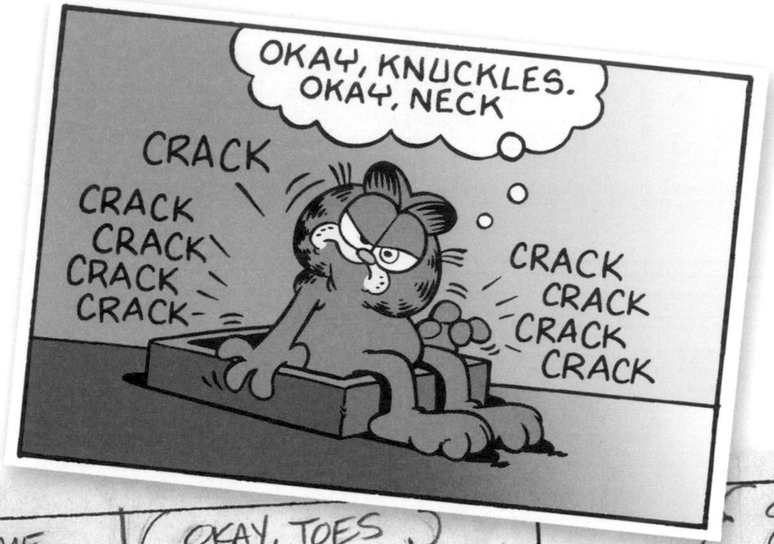
OKAY, KNUCKLES. OKAY, NECK
CRACK
CRACK CRACK CRACK CRACK
CRACK CRACK CRACK CRACK

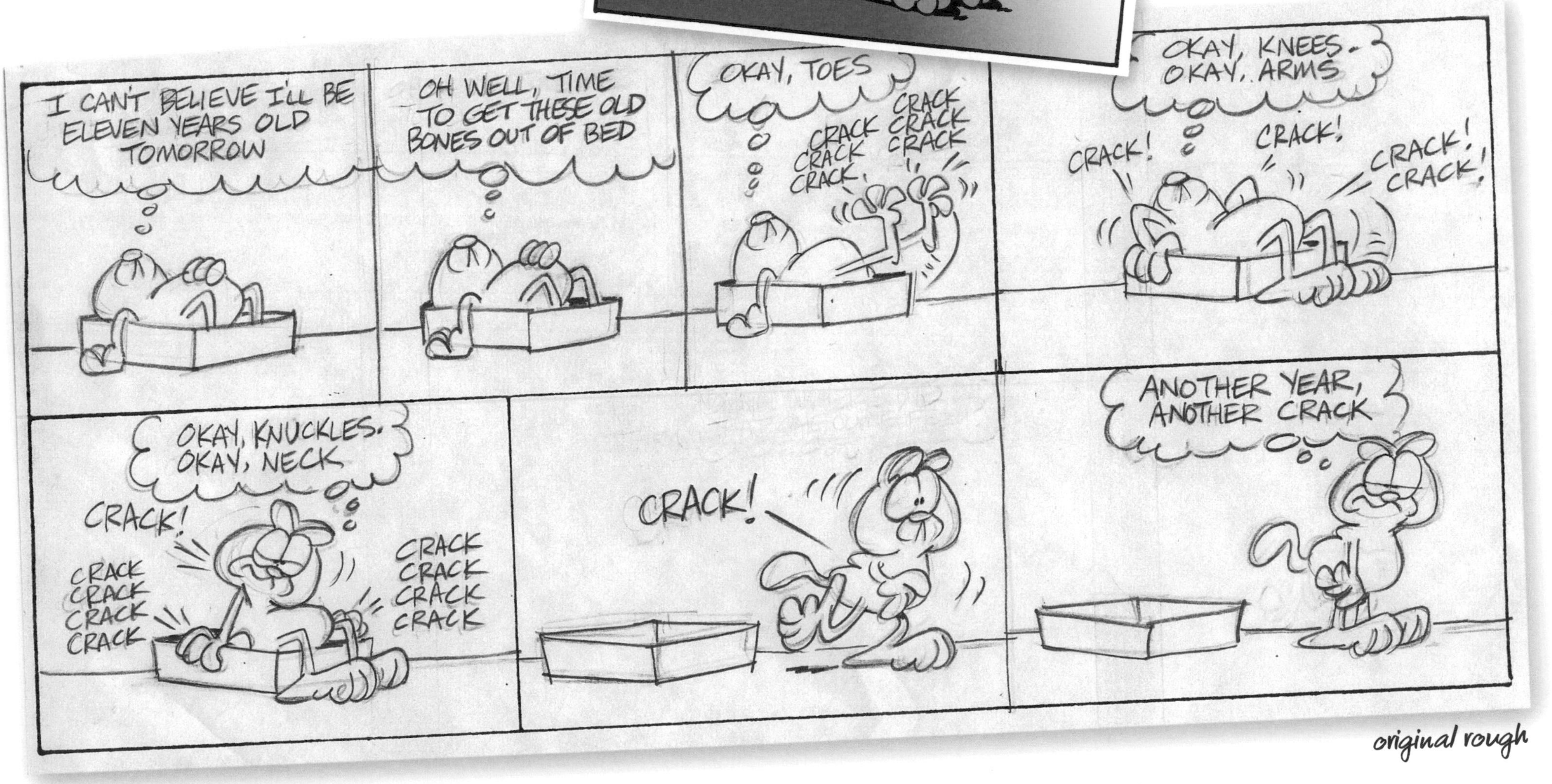
I CAN'T BELIEVE I'LL BE ELEVEN YEARS OLD TOMORROW
OH WELL, TIME TO GET THESE OLD BONES OUT OF BED
OKAY, TOES
CRACK CRACK CRACK
CRACK CRACK CRACK
OKAY, KNEES. OKAY, ARMS
CRACK!
CRACK!
CRACK! CRACK!
OKAY, KNUCKLES. OKAY, NECK
CRACK!
CRACK CRACK CRACK CRACK
CRACK CRACK CRACK CRACK
CRACK!
ANOTHER YEAR, ANOTHER CRACK

original rough

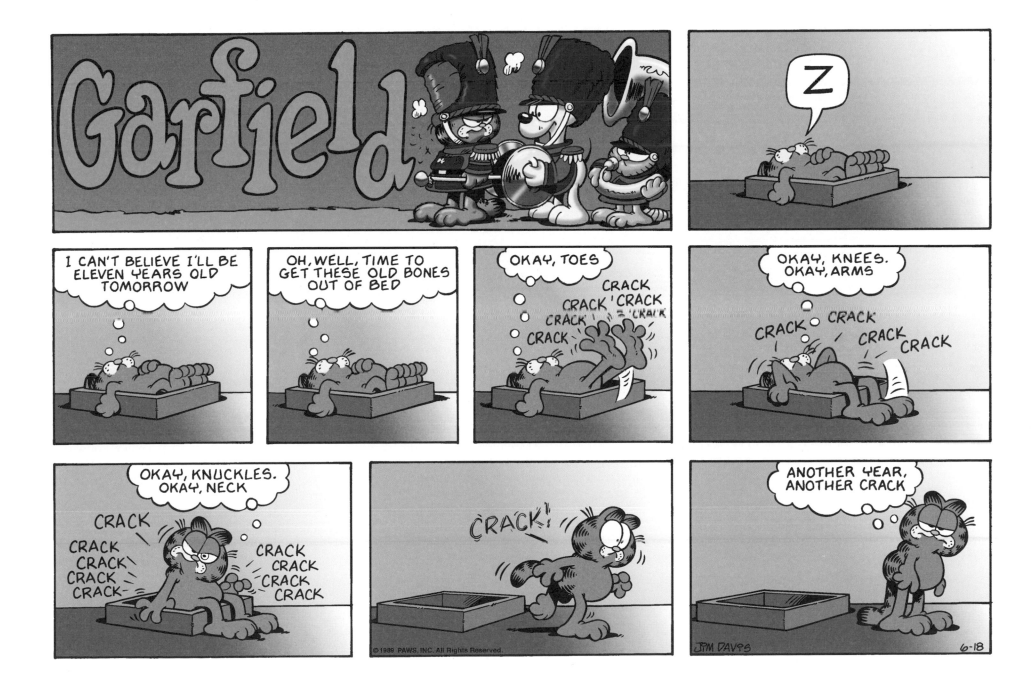

GARFIELD
OH! I SEE THAT YOU'VE FOUND MY RUBBER MOUSEY
SWOOSH
THUD!
OUCH!
WHIMPER WHIMPER
POKE POKE
THANKS, BUDDY

SWOOSH
THUD!
OUCH!
WHIMPER WHIMPER
POKE POKE
THANKS, BUDDY

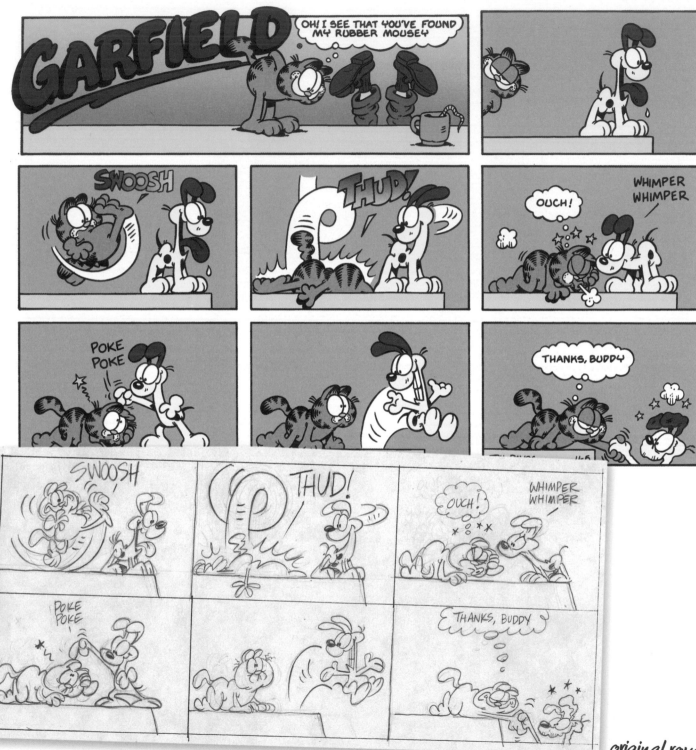

original rough

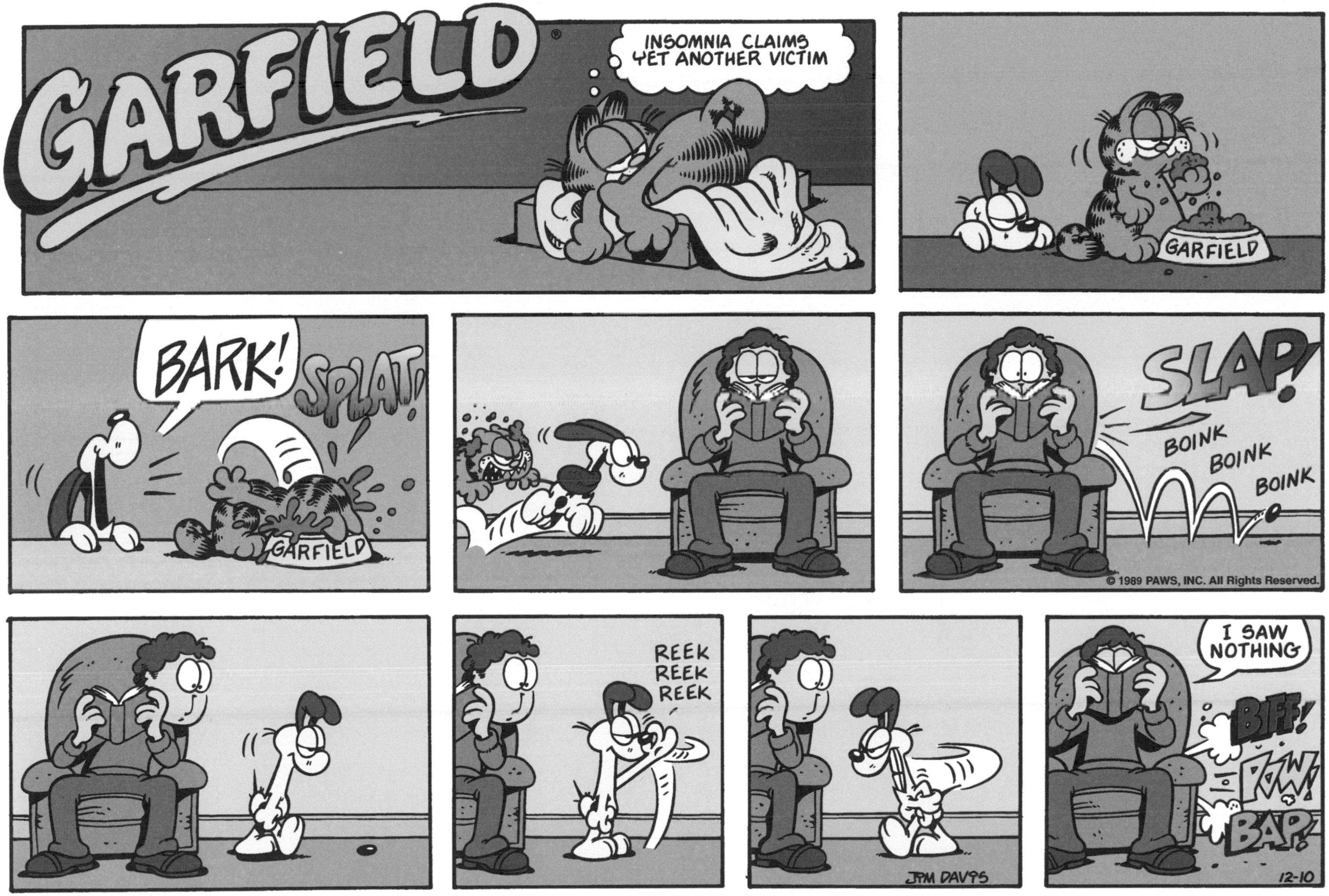
GARFIELD
INSOMNIA CLAIMS YET ANOTHER VICTIM
GARFIELD
BARK!
SPLAT!
GARFIELD
SLAP!
BOINK
BOINK
BOINK
© 1989 PAWS, INC. All Rights Reserved.
REEK
REEK
REEK
JIM DAVIS
I SAW NOTHING
BIFF!
POW!
BAP!
12-10

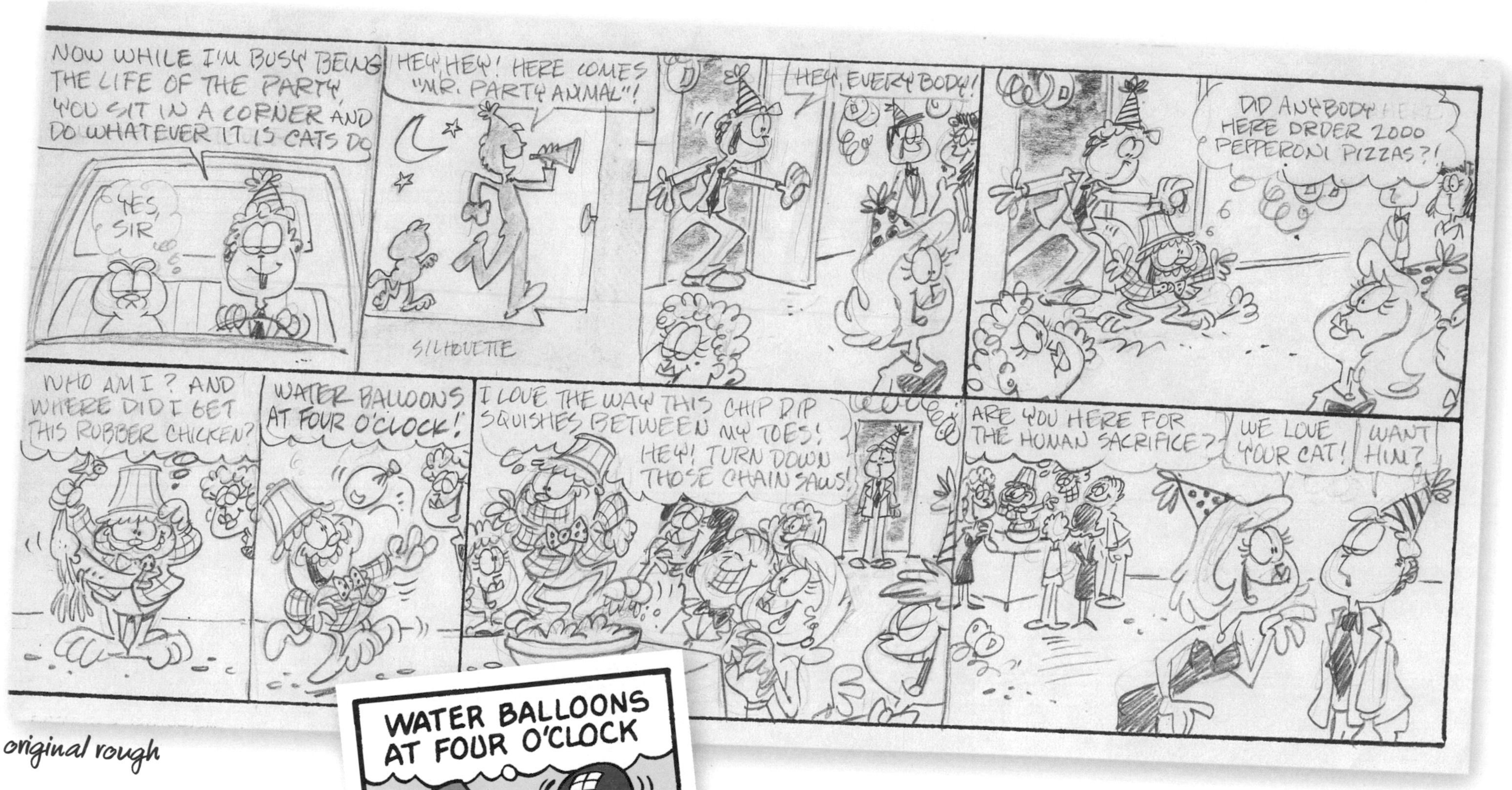
NOW WHILE I'M BUSY BEING THE LIFE OF THE PARTY, YOU SIT IN A CORNER AND DO WHATEVER IT IS CATS DO
YES, SIR
HEY, HEY! HERE COMES "MR. PARTY ANIMAL"!
SILHOUETTE
HEY, EVERYBODY!
DID ANYBODY HERE ORDER 2000 PEPPERONI PIZZAS?!
WHO AM I? AND WHERE DID I GET THIS RUBBER CHICKEN?
WATER BALLOONS AT FOUR O'CLOCK!
I LOVE THE WAY THIS CHIP DIP SQUISHES BETWEEN MY TOES!
HEY! TURN DOWN THOSE CHAIN SAWS!
ARE YOU HERE FOR THE HUMAN SACRIFICE?
WE LOVE YOUR CAT!
WANT HIM?

original rough

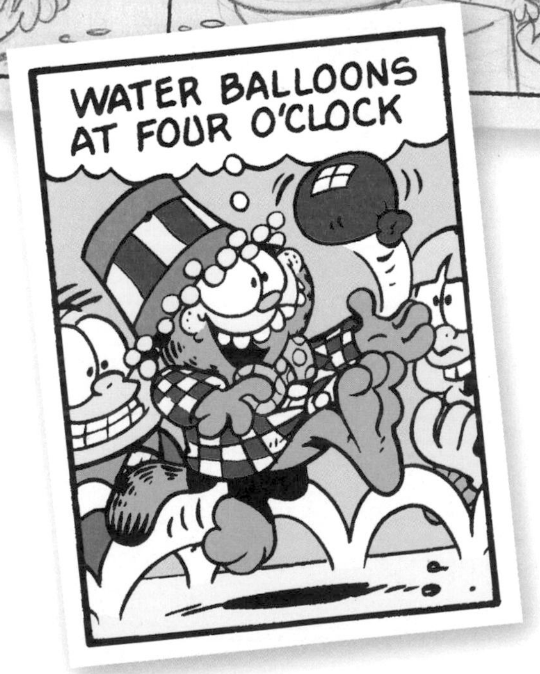
WATER BALLOONS AT FOUR O'CLOCK

This strip was inspired by an episode of The Dick Van Dyke Show where Dick's shy brother nightly became a sleepwalking life of the party.

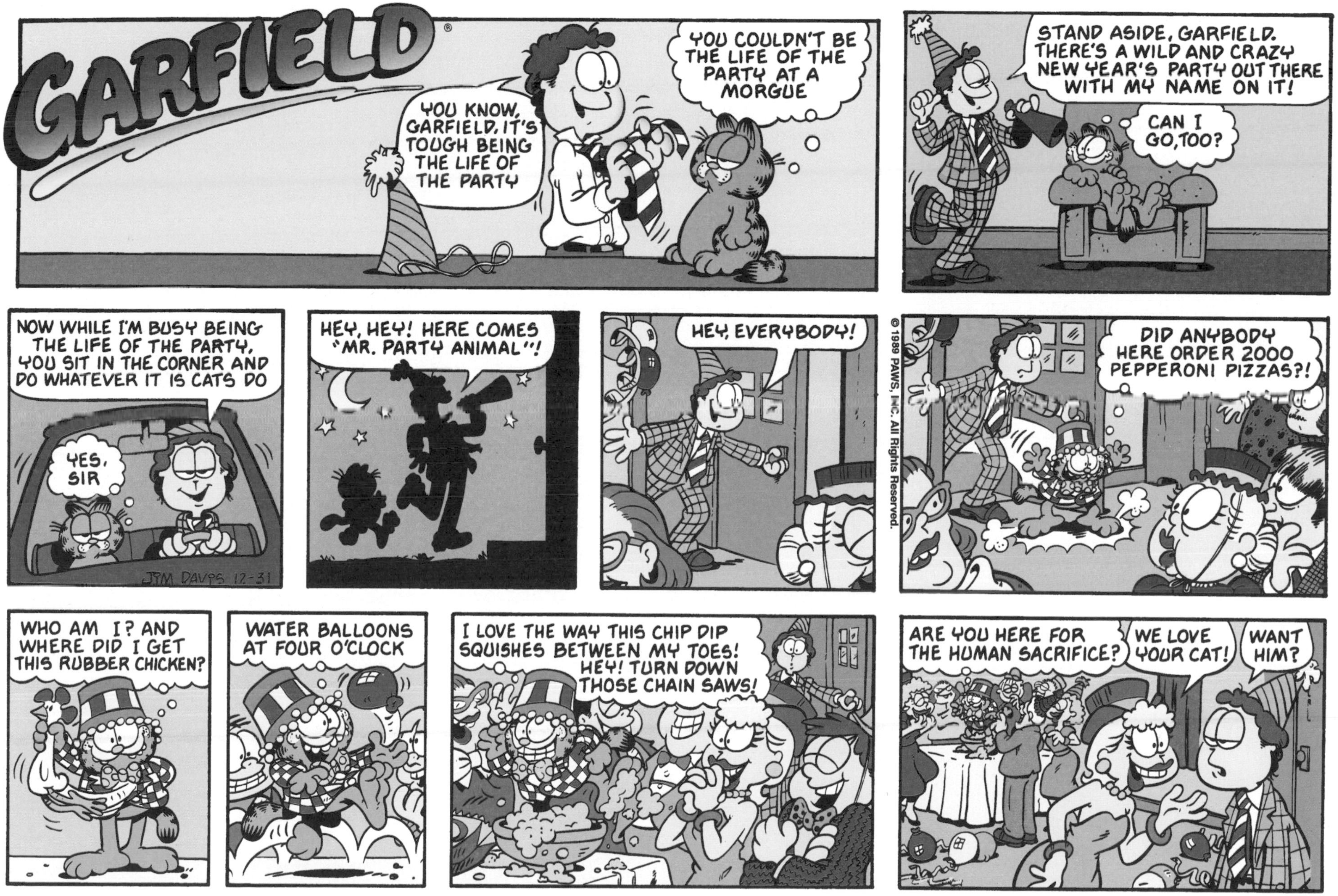
GARFIELD
YOU KNOW, GARFIELD, IT'S TOUGH BEING THE LIFE OF THE PARTY
YOU COULDN'T BE THE LIFE OF THE PARTY AT A MORGUE
STAND ASIDE, GARFIELD. THERE'S A WILD AND CRAZY NEW YEAR'S PARTY OUT THERE WITH MY NAME ON IT!
CAN I GO, TOO?
NOW WHILE I'M BUSY BEING THE LIFE OF THE PARTY, YOU SIT IN THE CORNER AND DO WHATEVER IT IS CATS DO
YES, SIR
JIM DAVIS 12-31
HEY, HEY! HERE COMES "MR. PARTY ANIMAL"!
HEY, EVERYBODY!
© 1989 PAWS, INC. All Rights Reserved.
DID ANYBODY HERE ORDER 2000 PEPPERONI PIZZAS?!
WHO AM I? AND WHERE DID I GET THIS RUBBER CHICKEN?
WATER BALLOONS AT FOUR O'CLOCK
I LOVE THE WAY THIS CHIP DIP SQUISHES BETWEEN MY TOES!
HEY! TURN DOWN THOSE CHAIN SAWS!
ARE YOU HERE FOR THE HUMAN SACRIFICE?
WE LOVE YOUR CAT!
WANT HIM?

The beauty of writing a Sunday page is that I get the luxury of space and time to craft the gag. Garfield took his sweet time performing a gag that could not have been done as a daily.

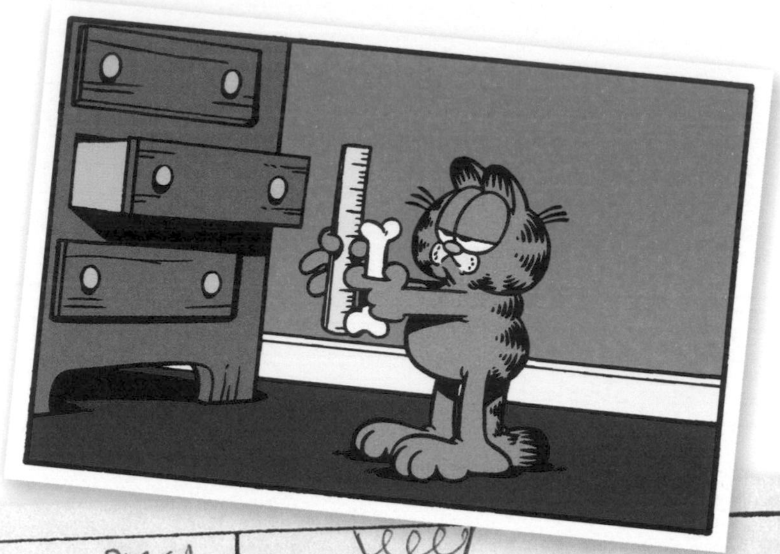

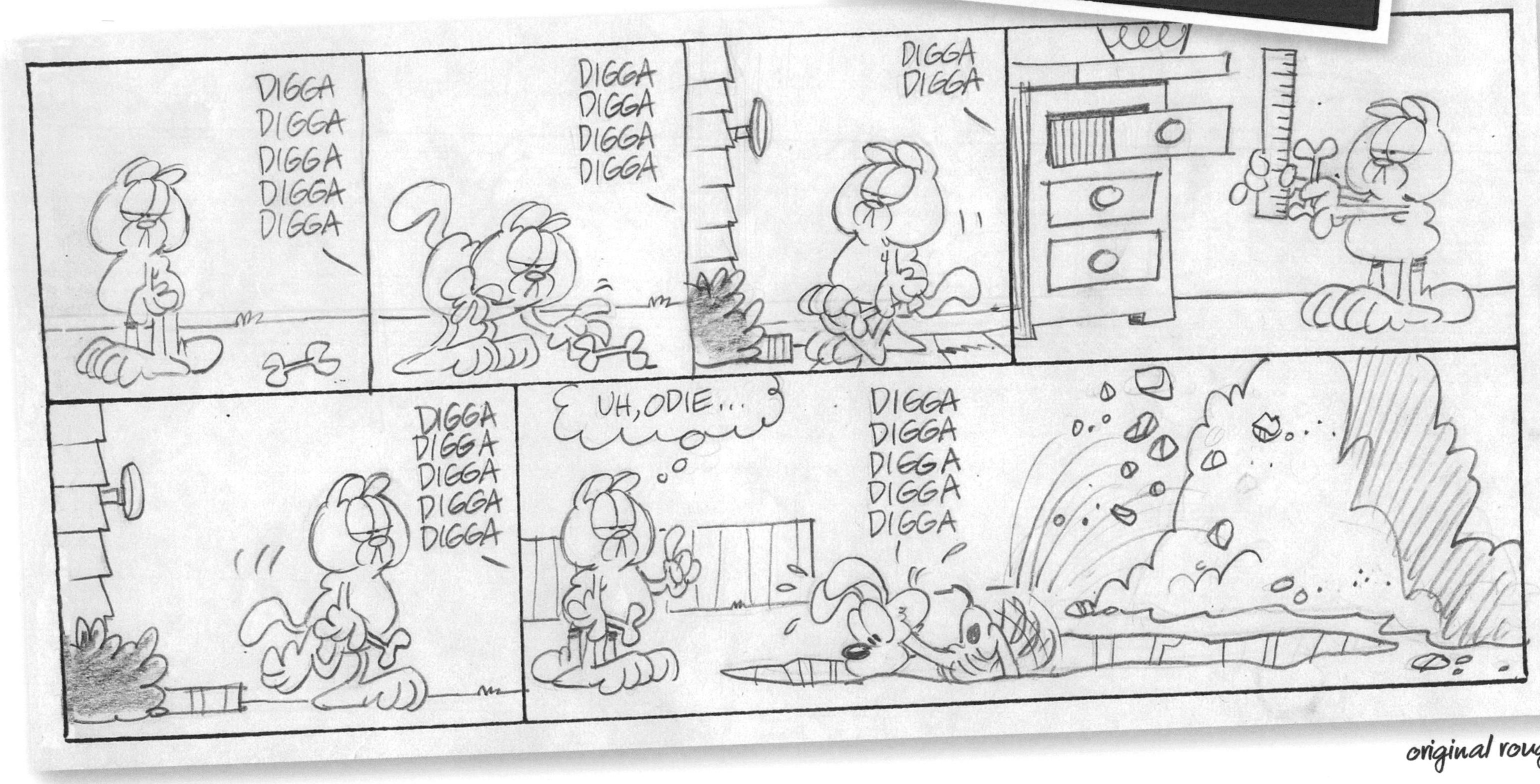

DIGGA DIGGA DIGGA DIGGA DIGGA
DIGGA DIGGA DIGGA DIGGA
DIGGA DIGGA
DIGGA DIGGA DIGGA DIGGA DIGGA
UH, ODIE...
DIGGA DIGGA DIGGA DIGGA DIGGA

original rough

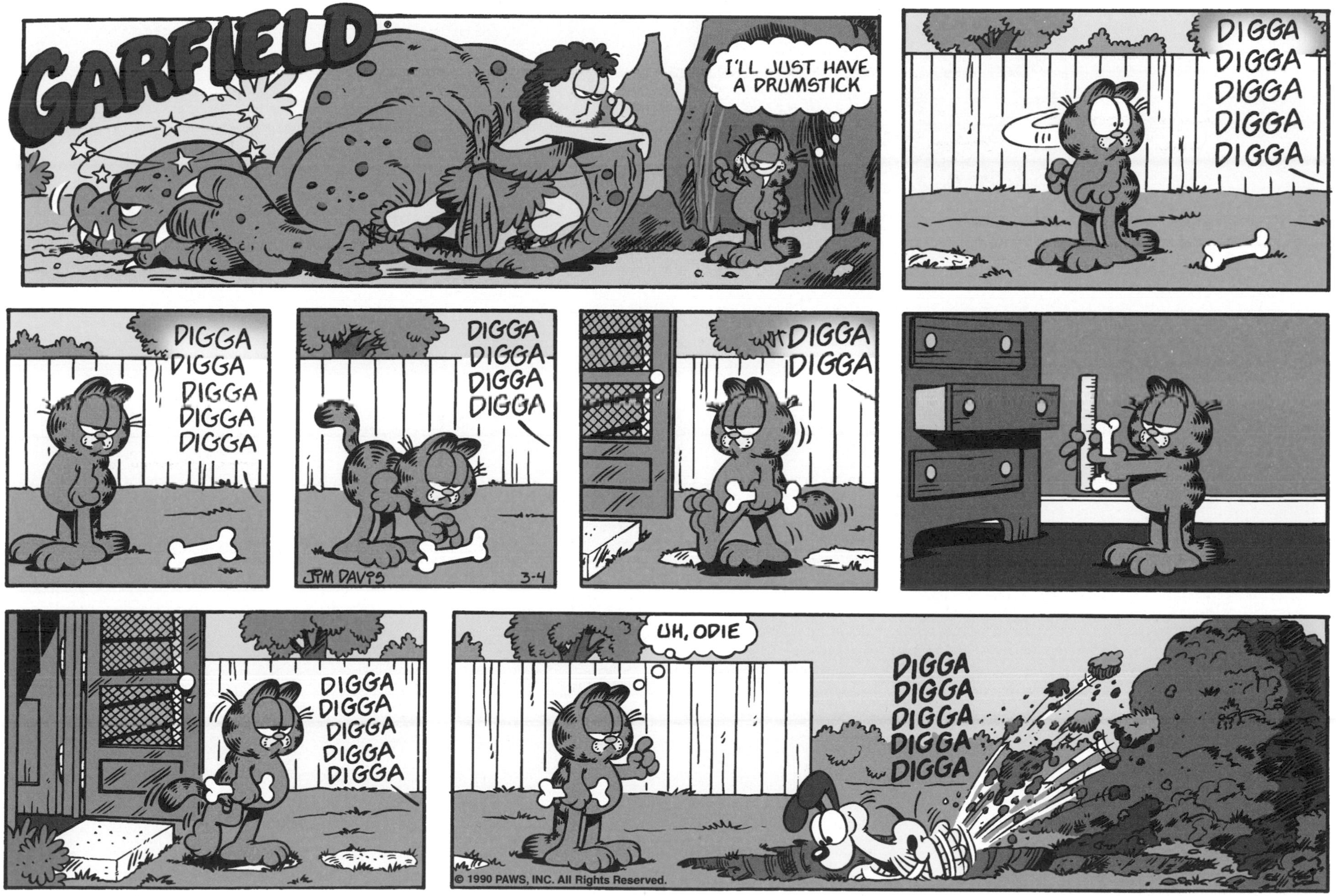
GARFIELD
I'LL JUST HAVE A DRUMSTICK
DIGGA DIGGA DIGGA DIGGA DIGGA
DIGGA DIGGA DIGGA DIGGA DIGGA
DIGGA DIGGA DIGGA DIGGA
JIM DAVIS 3-4
DIGGA DIGGA
DIGGA DIGGA DIGGA DIGGA DIGGA
UH, ODIE
DIGGA DIGGA DIGGA DIGGA DIGGA
© 1990 PAWS, INC. All Rights Reserved.

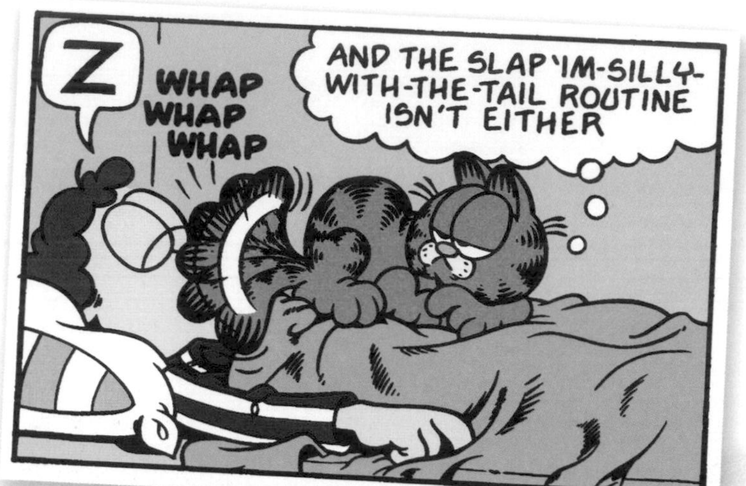
Z
WHAP
WHAP
WHAP
AND THE SLAP'IM-SILLY-WITH-THE-TAIL ROUTINE ISN'T EITHER

What pet owner hasn't suffered this abuse? Gags that strike a familiar chord seem to elicit the most fan mail.

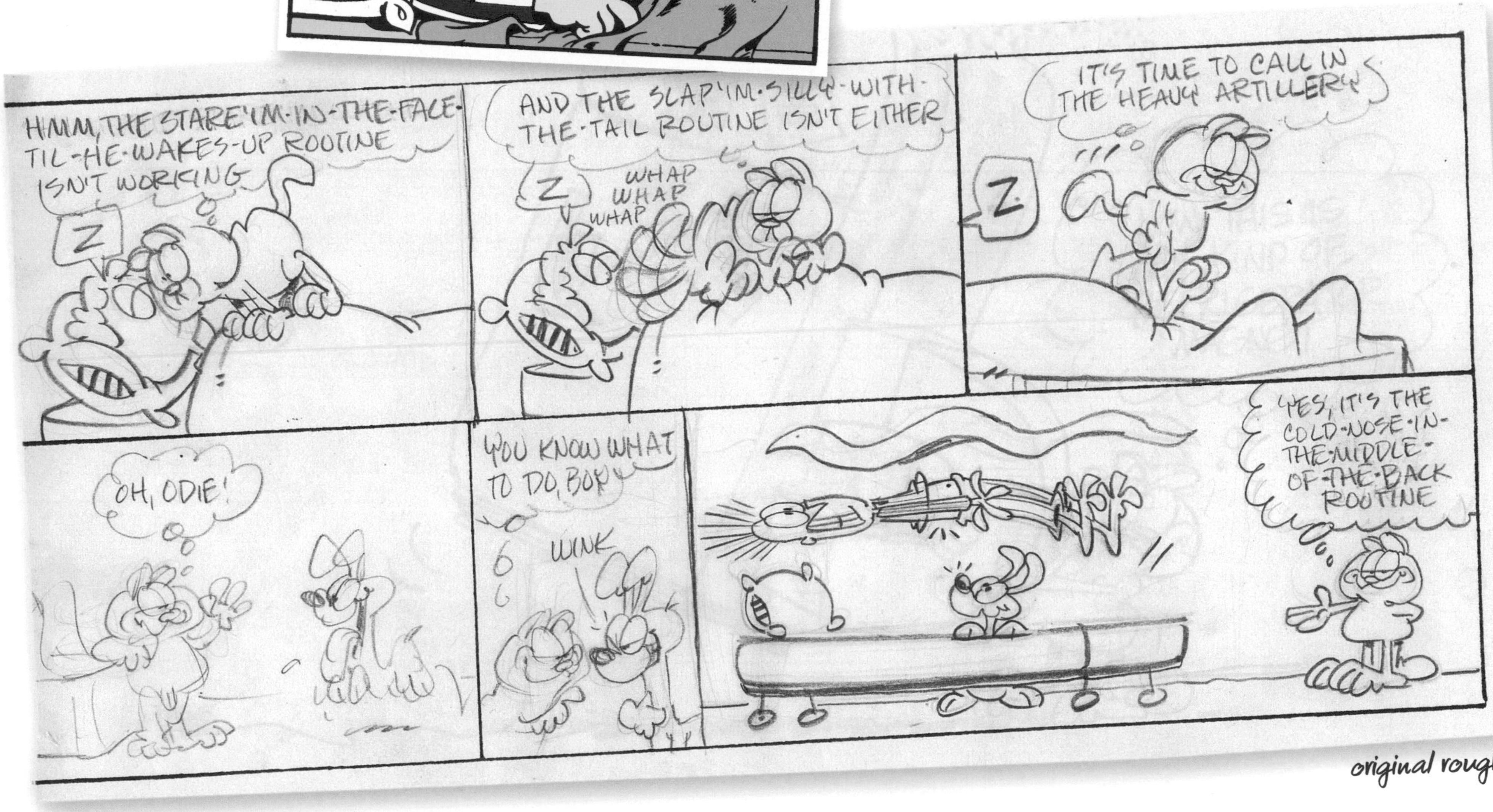
HMM, THE STARE'IM-IN-THE-FACE-TIL-HE-WAKES-UP ROUTINE ISN'T WORKING
Z
AND THE SLAP'IM-SILLY-WITH-THE-TAIL ROUTINE ISN'T EITHER
Z
WHAP
WHAP
WHAP
IT'S TIME TO CALL IN THE HEAVY ARTILLERY
Z
OH, ODIE!
YOU KNOW WHAT TO DO, BOY
WINK
YES, IT'S THE COLD-NOSE-IN-THE-MIDDLE-OF-THE-BACK ROUTINE

original rough

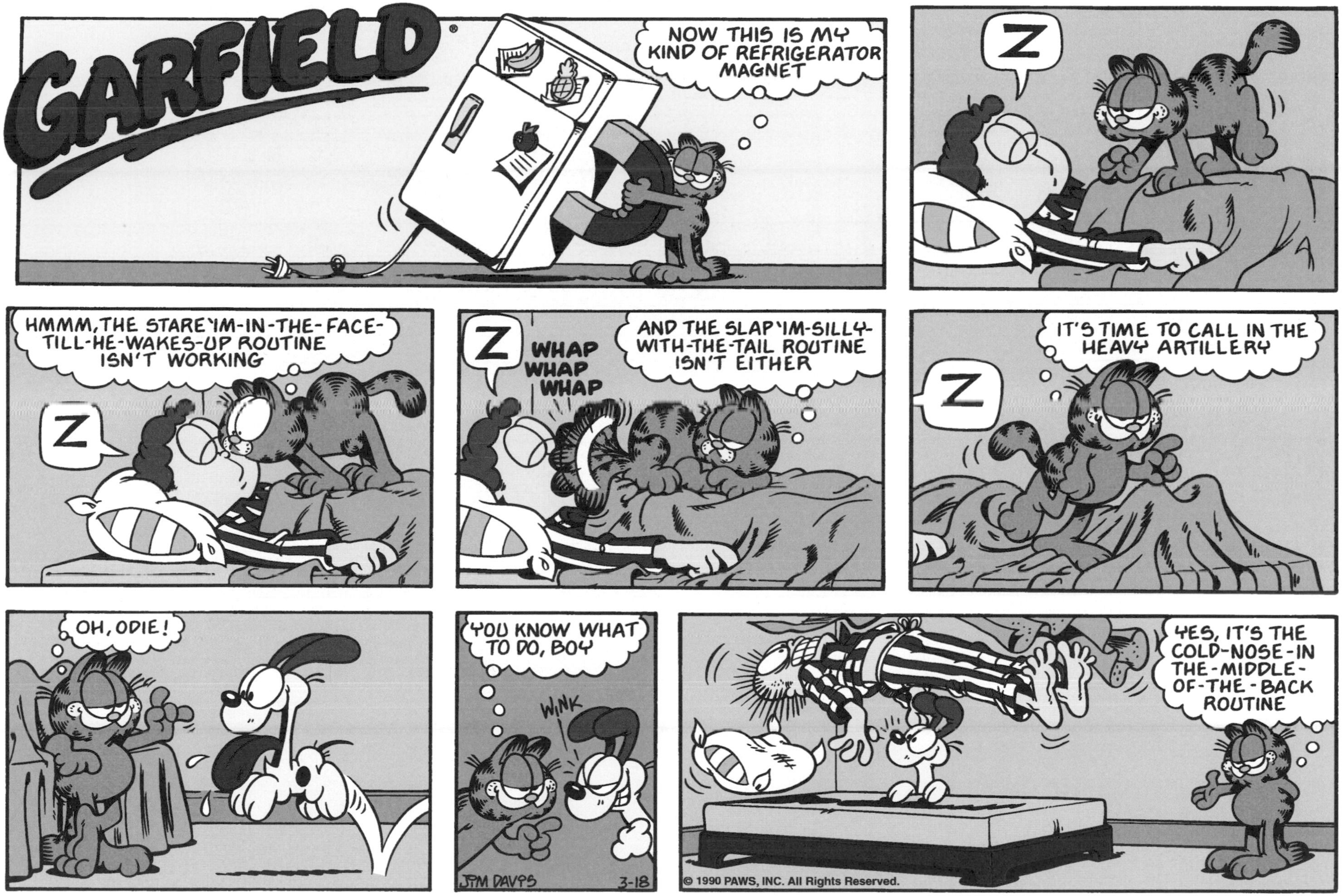
GARFIELD
NOW THIS IS MY KIND OF REFRIGERATOR MAGNET
Z
HMMM, THE STARE 'IM-IN-THE-FACE-TILL-HE-WAKES-UP ROUTINE ISN'T WORKING
Z
Z
WHAP WHAP WHAP
AND THE SLAP 'IM-SILLY-WITH-THE-TAIL ROUTINE ISN'T EITHER
Z
IT'S TIME TO CALL IN THE HEAVY ARTILLERY
OH, ODIE!
YOU KNOW WHAT TO DO, BOY
WINK
JIM DAVIS 3-18
YES, IT'S THE COLD-NOSE-IN-THE-MIDDLE-OF-THE-BACK ROUTINE

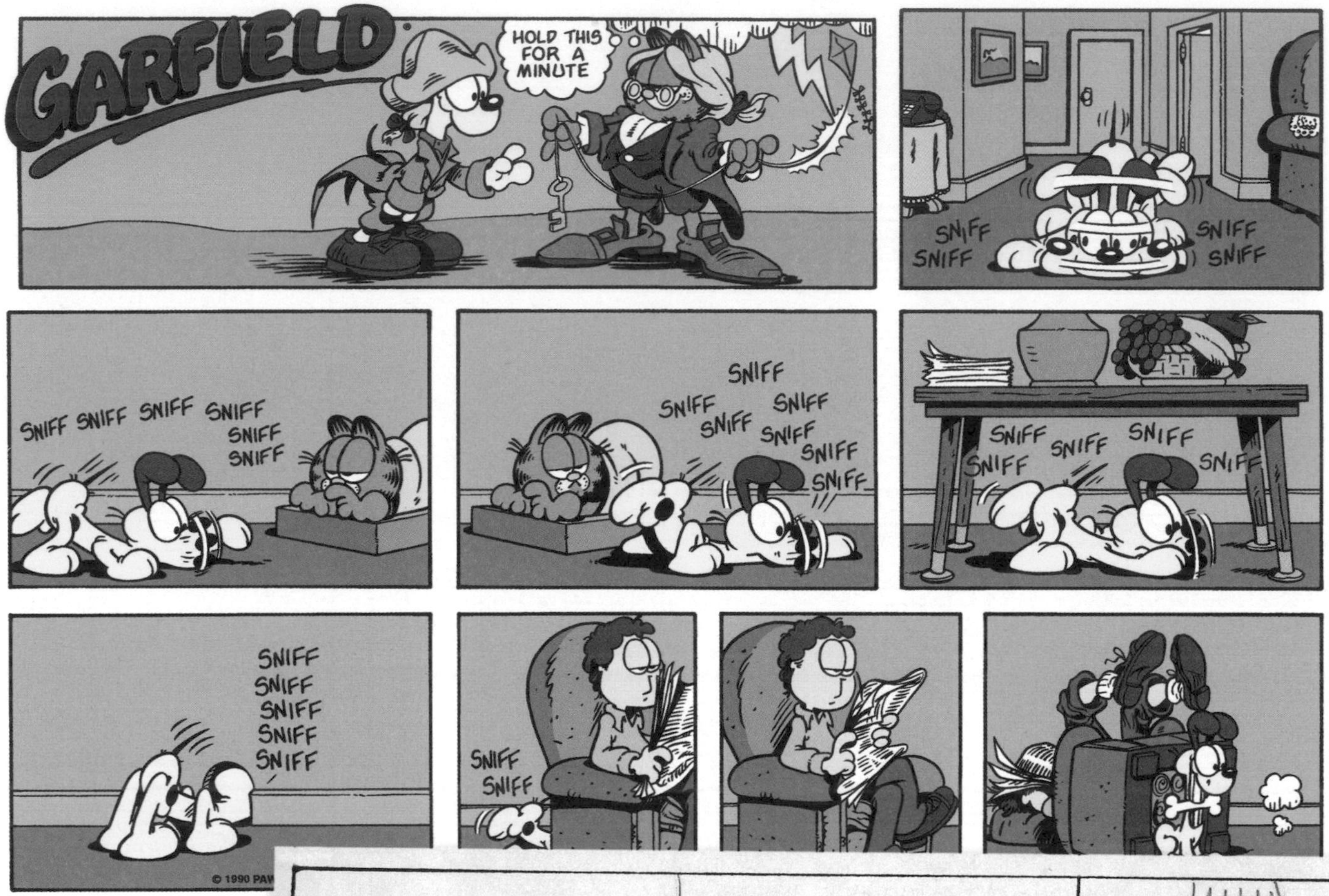
GARFIELD
HOLD THIS FOR A MINUTE
SNIFF SNIFF
SNIFF SNIFF
SNIFF SNIFF SNIFF SNIFF SNIFF SNIFF
SNIFF SNIFF SNIFF SNIFF SNIFF SNIFF SNIFF
SNIFF SNIFF SNIFF SNIFF SNIFF
SNIFF SNIFF SNIFF SNIFF SNIFF
SNIFF SNIFF
© 1990 PAW

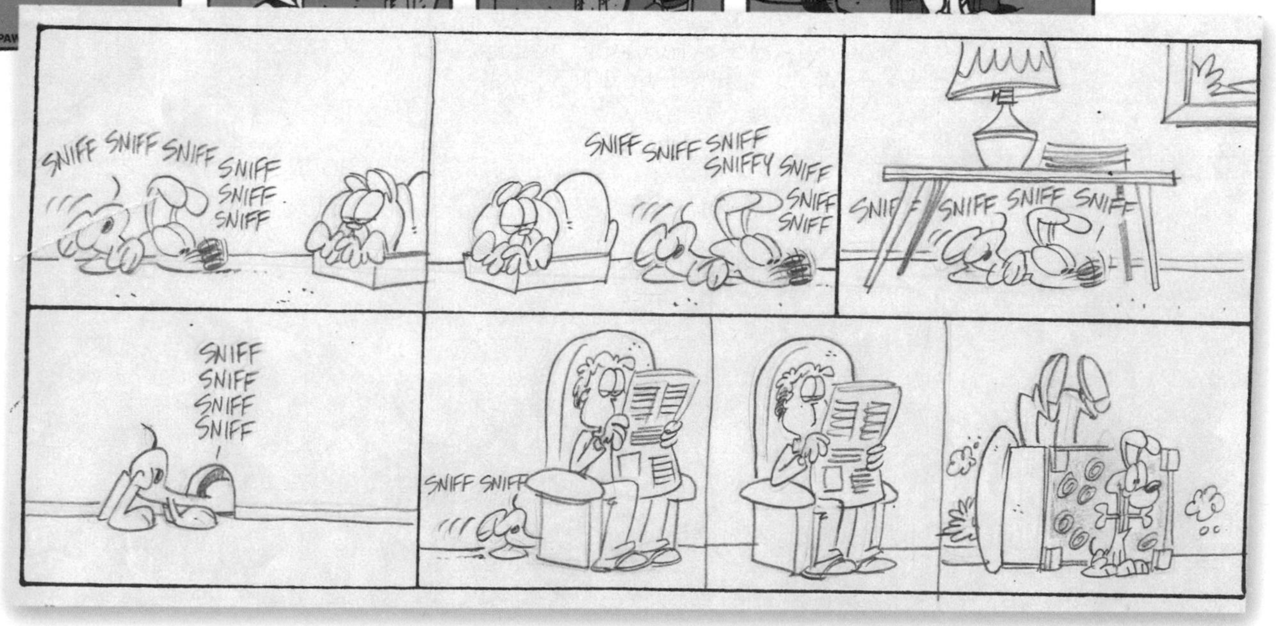
SNIFF SNIFF SNIFF SNIFF SNIFF SNIFF
SNIFF SNIFF SNIFF SNIFFY SNIFF SNIFF SNIFF
SNIFF SNIFF SNIFF SNIFF
SNIFF SNIFF SNIFF SNIFF
SNIFF SNIFF

original rough

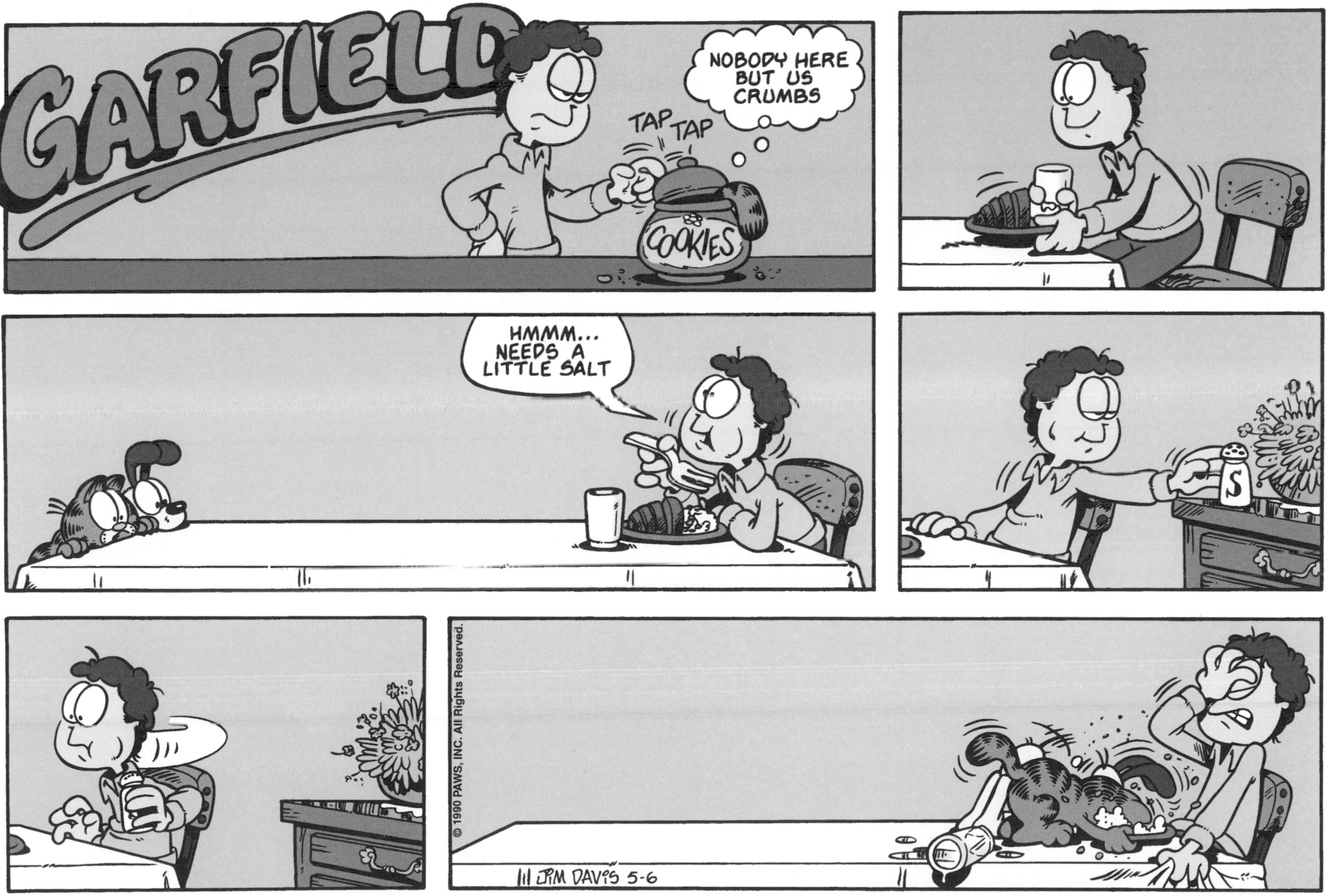
GARFIELD
TAP TAP
NOBODY HERE BUT US CRUMBS
COOKIES
HMMM... NEEDS A LITTLE SALT
S
© 1990 PAWS, INC. All Rights Reserved.
JIM DAVIS 5-6

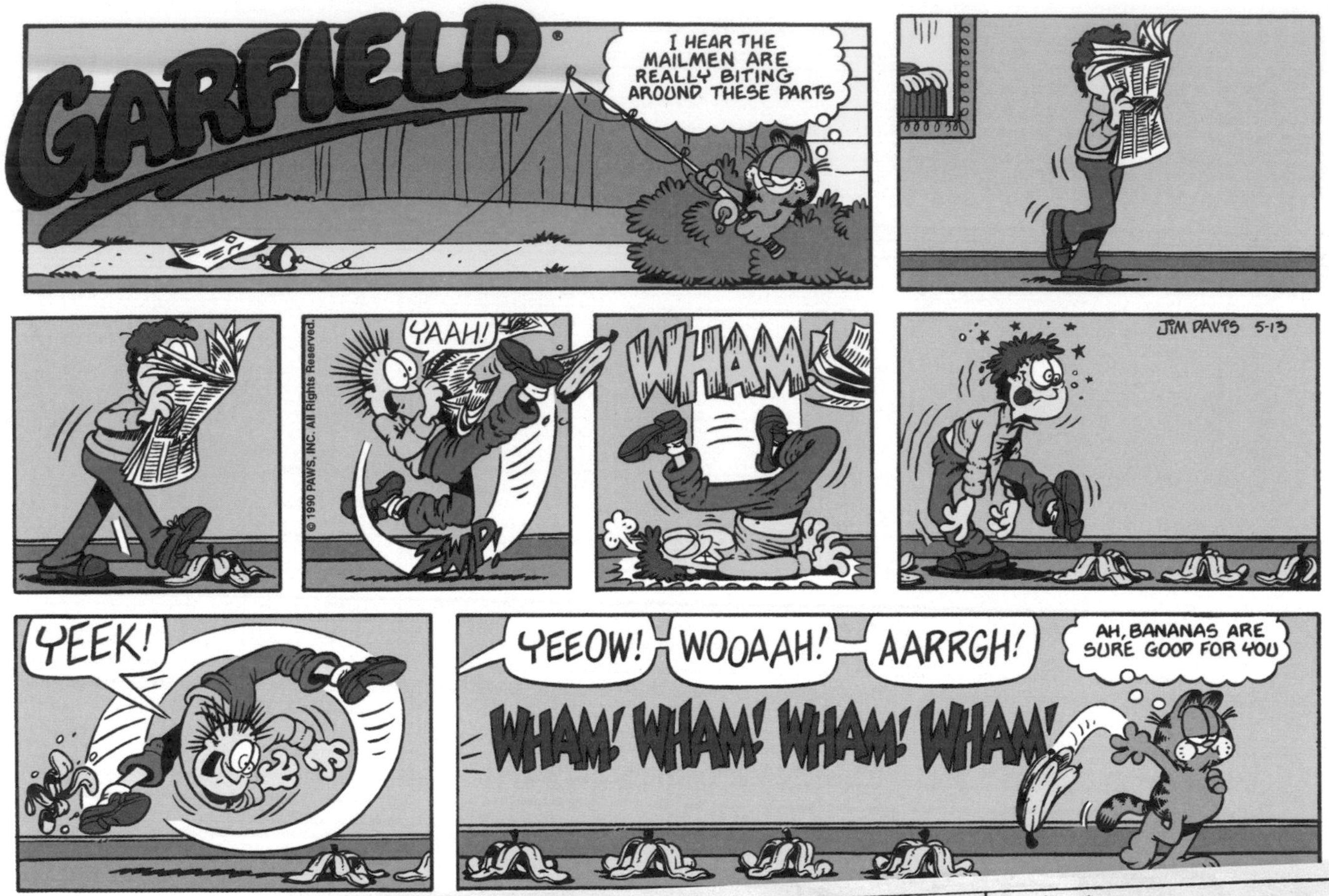
GARFIELD
I HEAR THE MAILMEN ARE REALLY BITING AROUND THESE PARTS
YAAH!
© 1990 PAWS, INC. All Rights Reserved.
ZWIP!
WHAM!
JIM DAVIS 5-13
YEEK!
YEEOW!
WOOAAH!
AARRGH!
AH, BANANAS ARE SURE GOOD FOR YOU
WHAM! WHAM! WHAM! WHAM!

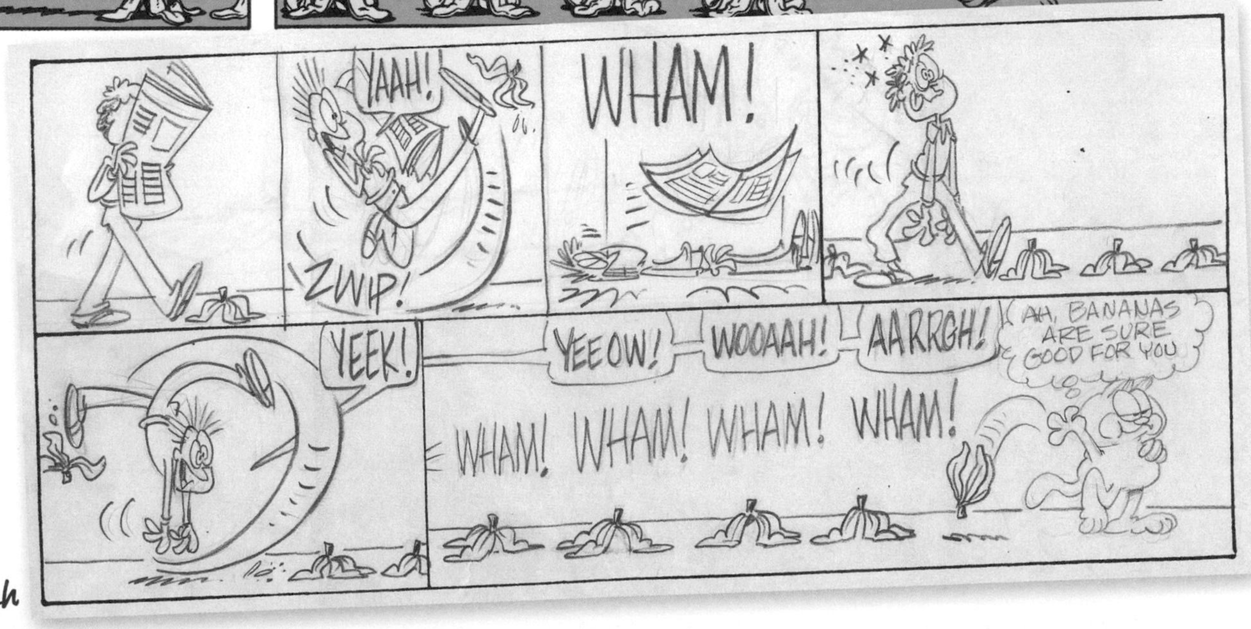
YAAH!
ZWIP!
WHAM!
YEEK!
YEEOW!
WOOAAH!
AARRGH!
AH, BANANAS ARE SURE GOOD FOR YOU
WHAM! WHAM! WHAM! WHAM!

original rough

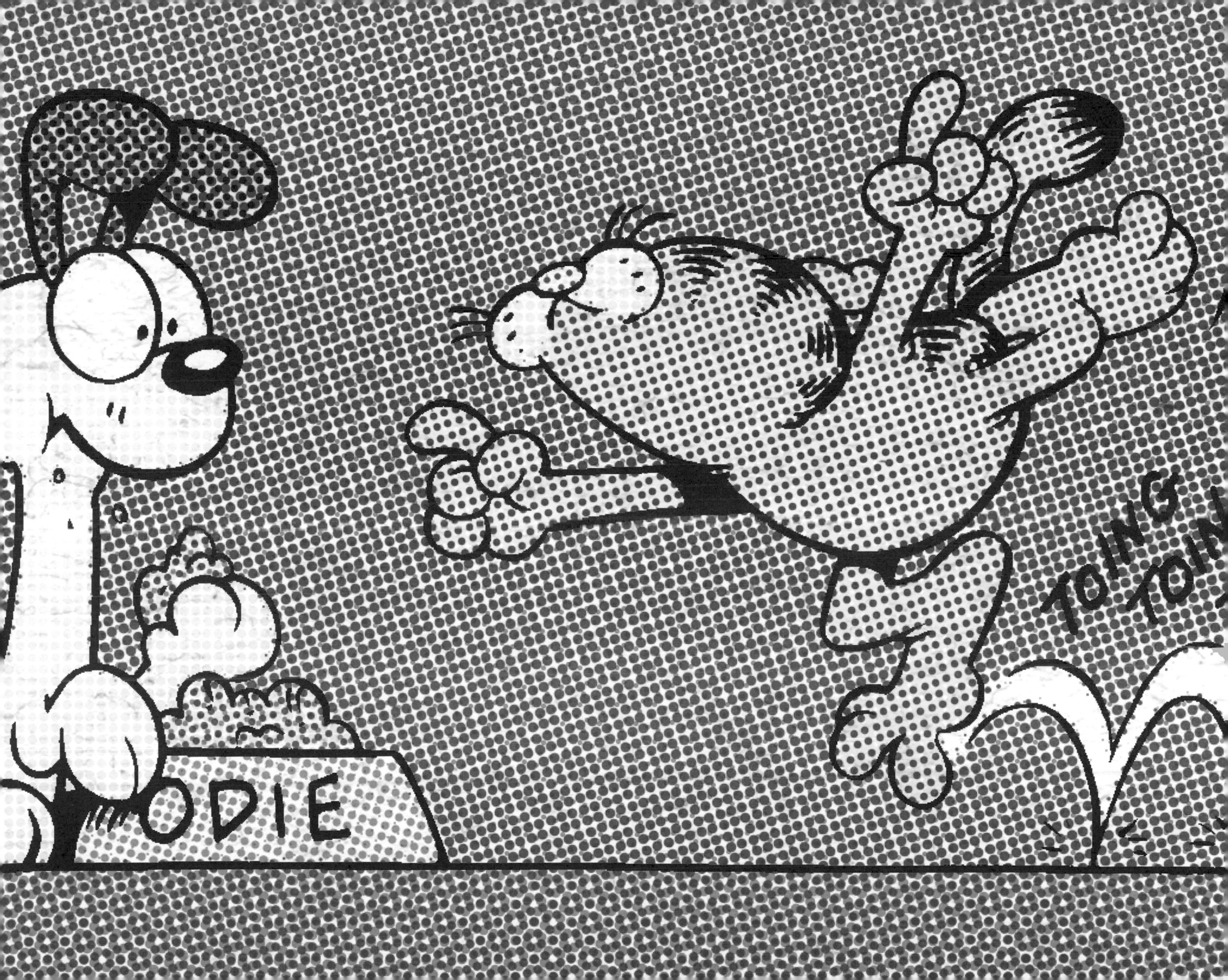
ODIE
TOING

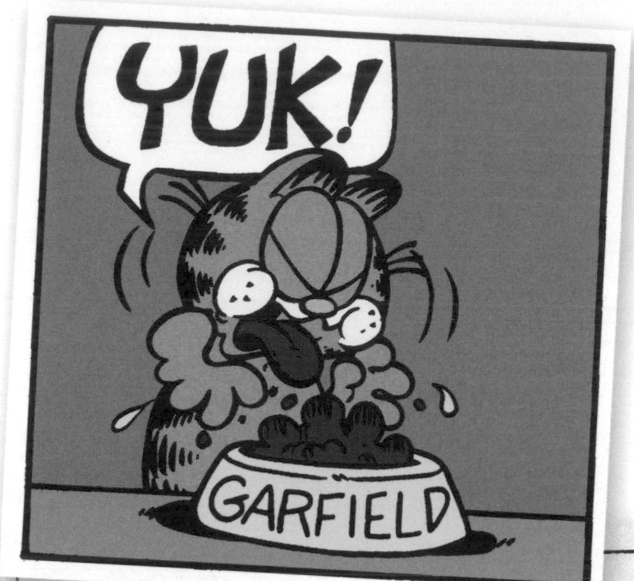
YUK!
GARFIELD

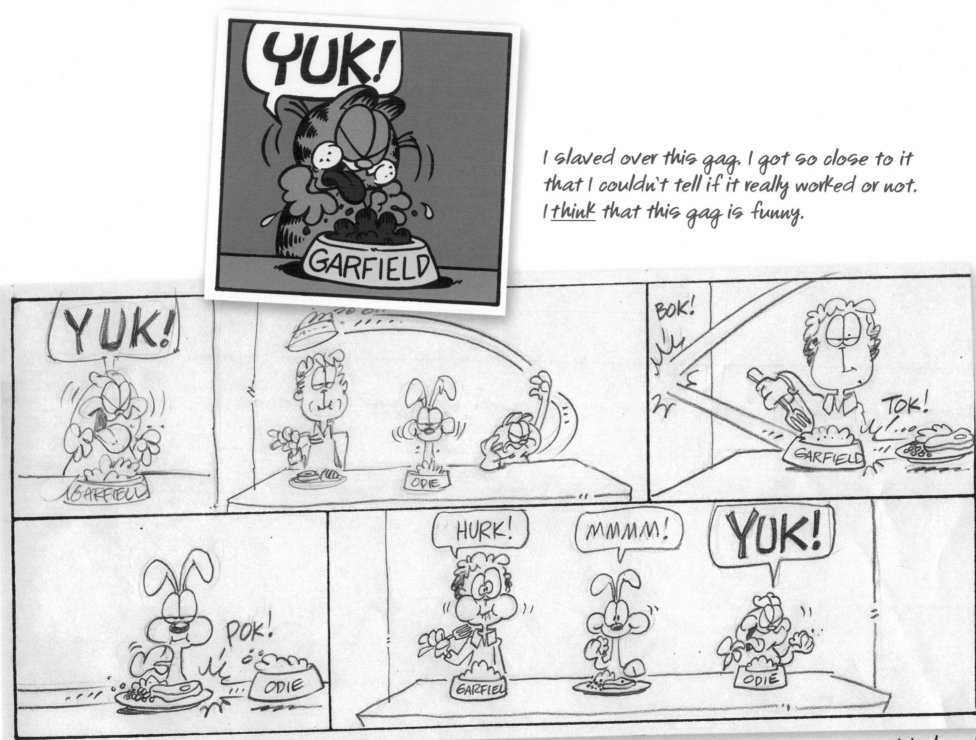

I slaved over this gag. I got so close to it that I couldn't tell if it really worked or not. I think that this gag is funny.

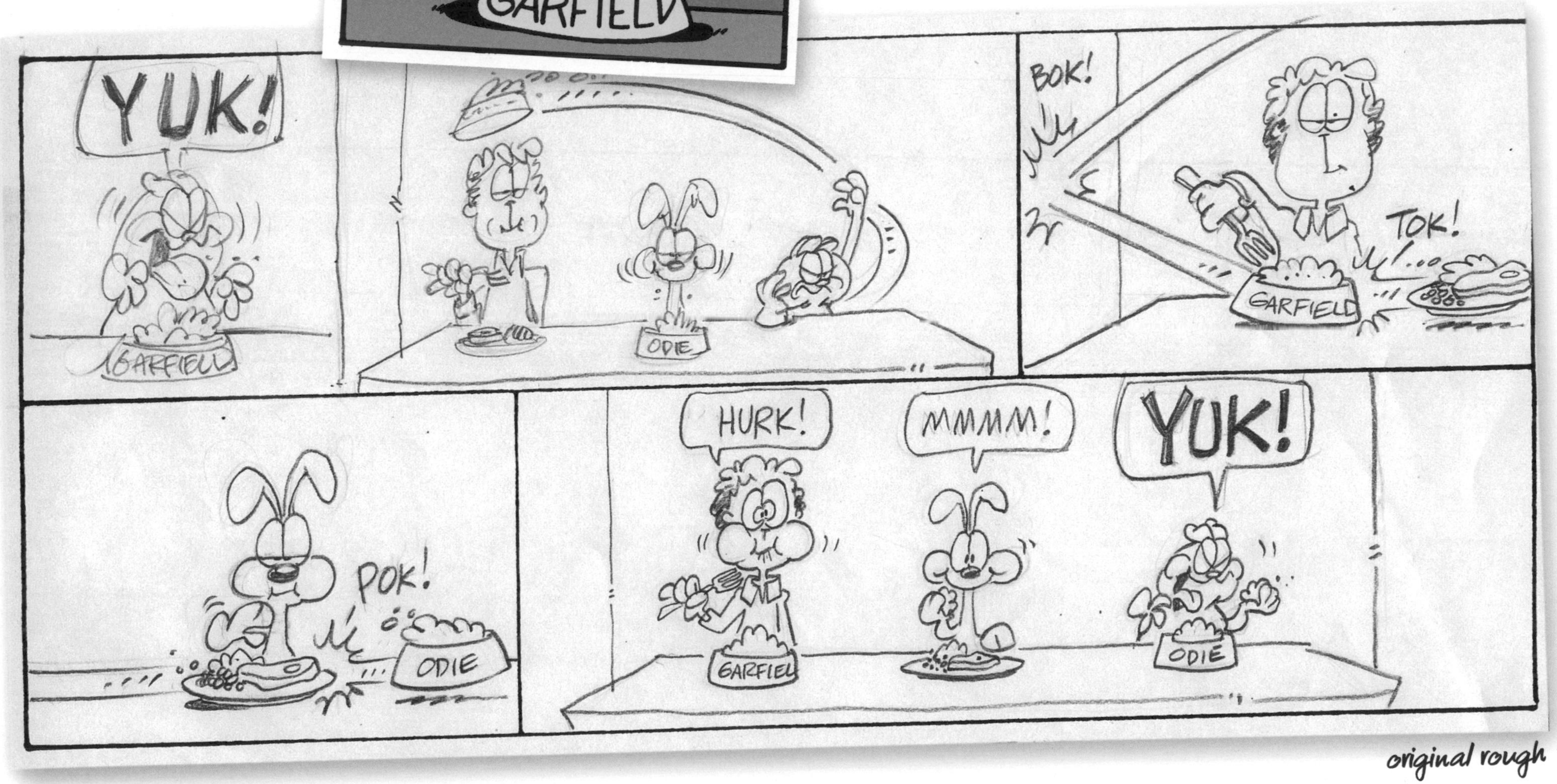
YUK!
GARFIELD
ODIE
BOK!
TOK!
GARFIELD
POK!
ODIE
HURK!
MMMM!
YUK!
GARFIELD
ODIE

original rough

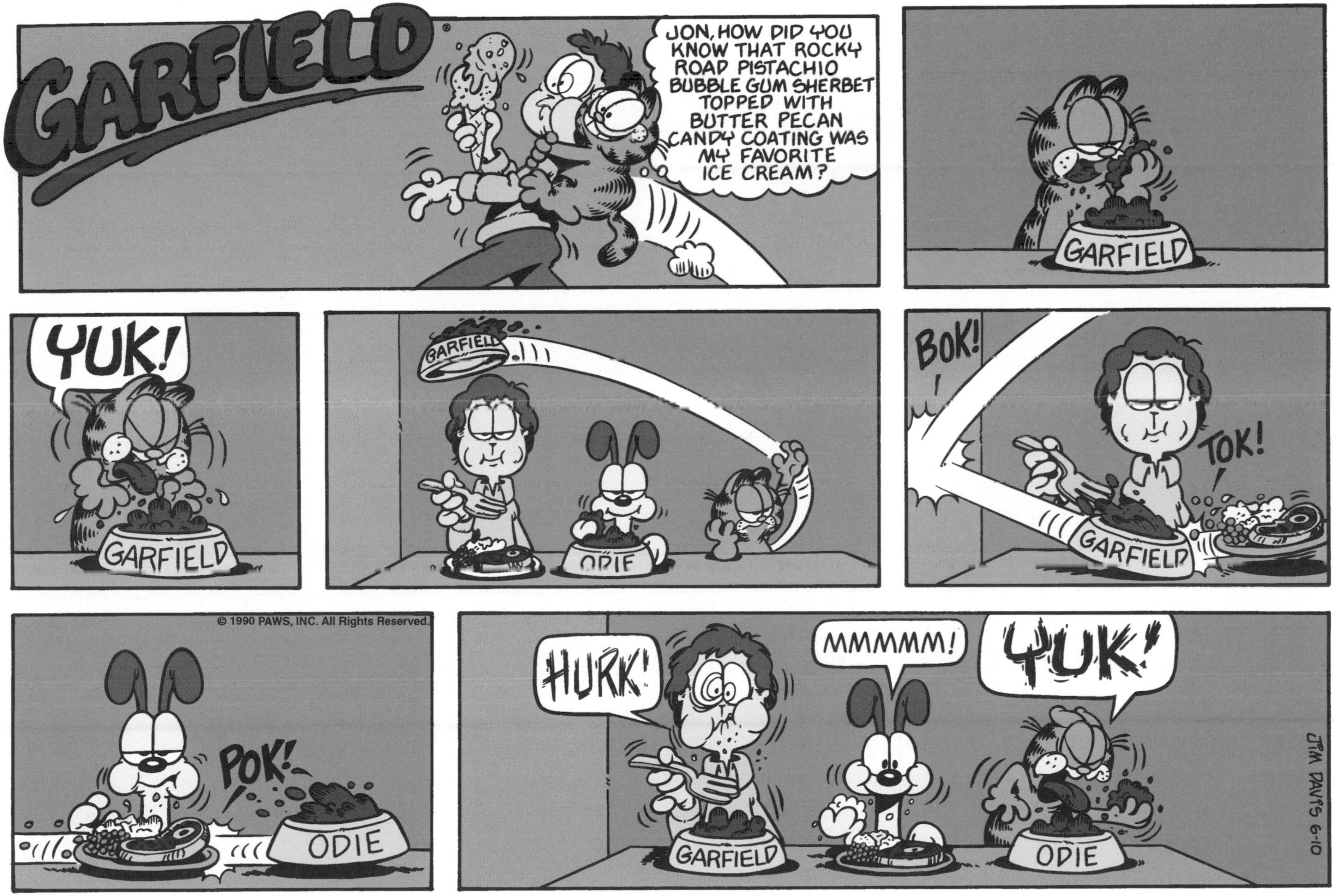
GARFIELD
JON, HOW DID YOU KNOW THAT ROCKY ROAD PISTACHIO BUBBLE GUM SHERBET TOPPED WITH BUTTER PECAN CANDY COATING WAS MY FAVORITE ICE CREAM?
GARFIELD
YUK!
GARFIELD
GARFIELD
ODIE
BOK!
TOK!
GARFIELD
© 1990 PAWS, INC. All Rights Reserved.
POK!
ODIE
HURK!
MMMMM!
YUK!
GARFIELD
ODIE
JIM DAVIS 6-10

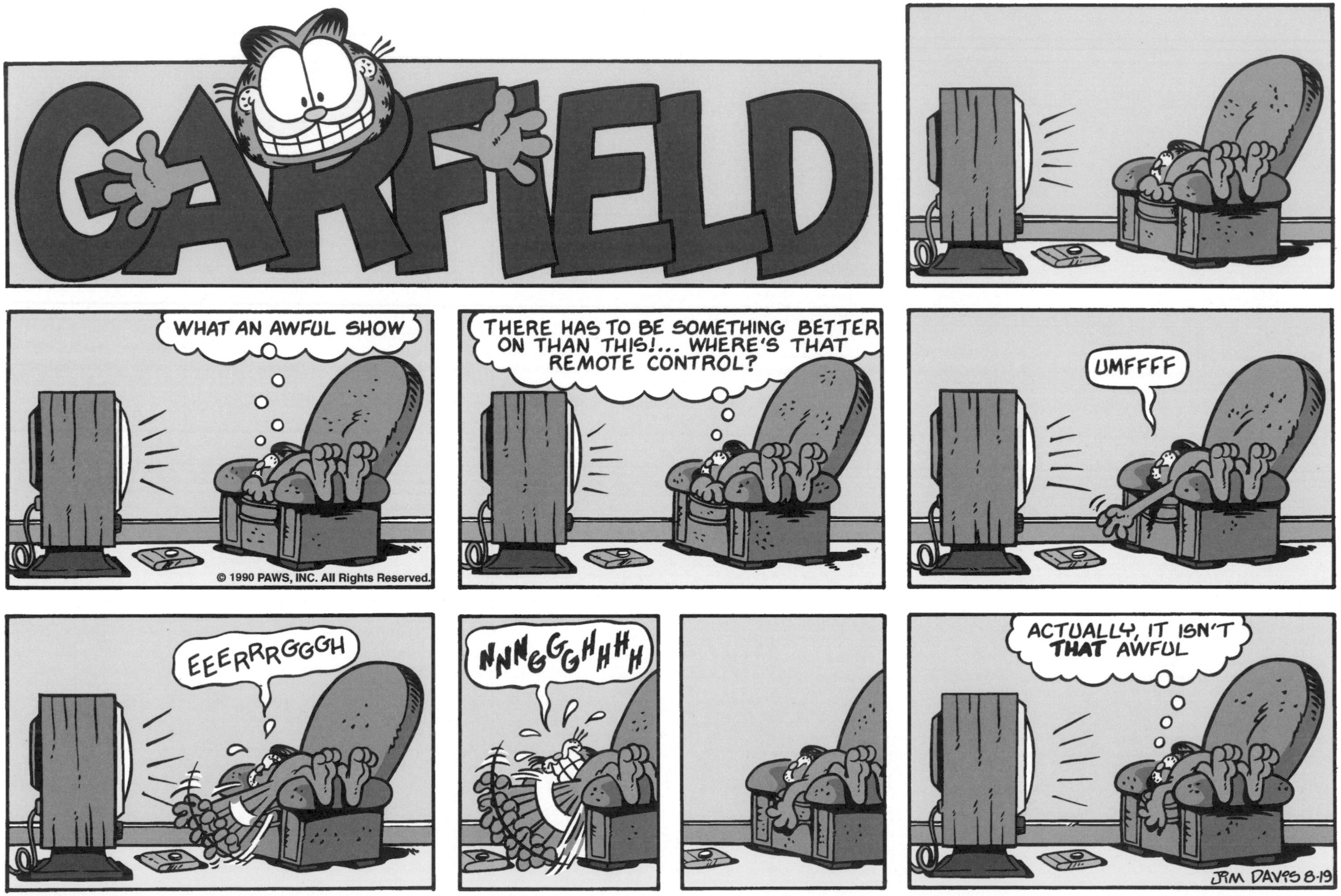
GARFIELD
WHAT AN AWFUL SHOW
© 1990 PAWS, INC. All Rights Reserved.
THERE HAS TO BE SOMETHING BETTER ON THAN THIS!... WHERE'S THAT REMOTE CONTROL?
UMFFFF
EEERRRRGGGH
NNNGGGHHHH
ACTUALLY, IT ISN'T **THAT** AWFUL
JIM DAVIS 8-19

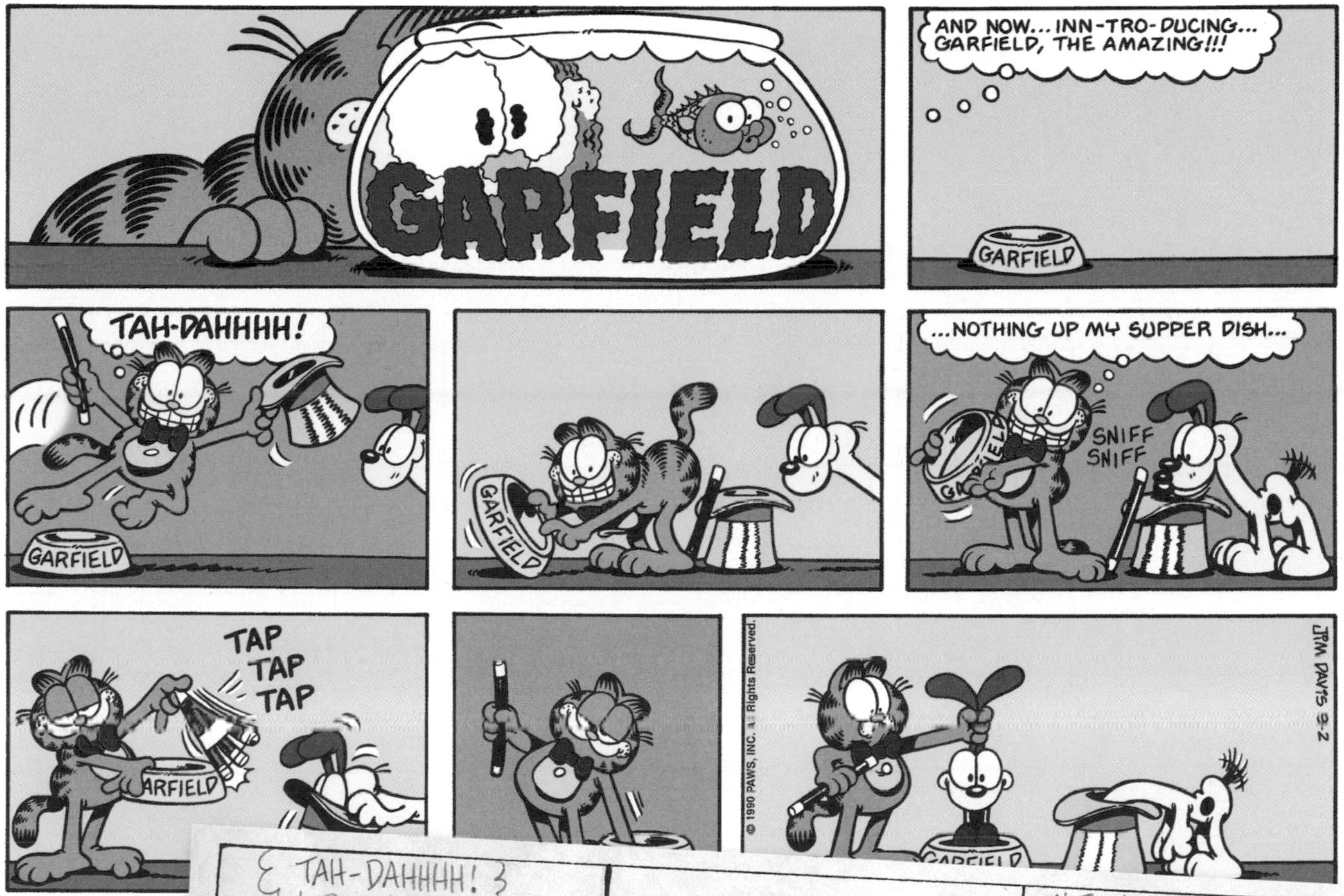
GARFIELD
AND NOW... INN-TRO-DUCING... GARFIELD, THE AMAZING!!!
GARFIELD
TAH-DAHHHH!
GARFIELD
GARFIELD
...NOTHING UP MY SUPPER DISH...
SNIFF SNIFF
GARFIELD
TAP TAP TAP
ARFIELD
© 1990 PAWS, INC. All Rights Reserved.

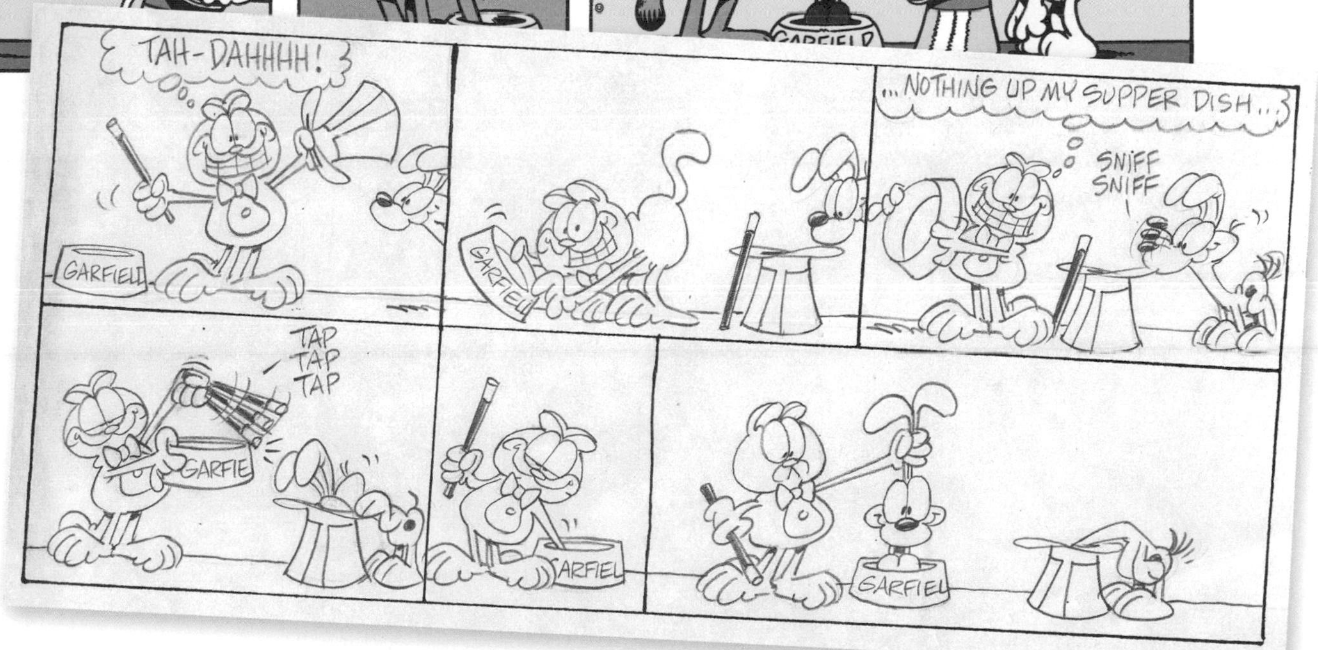
TAH-DAHHHH!
GARFIELD
GARFIEL
...NOTHING UP MY SUPPER DISH...
SNIFF SNIFF
TAP TAP TAP
GARFIE
GARFIEL
GARFIEL

original rough

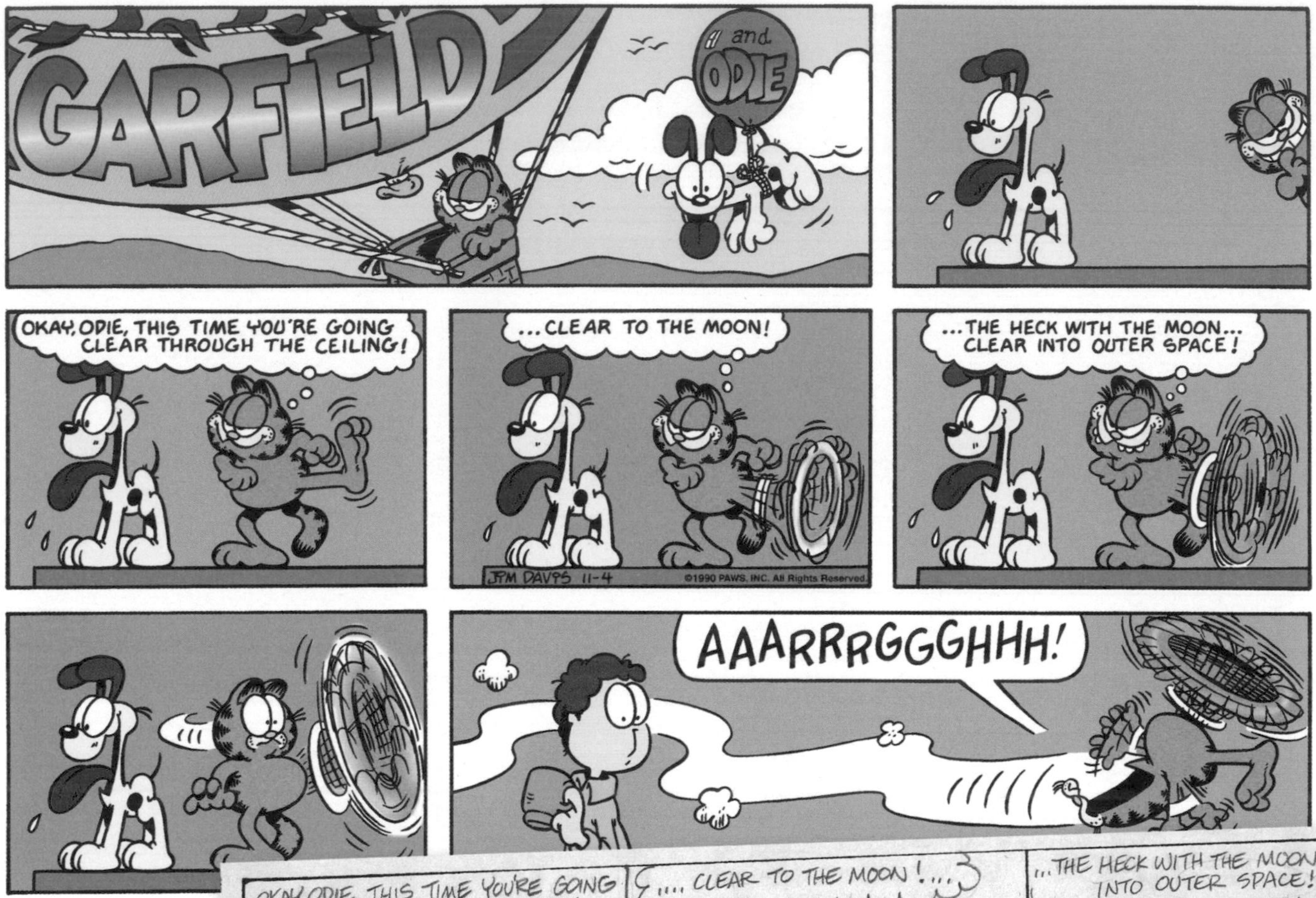
GARFIELD
and
ODIE
OKAY, ODIE, THIS TIME YOU'RE GOING CLEAR THROUGH THE CEILING!
...CLEAR TO THE MOON!
JIM DAVIS 11-4
©1990 PAWS, INC. All Rights Reserved.
...THE HECK WITH THE MOON... CLEAR INTO OUTER SPACE!
AAARRRGGGHHH!

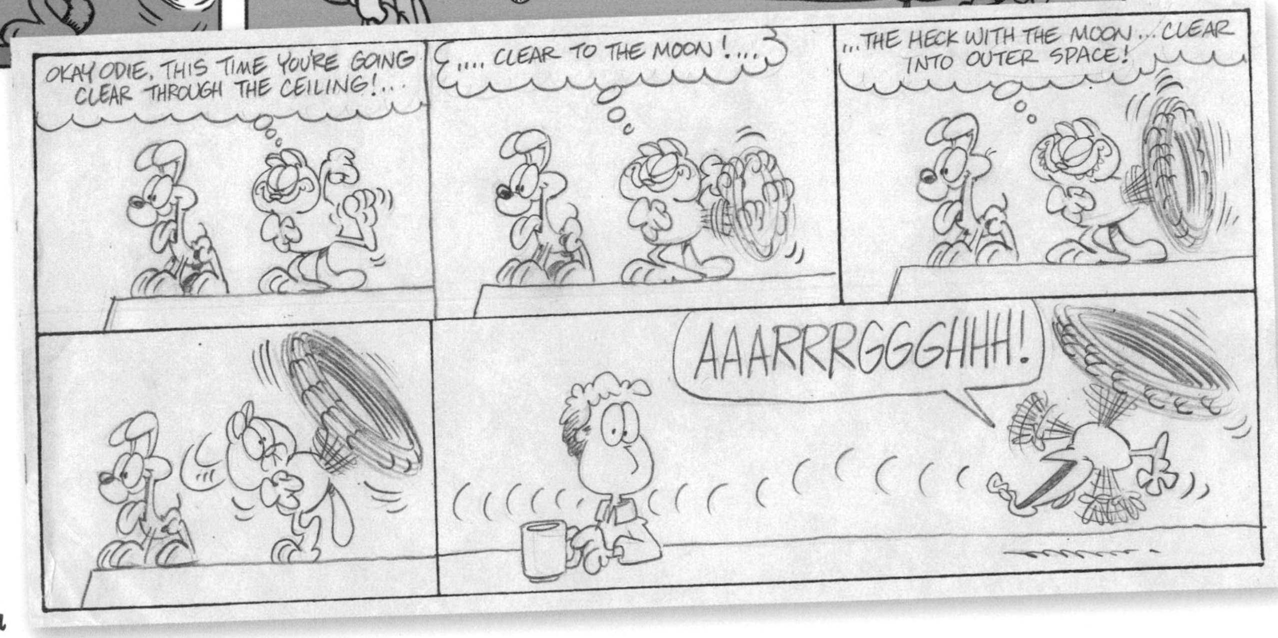
OKAY ODIE, THIS TIME YOU'RE GOING CLEAR THROUGH THE CEILING!...
.... CLEAR TO THE MOON!....
...THE HECK WITH THE MOON... CLEAR INTO OUTER SPACE!
AAARRRGGGHHH!

original rough

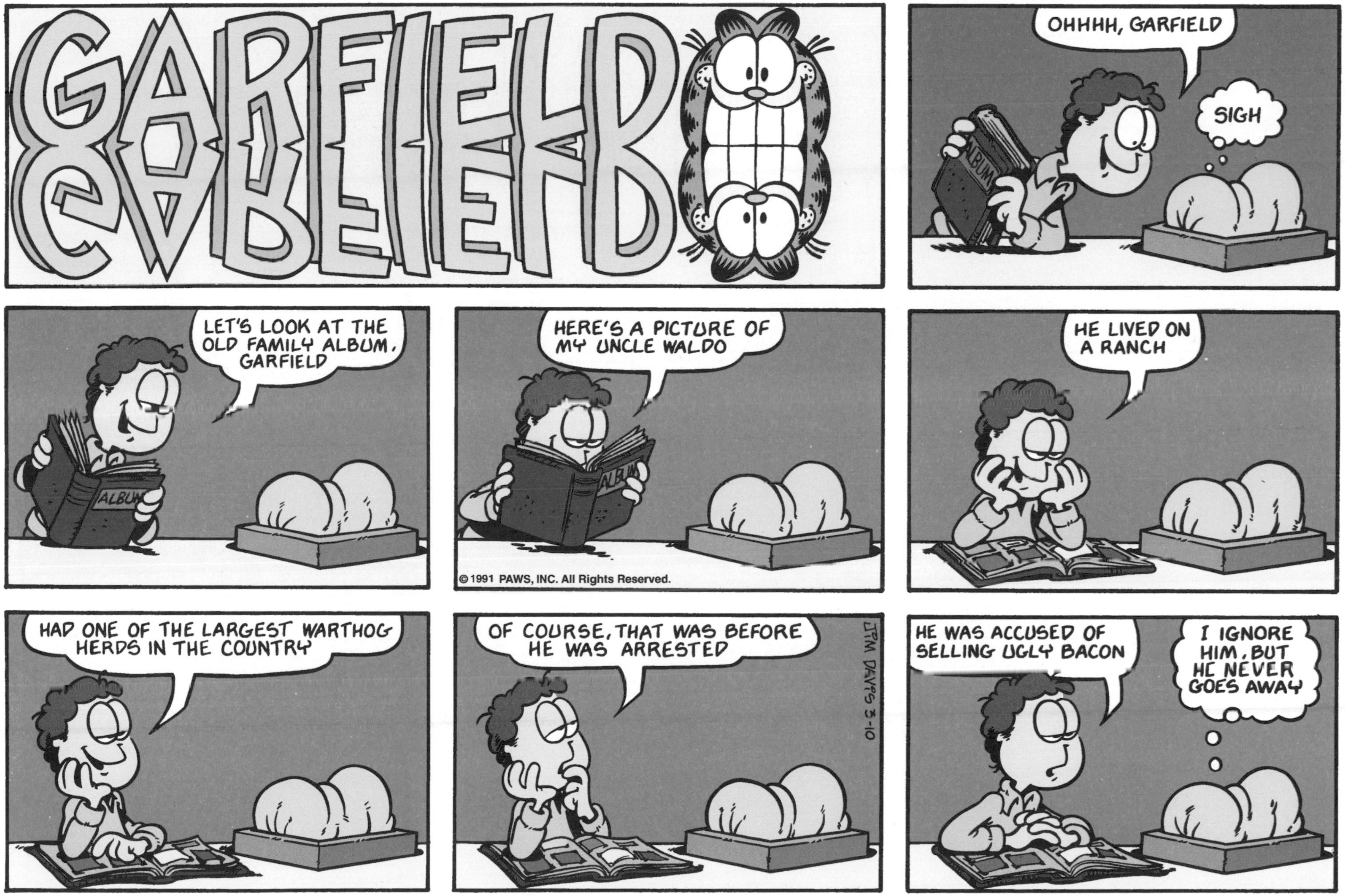
GARFIELD
OHHHH, GARFIELD
SIGH
LET'S LOOK AT THE OLD FAMILY ALBUM, GARFIELD
ALBUM
HERE'S A PICTURE OF MY UNCLE WALDO
ALBUM
© 1991 PAWS, INC. All Rights Reserved.
HE LIVED ON A RANCH
HAD ONE OF THE LARGEST WARTHOG HERDS IN THE COUNTRY
OF COURSE, THAT WAS BEFORE HE WAS ARRESTED
JIM DAVIS 3-10
HE WAS ACCUSED OF SELLING UGLY BACON
I IGNORE HIM, BUT HE NEVER GOES AWAY

I love sight gags, Mad magazine, and the Three Stooges . . . enough said.

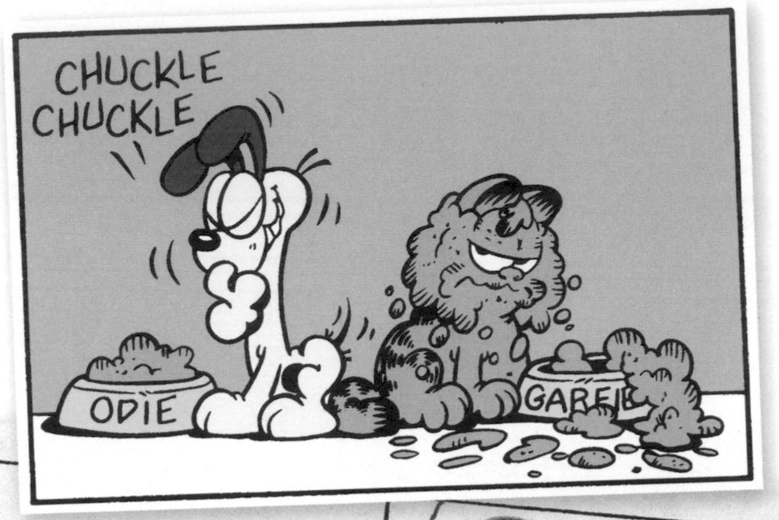
CHUCKLE
CHUCKLE
ODIE
GARFI

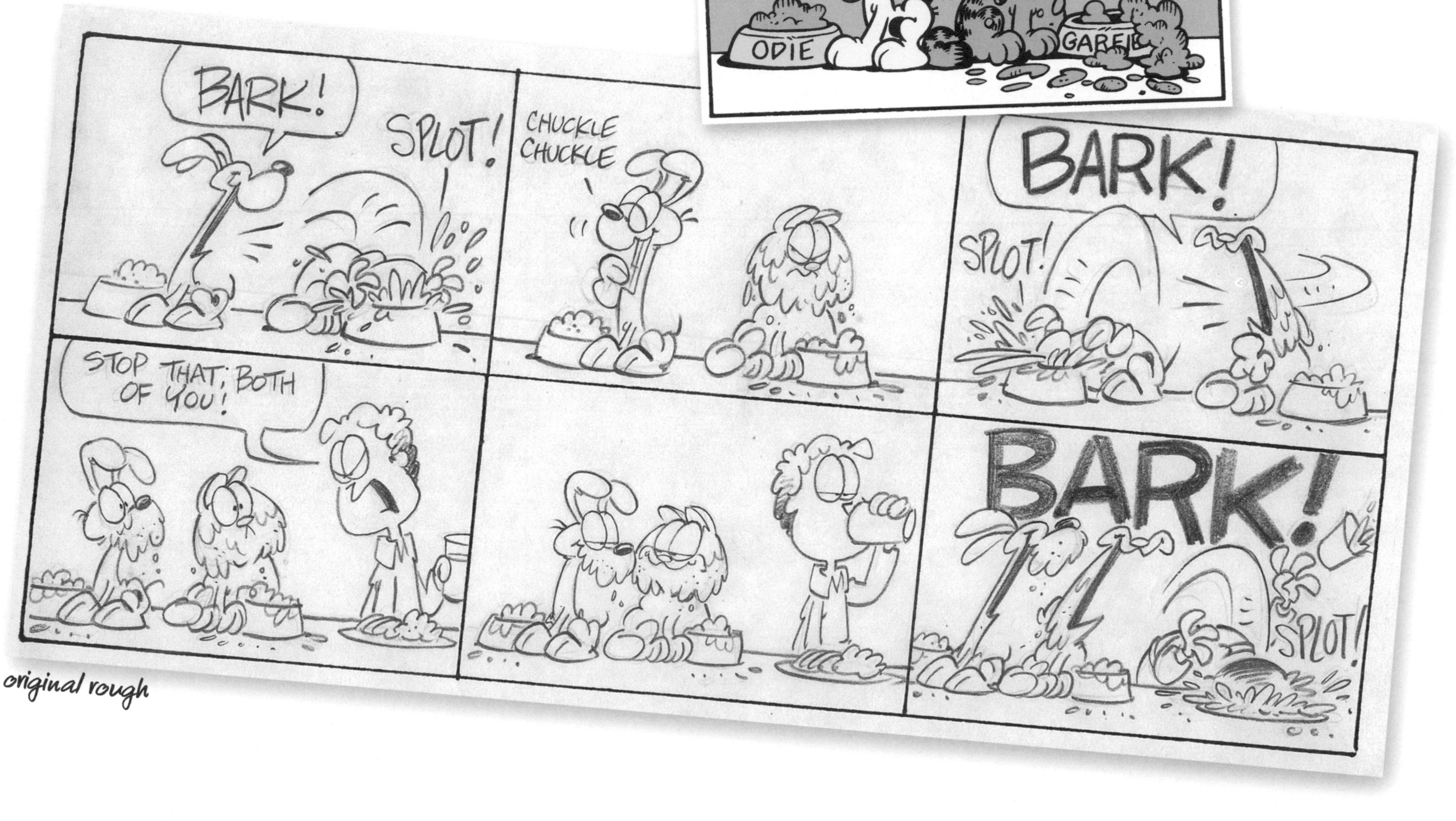
BARK!
SPLOT!
CHUCKLE
CHUCKLE
BARK!
SPLOT!
STOP THAT; BOTH OF YOU!
BARK!
SPLOT!

original rough

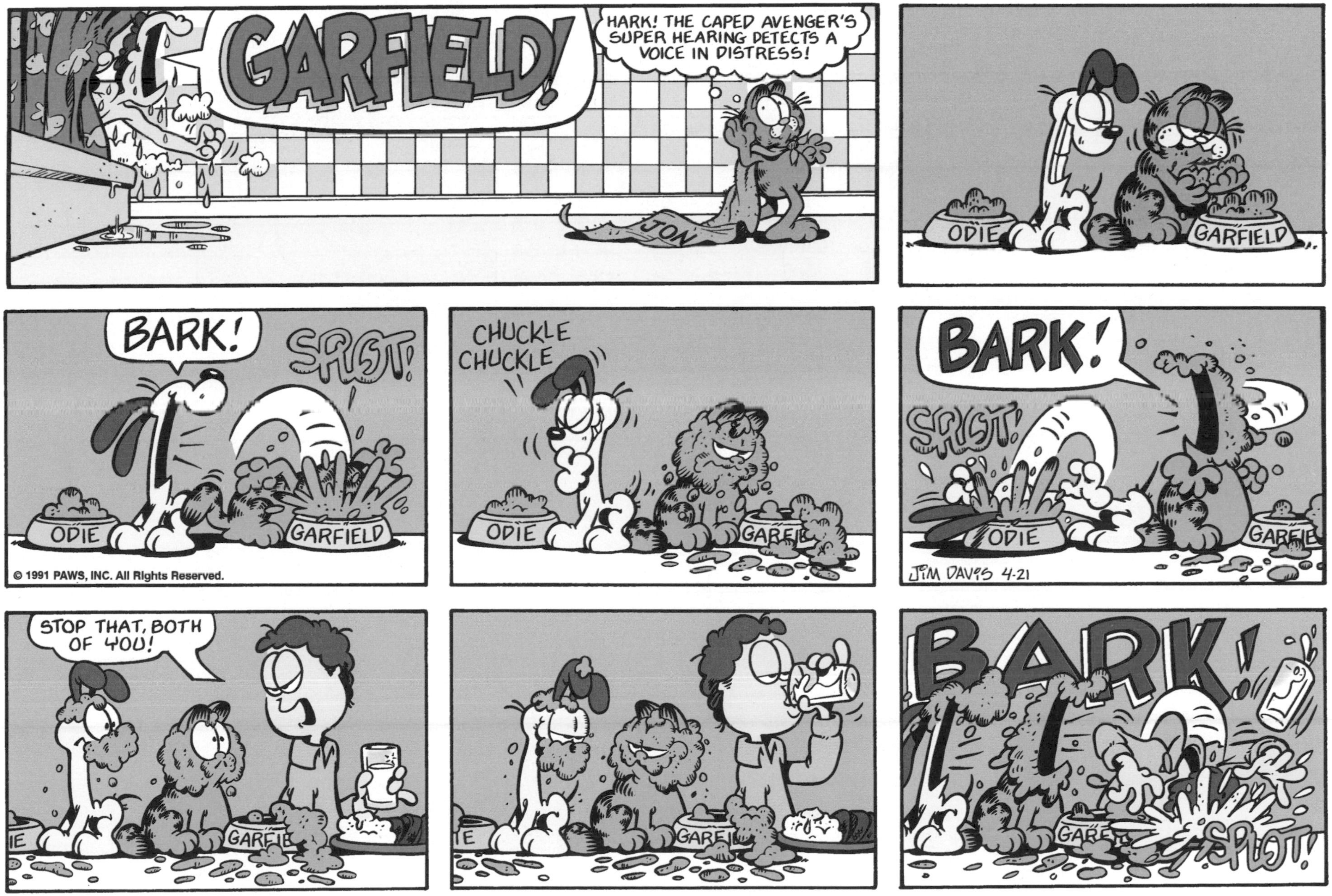
GARFIELD!
HARK! THE CAPED AVENGER'S SUPER HEARING DETECTS A VOICE IN DISTRESS!
JON
ODIE
GARFIELD
BARK!
SPLOT!
ODIE
GARFIELD
© 1991 PAWS, INC. All Rights Reserved.
CHUCKLE CHUCKLE
ODIE
BARK!
SPLOT!
ODIE
JIM DAVIS 4-21
STOP THAT, BOTH OF YOU!
BARK!
SPLOT!

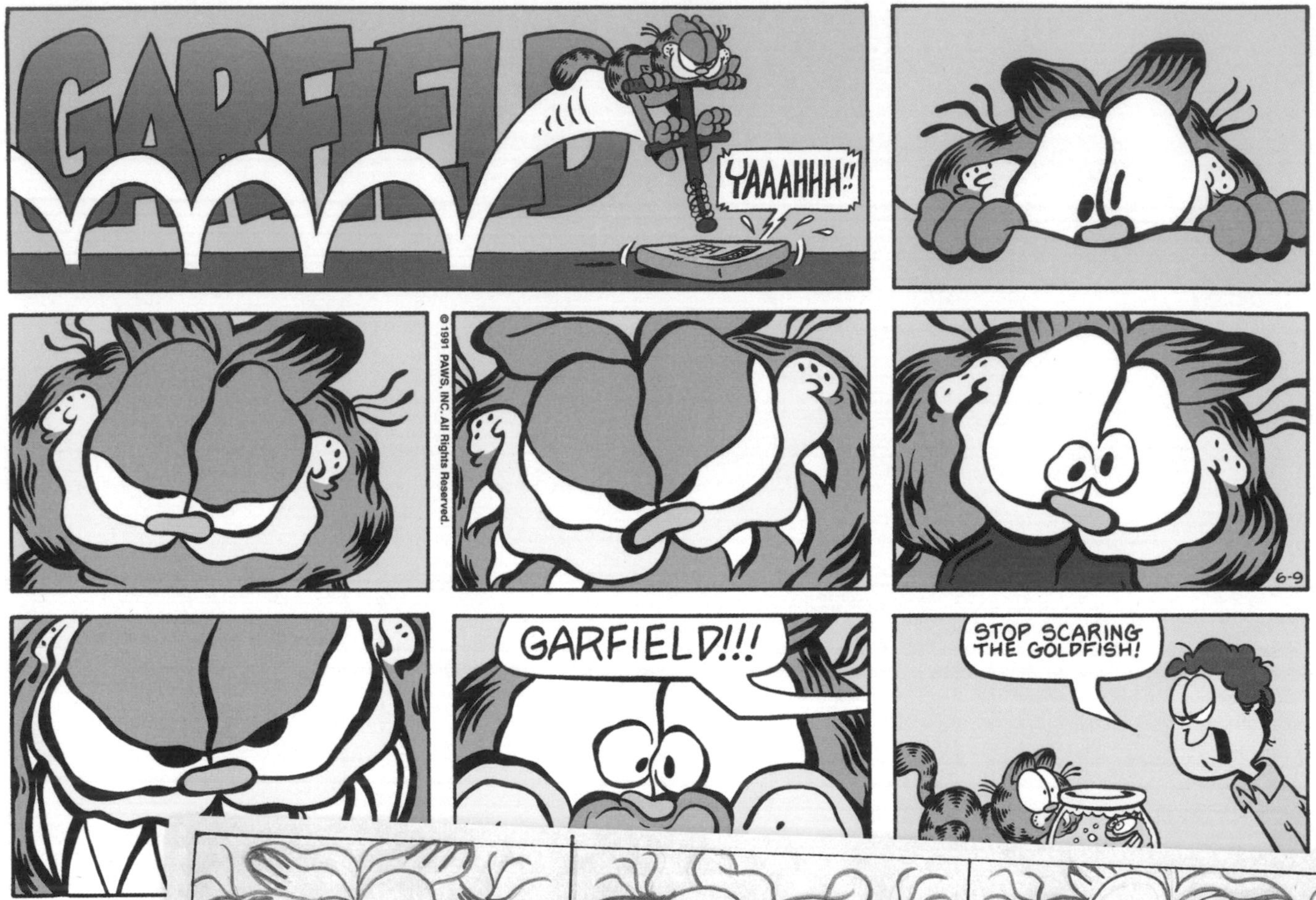
GARFIELD
YAAAHHH!!
© 1991 PAWS, INC. All Rights Reserved.
6-9
GARFIELD!!!
STOP SCARING THE GOLDFISH!

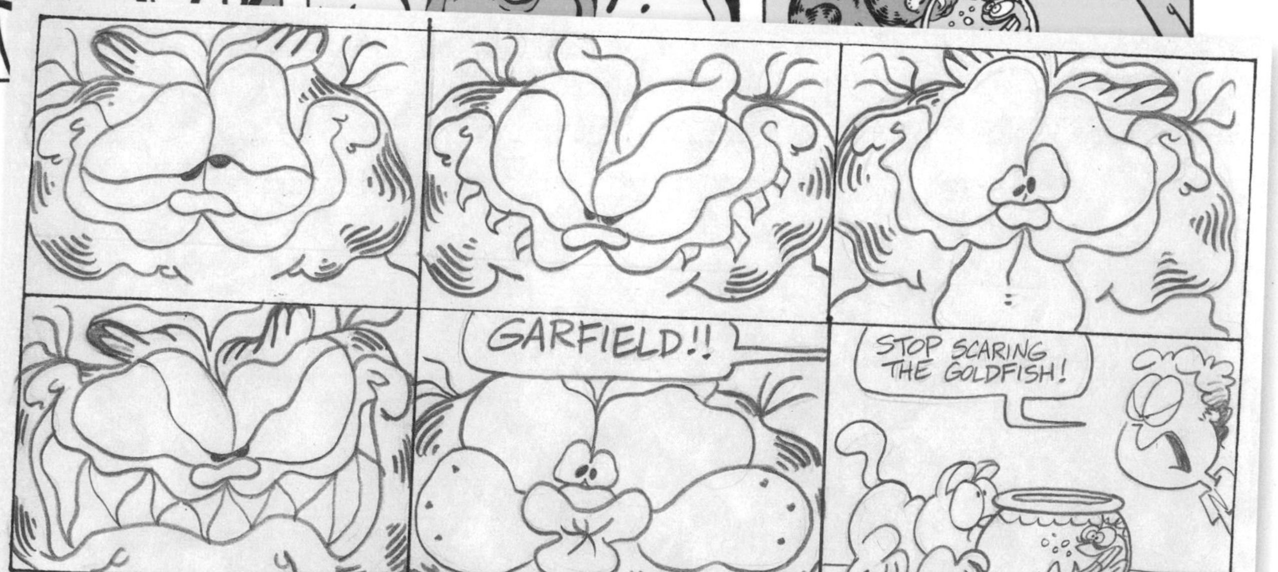
GARFIELD!!
STOP SCARING THE GOLDFISH!

original rough

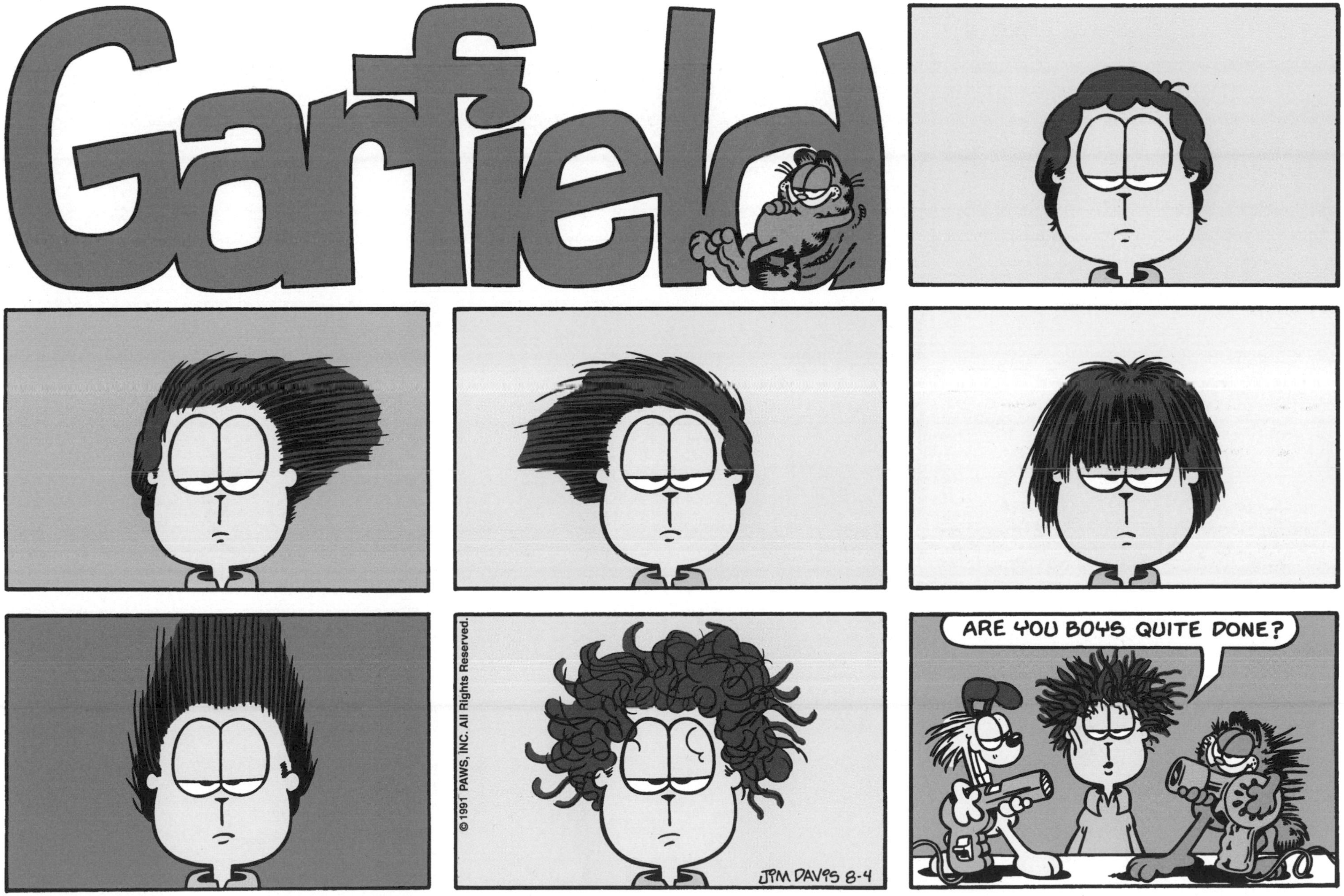
Garfield
© 1991 PAWS, INC. All Rights Reserved.
JIM DAVIS 8-4
ARE YOU BOYS QUITE DONE?

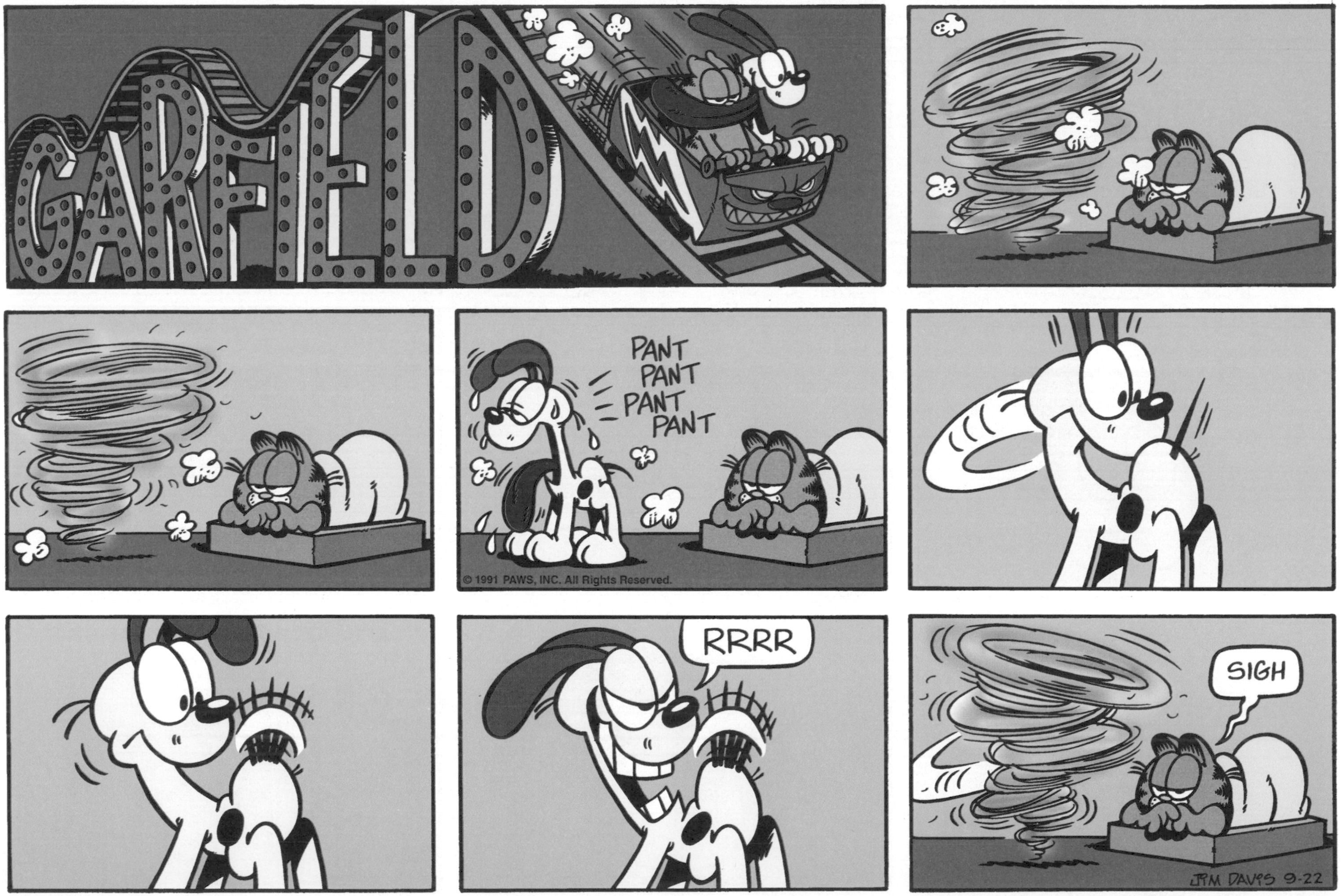
GARFIELD
PANT PANT PANT PANT
© 1991 PAWS, INC. All Rights Reserved.
RRRR
SIGH
JIM DAVIS 9-22

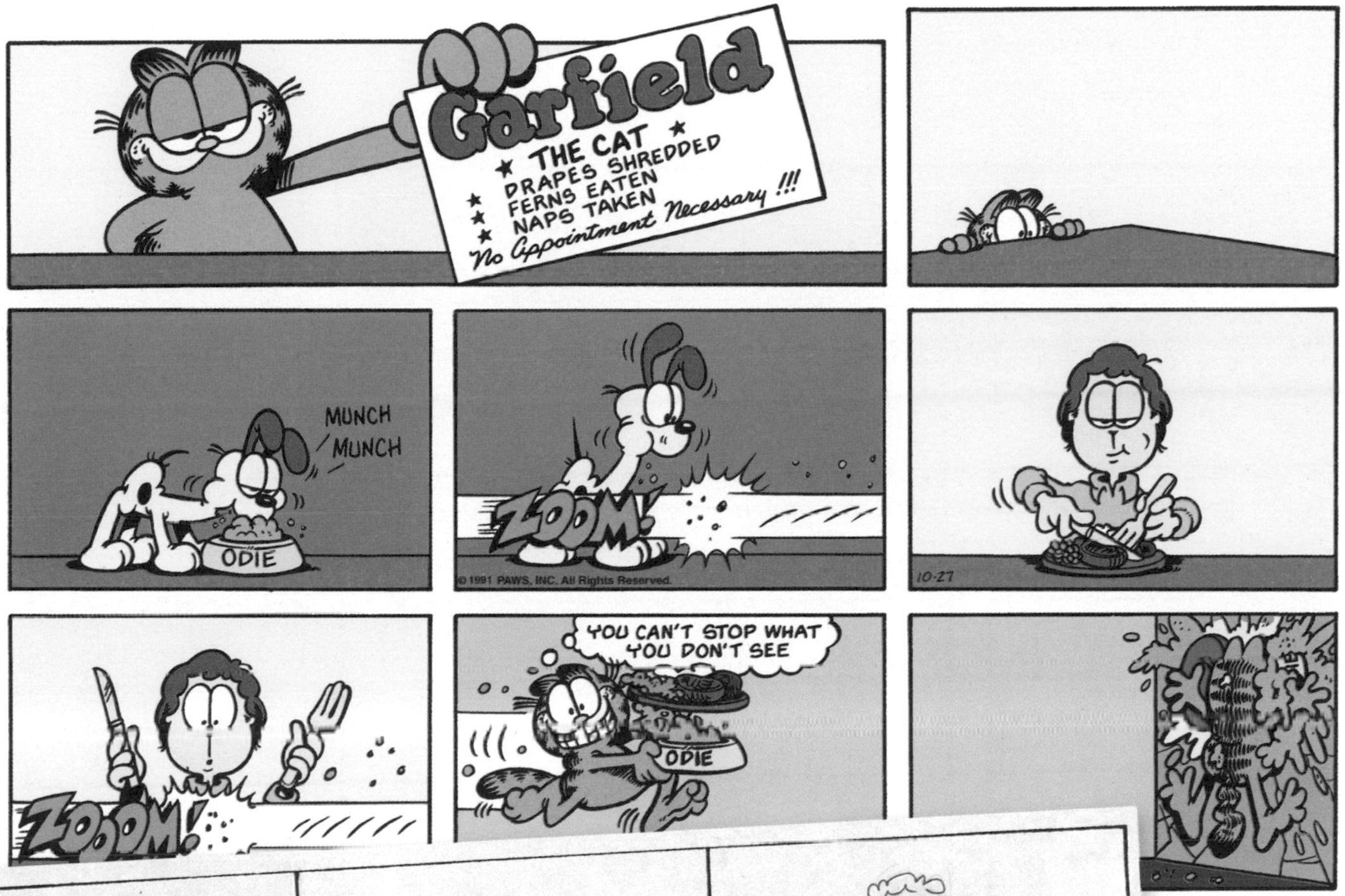
Garfield
THE CAT
DRAPES SHREDDED
FERNS EATEN
NAPS TAKEN
No Appointment Necessary !!!
MUNCH MUNCH
ODIE
ZOOM!
© 1991 PAWS, INC. All Rights Reserved.
10-27
ZOOOM!
YOU CAN'T STOP WHAT YOU DON'T SEE
ODIE

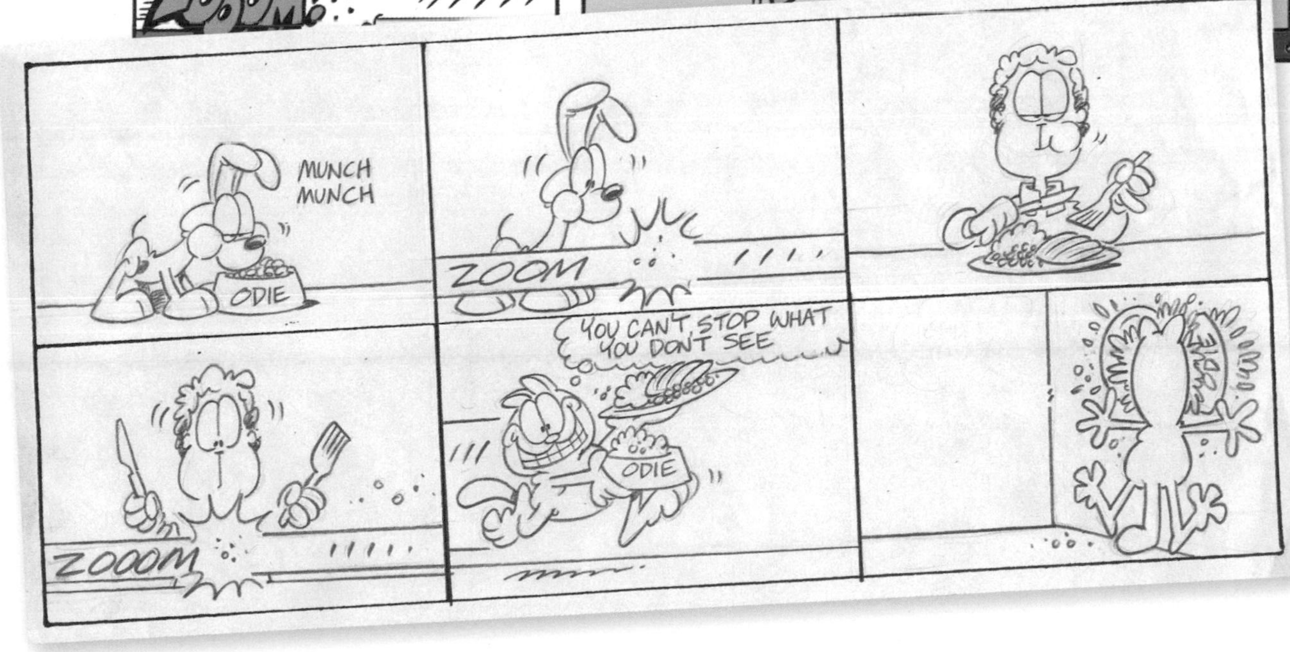
MUNCH MUNCH
ODIE
ZOOM
ZOOOM
YOU CAN'T STOP WHAT YOU DON'T SEE
ODIE
ODIE

original rough

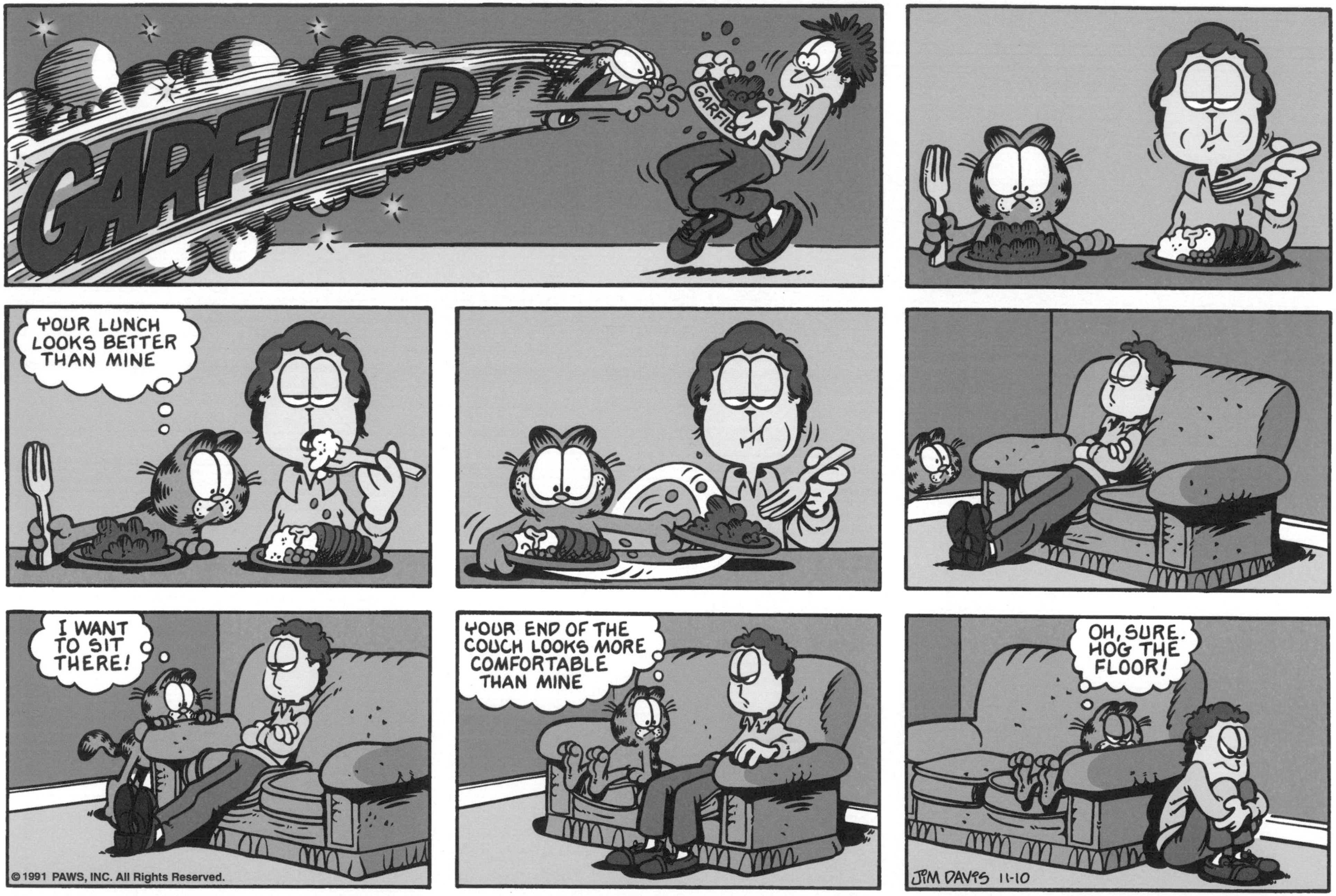
GARFIELD
GARFIELD
YOUR LUNCH LOOKS BETTER THAN MINE
I WANT TO SIT THERE!
YOUR END OF THE COUCH LOOKS MORE COMFORTABLE THAN MINE
OH, SURE. HOG THE FLOOR!
© 1991 PAWS, INC. All Rights Reserved.
JIM DAVIS 11-10

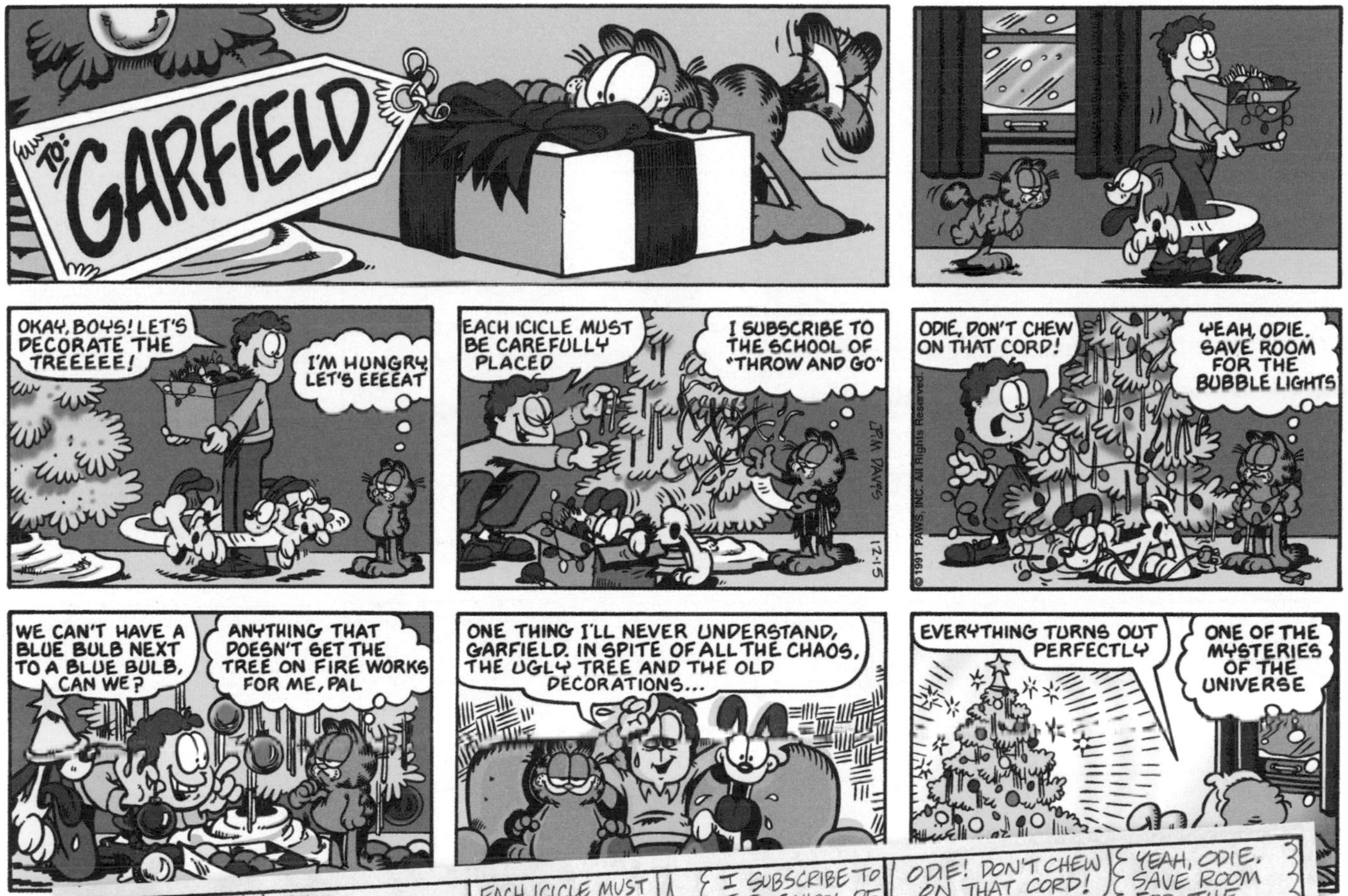
TO: GARFIELD
OKAY, BOYS! LET'S DECORATE THE TREEEEE!
I'M HUNGRY. LET'S EEEEAT
EACH ICICLE MUST BE CAREFULLY PLACED
I SUBSCRIBE TO THE SCHOOL OF "THROW AND GO"
JPM DAVIS 12-15
© 1991 PAWS, INC. All Rights Reserved.
ODIE, DON'T CHEW ON THAT CORD!
YEAH, ODIE. SAVE ROOM FOR THE BUBBLE LIGHTS
WE CAN'T HAVE A BLUE BULB NEXT TO A BLUE BULB, CAN WE?
ANYTHING THAT DOESN'T SET THE TREE ON FIRE WORKS FOR ME, PAL
ONE THING I'LL NEVER UNDERSTAND, GARFIELD. IN SPITE OF ALL THE CHAOS, THE UGLY TREE AND THE OLD DECORATIONS...
EVERYTHING TURNS OUT PERFECTLY
ONE OF THE MYSTERIES OF THE UNIVERSE

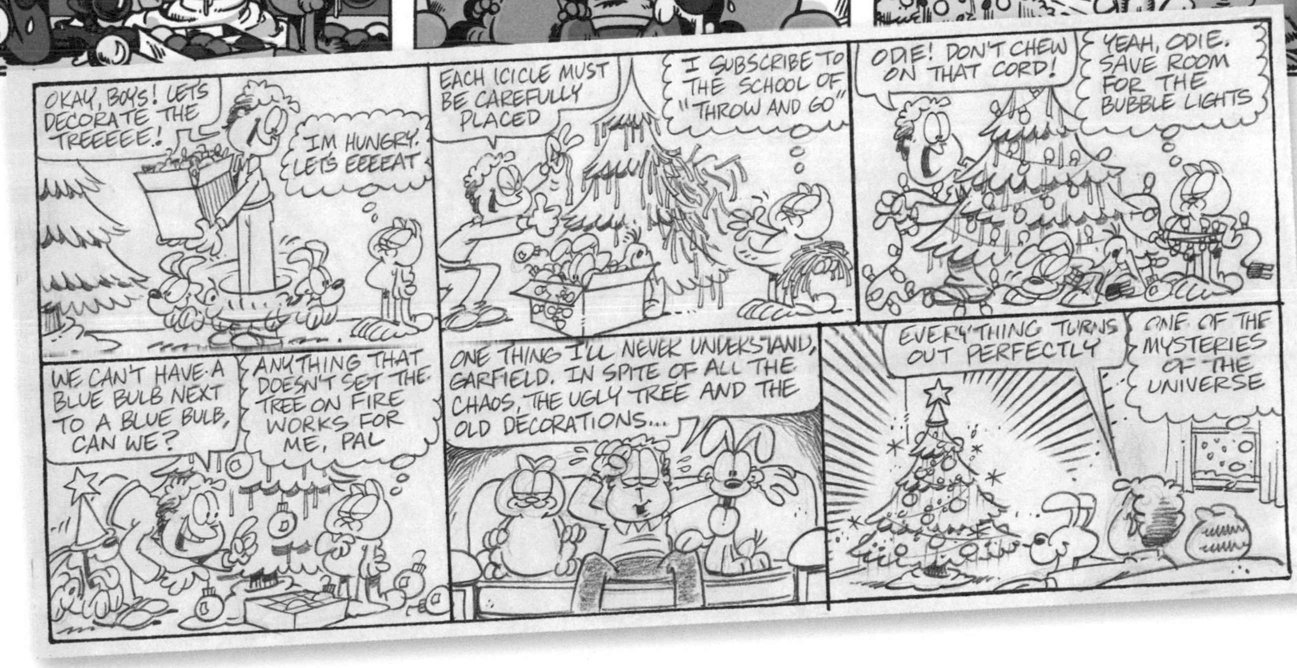
OKAY, BOYS! LET'S DECORATE THE TREEEEE!
I'M HUNGRY. LET'S EEEEAT
EACH ICICLE MUST BE CAREFULLY PLACED
I SUBSCRIBE TO THE SCHOOL OF "THROW AND GO"
ODIE! DON'T CHEW ON THAT CORD!
YEAH, ODIE. SAVE ROOM FOR THE BUBBLE LIGHTS
WE CAN'T HAVE A BLUE BULB NEXT TO A BLUE BULB, CAN WE?
ANYTHING THAT DOESN'T SET THE TREE ON FIRE WORKS FOR ME, PAL
ONE THING I'LL NEVER UNDERSTAND, GARFIELD. IN SPITE OF ALL THE CHAOS, THE UGLY TREE AND THE OLD DECORATIONS...
EVERYTHING TURNS OUT PERFECTLY
ONE OF THE MYSTERIES OF THE UNIVERSE

original rough

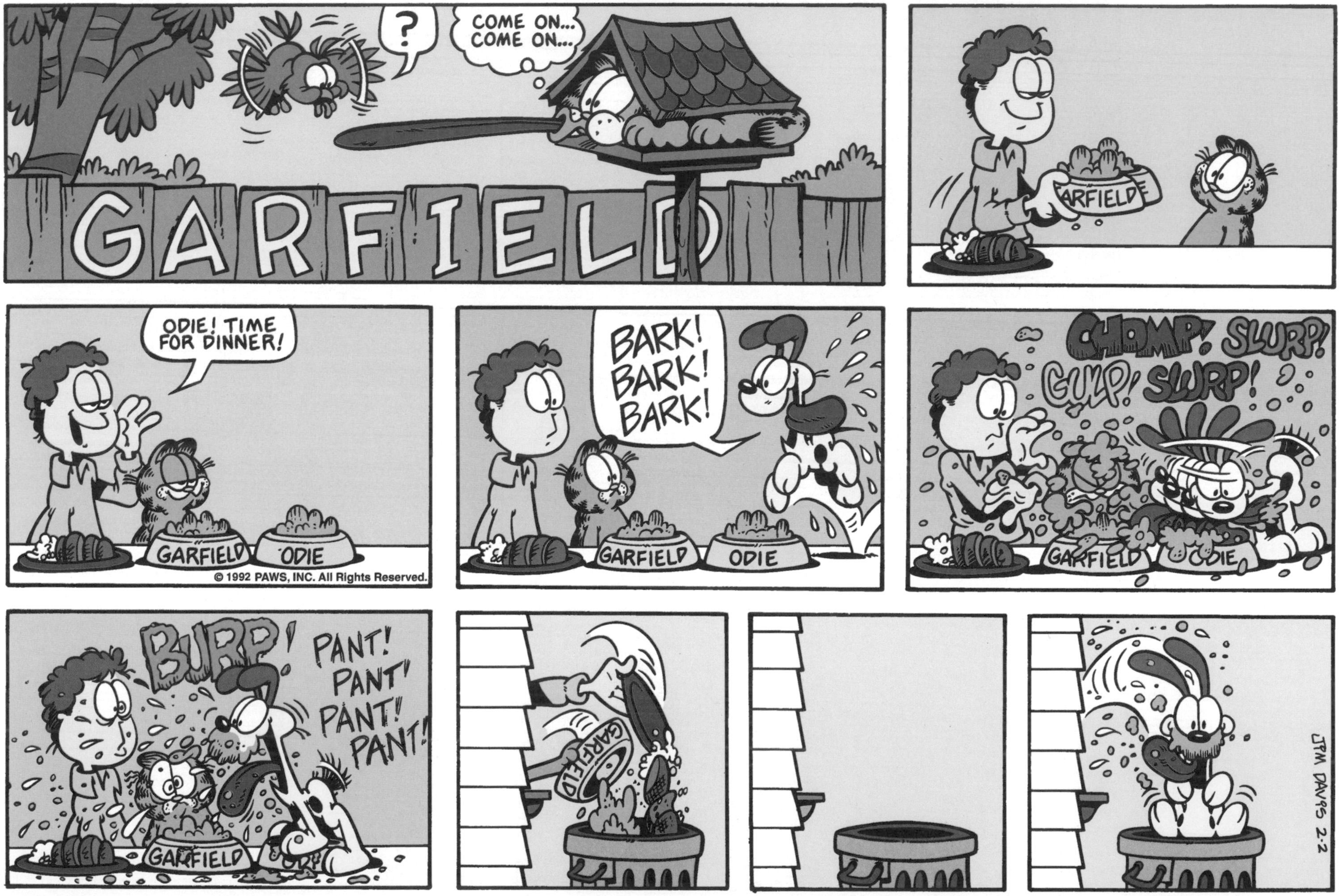
?
COME ON... COME ON...
GARFIELD
GARFIELD
ODIE! TIME FOR DINNER!
GARFIELD
ODIE
© 1992 PAWS, INC. All Rights Reserved.
BARK! BARK! BARK!
GARFIELD
ODIE
CHOMP! SLURP!
GULP! SLURP!
GARFIELD
ODIE
BURP!
PANT! PANT! PANT! PANT!
GARFIELD
GARFIELD
JPM DAVIS 2-2

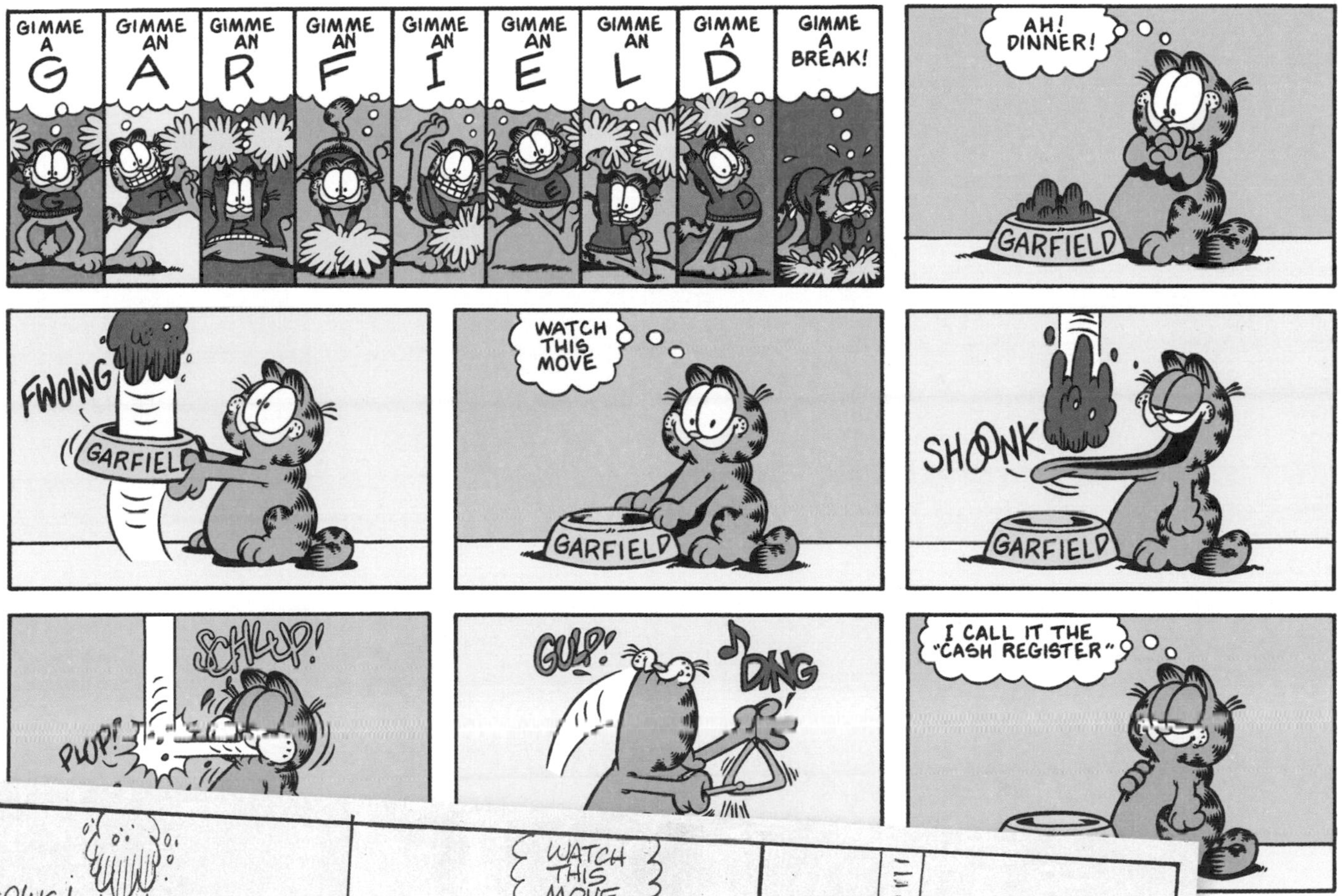
GIMME A G
GIMME AN A
GIMME AN R
GIMME AN F
GIMME AN I
GIMME AN E
GIMME AN L
GIMME A D
GIMME A BREAK!
AH! DINNER!
GARFIELD
FWOING
GARFIELD
WATCH THIS MOVE
GARFIELD
SHOONK
GARFIELD
SCHLUP!
PLOP!
GULP!
DING
I CALL IT THE "CASH REGISTER"

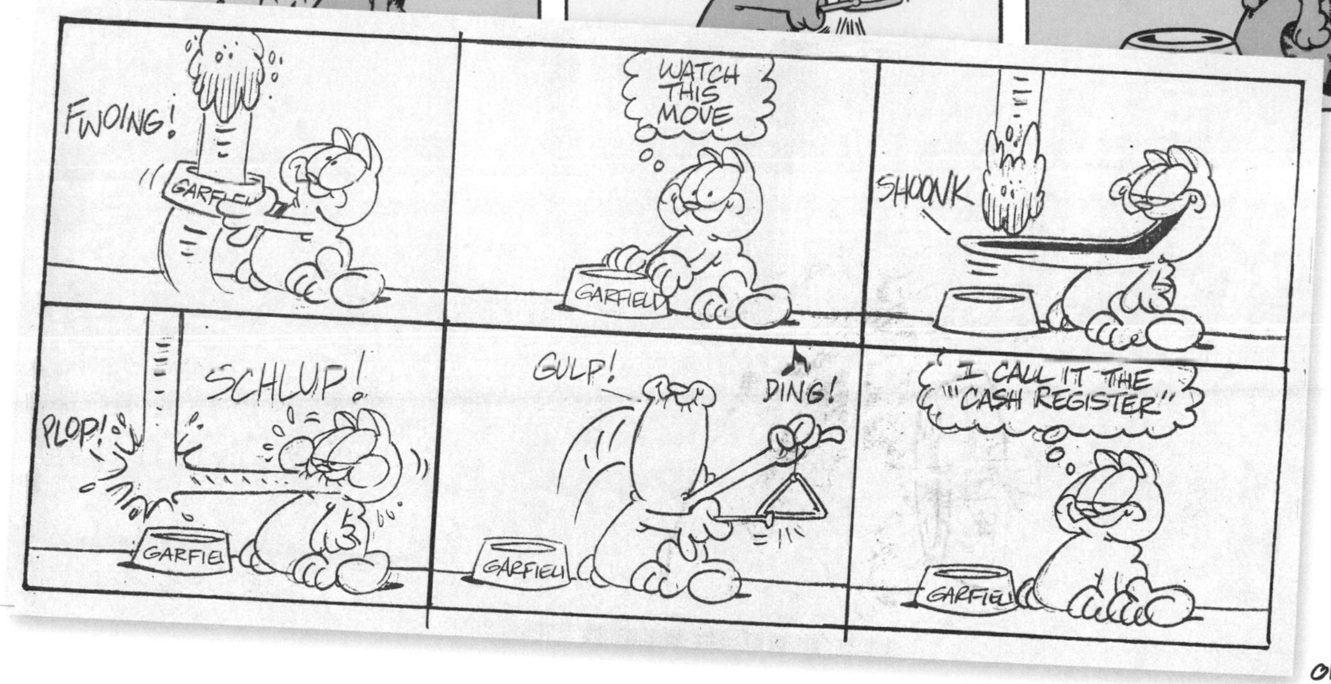
FWOING!
WATCH THIS MOVE
GARFIELD
SHOONK
SCHLUP!
PLOP!
GARFIEL
GULP!
DING!
GARFIELL
I CALL IT THE "CASH REGISTER"
GARFIEL

original rough

I've always loved story lines that end with the moral, "Be careful what you wish for."

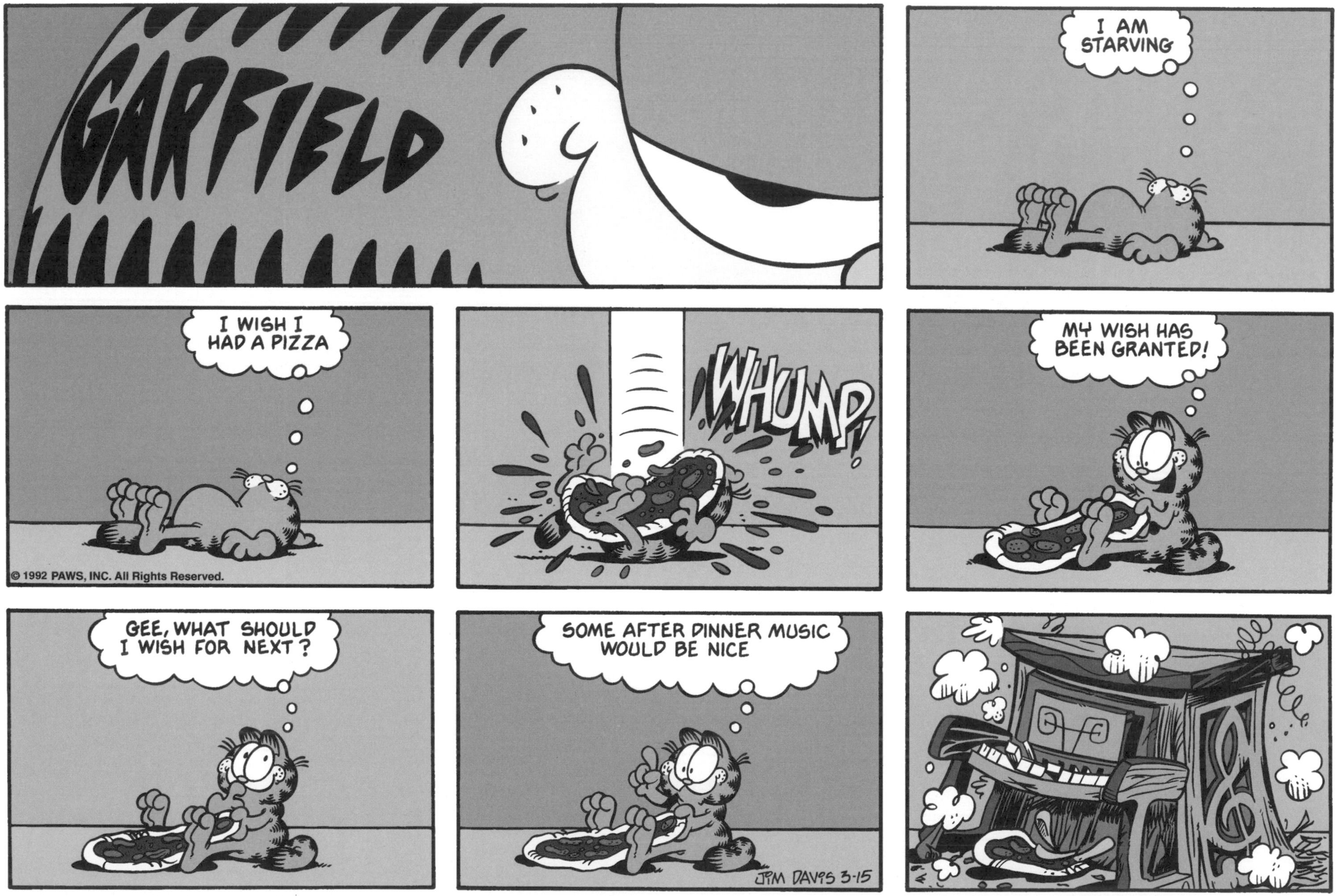
GARFIELD
I AM STARVING
I WISH I HAD A PIZZA
© 1992 PAWS, INC. All Rights Reserved.
WHUMP!
MY WISH HAS BEEN GRANTED!
GEE, WHAT SHOULD I WISH FOR NEXT?
SOME AFTER DINNER MUSIC WOULD BE NICE
JIM DAVIS 3-15

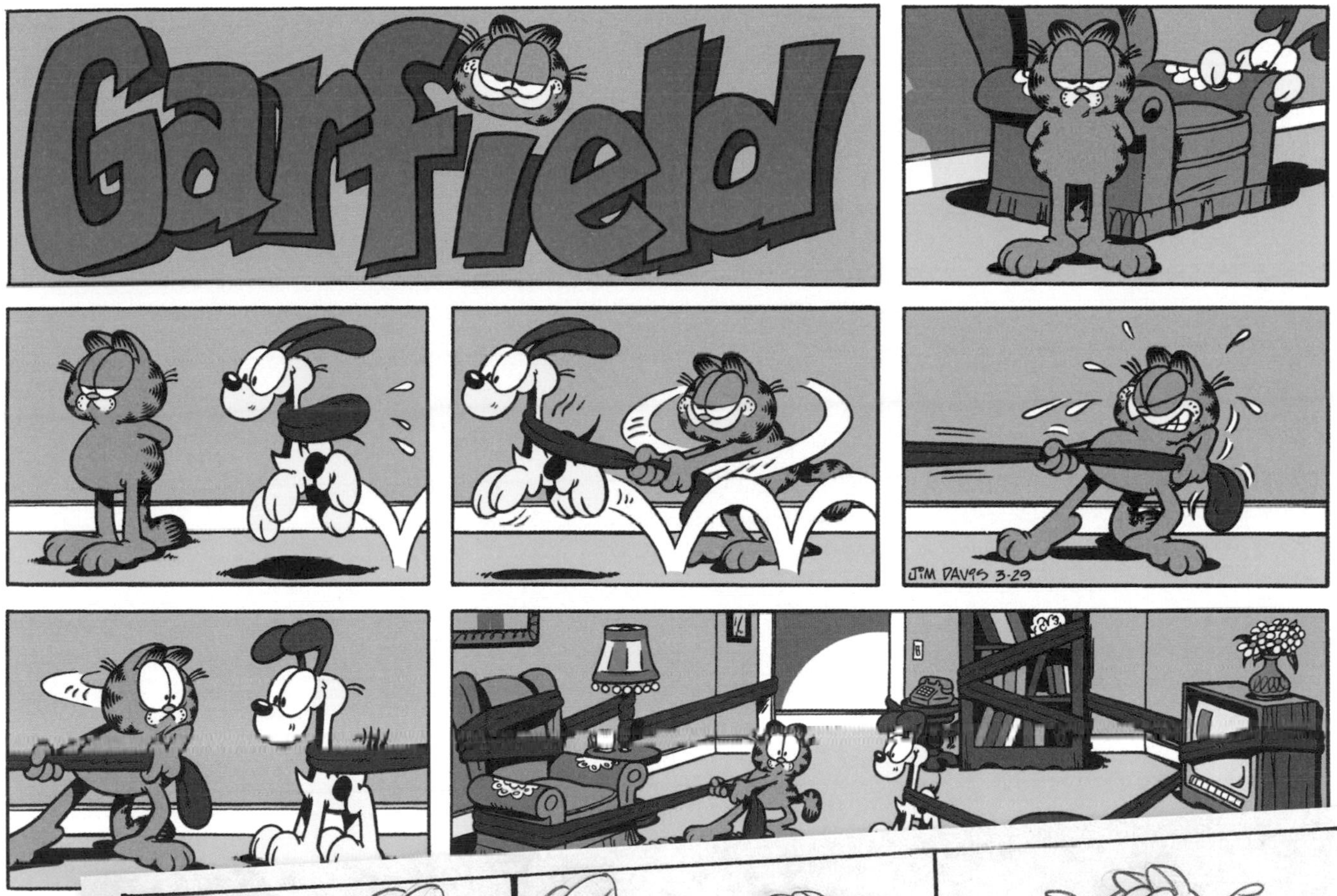
Garfield
JIM DAVIS 3-29

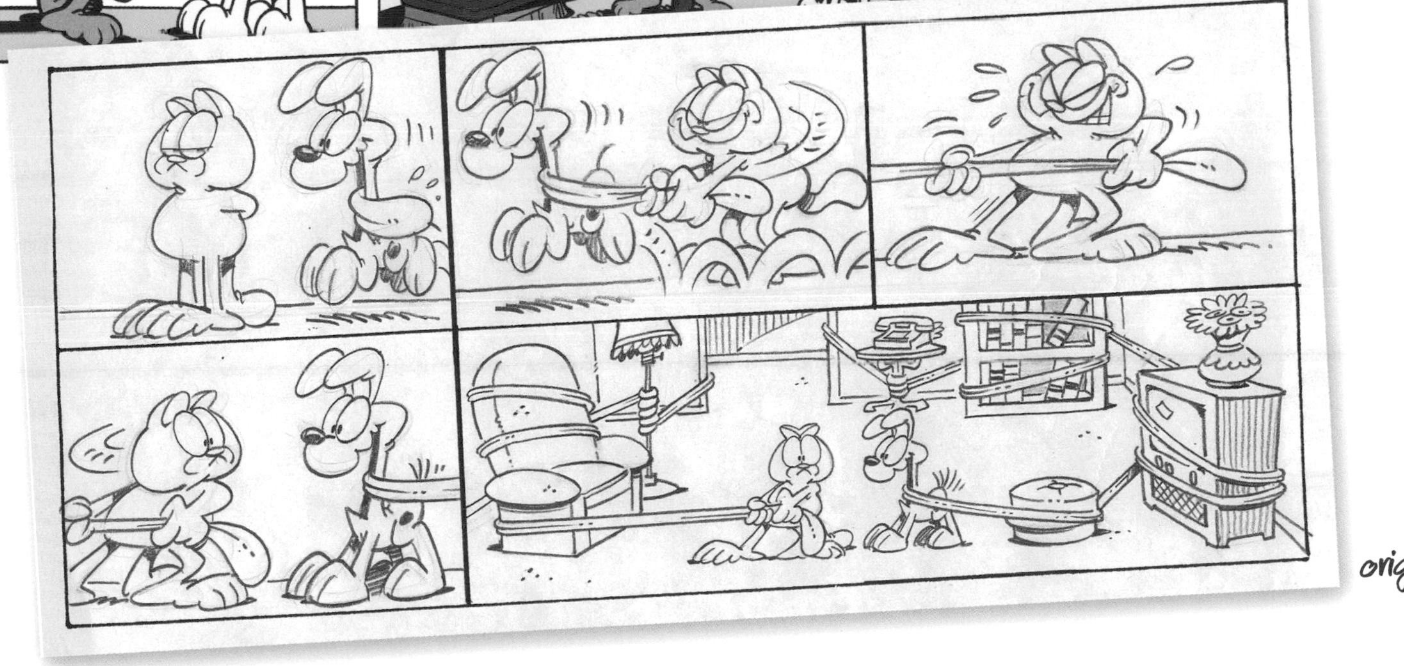

original rough

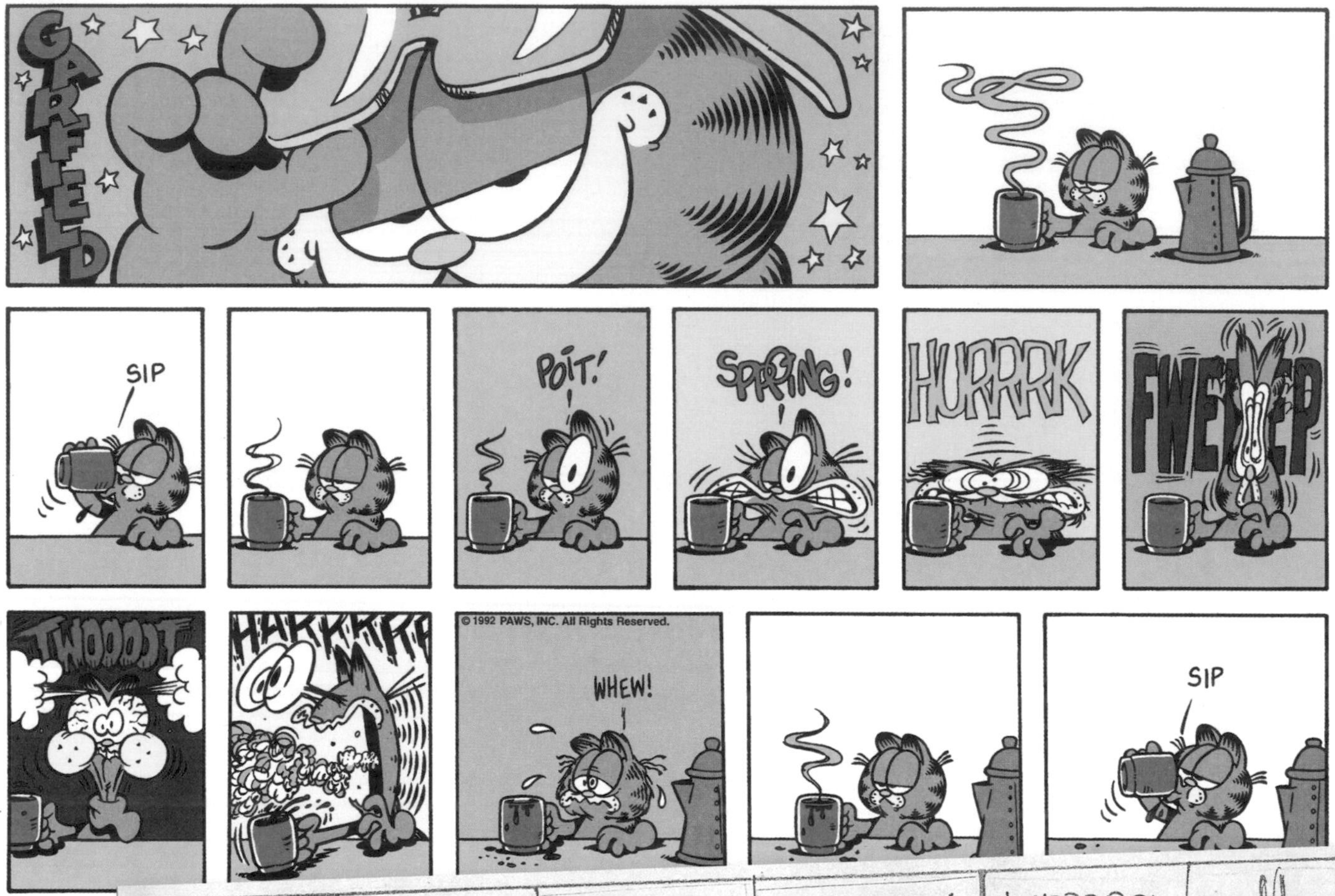
GARFIELD
SIP
POIT!
SPROING!
HURRRK
TWOOOOT
© 1992 PAWS, INC. All Rights Reserved.
WHEW!
SIP

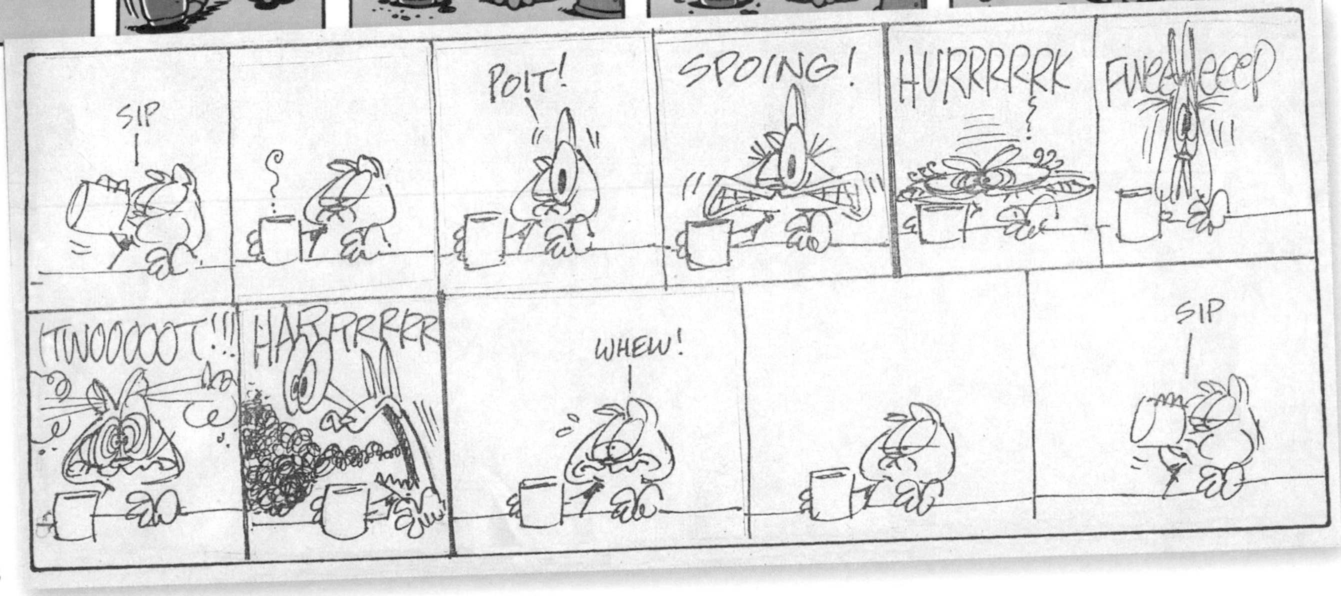
SIP
POIT!
SPOING!
HURRRRRK
TWOOOOOT!!!
WHEW!
SIP

original rough

When you do what I do for a living, you often have days like this.

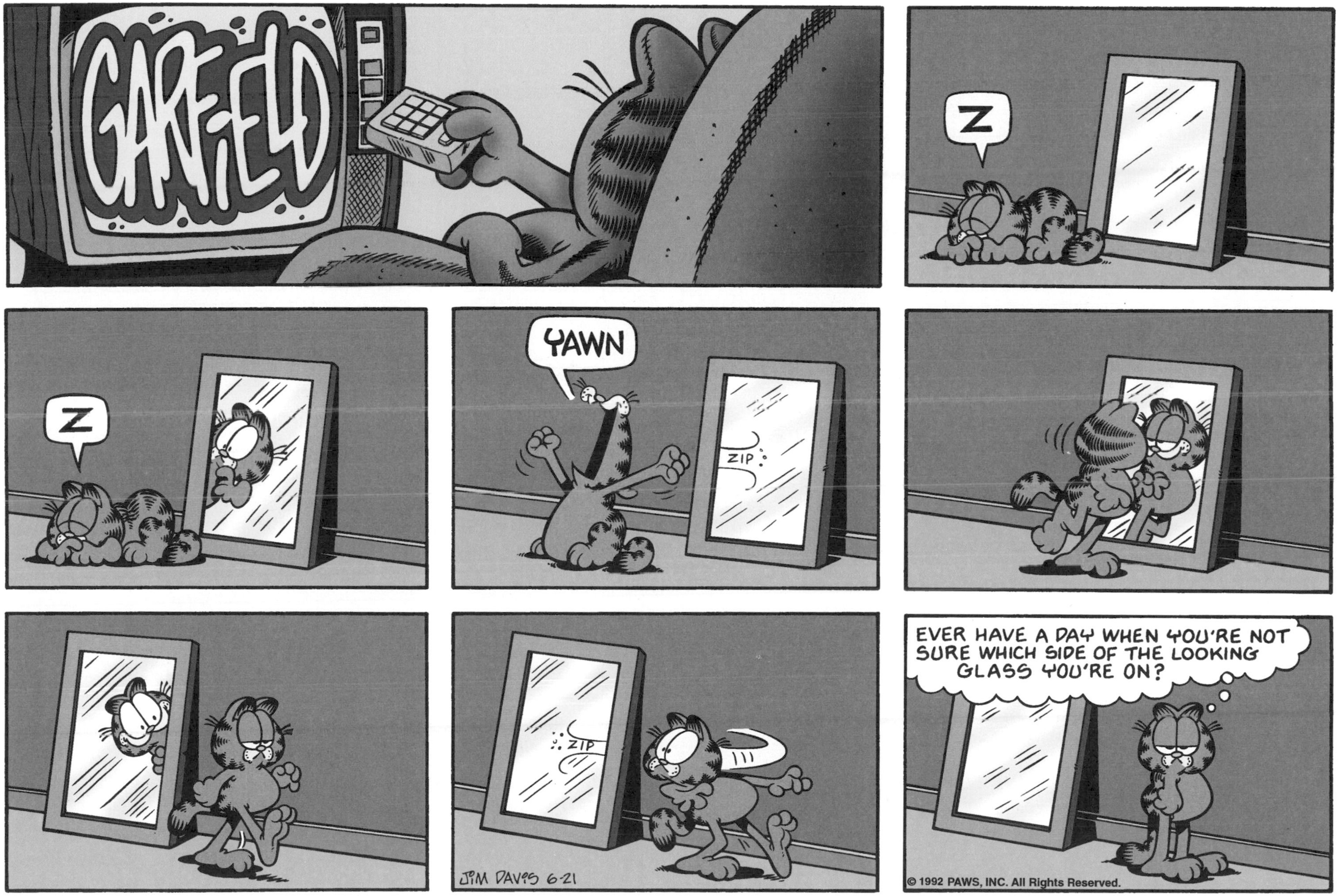
GARFIELD
Z
Z
YAWN
ZIP
ZIP
EVER HAVE A DAY WHEN YOU'RE NOT SURE WHICH SIDE OF THE LOOKING GLASS YOU'RE ON?
JIM DAVIS 6-21
© 1992 PAWS, INC. All Rights Reserved.

This strip is funny because it's so true, which is a bit odd because it's not so funny when it really happens to you.

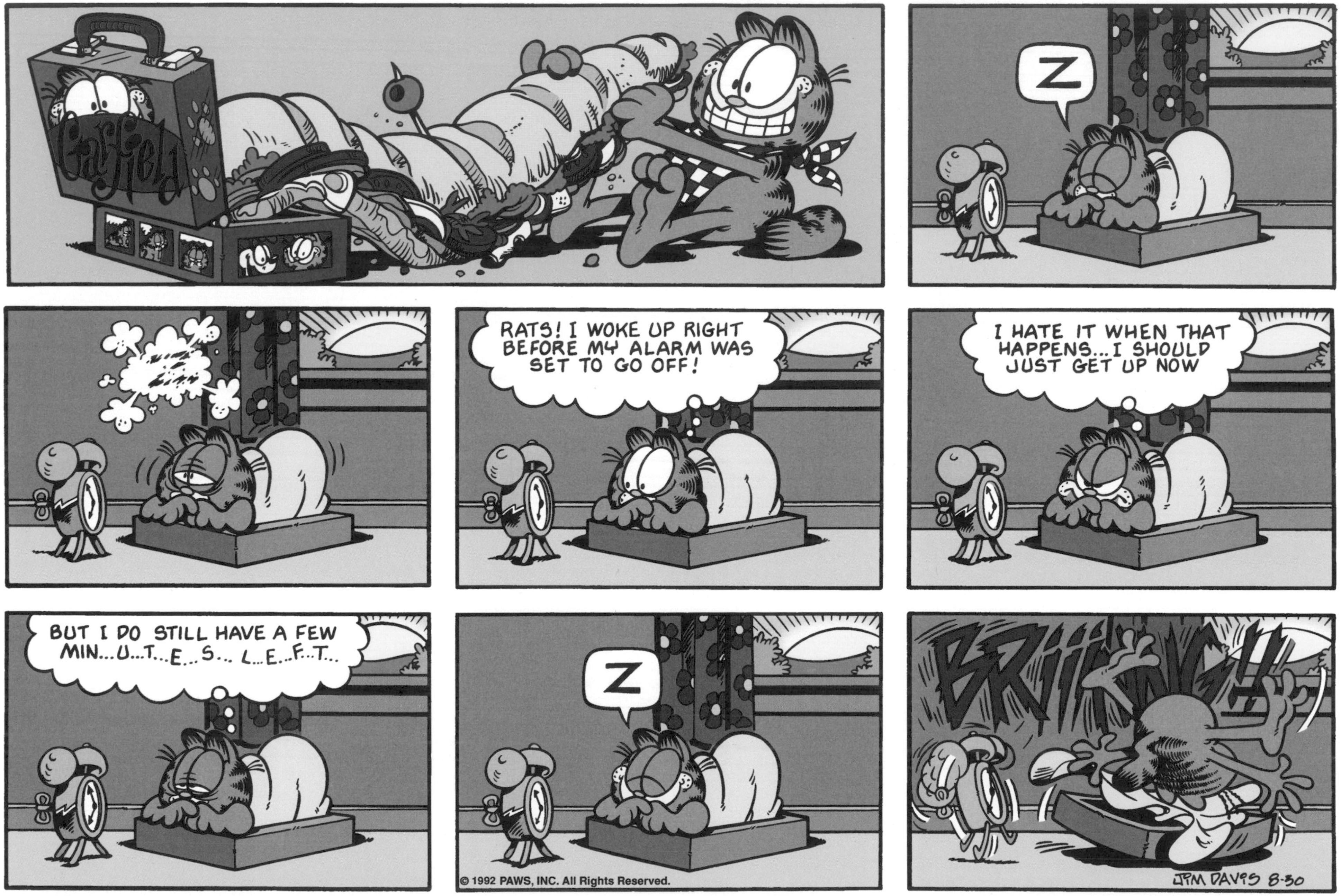

Garfield
Z
RATS! I WOKE UP RIGHT BEFORE MY ALARM WAS SET TO GO OFF!
I HATE IT WHEN THAT HAPPENS...I SHOULD JUST GET UP NOW
BUT I DO STILL HAVE A FEW MIN...U...T...E...S... L...E...F...T...
Z
© 1992 PAWS, INC. All Rights Reserved.
JIM DAVIS 8-30

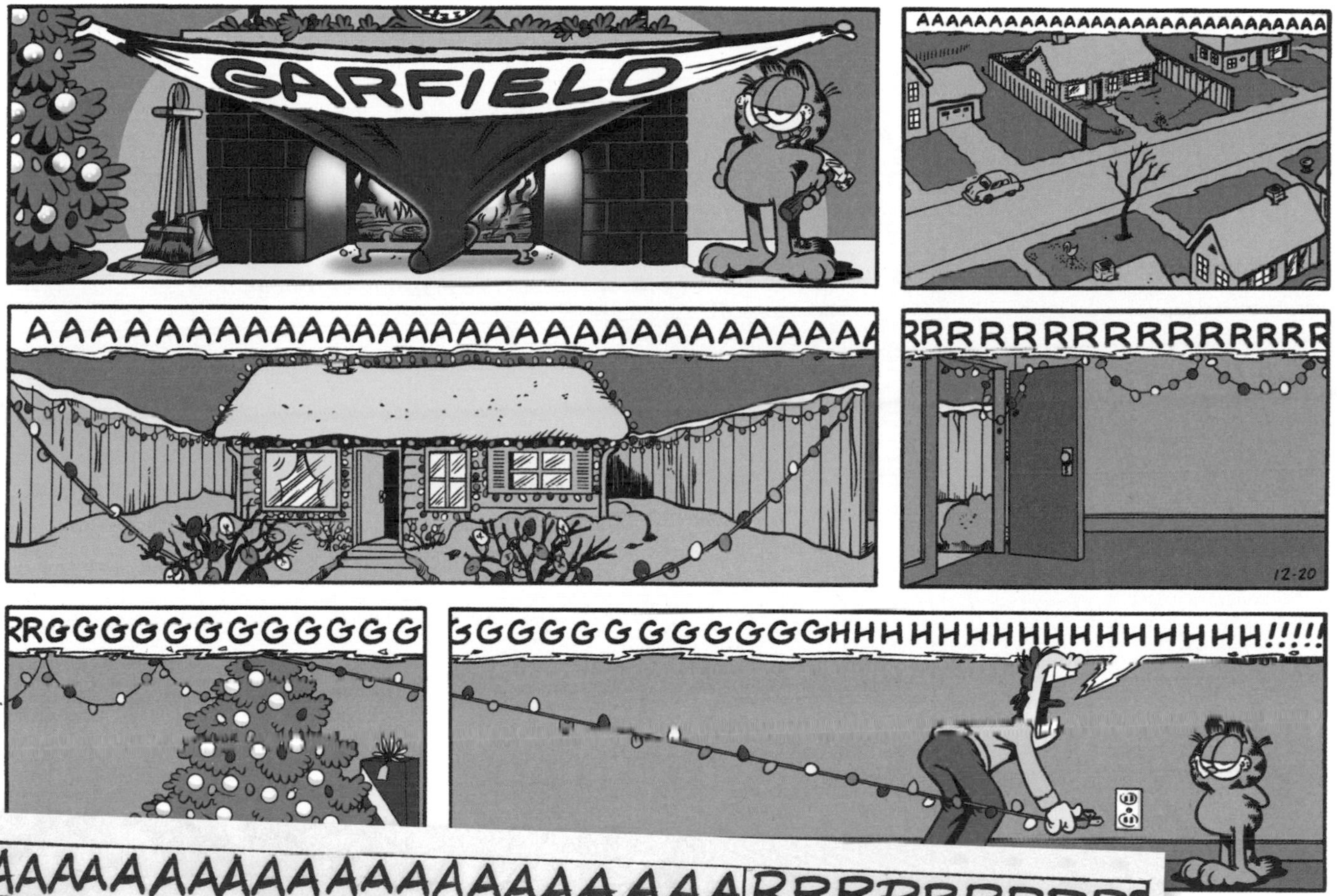
GARFIELD
AAAAAAAAAAAAAAAAAAAAAAAAAAAAAA
AAAAAAAAAAAAAAAAAAAAAAAAAAAAA
RRRRRRRRRRRRRRRRR
12-20
RRGGGGGGGGGGGGG
GGGGGGGGGGGGGHHHHHHHHHHHHHHHH!!!!!

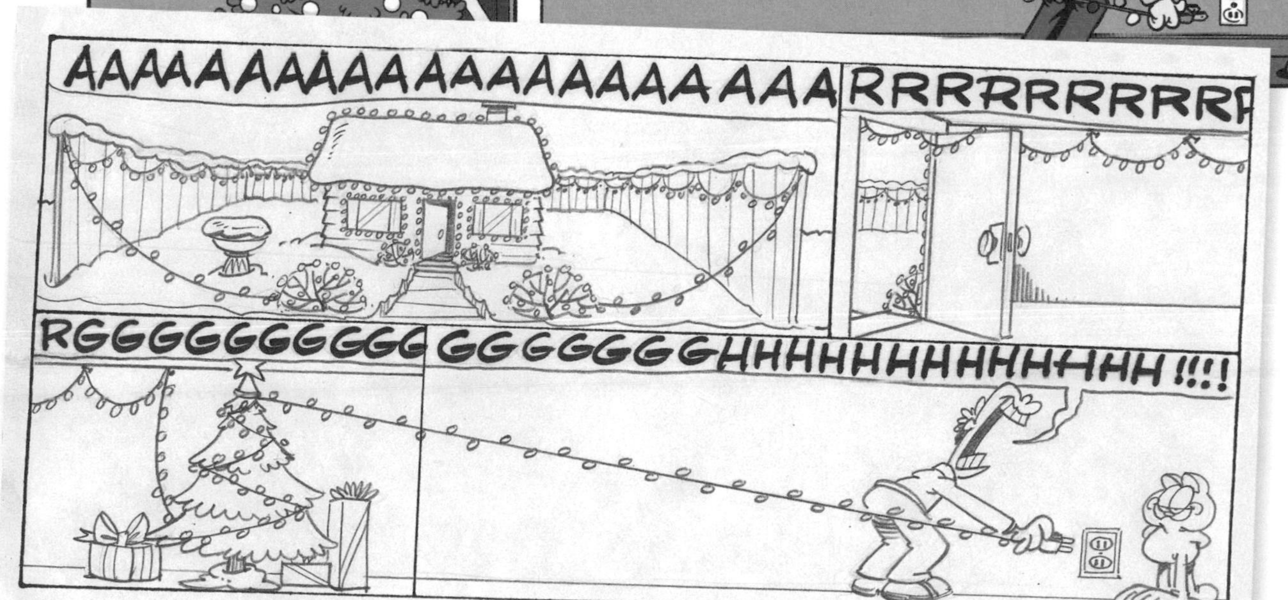
AAAAAAAAAAAAAAAAAAAAAA
RRRRRRRRRRR
RGGGGGGGGGGG
GGGGGGGHHHHHHHHHHHHHH!!!!

original rough

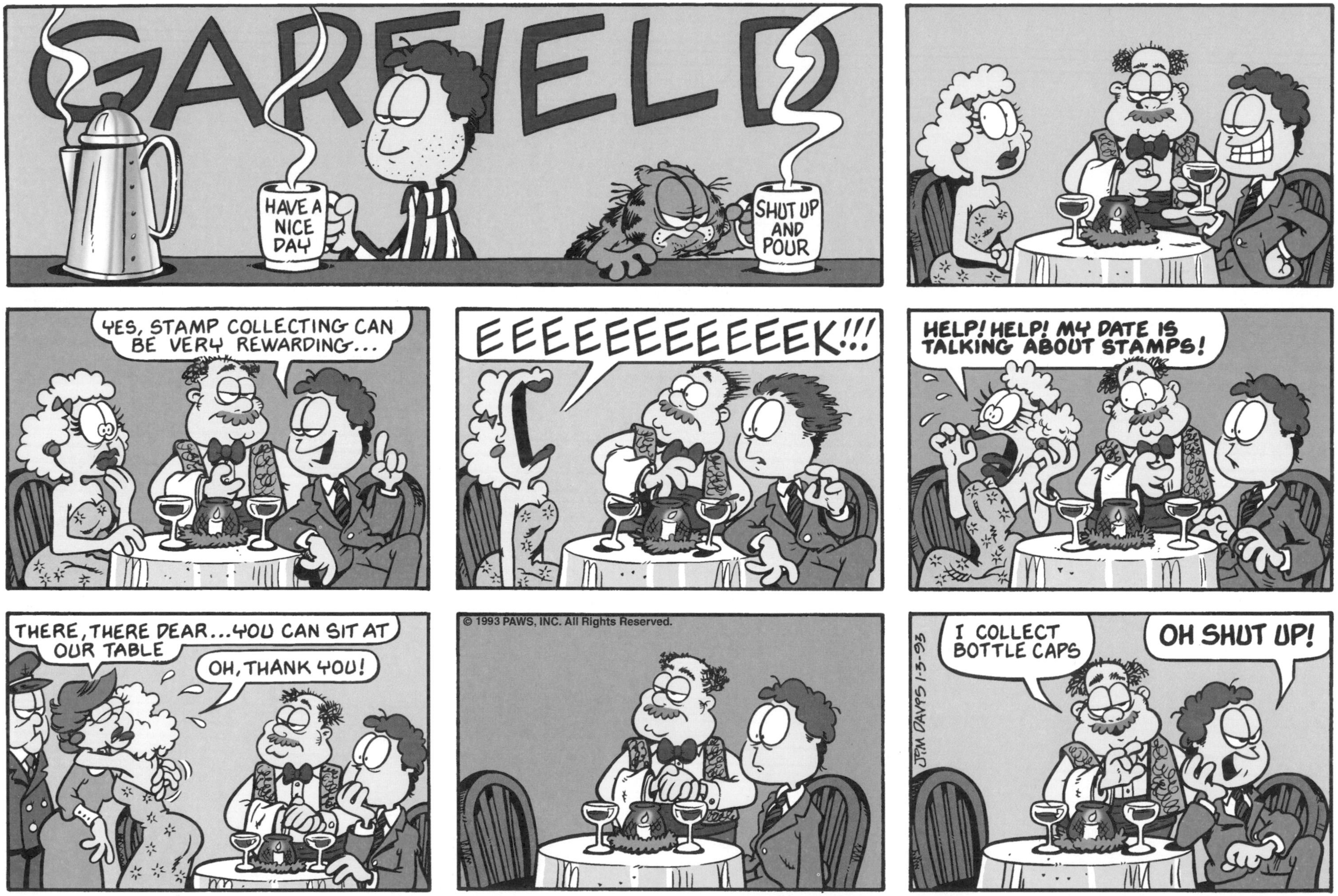
GARFIELD
HAVE A NICE DAY
SHUT UP AND POUR
YES, STAMP COLLECTING CAN BE VERY REWARDING...
EEEEEEEEEEEEK!!!
HELP! HELP! MY DATE IS TALKING ABOUT STAMPS!
THERE, THERE DEAR...YOU CAN SIT AT OUR TABLE
OH, THANK YOU!
© 1993 PAWS, INC. All Rights Reserved.
JIM DAVIS 1-3-93
I COLLECT BOTTLE CAPS
OH SHUT UP!

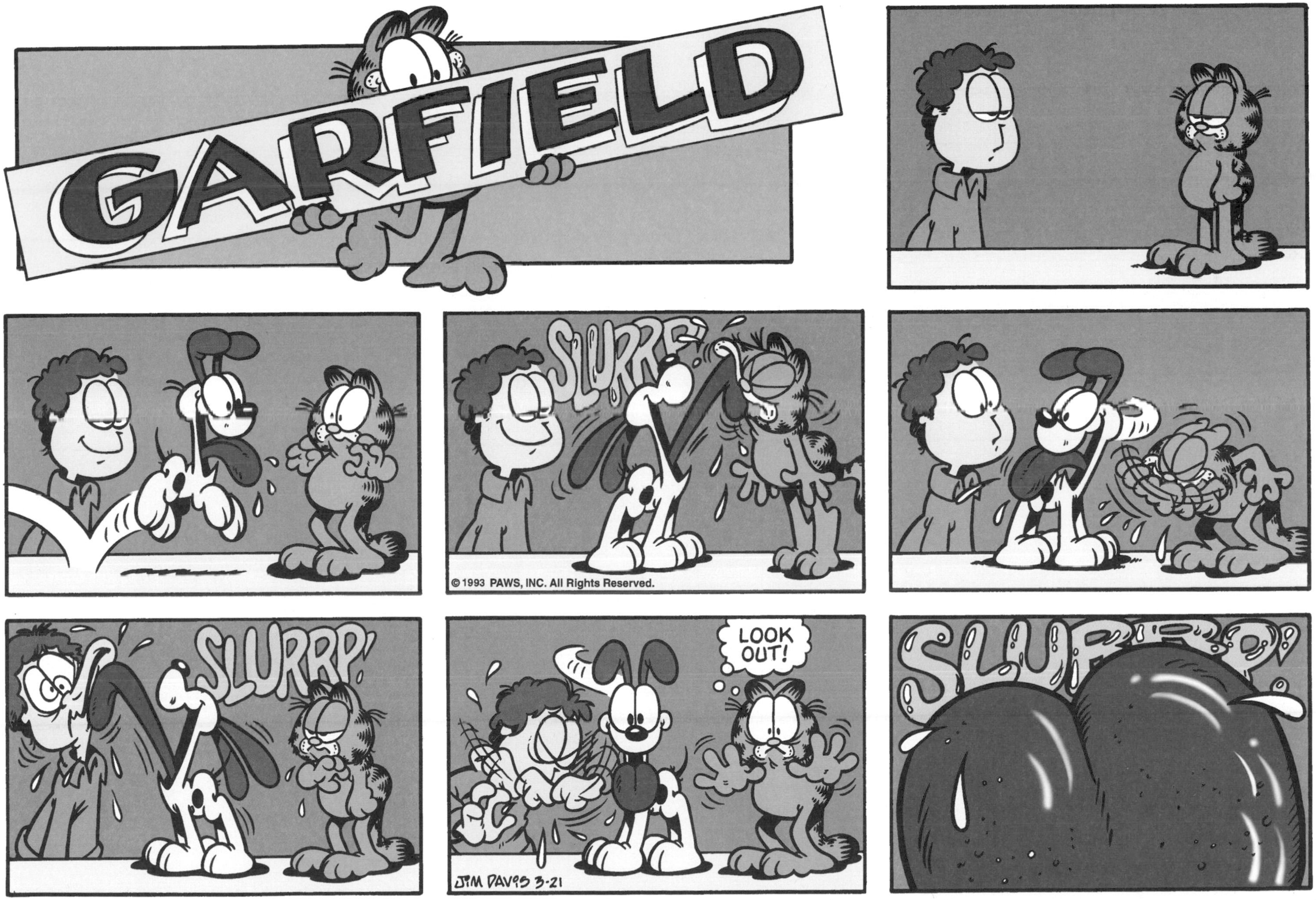
GARFIELD
SLURRP!
© 1993 PAWS, INC. All Rights Reserved.
SLURRP!
LOOK OUT!
JIM DAVIS 3-21
SLURRP!

If I got a dollar for every time this happened to me, I could buy a car . . . a nice car.

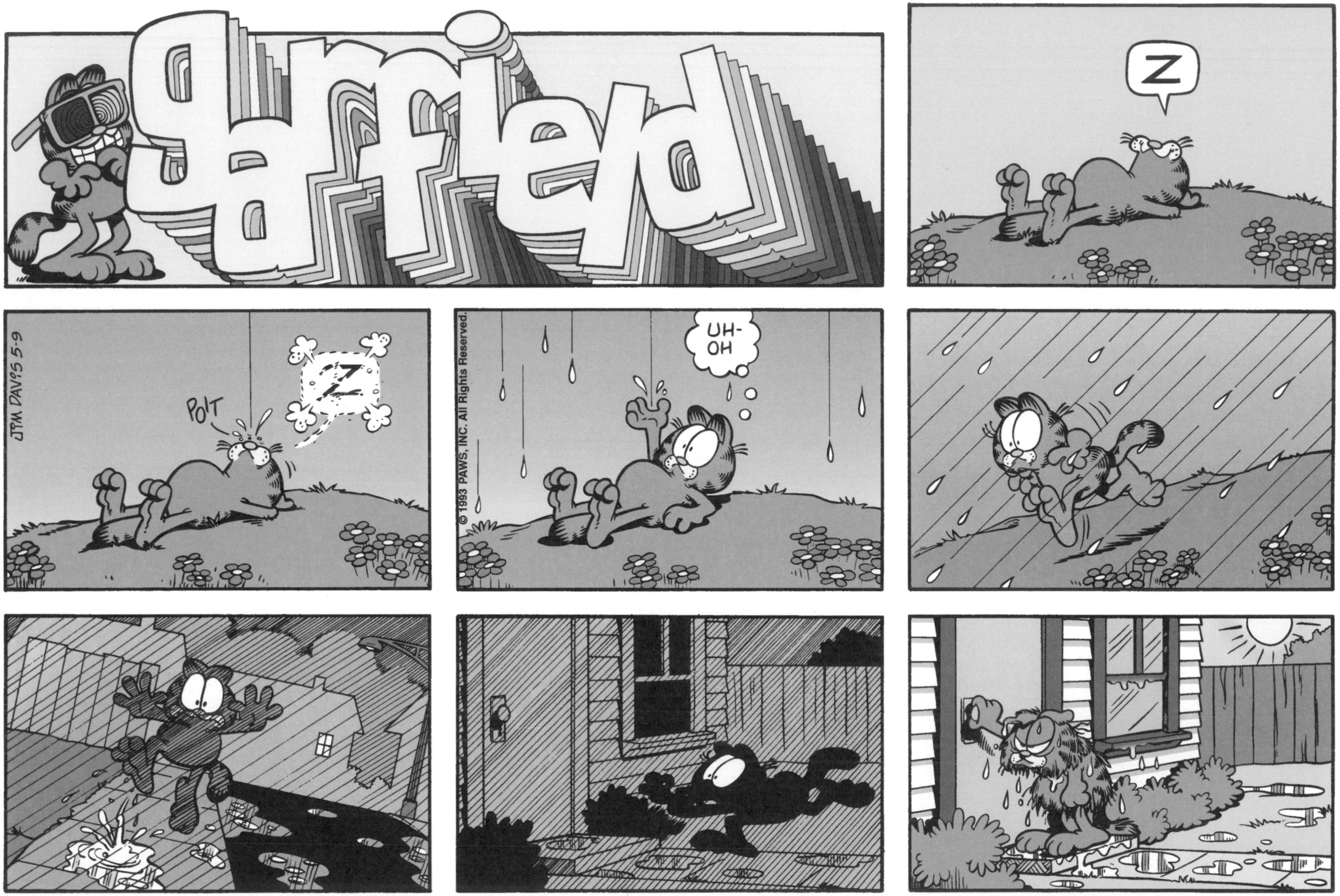
garfield
Z
JIM DAVIS 5-9
POIT
Z
© 1993 PAWS, INC. All Rights Reserved.
UH-OH

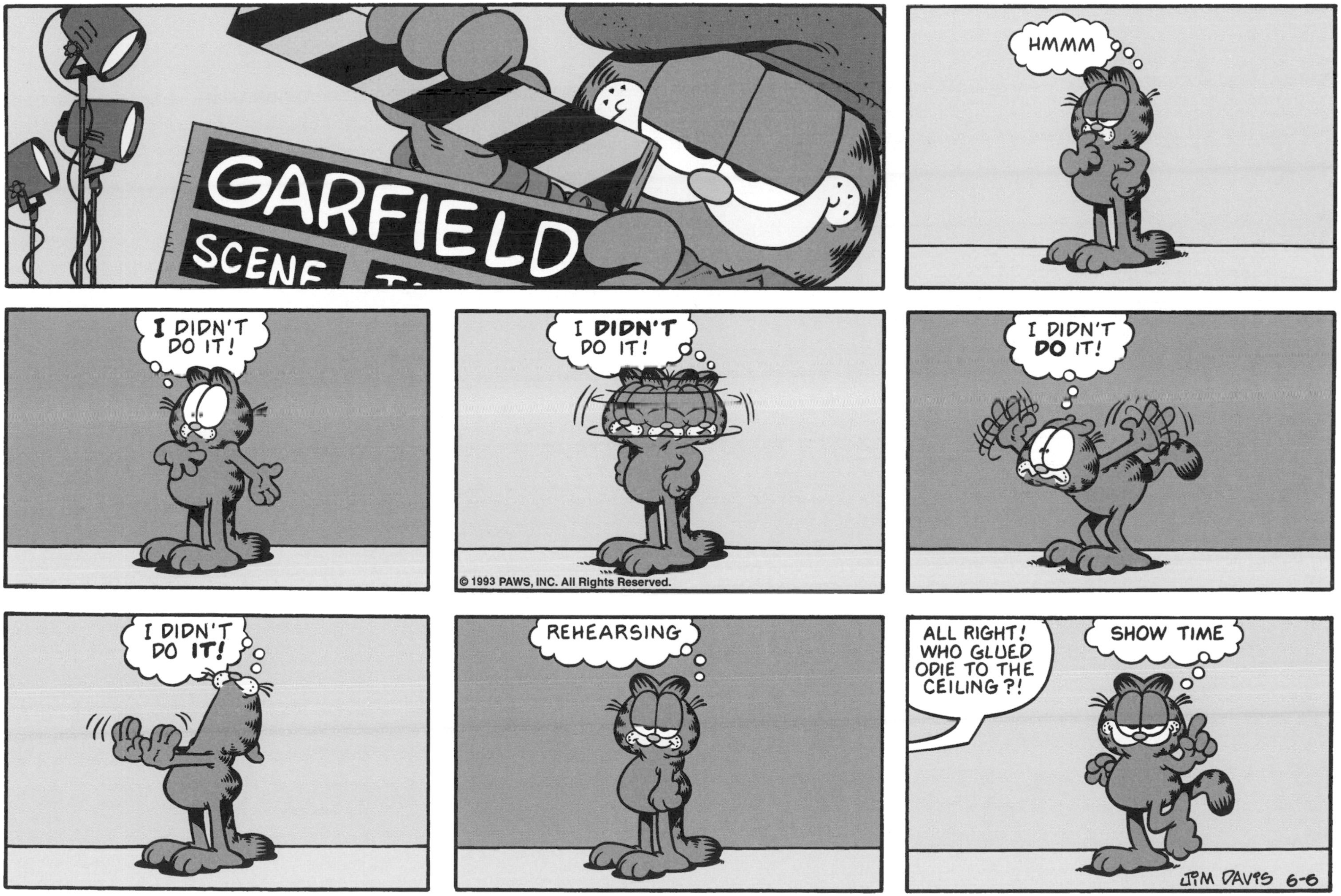

GARFIELD
SCENE
HMMM
I DIDN'T DO IT!
I DIDN'T DO IT!
I DIDN'T DO IT!
© 1993 PAWS, INC. All Rights Reserved.
I DIDN'T DO IT!
REHEARSING
ALL RIGHT! WHO GLUED ODIE TO THE CEILING?!
SHOW TIME
JIM DAVIS 6-6

This one might be considered a bit suggestive, but, hey, it's funny!

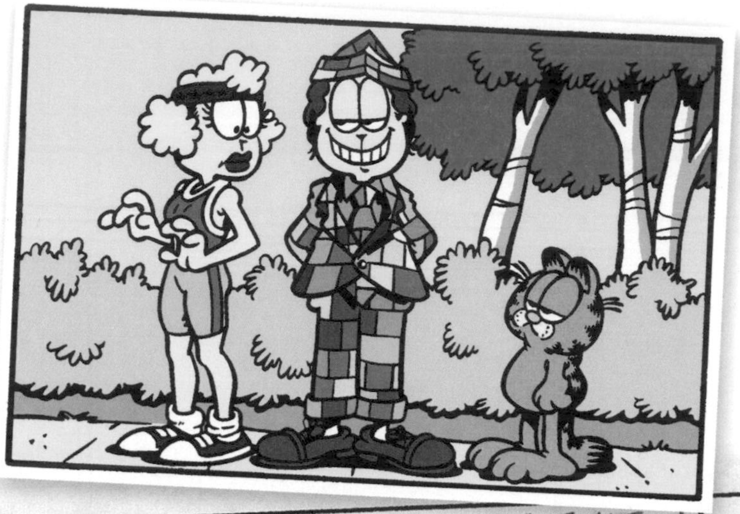

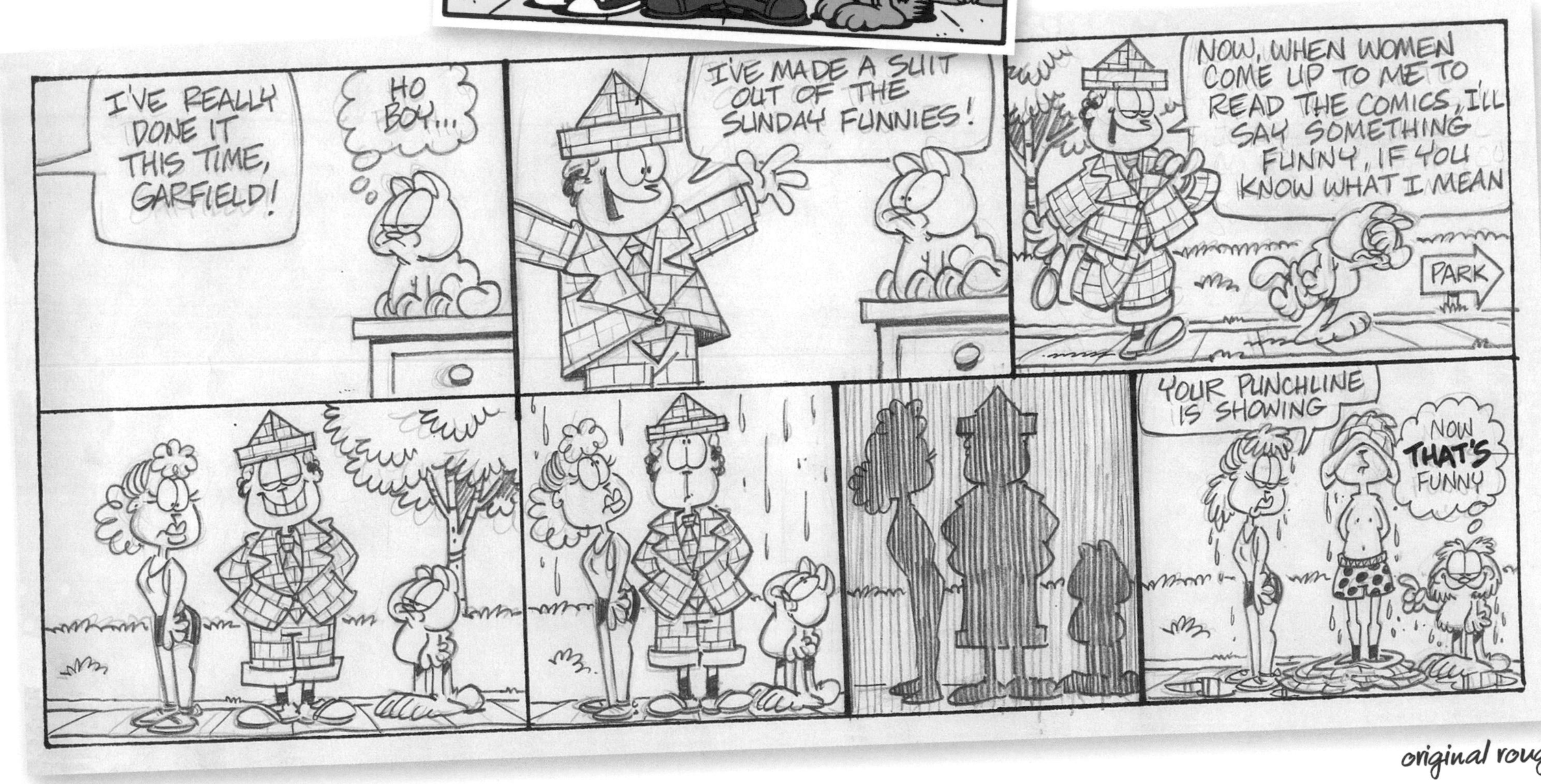

I'VE REALLY DONE IT THIS TIME, GARFIELD!
HO BOY....
I'VE MADE A SUIT OUT OF THE SUNDAY FUNNIES!
NOW, WHEN WOMEN COME UP TO ME TO READ THE COMICS, I'LL SAY SOMETHING FUNNY, IF YOU KNOW WHAT I MEAN
PARK
YOUR PUNCHLINE IS SHOWING
NOW THAT'S FUNNY

original rough

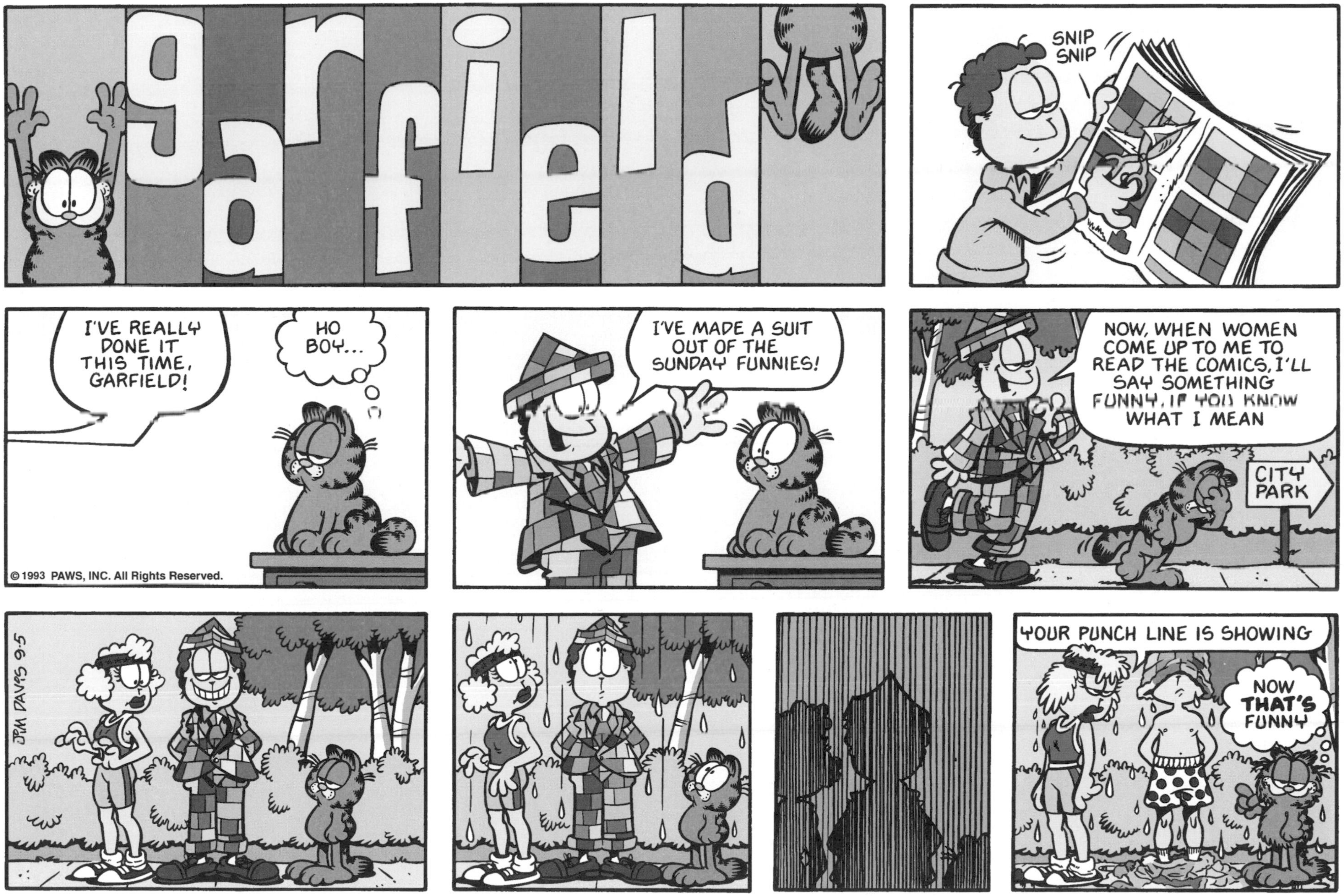
garfield
SNIP SNIP
I'VE REALLY DONE IT THIS TIME, GARFIELD!
HO BOY...
© 1993 PAWS, INC. All Rights Reserved.
I'VE MADE A SUIT OUT OF THE SUNDAY FUNNIES!
NOW, WHEN WOMEN COME UP TO ME TO READ THE COMICS, I'LL SAY SOMETHING FUNNY, IF YOU KNOW WHAT I MEAN
CITY PARK
JPM DAVIS 9-5
YOUR PUNCH LINE IS SHOWING
NOW THAT'S FUNNY

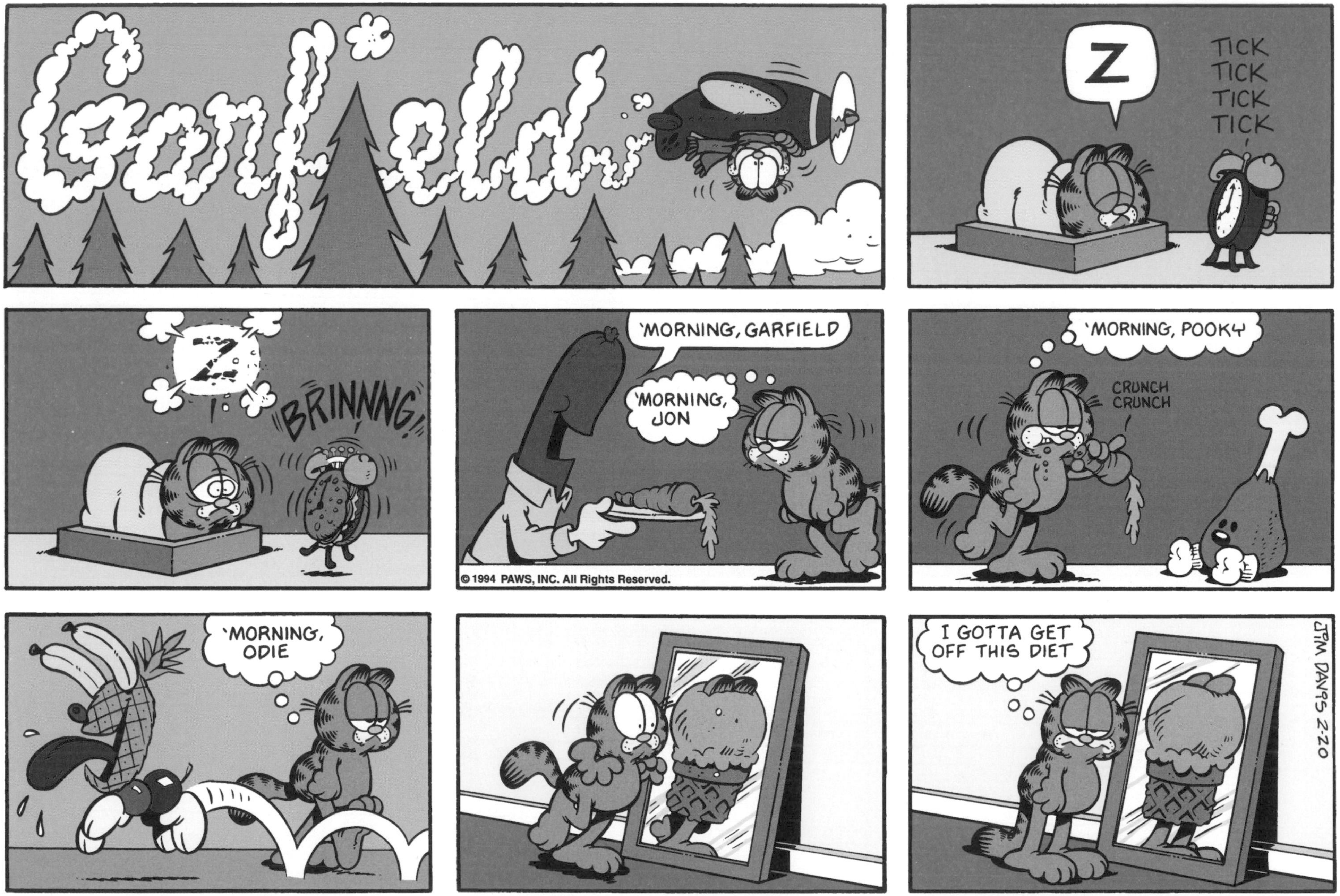
Garfield
Z
TICK
TICK
TICK
TICK
Z
BRINNNG!
'MORNING, GARFIELD
'MORNING, JON
© 1994 PAWS, INC. All Rights Reserved.
'MORNING, POOKY
CRUNCH
CRUNCH
'MORNING, ODIE
I GOTTA GET OFF THIS DIET
JIM DAVIS 2-20

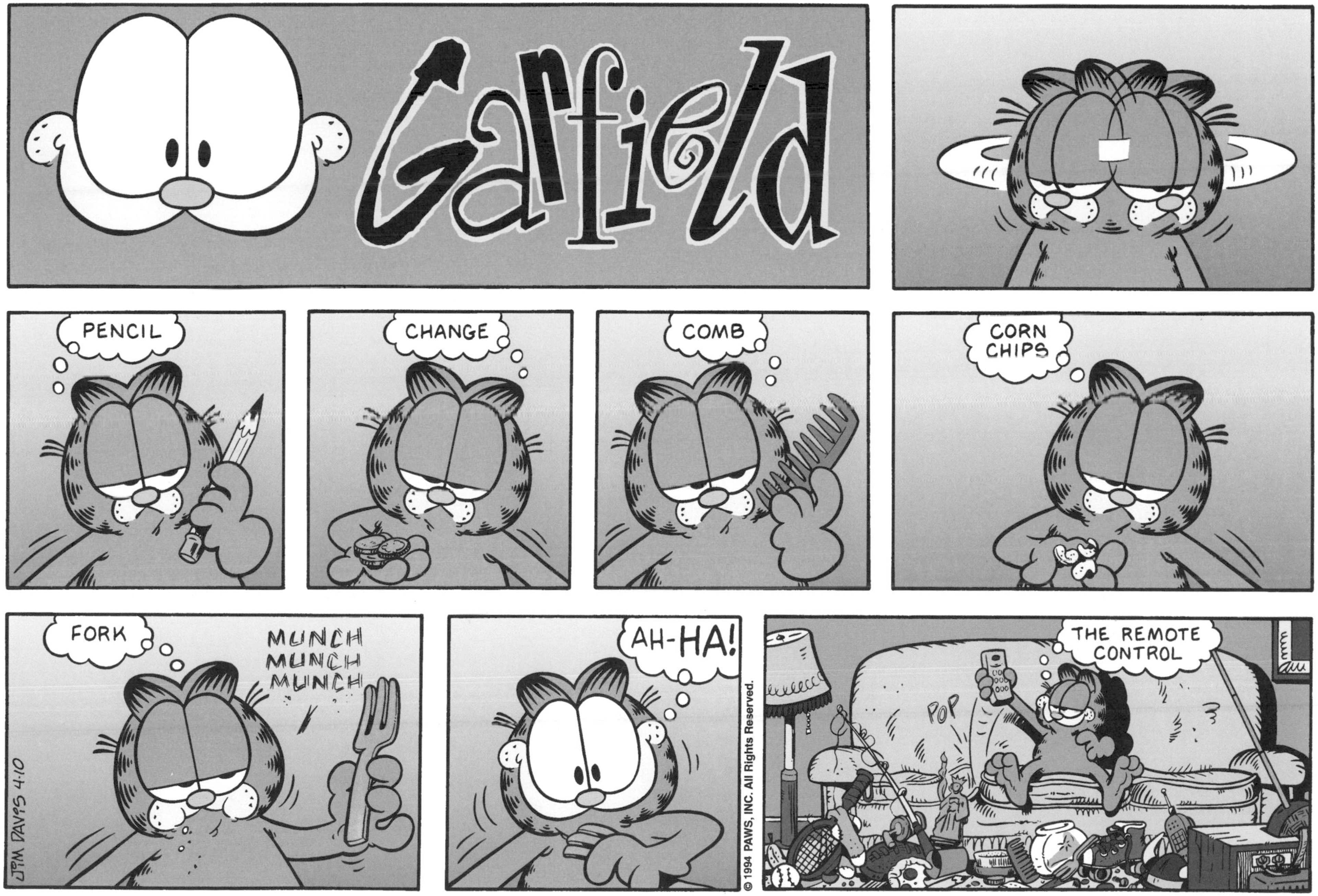
Garfield
PENCIL
CHANGE
COMB
CORN CHIPS
FORK
MUNCH MUNCH MUNCH
JPM DAVPS 4-10
AH-HA!
© 1994 PAWS, INC. All Rights Reserved.
POP
THE REMOTE CONTROL

Words are overrated. It's fun when Garfield makes silly faces.

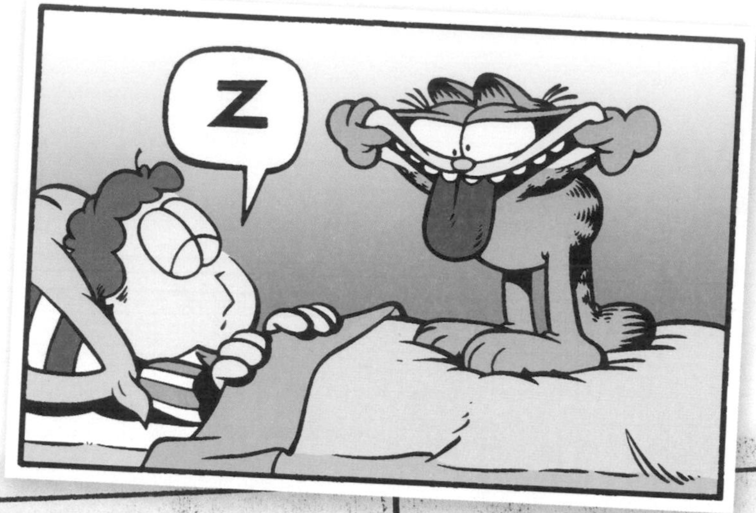
Z

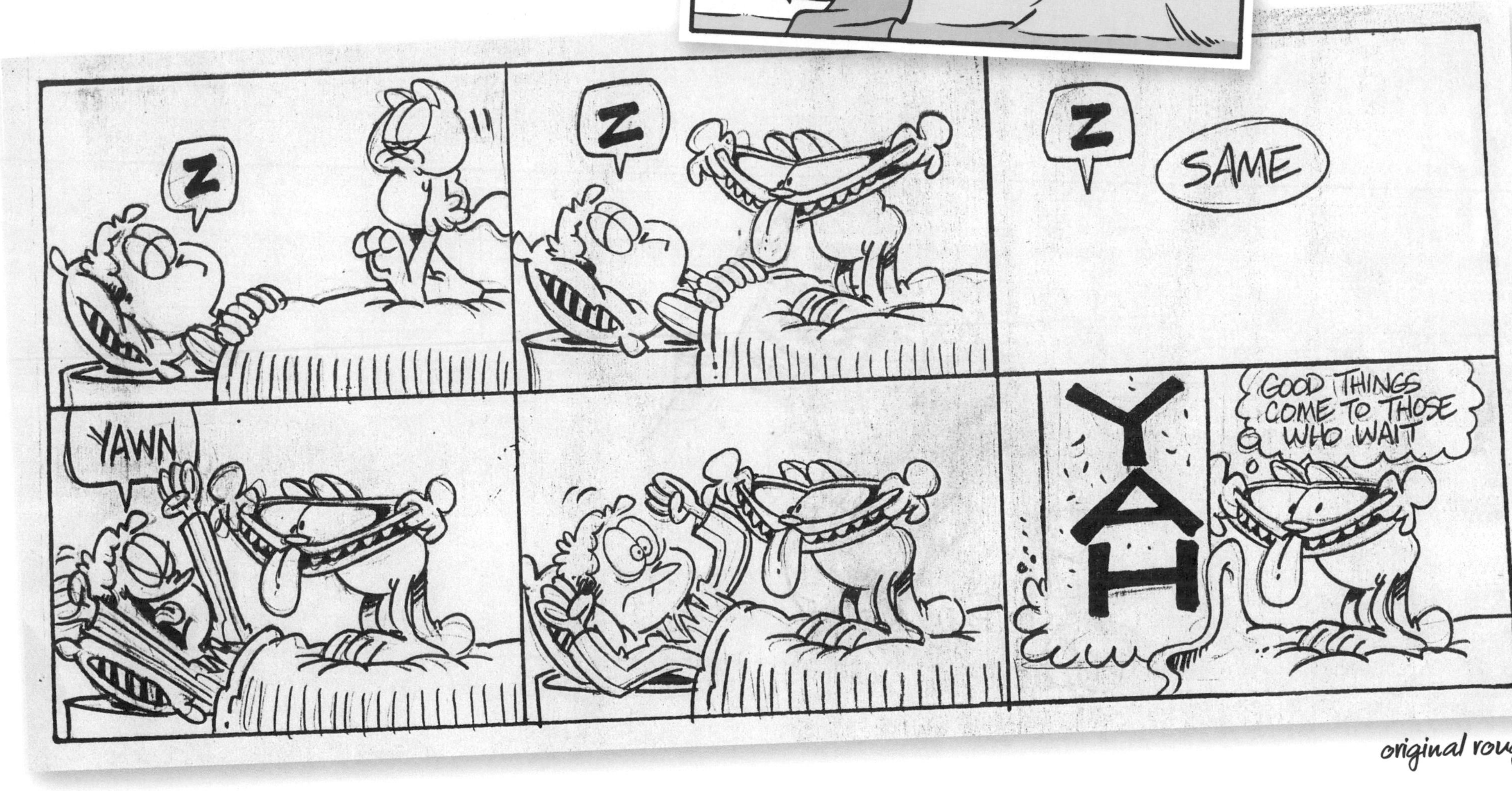
Z
Z
Z
SAME
YAWN
YAH
GOOD THINGS COME TO THOSE WHO WAIT

original rough

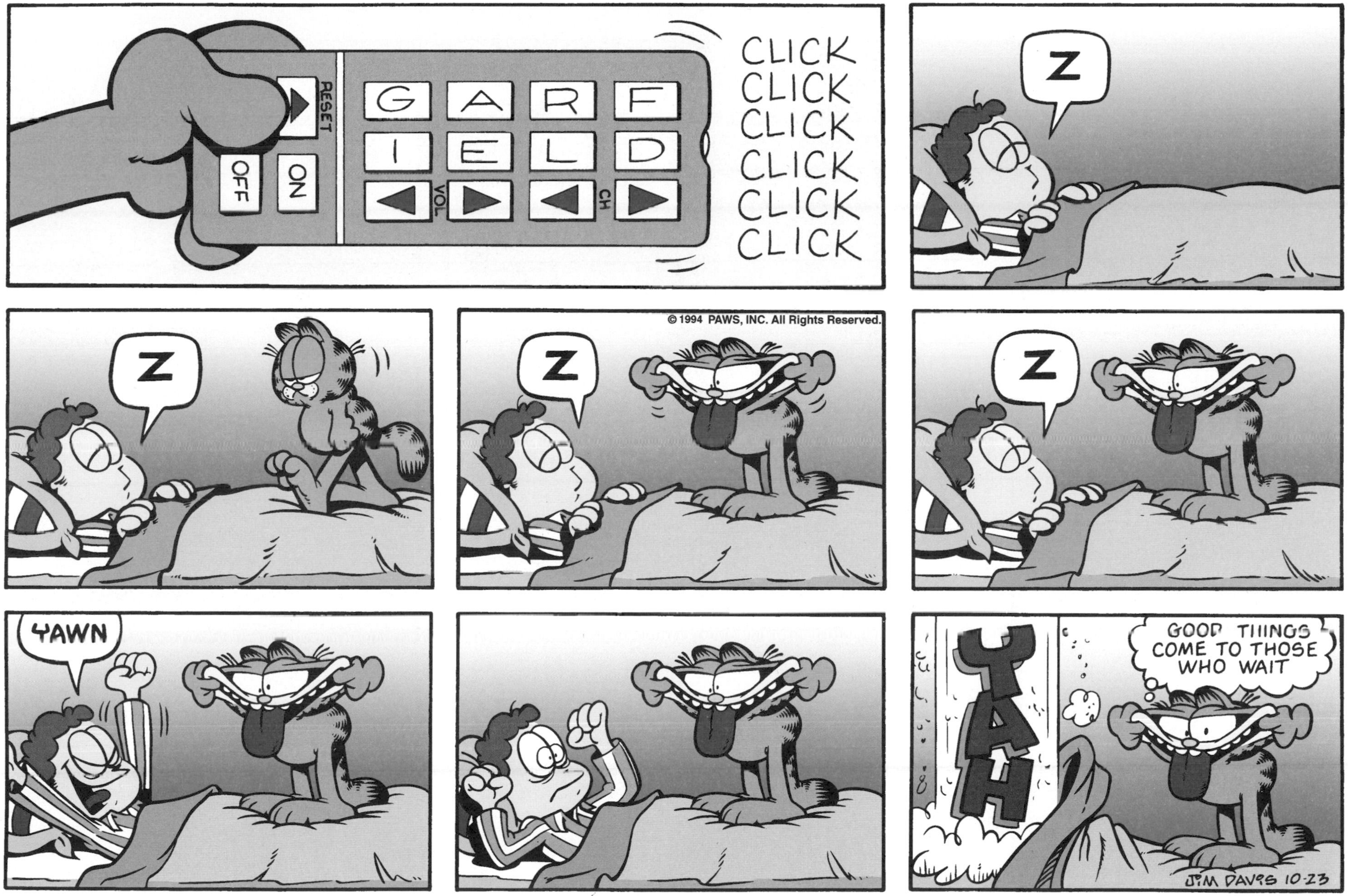
RESET
G A R F
I E L D
ON
OFF
VOL
CH
CLICK
CLICK
CLICK
CLICK
CLICK
CLICK
Z
Z
© 1994 PAWS, INC. All Rights Reserved.
Z
Z
YAWN
YAAH
GOOD THINGS COME TO THOSE WHO WAIT
JIM DAVIS 10-23

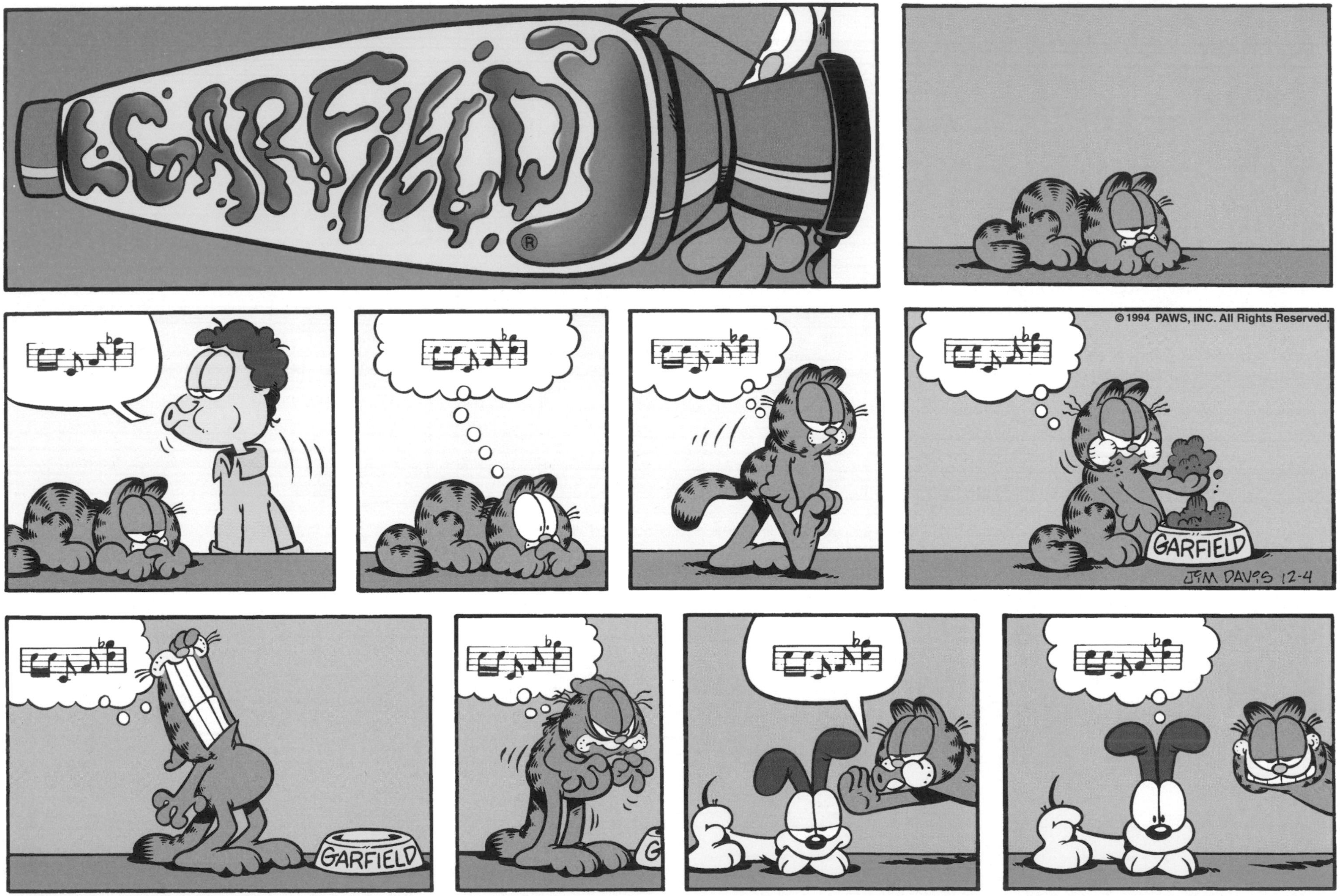
GARFIELD®
© 1994 PAWS, INC. All Rights Reserved.
GARFIELD
JIM DAVIS 12-4
GARFIELD

I get lots of suggestions for strip situations. One day someone said, "Hey, what if everyone confides in Pooky?" The gag was in my head before I could get to the drawing pad!

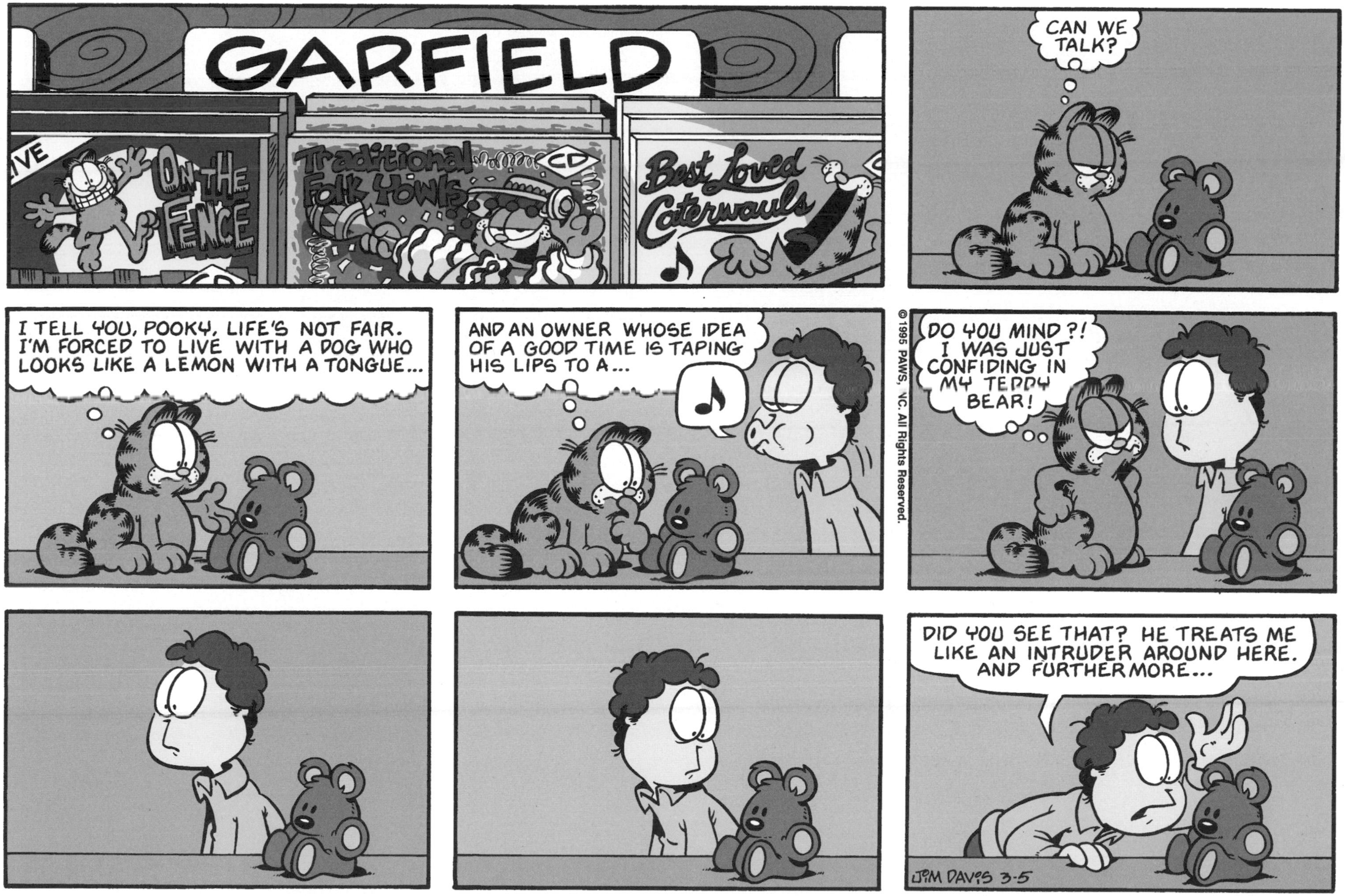

GARFIELD
ON THE FENCE
Traditional Folk Yowls
CD
Best Loved Caterwauls
CAN WE TALK?
I TELL YOU, POOKY, LIFE'S NOT FAIR. I'M FORCED TO LIVE WITH A DOG WHO LOOKS LIKE A LEMON WITH A TONGUE...
AND AN OWNER WHOSE IDEA OF A GOOD TIME IS TAPING HIS LIPS TO A...
© 1995 PAWS, INC. All Rights Reserved.
DO YOU MIND?! I WAS JUST CONFIDING IN MY TEDDY BEAR!
DID YOU SEE THAT? HE TREATS ME LIKE AN INTRUDER AROUND HERE. AND FURTHERMORE...
JIM DAVIS 3-5

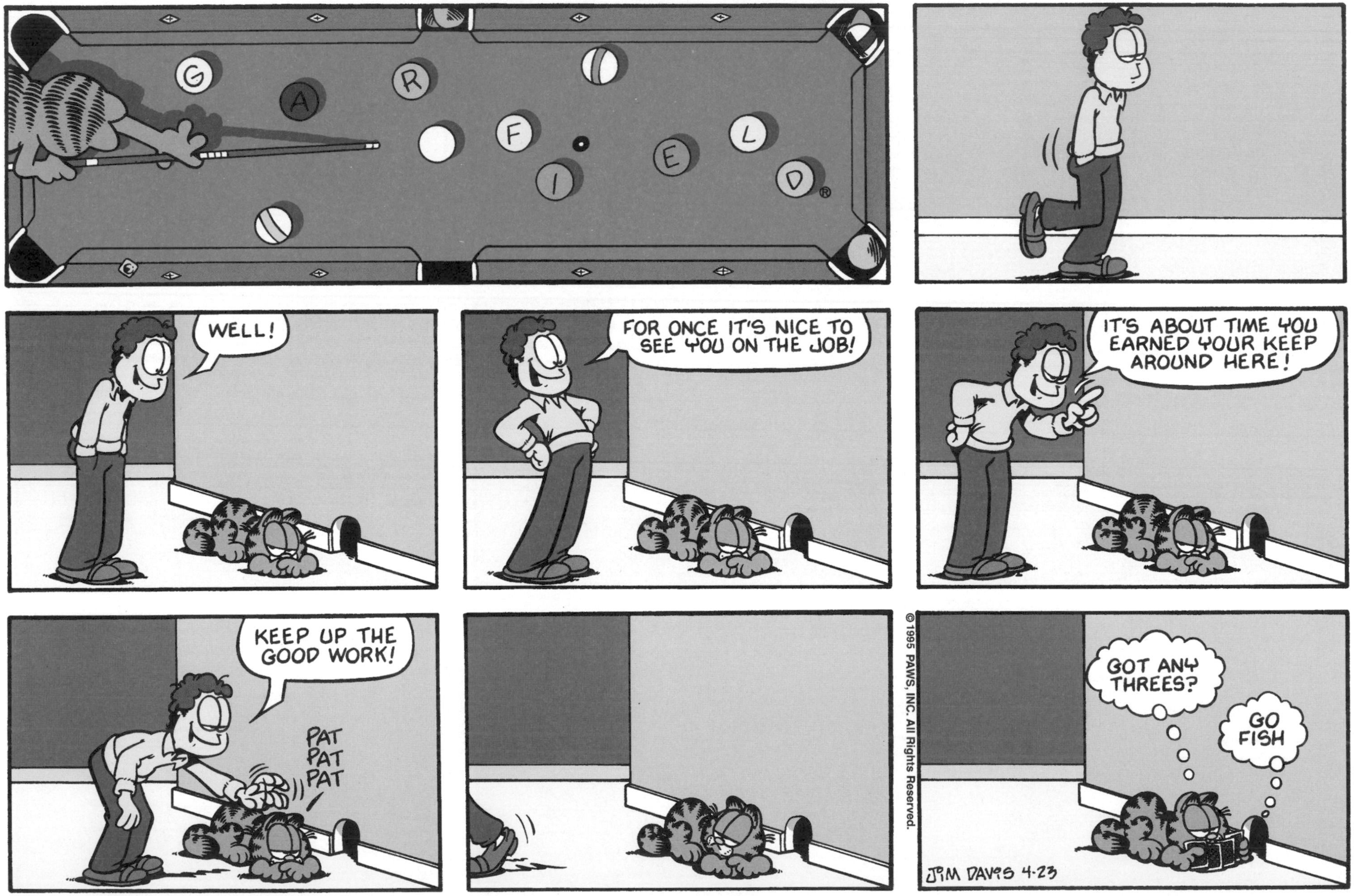
GARFIELD®
WELL!
FOR ONCE IT'S NICE TO SEE YOU ON THE JOB!
IT'S ABOUT TIME YOU EARNED YOUR KEEP AROUND HERE!
KEEP UP THE GOOD WORK!
PAT PAT PAT
GOT ANY THREES?
GO FISH
JIM DAVIS 4-23
© 1995 PAWS, INC. All Rights Reserved.

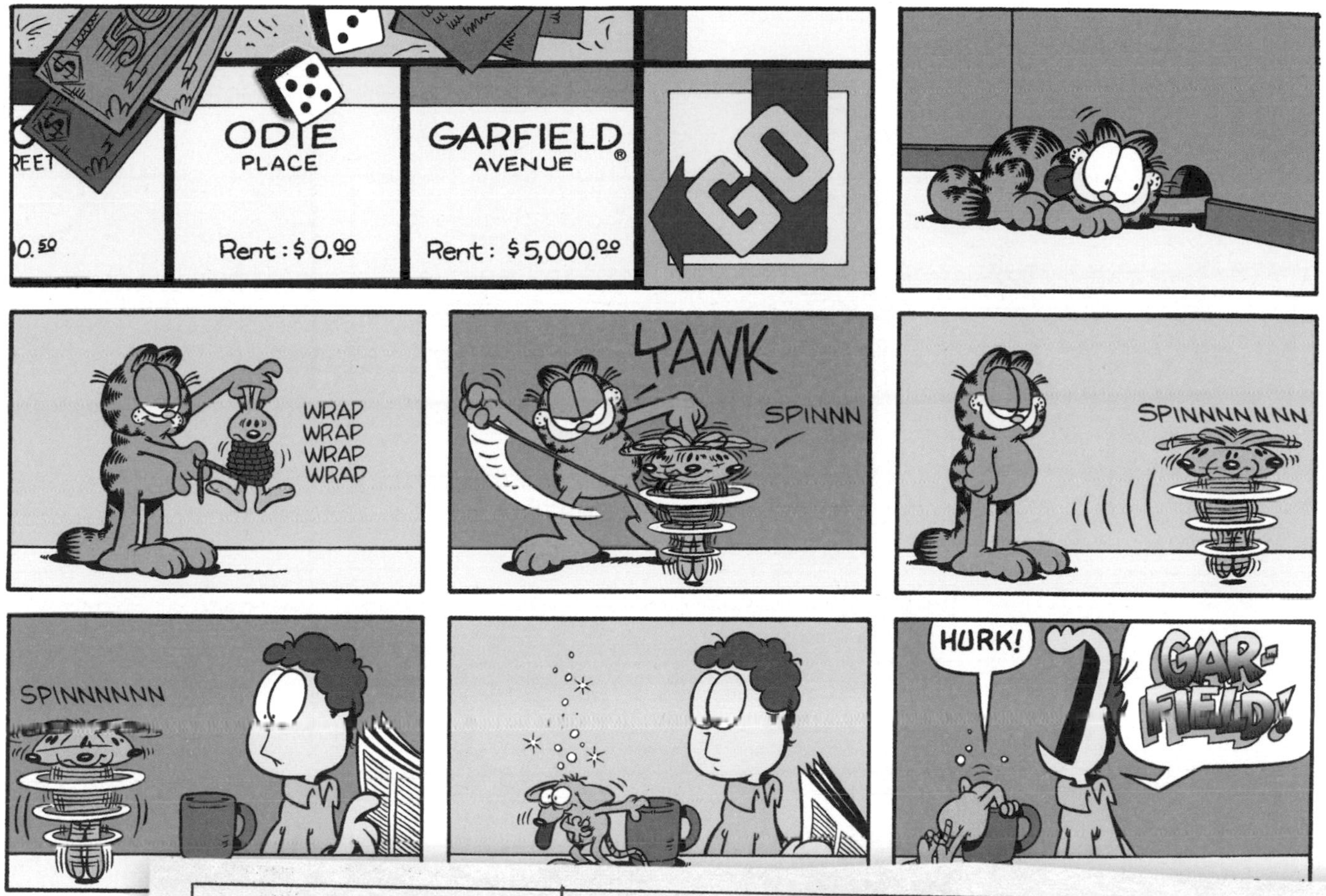
ODIE
PLACE
Rent: $ 0.00
GARFIELD
AVENUE
Rent: $ 5,000.00
GO
WRAP
WRAP
WRAP
WRAP
YANK
SPINNN
SPINNNNNNNN
SPINNNNNNN
HURK!
GAR-FIELD!

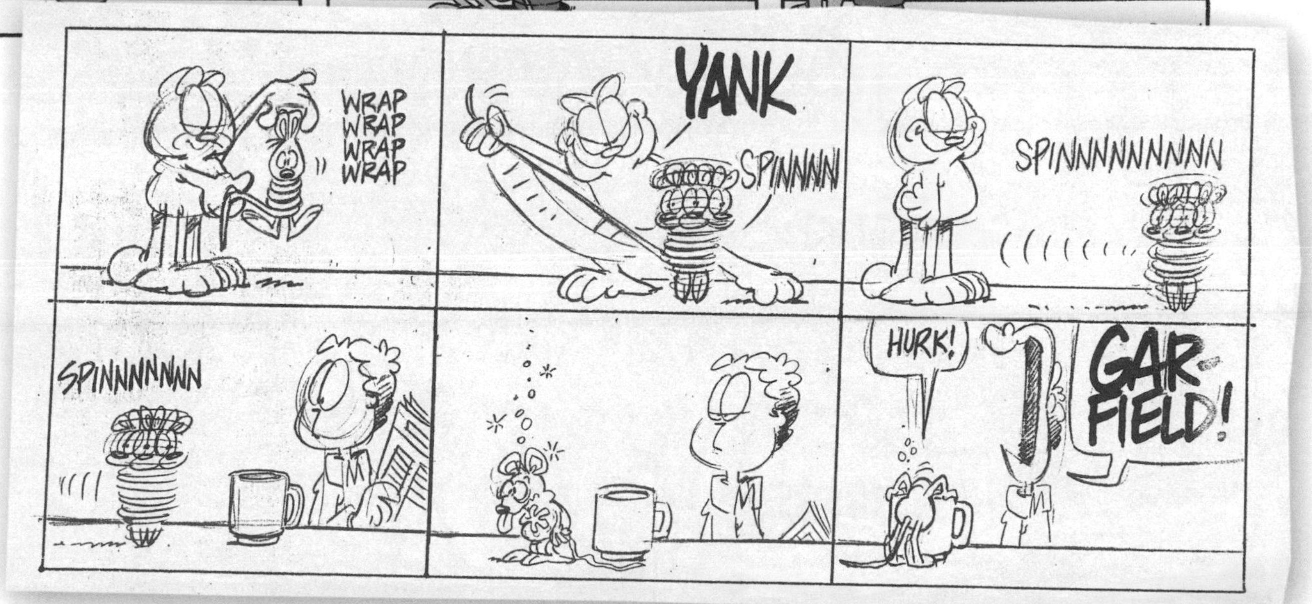
WRAP
WRAP
WRAP
WRAP
YANK
SPINNNN
SPINNNNNNNNNN
SPINNNNNNN
HURK!
GAR-FIELD!

original rough

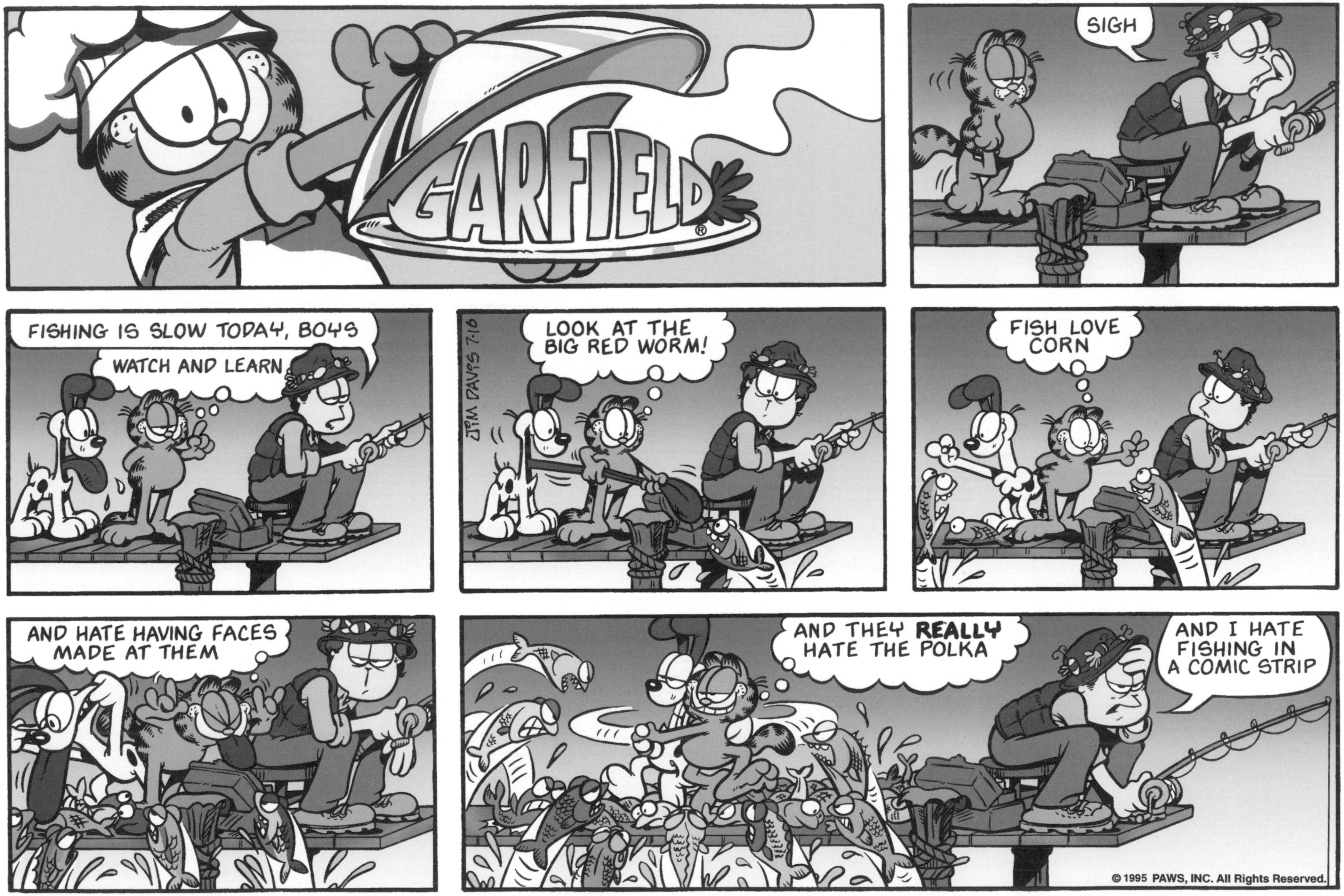
GARFIELD
SIGH
FISHING IS SLOW TODAY, BOYS
WATCH AND LEARN
JIM DAVIS 7-16
LOOK AT THE BIG RED WORM!
FISH LOVE CORN
AND HATE HAVING FACES MADE AT THEM
AND THEY **REALLY** HATE THE POLKA
AND I HATE FISHING IN A COMIC STRIP
© 1995 PAWS, INC. All Rights Reserved.

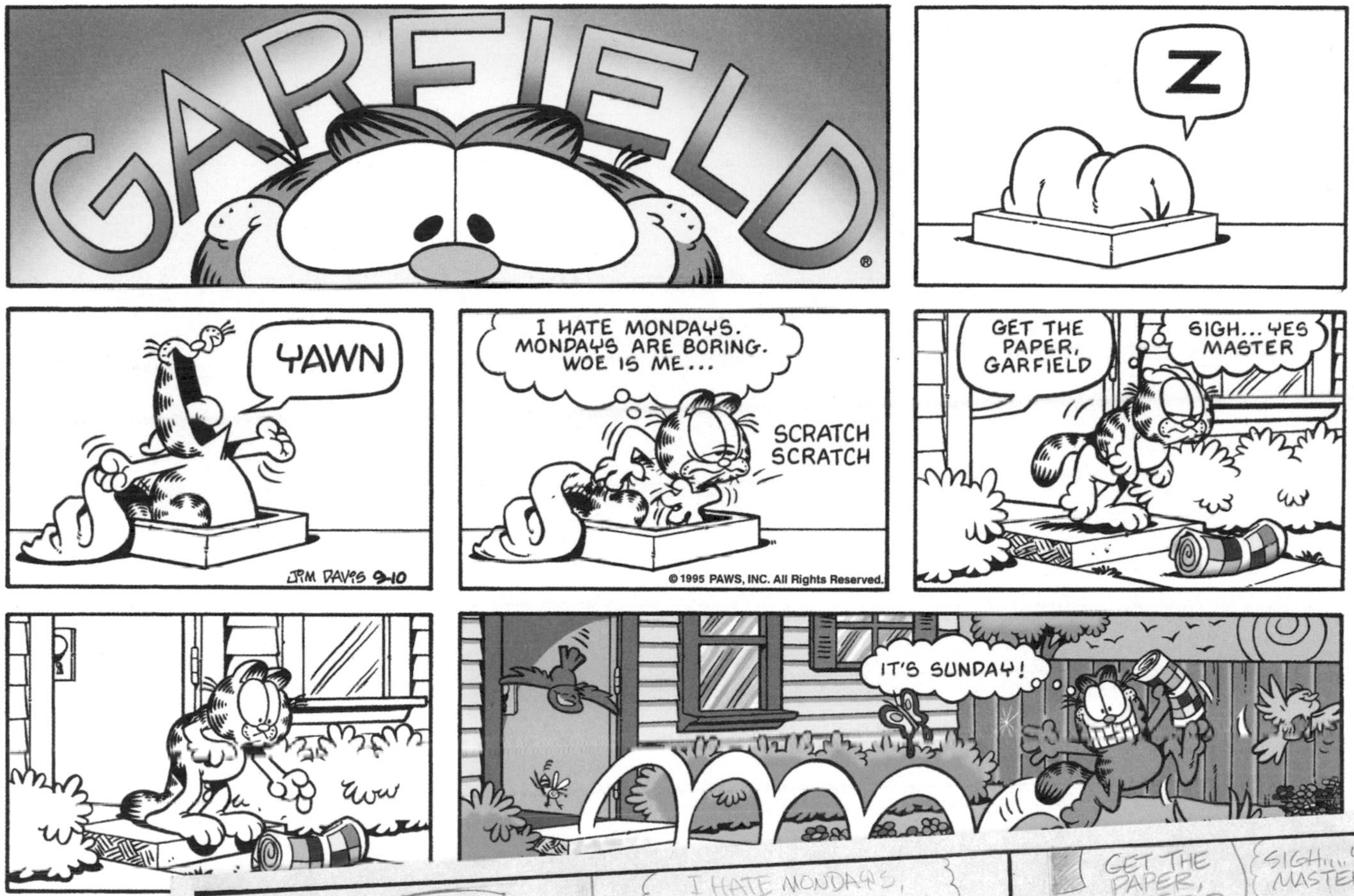
GARFIELD
Z
YAWN
I HATE MONDAYS. MONDAYS ARE BORING. WOE IS ME...
SCRATCH SCRATCH
JIM DAVIS 9-10
© 1995 PAWS, INC. All Rights Reserved.
GET THE PAPER, GARFIELD
SIGH... YES MASTER
IT'S SUNDAY!

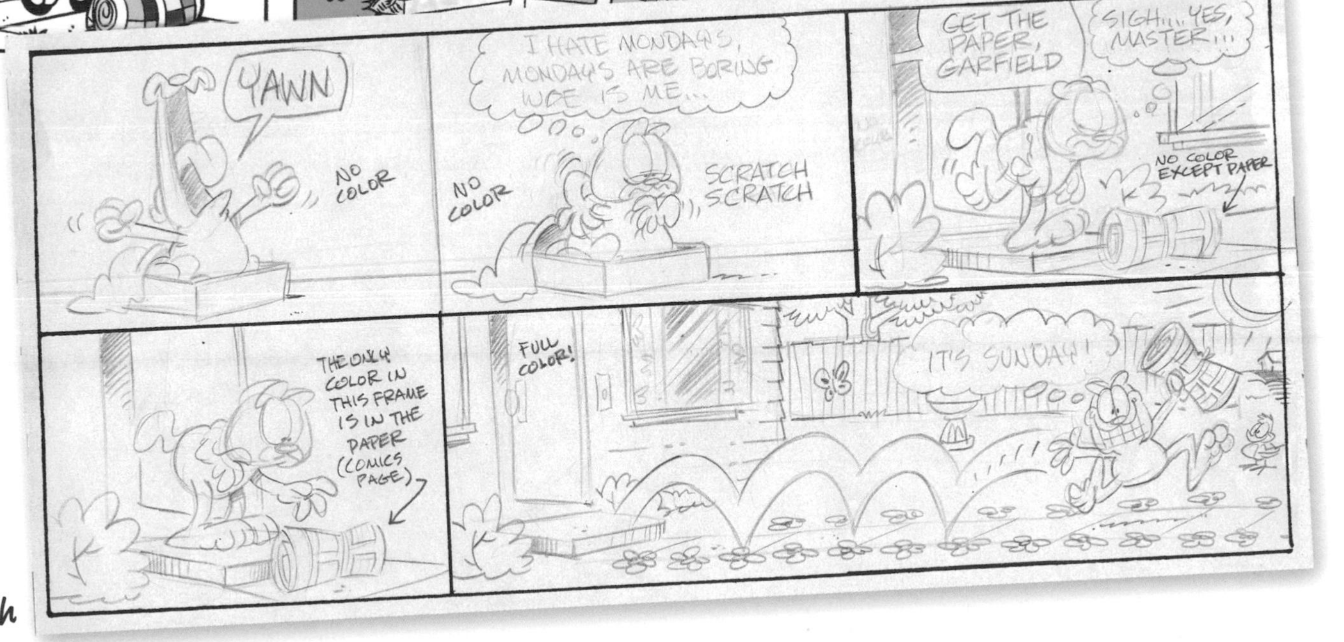
YAWN
NO COLOR
I HATE MONDAYS, MONDAYS ARE BORING WOE IS ME...
NO COLOR
SCRATCH SCRATCH
GET THE PAPER, GARFIELD
SIGH... YES, MASTER...
NO COLOR EXCEPT PAPER
THE ONLY COLOR IN THIS FRAME IS IN THE PAPER (COMICS PAGE)
FULL COLOR!
IT'S SUNDAY!

original rough

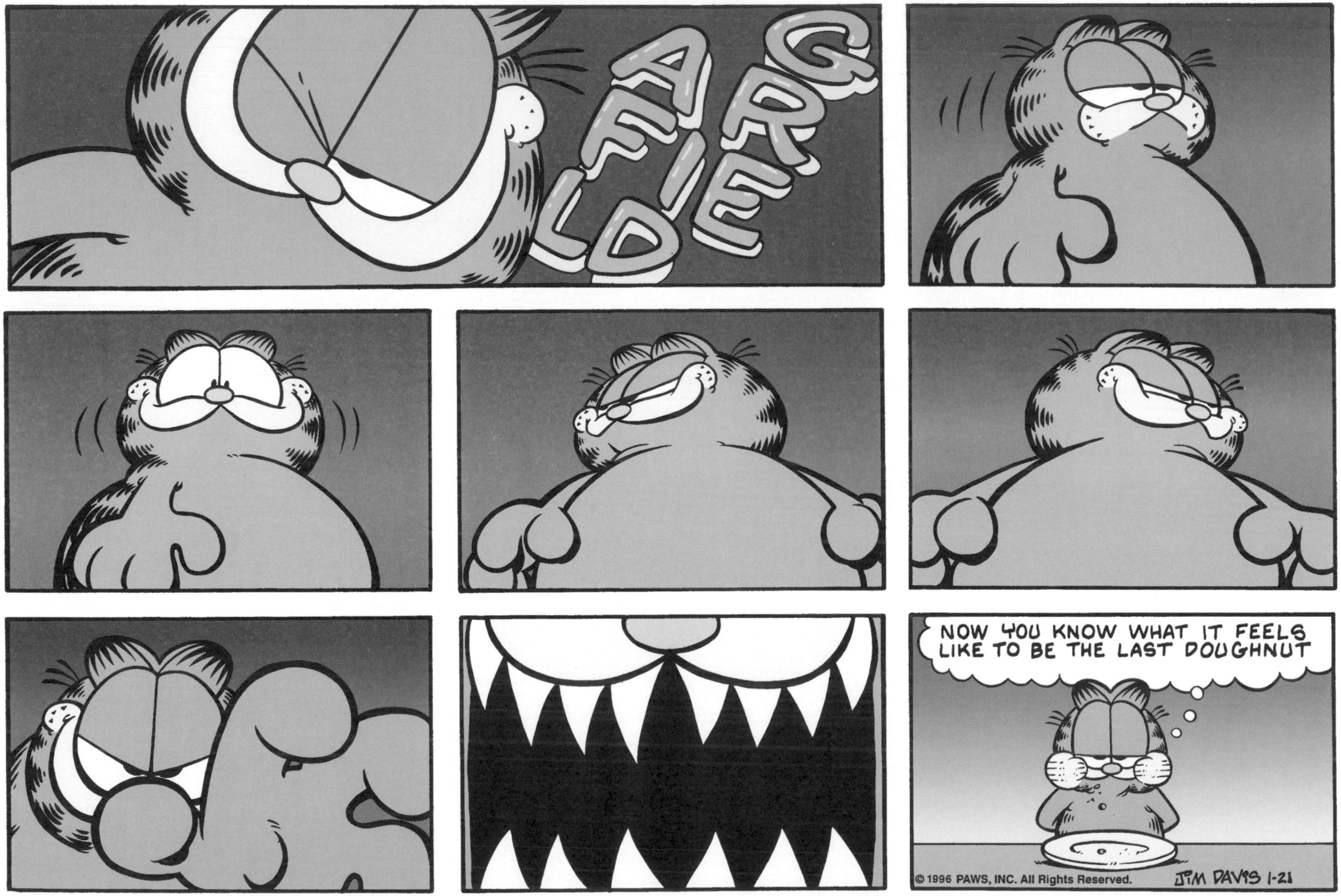
GARFIELD
NOW YOU KNOW WHAT IT FEELS LIKE TO BE THE LAST DOUGHNUT
© 1996 PAWS, INC. All Rights Reserved.
JIM DAVIS 1-21

"SQUIRRRT," "SPLORT," and "PLOOT" may not be in the dictionary, but that doesn't mean that they're not funny as heck!

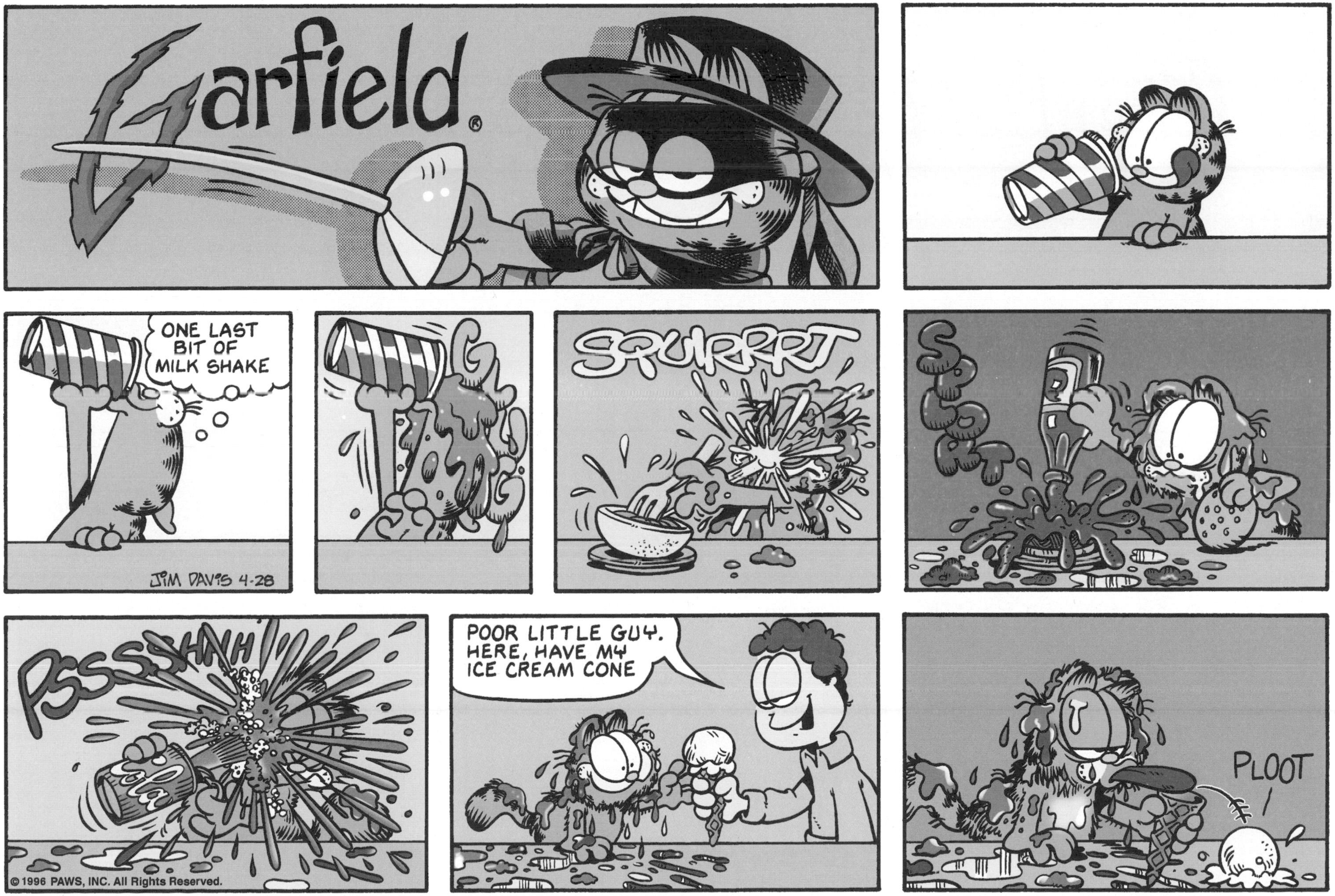
Garfield®
ONE LAST BIT OF MILK SHAKE
JIM DAVIS 4-28
SQUIRRRT
SPLORT
PSSSSHHH
© 1996 PAWS, INC. All Rights Reserved.
POOR LITTLE GUY. HERE, HAVE MY ICE CREAM CONE
PLOOT

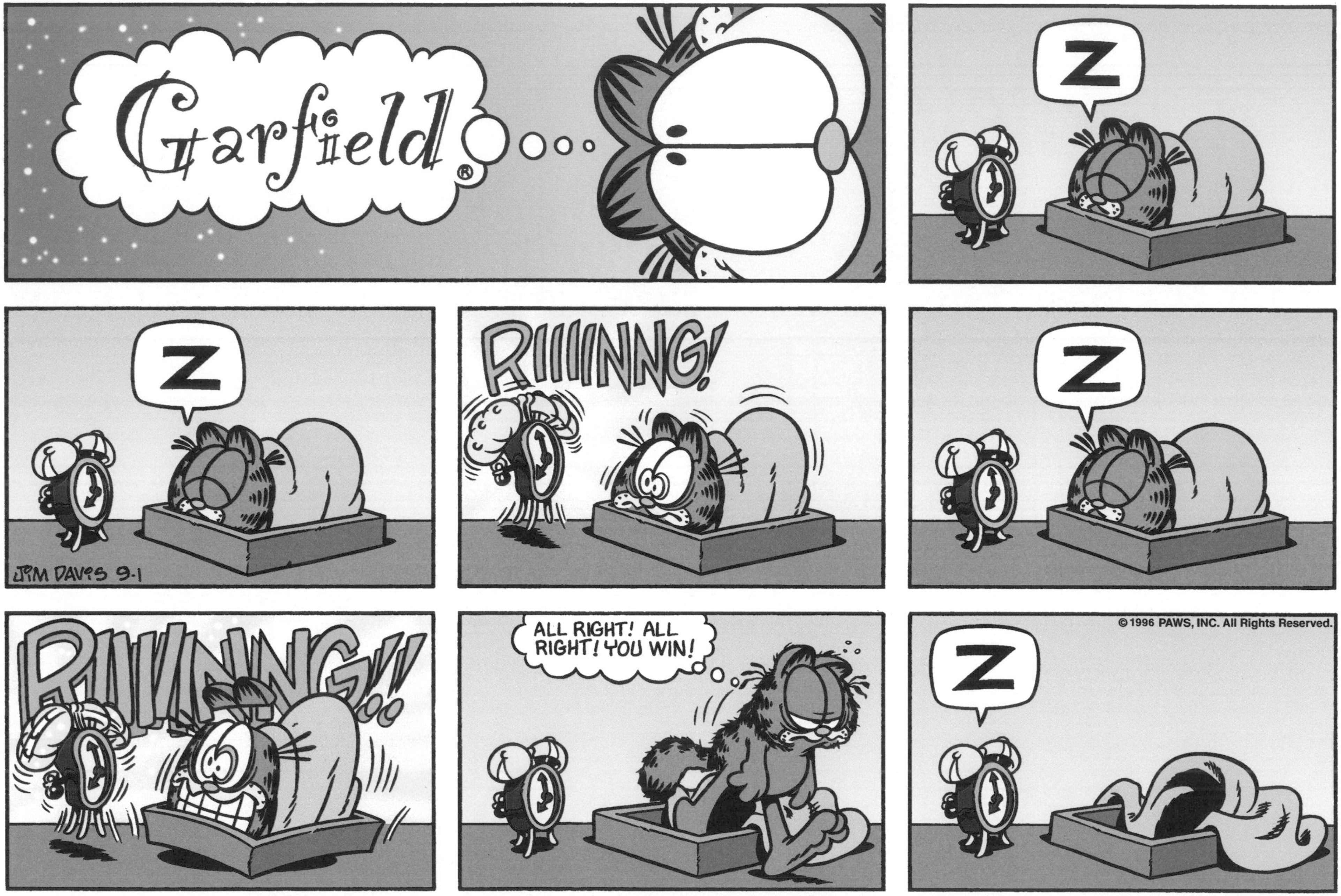
Garfield®
Z
Z
JIM DAVIS 9-1
RIIIINNG!
Z
RIIIINNG!!
ALL RIGHT! ALL RIGHT! YOU WIN!
© 1996 PAWS, INC. All Rights Reserved.
Z

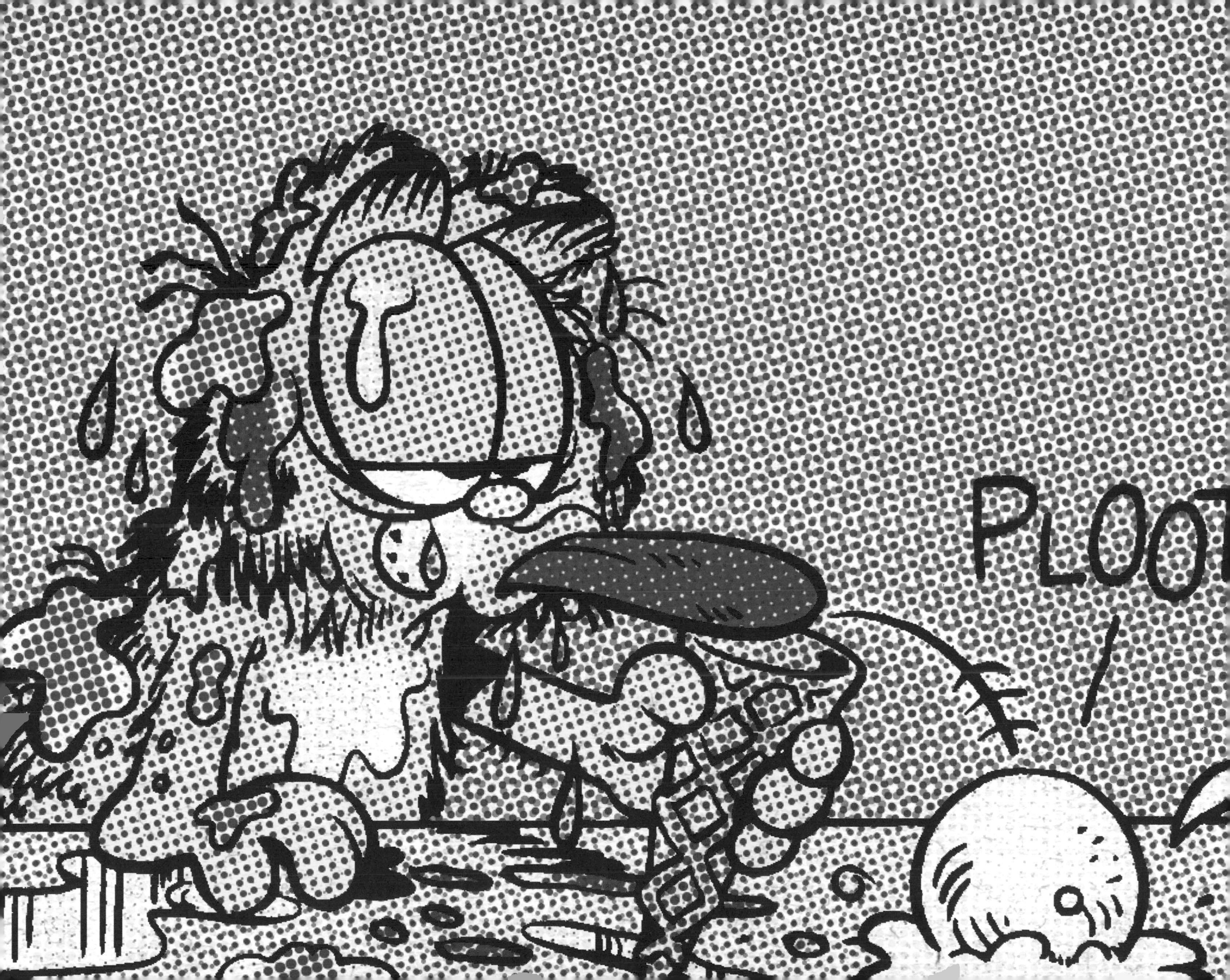
PLOOT!

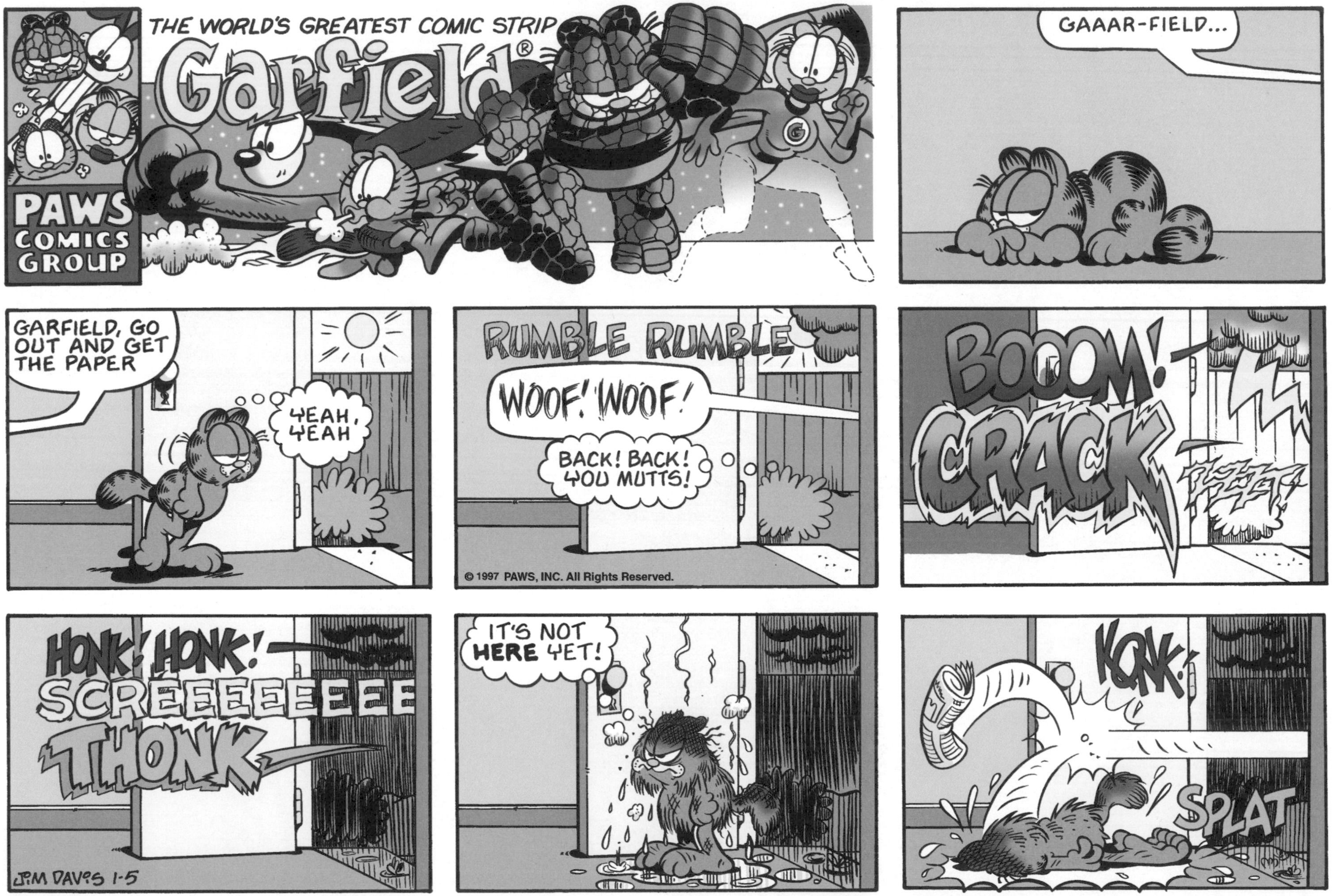
THE WORLD'S GREATEST COMIC STRIP
Garfield®
PAWS COMICS GROUP
GAAAR-FIELD...
GARFIELD, GO OUT AND GET THE PAPER
YEAH, YEAH
RUMBLE RUMBLE
WOOF! WOOF!
BACK! BACK! YOU MUTTS!
© 1997 PAWS, INC. All Rights Reserved.
BOOOM!
CRACK
HONK! HONK!
SCREEEEEEEEEE
THONK
JIM DAVIS 1-5
IT'S NOT **HERE** YET!
KONK!
SPLAT

This gag rides that fine line between funny and disturbing. I hope that it's the former.

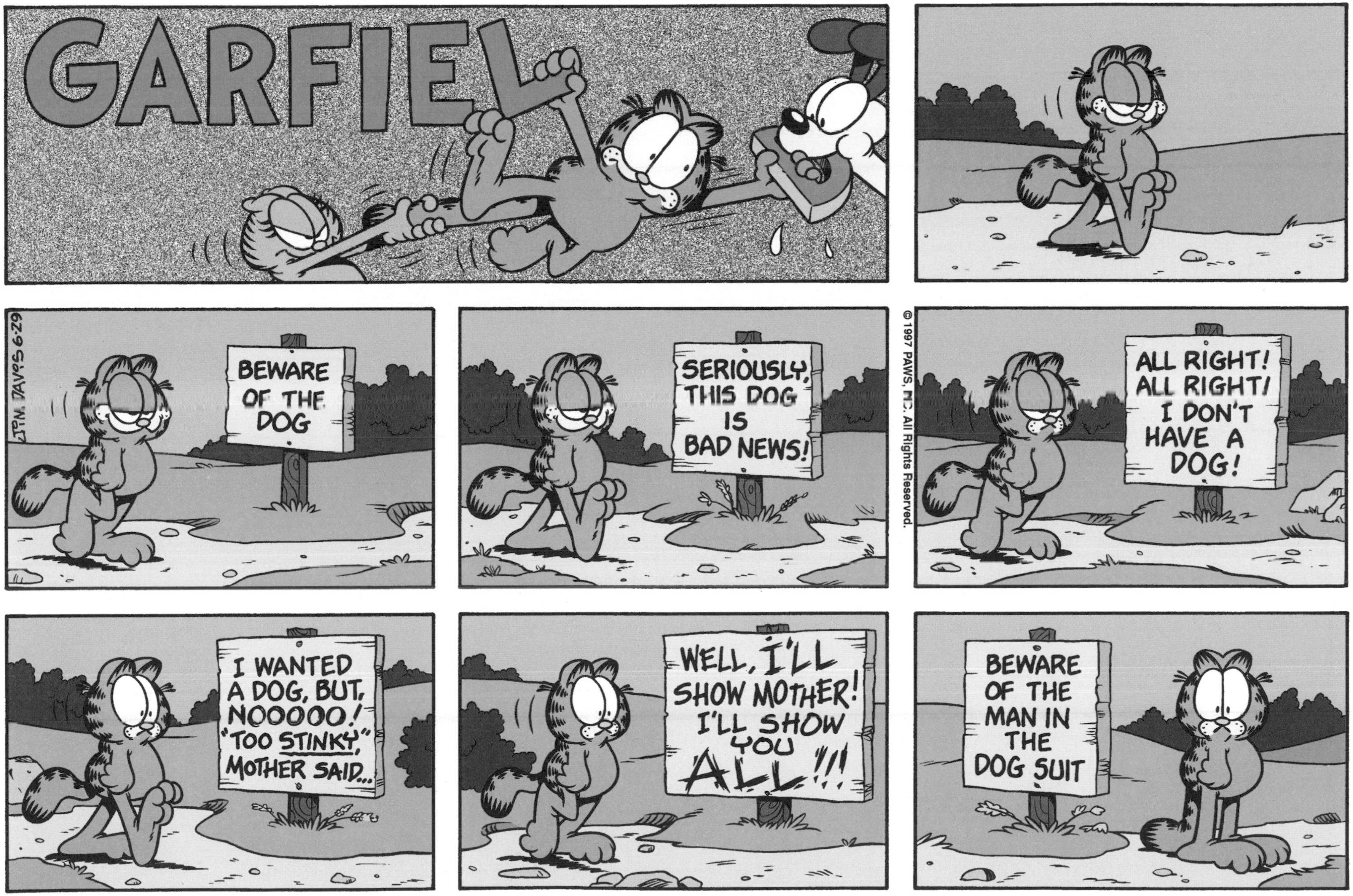
GARFIEL
JPM DAVIS 6·29
BEWARE OF THE DOG
SERIOUSLY, THIS DOG IS BAD NEWS!
© 1997 PAWS, INC. All Rights Reserved.
ALL RIGHT! ALL RIGHT! I DON'T HAVE A DOG!
I WANTED A DOG, BUT, NOOOOO! "TOO STINKY," MOTHER SAID...
WELL, I'LL SHOW MOTHER! I'LL SHOW YOU ALL!!!
BEWARE OF THE MAN IN THE DOG SUIT

Someone said, "Humor is when something bad happens to someone else." Enjoy . . .

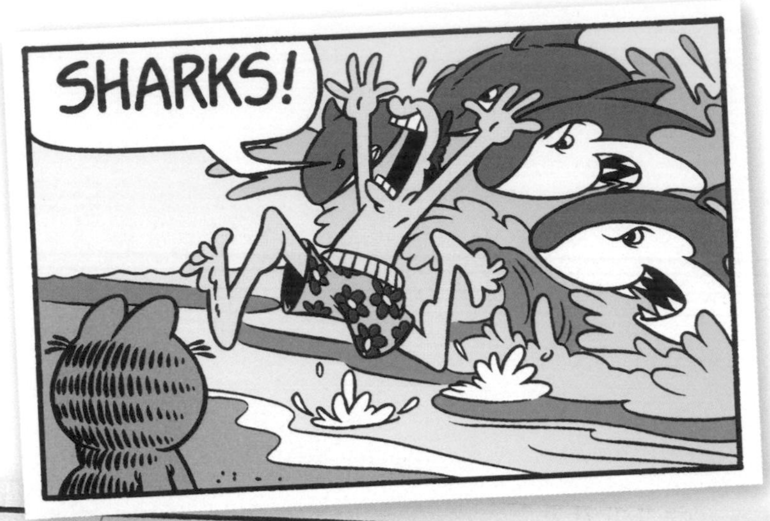
SHARKS!

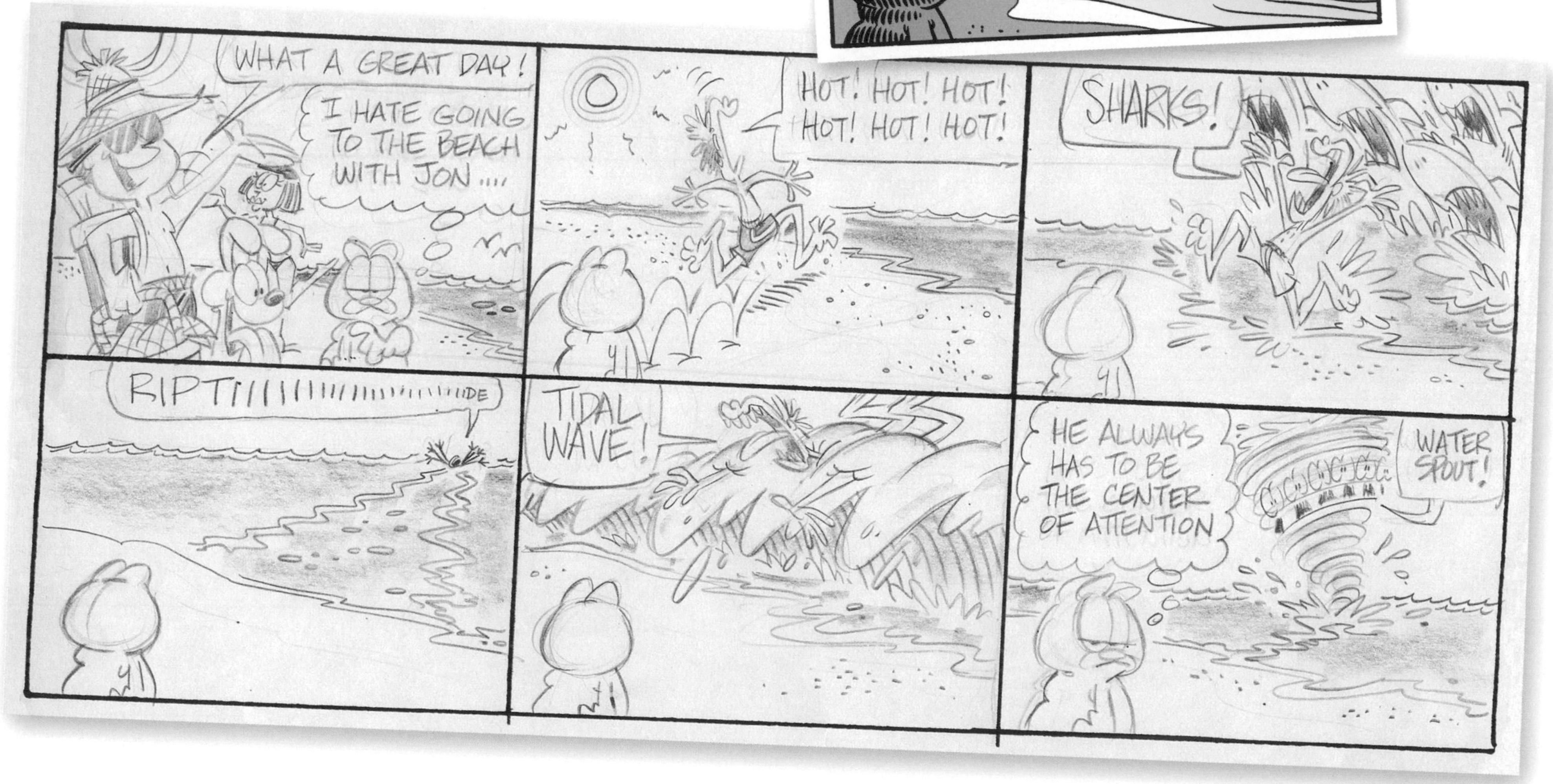
WHAT A GREAT DAY!
I HATE GOING TO THE BEACH WITH JON....
HOT! HOT! HOT! HOT! HOT! HOT!
SHARKS!
RIPTIIIIIIIIIIIIIIIIIIIIIIDE
TIDAL WAVE!
HE ALWAYS HAS TO BE THE CENTER OF ATTENTION
WATER SPOUT!

original rough

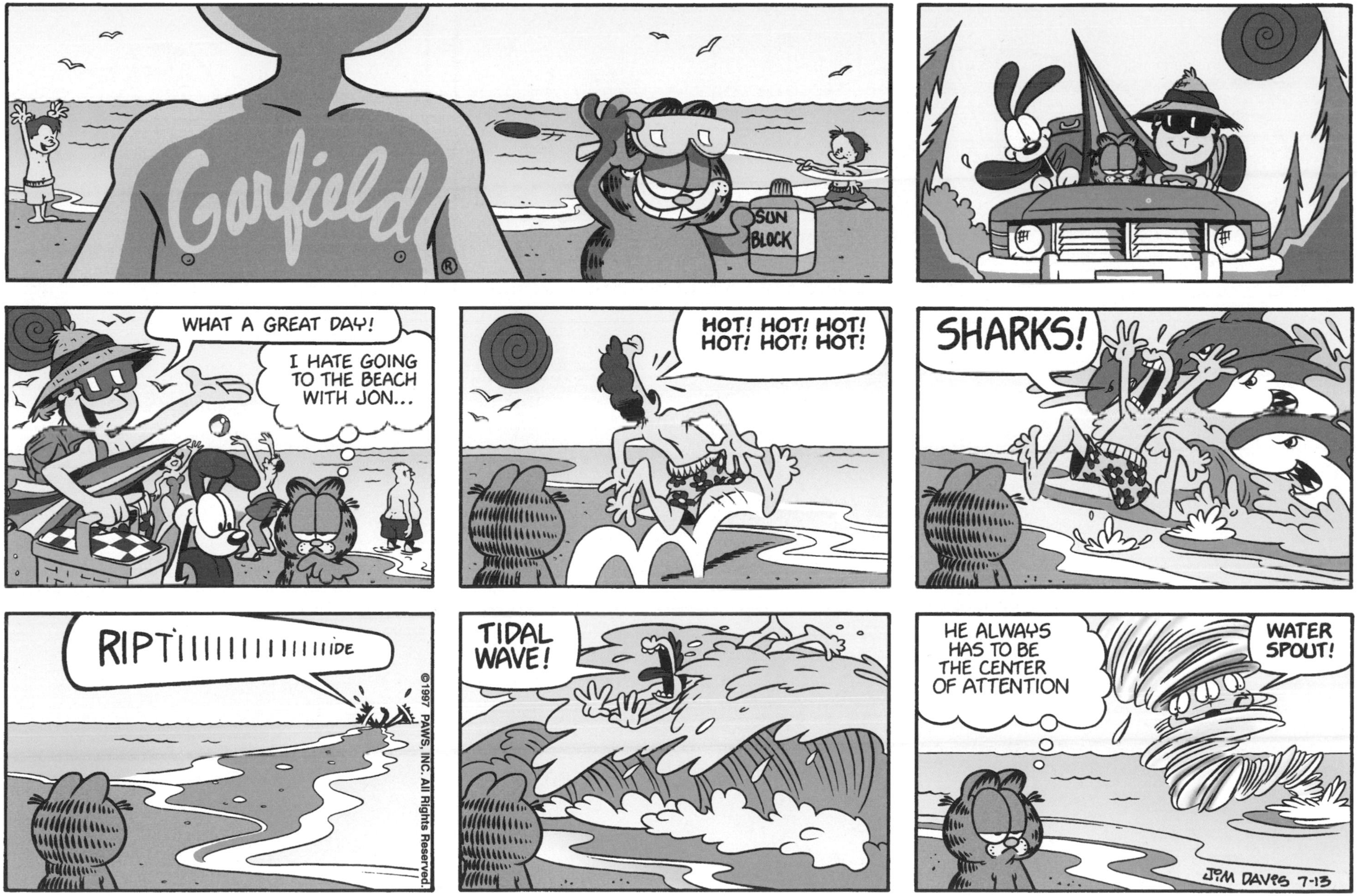
Garfield®
SUN BLOCK
WHAT A GREAT DAY!
I HATE GOING TO THE BEACH WITH JON...
HOT! HOT! HOT! HOT! HOT! HOT!
SHARKS!
RIPTIIIIIIIIIIIIIIIIIDE
©1997 PAWS, INC. All Rights Reserved.
TIDAL WAVE!
HE ALWAYS HAS TO BE THE CENTER OF ATTENTION
WATER SPOUT!
JIM DAVIS 7-13

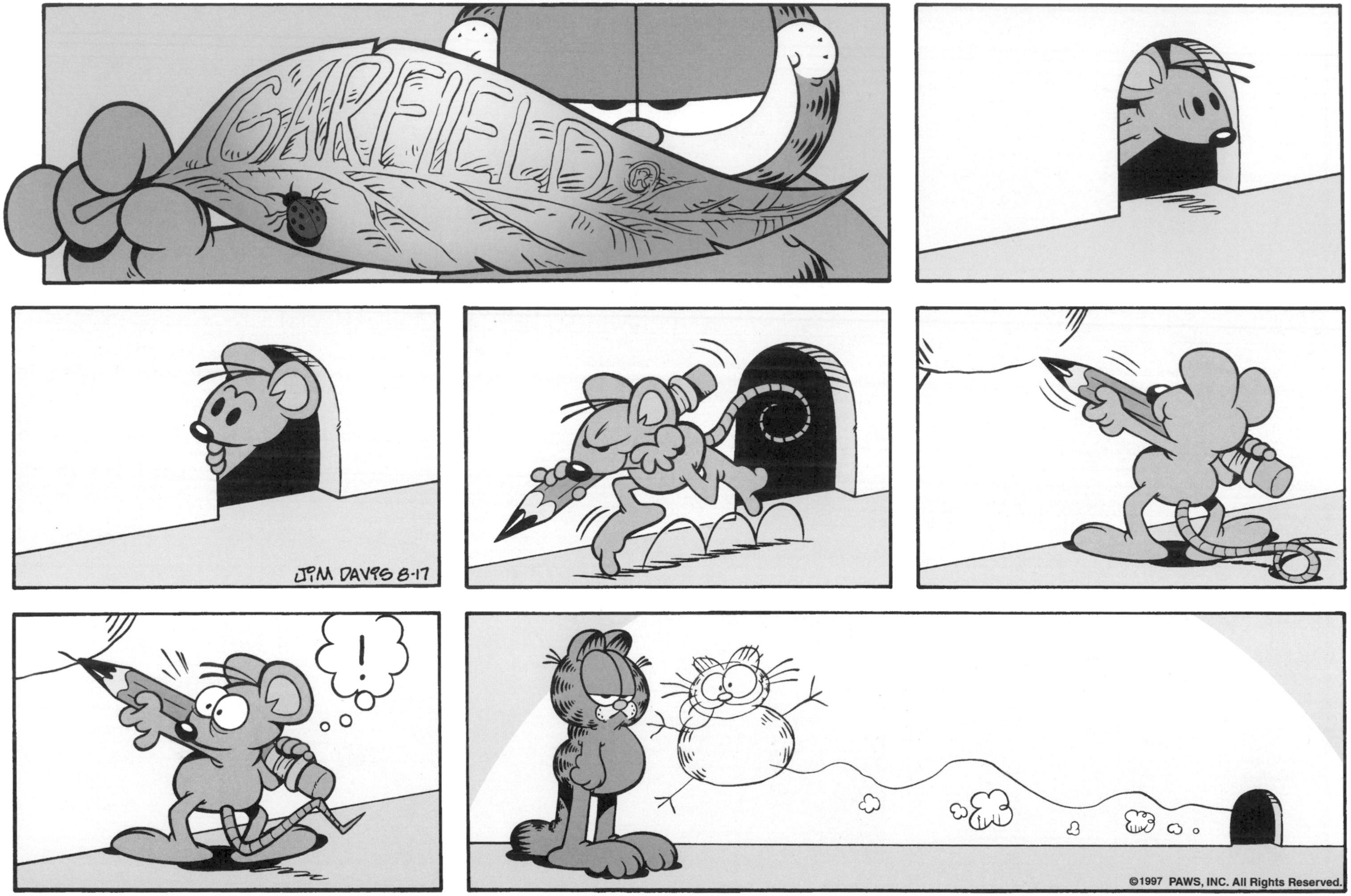
GARFIELD®
JIM DAVIS 8-17
!
©1997 PAWS, INC. All Rights Reserved.

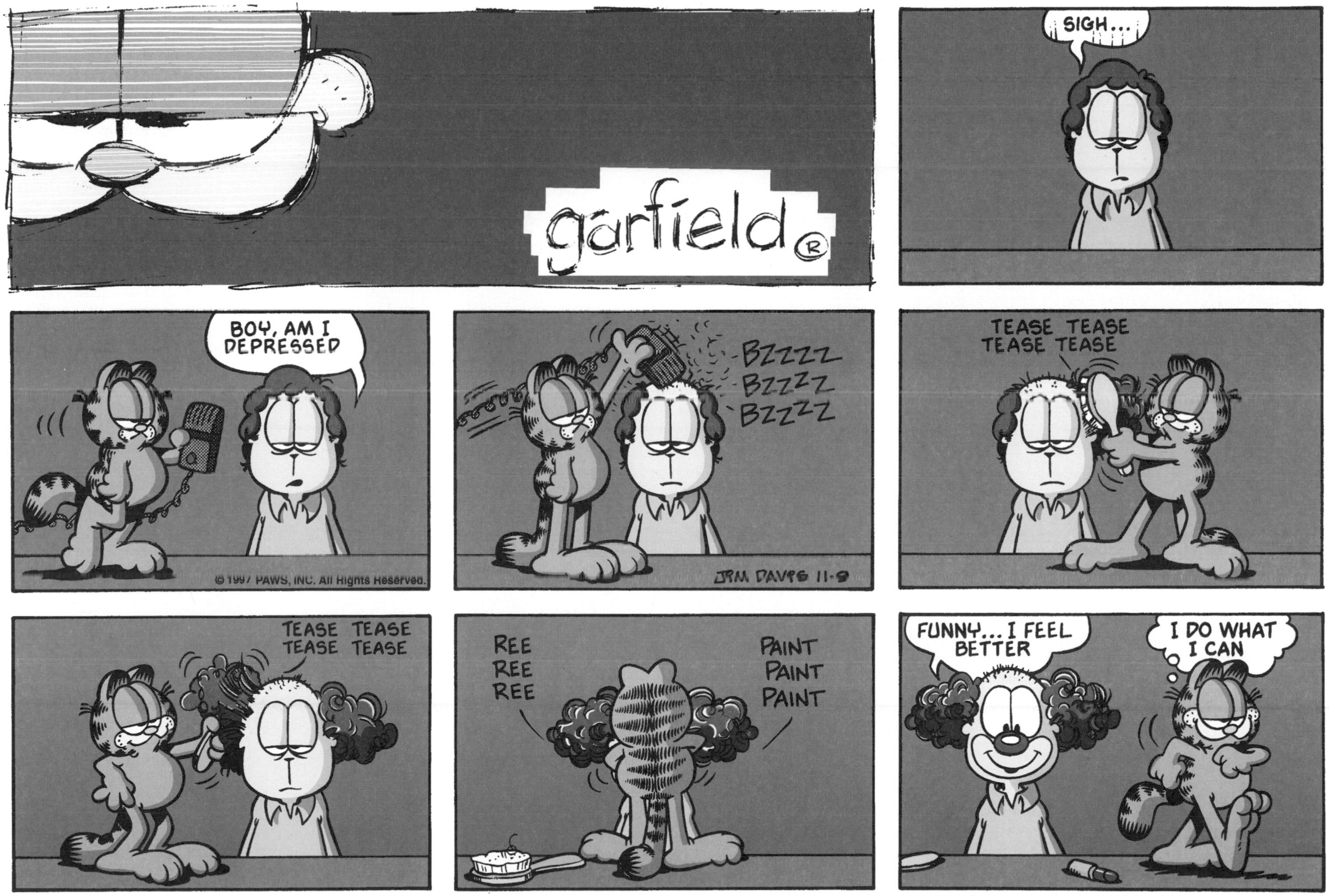
garfield®
SIGH...
BOY, AM I DEPRESSED
© 1997 PAWS, INC. All Rights Reserved.
BZZZZ
BZZZZ
BZZZZ
JIM DAVIS 11-9
TEASE TEASE
TEASE TEASE
TEASE TEASE
TEASE TEASE
REE
REE
REE
PAINT
PAINT
PAINT
FUNNY... I FEEL BETTER
I DO WHAT I CAN

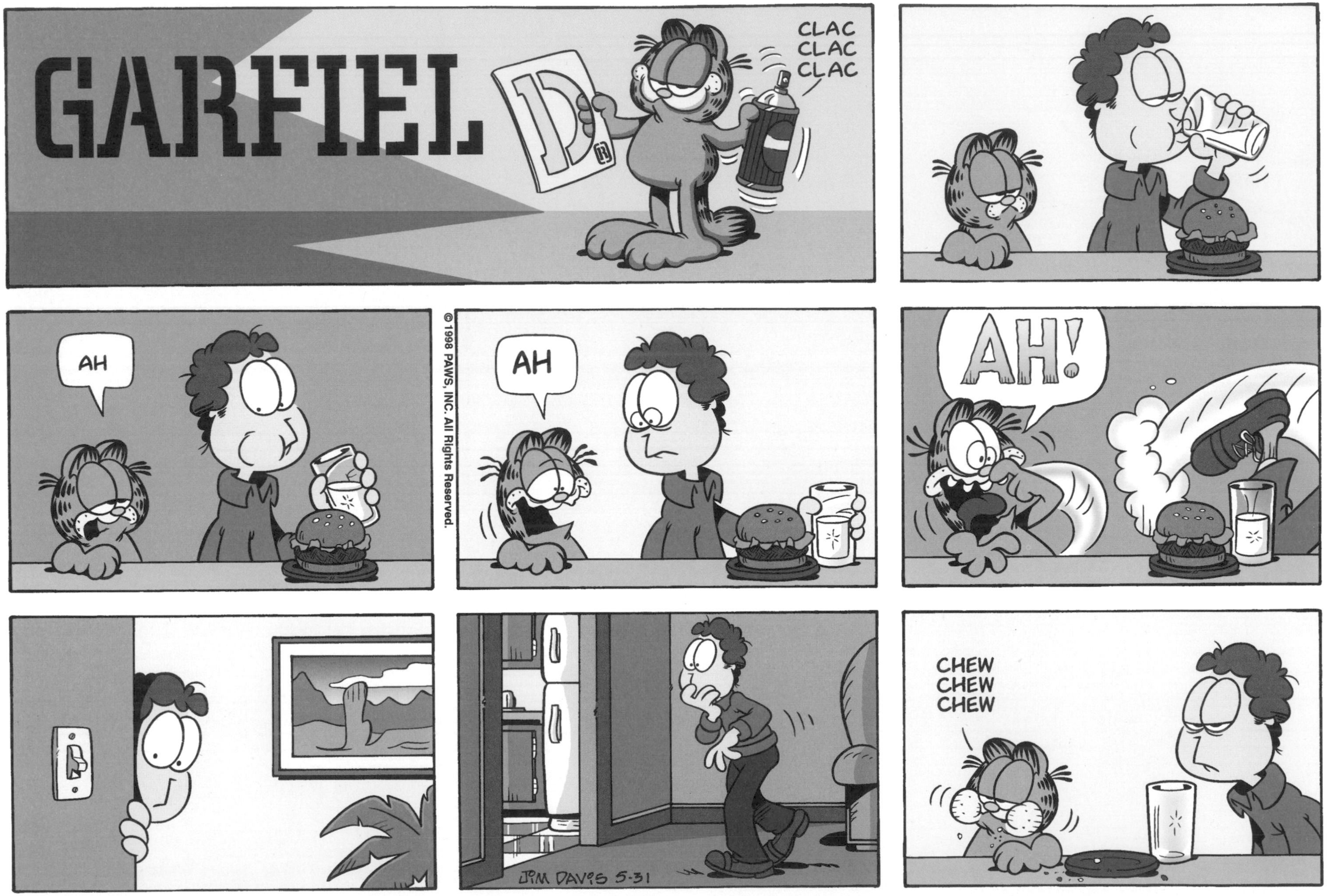
GARFIEL
CLAC
CLAC
CLAC
AH
AH
AH!
JIM DAVIS 5-31
CHEW
CHEW
CHEW

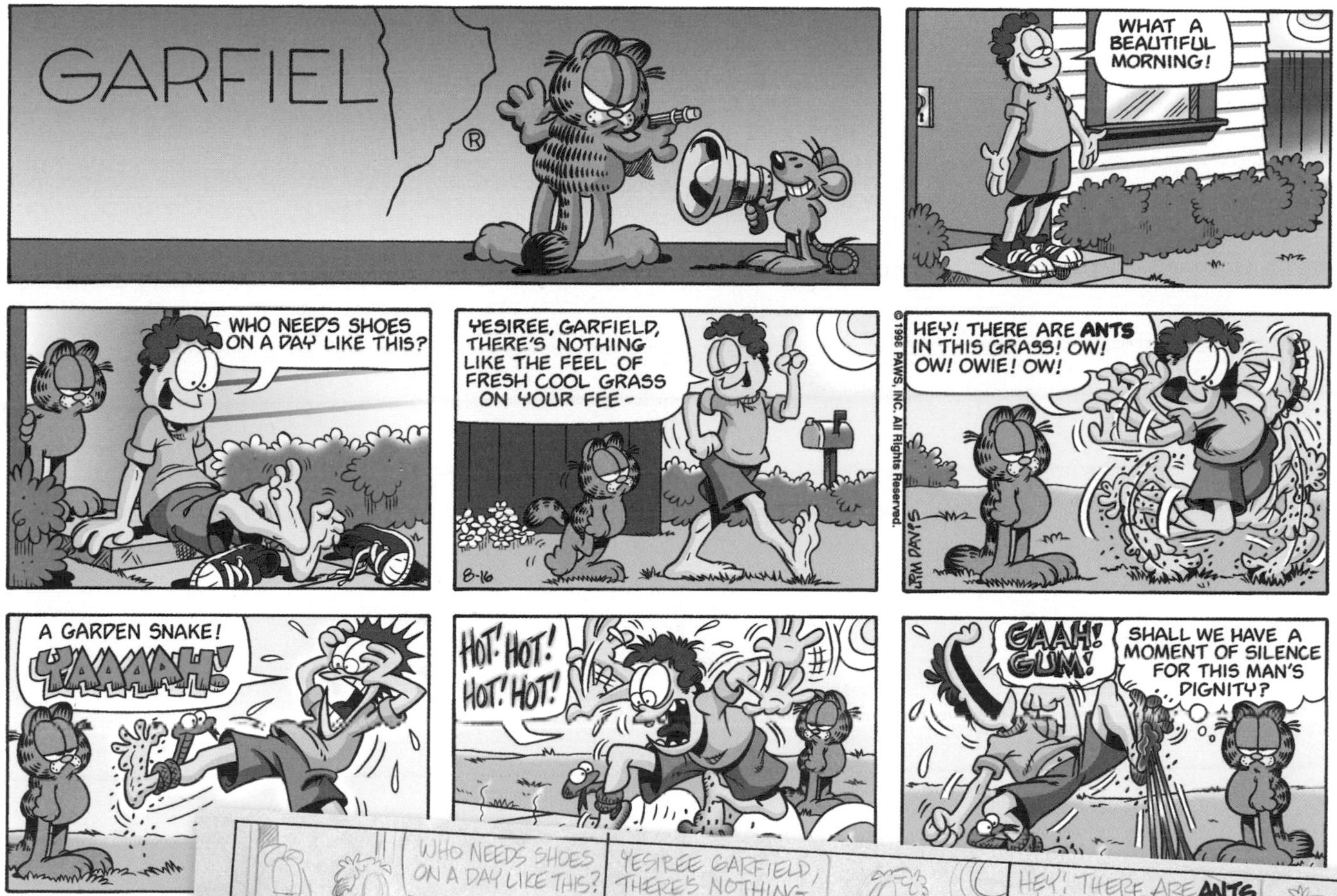
GARFIEL
®
WHAT A BEAUTIFUL MORNING!
WHO NEEDS SHOES ON A DAY LIKE THIS?
YESIREE, GARFIELD, THERE'S NOTHING LIKE THE FEEL OF FRESH COOL GRASS ON YOUR FEE-
8-16
© 1998 PAWS, INC. All Rights Reserved.
JIM DAVIS
HEY! THERE ARE **ANTS** IN THIS GRASS! OW! OW! OWIE! OW!
A GARDEN SNAKE!
YAAAAH!
HOT! HOT! HOT! HOT!
GAAH! GUM!
SHALL WE HAVE A MOMENT OF SILENCE FOR THIS MAN'S DIGNITY?

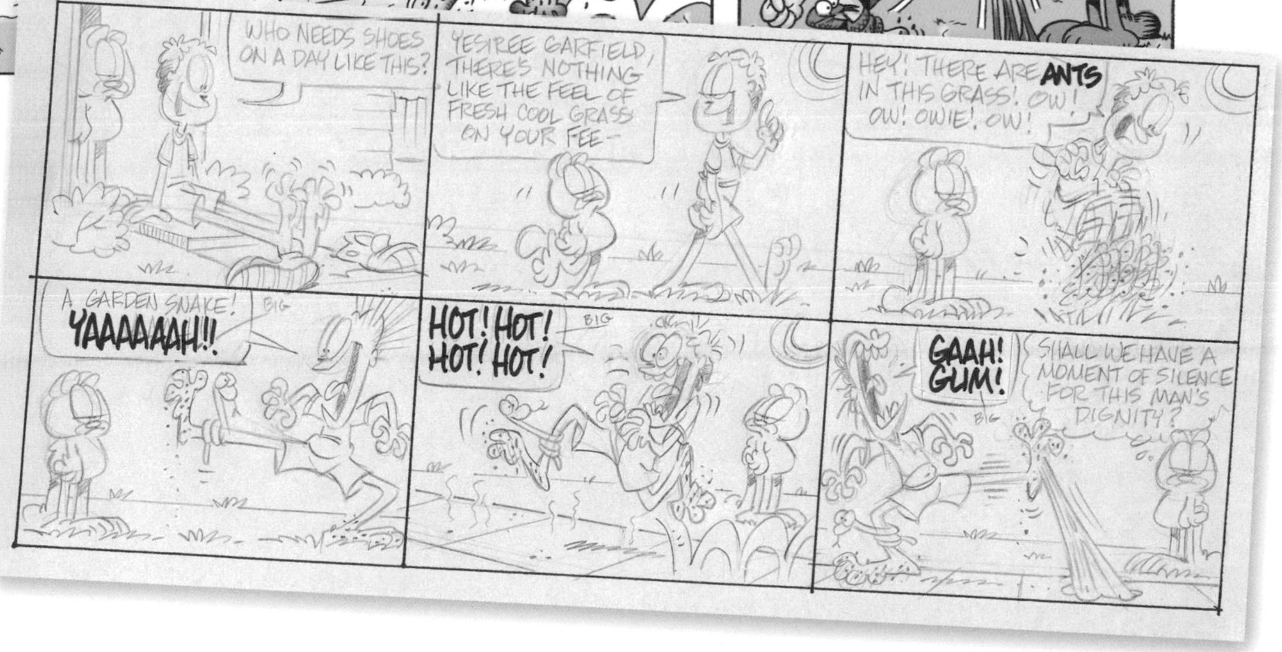
WHO NEEDS SHOES ON A DAY LIKE THIS?
YESIREE GARFIELD, THERE'S NOTHING LIKE THE FEEL OF FRESH COOL GRASS ON YOUR FEE-
HEY! THERE ARE **ANTS** IN THIS GRASS! OW! OW! OWIE! OW!
A GARDEN SNAKE!
BIG
YAAAAAAH!!
HOT! HOT! HOT! HOT!
BIG
GAAH! GUM!
BIG
SHALL WE HAVE A MOMENT OF SILENCE FOR THIS MAN'S DIGNITY?

original rough

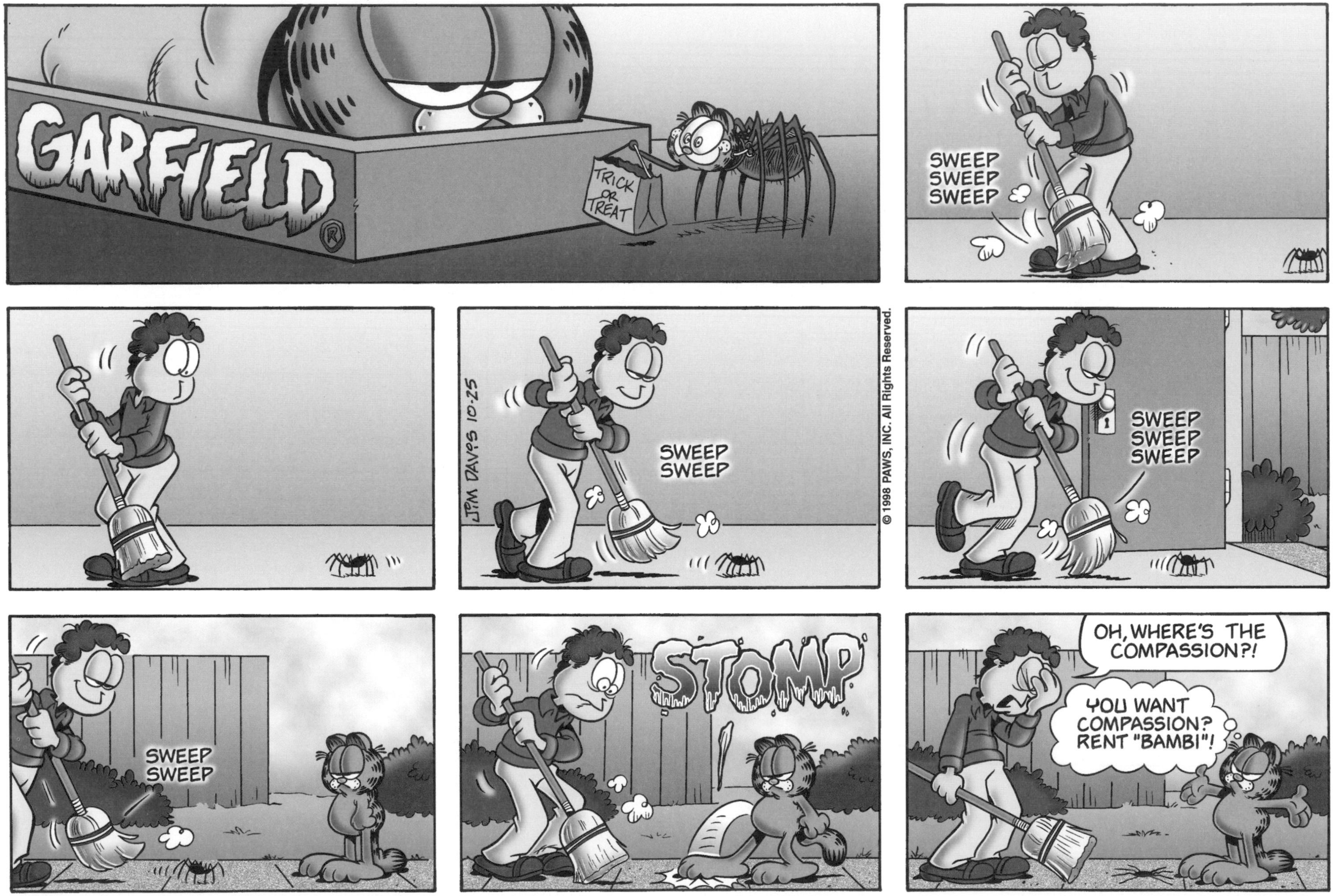
GARFIELD
TRICK OR TREAT
SWEEP SWEEP SWEEP
JPM DAVPS 10-25
SWEEP SWEEP
© 1998 PAWS, INC. All Rights Reserved.
SWEEP SWEEP SWEEP
SWEEP SWEEP
STOMP
OH, WHERE'S THE COMPASSION?!
YOU WANT COMPASSION? RENT "BAMBI"!

"Anthropomorphism" is the word used to describe giving human traits to animals . . . always a crowd pleaser.

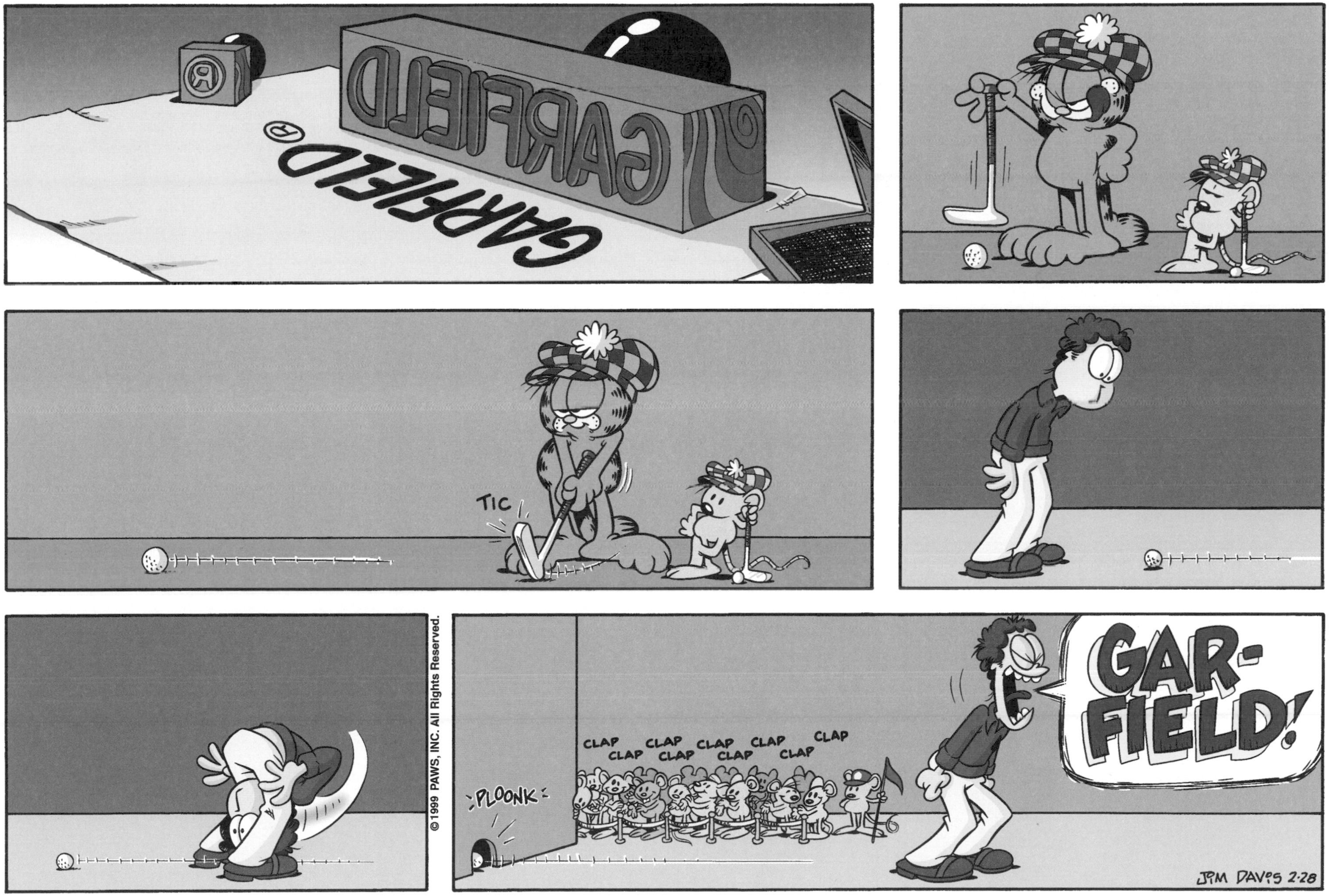

GARFIELD®
TIC
PLOONK
CLAP CLAP CLAP CLAP CLAP CLAP CLAP CLAP CLAP
GAR-FIELD!
©1999 PAWS, INC. All Rights Reserved.
JIM DAVIS 2-28

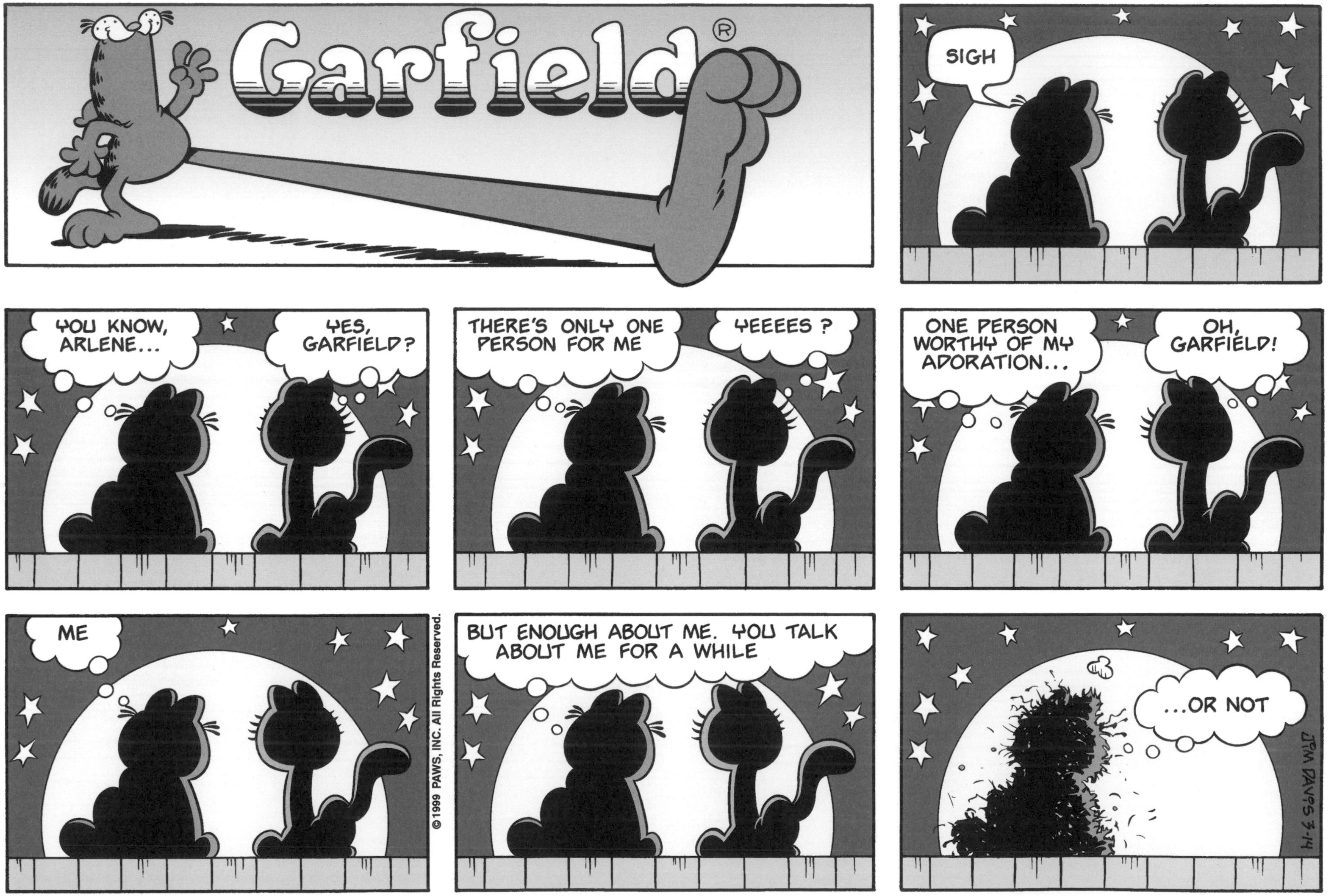
Garfield®
SIGH
YOU KNOW, ARLENE...
YES, GARFIELD?
THERE'S ONLY ONE PERSON FOR ME
YEEEES ?
ONE PERSON WORTHY OF MY ADORATION...
OH, GARFIELD!
ME
©1999 PAWS, INC. All Rights Reserved.
BUT ENOUGH ABOUT ME. YOU TALK ABOUT ME FOR A WHILE
...OR NOT
JIM DAVIS 3-14

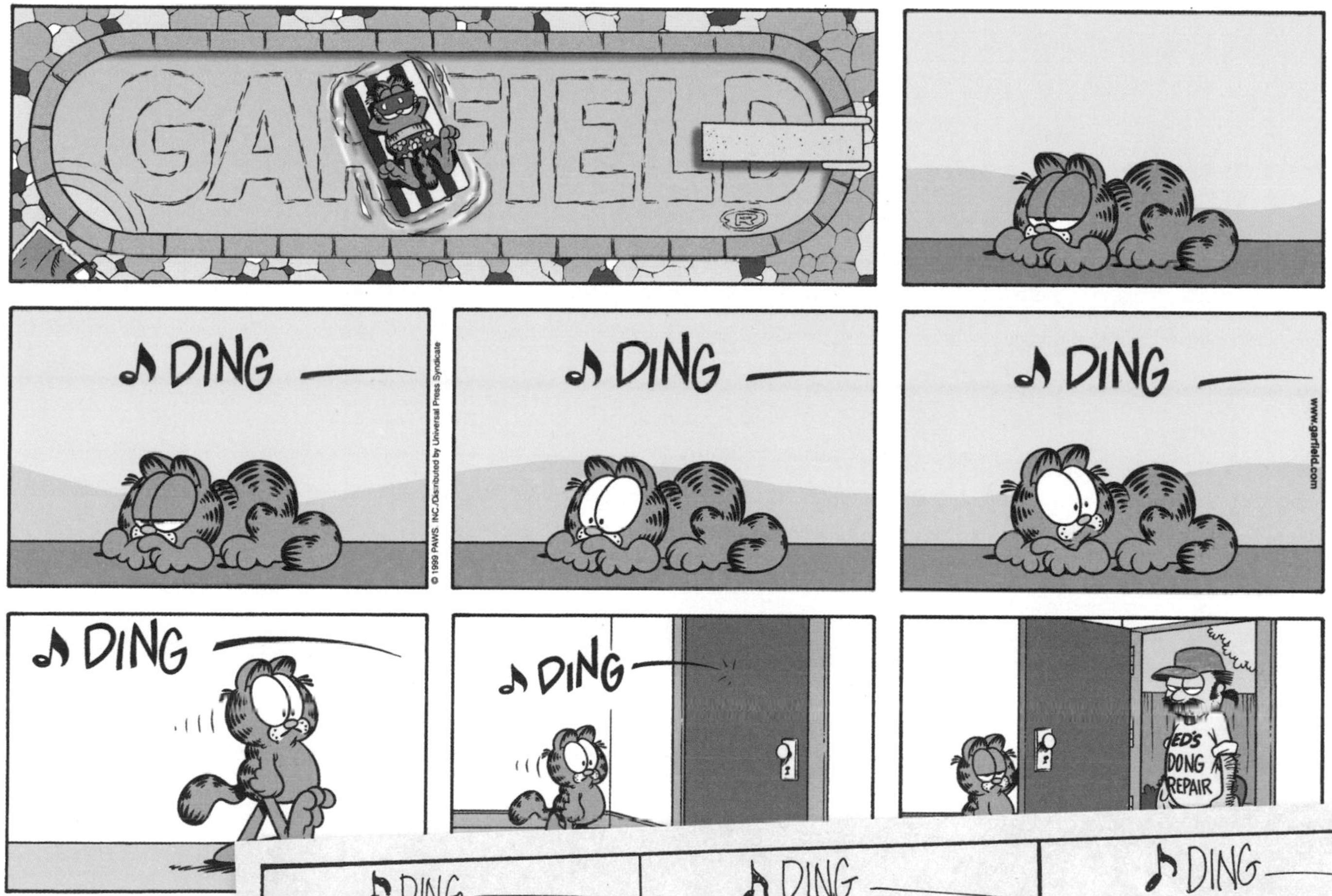
GARFIELD
DING
DING
DING
DING
DING
ED'S DONG REPAIR
© 1999 PAWS, INC./Distributed by Universal Press Syndicate
www.garfield.com

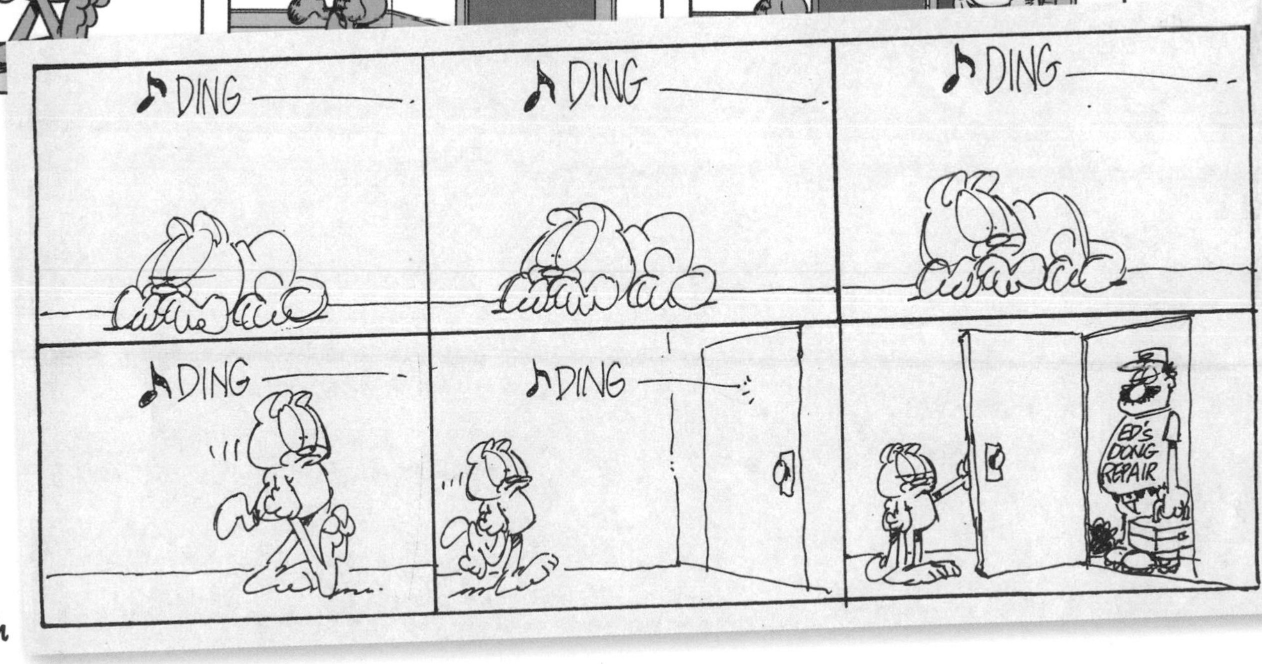
DING
DING
DING
DING
DING
ED'S DONG REPAIR

original rough

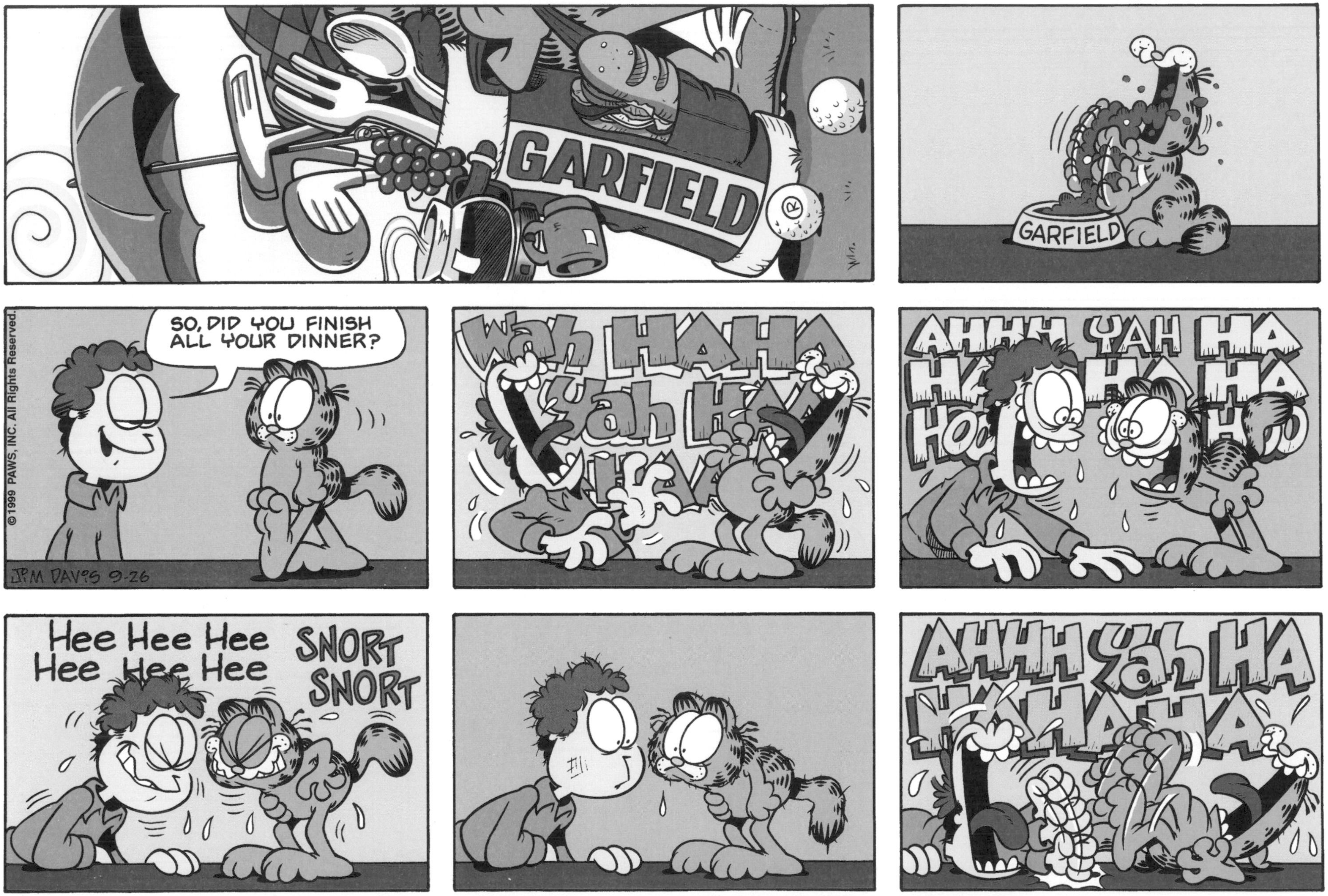
GARFIELD
GARFIELD
©1999 PAWS, INC. All Rights Reserved.
JIM DAVIS 9-26
SO, DID YOU FINISH ALL YOUR DINNER?
Wah HAHA
Yah
AHHH YAH HA
HA HA HA
Hee Hee Hee
Hee Hee Hee
SNORT
SNORT
AHHH Yah HA

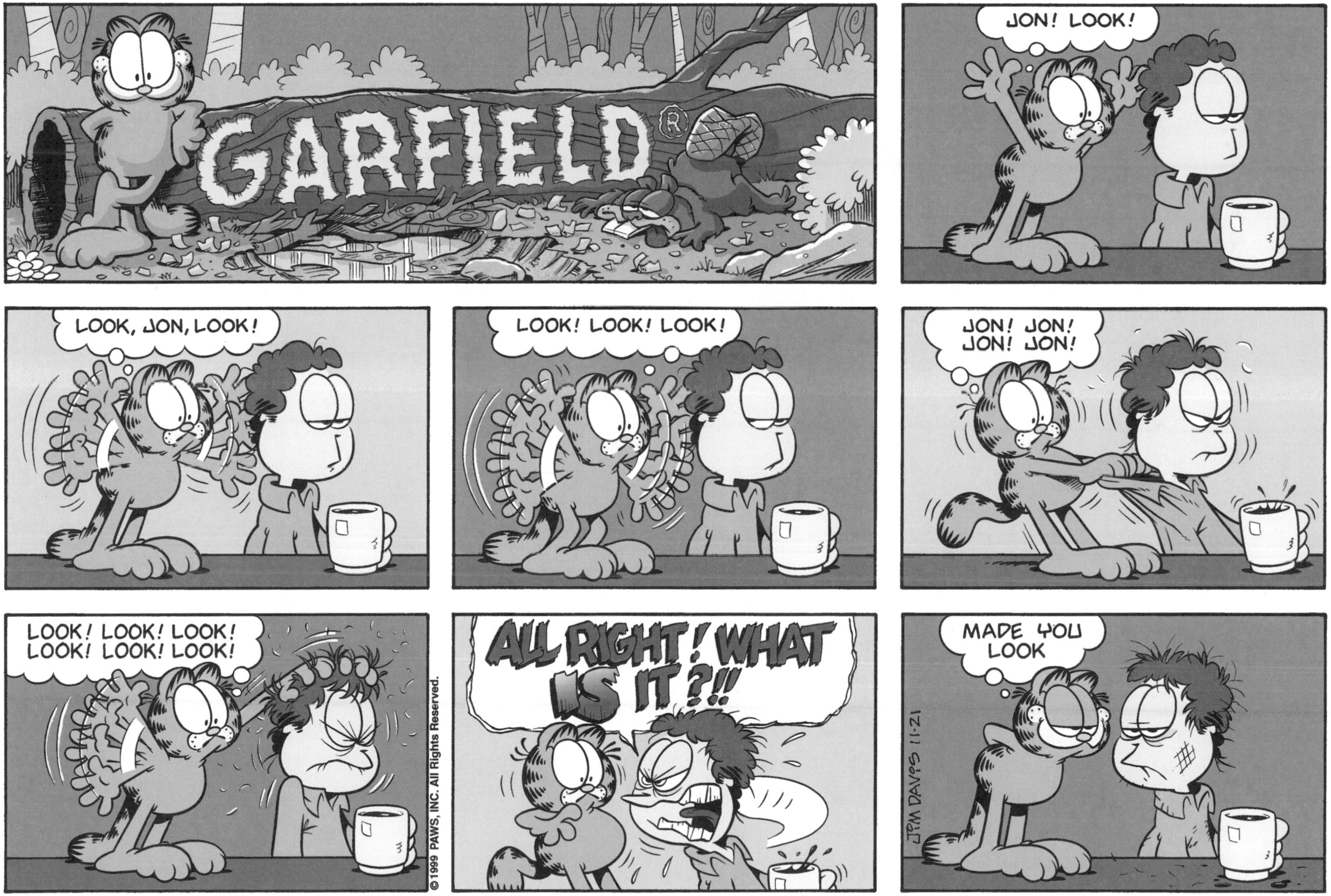

GARFIELD®
JON! LOOK!
LOOK, JON, LOOK!
LOOK! LOOK! LOOK!
JON! JON! JON! JON!
LOOK! LOOK! LOOK! LOOK! LOOK! LOOK!
ALL RIGHT! WHAT IS IT?!!
MADE YOU LOOK
JPM DAVPS 11·21

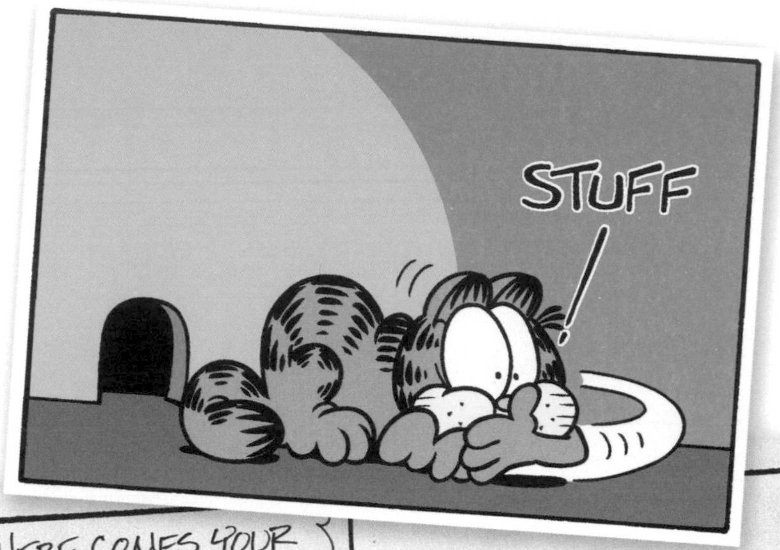
STUFF

This strip features what has to be the oddest punch line in the history of cartooning!

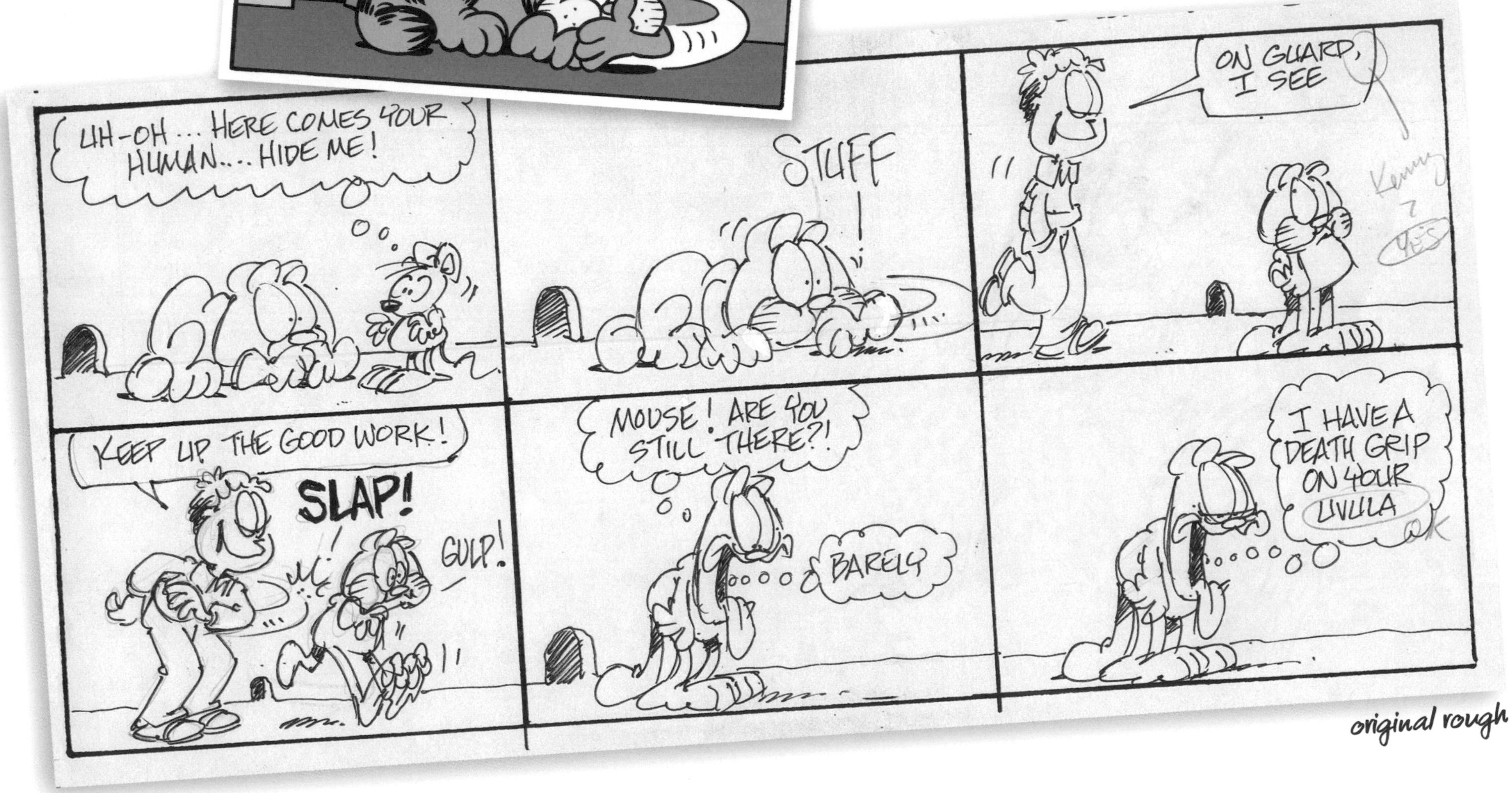
UH-OH... HERE COMES YOUR HUMAN.... HIDE ME!
STUFF
ON GUARD, I SEE
KEEP UP THE GOOD WORK!
SLAP!
GULP!
MOUSE! ARE YOU STILL THERE?!
BARELY
I HAVE A DEATH GRIP ON YOUR UVULA

original rough

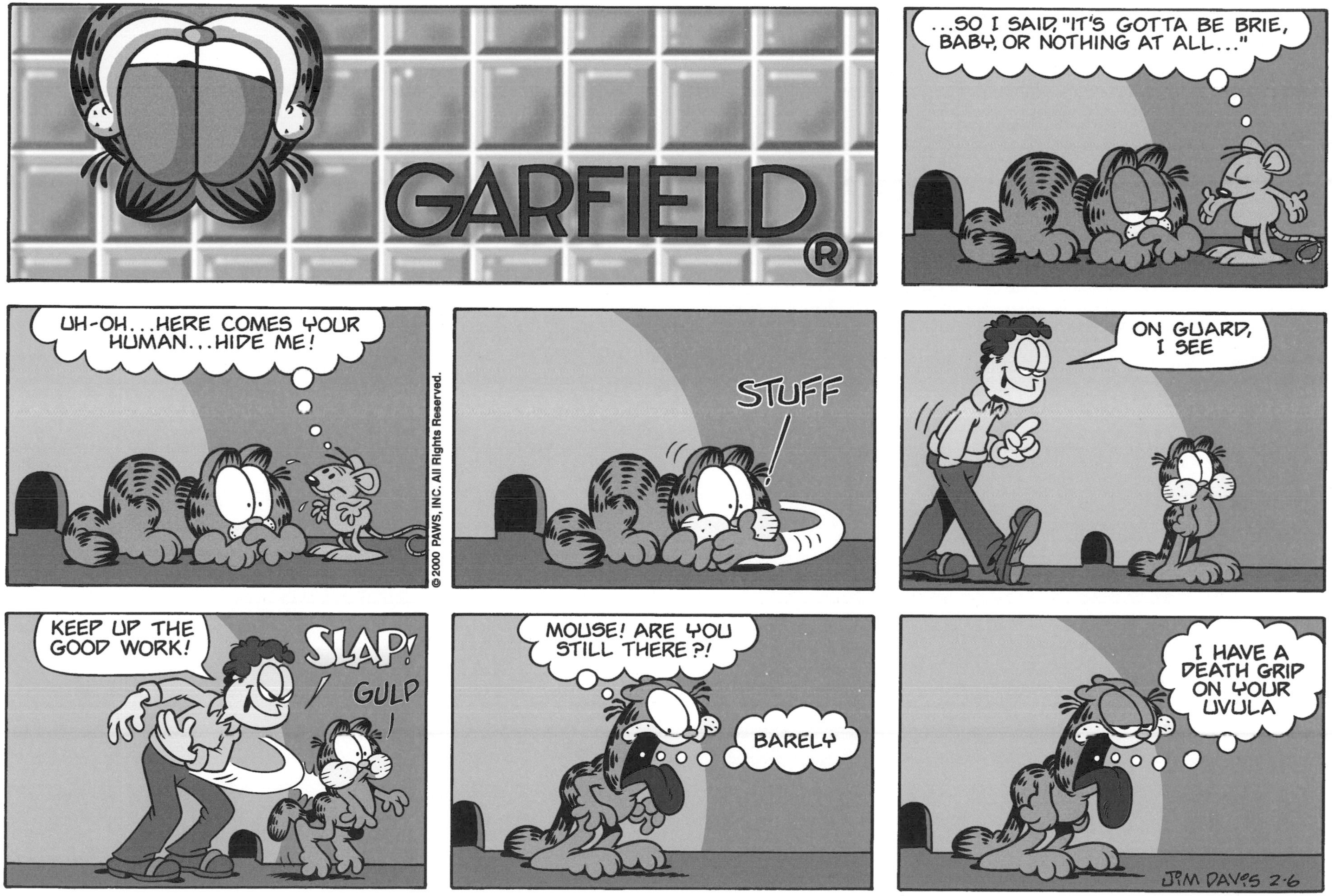
GARFIELD ®
...SO I SAID, "IT'S GOTTA BE BRIE, BABY, OR NOTHING AT ALL..."
UH-OH...HERE COMES YOUR HUMAN...HIDE ME!
© 2000 PAWS, INC. All Rights Reserved.
STUFF
ON GUARD, I SEE
KEEP UP THE GOOD WORK!
SLAP!
GULP
MOUSE! ARE YOU STILL THERE?!
BARELY
I HAVE A DEATH GRIP ON YOUR UVULA
JIM DAVIS 2·6

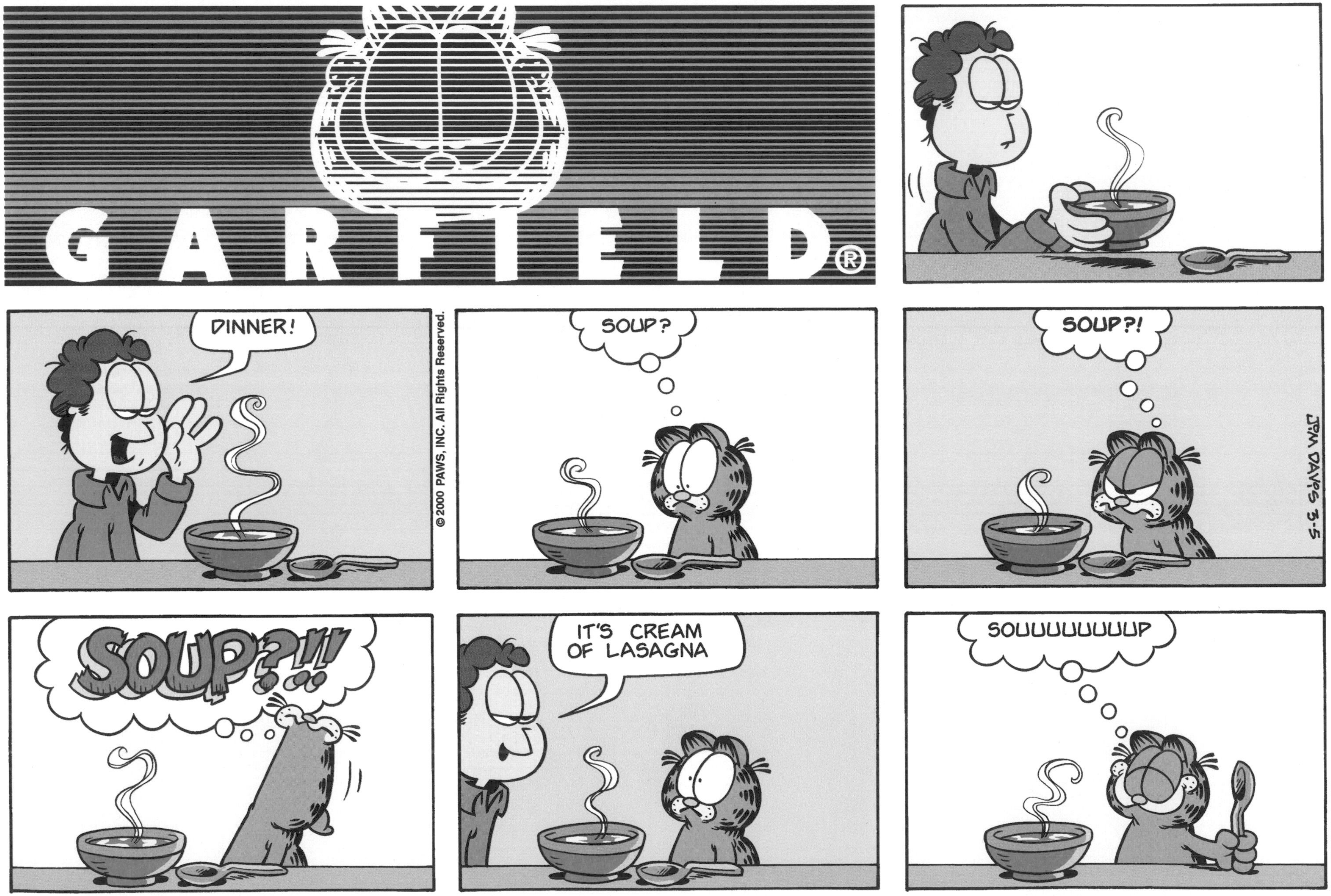
GARFIELD®
DINNER!
© 2000 PAWS, INC. All Rights Reserved.
SOUP?
SOUP?!
JIM DAVIS 3-5
SOUP?!!
IT'S CREAM OF LASAGNA
SOUUUUUUUUP

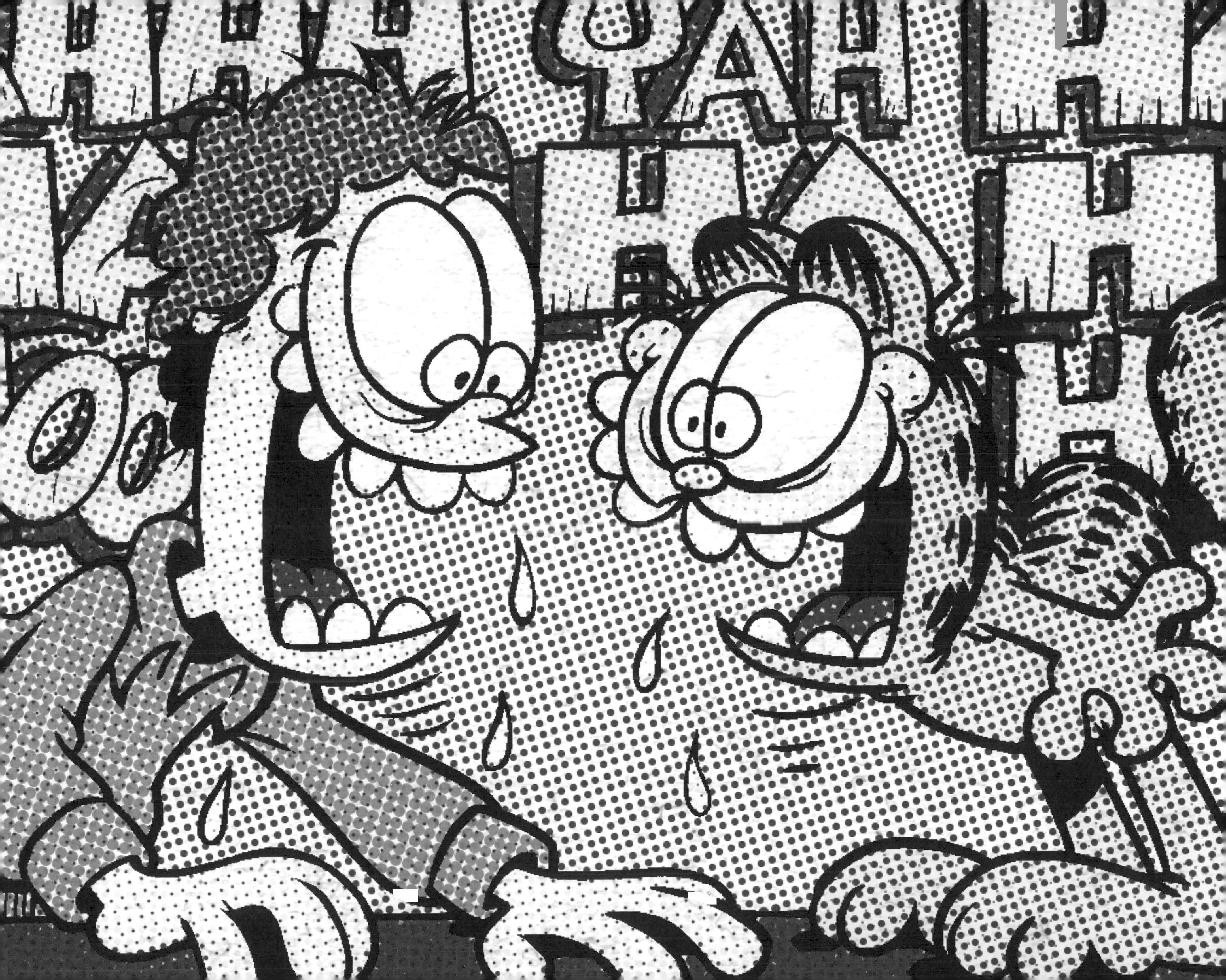

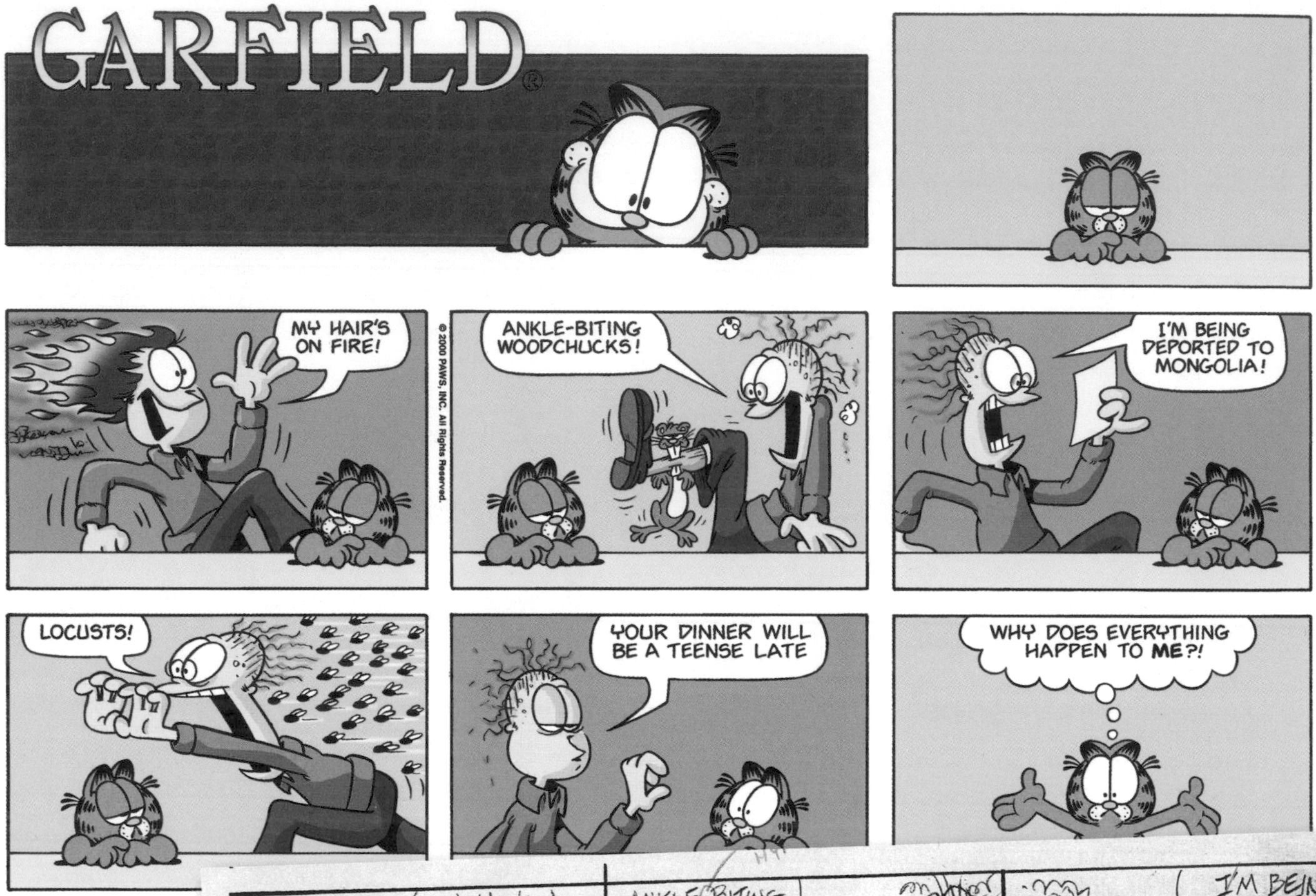
GARFIELD
MY HAIR'S ON FIRE!
© 2000 PAWS, INC. All Rights Reserved.
ANKLE-BITING WOODCHUCKS!
I'M BEING DEPORTED TO MONGOLIA!
LOCUSTS!
YOUR DINNER WILL BE A TEENSE LATE
WHY DOES EVERYTHING HAPPEN TO **ME**?!

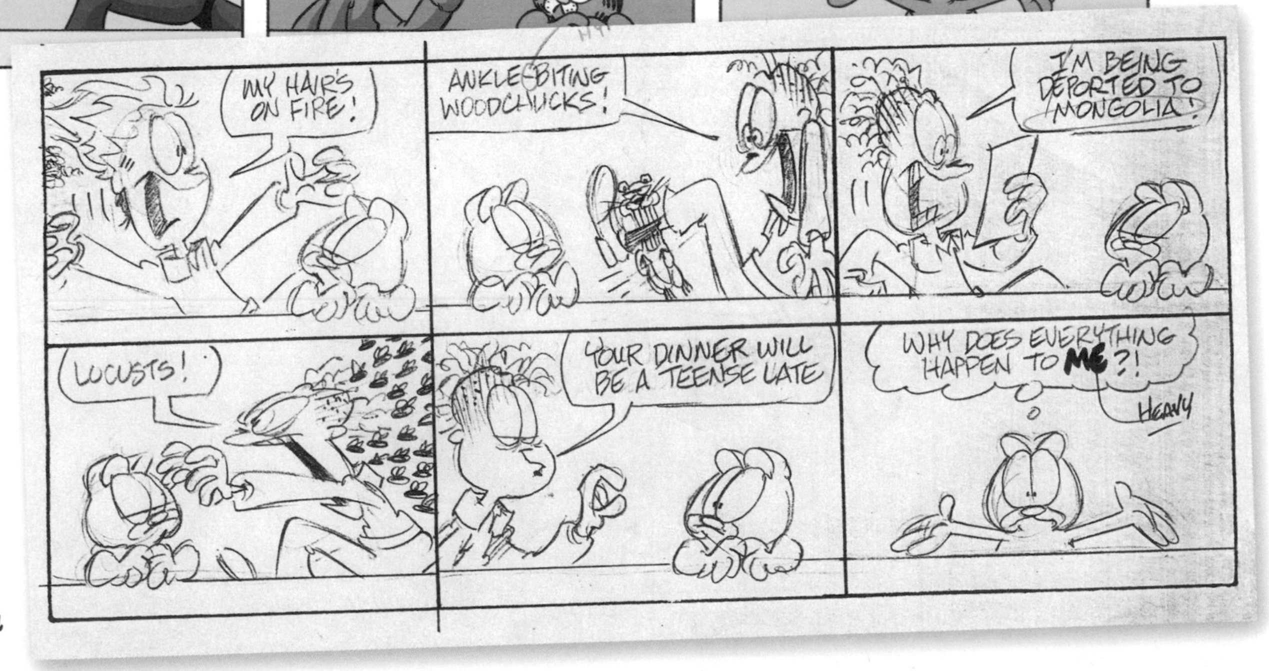
MY HAIR'S ON FIRE!
ANKLE-BITING WOODCHUCKS!
I'M BEING DEPORTED TO MONGOLIA!
LOCUSTS!
YOUR DINNER WILL BE A TEENSE LATE
WHY DOES EVERYTHING HAPPEN TO **ME**?!
HEAVY

original rough

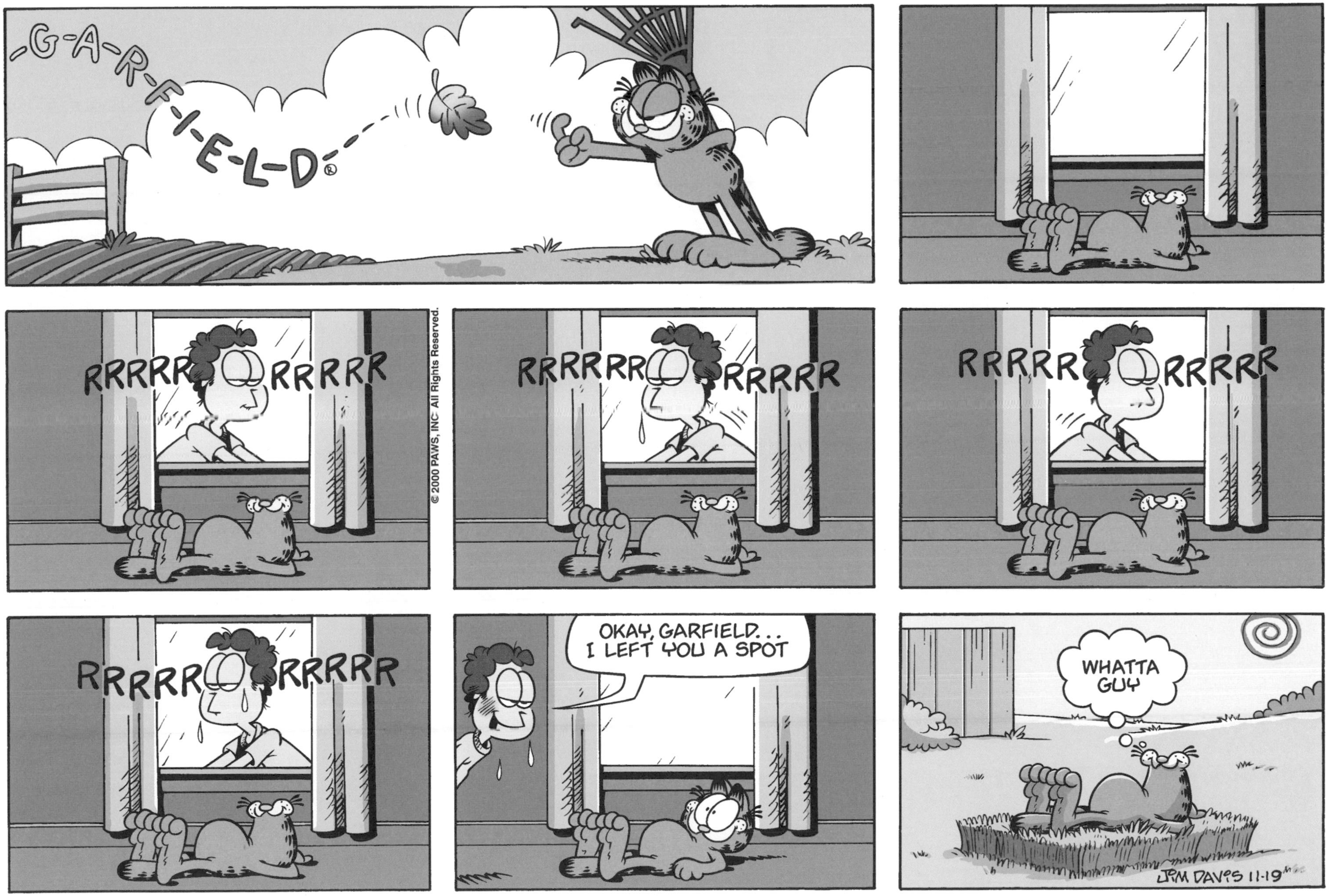

-G-A-R-F-I-E-L-D-®
RRRRR RRRRR
RRRRRR RRRRR
RRRRR RRRRR
RRRRR RRRRRR
OKAY, GARFIELD... I LEFT YOU A SPOT
WHATTA GUY
JIM DAVIS 11-19
© 2000 PAWS, INC. All Rights Reserved.

Just my whole philosophy of life, that's all.

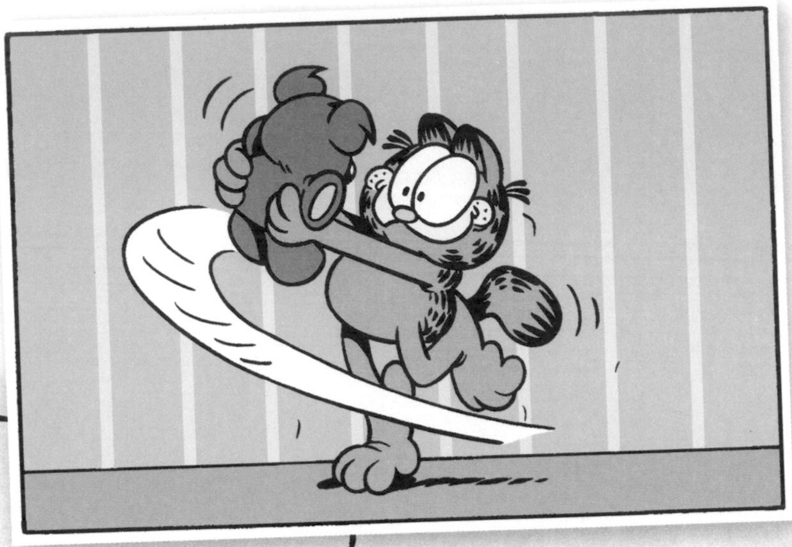

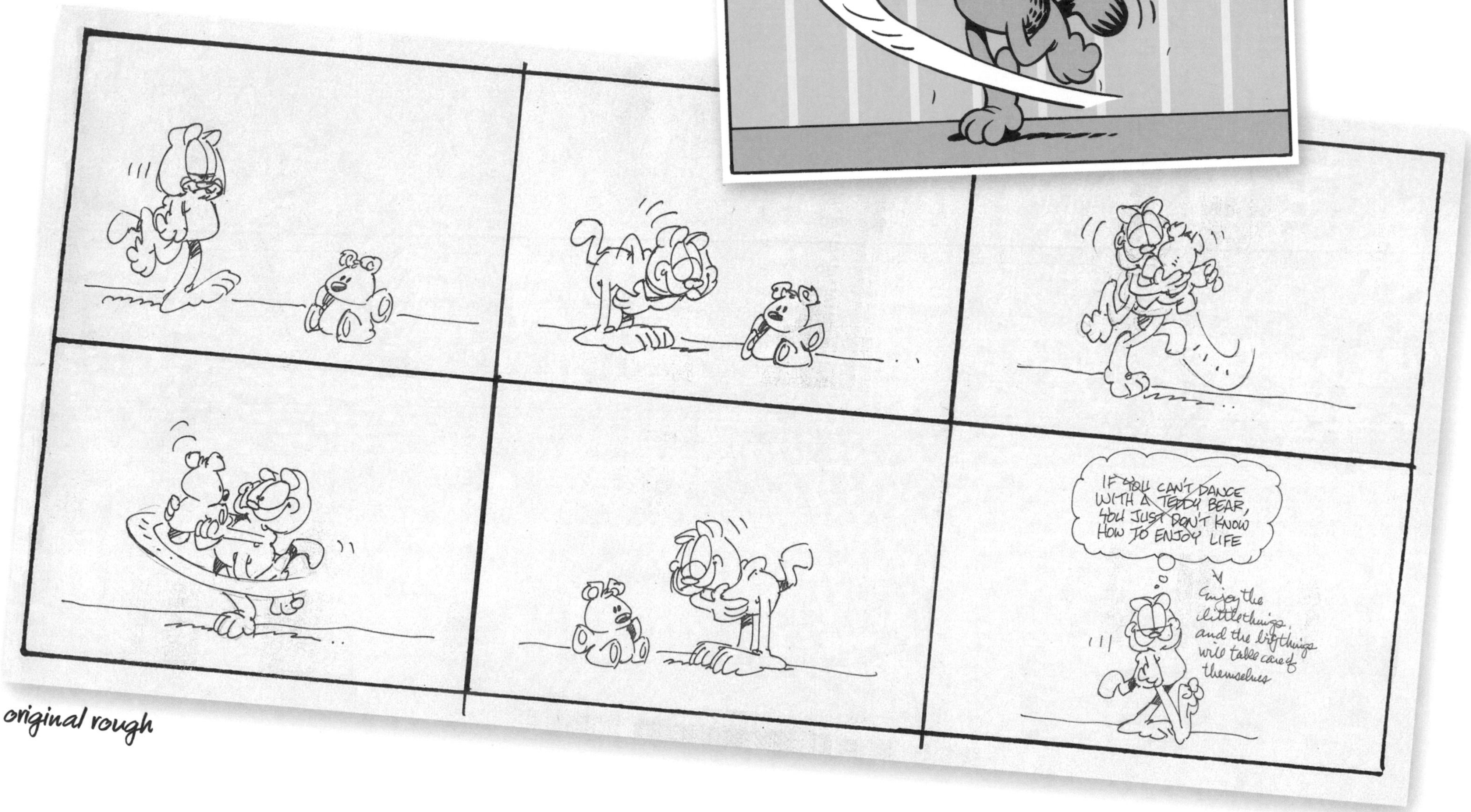
IF YOU CAN'T DANCE WITH A TEDDY BEAR, YOU JUST DON'T KNOW HOW TO ENJOY LIFE
Enjoy the little things, and the big things will take care of themselves

original rough

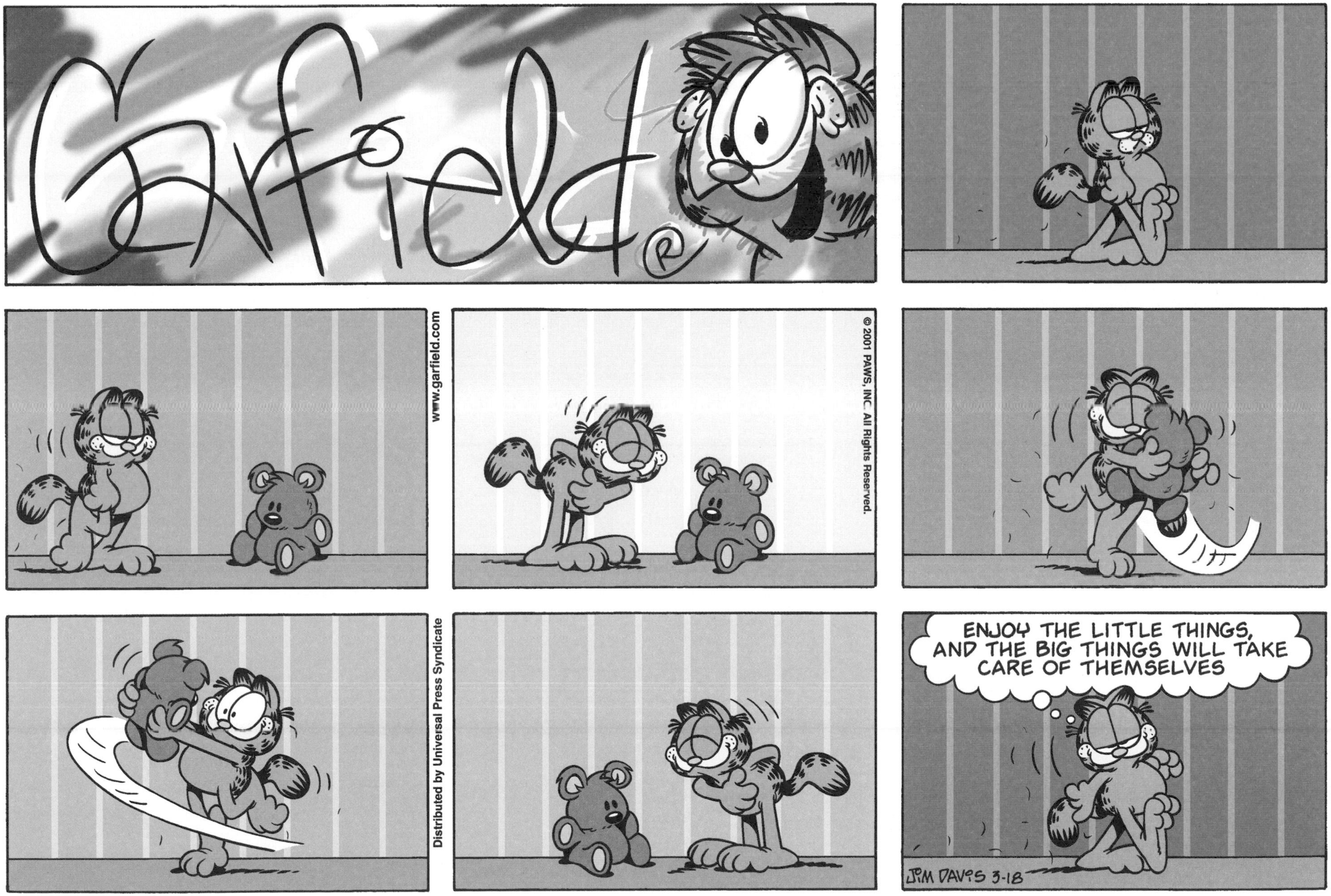
Garfield®
www.garfield.com
© 2001 PAWS, INC. All Rights Reserved.
Distributed by Universal Press Syndicate
ENJOY THE LITTLE THINGS, AND THE BIG THINGS WILL TAKE CARE OF THEMSELVES
JIM DAVIS 3-18

JIM DAVIS   5·13

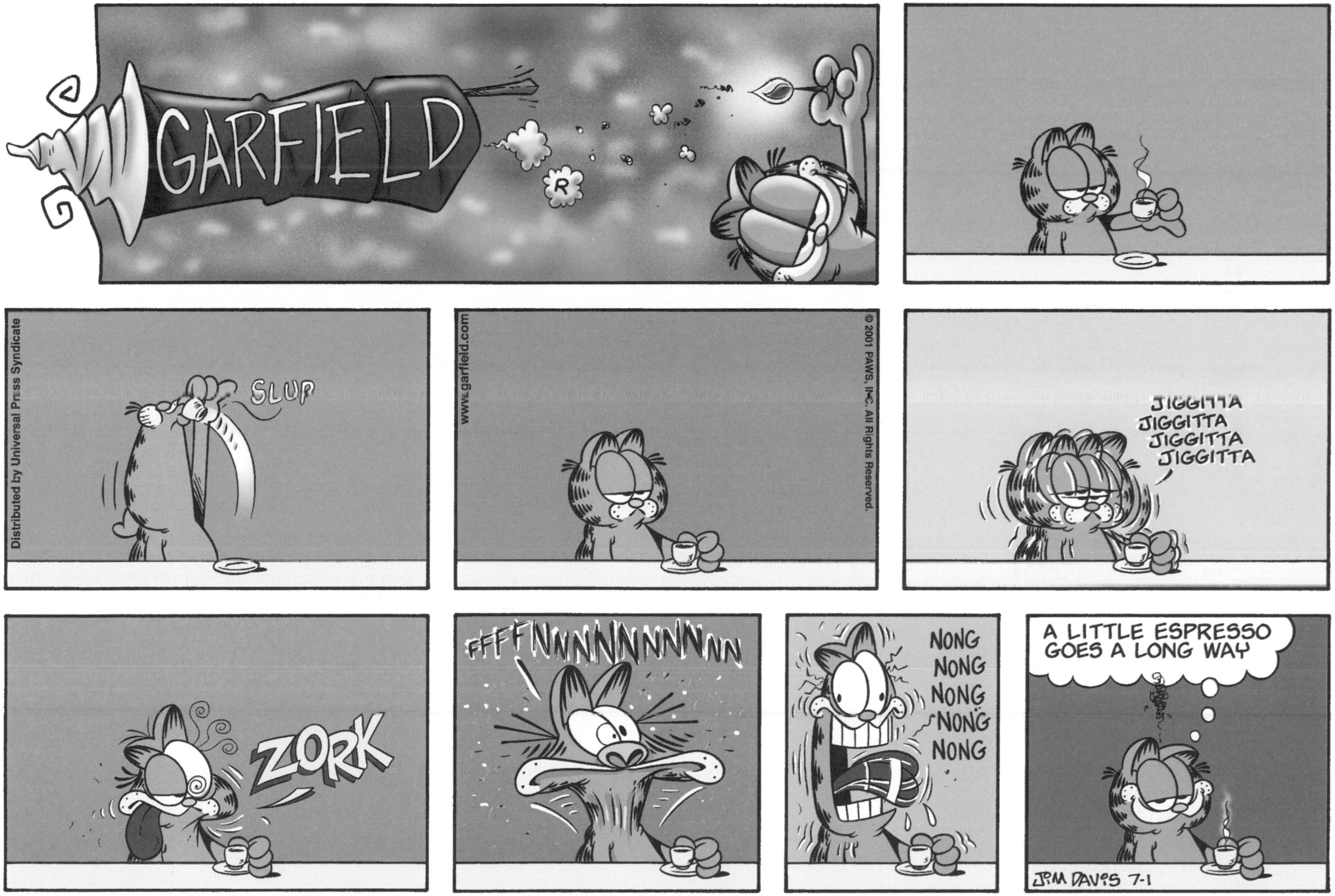
GARFIELD
SLUP
Distributed by Universal Press Syndicate
www.garfield.com
© 2001 PAWS, INC. All Rights Reserved.
JIGGITTA
JIGGITTA
JIGGITTA
JIGGITTA
ZORK
FFFFNNNNNNNNNNN
NONG
NONG
NONG
NONG
NONG
A LITTLE ESPRESSO GOES A LONG WAY
JIM DAVIS 7-1

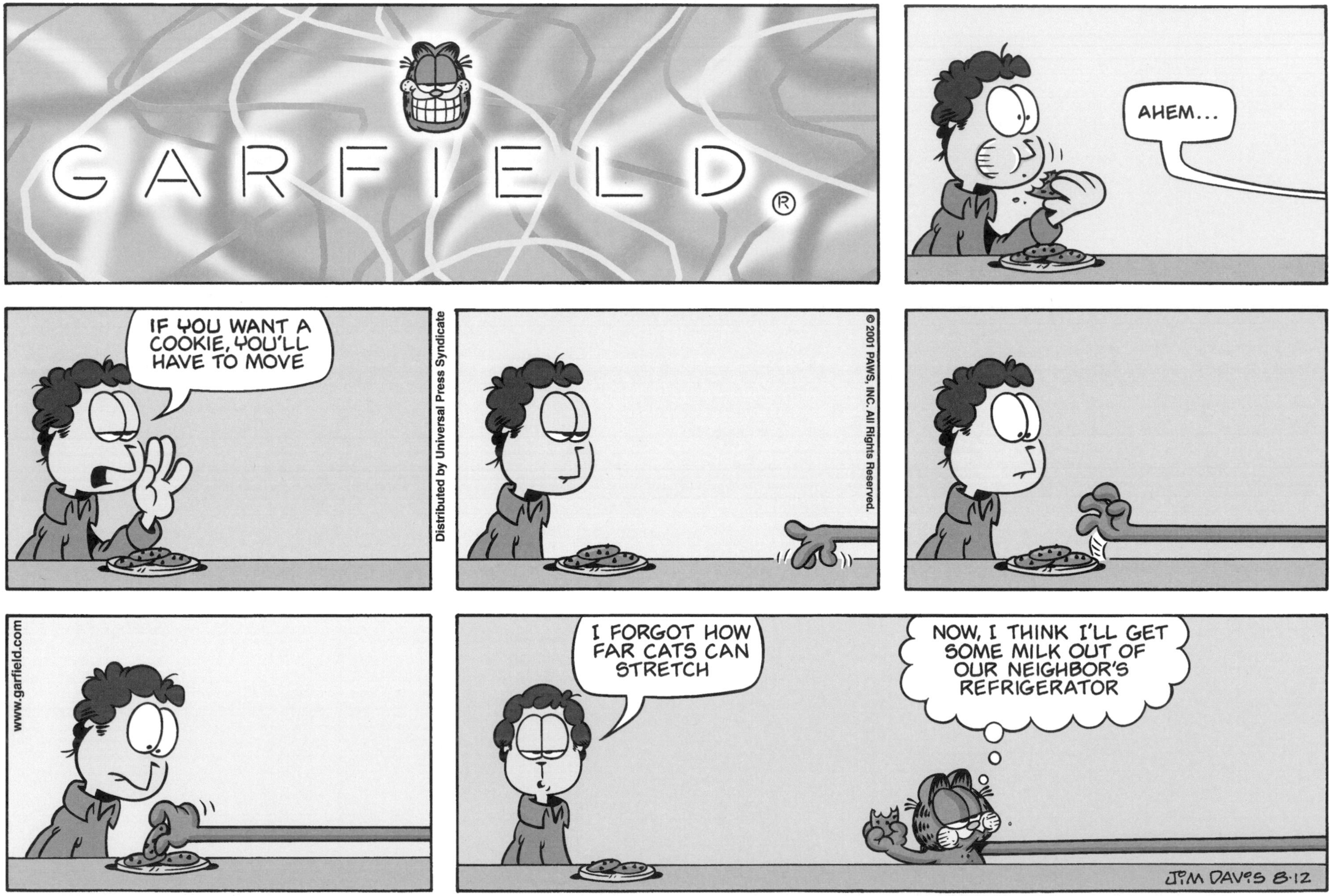
GARFIELD®
AHEM...
IF YOU WANT A COOKIE, YOU'LL HAVE TO MOVE
Distributed by Universal Press Syndicate
© 2001 PAWS, INC. All Rights Reserved.
www.garfield.com
I FORGOT HOW FAR CATS CAN STRETCH
NOW, I THINK I'LL GET SOME MILK OUT OF OUR NEIGHBOR'S REFRIGERATOR
JIM DAVIS 8·12

This is my life . . . I wouldn't trade it for anything.

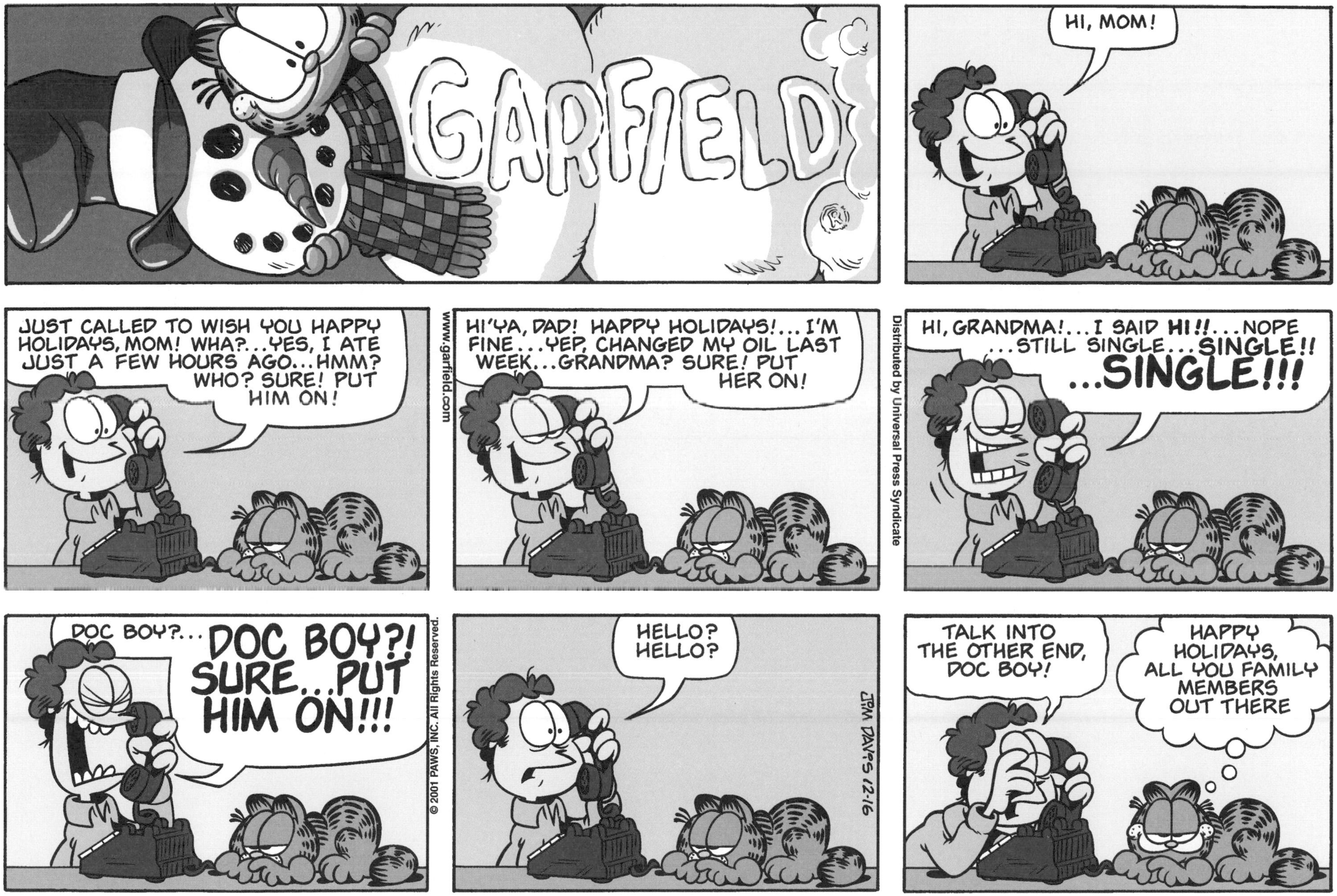

GARFIELD
HI, MOM!
JUST CALLED TO WISH YOU HAPPY HOLIDAYS, MOM! WHA?...YES, I ATE JUST A FEW HOURS AGO...HMM? WHO? SURE! PUT HIM ON!
www.garfield.com
HI'YA, DAD! HAPPY HOLIDAYS!... I'M FINE...YEP, CHANGED MY OIL LAST WEEK...GRANDMA? SURE! PUT HER ON!
Distributed by Universal Press Syndicate
HI, GRANDMA!...I SAID HI!!...NOPE ...STILL SINGLE...SINGLE!! ...SINGLE!!!
DOC BOY?... DOC BOY?! SURE...PUT HIM ON!!!
© 2001 PAWS, INC. All Rights Reserved.
HELLO? HELLO?
JIM DAVIS 12-16
TALK INTO THE OTHER END, DOC BOY!
HAPPY HOLIDAYS, ALL YOU FAMILY MEMBERS OUT THERE

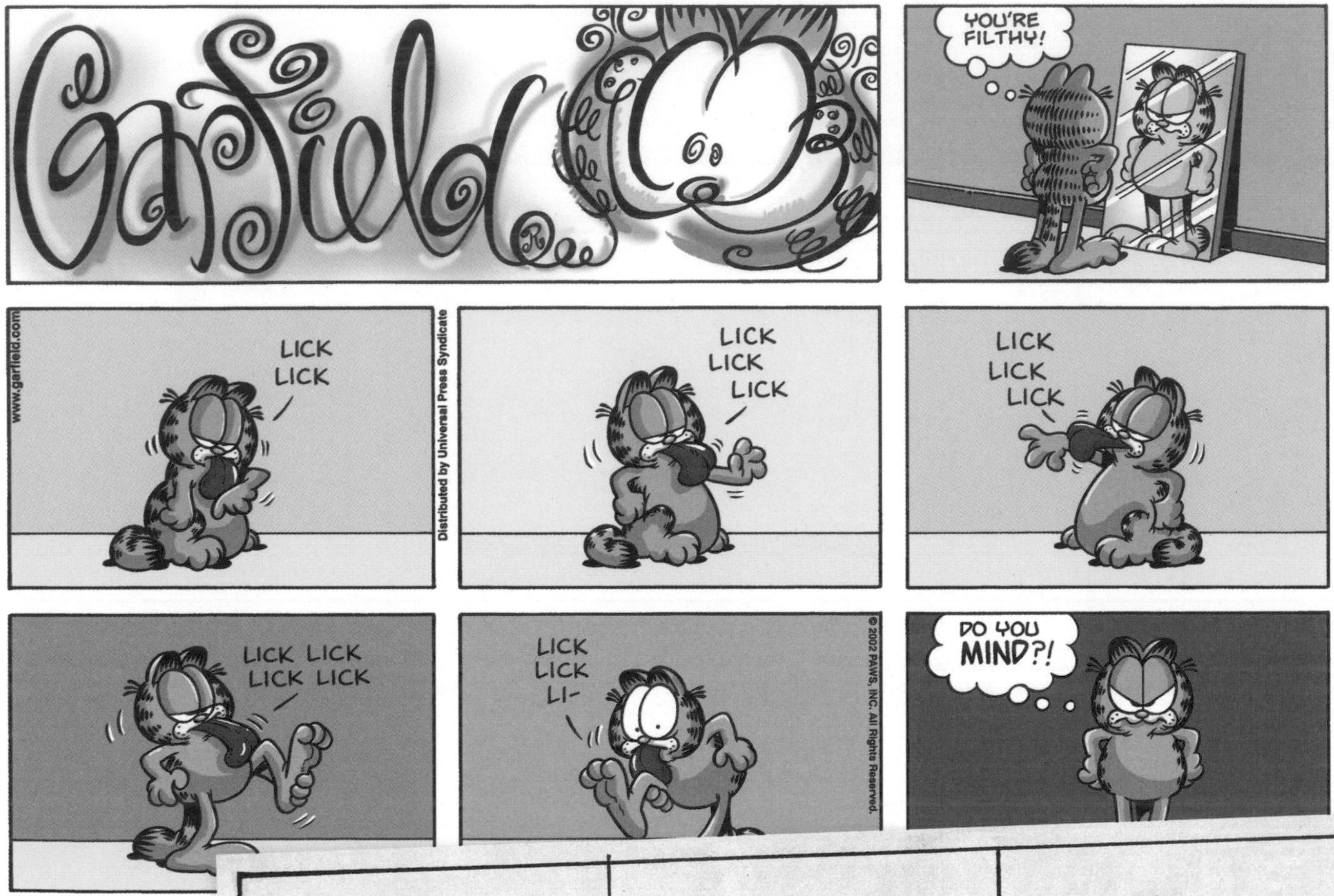
Garfield
YOU'RE FILTHY!
LICK LICK
LICK LICK LICK
LICK LICK LICK
LICK LICK LICK LICK
LICK LICK LI-
DO YOU MIND?!
www.garfield.com
Distributed by Universal Press Syndicate
© 2002 PAWS, INC. All Rights Reserved.

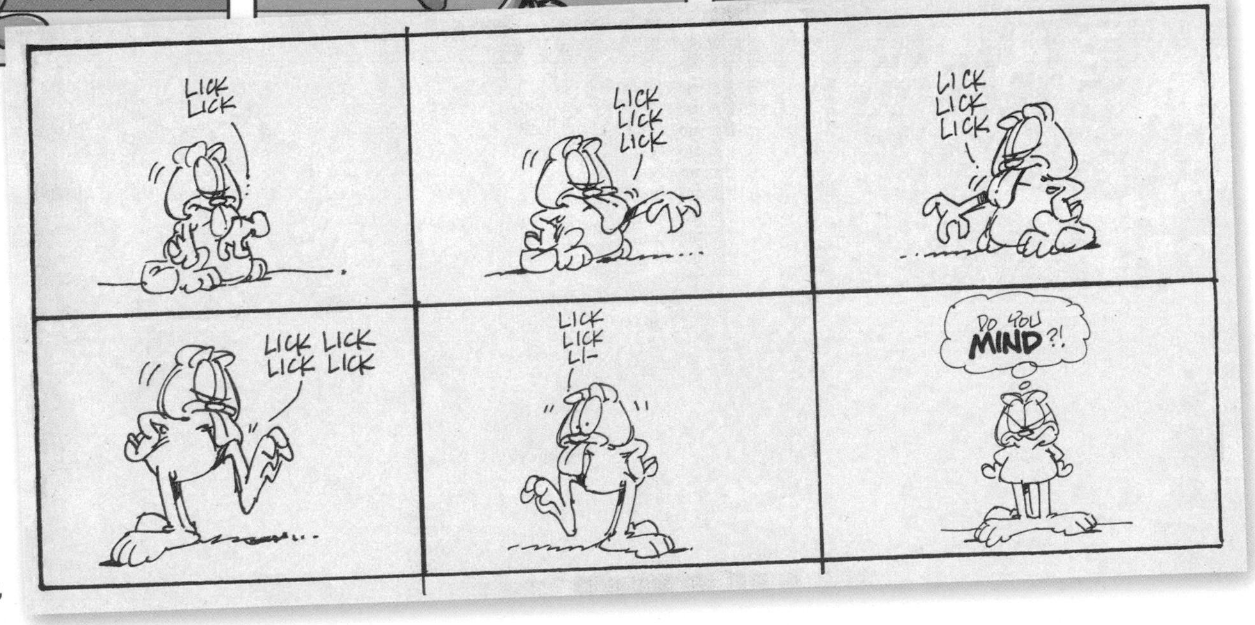
LICK LICK
LICK LICK LICK
LICK LICK LICK
LICK LICK LICK LICK
LICK LICK LI-
DO YOU MIND?!

original rough

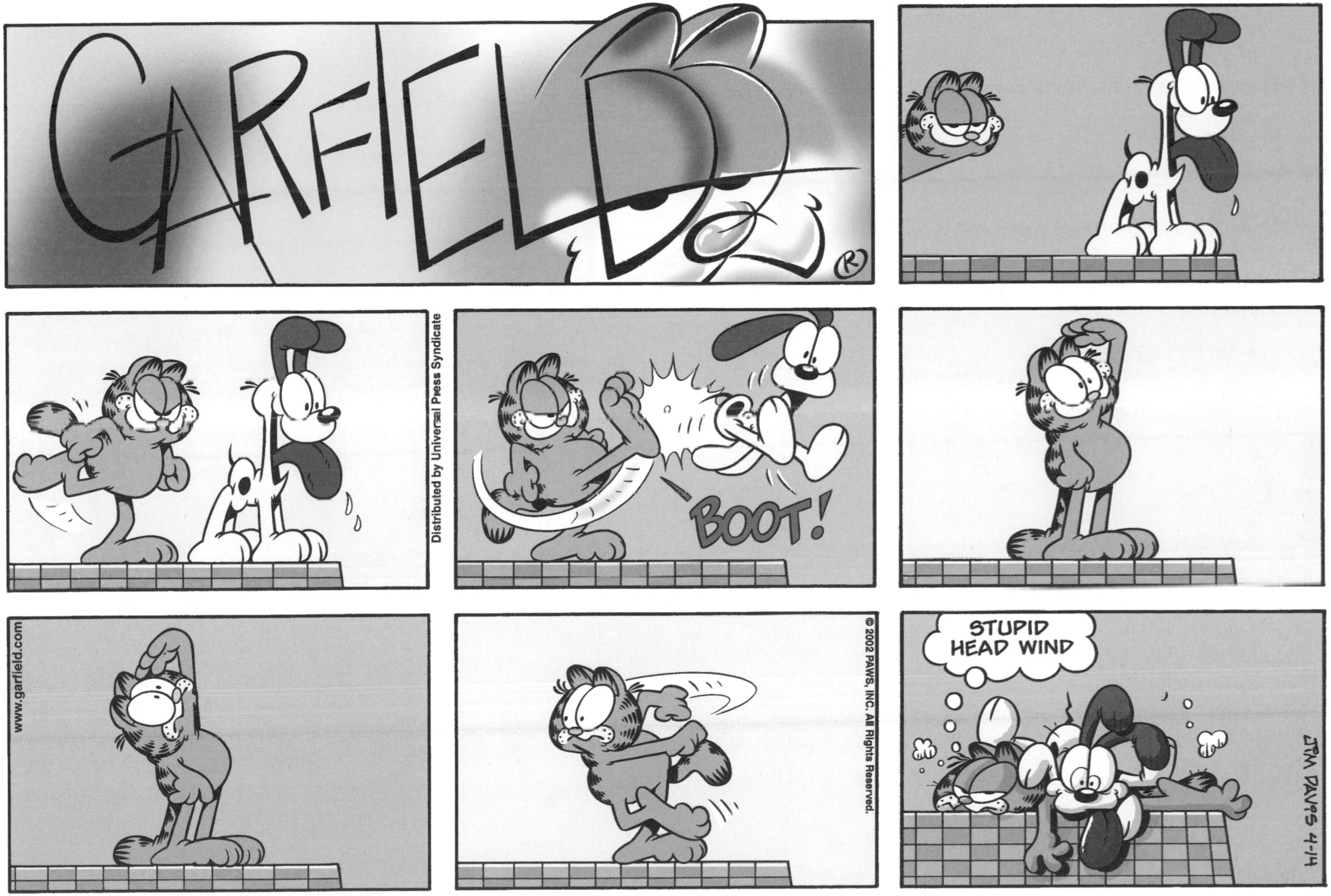
GARFIELD ®
Distributed by Universal Press Syndicate
BOOT!
www.garfield.com
© 2002 PAWS, INC. All Rights Reserved.
STUPID HEAD WIND
JIM DAVIS 4-14

Garfield shares a rare moment of catharsis here, proving that even lazy cats can stress out.

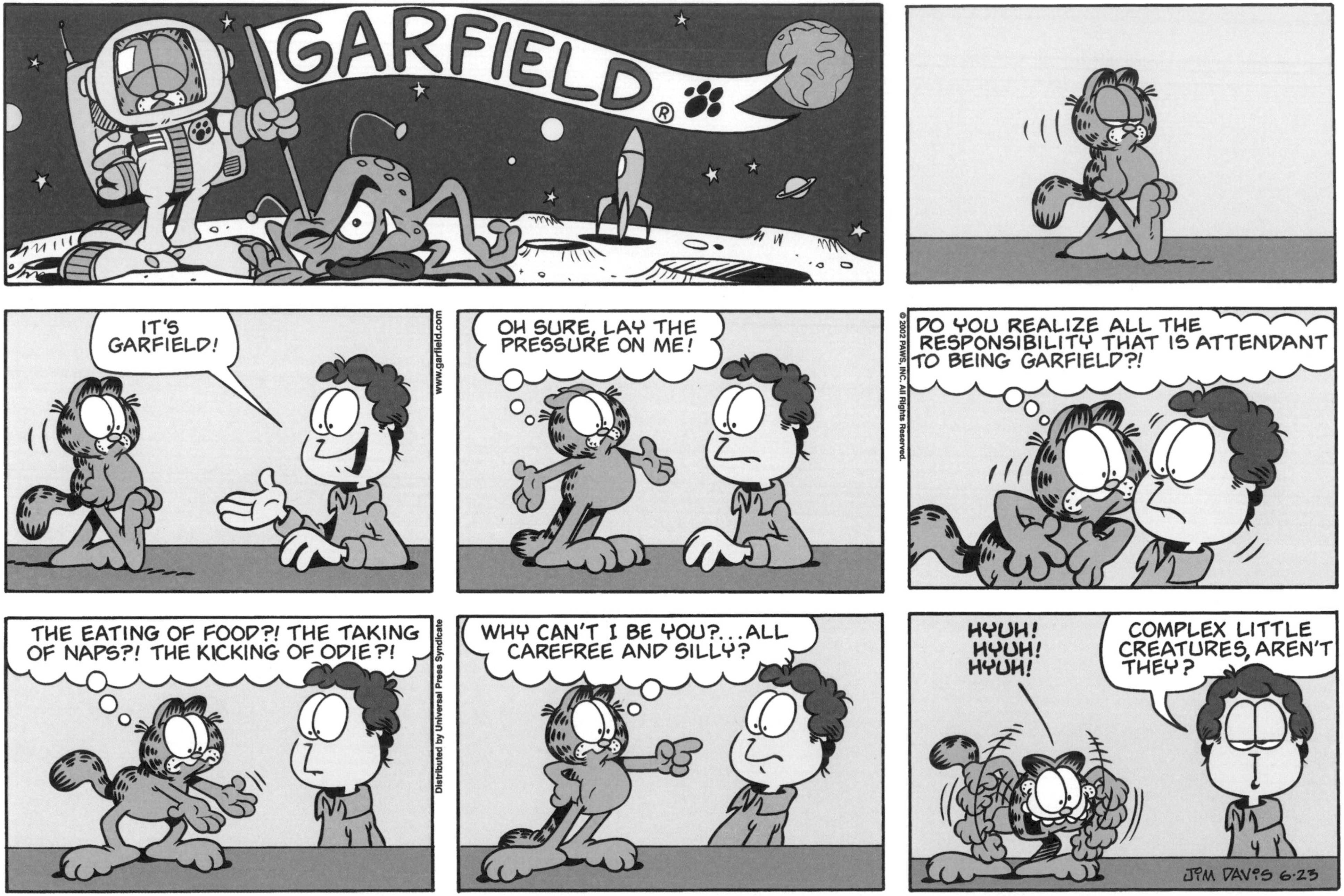

GARFIELD®
IT'S GARFIELD!
www.garfield.com
OH SURE, LAY THE PRESSURE ON ME!
© 2002 PAWS, INC. All Rights Reserved.
DO YOU REALIZE ALL THE RESPONSIBILITY THAT IS ATTENDANT TO BEING GARFIELD?!
THE EATING OF FOOD?! THE TAKING OF NAPS?! THE KICKING OF ODIE?!
Distributed by Universal Press Syndicate
WHY CAN'T I BE YOU?...ALL CAREFREE AND SILLY?
HYUH! HYUH! HYUH!
COMPLEX LITTLE CREATURES, AREN'T THEY?
JIM DAVIS 6-23

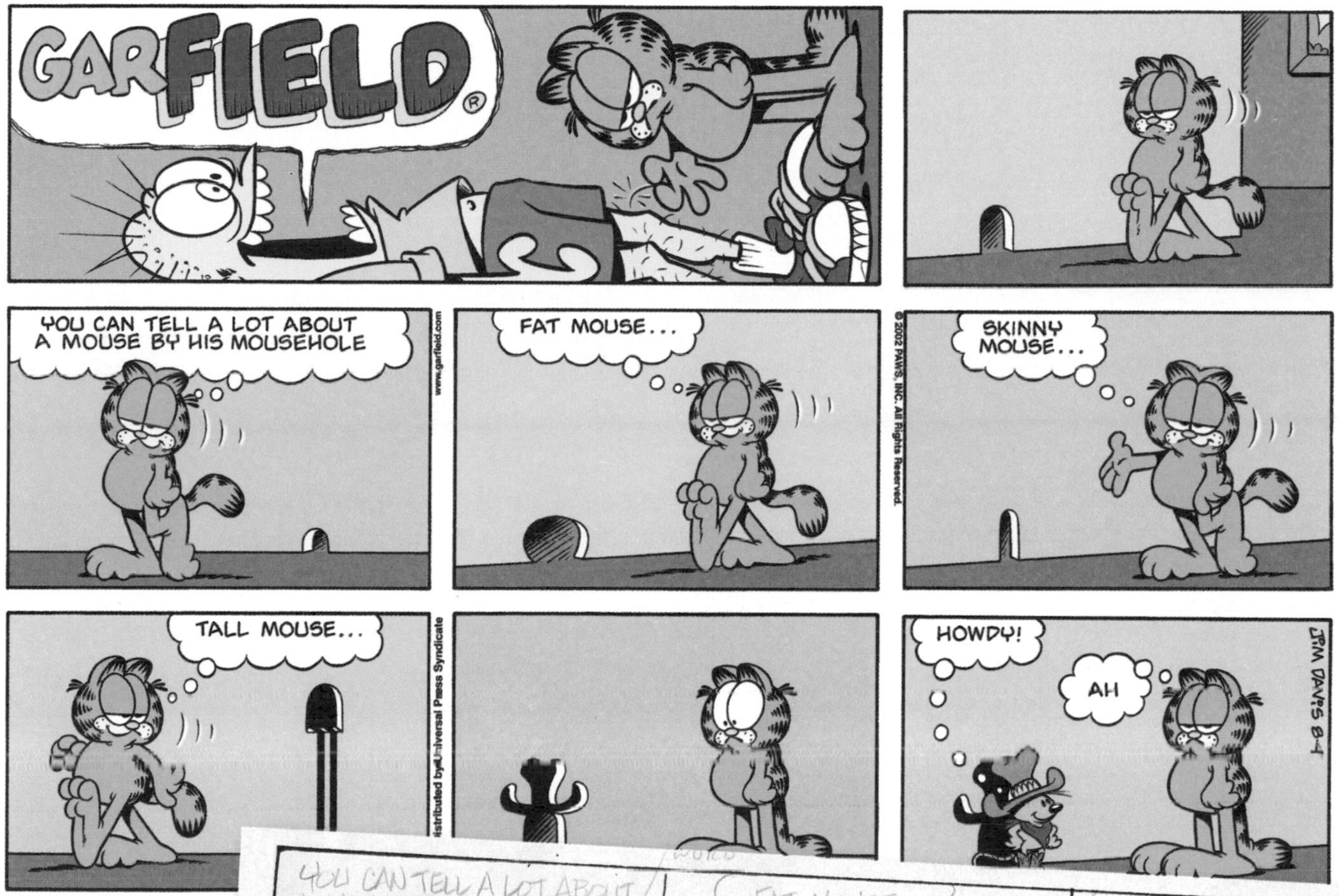
GARFIELD®
YOU CAN TELL A LOT ABOUT A MOUSE BY HIS MOUSEHOLE
FAT MOUSE...
SKINNY MOUSE...
TALL MOUSE...
HOWDY!
AH
JIM DAVIS 8-4
© 2002 PAWS, INC. All Rights Reserved.
www.garfield.com
Distributed by Universal Press Syndicate

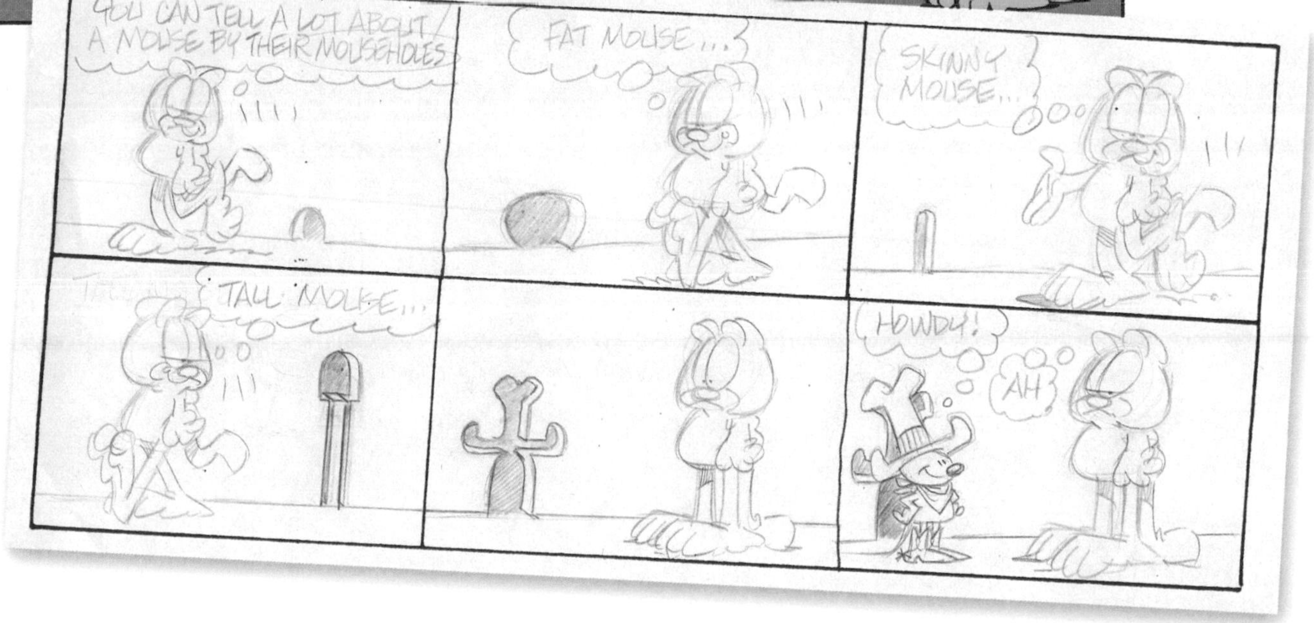
YOU CAN TELL A LOT ABOUT A MOUSE BY THEIR MOUSEHOLES
FAT MOUSE...
SKINNY MOUSE...
TALL MOUSE...
HOWDY!
AH

original rough

I took some poetic license with this classic seasonal situation. I think I'll keep my day job.

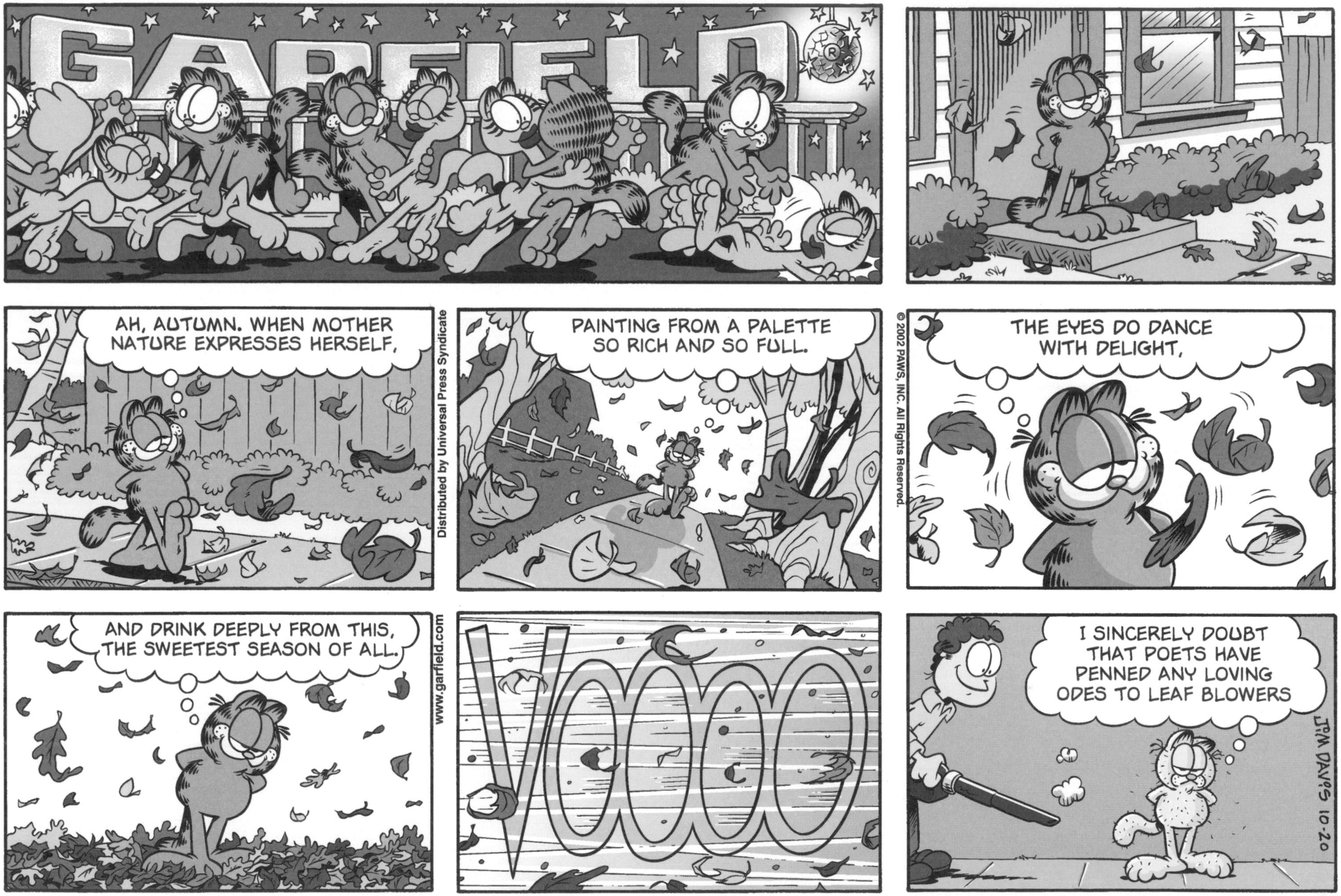
GARFIELD
AH, AUTUMN. WHEN MOTHER NATURE EXPRESSES HERSELF,
Distributed by Universal Press Syndicate
PAINTING FROM A PALETTE SO RICH AND SO FULL.
© 2002 PAWS, INC. All Rights Reserved.
THE EYES DO DANCE WITH DELIGHT,
AND DRINK DEEPLY FROM THIS, THE SWEETEST SEASON OF ALL.
www.garfield.com
VOOOOO
I SINCERELY DOUBT THAT POETS HAVE PENNED ANY LOVING ODES TO LEAF BLOWERS
JPM DAVIS 10-20

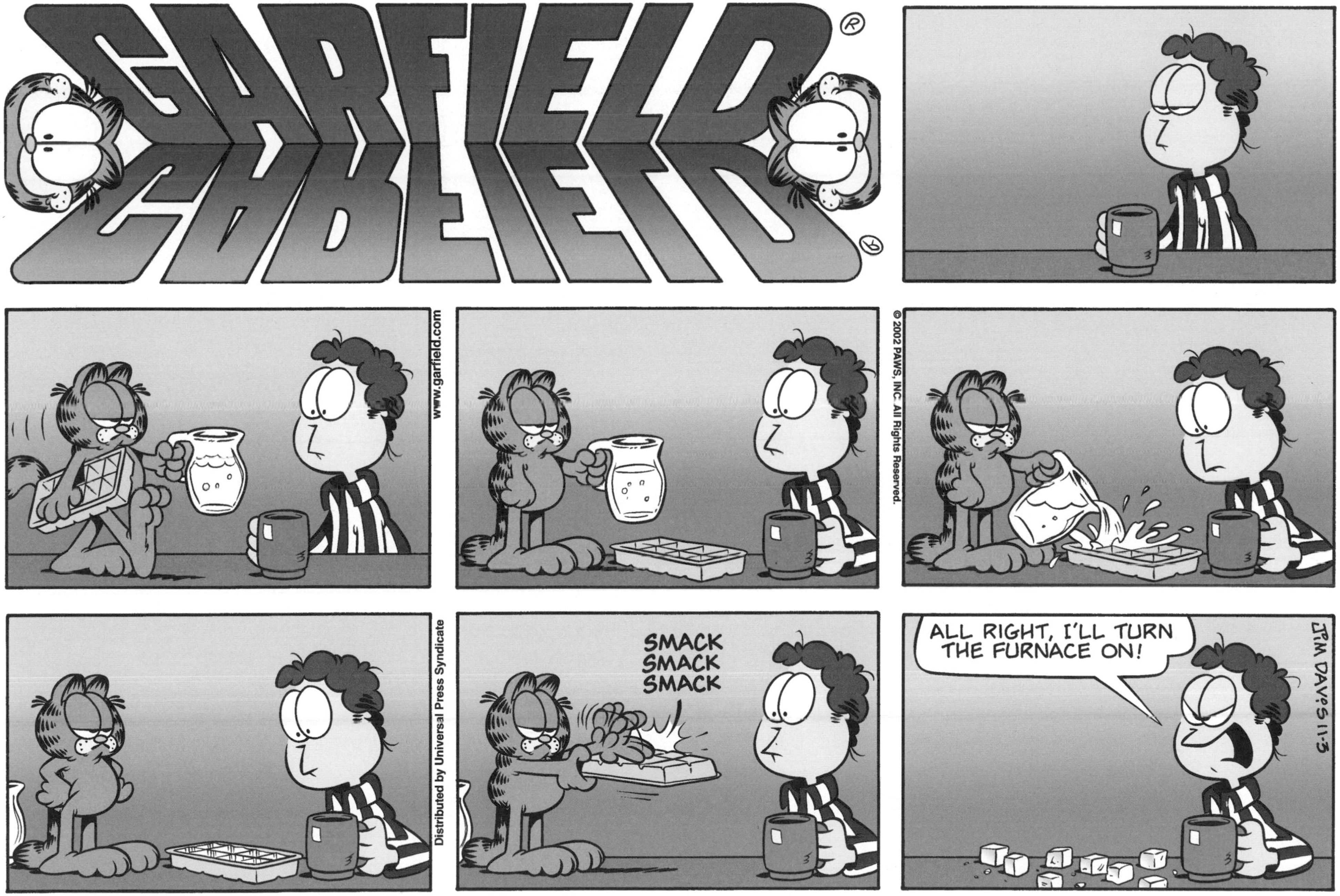
GARFIELD
www.garfield.com
© 2002 PAWS, INC. All Rights Reserved.
Distributed by Universal Press Syndicate
SMACK
SMACK
SMACK
ALL RIGHT, I'LL TURN THE FURNACE ON!
JIM DAVIS 11-3

I got so much grief for doing fat jokes during Bertha's first appearance that I decided to give her life a happy twist. Garfield doesn't concur.

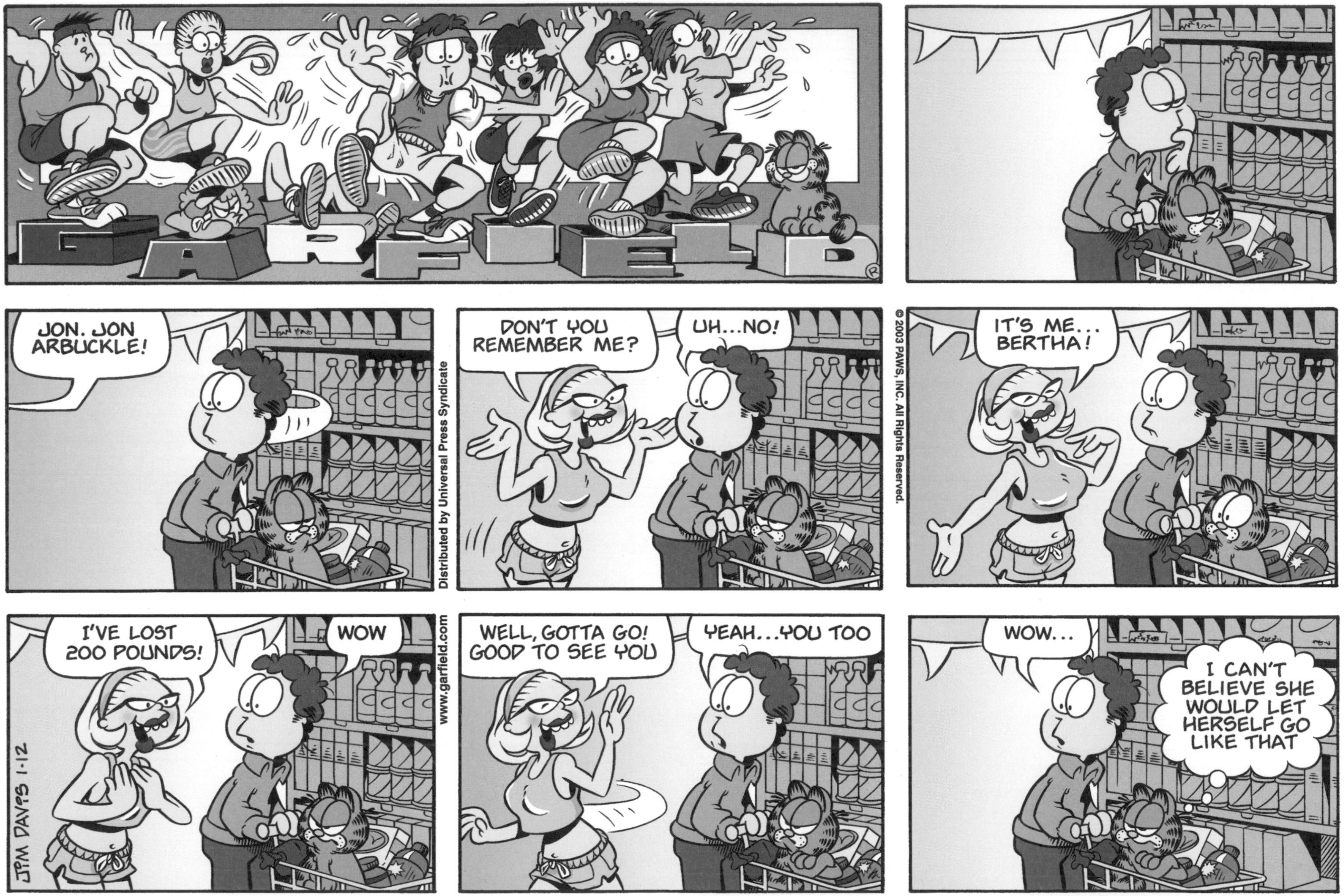

GARFIELD
JON. JON ARBUCKLE!
Distributed by Universal Press Syndicate
DON'T YOU REMEMBER ME?
UH...NO!
© 2003 PAWS, INC. All Rights Reserved.
IT'S ME... BERTHA!
JPM DAVPS 1-12
I'VE LOST 200 POUNDS!
WOW
www.garfield.com
WELL, GOTTA GO! GOOD TO SEE YOU
YEAH...YOU TOO
WOW...
I CAN'T BELIEVE SHE WOULD LET HERSELF GO LIKE THAT

I'm an avid people watcher. You just can't improve on those real-world conversations. People say the darndest things.

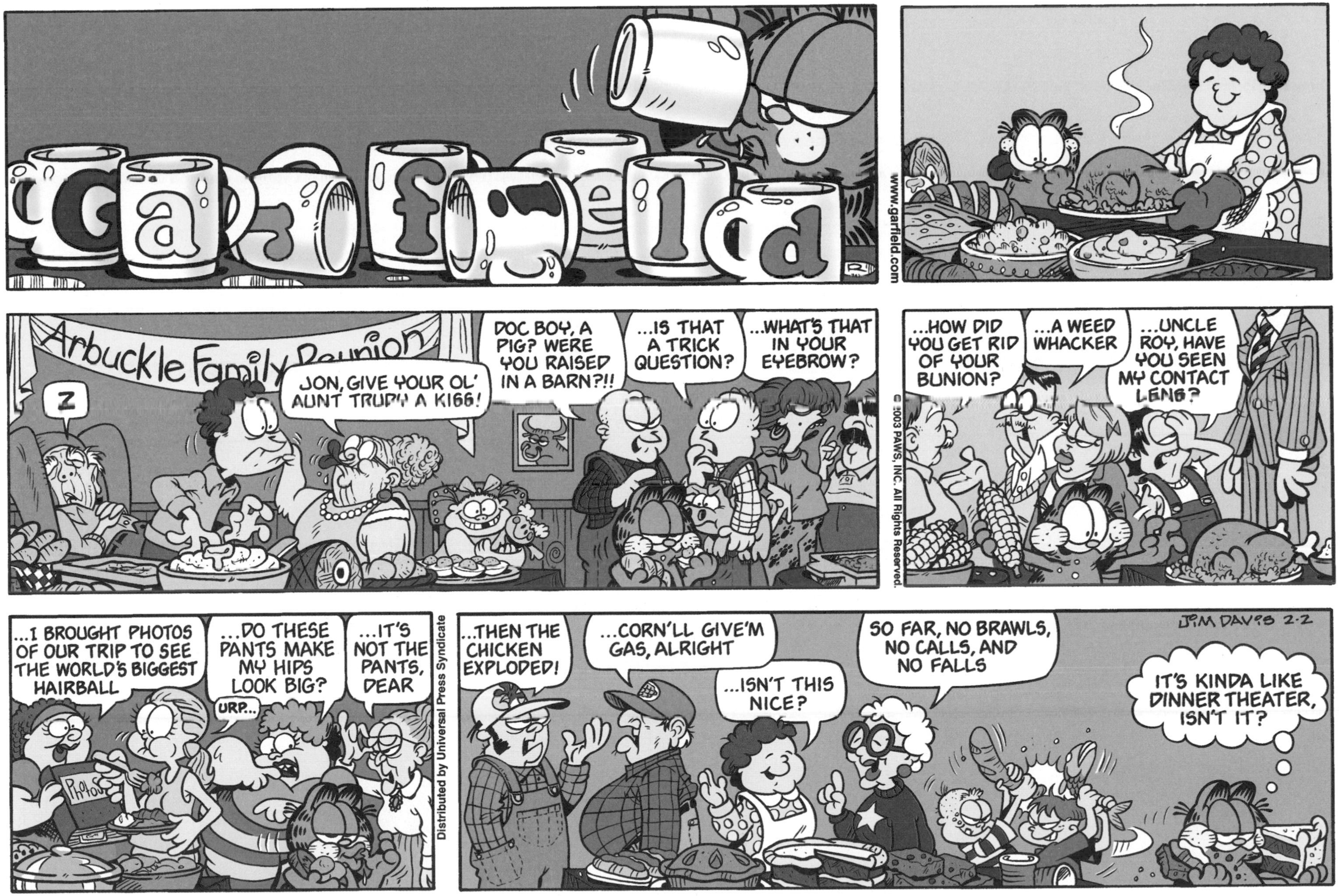
Garfield
www.garfield.com
Arbuckle Family Reunion
Z
JON, GIVE YOUR OL' AUNT TRUDY A KISS!
DOC BOY, A PIG? WERE YOU RAISED IN A BARN?!!
...IS THAT A TRICK QUESTION?
...WHAT'S THAT IN YOUR EYEBROW?
© 2003 PAWS, INC. All Rights Reserved.
...HOW DID YOU GET RID OF YOUR BUNION?
...A WEED WHACKER
...UNCLE ROY, HAVE YOU SEEN MY CONTACT LENS?
...I BROUGHT PHOTOS OF OUR TRIP TO SEE THE WORLD'S BIGGEST HAIRBALL
PHOTOS
...DO THESE PANTS MAKE MY HIPS LOOK BIG?
URP...
...IT'S NOT THE PANTS, DEAR
Distributed by Universal Press Syndicate
JIM DAVIS 2-2
...THEN THE CHICKEN EXPLODED!
...CORN'LL GIVE'M GAS, ALRIGHT
...ISN'T THIS NICE?
SO FAR, NO BRAWLS, NO CALLS, AND NO FALLS
IT'S KINDA LIKE DINNER THEATER, ISN'T IT?

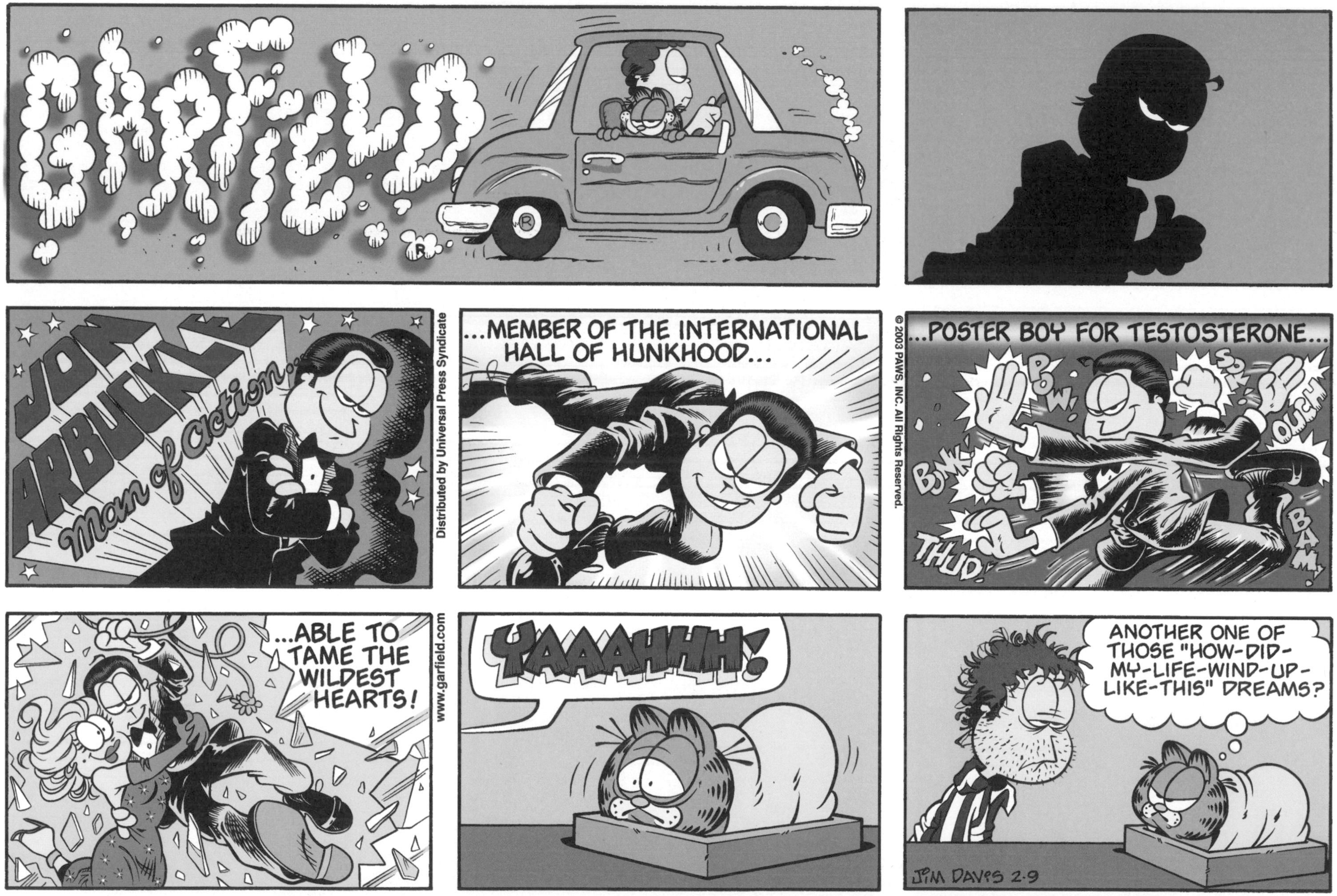
GARFIELD
JON ARBUCKLE
Man of action...
Distributed by Universal Press Syndicate
...MEMBER OF THE INTERNATIONAL HALL OF HUNKHOOD...
© 2003 PAWS, INC. All Rights Reserved.
...POSTER BOY FOR TESTOSTERONE...
POW!
OUCH
THUD!
BAM!
...ABLE TO TAME THE WILDEST HEARTS!
www.garfield.com
YAAAHHH!
ANOTHER ONE OF THOSE "HOW-DID-MY-LIFE-WIND-UP-LIKE-THIS" DREAMS?
JIM DAVIS 2-9

I call this strip a "smiler."
It doesn't make you laugh; it makes you feel all warm.

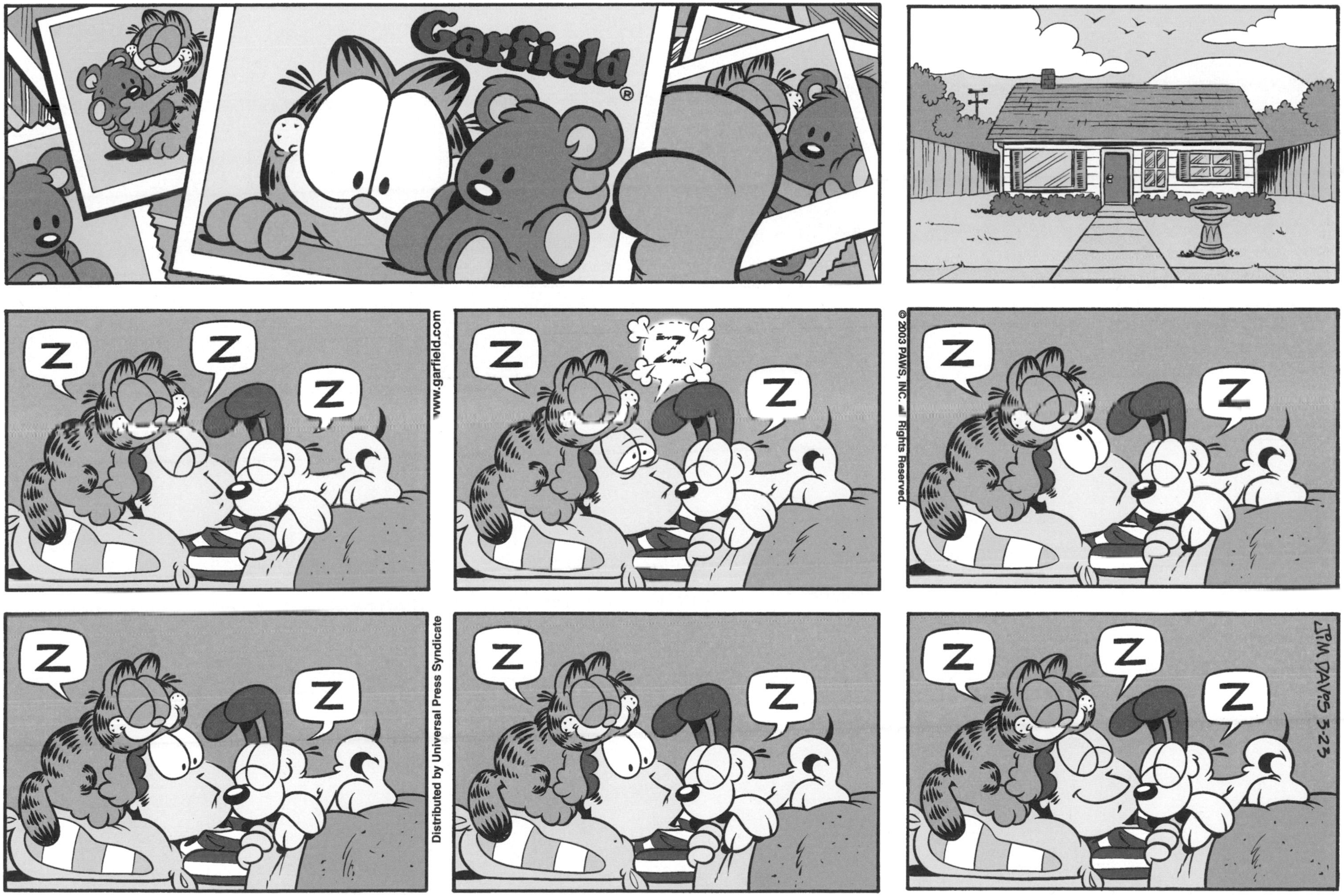

Garfield®
Z
Z
Z
www.garfield.com
Z
Z
Z
© 2003 PAWS, INC. All Rights Reserved.
Z
Z
Z
Z
Distributed by Universal Press Syndicate
Z
Z
Z
Z
Z
JIM DAVIS 3-23

I think that time travel is a cool plot; but then, when I think about it too hard, I get all confused.

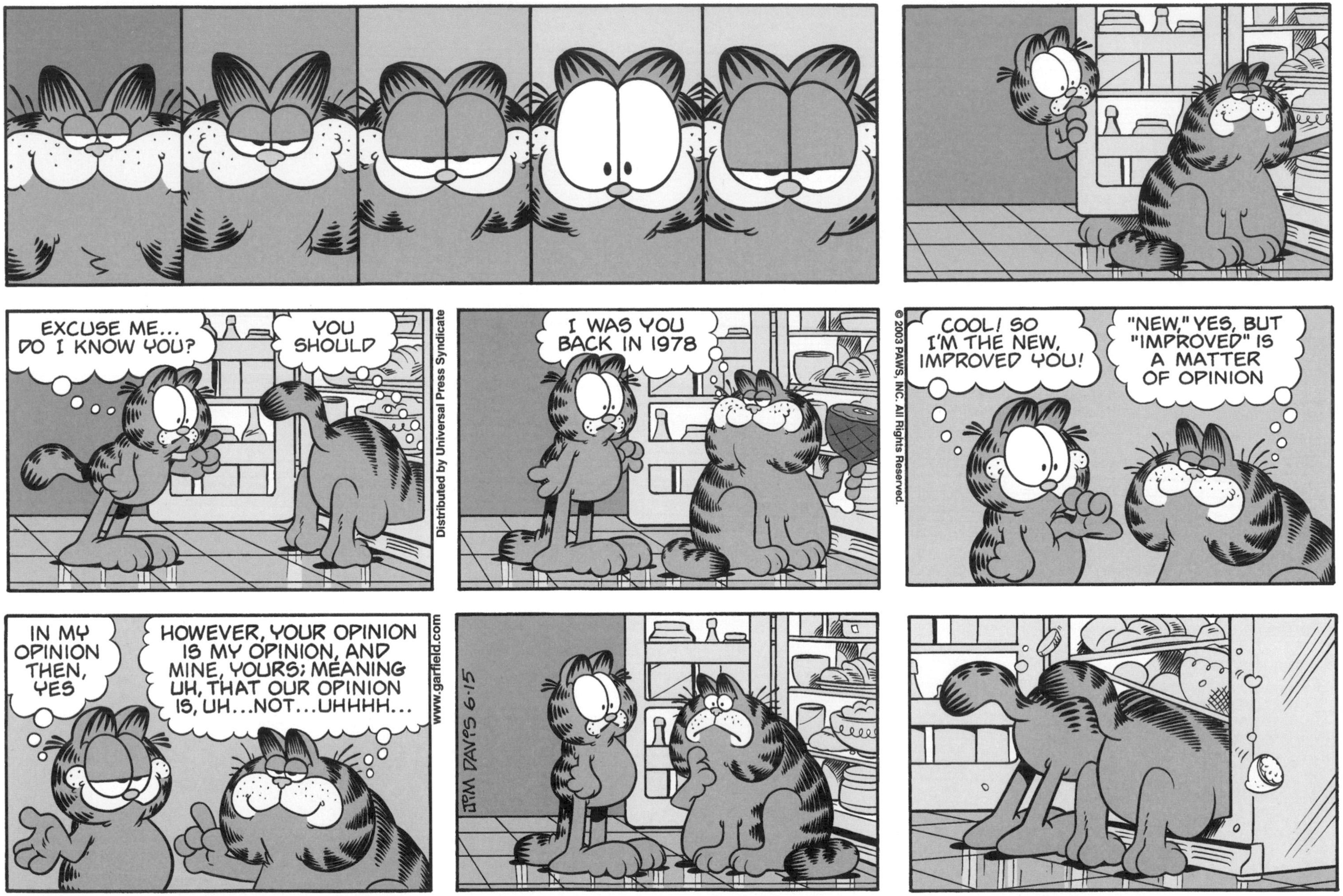
EXCUSE ME... DO I KNOW YOU?
YOU SHOULD
Distributed by Universal Press Syndicate
I WAS YOU BACK IN 1978
© 2003 PAWS, INC. All Rights Reserved.
COOL! SO I'M THE NEW, IMPROVED YOU!
"NEW," YES, BUT "IMPROVED" IS A MATTER OF OPINION
IN MY OPINION THEN, YES
HOWEVER, YOUR OPINION IS MY OPINION, AND MINE, YOURS; MEANING UH, THAT OUR OPINION IS, UH...NOT...UHHHH...
www.garfield.com
JPM DAVPS 6-15

Garfield loves Christmas . . . 'nuf said.

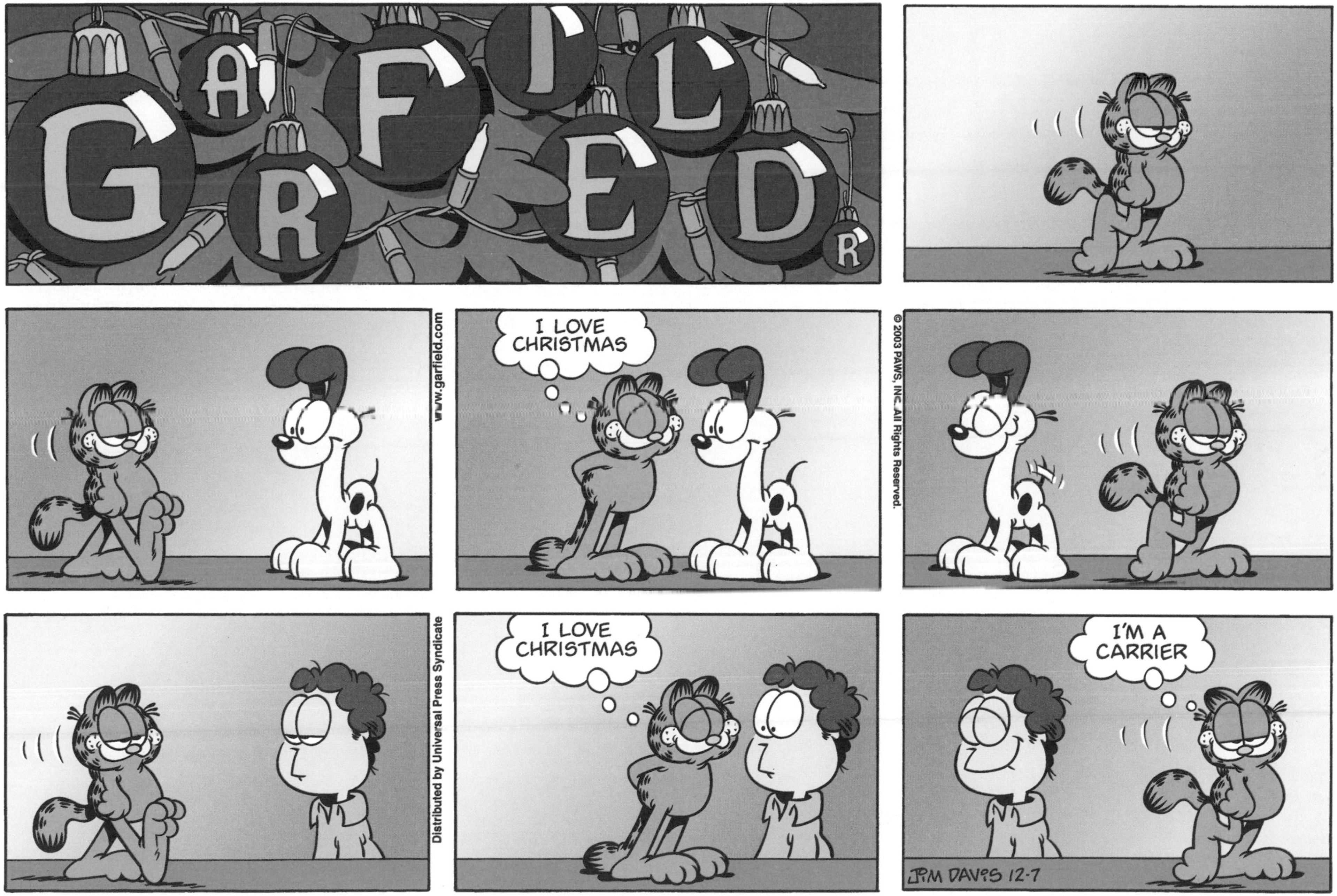
GARFIELD®
www.garfield.com
I LOVE CHRISTMAS
© 2003 PAWS, INC. All Rights Reserved.
Distributed by Universal Press Syndicate
I LOVE CHRISTMAS
I'M A CARRIER
JIM DAVIS 12-7

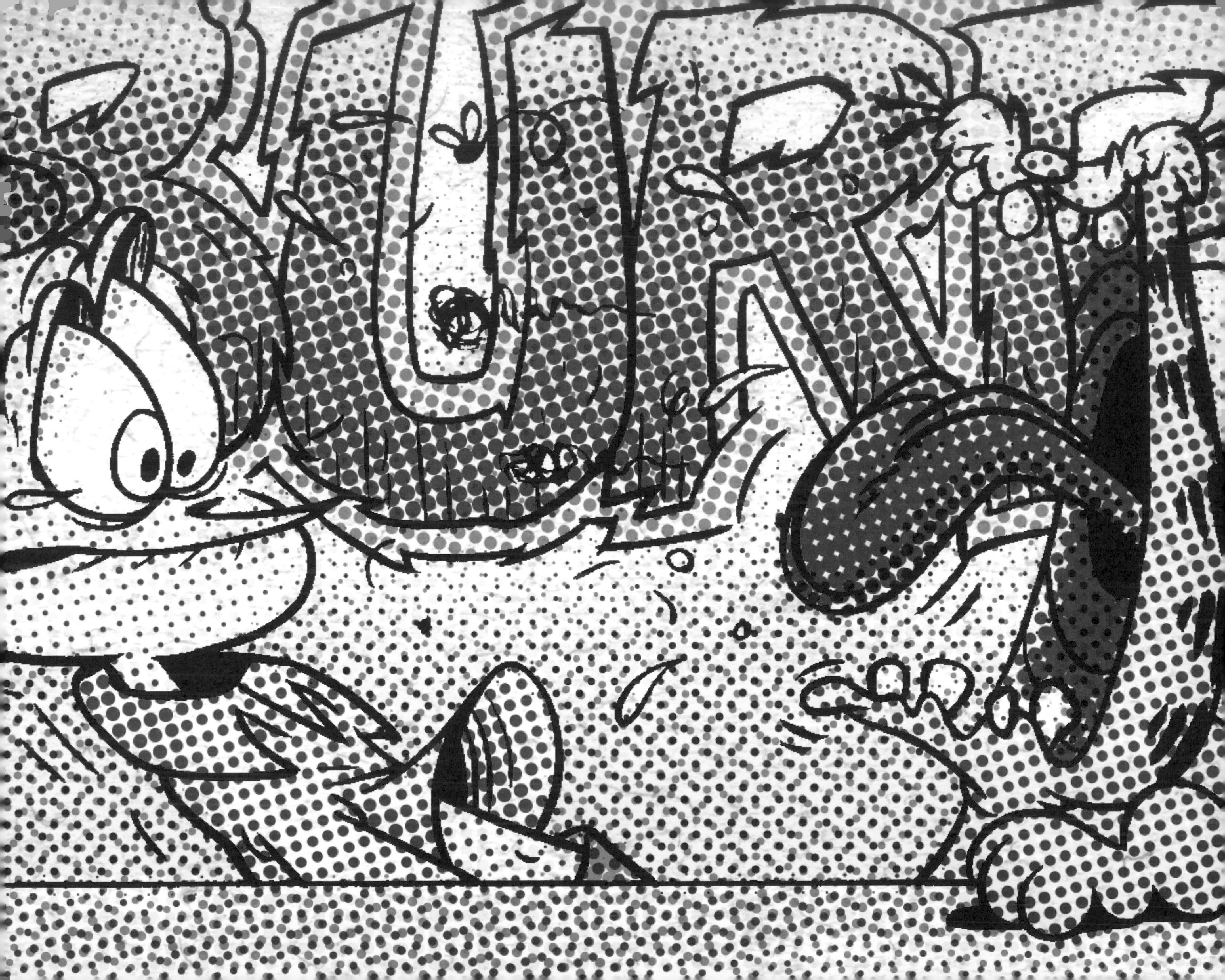

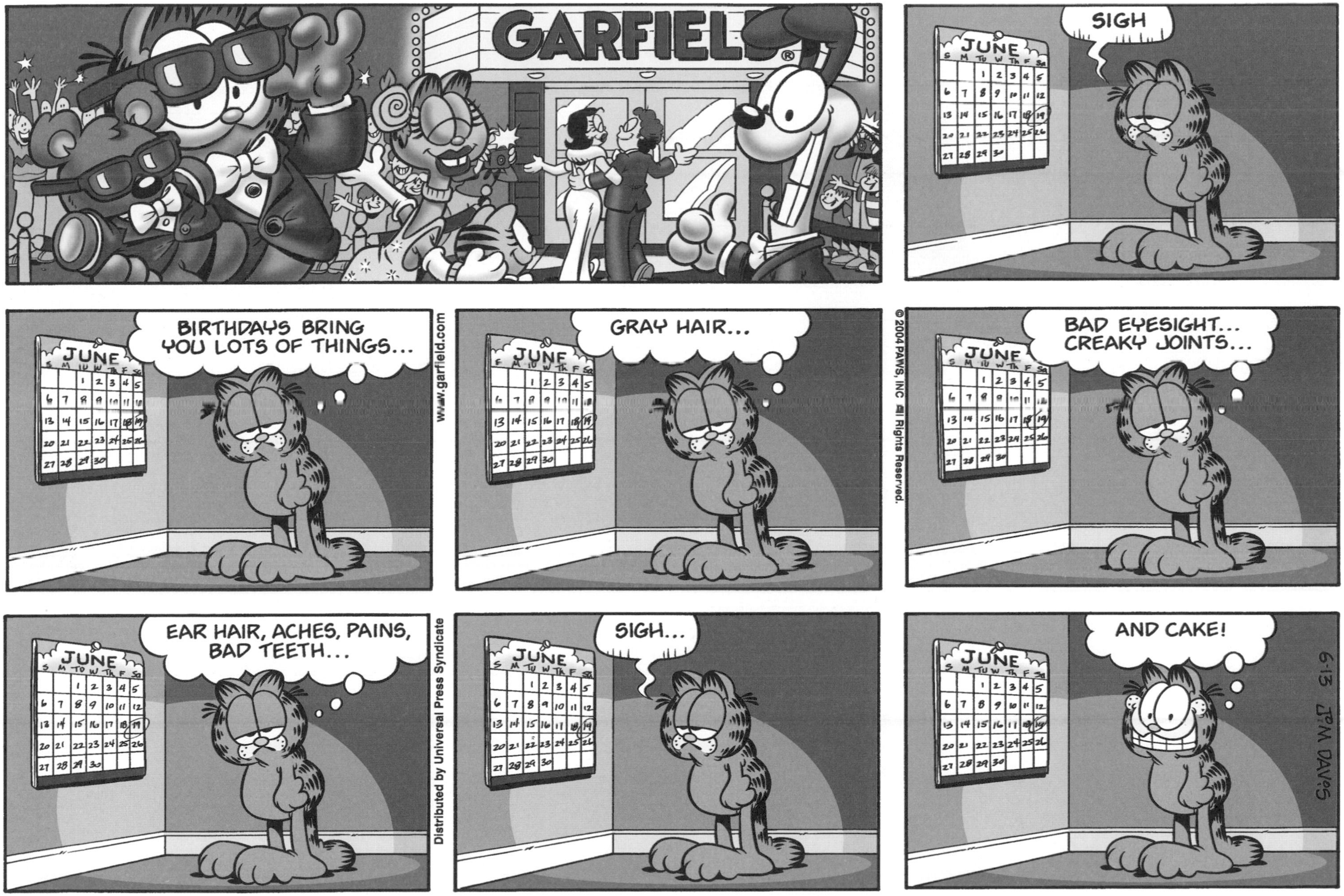
GARFIELD
SIGH
BIRTHDAYS BRING YOU LOTS OF THINGS...
GRAY HAIR...
BAD EYESIGHT... CREAKY JOINTS...
EAR HAIR, ACHES, PAINS, BAD TEETH...
SIGH...
AND CAKE!
www.garfield.com
© 2004 PAWS, INC All Rights Reserved.
Distributed by Universal Press Syndicate
JIM DAVIS 6-13

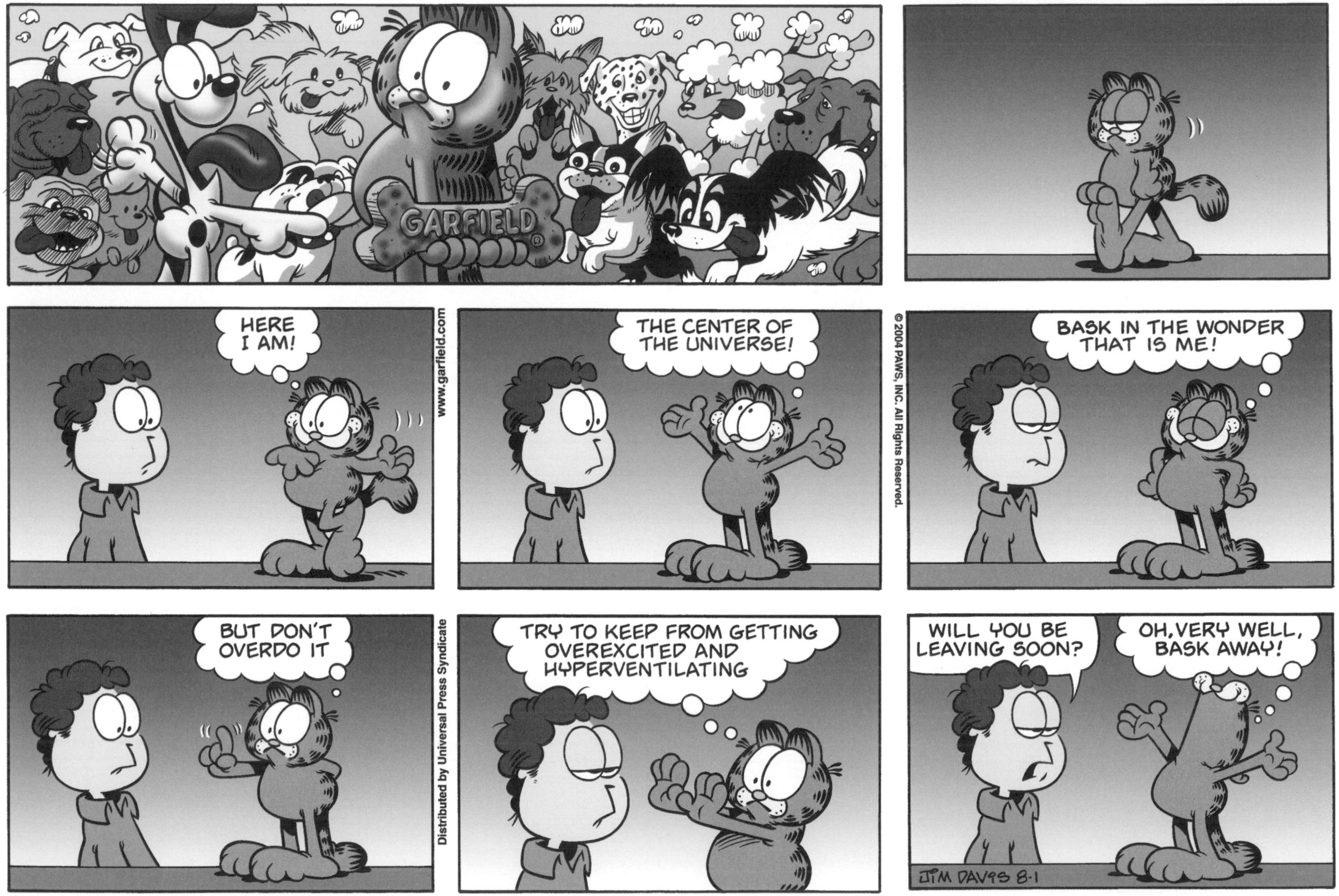
GARFIELD
HERE I AM!
www.garfield.com
THE CENTER OF THE UNIVERSE!
© 2004 PAWS, INC. All Rights Reserved.
BASK IN THE WONDER THAT IS ME!
BUT DON'T OVERDO IT
Distributed by Universal Press Syndicate
TRY TO KEEP FROM GETTING OVEREXCITED AND HYPERVENTILATING
WILL YOU BE LEAVING SOON?
OH, VERY WELL, BASK AWAY!
JIM DAVIS 8-1

Come on, admit it. We're all like this way down deep inside.

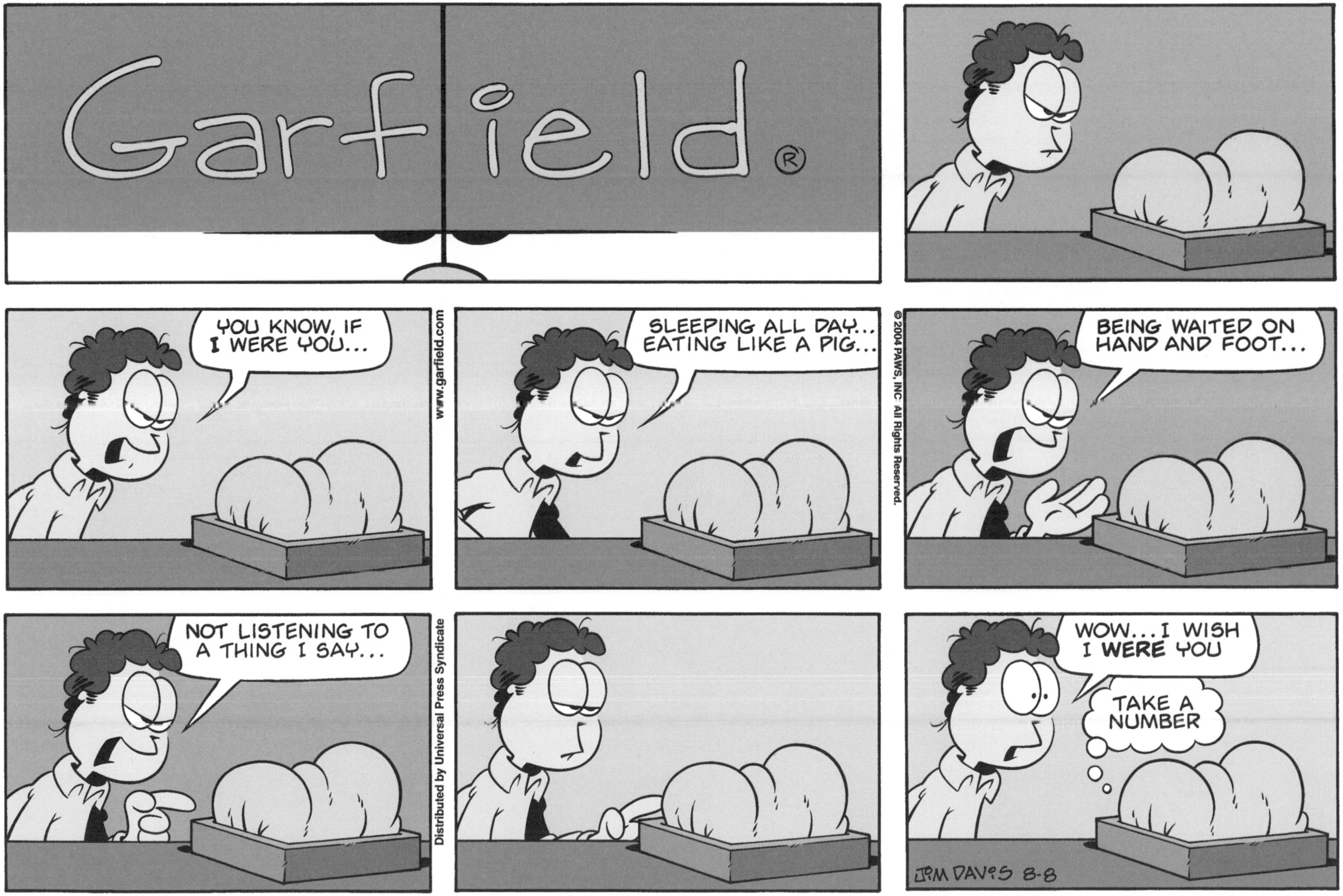
Garfield®
YOU KNOW, IF I WERE YOU...
SLEEPING ALL DAY... EATING LIKE A PIG...
BEING WAITED ON HAND AND FOOT...
NOT LISTENING TO A THING I SAY...
WOW... I WISH I WERE YOU
TAKE A NUMBER
JIM DAVIS 8-8
www.garfield.com
© 2004 PAWS, INC. All Rights Reserved.
Distributed by Universal Press Syndicate

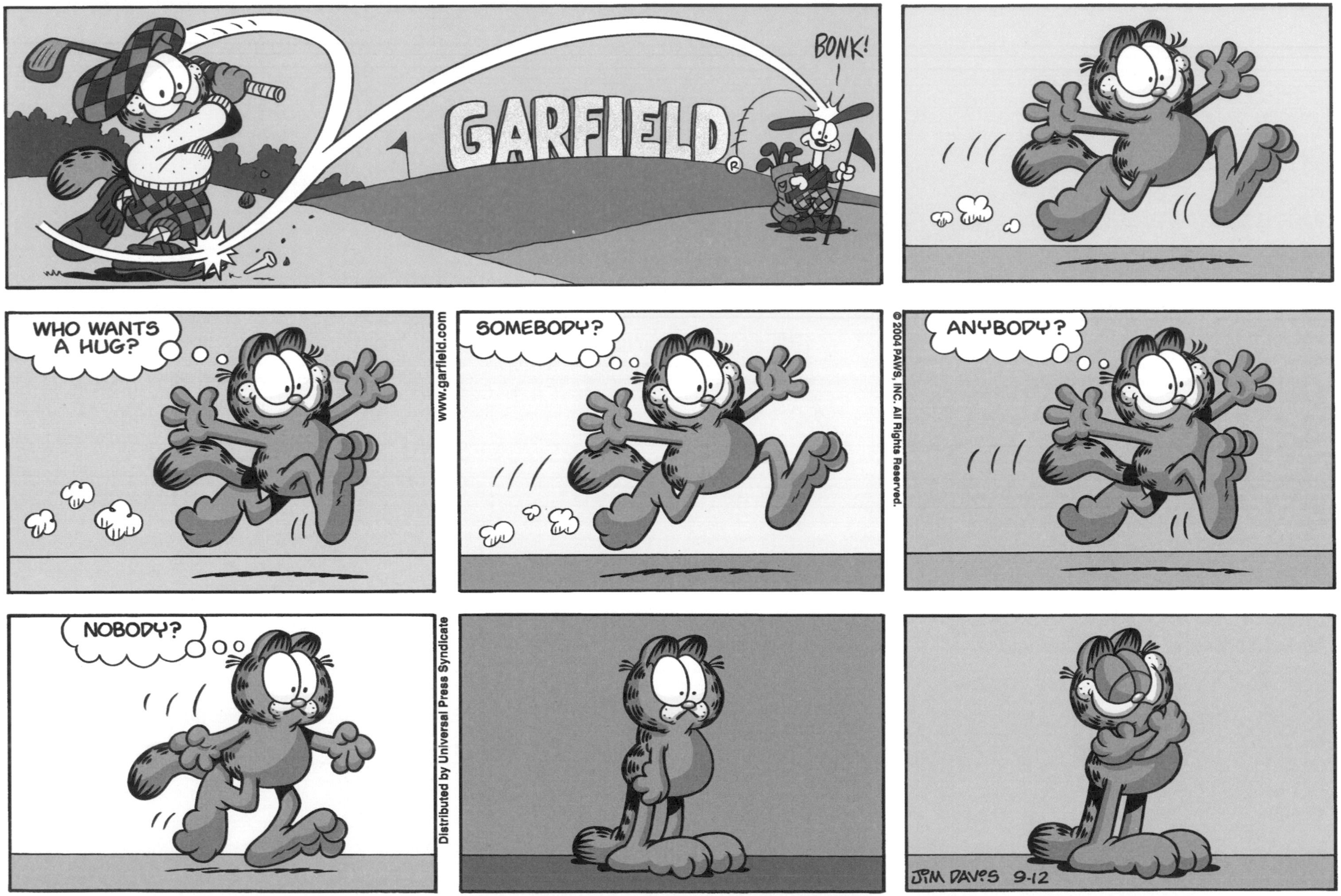

GARFIELD
BONK!
WHO WANTS A HUG?
www.garfield.com
SOMEBODY?
© 2004 PAWS, INC. All Rights Reserved.
ANYBODY?
NOBODY?
Distributed by Universal Press Syndicate
JIM DAVIS 9-12

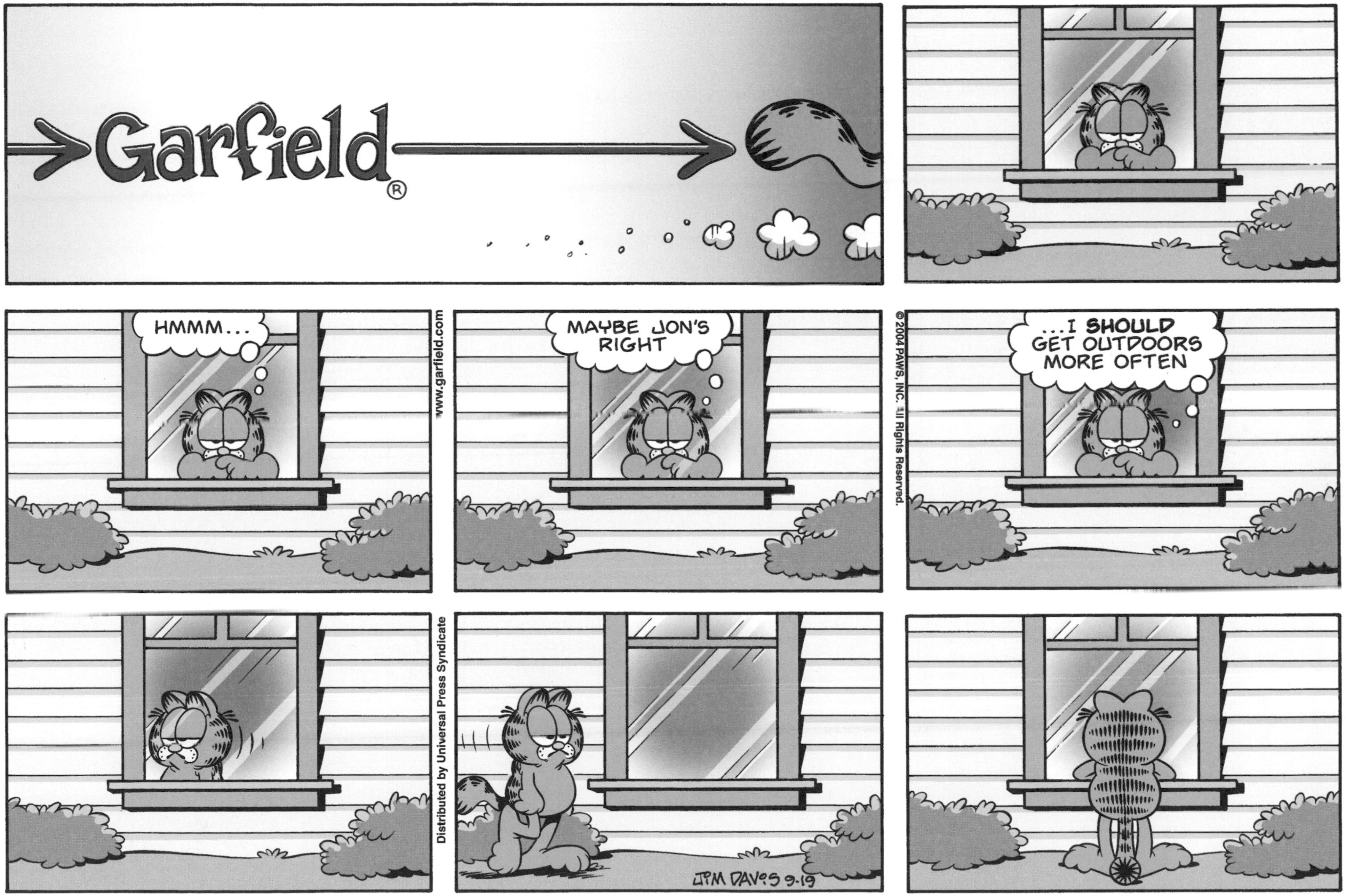
Garfield®
HMMM...
MAYBE JON'S RIGHT
...I SHOULD GET OUTDOORS MORE OFTEN
JPM DAVPS 9-19

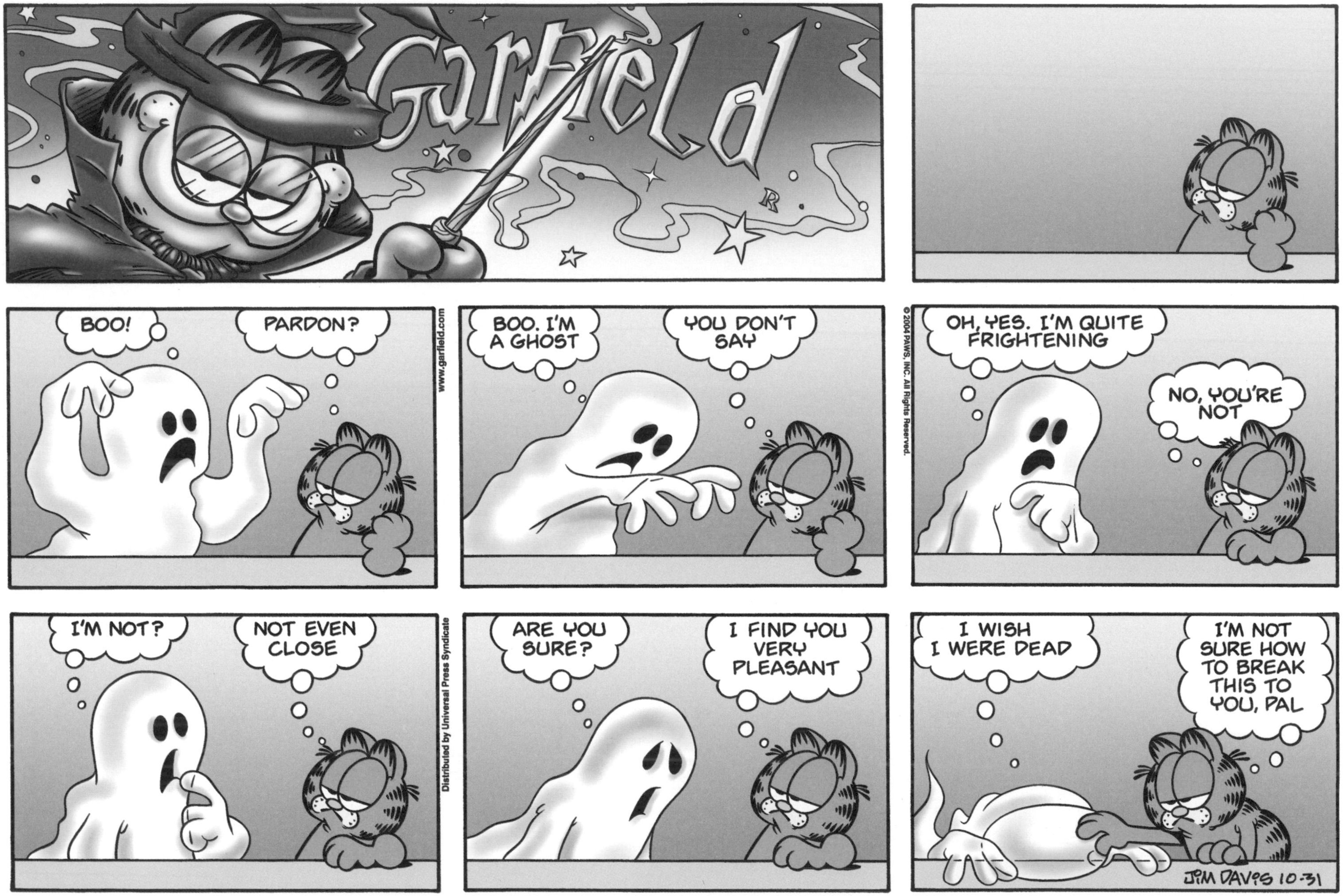
Garfield®
BOO!
PARDON?
BOO. I'M A GHOST
YOU DON'T SAY
OH, YES. I'M QUITE FRIGHTENING
NO, YOU'RE NOT
I'M NOT?
NOT EVEN CLOSE
ARE YOU SURE?
I FIND YOU VERY PLEASANT
I WISH I WERE DEAD
I'M NOT SURE HOW TO BREAK THIS TO YOU, PAL
JIM DAVIS 10-31
www.garfield.com
© 2004 PAWS, INC. All Rights Reserved.
Distributed by Universal Press Syndicate

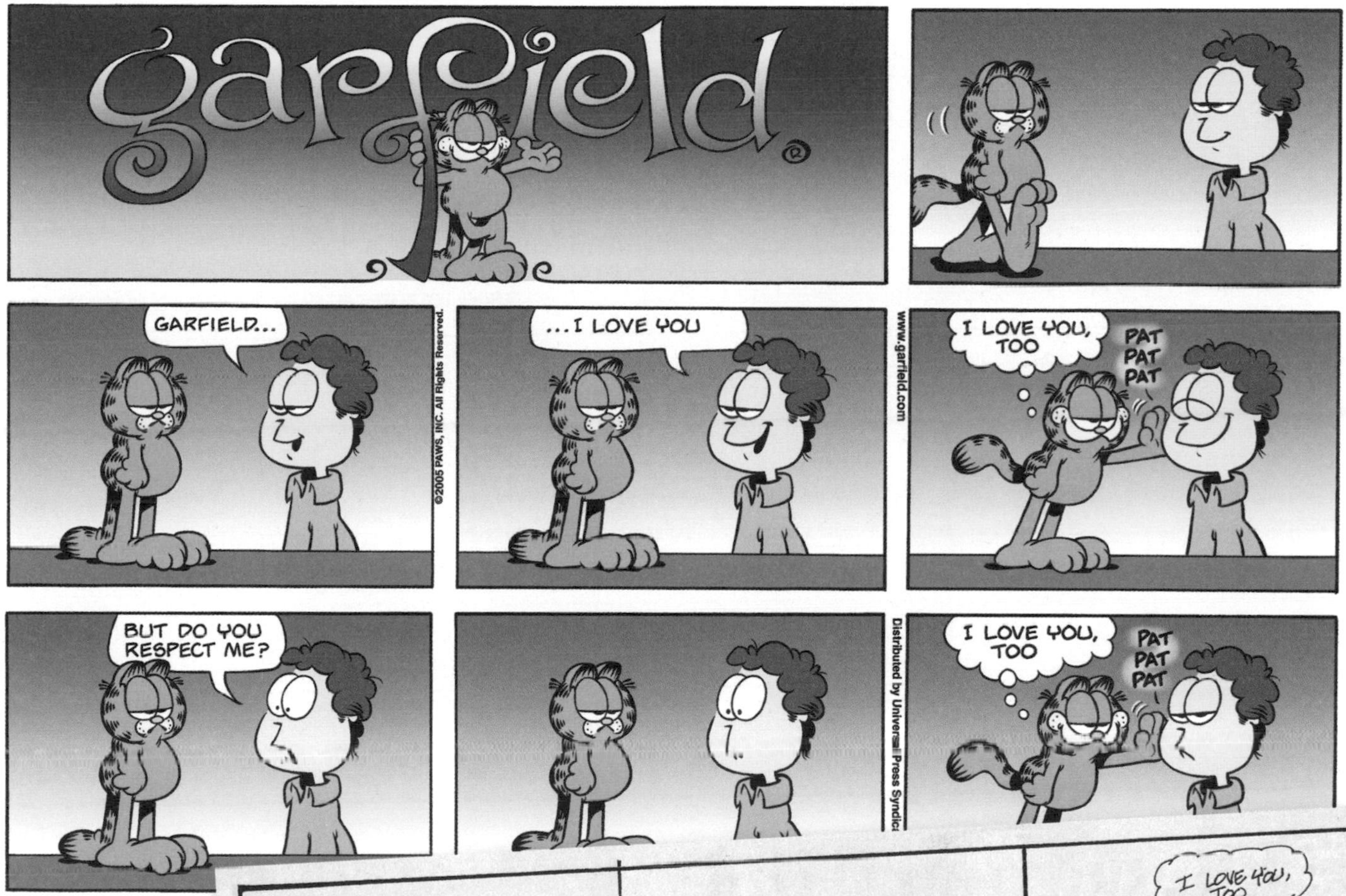
garfield
GARFIELD...
©2005 PAWS, INC. All Rights Reserved.
...I LOVE YOU
www.garfield.com
I LOVE YOU, TOO
PAT PAT PAT
BUT DO YOU RESPECT ME?
Distributed by Universal Press Syndic
I LOVE YOU, TOO
PAT PAT PAT

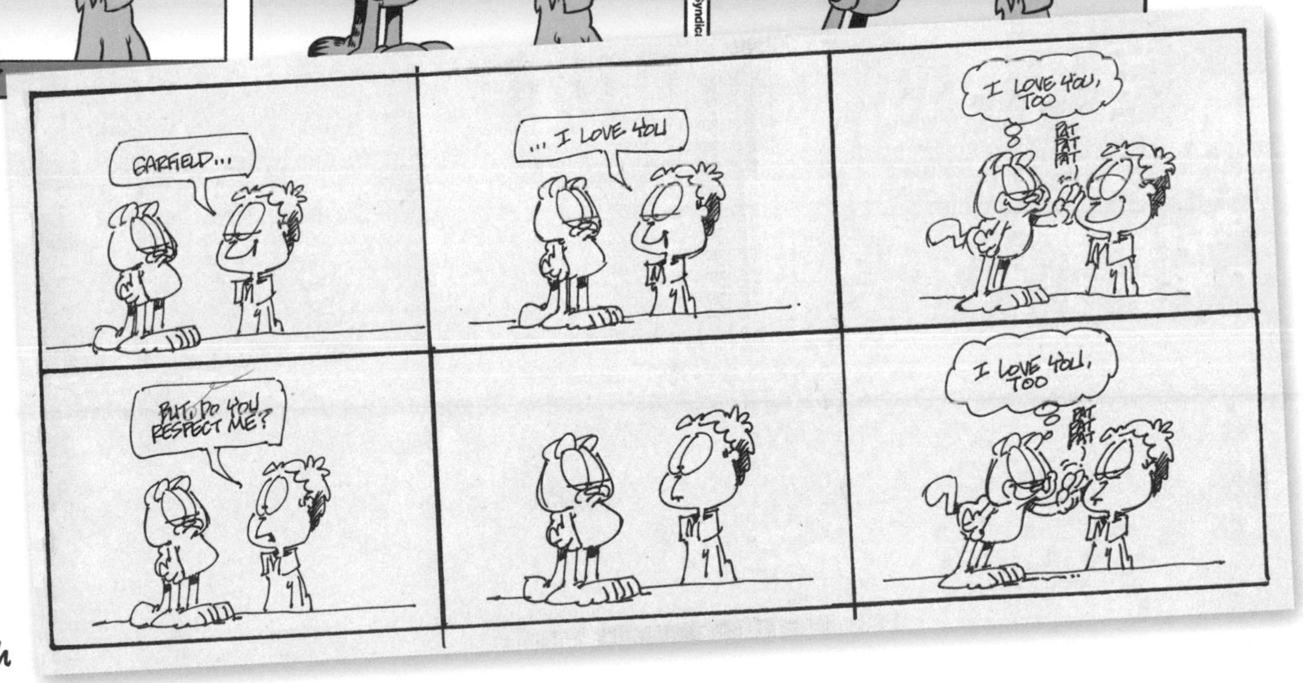
GARFIELD...
... I LOVE YOU
I LOVE YOU, TOO
PAT PAT PAT
BUT DO YOU RESPECT ME?
I LOVE YOU, TOO
PAT PAT PAT

original rough

Who cares about world peace if you can't have a pickle?

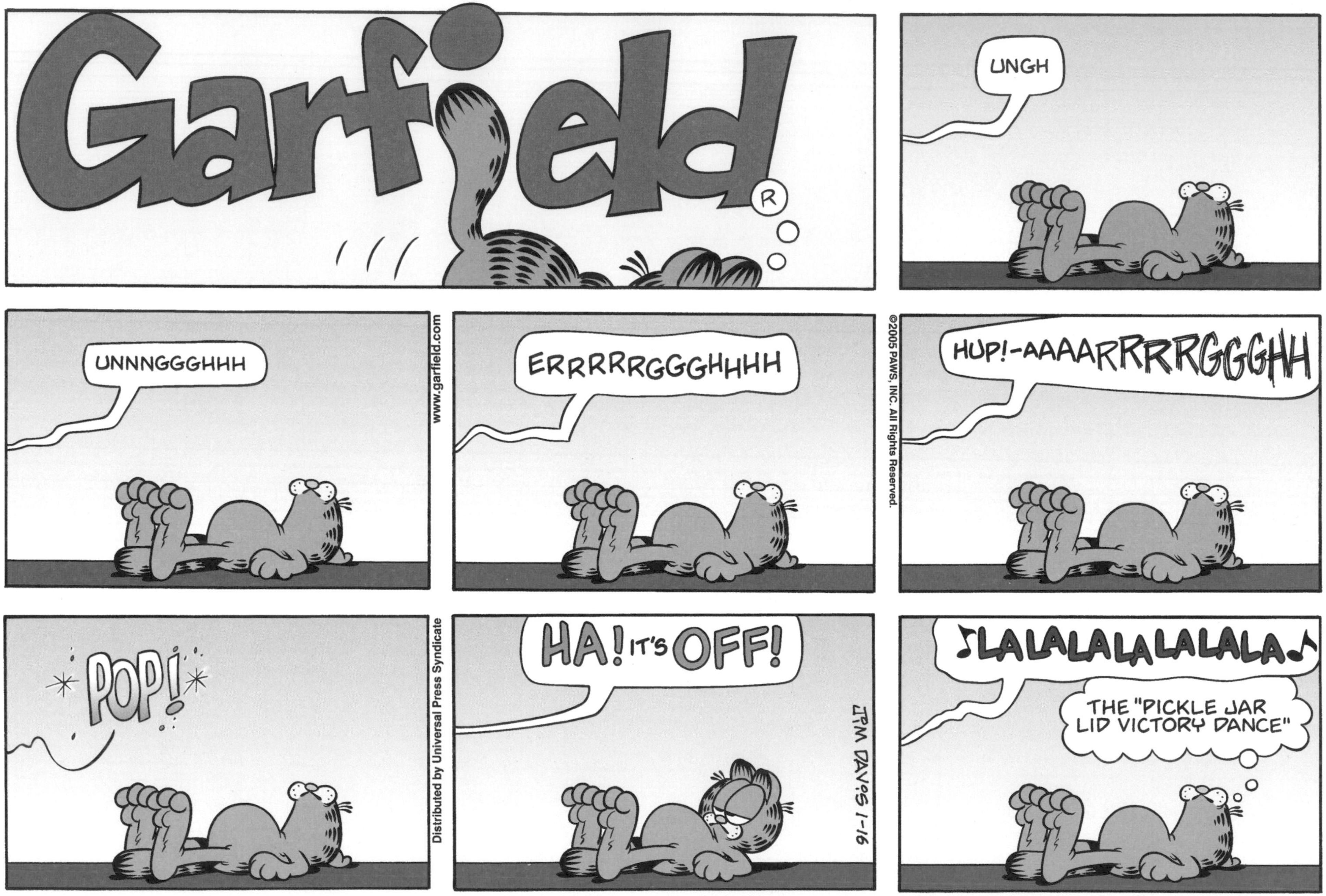
Garfield
UNGH
UNNNGGGHHH
ERRRRRGGGHHHH
HUP!-AAAARRRRGGGHH
POP!
HA! IT'S OFF!
LALALALALALALA
THE "PICKLE JAR LID VICTORY DANCE"
www.garfield.com
©2005 PAWS, INC. All Rights Reserved.
Distributed by Universal Press Syndicate
JIM DAVIS 1-16

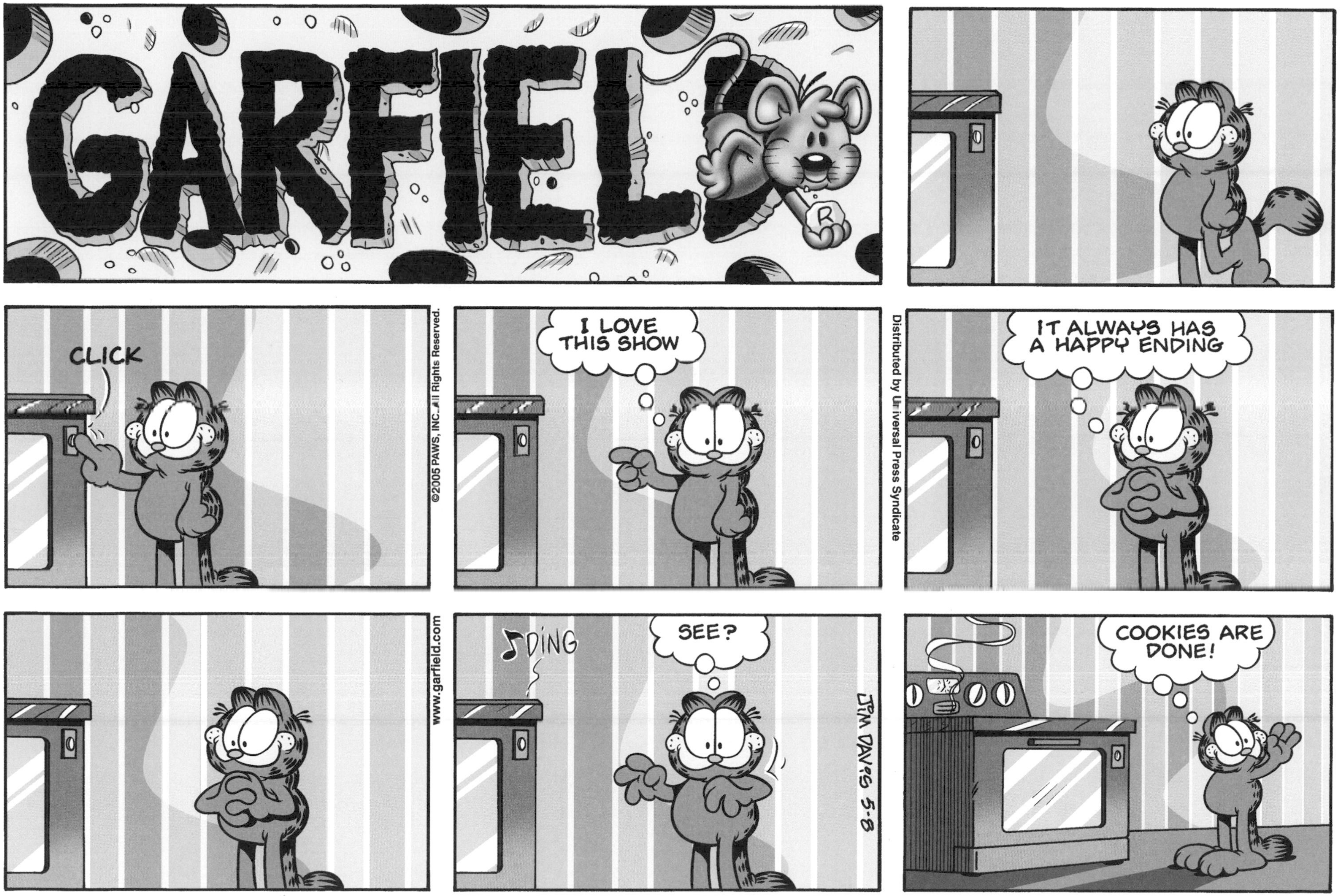
GARFIELD
CLICK
I LOVE THIS SHOW
IT ALWAYS HAS A HAPPY ENDING
DING
SEE?
COOKIES ARE DONE!
JIM DAVIS 5-8
©2005 PAWS, INC. All Rights Reserved.
Distributed by Universal Press Syndicate
www.garfield.com

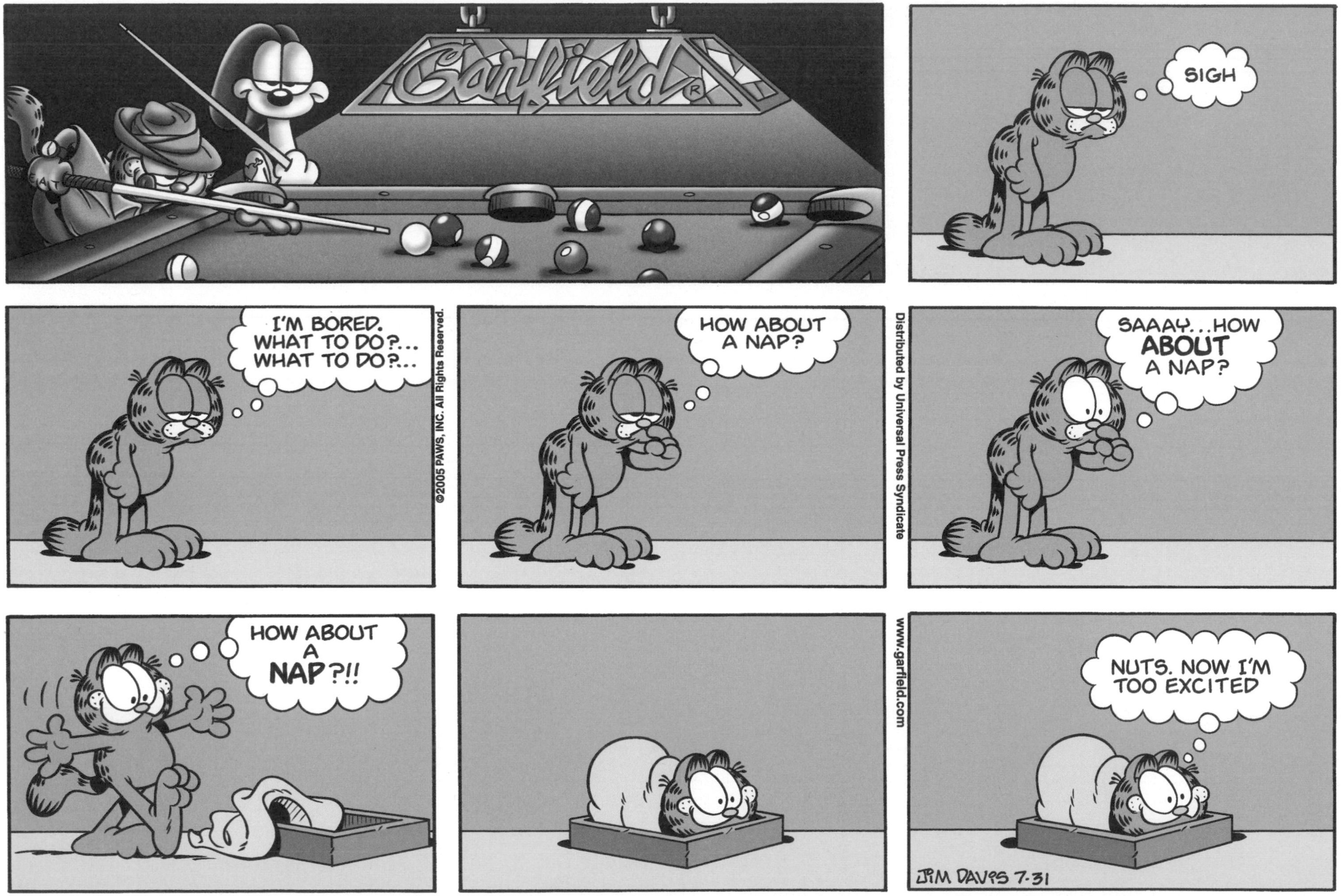

Garfield
SIGH
I'M BORED. WHAT TO DO?... WHAT TO DO?...
©2005 PAWS, INC. All Rights Reserved.
HOW ABOUT A NAP?
Distributed by Universal Press Syndicate
SAAAY...HOW ABOUT A NAP?
HOW ABOUT A NAP?!!
www.garfield.com
NUTS. NOW I'M TOO EXCITED
JIM DAVIS 7-31

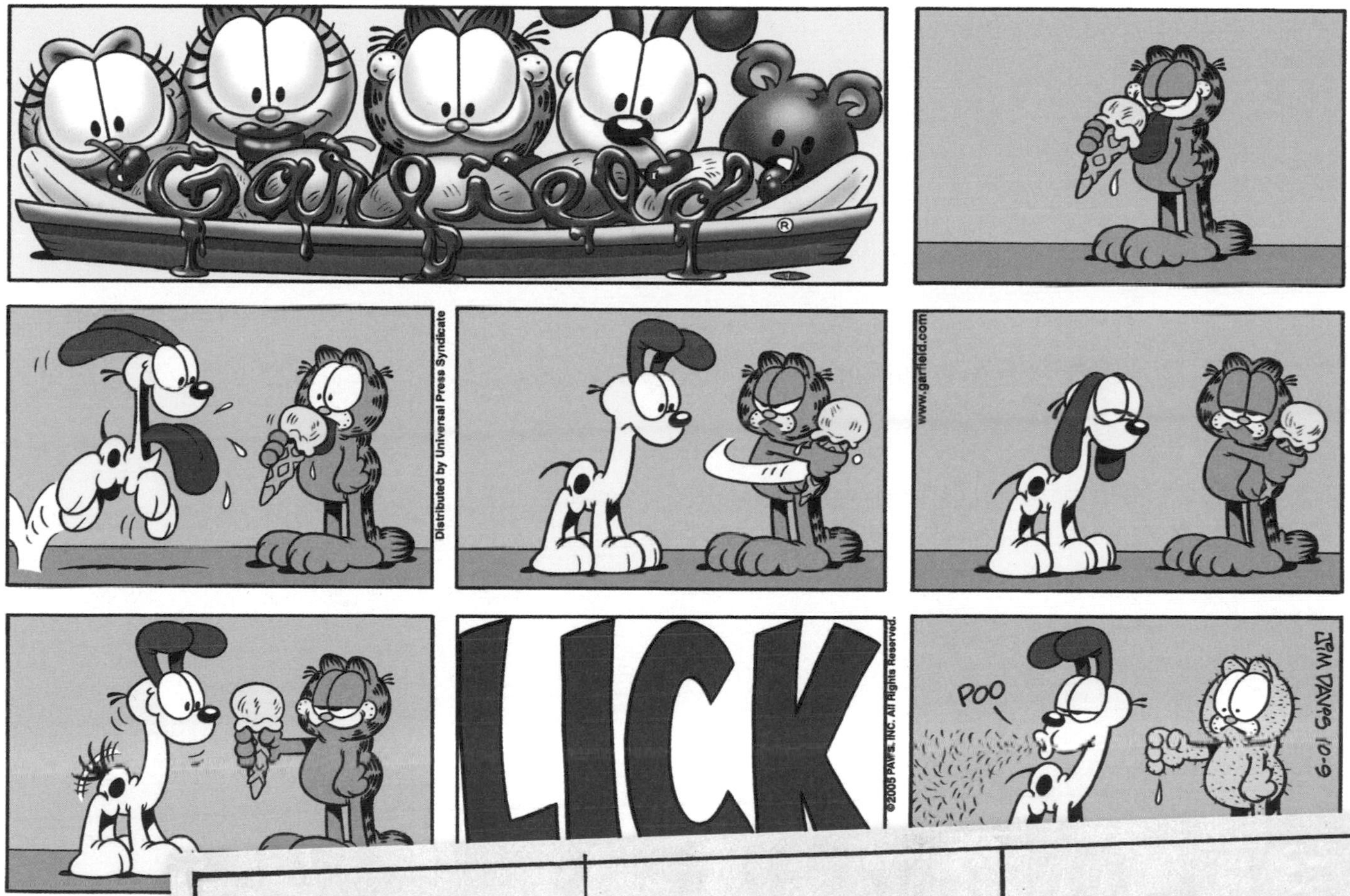
Garfield
Distributed by Universal Press Syndicate
www.garfield.com
LICK
©2005 PAWS, INC. All Rights Reserved.
POO

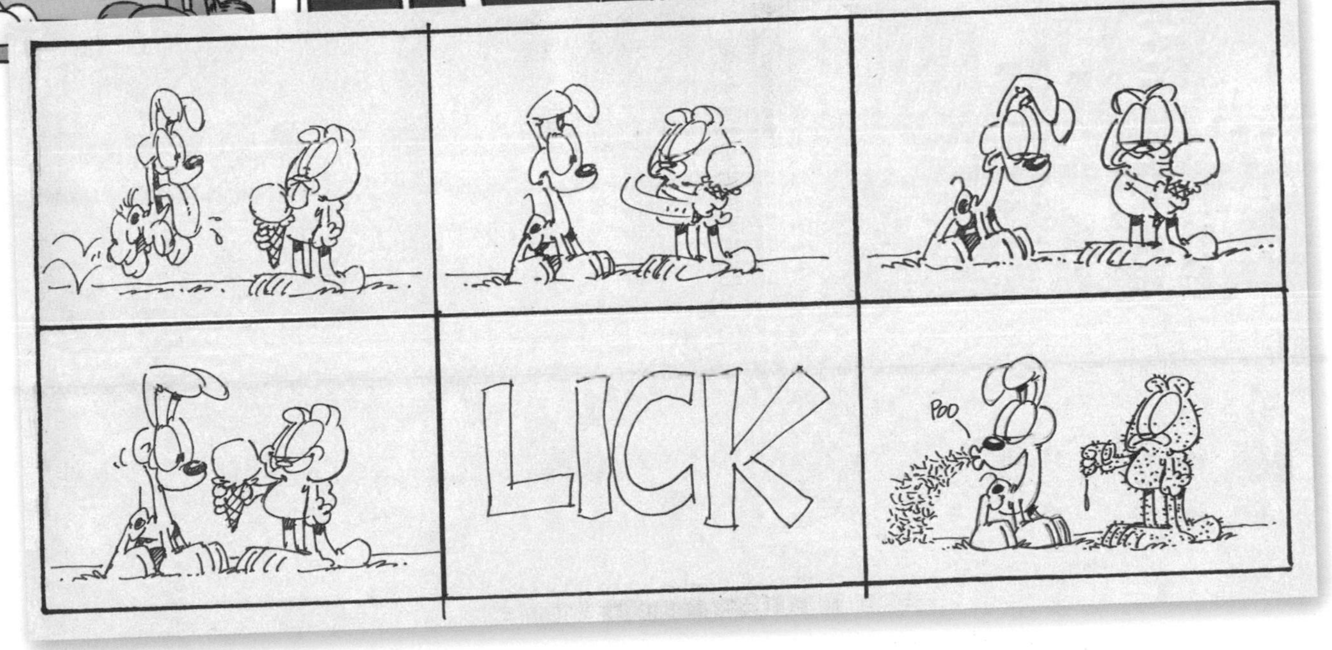
LICK
POO

original rough

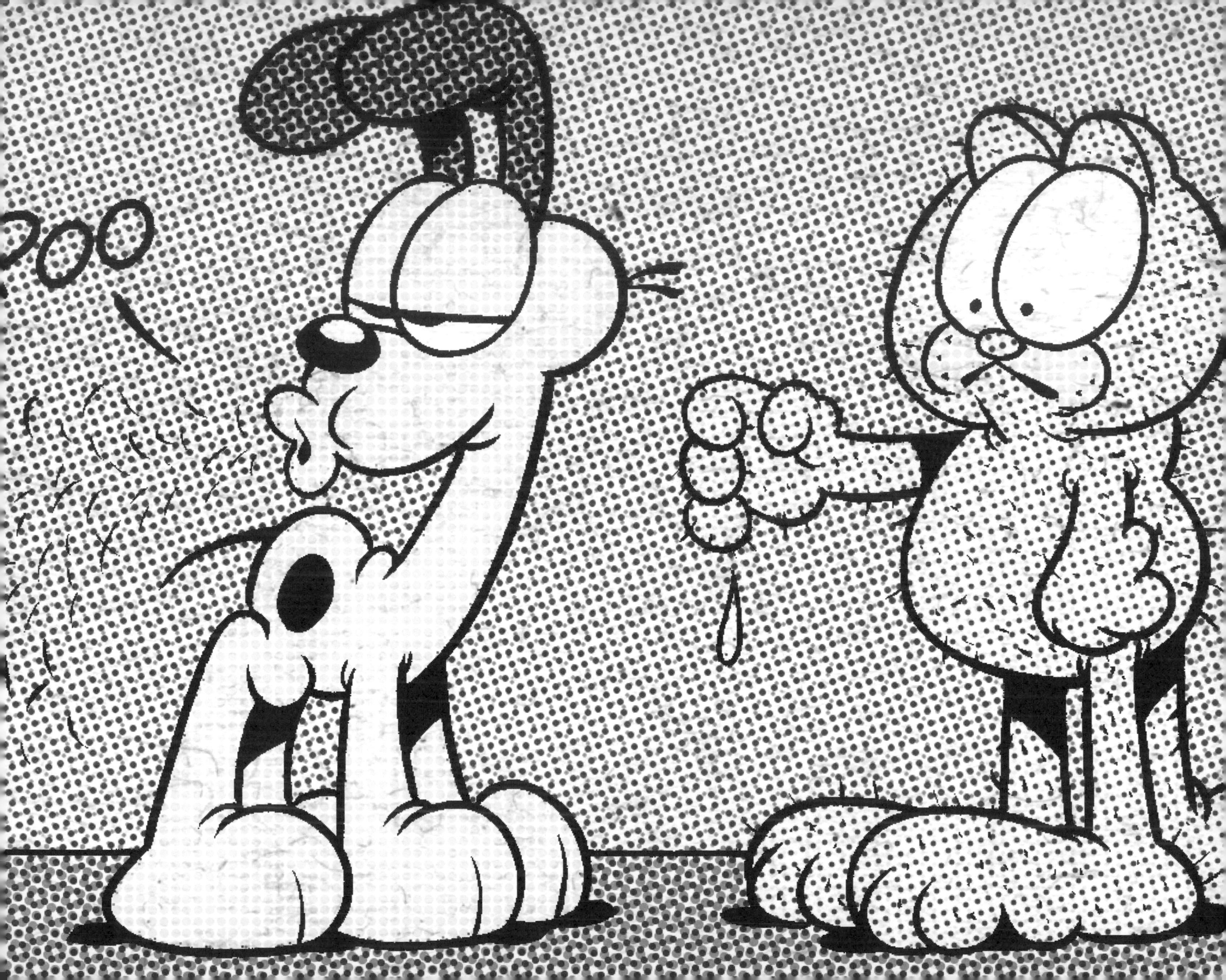

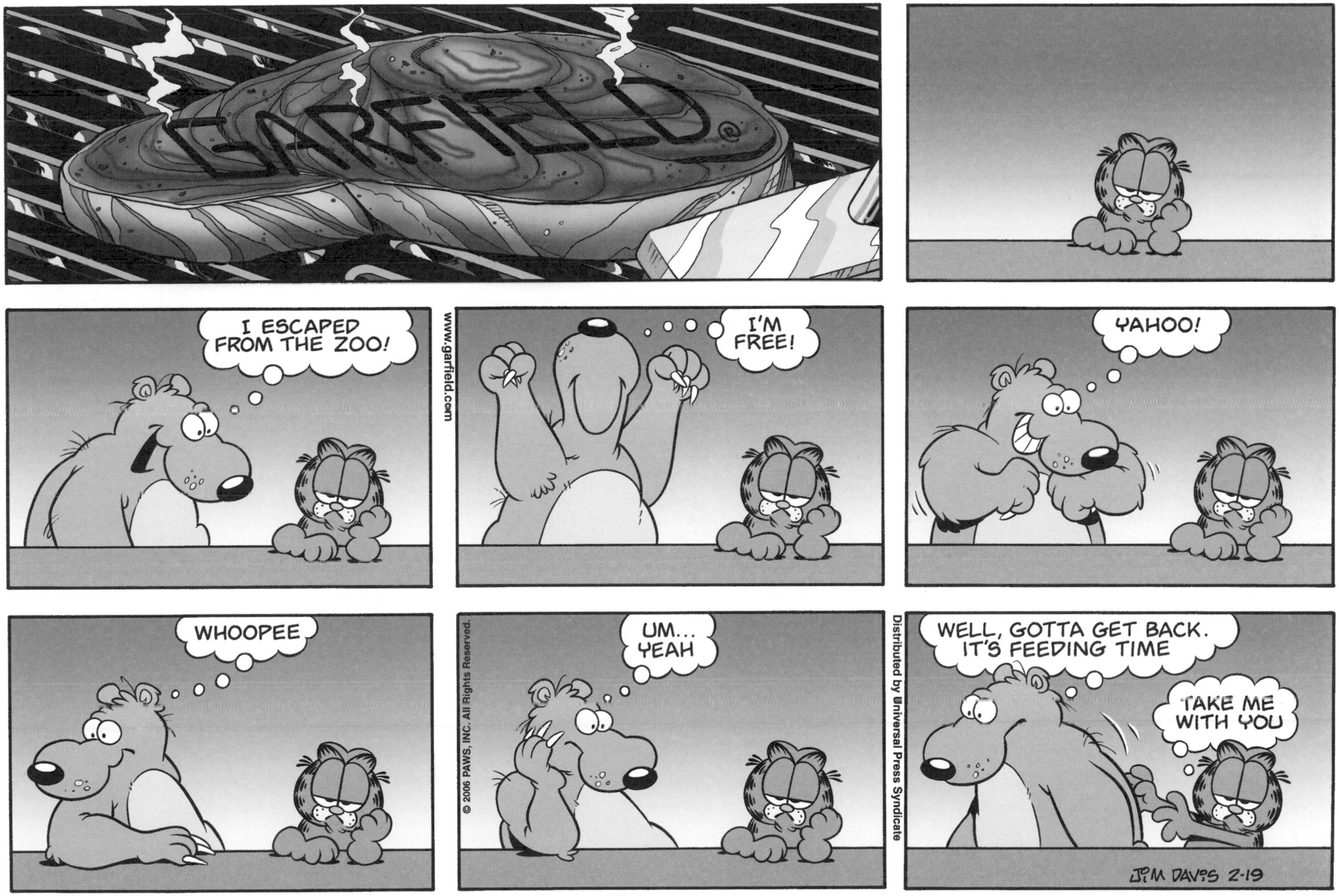
GARFIELD®
I ESCAPED FROM THE ZOO!
www.garfield.com
I'M FREE!
YAHOO!
WHOOPEE
UM... YEAH
WELL, GOTTA GET BACK. IT'S FEEDING TIME
TAKE ME WITH YOU
JIM DAVIS 2-19

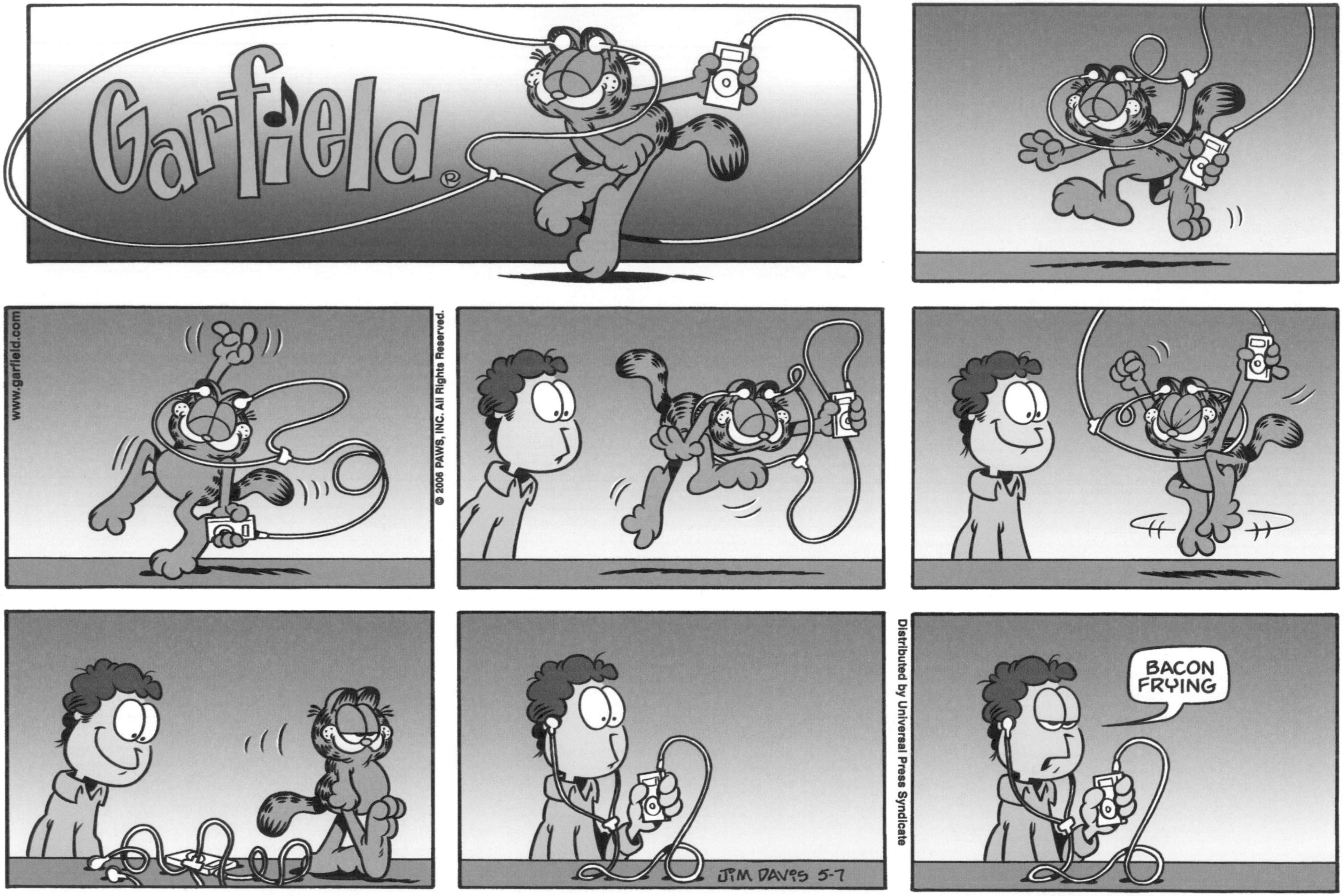
Garfield
www.garfield.com
© 2006 PAWS, INC. All Rights Reserved.
Distributed by Universal Press Syndicate
JIM DAVIS 5-7
BACON FRYING

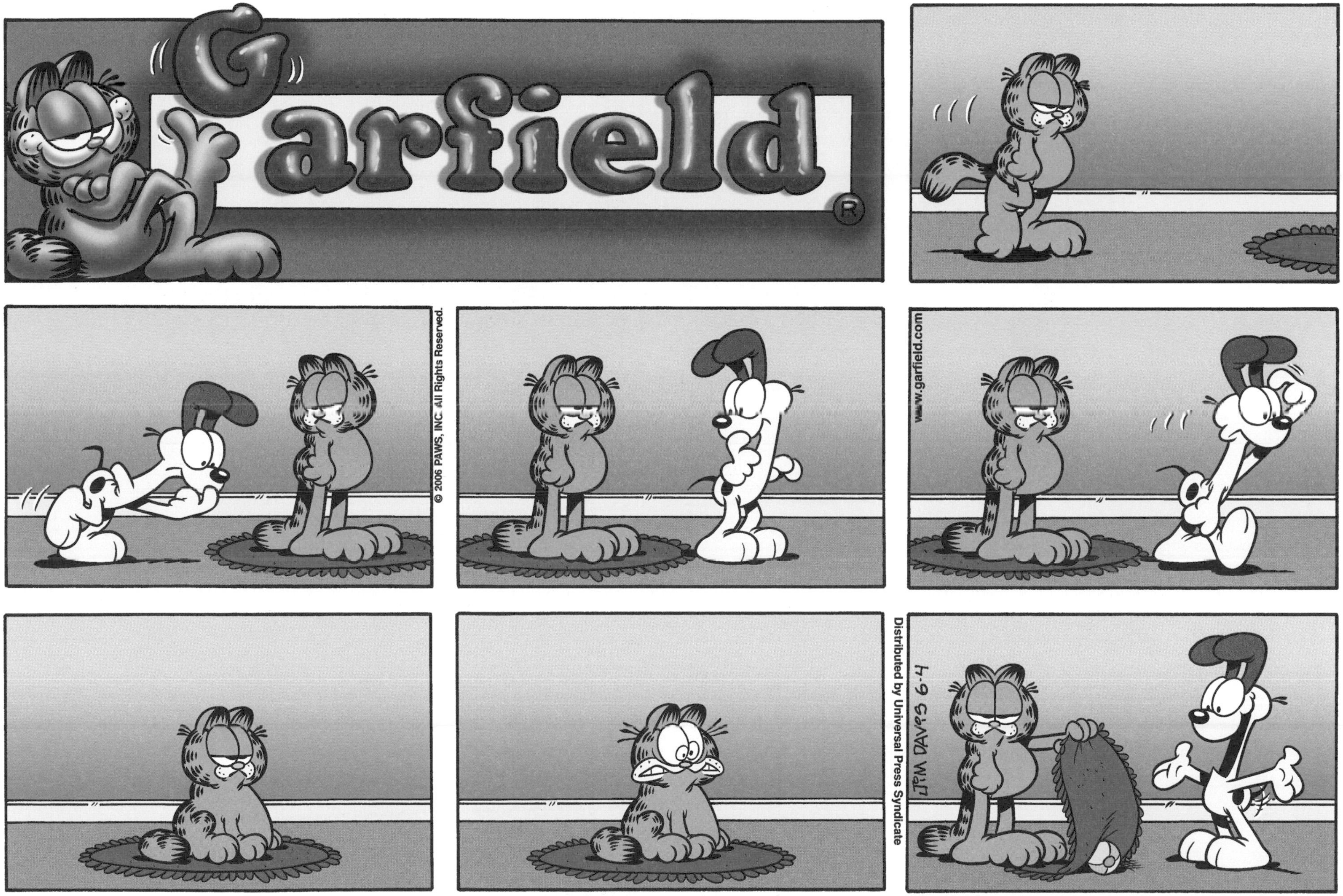
Garfield
© 2006 PAWS, INC. All Rights Reserved.
www.garfield.com
Distributed by Universal Press Syndicate
JPM DAVIS 6-4

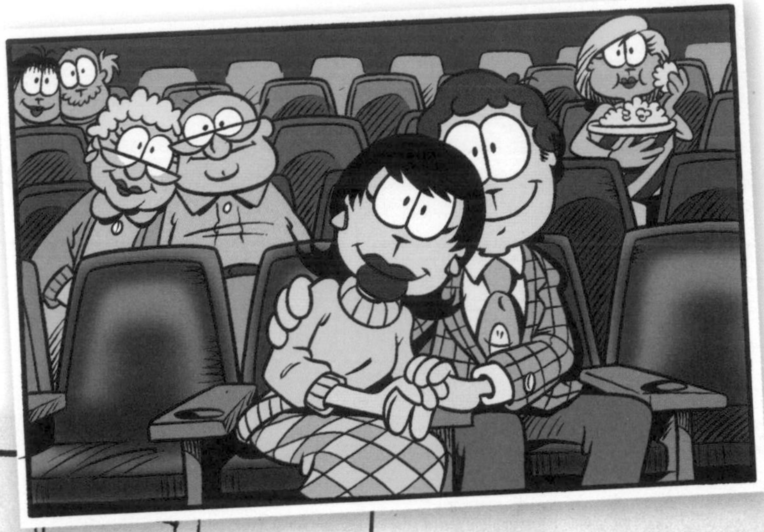

After twenty-five years of doing the strip, I asked the fans if there was anything more they'd like to see. I got a resounding, "Give Jon a life!"

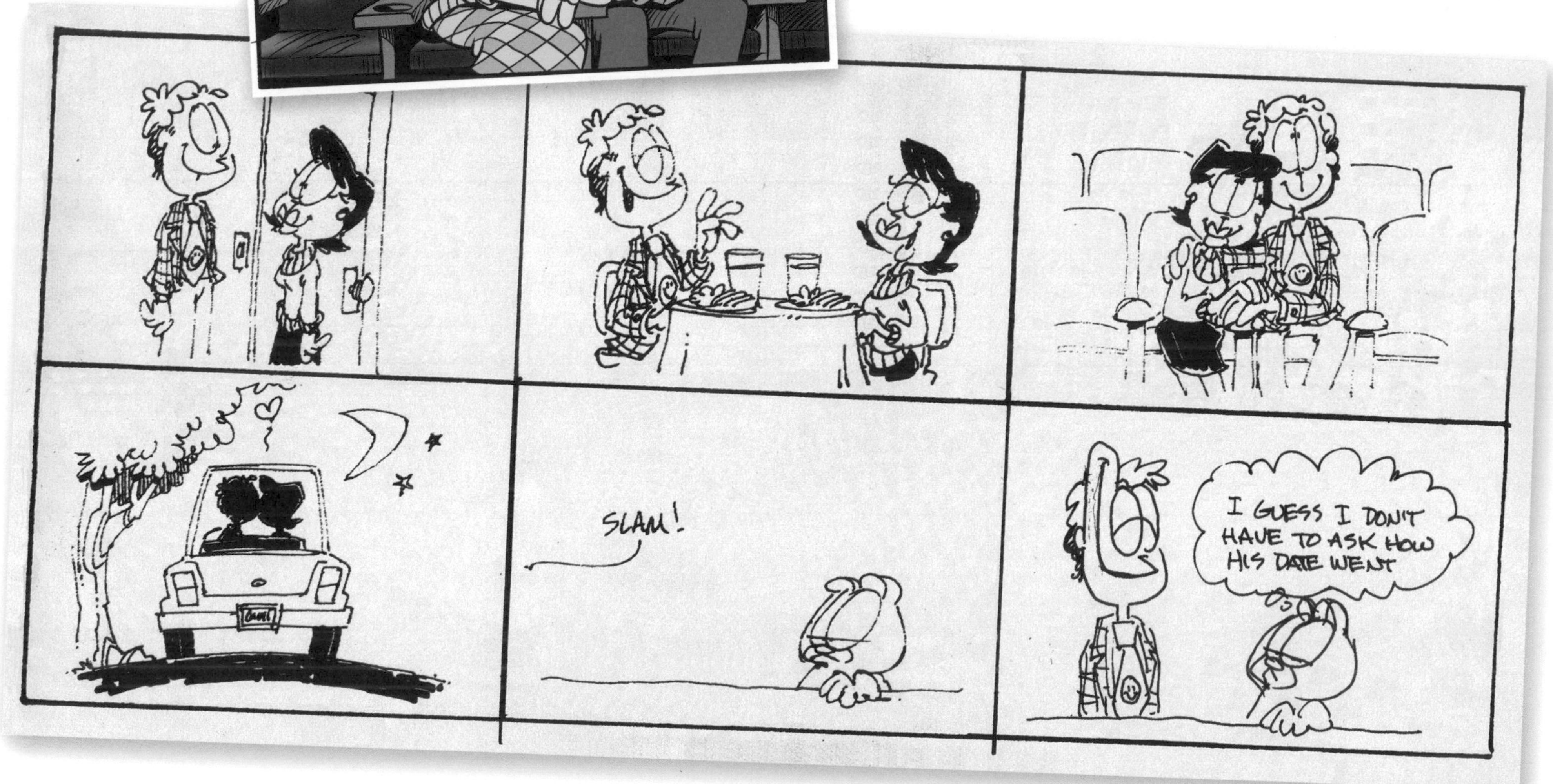

SLAM!
I GUESS I DON'T HAVE TO ASK HOW HIS DATE WENT

original rough

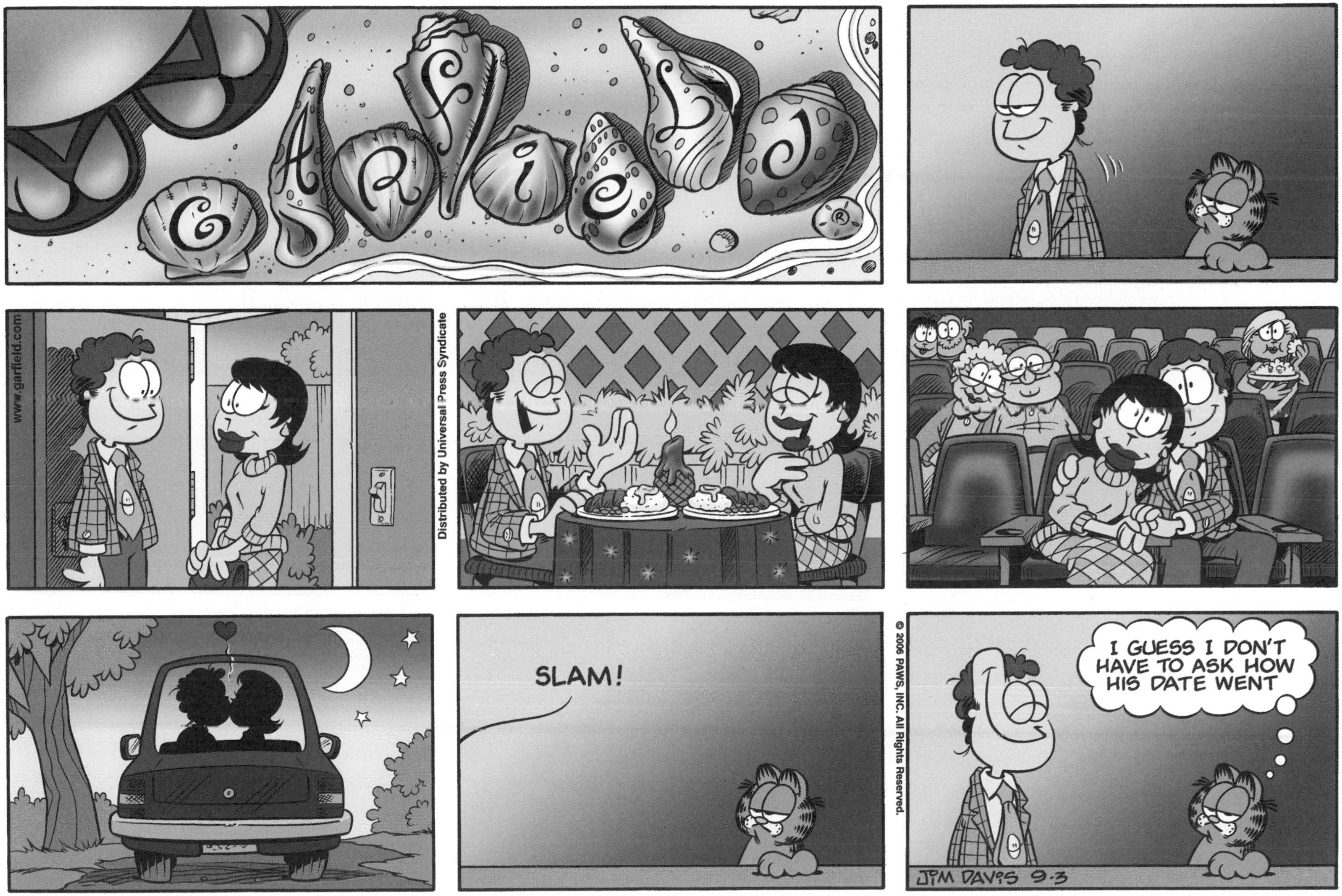
GARFIELD ®
www.garfield.com
Distributed by Universal Press Syndicate
SLAM!
© 2006 PAWS, INC. All Rights Reserved.
I GUESS I DON'T HAVE TO ASK HOW HIS DATE WENT
JIM DAVIS 9-3

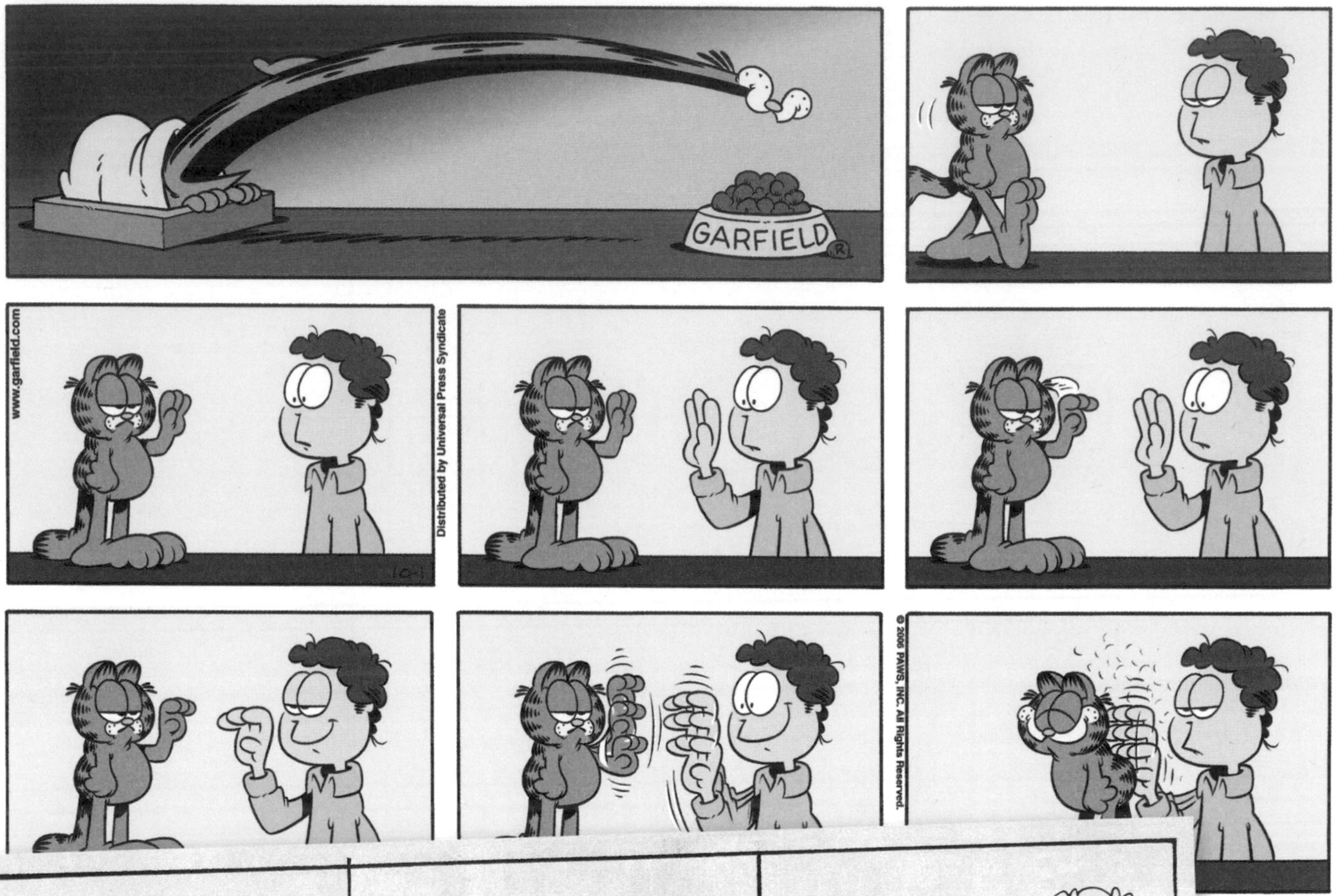
GARFIELD
www.garfield.com
Distributed by Universal Press Syndicate
10-1
© 2006 PAWS, INC. All Rights Reserved.

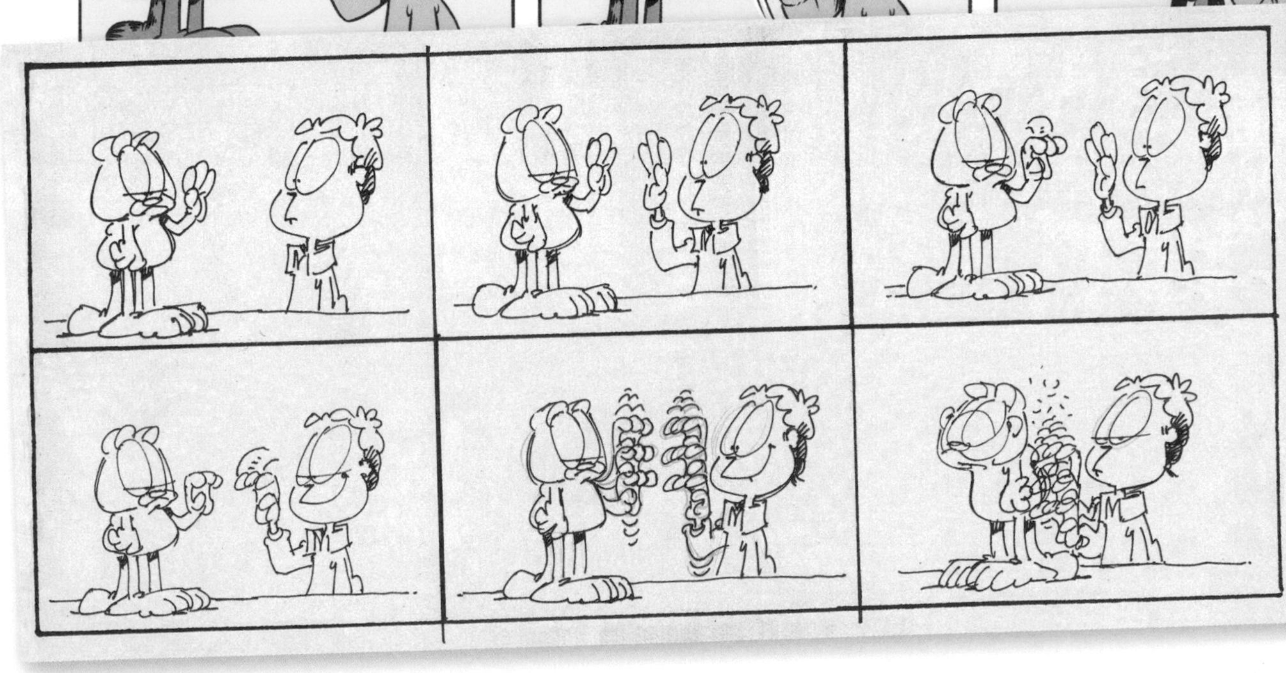

original rough

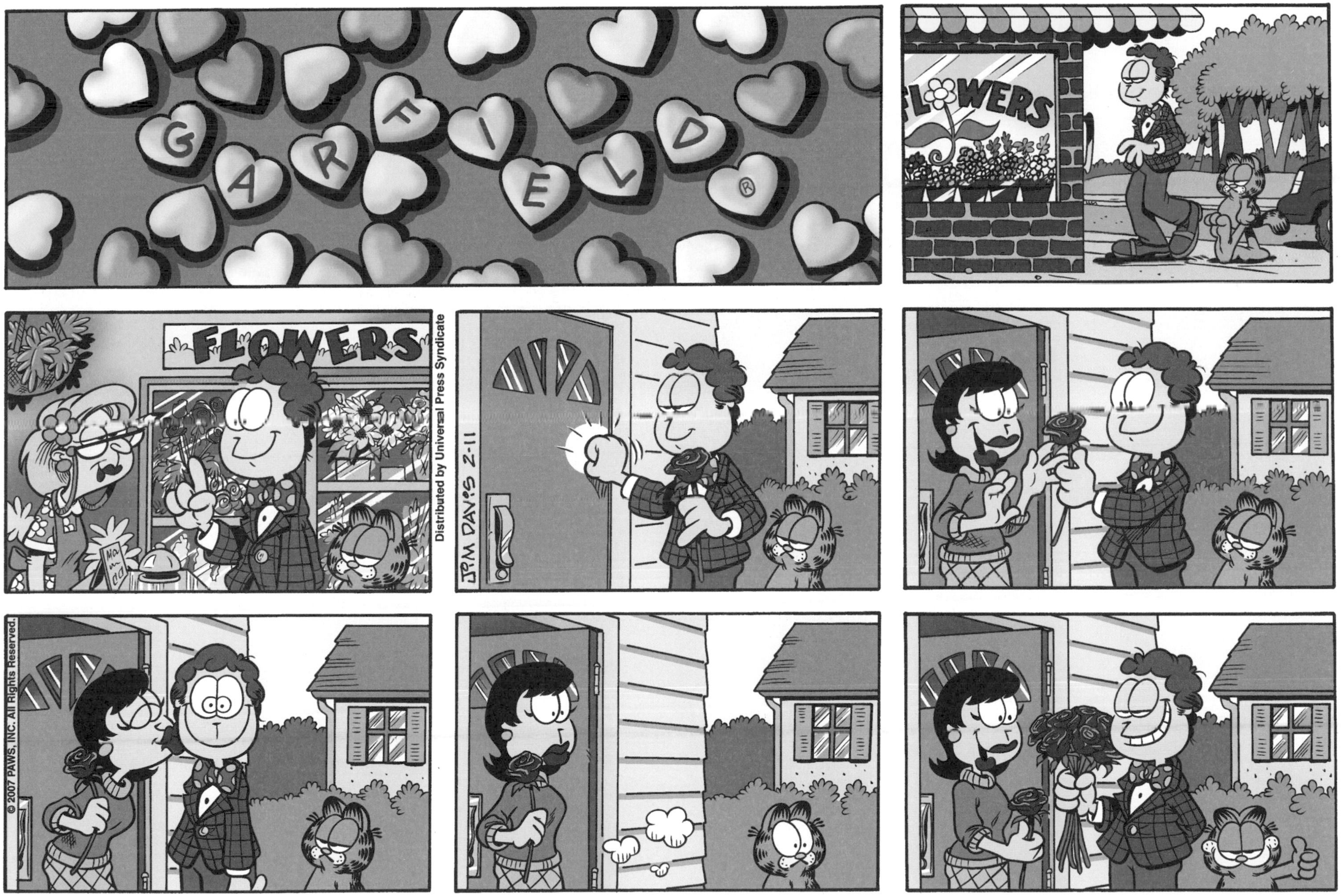
GARFIELD®
FLOWERS
Distributed by Universal Press Syndicate
JIM DAVIS 2-11
© 2007 PAWS, INC. All Rights Reserved.

DOINGA DOINGA DOINGA

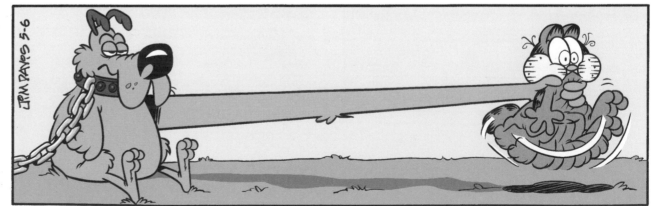

Distributed by Universal Press Syndicate

JIM DAVIS 5-6

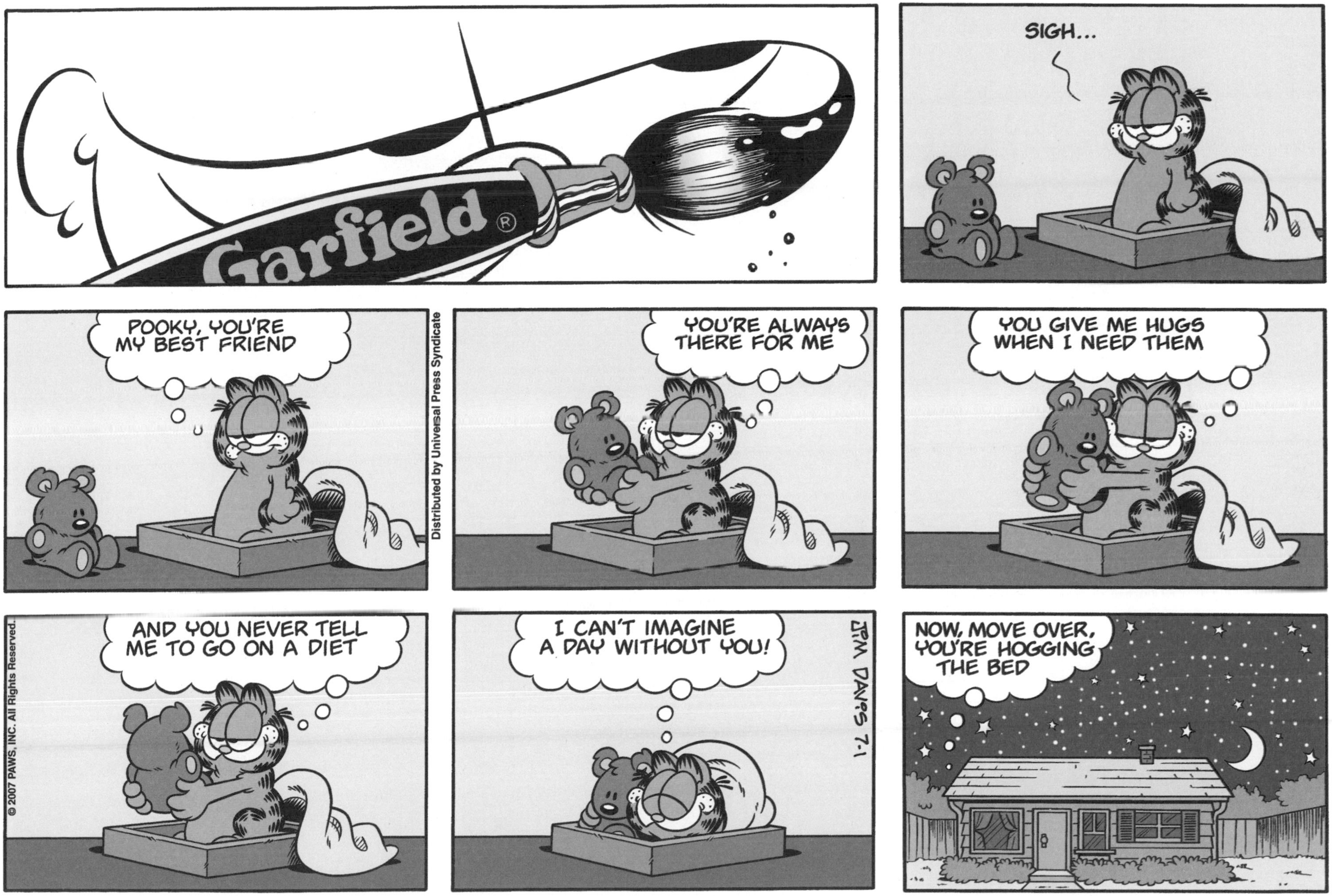
Garfield ®
SIGH...
POOKY, YOU'RE MY BEST FRIEND
Distributed by Universal Press Syndicate
YOU'RE ALWAYS THERE FOR ME
YOU GIVE ME HUGS WHEN I NEED THEM
© 2007 PAWS, INC. All Rights Reserved.
AND YOU NEVER TELL ME TO GO ON A DIET
I CAN'T IMAGINE A DAY WITHOUT YOU!
JIM DAVIS 7-1
NOW, MOVE OVER, YOU'RE HOGGING THE BED

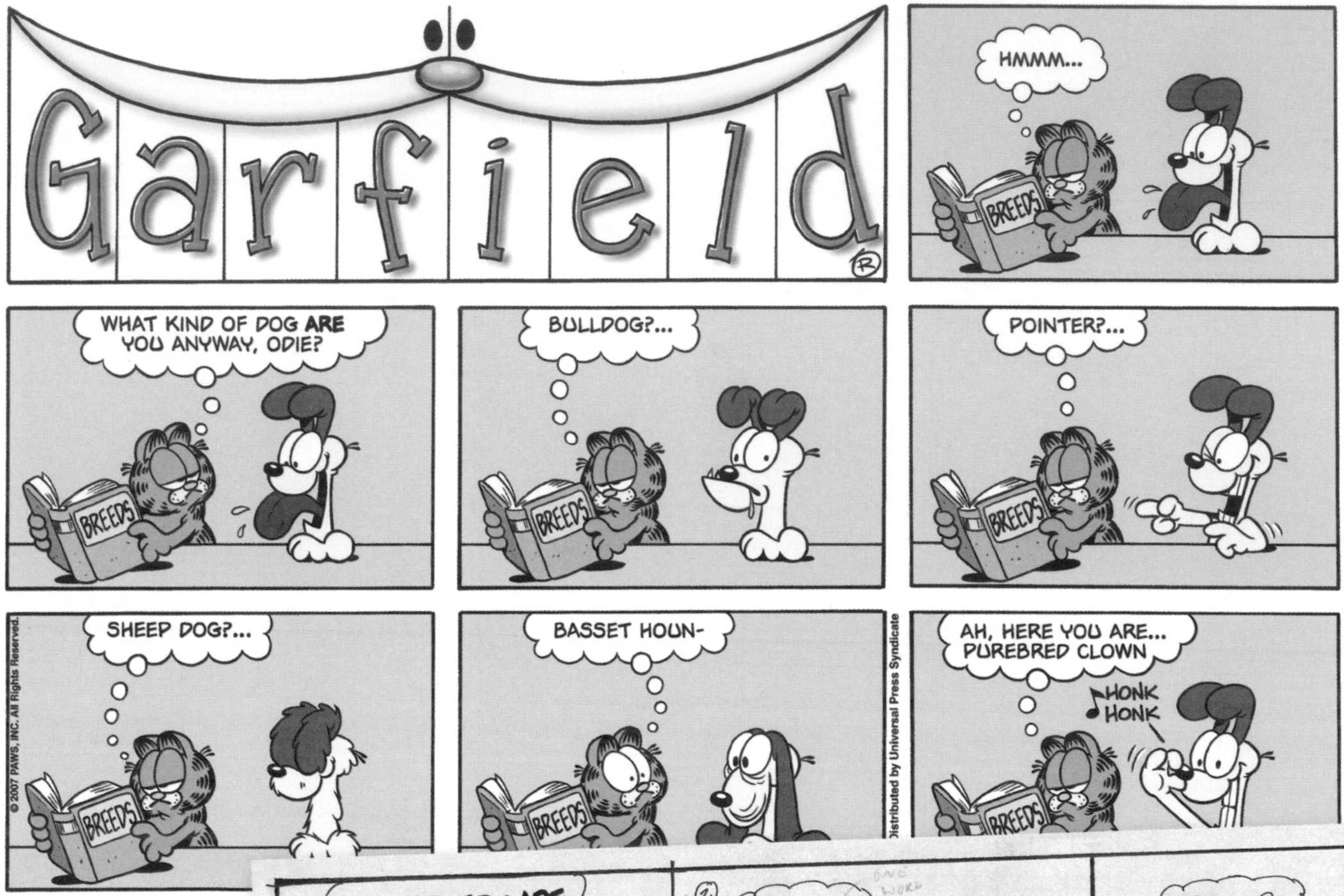
Garfield
HMMM...
WHAT KIND OF DOG ARE YOU ANYWAY, ODIE?
BREEDS
BULLDOG?...
POINTER?...
SHEEP DOG?...
BASSET HOUN-
AH, HERE YOU ARE... PUREBRED CLOWN
HONK HONK
© 2007 PAWS, INC. All Rights Reserved.
Distributed by Universal Press Syndicate

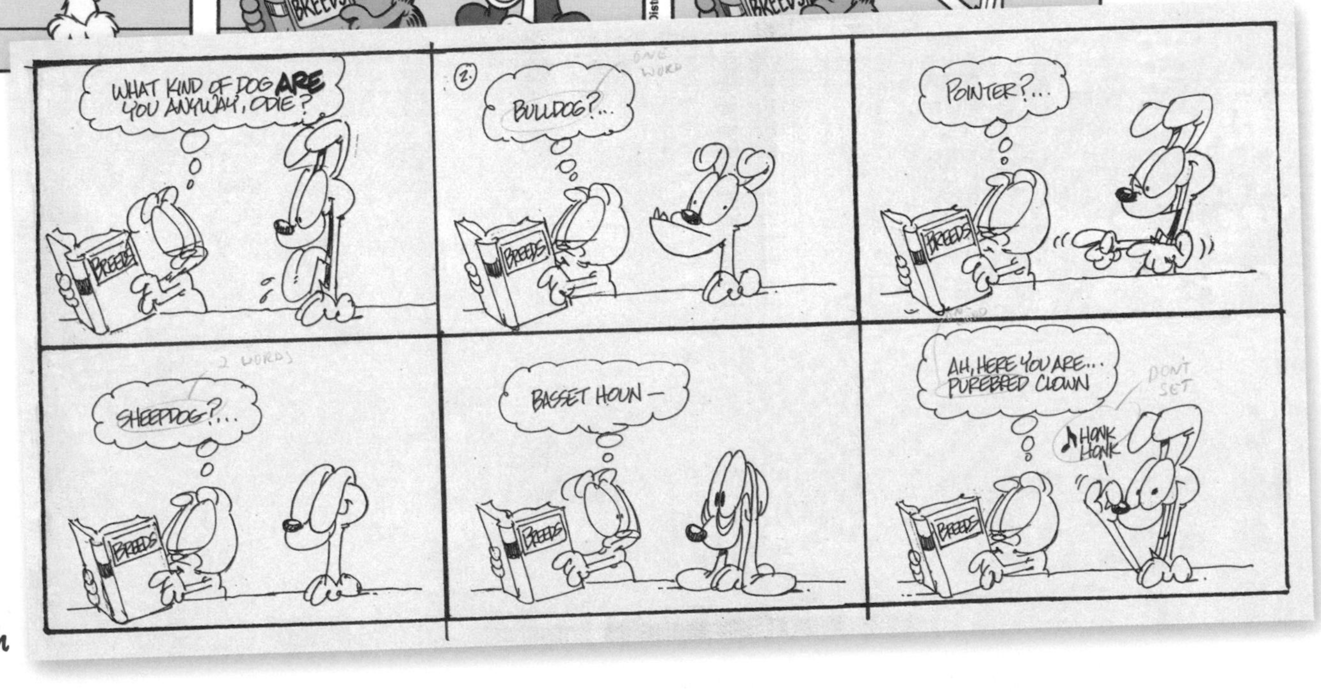
WHAT KIND OF DOG ARE YOU ANYWAY, ODIE?
BREEDS
2.
ONE WORD
BULLDOG?...
POINTER?...
2 WORDS
SHEEPDOG?...
BASSET HOUN –
AH, HERE YOU ARE... PUREBRED CLOWN
DON'T SET
HONK HONK

original rough

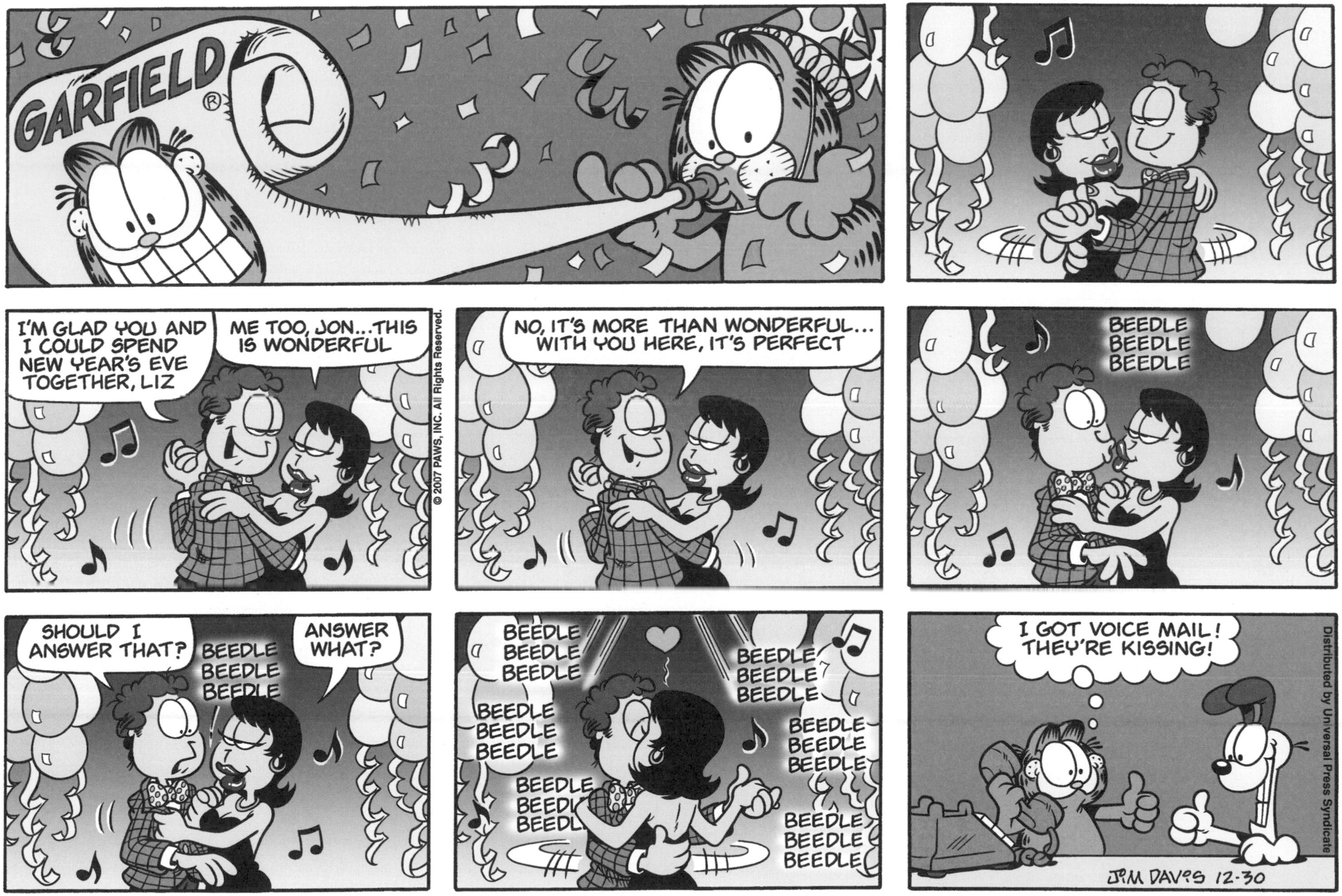
GARFIELD®
I'M GLAD YOU AND I COULD SPEND NEW YEAR'S EVE TOGETHER, LIZ
ME TOO, JON...THIS IS WONDERFUL
© 2007 PAWS, INC. All Rights Reserved.
NO, IT'S MORE THAN WONDERFUL... WITH YOU HERE, IT'S PERFECT
BEEDLE BEEDLE BEEDLE
SHOULD I ANSWER THAT?
BEEDLE BEEDLE BEEDLE
ANSWER WHAT?
BEEDLE BEEDLE BEEDLE
BEEDLE BEEDLE BEEDLE
BEEDLE BEEDLE BEEDLE
BEEDLE BEEDLE BEEDLE
BEEDLE BEEDLE BEEDLE
I GOT VOICE MAIL! THEY'RE KISSING!
Distributed by Universal Press Syndicate
JIM DAVIS 12-30

I did this one for me. I love the wordplay.

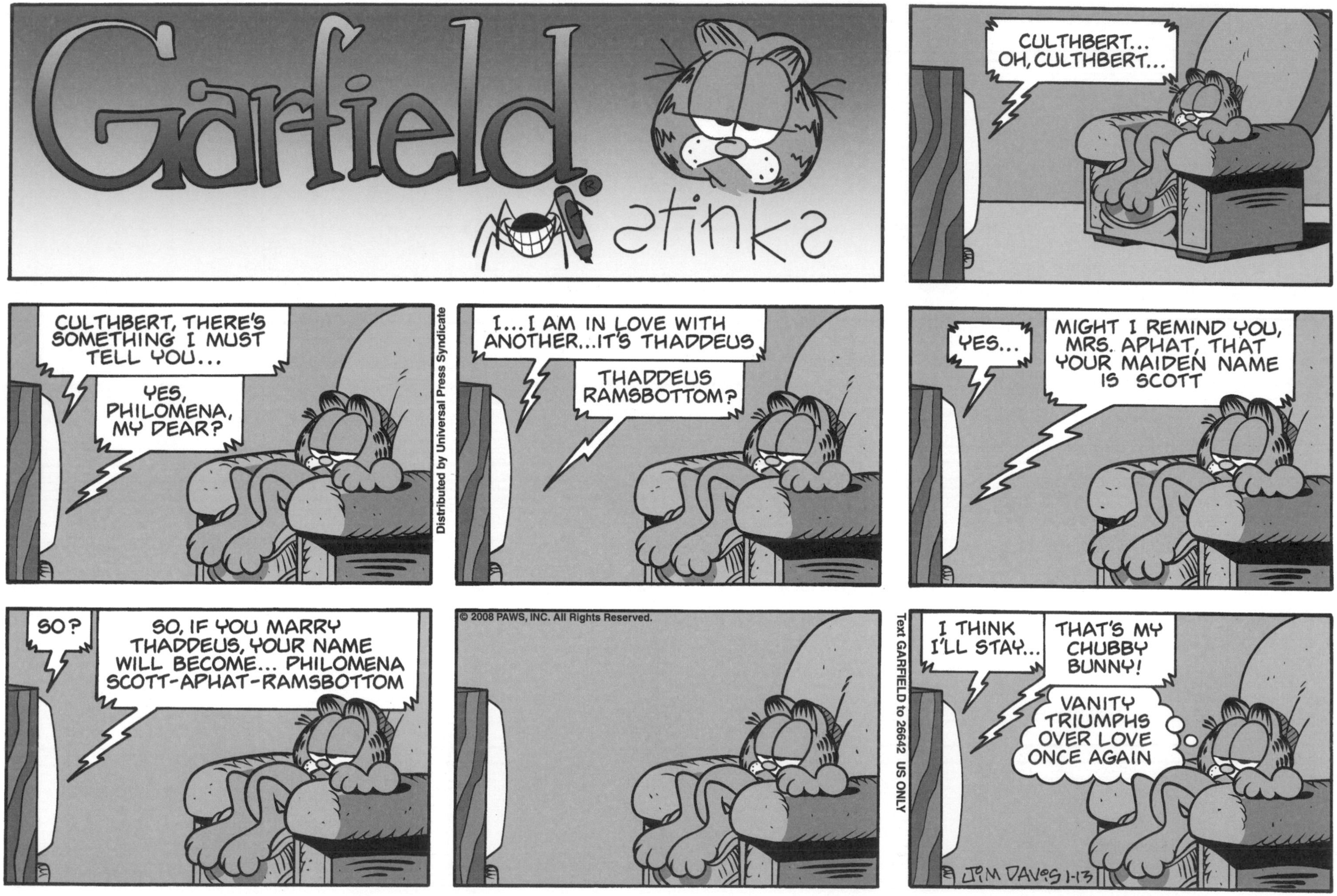

Garfield
stinks
CULTHBERT... OH, CULTHBERT...
CULTHBERT, THERE'S SOMETHING I MUST TELL YOU...
YES, PHILOMENA, MY DEAR?
Distributed by Universal Press Syndicate
I... I AM IN LOVE WITH ANOTHER... IT'S THADDEUS
THADDEUS RAMSBOTTOM?
YES...
MIGHT I REMIND YOU, MRS. APHAT, THAT YOUR MAIDEN NAME IS SCOTT
SO?
SO, IF YOU MARRY THADDEUS, YOUR NAME WILL BECOME... PHILOMENA SCOTT-APHAT-RAMSBOTTOM
© 2008 PAWS, INC. All Rights Reserved.
Text GARFIELD to 26642 US ONLY
I THINK I'LL STAY...
THAT'S MY CHUBBY BUNNY!
VANITY TRIUMPHS OVER LOVE ONCE AGAIN
JIM DAVIS 1-13

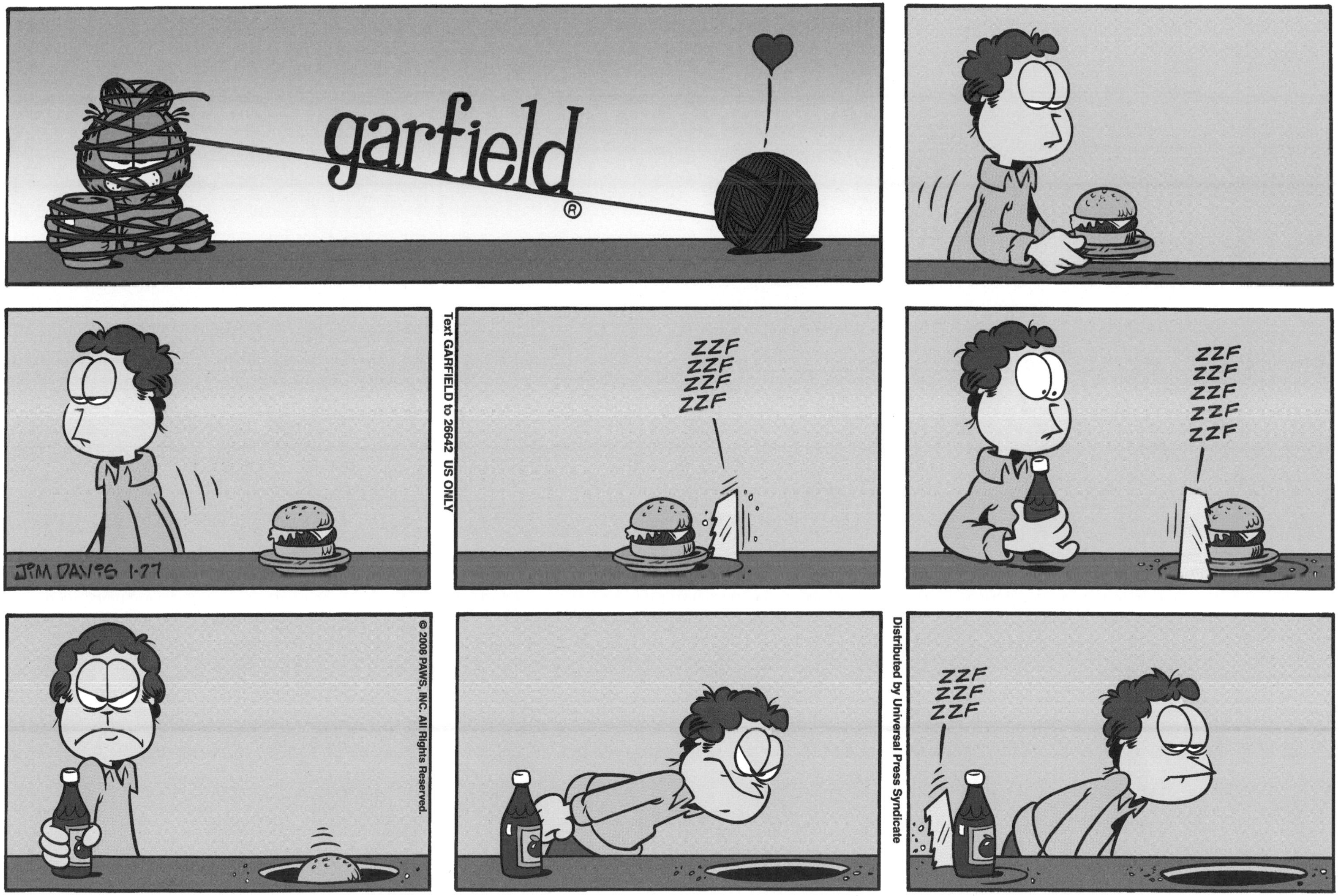
garfield
JIM DAVIS 1-27
ZZF
ZZF
ZZF
ZZF
ZZF
ZZF
ZZF
ZZF
ZZF
ZZF
ZZF
ZZF

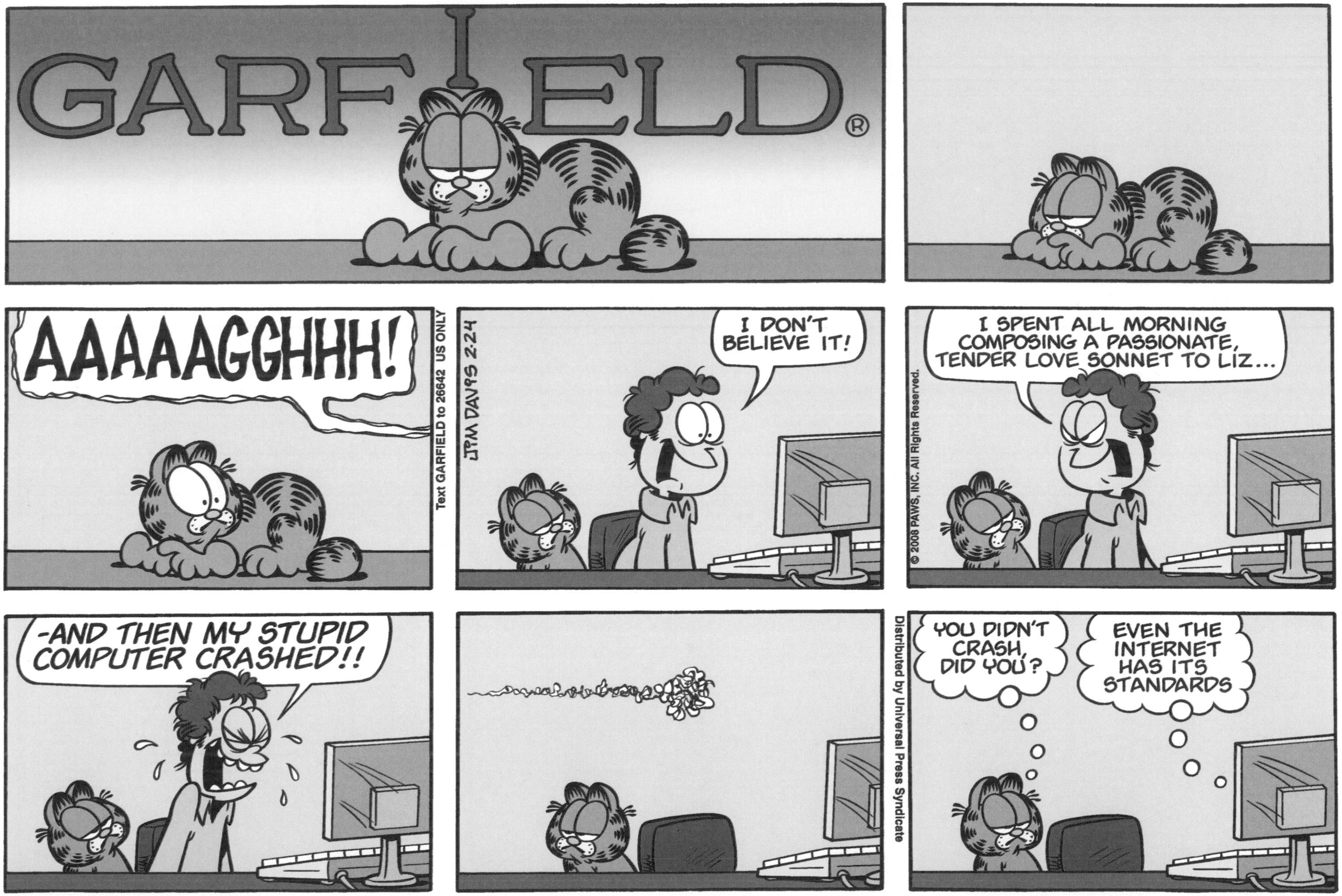
GARFIELD®
AAAAAGGHHH!
Text GARFIELD to 26642 US ONLY
JIM DAVIS 2-24
I DON'T BELIEVE IT!
I SPENT ALL MORNING COMPOSING A PASSIONATE, TENDER LOVE SONNET TO LIZ...
© 2008 PAWS, INC. All Rights Reserved.
-AND THEN MY STUPID COMPUTER CRASHED!!
Distributed by Universal Press Syndicate
YOU DIDN'T CRASH, DID YOU?
EVEN THE INTERNET HAS ITS STANDARDS

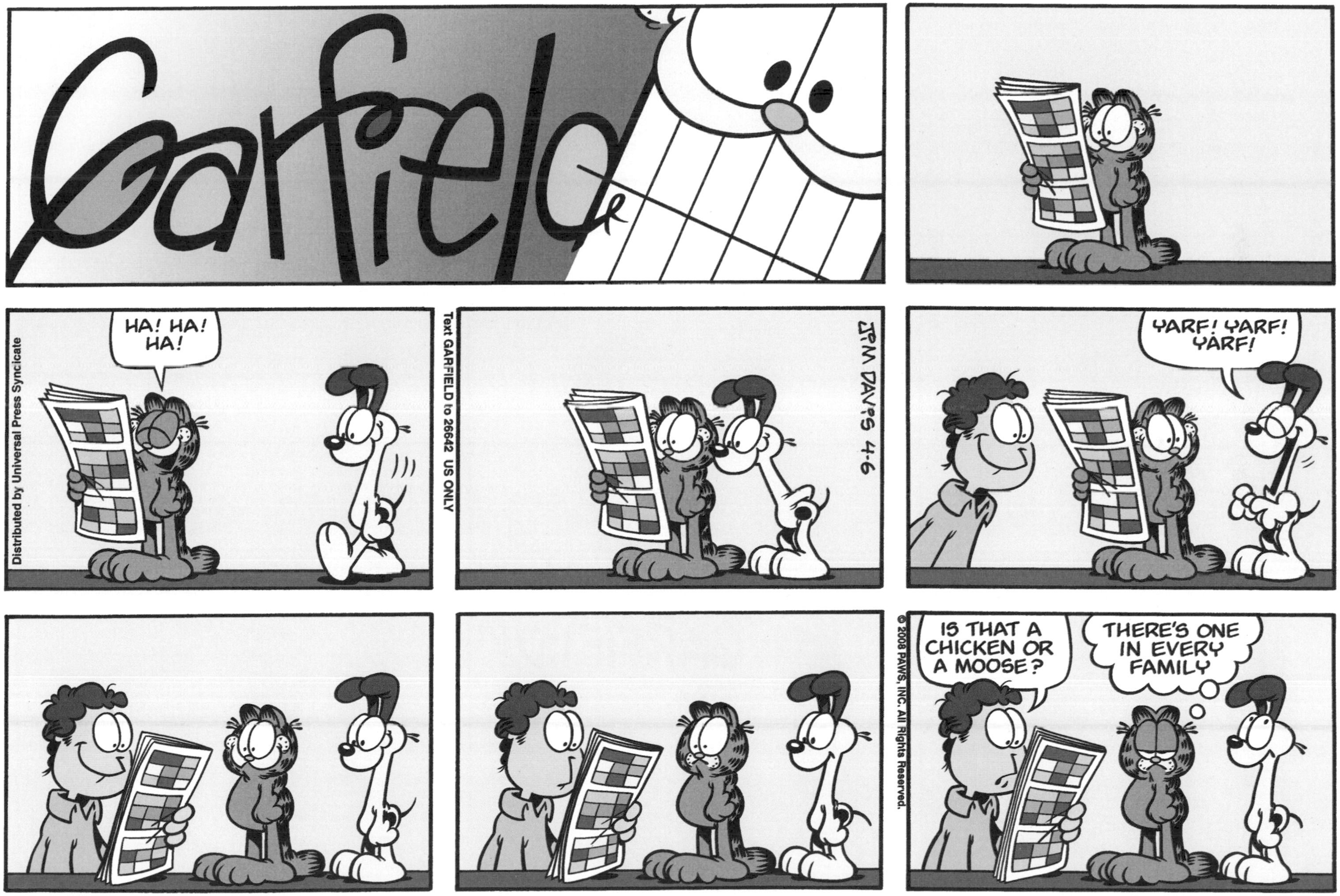
Garfield
Distributed by Universal Press Syncicate
HA! HA! HA!
Text GARFIELD to 26642 US ONLY
JIM DAVIS 4-6
YARF! YARF! YARF!
© 2008 PAWS, INC. All Rights Reserved.
IS THAT A CHICKEN OR A MOOSE?
THERE'S ONE IN EVERY FAMILY

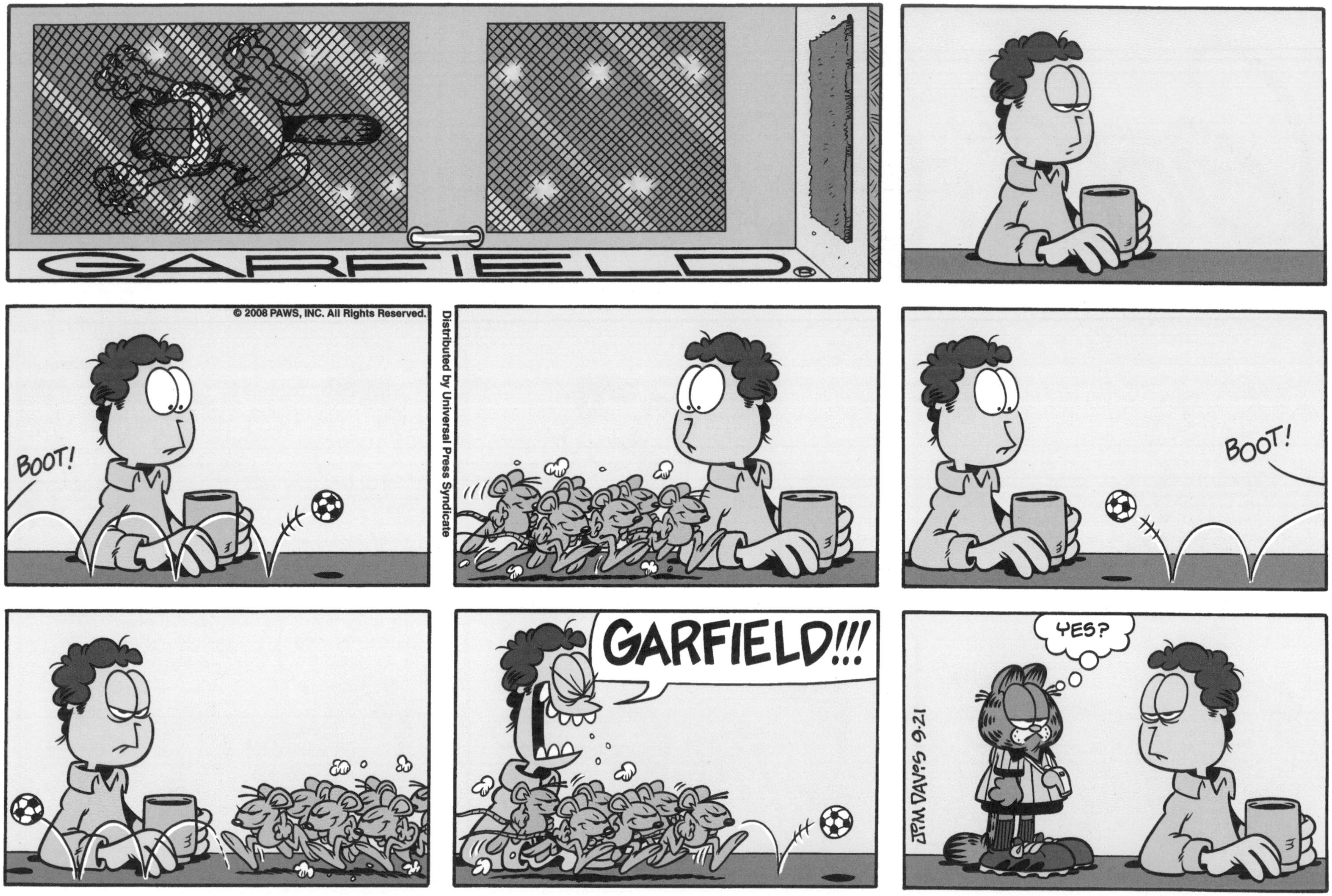
GARFIELD
© 2008 PAWS, INC. All Rights Reserved.
Distributed by Universal Press Syndicate
BOOT!
BOOT!
GARFIELD!!!
JPM DAVIS 9-21
YES?

That odie . . . you have to love him.

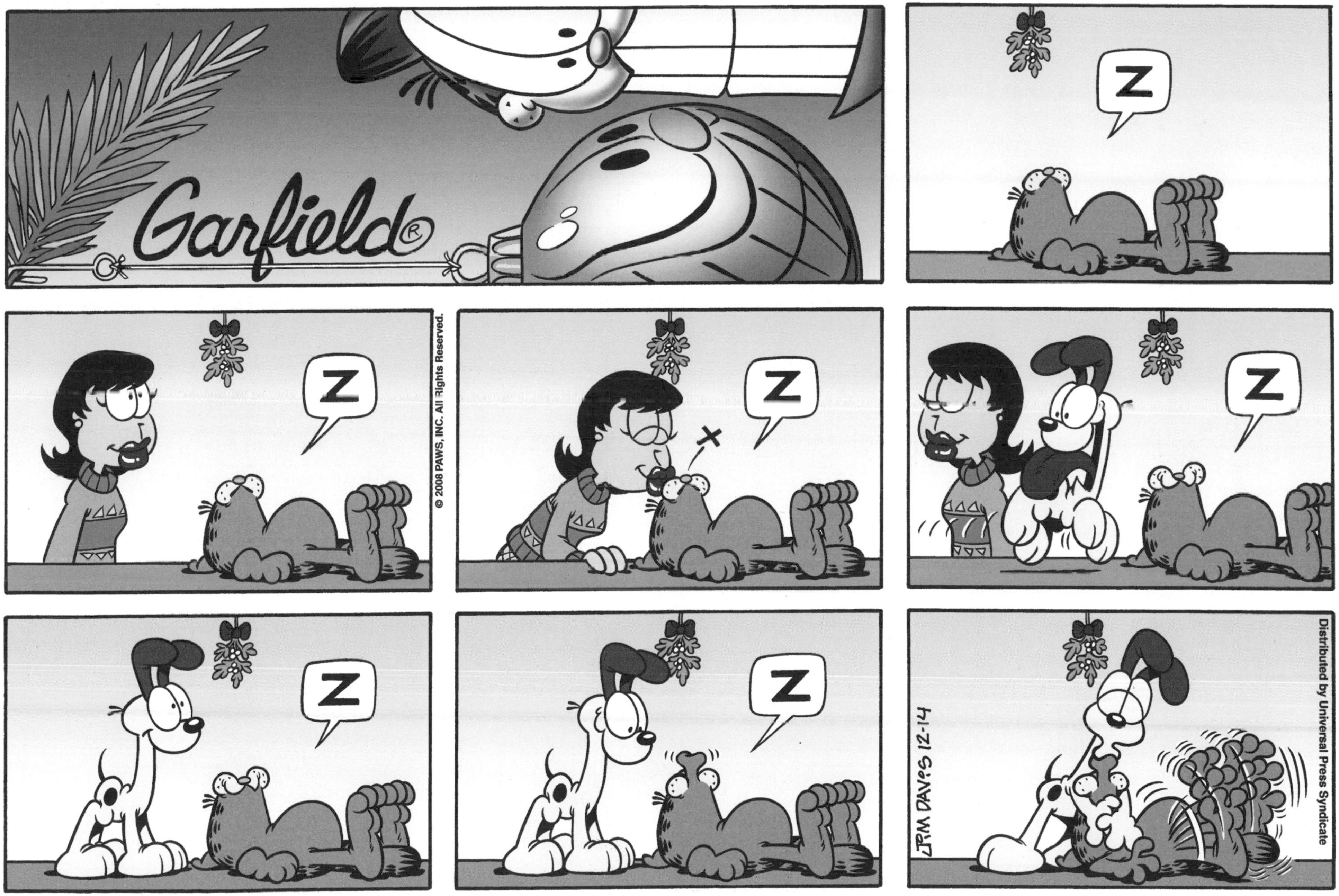
Garfield®
Z
Z
© 2008 PAWS, INC. All Rights Reserved.
Z
Z
Z
JPM DAVIS 12-14
Z
Distributed by Universal Press Syndicate

A great national pastime.

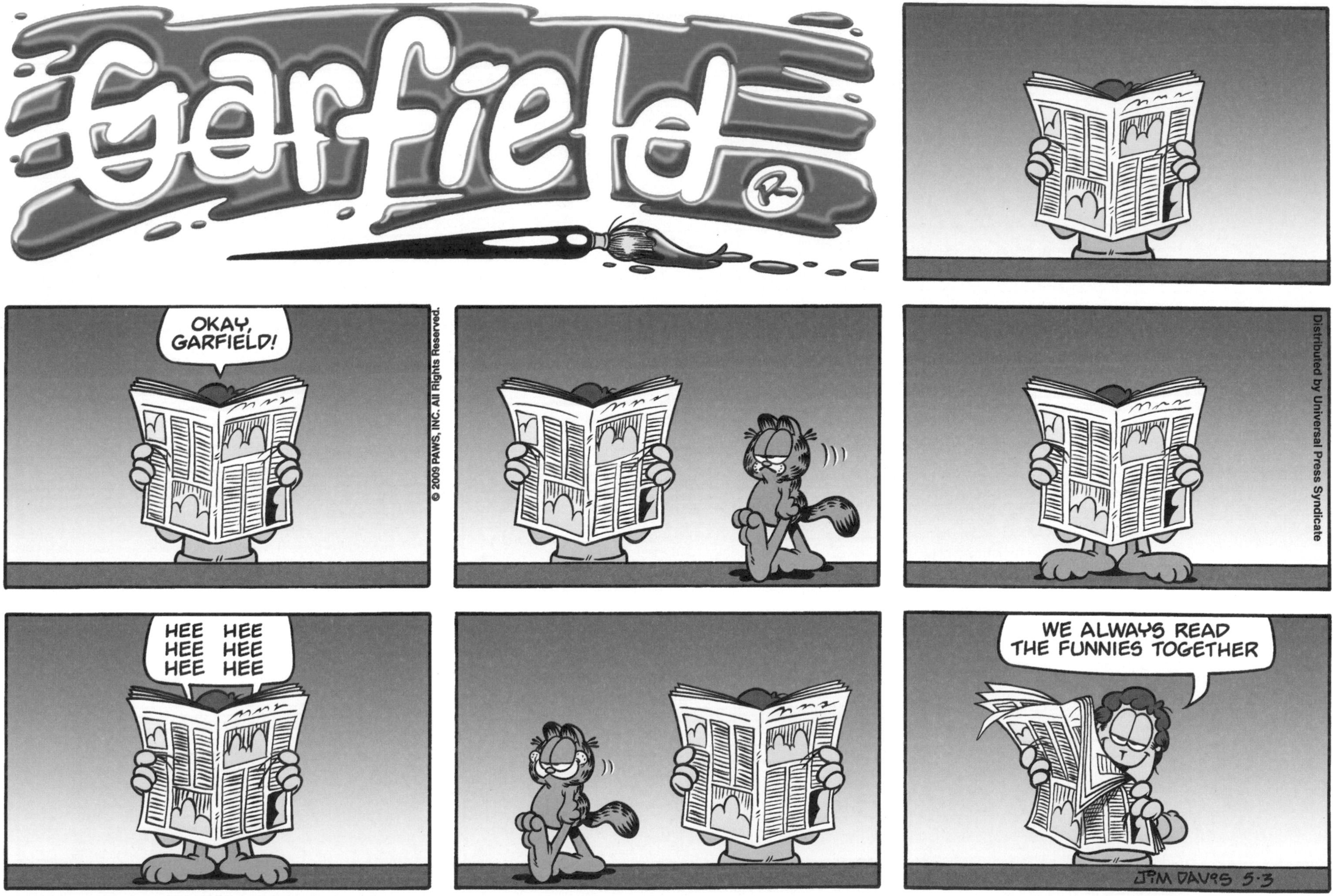

Garfield
OKAY, GARFIELD!
© 2009 PAWS, INC. All Rights Reserved.
Distributed by Universal Press Syndicate
HEE HEE HEE HEE HEE HEE
WE ALWAYS READ THE FUNNIES TOGETHER
JIM DAVIS 5-3

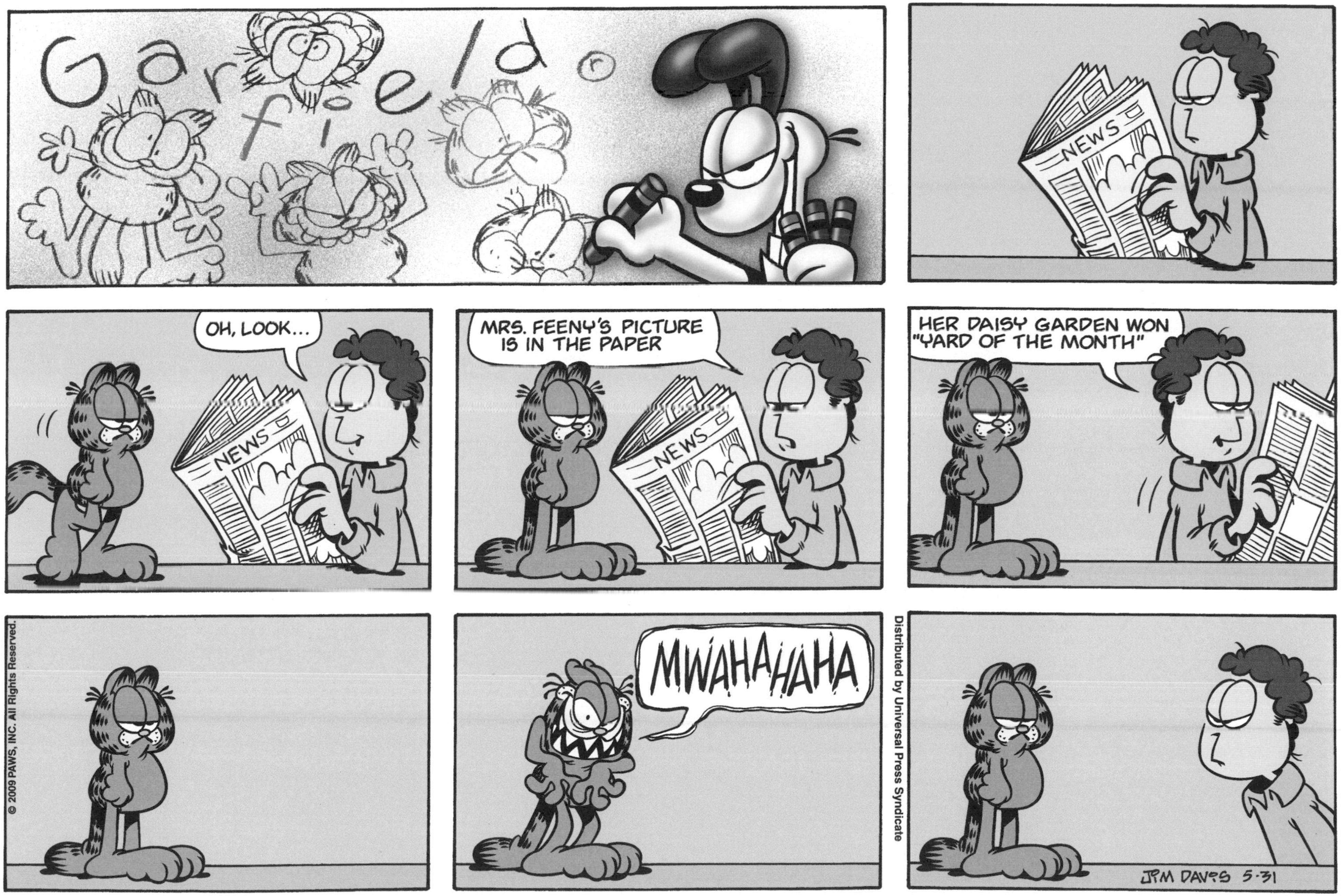
Garfield®
NEWS
OH, LOOK...
NEWS
MRS. FEENY'S PICTURE IS IN THE PAPER
NEWS
HER DAISY GARDEN WON "YARD OF THE MONTH"
© 2009 PAWS, INC. All Rights Reserved.
MWAHAHAHA
Distributed by Universal Press Syndicate
JIM DAVIS 5-31

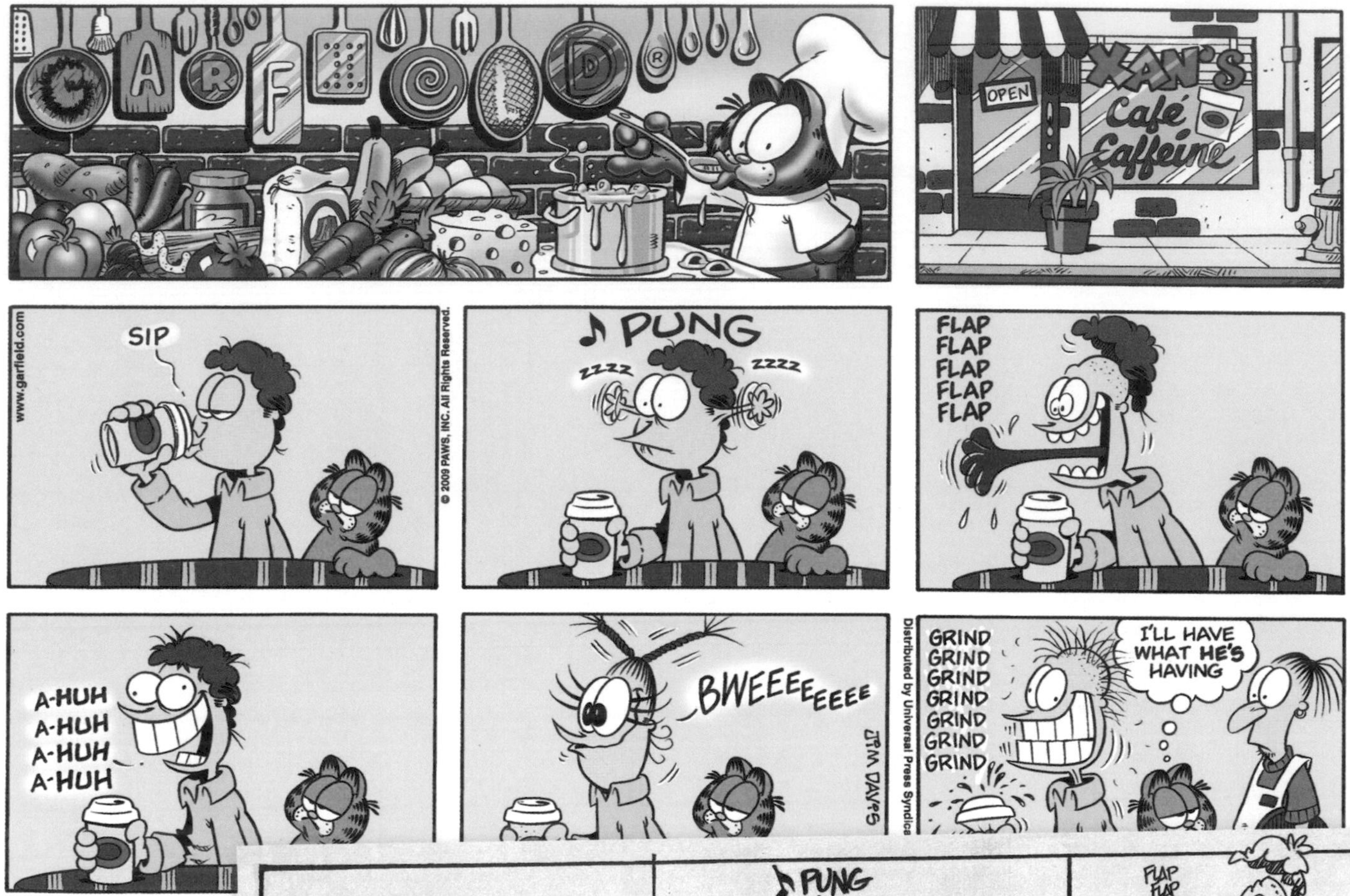
GARFIELD
OPEN
XAN'S Café Caffeine
SIP
www.garfield.com
© 2009 PAWS, INC. All Rights Reserved.
♪ PUNG
ZZZZ
ZZZZ
FLAP FLAP FLAP FLAP FLAP
A-HUH A-HUH A-HUH A-HUH
BWEEEEEEEE
JIM DAVIS
GRIND GRIND GRIND GRIND GRIND GRIND GRIND
I'LL HAVE WHAT **HE'S** HAVING

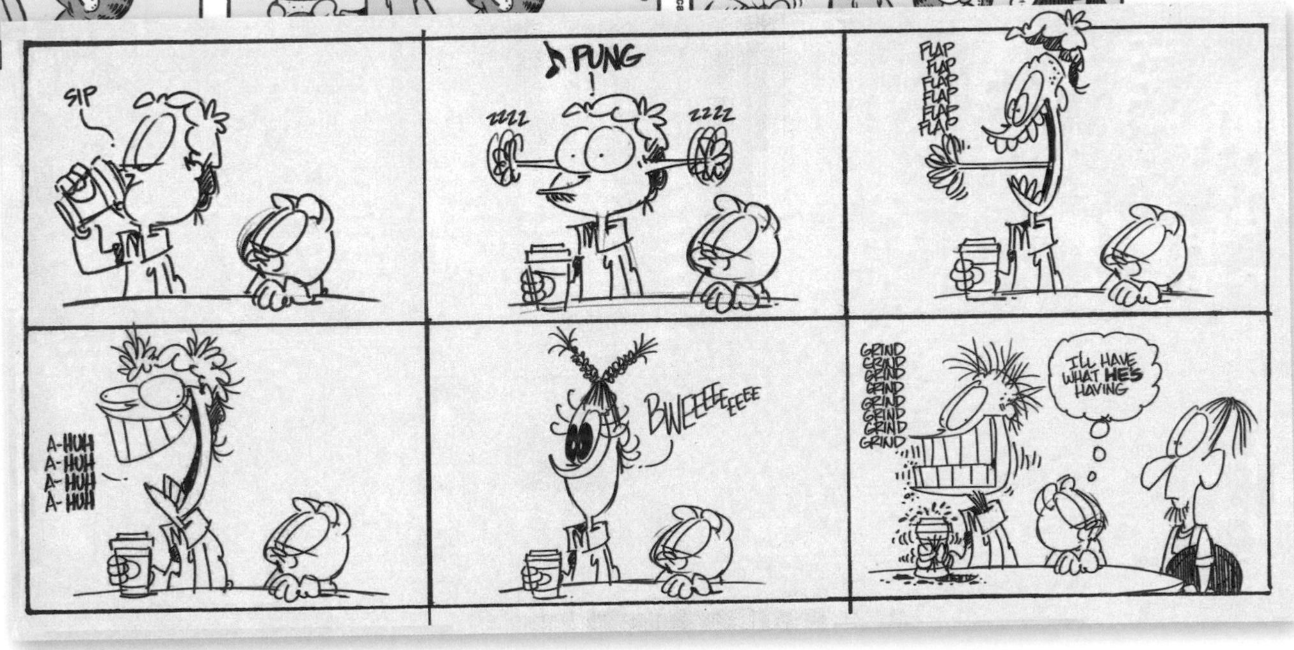
SIP
♪ PUNG
ZZZZ
ZZZZ
FLAP FLAP FLAP FLAP FLAP FLAP
A-HUH A-HUH A-HUH A-HUH
BWEEEEEEEE
I'LL HAVE WHAT **HE'S** HAVING

original rough

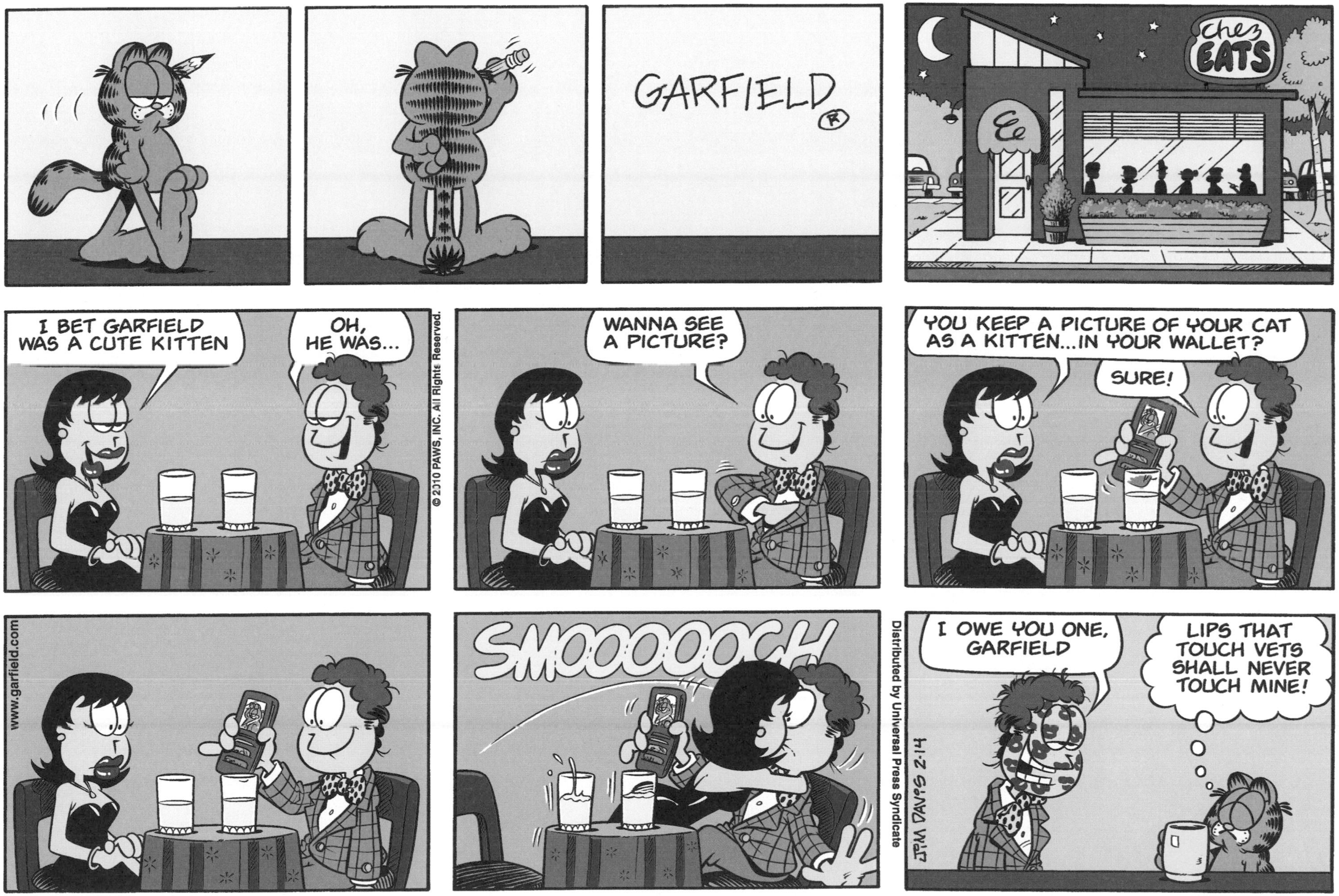
GARFIELD ®
Chez EATS
I BET GARFIELD WAS A CUTE KITTEN
OH, HE WAS...
WANNA SEE A PICTURE?
YOU KEEP A PICTURE OF YOUR CAT AS A KITTEN...IN YOUR WALLET?
SURE!
SMOOOOOCH
I OWE YOU ONE, GARFIELD
LIPS THAT TOUCH VETS SHALL NEVER TOUCH MINE!
JPM DAVIS 2-14
© 2010 PAWS, INC. All Rights Reserved.
www.garfield.com
Distributed by Universal Press Syndicate

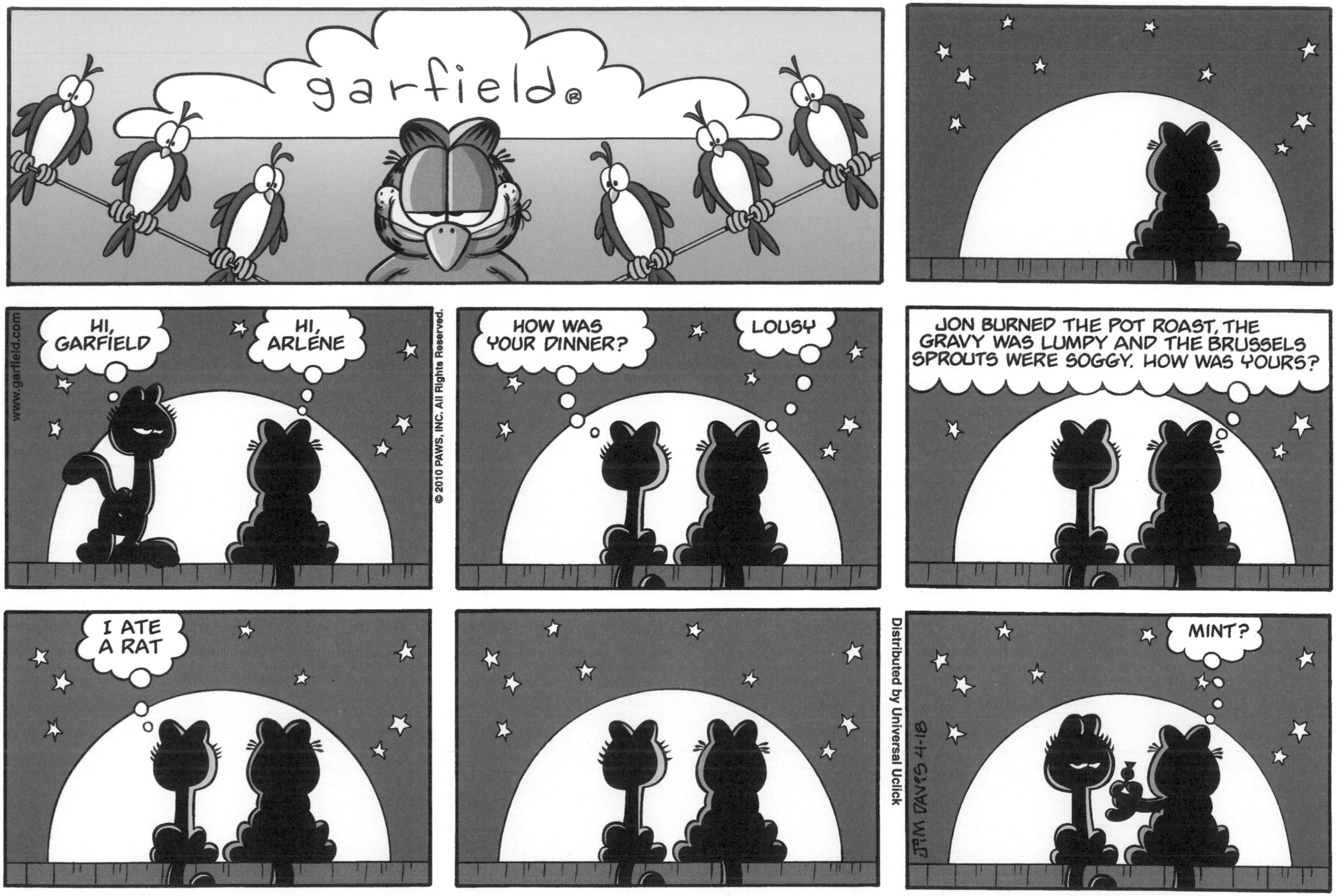
garfield®
www.garfield.com
HI, GARFIELD
HI, ARLENE
© 2010 PAWS, INC. All Rights Reserved.
HOW WAS YOUR DINNER?
LOUSY
JON BURNED THE POT ROAST, THE GRAVY WAS LUMPY AND THE BRUSSELS SPROUTS WERE SOGGY. HOW WAS YOURS?
I ATE A RAT
Distributed by Universal Uclick
JPM DAVIS 4-18
MINT?

I did this in honor of National Cartoonists Day, which is May 5.

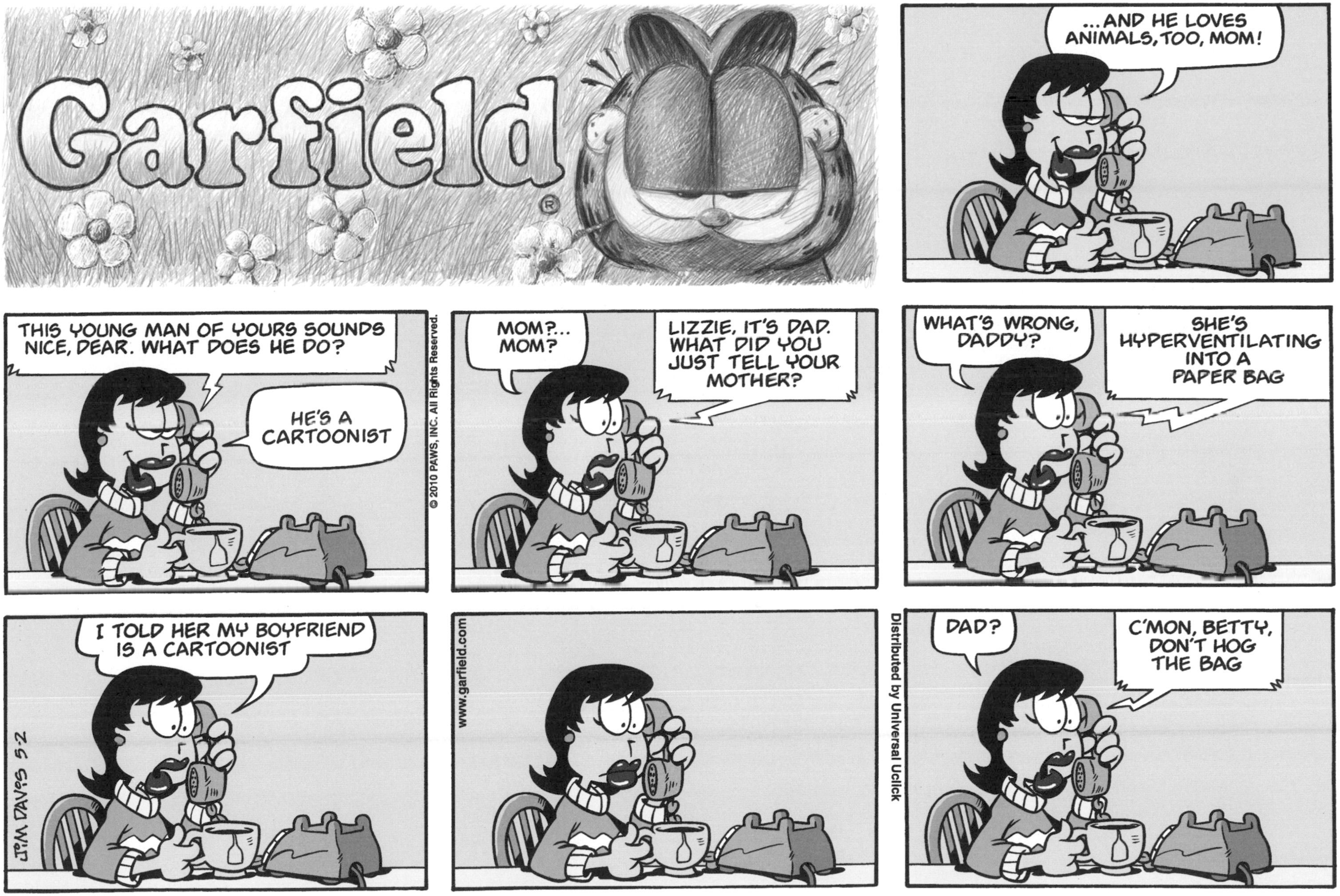

Garfield
...AND HE LOVES ANIMALS, TOO, MOM!
THIS YOUNG MAN OF YOURS SOUNDS NICE, DEAR. WHAT DOES HE DO?
HE'S A CARTOONIST
© 2010 PAWS, INC. All Rights Reserved.
MOM?... MOM?
LIZZIE, IT'S DAD. WHAT DID YOU JUST TELL YOUR MOTHER?
WHAT'S WRONG, DADDY?
SHE'S HYPERVENTILATING INTO A PAPER BAG
I TOLD HER MY BOYFRIEND IS A CARTOONIST
JPM DAVIS 5-2
www.garfield.com
Distributed by Universal Uclick
DAD?
C'MON, BETTY, DON'T HOG THE BAG

With a relationship like this, can marriage be far down the road?

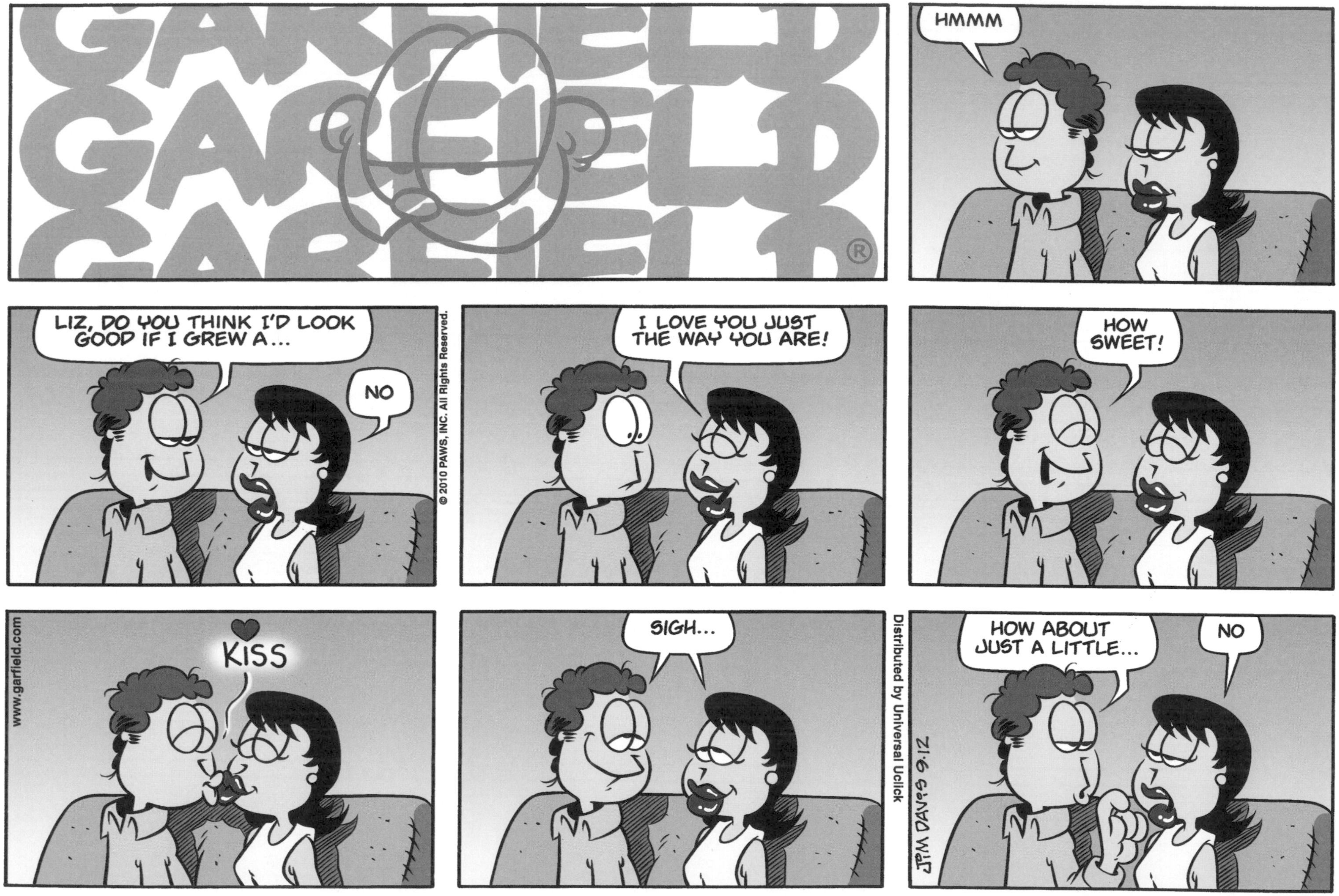
GARFIELD
HMMM
LIZ, DO YOU THINK I'D LOOK GOOD IF I GREW A...
NO
I LOVE YOU JUST THE WAY YOU ARE!
HOW SWEET!
KISS
SIGH...
HOW ABOUT JUST A LITTLE...
NO
© 2010 PAWS, INC. All Rights Reserved.
www.garfield.com
Distributed by Universal Uclick
JPM DAVIS 9.12

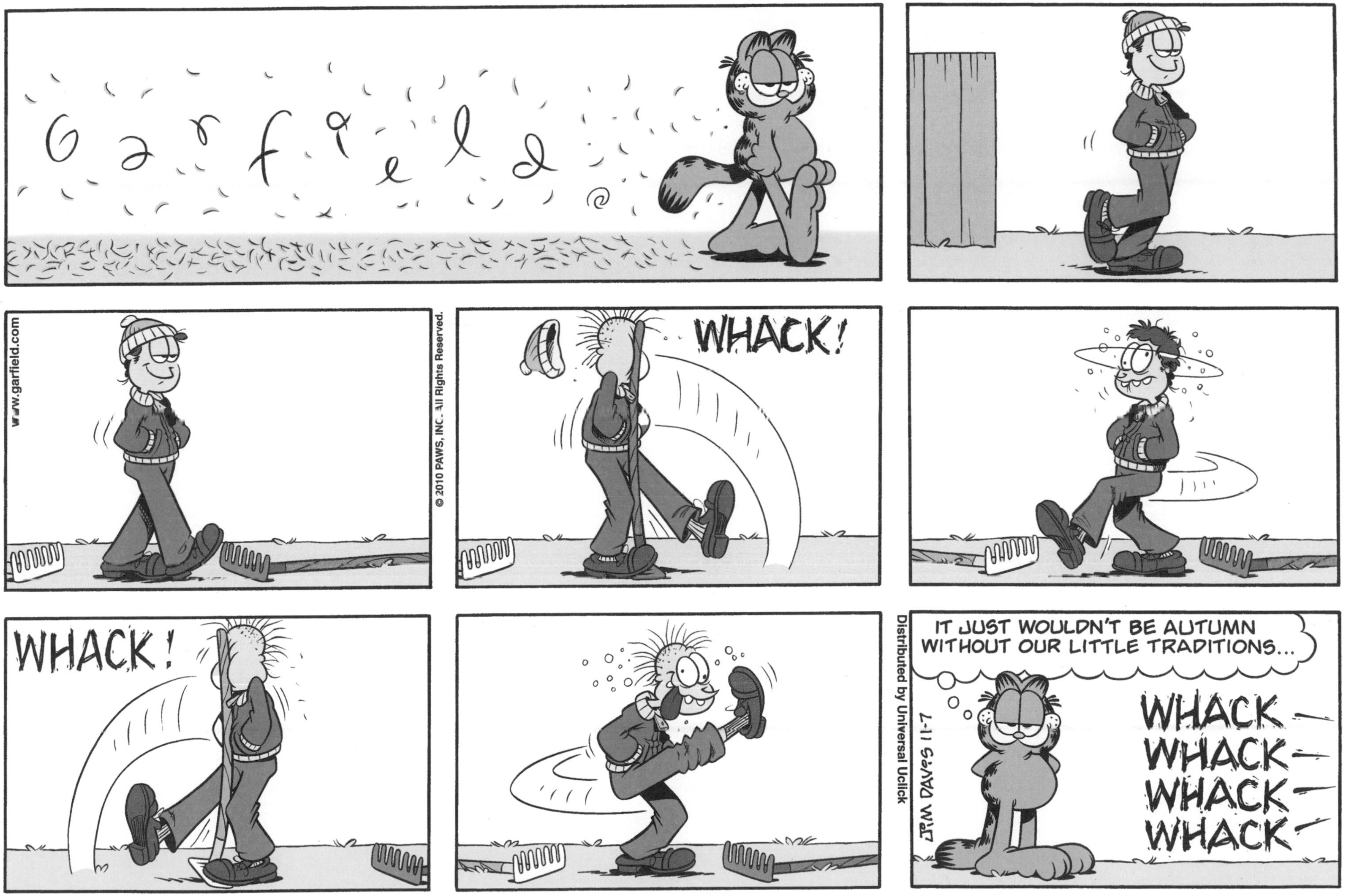
garfield
www.garfield.com
© 2010 PAWS, INC. All Rights Reserved.
WHACK!
WHACK!
Distributed by Universal Uclick
JPM DAVPS 11-7
IT JUST WOULDN'T BE AUTUMN WITHOUT OUR LITTLE TRADITIONS...
WHACK
WHACK
WHACK
WHACK

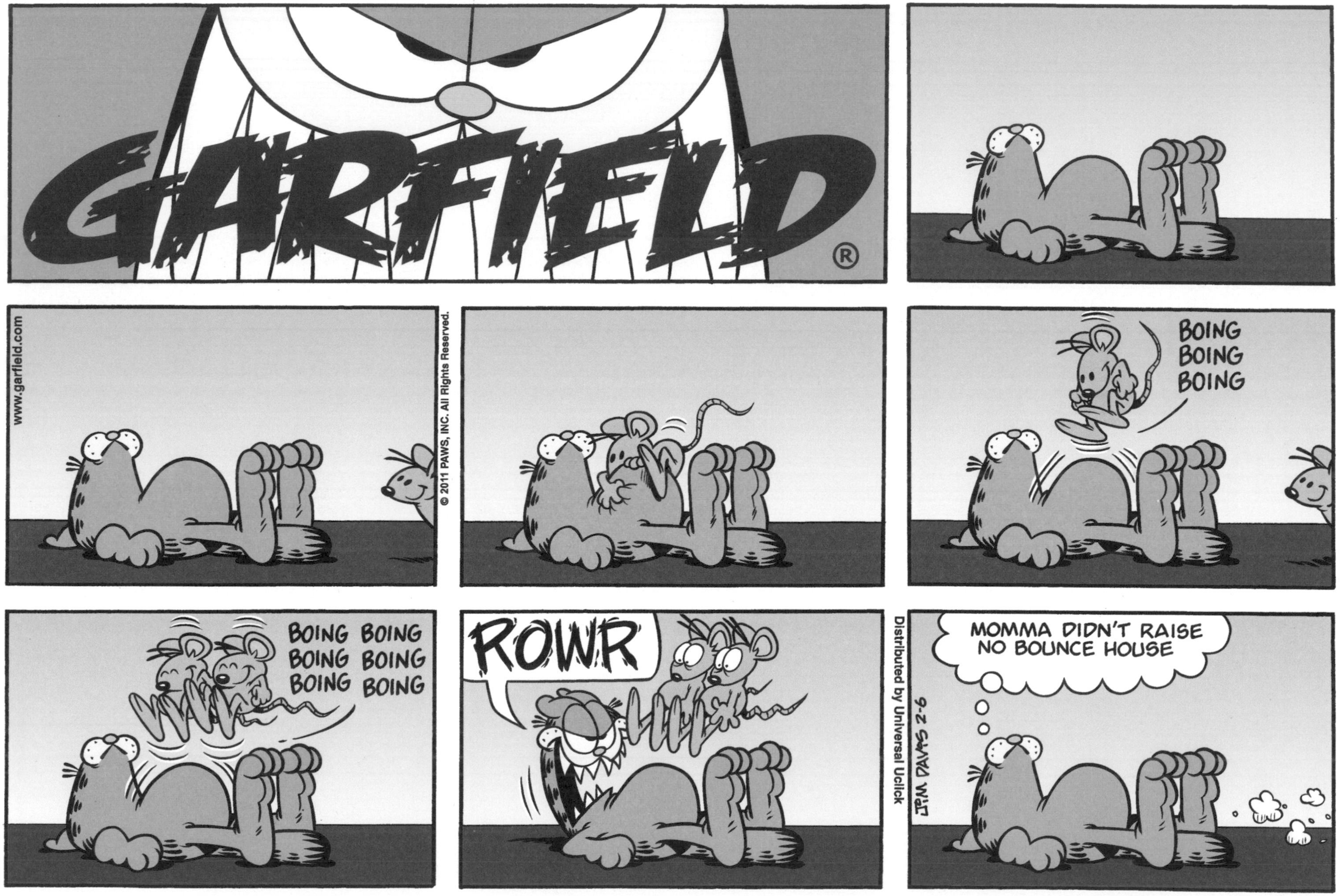
GARFIELD®
www.garfield.com
© 2011 PAWS, INC. All Rights Reserved.
BOING
BOING
BOING
BOING BOING
BOING BOING
BOING BOING
ROWR
Distributed by Universal Uclick
JPM DAVIS 2-6
MOMMA DIDN'T RAISE
NO BOUNCE HOUSE

People believe too much of what they hear and read.
And there's that "ignorance is bliss" thing, too.

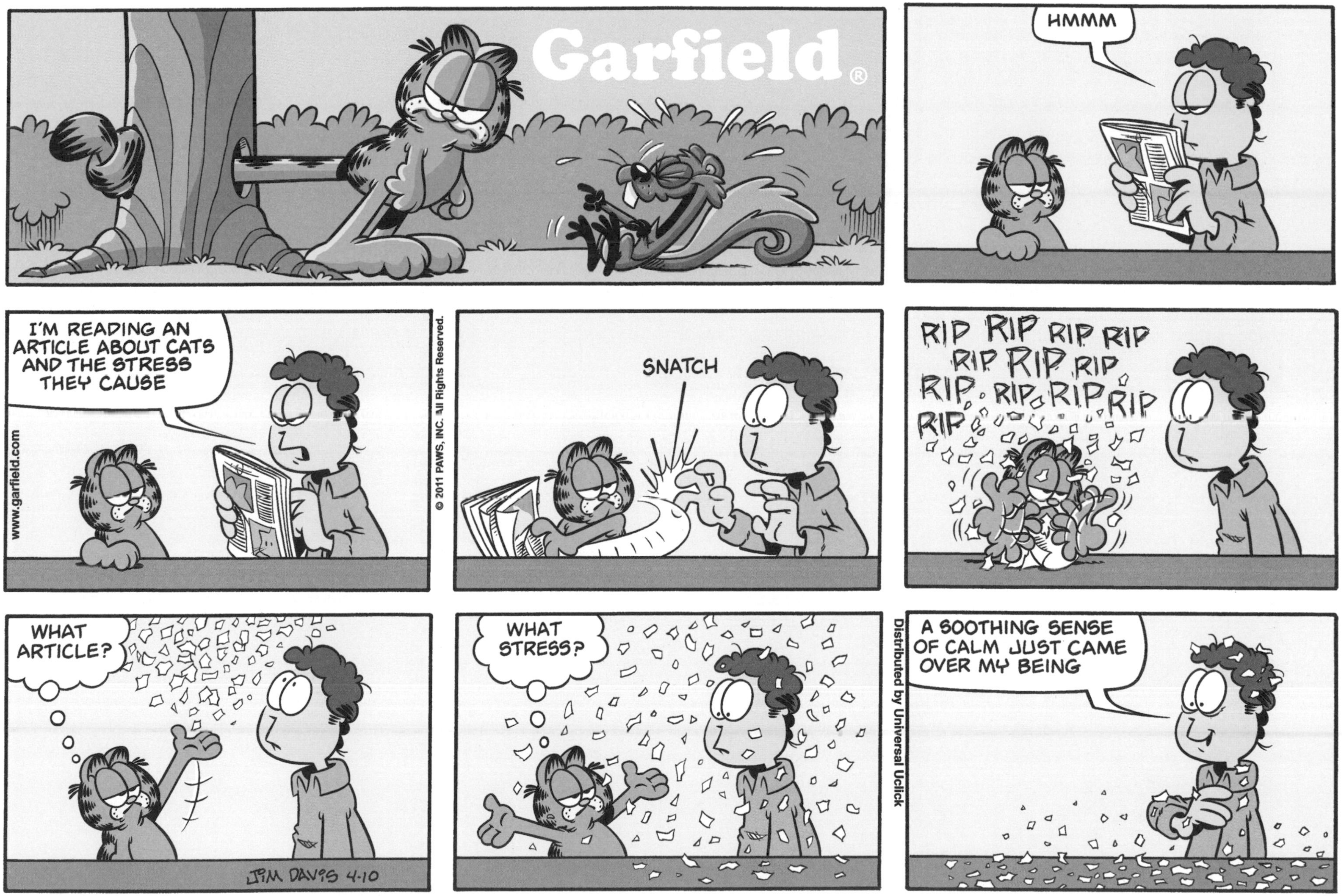

Garfield®
HMMM
I'M READING AN ARTICLE ABOUT CATS AND THE STRESS THEY CAUSE
www.garfield.com
© 2011 PAWS, INC. All Rights Reserved.
SNATCH
RIP RIP RIP RIP RIP RIP RIP RIP RIP RIP RIP RIP
WHAT ARTICLE?
JIM DAVIS 4-10
WHAT STRESS?
Distributed by Universal Uclick
A SOOTHING SENSE OF CALM JUST CAME OVER MY BEING

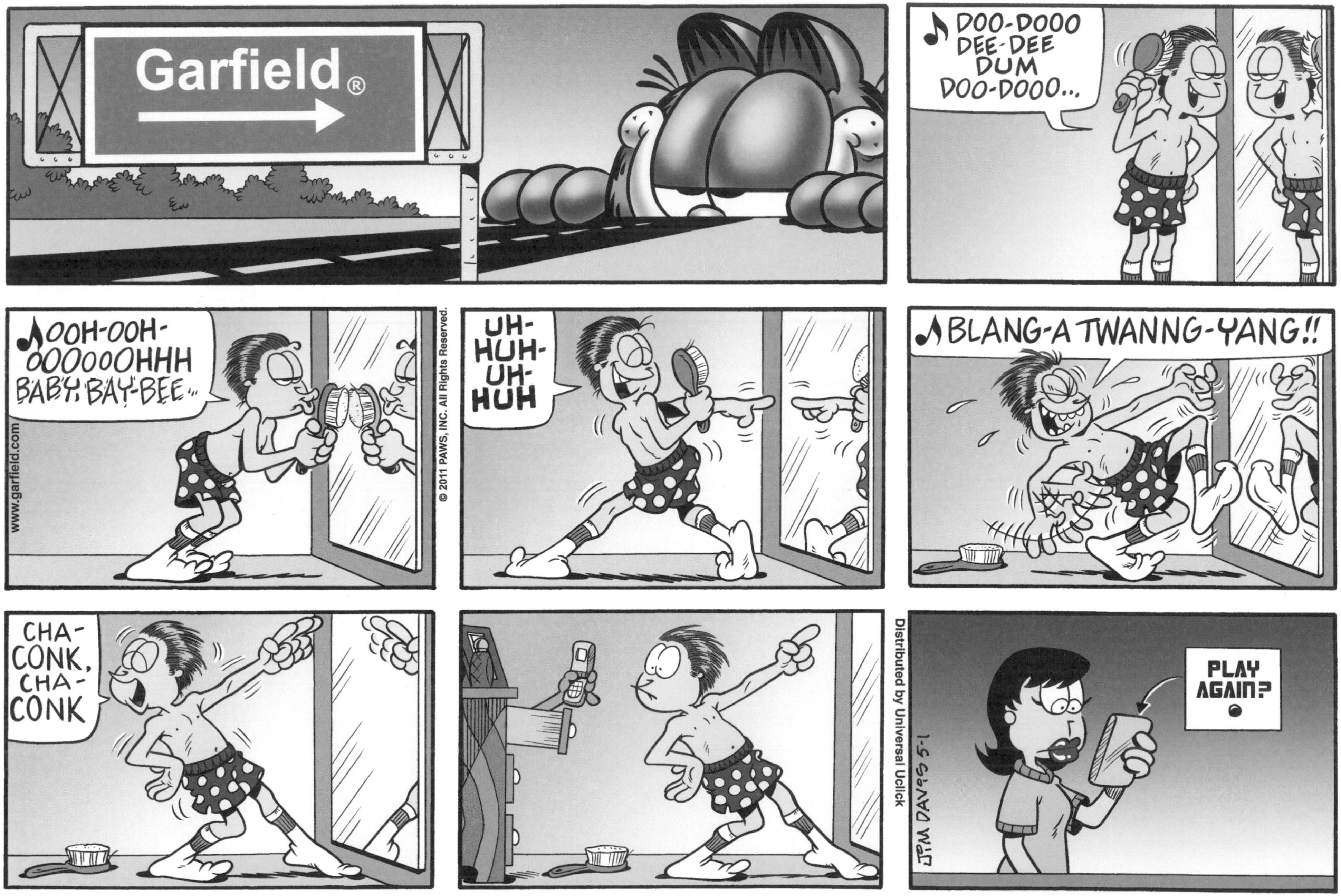
Garfield®
♪ DOO-DOOO DEE-DEE DUM DOO-DOOO...
♪ OOH-OOH-OOOOOOHHH BABY, BAY-BEE...
www.garfield.com
© 2011 PAWS, INC. All Rights Reserved.
UH-HUH-UH-HUH
♪ BLANG-A TWANNG-YANG!!
CHA-CONK, CHA-CONK
Distributed by Universal Uclick
JPM DAVIS 5-1
PLAY AGAIN?

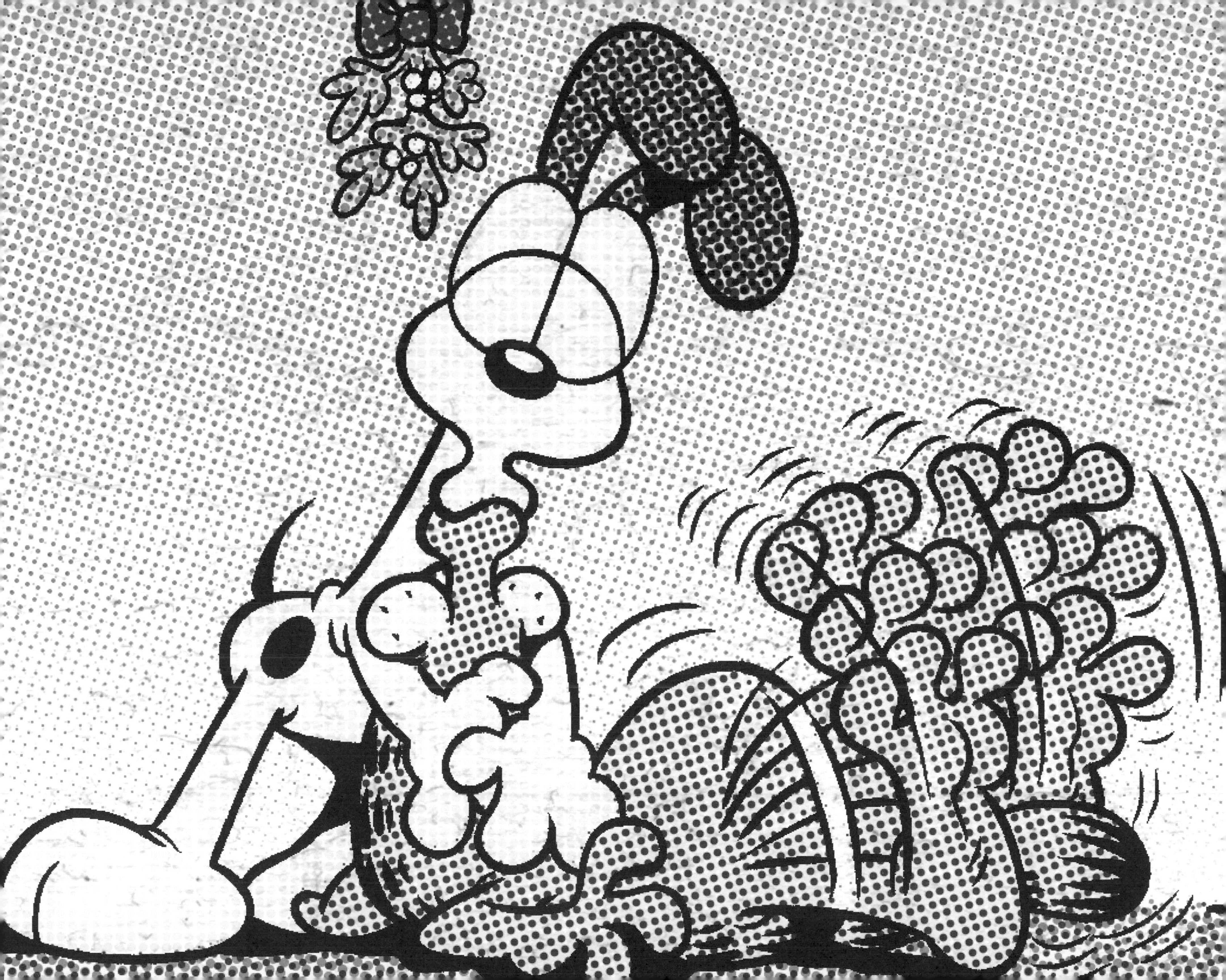

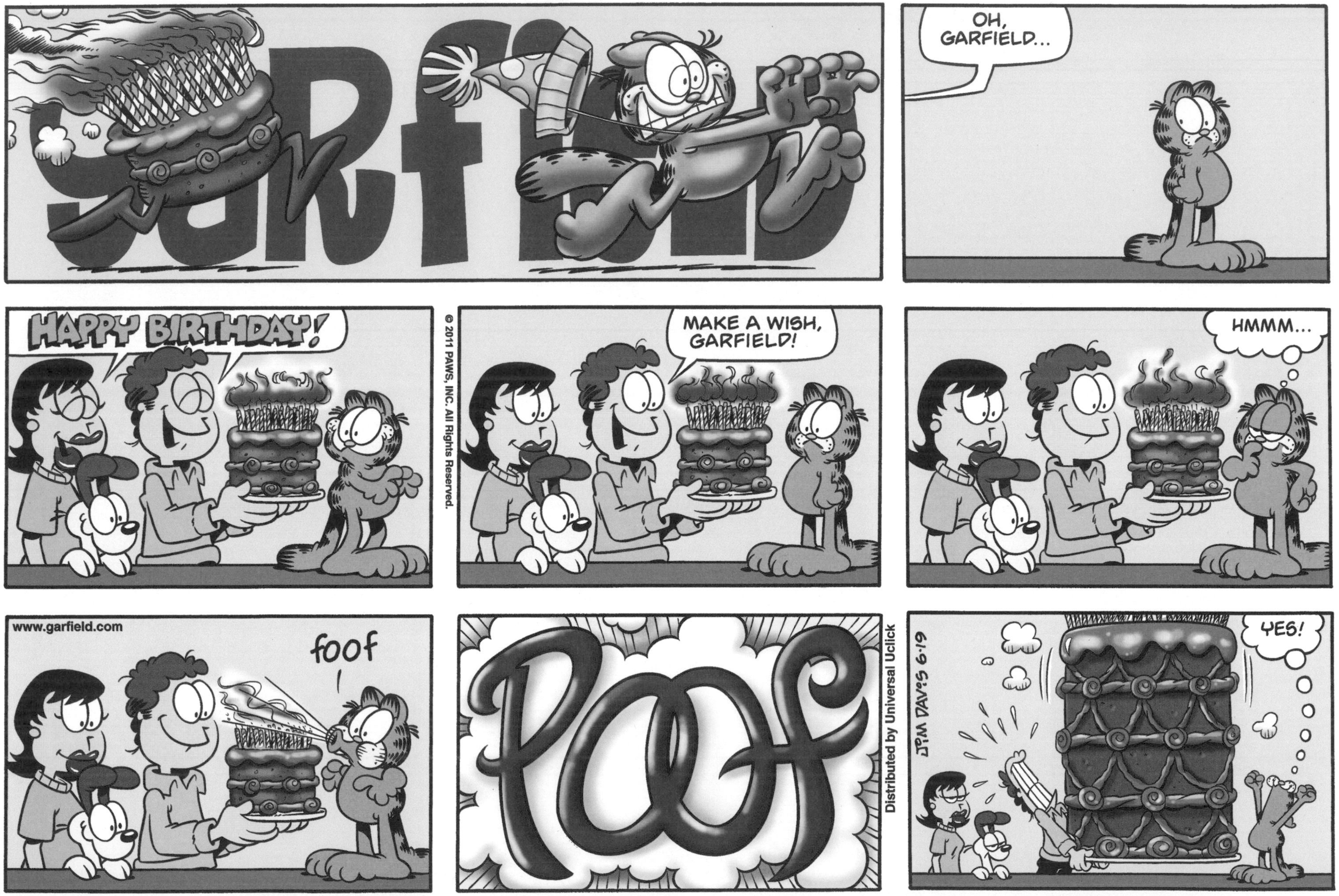
OH, GARFIELD...
HAPPY BIRTHDAY!
© 2011 PAWS, INC. All Rights Reserved.
MAKE A WISH, GARFIELD!
HMMM...
www.garfield.com
foof
POOF
Distributed by Universal Uclick
JIM DAVIS 6-19
YES!

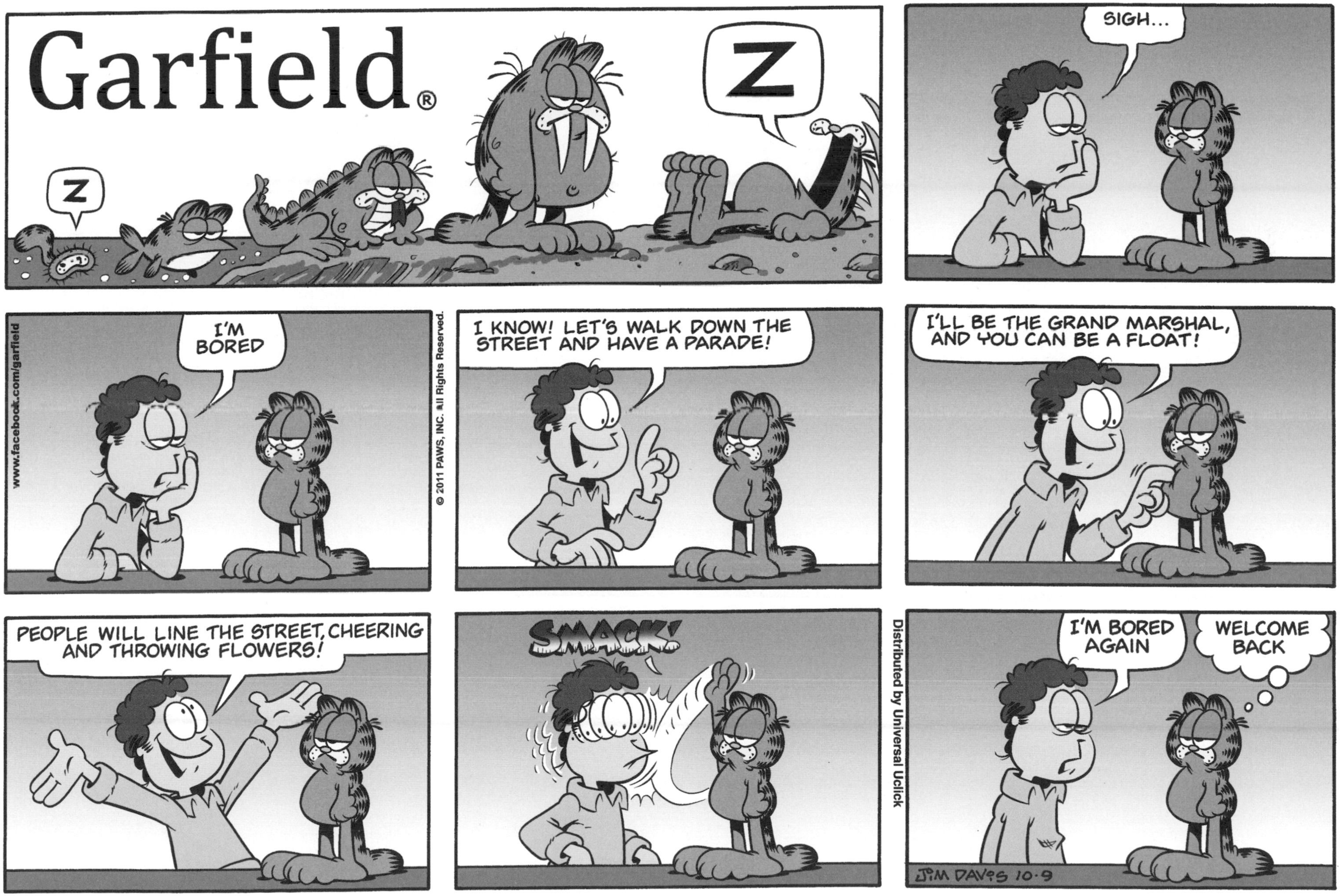
Garfield®
Z
Z
SIGH...
www.facebook.com/garfield
I'M BORED
© 2011 PAWS, INC. All Rights Reserved.
I KNOW! LET'S WALK DOWN THE STREET AND HAVE A PARADE!
I'LL BE THE GRAND MARSHAL, AND YOU CAN BE A FLOAT!
PEOPLE WILL LINE THE STREET, CHEERING AND THROWING FLOWERS!
SMACK!
Distributed by Universal Uclick
I'M BORED AGAIN
WELCOME BACK
JIM DAVIS 10-9

This is as close as I've ever been to doing a rim shot.

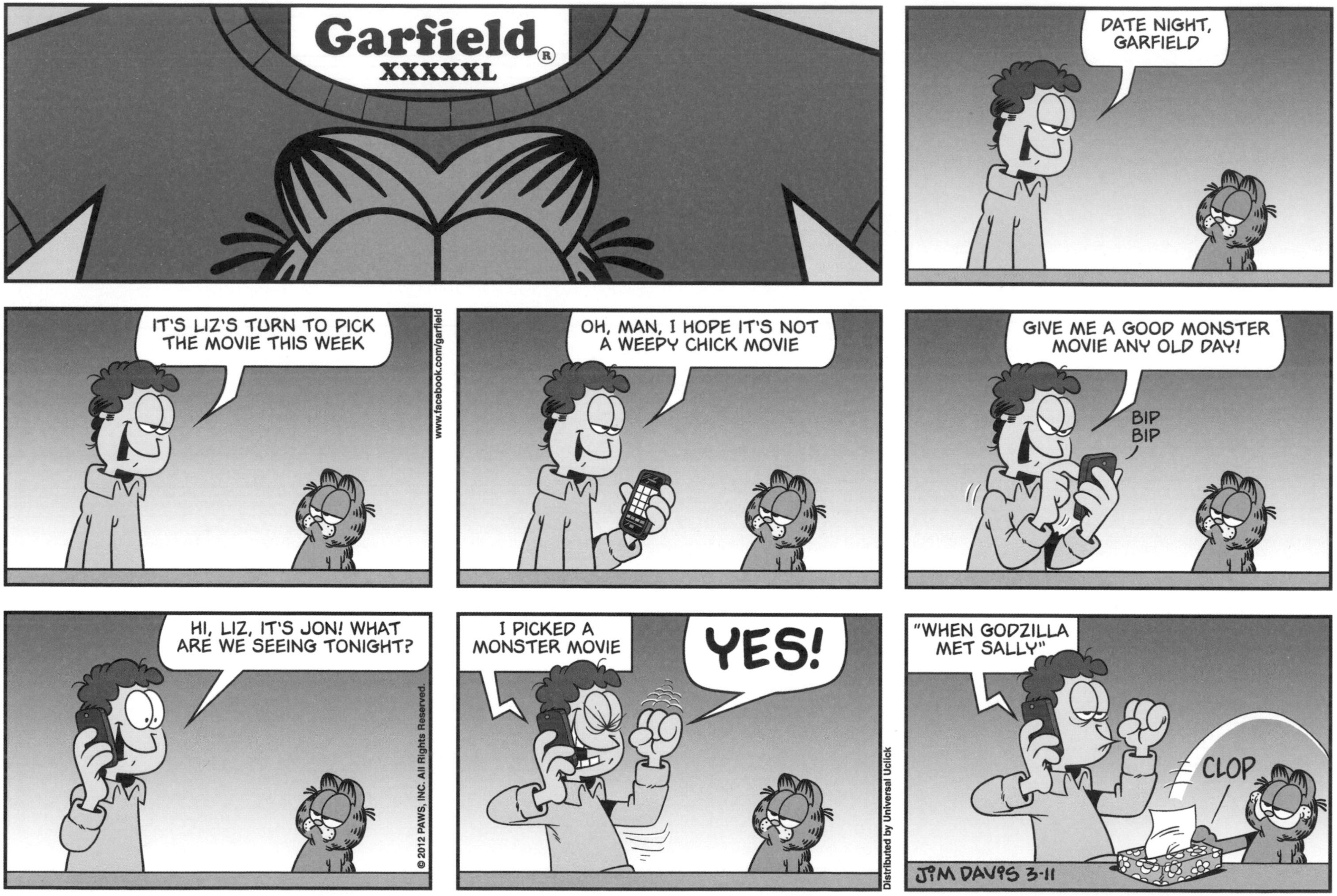
Garfield®
XXXXXL
DATE NIGHT, GARFIELD
IT'S LIZ'S TURN TO PICK THE MOVIE THIS WEEK
www.facebook.com/garfield
OH, MAN, I HOPE IT'S NOT A WEEPY CHICK MOVIE
GIVE ME A GOOD MONSTER MOVIE ANY OLD DAY!
BIP BIP
HI, LIZ, IT'S JON! WHAT ARE WE SEEING TONIGHT?
© 2012 PAWS, INC. All Rights Reserved.
I PICKED A MONSTER MOVIE
YES!
Distributed by Universal Uclick
"WHEN GODZILLA MET SALLY"
CLOP
JIM DAVIS 3-11

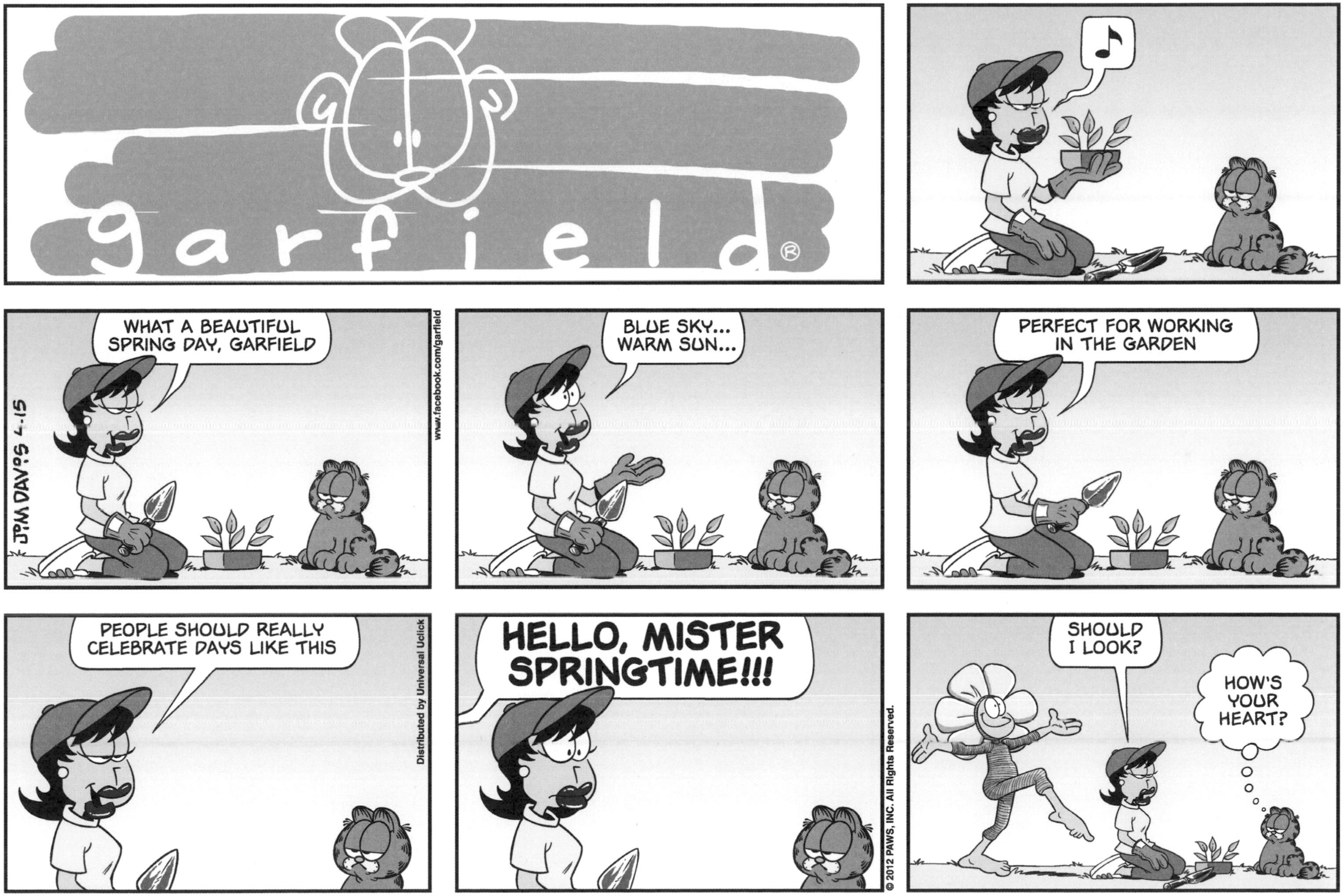

garfield®
♪
WHAT A BEAUTIFUL SPRING DAY, GARFIELD
JPM DAVPS 4-15
www.facebook.com/garfield
BLUE SKY... WARM SUN...
PERFECT FOR WORKING IN THE GARDEN
PEOPLE SHOULD REALLY CELEBRATE DAYS LIKE THIS
Distributed by Universal Uclick
HELLO, MISTER SPRINGTIME!!!
© 2012 PAWS, INC. All Rights Reserved.
SHOULD I LOOK?
HOW'S YOUR HEART?

A funny expression is worth ten thousand words.

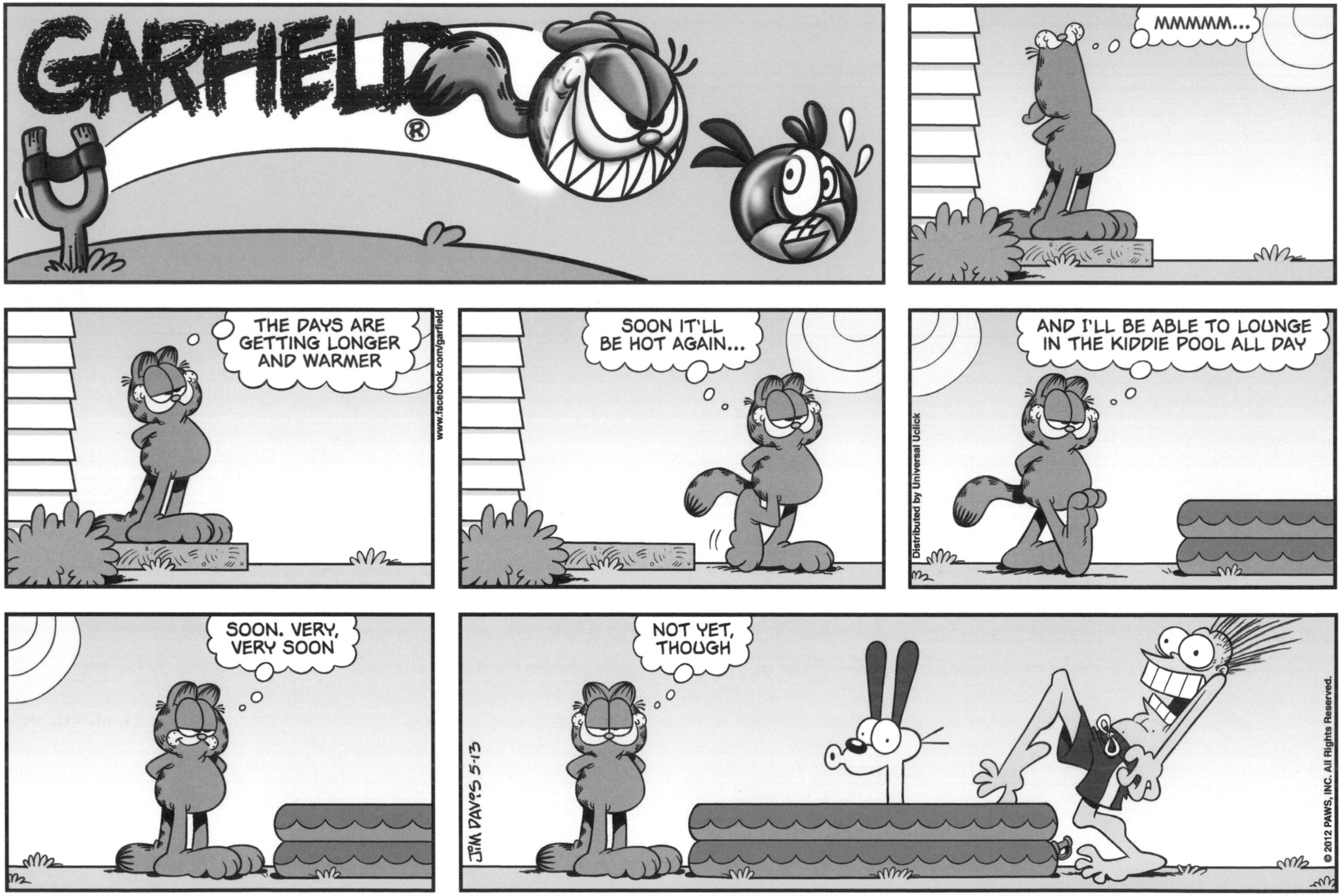

GARFIELD®
MMMMM...
THE DAYS ARE GETTING LONGER AND WARMER
www.facebook.com/garfield
SOON IT'LL BE HOT AGAIN...
Distributed by Universal Uclick
AND I'LL BE ABLE TO LOUNGE IN THE KIDDIE POOL ALL DAY
SOON. VERY, VERY SOON
NOT YET, THOUGH
JIM DAVIS 5-13
© 2012 PAWS, INC. All Rights Reserved.

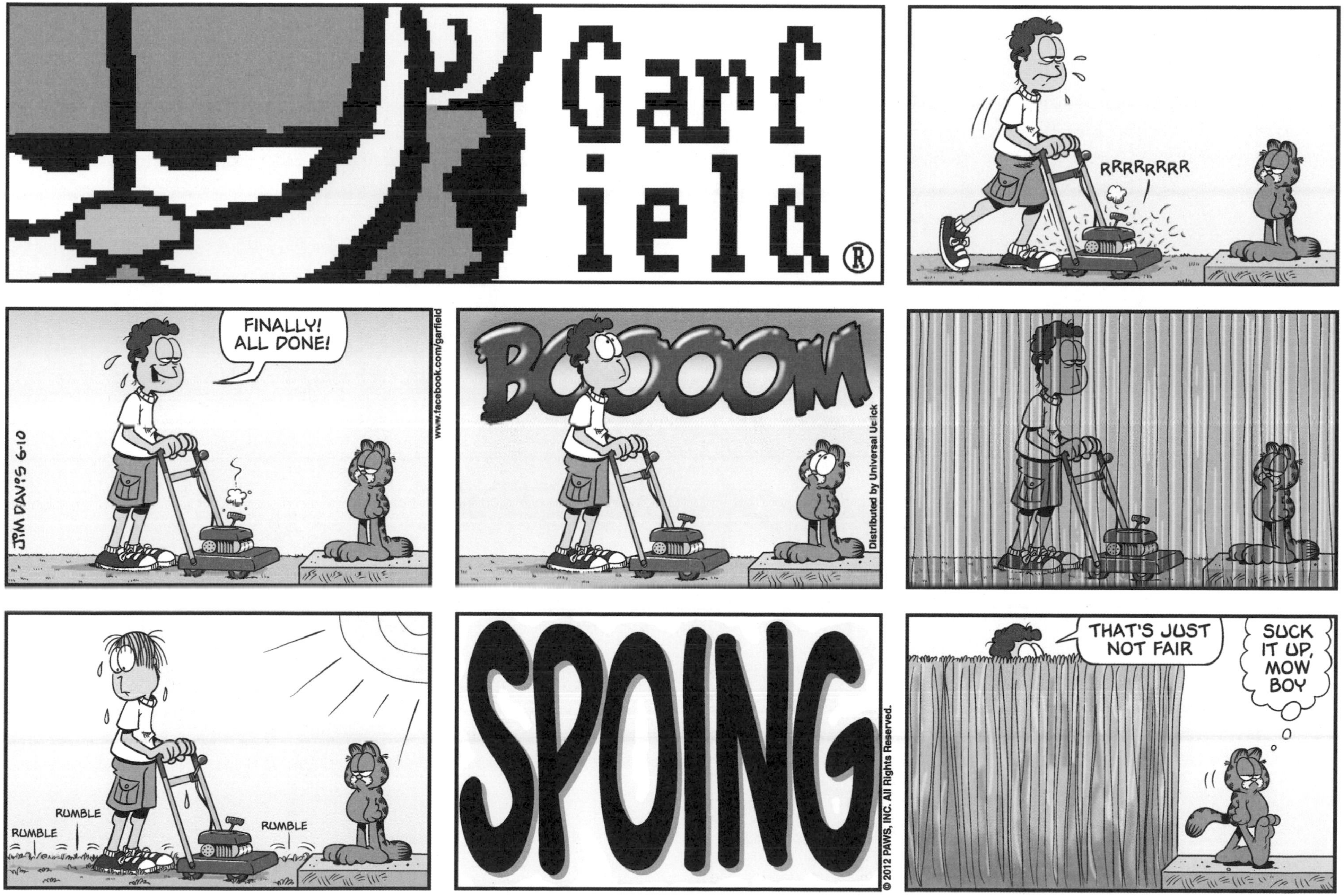
Garfield®
RRRRRRRR
JIM DAVIS 6-10
FINALLY! ALL DONE!
www.facebook.com/garfield
BOOOOOM
Distributed by Universal Uclick
RUMBLE
RUMBLE
RUMBLE
SPOING
© 2012 PAWS, INC. All Rights Reserved.
THAT'S JUST NOT FAIR
SUCK IT UP, MOW BOY

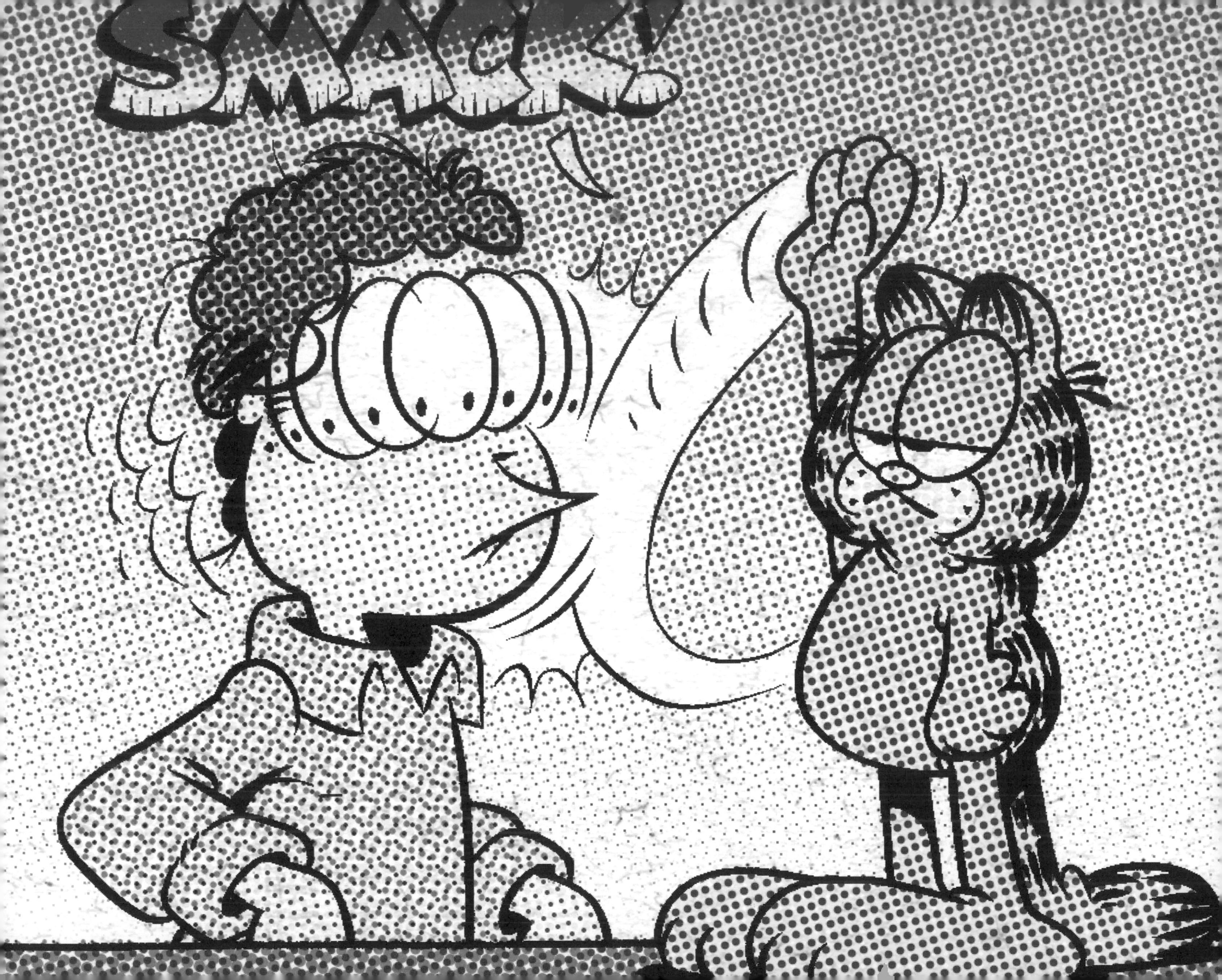
SMACK!

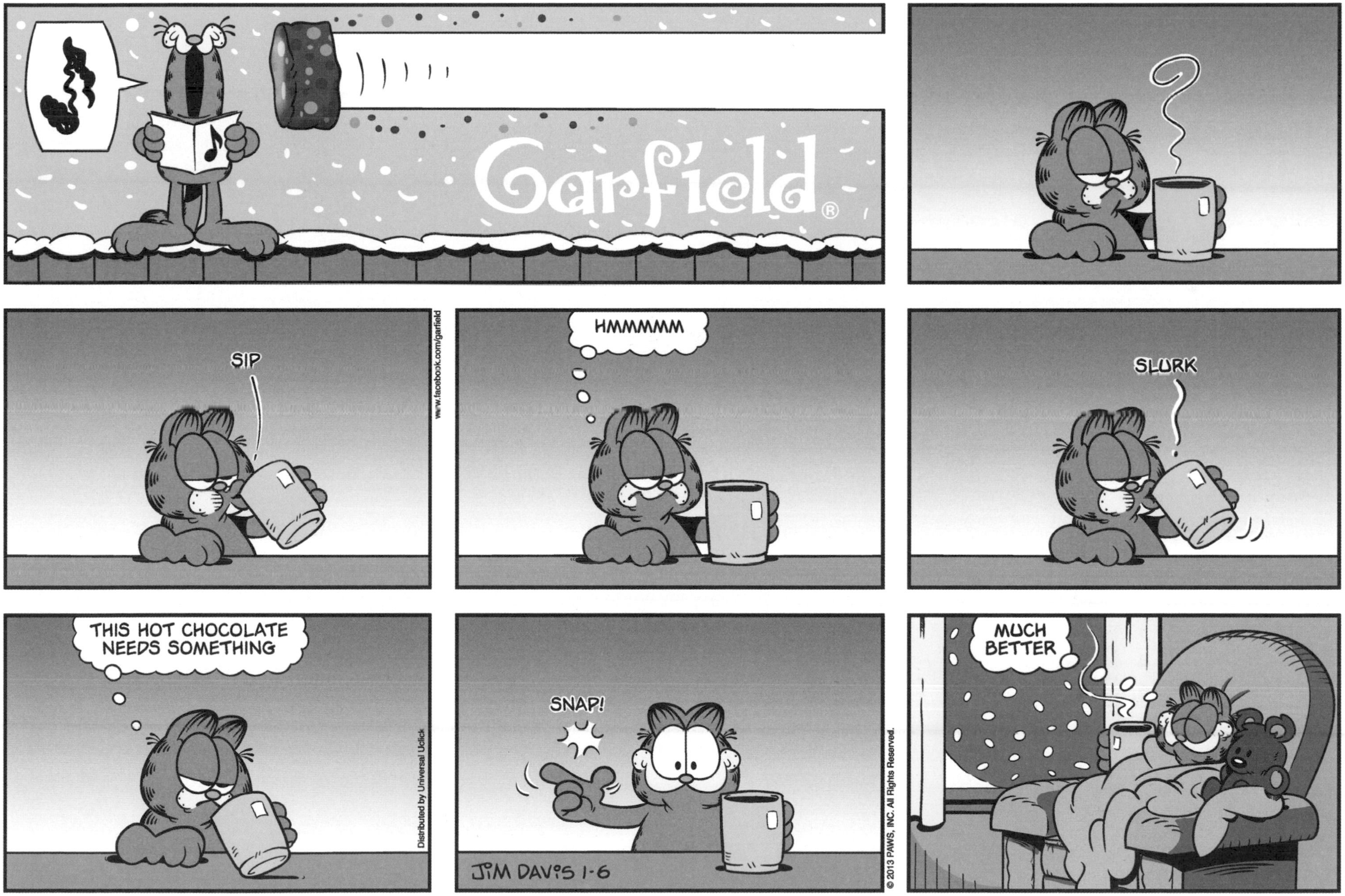
Garfield®
www.facebook.com/garfield
SIP
HMMMMM
SLURK
THIS HOT CHOCOLATE NEEDS SOMETHING
Distributed by Universal Uclick
SNAP!
JIM DAVIS 1-6
© 2013 PAWS, INC. All Rights Reserved.
MUCH BETTER

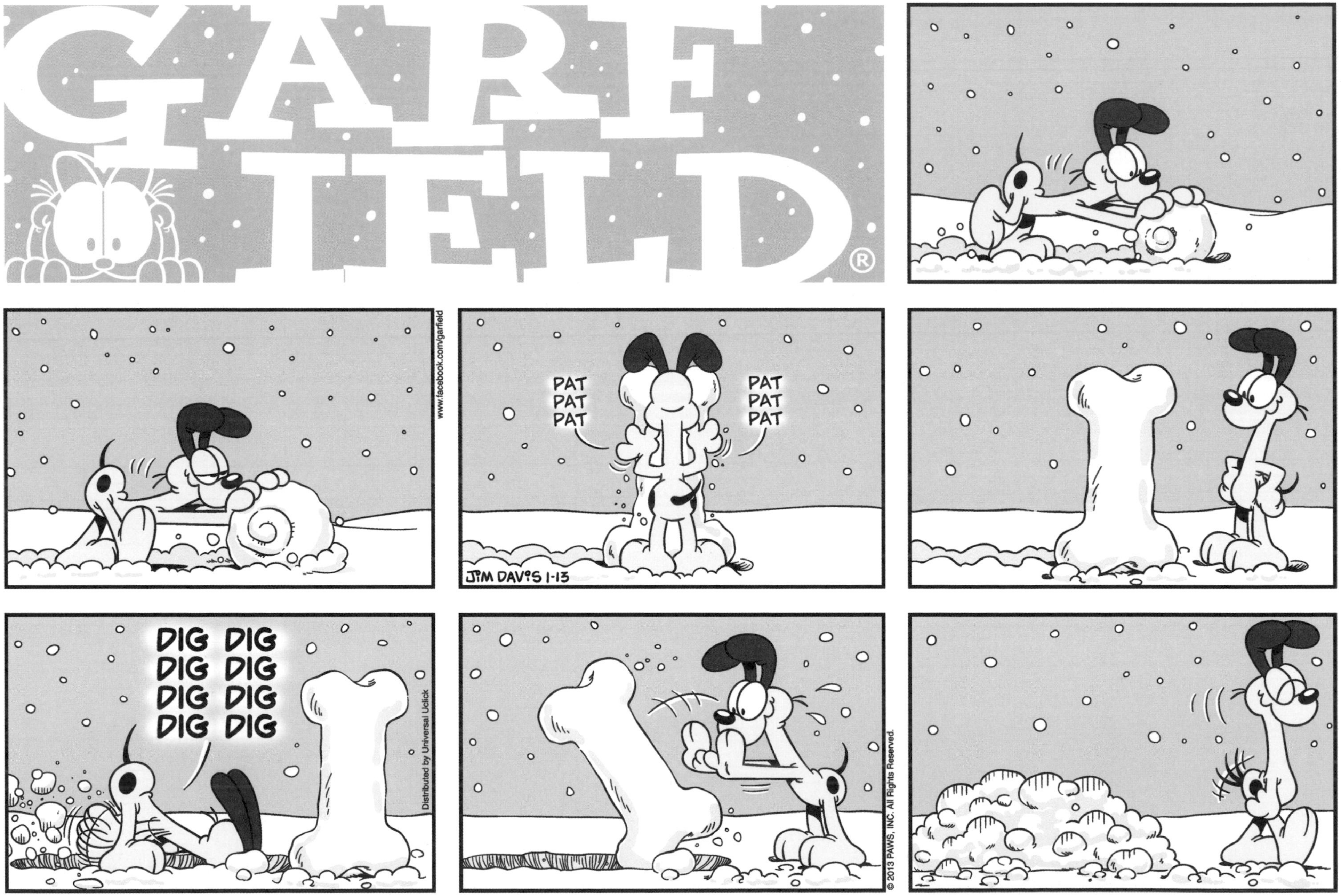
GARFIELD®
www.facebook.com/garfield
PAT
PAT
PAT
PAT
PAT
PAT
JIM DAVIS 1-13
DIG DIG
DIG DIG
DIG DIG
DIG DIG
Distributed by Universal Uclick
© 2013 PAWS, INC. All Rights Reserved.

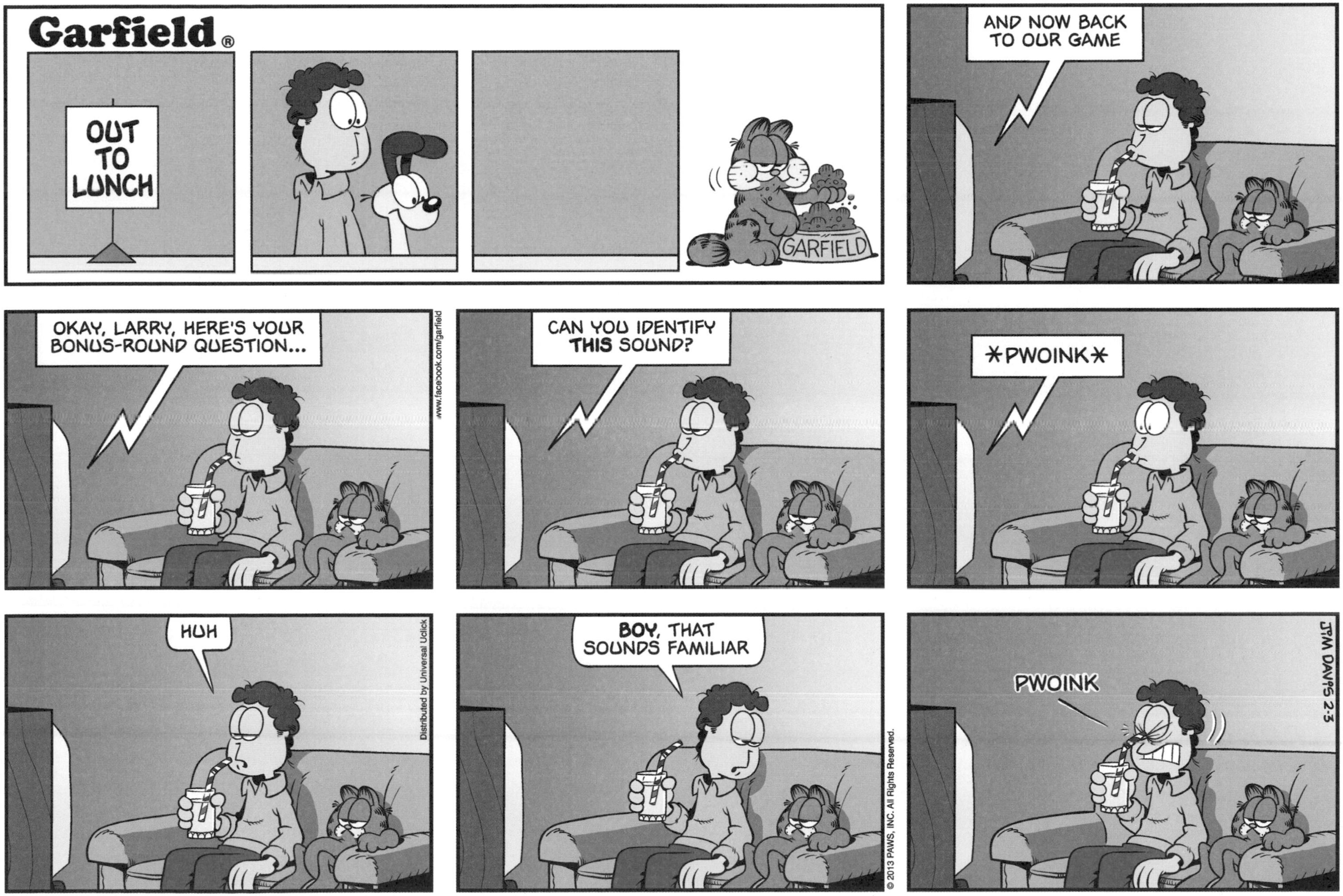
Garfield®
OUT TO LUNCH
GARFIELD
AND NOW BACK TO OUR GAME
OKAY, LARRY, HERE'S YOUR BONUS-ROUND QUESTION...
www.facebook.com/garfield
CAN YOU IDENTIFY THIS SOUND?
PWOINK
HUH
Distributed by Universal Uclick
BOY, THAT SOUNDS FAMILIAR
© 2013 PAWS, INC. All Rights Reserved.
JIM DAVIS 2-3
PWOINK

I think that it's the relationship gags that have sustained the strip over the years. You have to love these guys.

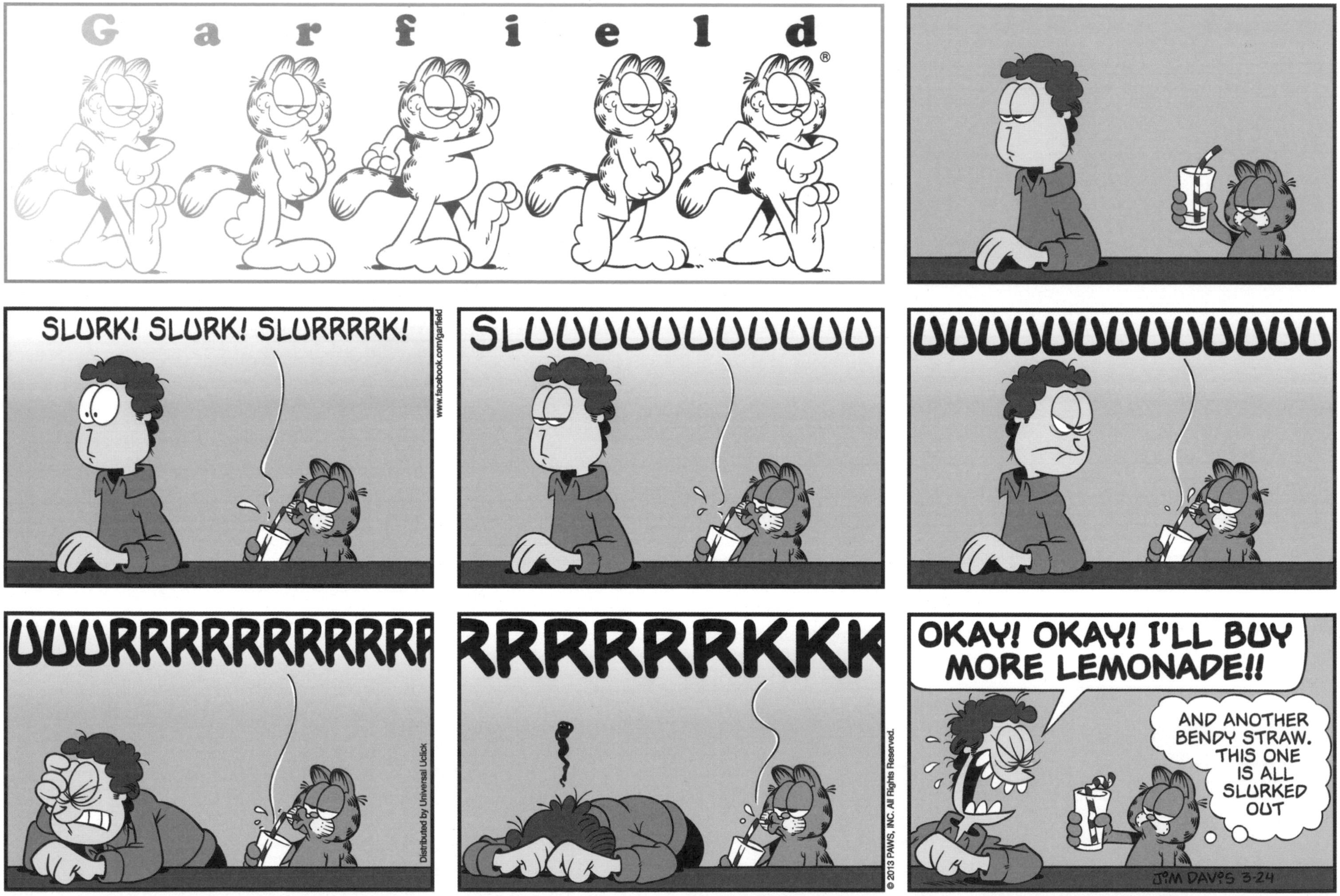

Garfield®
SLURK! SLURK! SLURRRRK!
www.facebook.com/garfield
SLUUUUUUUUUUUU
UUUUUUUUUUUUUU
UUURRRRRRRRRRRR
RRRRRRRRKKK
Distributed by Universal Uclick
© 2013 PAWS, INC. All Rights Reserved.
OKAY! OKAY! I'LL BUY MORE LEMONADE!!
AND ANOTHER BENDY STRAW. THIS ONE IS ALL SLURKED OUT
JIM DAVIS 3-24

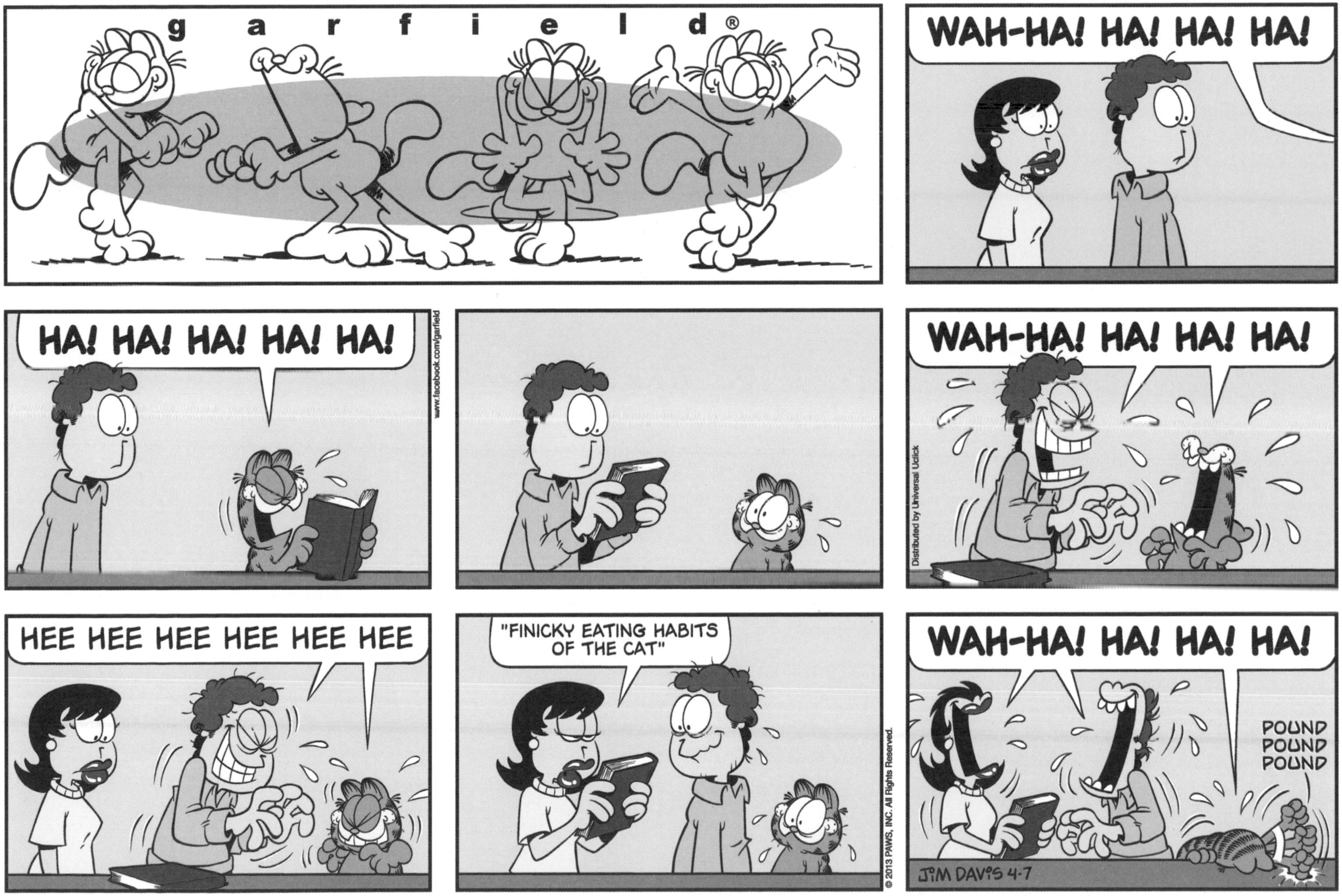
garfield®
WAH-HA! HA! HA! HA!
HA! HA! HA! HA! HA!
www.facebook.com/garfield
WAH-HA! HA! HA! HA!
Distributed by Universal Uclick
HEE HEE HEE HEE HEE HEE
"FINICKY EATING HABITS OF THE CAT"
© 2013 PAWS, INC. All Rights Reserved.
WAH-HA! HA! HA! HA!
POUND
POUND
POUND
JIM DAVIS 4-7

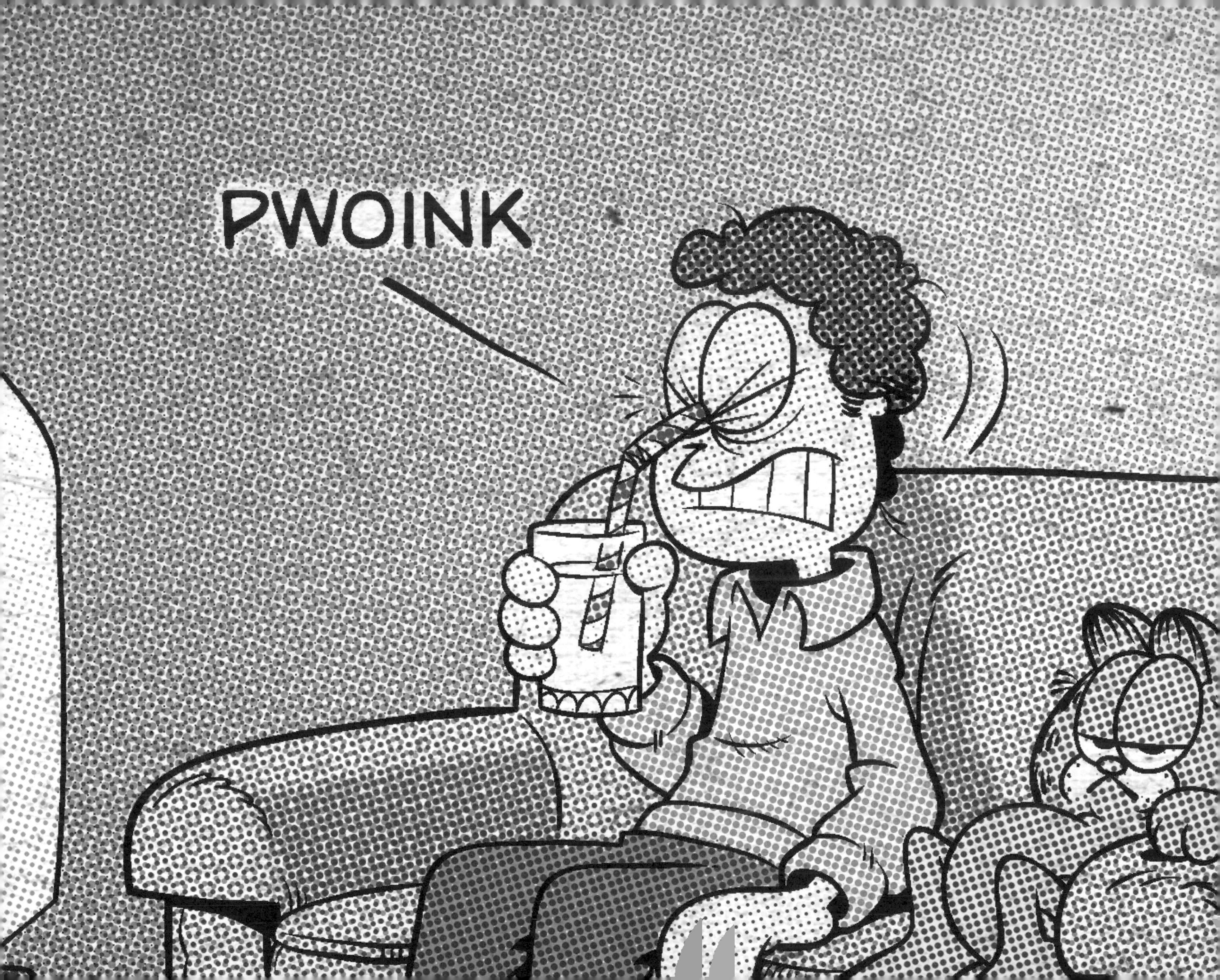
PWOINK

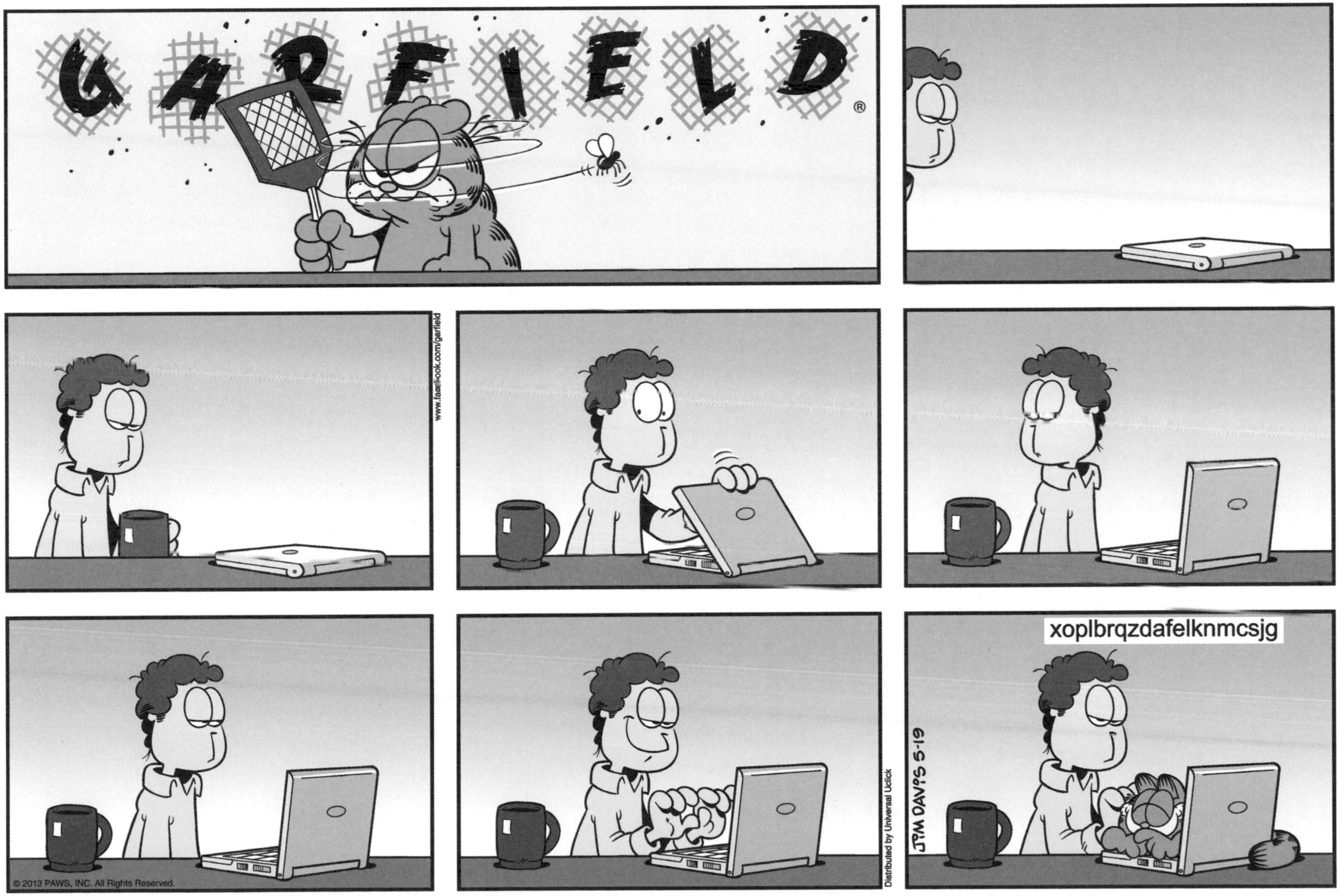
GARFIELD®
www.facebook.com/garfield
xoplbrqzdafelknmcsjg
© 2013 PAWS, INC. All Rights Reserved.
Distributed by Universal Uclick
JIM DAVIS 5-19

LOGO EXPO

Sunday title panels or "logo boxes" as we call them in-house.

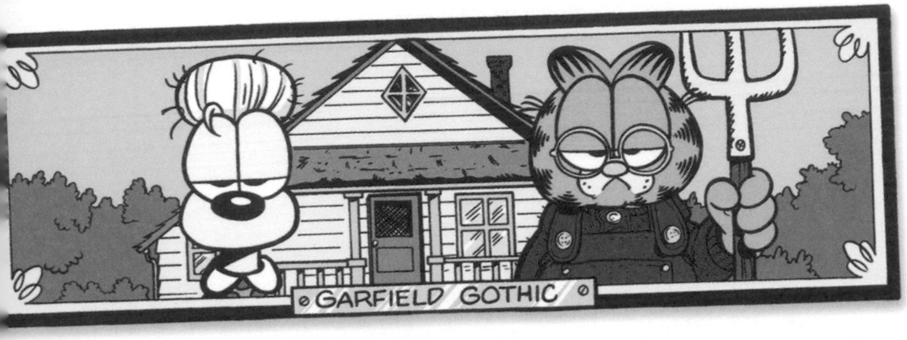
GARFIELD GOTHIC

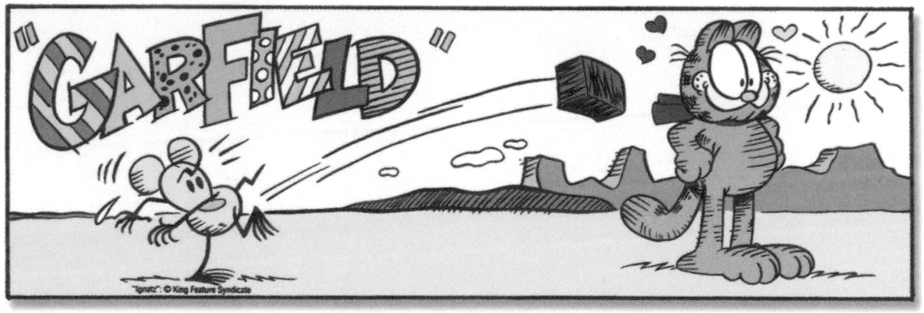
"GARFIELD"
"Ignatz": © King Feature Syndicate

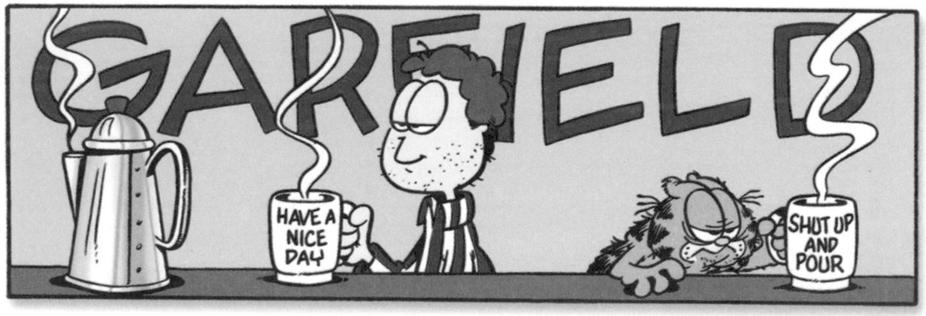
GARFIELD
HAVE A NICE DAY
SHUT UP AND POUR

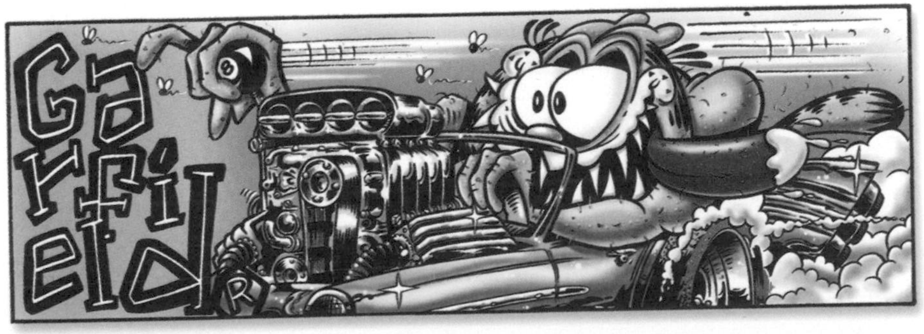
Garfield

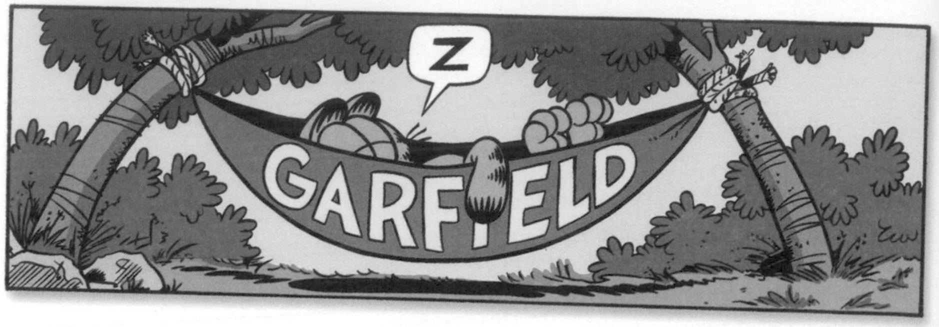
Z
GARFIELD

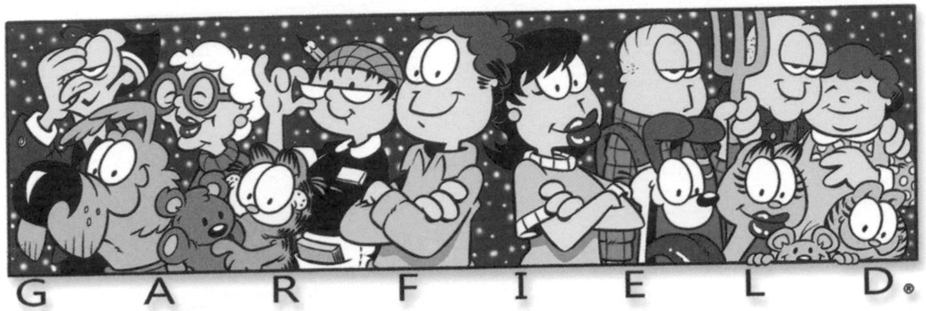
G A R F I E L D®

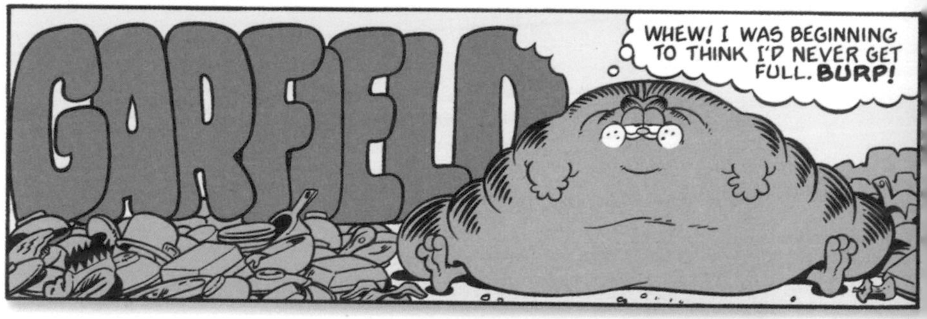
GARFIELD
WHEW! I WAS BEGINNING TO THINK I'D NEVER GET FULL. BURP!

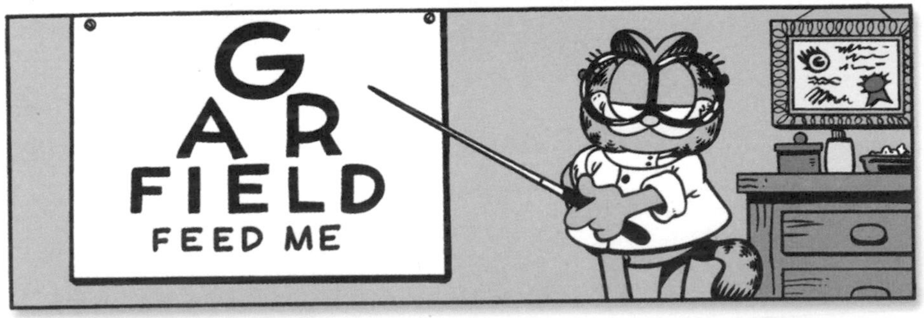
G
AR
FIELD
FEED ME

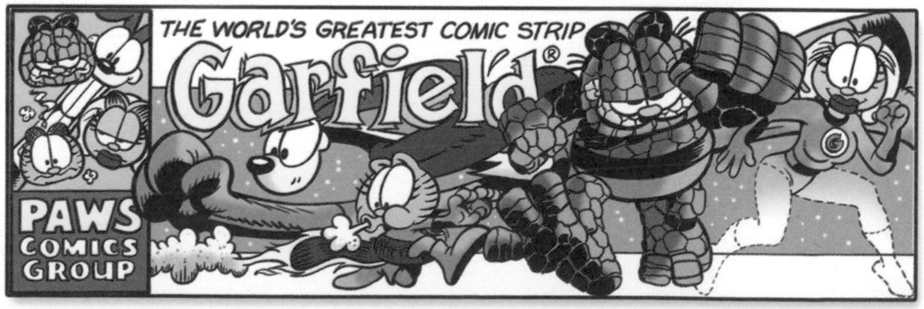
THE WORLD'S GREATEST COMIC STRIP
Garfield®
PAWS COMICS GROUP

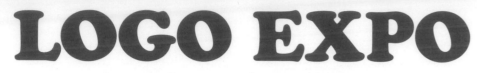

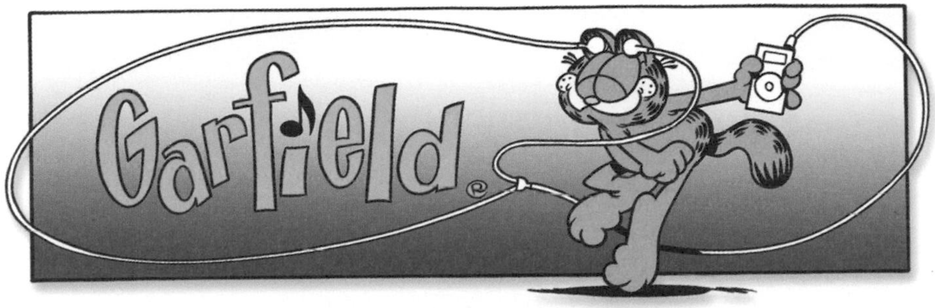
Garfield®

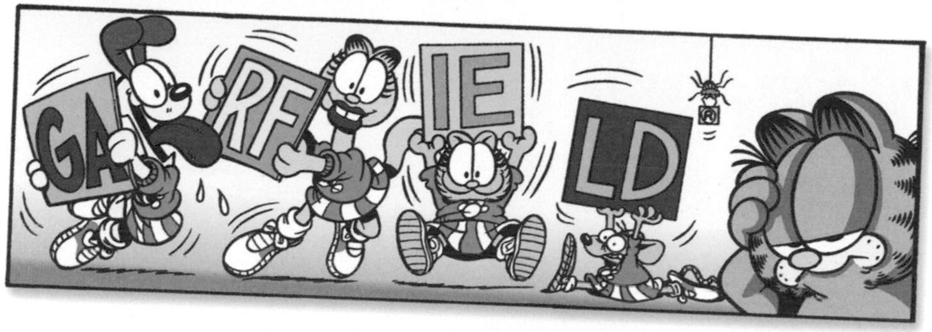
GA
RF
IE
LD

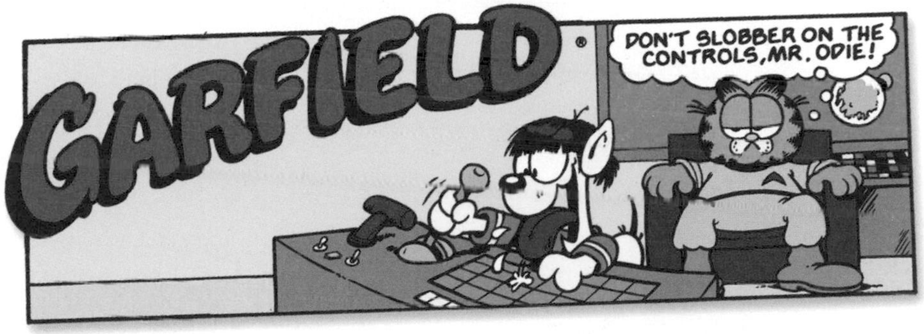
GARFIELD®
DON'T SLOBBER ON THE CONTROLS, MR. ODIE!

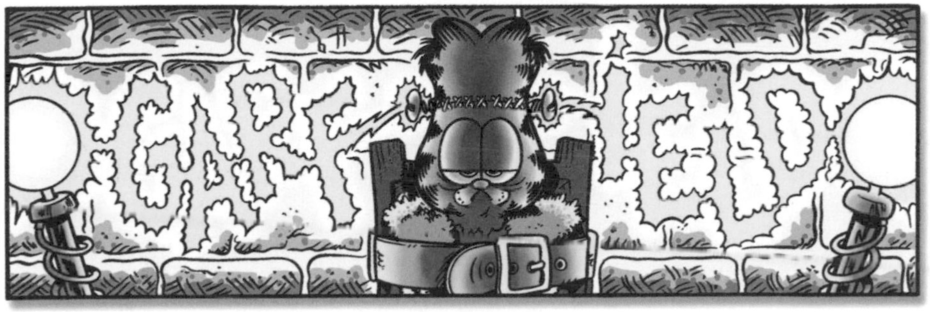
GARFIELD

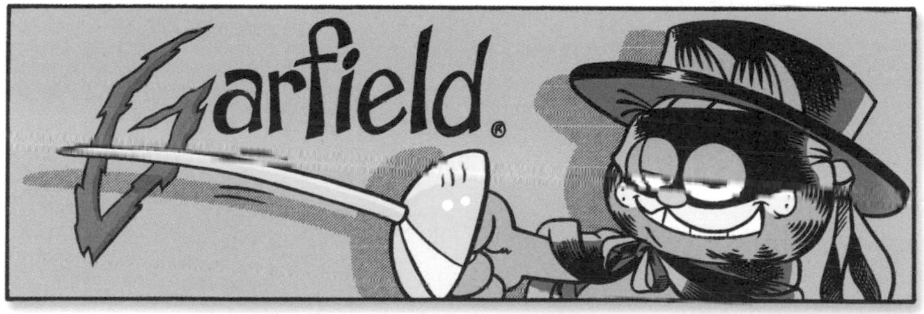
Garfield®

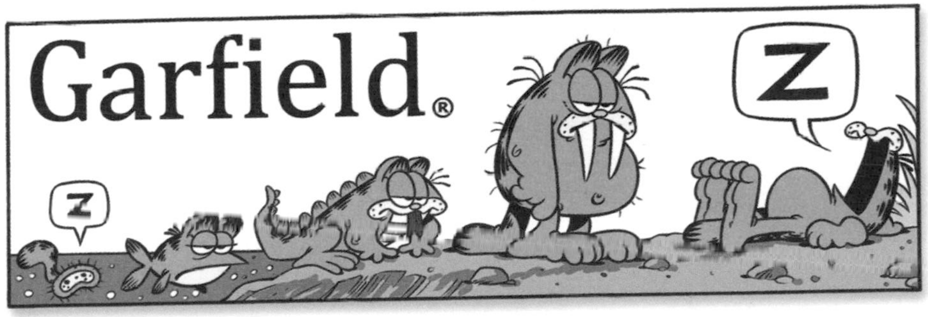
Garfield®
Z
Z

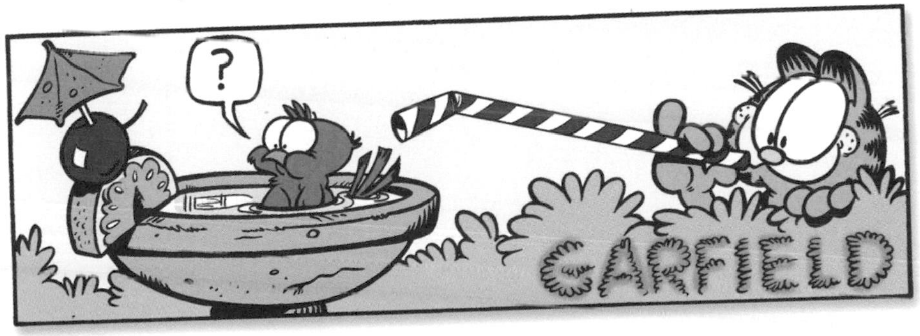
?
GARFIELD

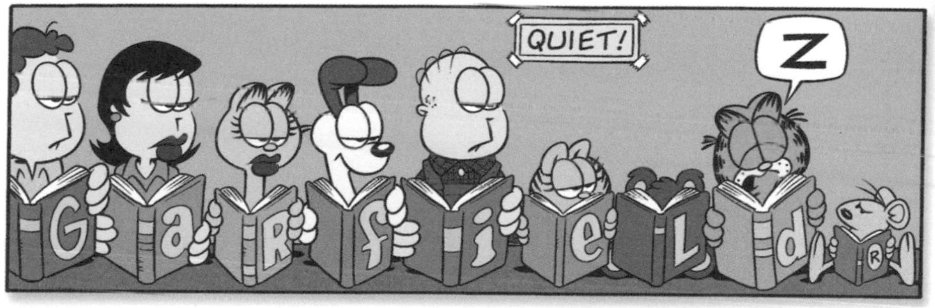
QUIET!
Z
G a R f i e L d ®

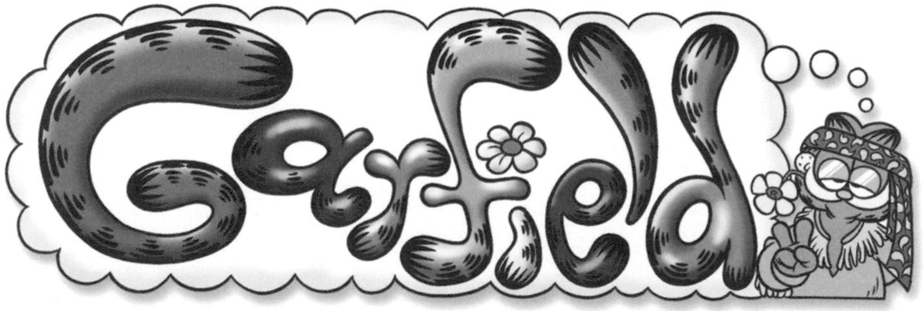
Garfield

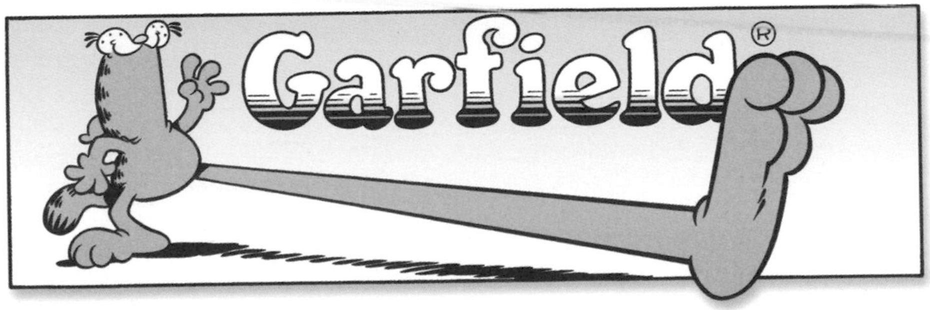
Garfield®

EJECT THE REJECTS!

These strips were jettisoned before they could land in the newspaper.

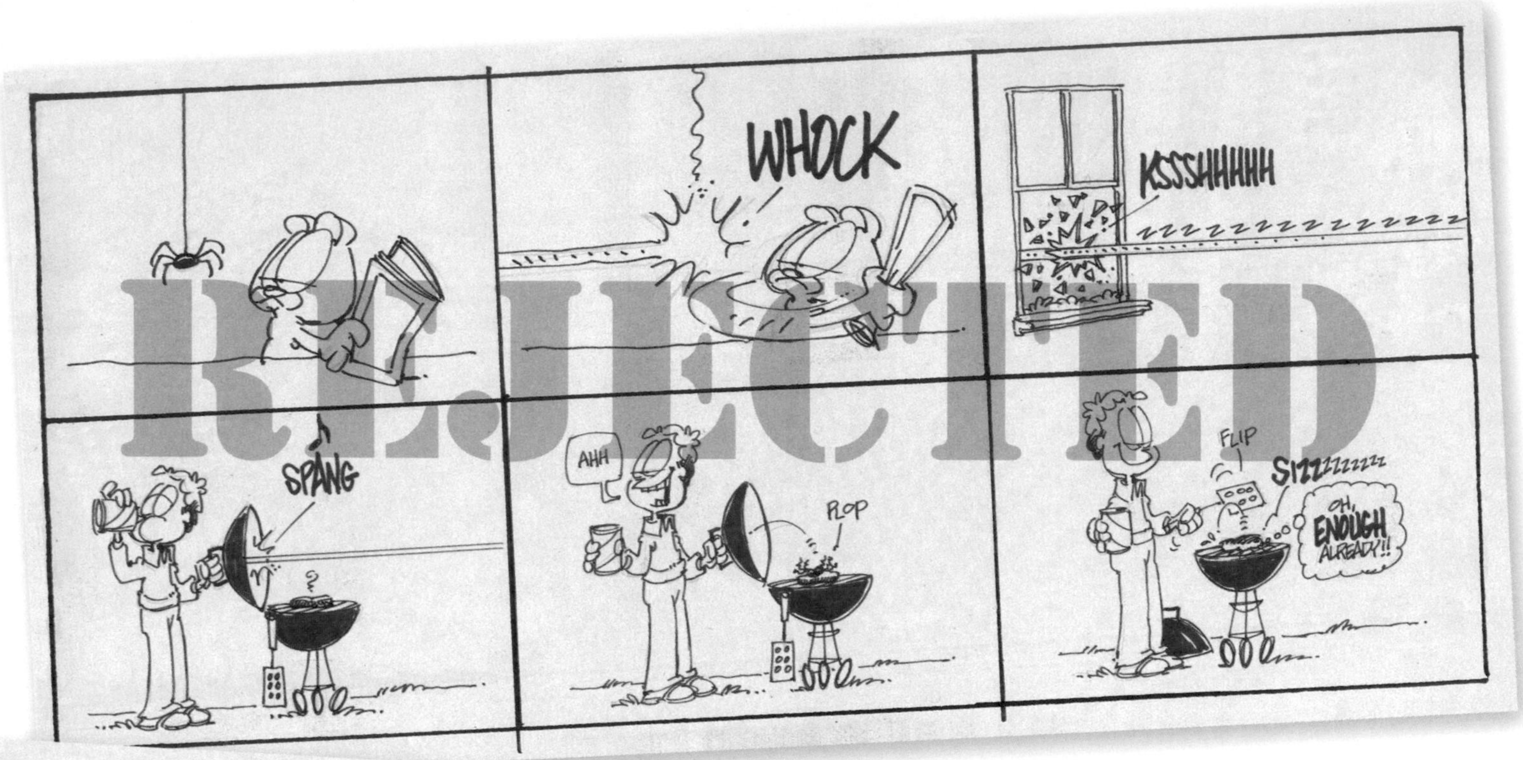
WHOCK
KSSSHHHHH
zzzzzzzzzzzzzz
REJECTED
SPANG
AHH
PLOP
FLIP
SIZZzzzzzz
OH, ENOUGH ALREADY?!!

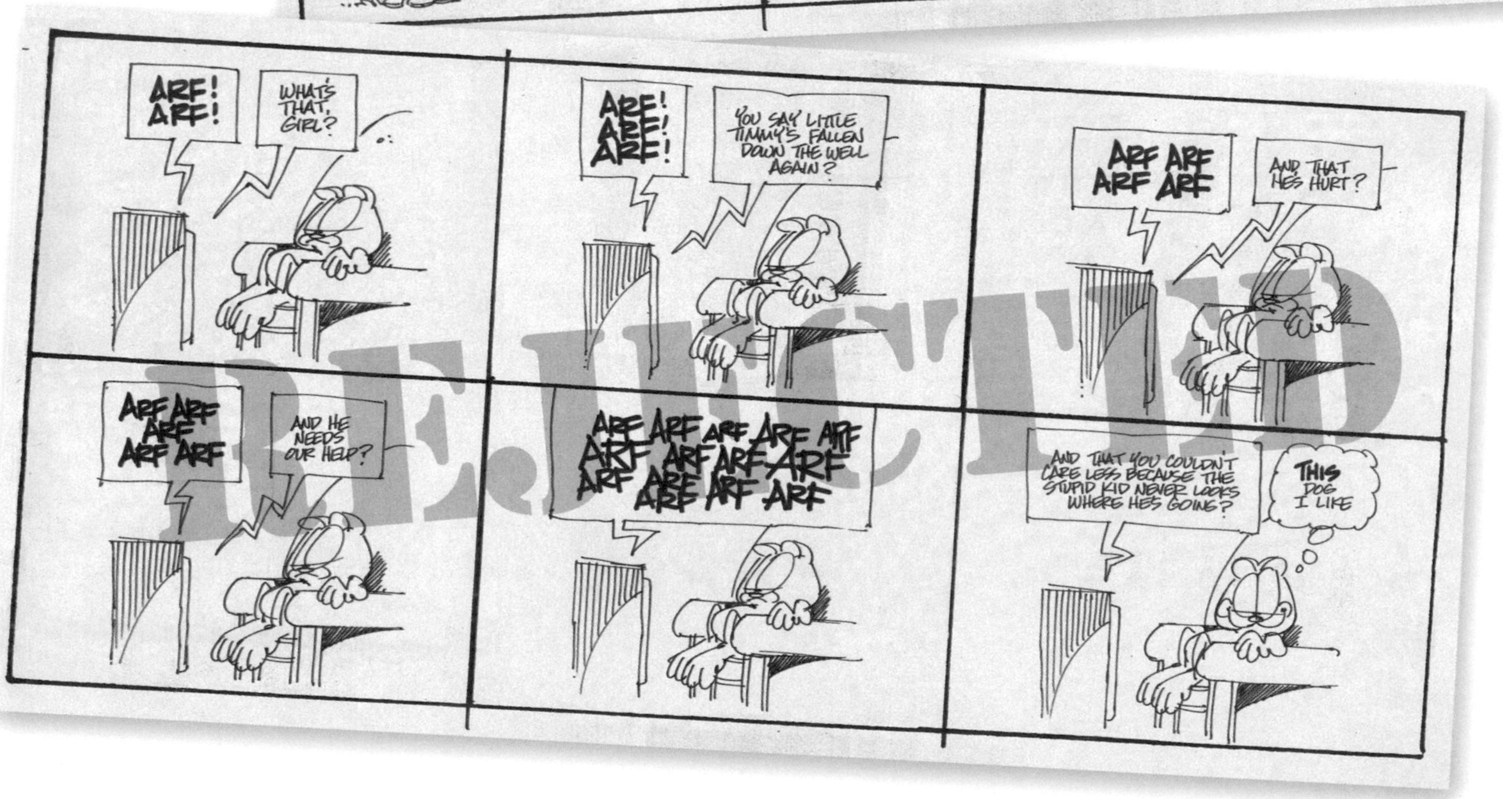
ARF! ARF!
WHAT'S THAT, GIRL?
ARF! ARF! ARF!
YOU SAY LITTLE TIMMY'S FALLEN DOWN THE WELL AGAIN?
ARF ARF ARF ARF
AND THAT HE'S HURT?
ARF ARF ARF ARF ARF
AND HE NEEDS OUR HELP?
ARF ARF ARF ARF ARF ARF ARF ARF ARF ARF ARF ARF ARF ARF ARF
AND THAT YOU COULDN'T CARE LESS BECAUSE THE STUPID KID NEVER LOOKS WHERE HE'S GOING?
THIS DOG I LIKE
REJECTED

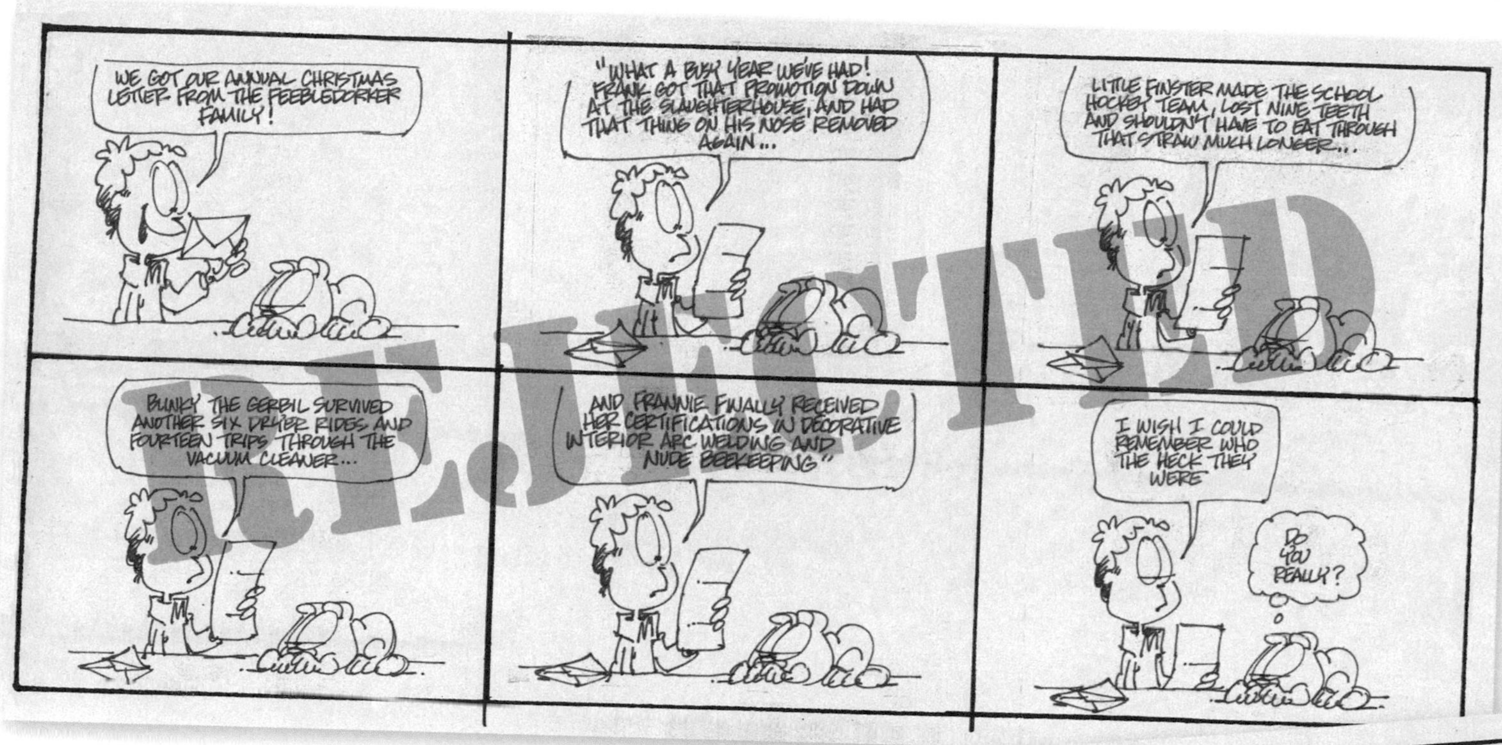
WE GOT OUR ANNUAL CHRISTMAS LETTER FROM THE FEEBLEDORKER FAMILY!
"WHAT A BUSY YEAR WE'VE HAD! FRANK GOT THAT PROMOTION DOWN AT THE SLAUGHTERHOUSE, AND HAD THAT THING ON HIS NOSE REMOVED AGAIN...
LITTLE FINSTER MADE THE SCHOOL HOCKEY TEAM, LOST NINE TEETH AND SHOULDN'T HAVE TO EAT THROUGH THAT STRAW MUCH LONGER...
BUNKY THE GERBIL SURVIVED ANOTHER SIX DRYER RIDES AND FOURTEEN TRIPS THROUGH THE VACUUM CLEANER...
AND FRANNIE FINALLY RECEIVED HER CERTIFICATIONS IN DECORATIVE INTERIOR ARC WELDING AND NUDE BEEKEEPING"
I WISH I COULD REMEMBER WHO THE HECK THEY WERE
DO YOU REALLY?
REJECTED

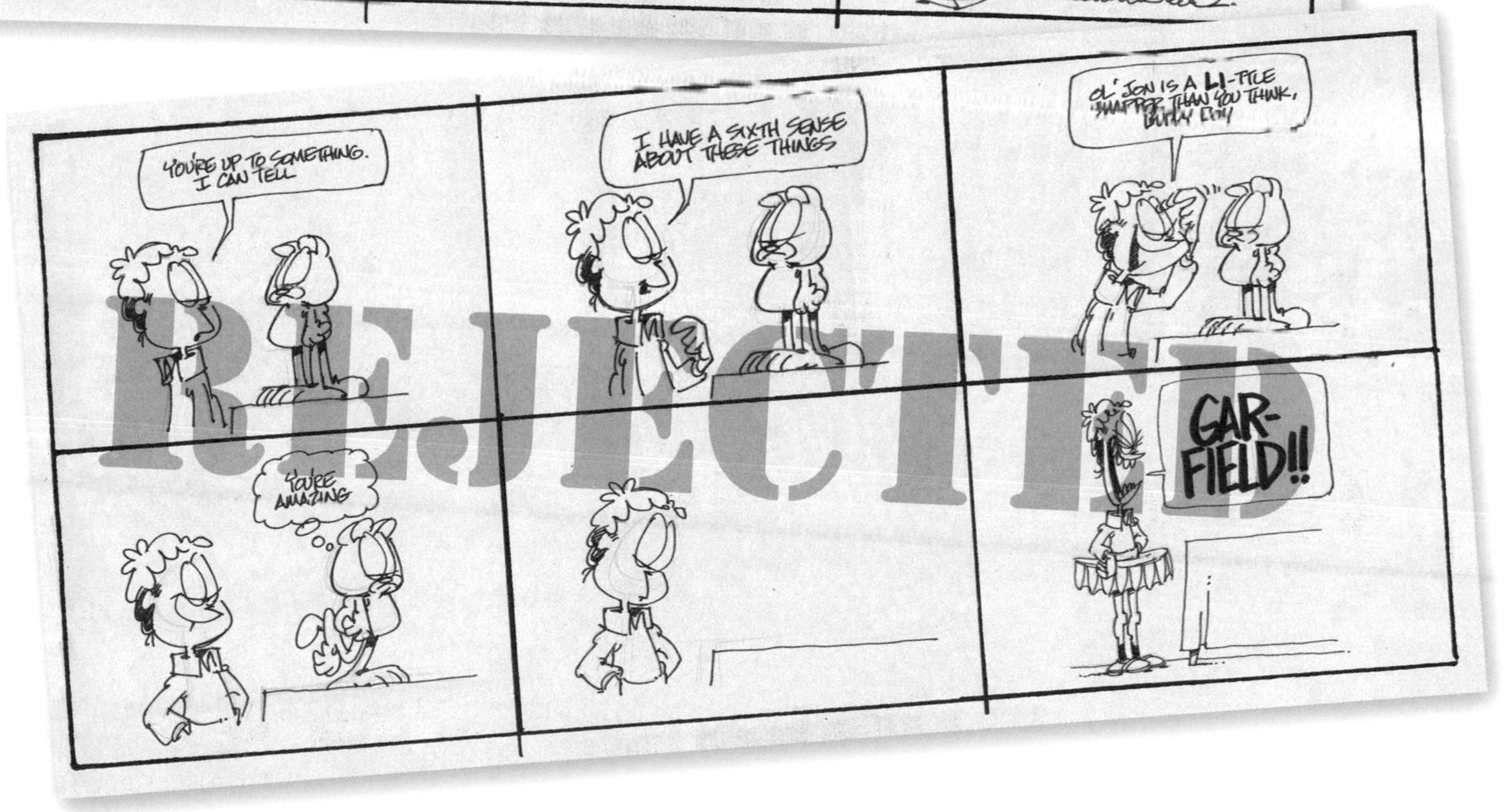
YOU'RE UP TO SOMETHING. I CAN TELL
I HAVE A SIXTH SENSE ABOUT THESE THINGS
OL' JON IS A LI-TTLE SHARPER THAN YOU THINK,
YOU'RE AMAZING
GAR-FIELD!!
REJECTED

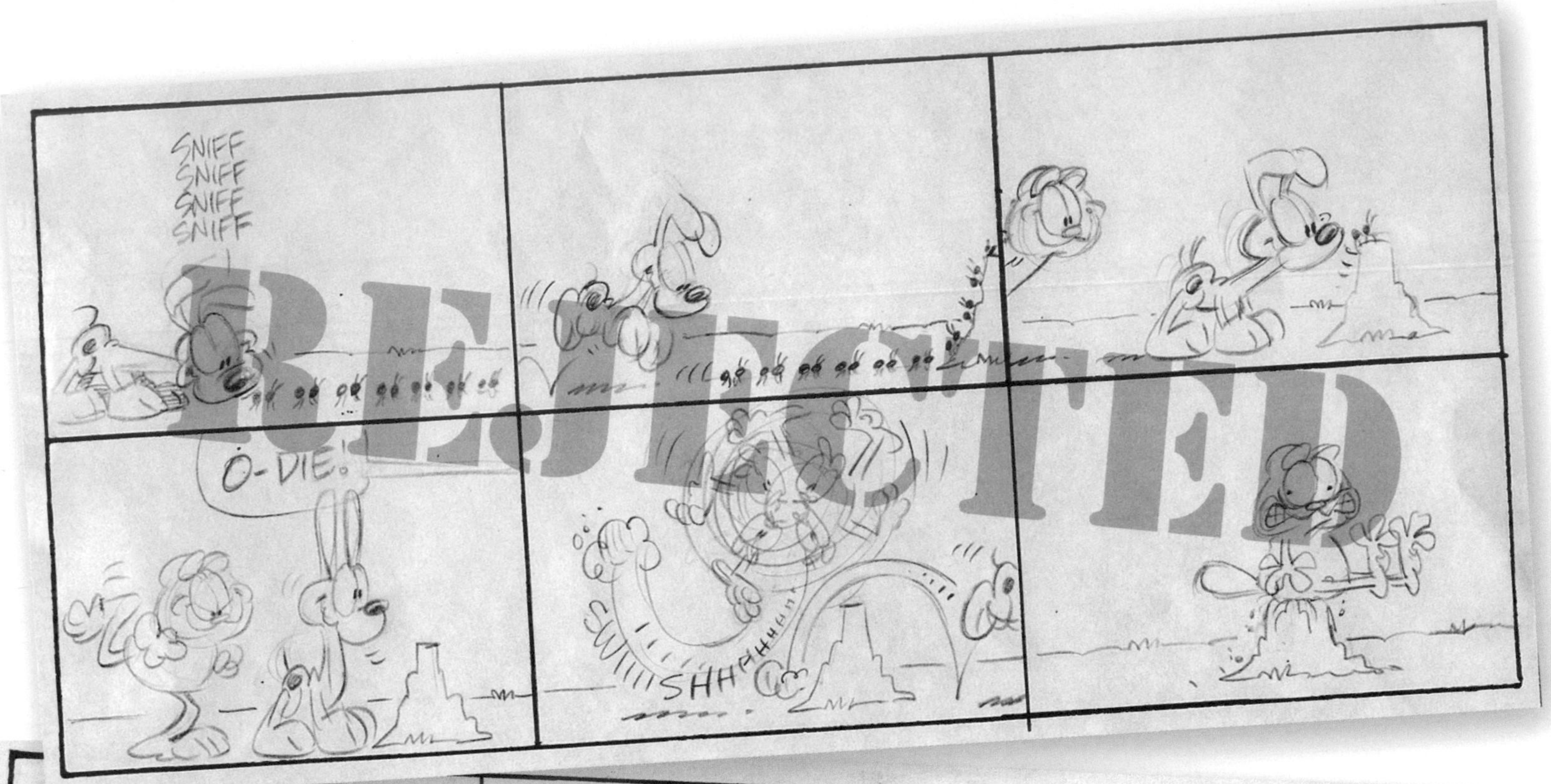
SNIFF
SNIFF
SNIFF
SNIFF
O-DIE!
SHHHHHH
REJECTED

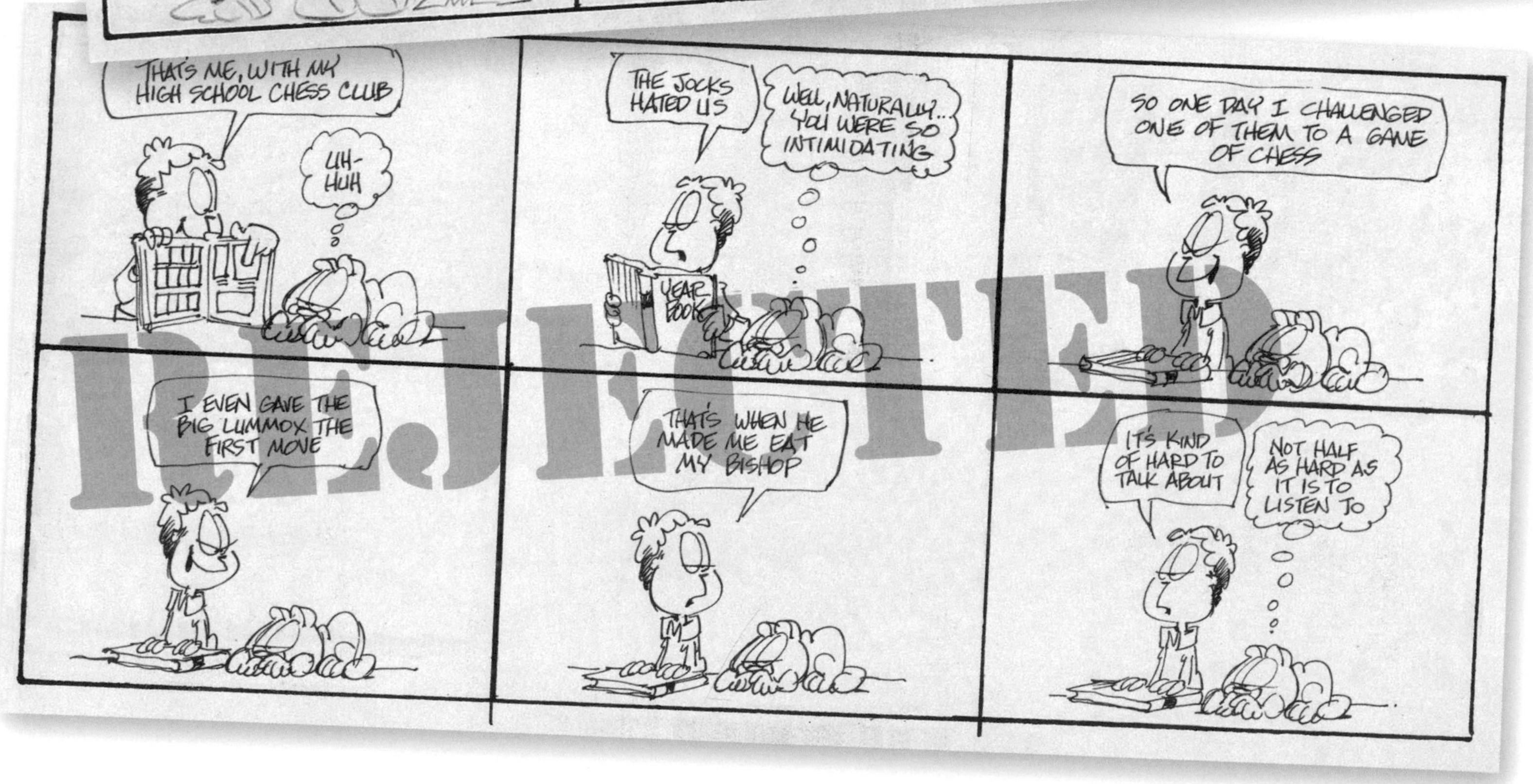
THAT'S ME, WITH MY HIGH SCHOOL CHESS CLUB
UH-HUH
THE JOCKS HATED US
WELL, NATURALLY... YOU WERE SO INTIMIDATING
YEAR BOOK
SO ONE DAY I CHALLENGED ONE OF THEM TO A GAME OF CHESS
I EVEN GAVE THE BIG LUMMOX THE FIRST MOVE
THAT'S WHEN HE MADE ME EAT MY BISHOP
IT'S KIND OF HARD TO TALK ABOUT
NOT HALF AS HARD AS IT IS TO LISTEN TO
REJECTED

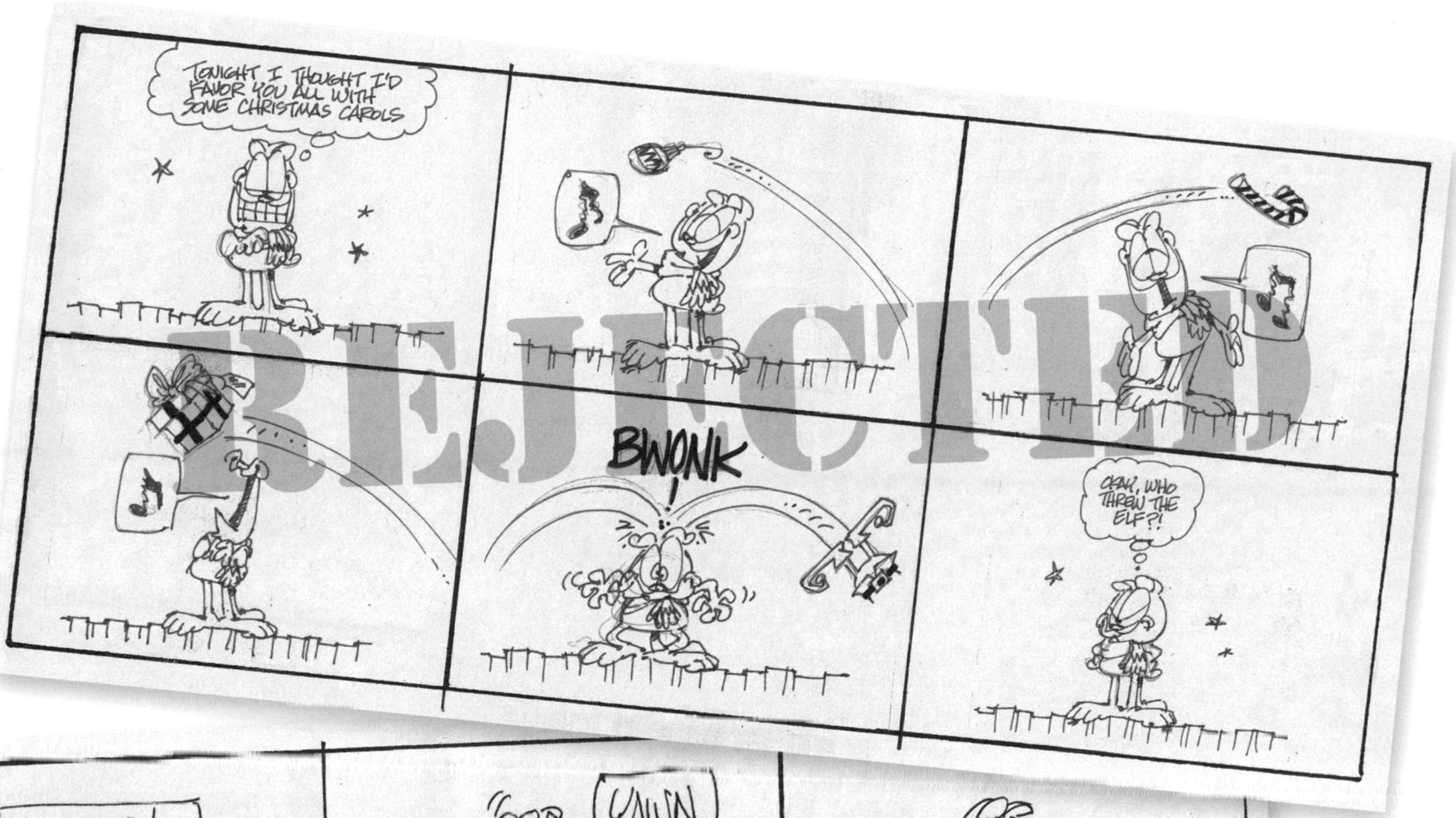
TONIGHT I THOUGHT I'D FAVOR YOU ALL WITH SOME CHRISTMAS CAROLS
BWONK
OKAY, WHO THREW THE ELF?!
REJECTED

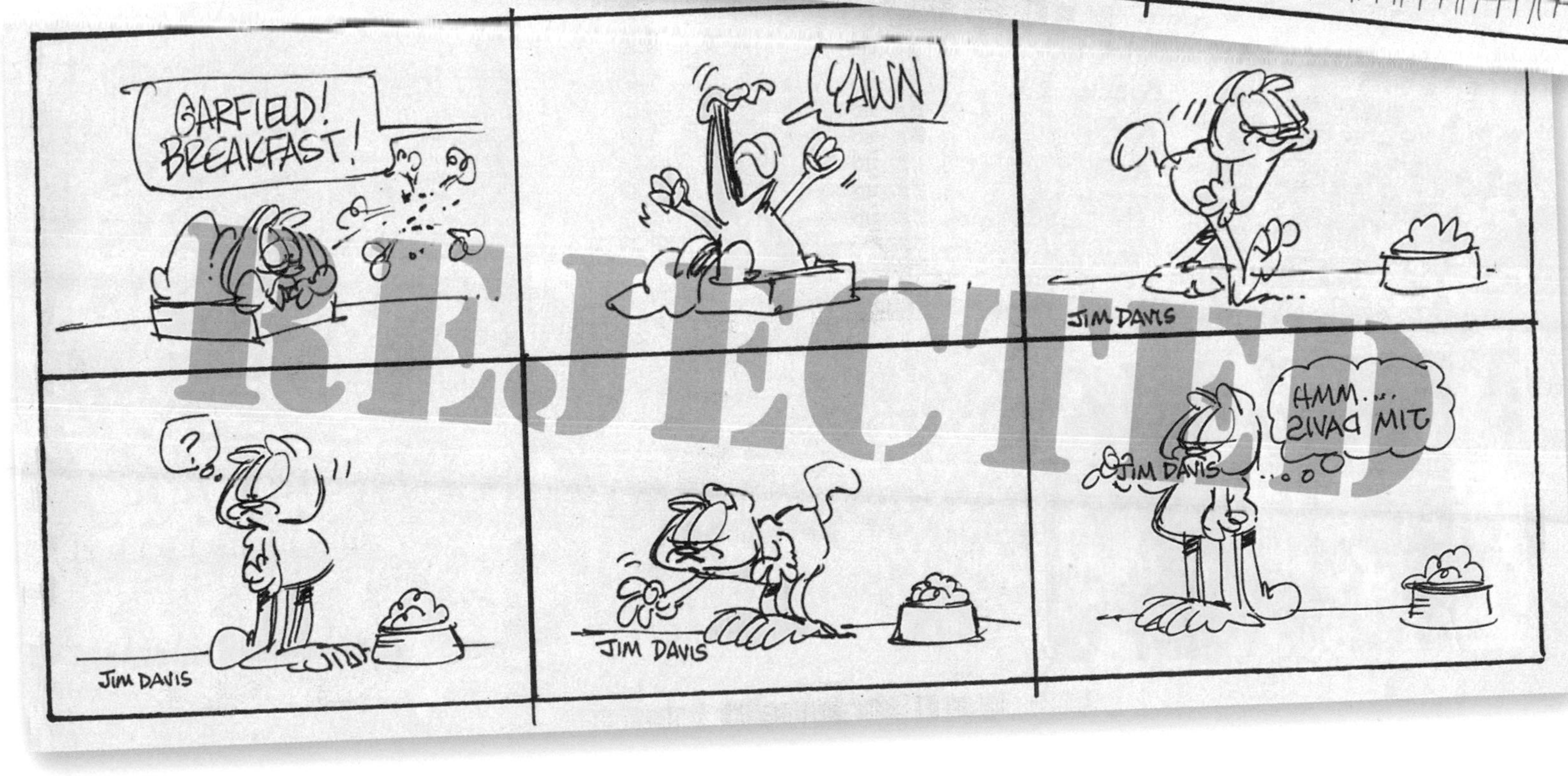
GARFIELD! BREAKFAST!
YAWN
JIM DAVIS
?
JIM DAVIS
JIM DAVIS
JIM DAVIS
HMM... SIVAD MIT
REJECTED

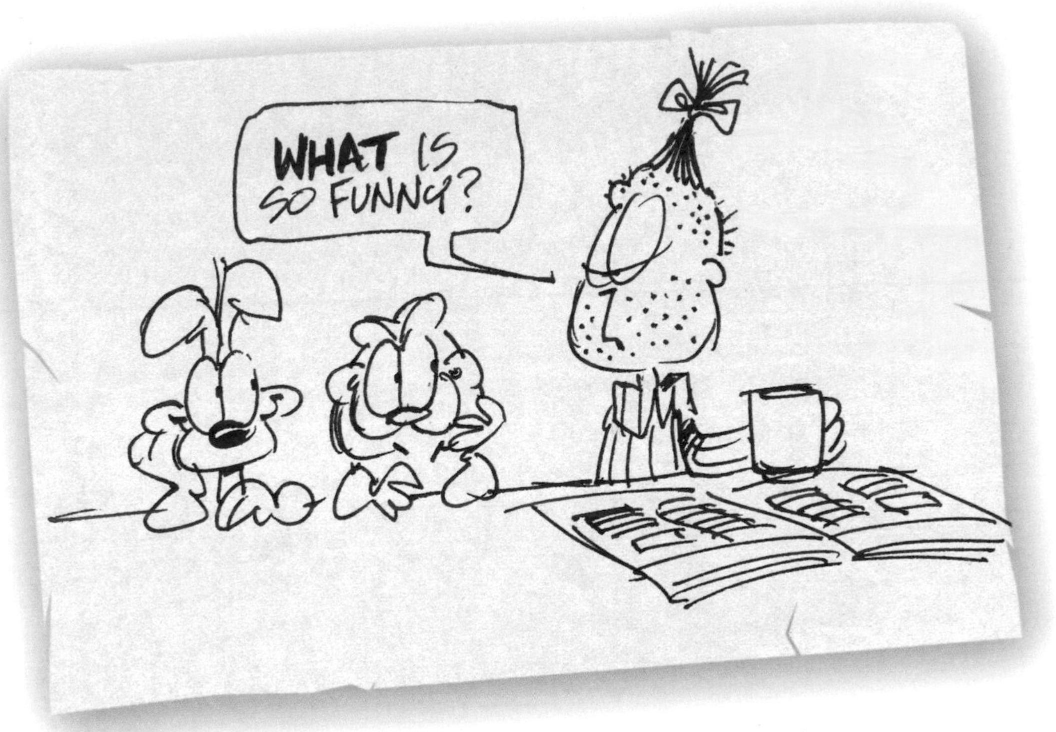
WHAT IS SO FUNNY?